MW01097215

Remembrances in Black

Remembrances in Black

Personal Perspectives
of the African American Experience
at the University of Arkansas, 1940s–2000s

■ ■ ■

Charles F. Robinson II
Lonnie R. Williams

The University of Arkansas Press
Fayetteville ■ 2010

ISBN-10: 1-55728-953-0
ISBN-13: 978-1-55728-953-7

14 13 12 11 10   5 4 3 2 1

Text design by Ellen Beeler

⊗ The paper used in this publication meets the minimum requirements
of the American National Standard for Permanence of
Paper for Printed Library Materials Z39.48-1984.

Library of Congress Cataloging-in-Publication Data

Robinson, Charles F. (Charles Frank)
Remembrances in Black : personal perspectives of the African American experience at the
University of Arkansas, 1940s-2000s / Charles F. Robinson II, Lonnie R. Williams.
p. cm.
Includes bibliographical references.
ISBN 978-1-55728-953-7 (cloth : alk. paper)
1. University of Arkansas, Fayetteville—Students--Interviews. 2. University of Arkansas,
Fayetteville—Employees—Interviews. 3. African Americans—Education (Higher)—Arkansas—
Fayetteville—History—20th century. 4. African American college students—Arkansas—
Fayetteville—History—20th century. 5. African Americans—Arkansas—Fayetteville—Social
conditions—20th century. 6. Education, Higher—Social aspects—Arkansas—Fayetteville—
History—20th century. 7. Discrimination in education—Arkansas—Fayetteville—History—
20th century. 8. College integration—Arkansas—Fayetteville—History—20th century.
I. Williams, Lonnie R., 1954– II. Title.
LD233.R63 2010
378.767'14--dc22   2010031530

This book is dedicated to the memory of Dr. Nudie Williams, former associate professor of history at the University of Arkansas, Fayetteville. Dr. Williams was a friend and mentor to both authors as well as many others during his tenure at the University of Arkansas, 1976–2003.

DR. NUDIE EUGENE WILLIAMS
OCTOBER 16, 1936 – JULY 16, 2003

Contents

Chapter 4: BAD Challenges Desegregation in the 1970s

Acknowledgments

This oral history is largely the idea of my friend and coeditor, Dr. Lonnie Williams. Some years ago when I approached him about my interest in writing a new historical monograph about desegregation at the University of Arkansas, Lonnie suggested that we first gather the stories of the participants in that history. Without Lonnie, this project would have been virtually impossible because he had the connections to the historical characters in this work to bring it to fruition. I am very grateful Lonnie allowed me to take this journey with him. Also, I would like to thank all of those wonderful people who shared their truly remarkable stories with us. Furthermore, I extend my gratitude to Andrea Cantrell, Dr. Tom Kennedy, and Jason Blankenship for their assistance in helping me to find the historical resources that comprise the introductions to each chapter. With regard to underwriting the considerable costs associated with the transcribing, I am deeply indebted to Dr. Todd Shields and the Diane D. Blair Center for Southern Politics and Societies at the University of Arkansas. Finally, I thank God for giving me the power to do anything that serves to help, heal, and constructively inform humanity. I believe that this work fits that category.

—Charles Robinson, PhD

I thank God for allowing this project to happen and for His continuous blessings. I am very grateful for the friendship and collaboration of Dr. Charles Robinson in bringing this project to life. To those who unselfishly, and for some painfully, provided the interviews, I cannot thank you enough. Special thanks to Mary and my family for their constant support and belief; Drs. Gordon Morgan and Izola Preston for their earlier work on the black experience at the U of A and their friendship; Gigi for transcription services; Angela, Kelley, and Laura for their technical support; Larry Malley and the University of Arkansas Press for accepting this project; and the many friends and colleagues who are constantly encouraging, particularly "the crew."

—Lonnie R. Williams, EdD

Foreword

As I sit here, winding down from what has proven to be yet another rewarding and long day in academe, my evening ritual of checking the mail while intermittently watching the television set to see what the day's national news conveys has left me both intrigued and saddened. Roland S. Martin, CNN political analyst, is sandwiched between Soledad O'Brian, CNN anchor, and Peter Beinart, senior political writer for the *Daily Beast*—each is being interviewed on *Anderson Cooper 360*. The subject of their discussion is the contemporary revival of the seminal doll experiments conducted by Kenneth and Mamie Clark in the 1940s. Most shocking is that some seventy years later, African American children still find that the doll that most "looks like them" is at best bad and worst *evil*. Yet, from where did these constructions come? What makes being black or the representation of blackness *evil*? Have black people always felt this way? Have they (we) always had these misgivings about self-worth and value?

Fortunately, my sadness is tempered by my reflection on the words proffered by important black figures, who were able to share with me during my formative years powerful narratives and counternarratives that framed a different story about my blackness. Much like the stories and masterful accounts that are conveyed in *Remembrances in Black: Personal Perspectives of the African American Experience at the University of Arkansas, 1940s–2000s*, I have been able to frame an identity that is based on resilience and strength. As Robinson and Williams state, "This volume is an attempt to better understand the experiences of African Americans at the University of Arkansas on the Fayetteville campus." What each one of these personal accounts provides is background to the milestones and accomplishments that African Americans, not only at the University of Arkansas but also in other contexts within and outside of academe, have been able to enjoy in the foreground. As the editors so eloquently state, *Remembrances in Black* prompts the reader to work toward better comprehending not only the challenges to integration in our past, but the residual barriers that still remain.

A common refrain that is often echoed in the African American community, particularly among African American church-goers is, "Give me my flowers while I yet live." This mantra, with its simple yet profound meaning, is exactly what these editors have done for the men and women included in this volume—they have given them their flowers. They have provided these storytellers with the space to create and share their experiences as students, faculty, and staff at the University of Arkansas across a continuum that spans Jim Crow to millennial culture. In addition to a vivid recounting of what it has meant to matriculate at the university, both historically and contemporarily, this book also fills an important void in the literature; namely, the authentic narrative accounts of students of color who attend predominantly white institutions (PWIs).

Prepare to engage with these narratives—some will make you laugh, and some will make you cry. However, what they are best at doing is creating a context in which you can better understand the motivations, thoughts, challenges, and opportunities that have made these African American students successful. Robinson and Williams, in providing space for "former students of color to tell of their pain, challenges, opportunities, and triumphs as they travailed to forge a place for themselves at the university" is the best of American sagas, the classic tale of the testimony bookending the text.

—Fred A. Bonner II
University of Arkansas (1994–1997), EdD 1997
Texas A&M University

Introduction

On April 28, 2006, the University of Arkansas sponsored the Silas Hunt Legacy Awards Banquet at the Town Center in the heart of downtown Fayetteville. Attended by alumni and dignitaries from around the state and nation, this event was advertised by university officials as an opportunity to recognize African American students, faculty, and staff who were instrumental in desegregating the university. In addition to commemorating the efforts of these black pioneers, the occasion also allowed the university to celebrate itself. Chancellor John White recognized the "special challenges" that black students experienced in the early days of school desegregation, yet he also proudly reminded those in attendance that the University of Arkansas was the first southern, public, institution of higher learning to voluntarily admit black students "in modern times."[1]

The University of Arkansas's touting of its unique desegregation history was warranted in part. Founded in 1871 during the Reconstruction period as the Arkansas Industrial University, neither the state legislature nor the school's first board of trustees made any provisions in the school's charter that denied access to students of color. In fact, the superintendent of public instruction in 1873, Joseph Carter Corbin, an African American from Pine Bluff, not only served as the first president ex-officio of the University of Arkansas Board of Trustees but also signed the contract that made possible the construction of University Hall (Old Main), the first building for the new institution. However, this did not mean that members of the board and other state officials expected blacks to attend the university. To the contrary, by placing the campus in Fayetteville, an area in the northwestern part of the state and far away from most of the black population, officials ensured that the institution would serve primarily white students. Furthermore, in 1873, Corbin and his board sought and received a $25,000 allocation from the state to construct a Branch Normal College in the eastern part of the state for "the education and fitting of persons as colored teachers." State officials assumed that this new institution would be attended by black students.[2] Thus, the board laid the foundation for the creation of a de facto segregated school system for higher education. As a result, although no official ban existed, the University of Arkansas had only one confirmed black student, James McGahee, prior to the twentieth century.[3]

After the establishment of the Branch Normal College in Pine Bluff, the University of Arkansas blatantly refused to allow black students to enroll in classes at the Fayetteville campus despite their apparent qualifications. In 1887, Scipio Africanus Jones, a black Arkansan who would later gain national acclaim as the attorney responsible for gaining reversals for some of the black men sentenced to death in the trials that followed the Elaine riots of 1919, attempted unsuccessfully to gain admittance into the university's Law School.[4] In 1938, Edward Lewis Jacko Jr., a black native of Little Rock who had earned an undergraduate degree from Talladega College in Alabama, also attempted to enroll in the university's Law School. University officials denied Jacko's application by arguing that since Talladega College was not a member of the Southern Association of Colleges and Secondary Schools, Jacko was not eligible to attend the Law School. The university held to this position despite the fact that Talladega had received an "A" rating from the Association of Colleges. Prior to the mid-twentieth century, the University of Arkansas would offer only correspondence and agricultural extension courses to black students.[5]

The United States Supreme Court's ruling in *Gaines v. Canada* (1938) brought pressure upon University of Arkansas officials to modify the school's practices with regard to black students. In that case, the Court ruled that the states must provide for graduate- and professional-level education for students of color within the states that they resided. In practice, the ruling meant that states that denied black students access to state colleges had to accommodate their pursuits of higher education in some way.[6] State institutions of higher learning could no longer simply ignore qualified black applicants. In 1941, Scipio Jones tested the power of the ruling by officially requesting that the university pay the out-of-state tuition of Prentice A. Hilburn, a black student who desired to attend Howard University. The university initially balked at the request, but after a conference with Jones, school officials agreed to pay $134.50 for Hilburn's tuition fees. Shortly thereafter, two other African American students, Louis M. Coggs and G. W. Stanley Ish Jr., also made tuition reimbursement requests on their own from the university and threatened to seek admission if the refunds were not granted. Although the university denied both requests, officials clearly recognized the urgency of developing a plan of action for what they perceived could become a quite expensive problem.[7] Within a month after agreeing to pay Hilburn's tuition, the university organized a conference in Little Rock attended by black leaders and representatives of the State Department of Education for the purpose of establishing an official policy for paying the out-of-state tuition costs for black students desiring graduate- or professional-level education. In 1943, the state allocated $5,000 for the policy developed at the conference.[8]

Despite this attempt by state officials to forestall any challenge to the university's segregation practice, by the late 1940s, some university officials could see the handwriting on the wall. With *Sipuel v. Board of Regents of the University of Oklahoma* (1947) and *Sweatt v. Painter* (1950), the Supreme Court delivered two crushing blows to state-sponsored segregation in higher education. Collectively, these rulings made it extremely difficult for state schools to deny qualified black students admission to in-state graduate or law programs.[9] Although, the state could still offer to pay out-of state tuition for black students, these students now had more power to demand entrance into the program offered by the state school.

Robert Leflar, dean of the Law School, was the first university official to deliberately address the university's policy toward black students. Shortly after Clifford Davis, an African American student at AM&N College (formally Branch Normal College), filed a petition for entry to the university's Law School in March 1946 for the coming fall semester. Leflar met with the chairman of the board of trustees, Herbert Thomas, and discussed possible responses to black students who sought admission to the university. Leflar suggested the university had several choices. It could continue to exclude blacks and face litigation; maintain its policy of paying the tuition of blacks to out-of-state schools and hope that sufficed; build a Law School for blacks at AM&N; or establish facilities at the university for teaching black students. Thomas took Leflar's ideas to the board, but it passed no recommendations. Instead, the board left the matter of how to handle the admission of blacks in the hands of the Law School dean.[10]

The fall 1946 came, but Davis did not show up to register. The delay gave Leflar time to consult with Lewis Webster Jones, the in-coming president, and the governor of Arkansas, Ben Laney. Jones, a native of Nebraska, had been educated in Oregon, New York, and London and had served as president of Bennington College in Vermont, yet his ideas about segregation mirrored those of most southerners. While serving as a member of President Harry S. Truman's Commission on Higher Education, Jones had opposed the commission's formal report, calling for the gradual abolition of segregation in the South. Jones had not yet arrived to the university, so Leflar wrote him a lengthy letter, apprising him of the board's deliberations. Jones responded succinctly that Leflar should follow the board's recommendations.[11]

Leflar then had a meeting with Governor Laney. Like Jones, Laney was a staunch segregationist. He had previously advocated the idea of southern states pooling their resources to establish regional schools that would serve the graduate and professional needs of blacks. In the session with the governor, Leflar presented many of the same points he had made to the board of trustees. However, with Laney, Leflar emphasized the costs, both monetary and social, of denying blacks access to the university. Leflar informed the governor that a court battle would not only be unsuccessful but also sully the state's relatively favorable public image with regard to race relations. Furthermore, Leflar suggested that building a separate Law School for blacks would be prohibitive, estimating the cost to the state at no less than $100,000 immediately and $20,000 annually. For Leflar, "setting up facilities" for blacks to attend the university was the only practical alternative. Grudgingly, Laney agreed and promised not to interfere with the university's actions on this matter.[12]

By January 1948, university officials had received word that two black students, Clifford Davis and Wiley Branton, had applied to the Law School and the business college, respectively. President Jones after consulting with board chairman Thomas issued a statement that the university would admit Davis with "special arrangements" to accommodate his presence but would submit Branton's application to the board of trustees for consideration. Subsequently, the board officially denied Branton's request for admission because of his undergraduate status.[13]

Jones's announcement indicated the university would admit blacks to graduate and professional schools at the university, but he did not intend for black students to be integrated into campus life. In response to a letter from an Arkansas resident criticizing him for allowing blacks to enroll, Jones explained that legal realities had forced him to make such a decision. Jones also offered assurances that every step would be taken to respect "state laws and traditions concerning segregation of the races in the schools of this state."[14] In practice, this meant that blacks would not be allowed to take classes with other students, use student restroom facilities, or live or eat in the dormitories. Clifford Davis balked at coming to the university with a separate facilities arrangement. Instead, Davis attended Howard University. Yet, another black student, Silas Hunt, a decorated veteran of WWII from Texarkana, Arkansas, applied and received admission in February 1948.

With the admittance of Silas Hunt, the University of Arkansas became the first southern public institution of higher education to officially desegregate without being required to do so by court order. However, it is important to highlight the reluctance demonstrated by the university in allowing black students on campus during this time in order to fully understand the historical significance of the Hunt admission. The university allowed Hunt to enroll, but it did not embrace him as one of its own. To the contrary, Hunt was forced to endure a campus-wide shunning that suggested that the University of Arkansas had no intention of immediately moving toward integration. The decision to let Hunt enroll was largely one of expediency. Hunt was not welcomed as a symbol of progress. He attended classes largely alone in the basement of the Law School. Although a few of the white law students sat with him during some of his classes, Hunt could not make decisions to join their classes. Neither could Hunt become a member of student organizations or participate in student-sponsored events. Furthermore, Hunt had to walk several miles to and from school. Denied access to the dorms, he lived off-campus in the home of a black family. This arrangement forced Hunt to have to endure the sometimes bone-chilling cold of the Fayetteville winter like no other Law School student at the time. Segregated, isolated, and largely ignored, one can only imagine the emotional malaise that such conditions forced upon Hunt. The experience may have also had a direct affect upon his health, for Hunt contracted tuberculosis in the summer of 1948, making it impossible for him to return to the school in the fall. In April 1949, Silas Hunt died.[15]

Hunt's death aroused little reaction on the Fayetteville campus in 1949. Few university students, faculty, or administrators seemed to take note. Yet, his decision to attend the University of Arkansas would have great repercussions on the future presence of African Americans at the university. The effects of Hunt's trailblazing could be seen even before his death. In the fall of 1948, Jackie Shropshire, another black law student, had arrived on campus. Other black students would soon follow Shropshire, signaling that the University of Arkansas would have to grapple with the continued and growing presence of blacks in its midst.[16]

By reading their sagas, the reader comes to better comprehend not only the challenges to desegregation in the university's past, but the residual barriers that still remain.

Key to the Organization of This Book

This volume is an attempt to better understand the experiences of African Americans at the University of Arkansas on the Fayetteville campus from Hunt's fateful decision to the present. It contains the stories of African American students, staff, and faculty who endured the largely racially homogenous university environment for a period that spanned more than fifty years.

Participants were first selected based on having a historical presence on the campus such as being the first or one of the first African American to enroll as a law student, graduate student, undergraduate student, first PhD, first faculty member, first black president of the student body, first football or basketball players, and first homecoming queen, and so forth. Other historical moments included events in African American history such as the suing of the university so African Americans could live in the residence halls, the protest of the playing of "Dixie" in 1969, and the first black sorority and fraternity. In addition, some participants were selected due to their leadership roles to speak about their experiences. The original thought was to interview as many "firsts" as we could. We realized that the "firsts" would start to diminish after the 1970s. Thus you will find fewer interviews with each decade past the 1970s. At that point, we would interview more leaders to speak of their experiences to ensure we had voices speaking from 1949 into the present century.

Participants in this volume were given the choice of being interviewed or responding to a list of questions about their experiences at the university. Those interviewed, either in person or over the telephone, tended to provide longer and fuller accounts than most who responded in writing to the pre-set questions. Everyone was asked the same pre-set questions; however, live interviews allowed for follow-up questions to get more details. The pre-set questions were:

1. What year did you enter the University of Arkansas and to obtain what degree or major?
2. Why did you select the University of Arkansas?
3. How long did you attend the university?
4. What was your role in the history of African Americans at the UA (one of first black law students, first or early graduates, first whatever, historical event, etc.)?
5. In your own words, and as many as you choose, describe your experience at the university including events, interaction, and points you feel would be of interest to an audience.
6. Describe your feelings toward the university during your time of study?
7. Have you returned to the university since your departure and if so, for what reasons and when?
8. Describe your present feelings toward the university. If they have changed from previous feelings, what made them change?
9. Discuss whatever you would like for us to know about you and your experience at the University of Arkansas.

The questions were selected to get basic information from the participants such as when they attended the university, why they selected the university, and their feelings while there and their feelings now. The questions were designed so as not to present any type of bias or to be leading in any way.

Initially, participants were contacted by letter or e-mail requesting their participation and given an option as to whether they wanted to respond in writing to the questions, live interview, or telephone interview. As each interview is introduced, it will state in the heading whether the interview was conducted as a telephone interview, written response to the interview questions, or if in person, where the interview was conducted such as in their home or other location. The heading of each interview will also tell you the timeframe the person being interviewed was at the university, and employment information (judge, attorney, educator, manager, and so forth). A more detailed biography on most (not all provided one) of those interviewed is provided in the appendix section of the manuscript.

After the interviews were received, and in some cases transcribed from the interview tape, the interviews were edited to read as if the interviewee was sitting and telling their story versus responding to the questions. In order to preserve the actual voice of those interviewed, minimal editing was done for spelling, consistency, punctuation, and sometimes for grammar and length, but we tried to keep the interviews as close to the original interview as possible with what was said and how it was spoken or written. The interviews were then returned to the participants for their editing, approval, and later edited to the state presented here. The transcribing of the tapes was funded by the Pryor Center for Arkansas Oral and Visual History, Special Collections Department of the University of Arkansas Libraries in Fayetteville. They are being stored and can be heard there.

The oral histories were also arranged chronologically by decades. By setting the stories in this fashion, we hope to provide the reader with a better feel for consistency and/or change at the university over time. In this work, former students, staff, and faculty of color tell of their pain, challenges, opportunities, and triumphs as they travailed to forge a place for themselves at the university.

Chapter 1

In the Beginning

The University of Arkansas is honestly and earnestly feeling its way toward the solution of a very difficult problem. In doing so, we have no roadmaps to follow . . . We do not know, and we cannot know, the pattern future [race] relationships will take, but we are seeking a pattern as we go along.

—William J. Good, October 15, 1948

William J. Good, the director of public relations for the University of Arkansas, wrote the above statement in response to a letter sent by James R. Goodrich, the assistant editor of *Ebony* magazine, who indicated that the black publication desired to run an article on the admission of Edith Mae Irby, an African American woman from Hot Springs, to the university's previously all-white medical school in the fall of 1948. In accordance with the thinking that had allowed Hunt and Shropshire to enroll in the Fayetteville campus, university officials had permitted the qualified Irby to become a medical student on the Little Rock campus. In couching his reply to Goodrich, Good expressed his willingness to speak "frankly" about Irby and desegregation at the University of Arkansas, but he distinguished "off the record" comments from those that could be published. Good also requested that the article never quote any specific university official nor state that "university personnel refused to be quoted."[1]

For the record, Good went on to give a brief overview of the university's historic efforts to provide educational opportunity for African American students. Good mentioned the establishment of the campus at Pine Bluff, the general extension courses, and the correspondence courses the university had made available to blacks even before the admission of Silas Hunt. With regard to Irby, Good described her fully integrated class arrangement. He explained that Irby sat with "no objection" at a table in the anatomy laboratory with three white students. Although Irby and the three white students worked well together, Good asserted they had not "evidenced any inclination to mingle with each other on a social basis outside the classroom and laboratory."[2]

Off the record, Good implored the black publication to be sensitive to the unique and difficult situation facing the University of Arkansas. He intimated that the university supported "improved relationship" between the races and "more nearly equalized opportunities" for blacks. However, Good cautioned the magazine not to overplay the desegregation developments for fear it would "inflame the extreme elements" of both races and "set back race relations many years." Good also candidly revealed the university had no fixed and established policy on how to implement desegregation. According to Good, the university had "no road maps" and was simply "feeling its way toward the solution to a very difficult problem."[3]

The letter of William Good very accurately described how the university handled desegregation prior to the Supreme Court's ruling in the *Brown* decision of 1954. University officials refused to admit black undergraduates regardless of their credentials, but continued providing graduate opportunity to black students in programs that were not offered by Arkansas AM&N. The actions of the university with regard to desegregation at this time seemed guided by three principles. First, the university did not welcome attention to its desegregation efforts. Good's response to *Ebony* implied the magazine should present the university's story in a very matter-of-fact way in order to decrease any interest the institution might receive. On another occasion when President Jones was asked by the Southern Conference Educational Fund, an interracial organization that favored integration in education, to serve as one of the sponsors for their regional conference, he declined. Jones emphasized the university had made reasonable progress by "working in a quiet way" to provide better educational opportunities for blacks in the state.[4]

The second principle guiding the university with regard to desegregation was that desegregation must be achieved slowly. As mentioned earlier, the university continued denying the admission of qualified black undergraduates. When James Miller, a black high school sophomore from Englewood, Colorado, wrote Jones in May 1951, inquiring about the prospect of attending the university's department of forestry and agriculture in the fall of 1953, Jones succinctly replied it was not the present policy of the university to admit undergraduates and that "it would be impossible" to predict future university policy.[5] Also in the fall of 1949, the university established a Residence Center in Little Rock to provide graduate training for black students, mostly in education. The vast majority of blacks enrolled in the university during this time attended and graduated from the Little Rock center.[6] University officials appear to have started the Little Rock program at least in part to reduce the number of black students who might enroll in classes in Fayetteville and thus slow down the pace of desegregation.[7]

The third principle that directed university desegregation actions was that the university followed legal mandates rather than choosing to set new social trends. Prior to 1951, the few black students who attended the Fayetteville campus encountered a rigid segregation that locked them out of university housing, dining facilities, student organizations, and activities.[8] Furthermore, in fall 1948, the university modified the separate-class policy for black students. Unlike Hunt, who was forced to take his classes in almost complete isolation, subsequent black students would be allowed to take some of their classes with whites, but they would be positioned away from white students in a conspicuous fashion.[9] The reasons for this subtle change had more to do with concerns about potential legal challenges to the complete segregation of black students and the exorbitant costs of providing segregated classroom instruction rather than the idea of furthering integration. Also, the university implemented the change out of a desire to better accommodate educating white students. In the fall of 1948, the Law School enrolled a record number of 125 first-year students. Under the old practice, all of these students would have been crowded together into classrooms designed for about sixty while Jackie Shropshire had his own class. In September 1948, Leflar issued a memorandum announcing the change. He wrote, "The Law School is continuing its segregation policy, but with a segregation system fairer to white students . . . Hereafter, the colored student will be seated in a separate section of a room, and white students will sit in other parts of the room."[10]

The *McLaurin v. Oklahoma State Regents for Higher Education* (1950) forced University of Arkansas officials to further revise their policies toward desegregation. In that case, the United States Supreme Court ruled the University of Oklahoma had to discontinue practices that required George McLaurin, a black graduate student in education, to endure segregation on the university campus. Prior to the ruling, University of Oklahoma officials had handled

McLaurin in a fashion similar to the way the University of Arkansas officials dealt with Shropshire. Oklahoma forced the sixty-eight-year-old McLaurin to sit at a desk by himself in an anteroom outside the regular classroom, to use a segregated desk in the mezzanine of the library behind old newspapers, and to eat in a dingy part of the cafeteria by himself at a different hour from whites.[11] Shortly after the *McLaurin* decision, the University of Arkansas began allowing black male students to live in Lloyd Halls, an all-male dormitory comprised of law and graduate students. Yet, the school continued segregating black females from white female students. In the summer of 1953, the institution purchased a large residence near the university and converted it into housing for black women.[12]

The university also officially opened all campus facilities, including the dining hall in the student union, to black students. After 1951, black students began attending musical events, dramatic productions, and other on-campus public gatherings on a nonsegregated basis.[13] However, this change did not mean that black students at the university ceased to experience exclusionary discrimination. Most student organizations remained off-limits to students of color. Also, black students continued to endure segregation practices when they ventured into the town of Fayetteville.[14]

There are no good records on the number of blacks who came to Fayetteville to pursue their education between the years 1948–1954. During this time, university officials did not keep official records indicating the race of students.[15] In fact, all state funds appropriated to the university went on state records "as funds for the education of white students."[16] Yet, evidence does suggest that changes in some of the institution's desegregation practices, along with the growing awareness of blacks in the state of the educational opportunities opened to them, positively affected the number of blacks who attended and graduated from the university. Most black students who came to the Fayetteville campus during this time attended summer classes, but returned to the Little Rock center during the fall and spring. In January 1954, Good guessed there were "upwards of 200 Negroes, possibly more" presently enrolled in the "various advance divisions of the University . . . most of them are part-time students in our Graduate Division in Little Rock."[17]

By the spring of 1954, the University of Arkansas had evolving policies and practices with regard to desegregation. The institution labored to limit the number of blacks on the Fayetteville campus and to avoid legal entanglements that might attract unwanted, negative, media attention. However, the university expended very little energy in attempting to create a better campus environment for black students. In this section, we hear from George Haley and Chris Mercer, two of the six "black pioneers," the first black students to enroll in the Law School. With their oral histories, Haley and Mercer give us vivid accounts of what it meant to be a black University of Arkansas student in the beginning years of desegregation.

■ George W. B. Haley (1949–1952), U.S. ambassador

Telephone interview by Lonnie R. Williams, September 24, 2007
For detailed biography, see Appendix A, page 285

I entered the University of Arkansas in the fall of 1949 and I was in the Law School there. I selected it [the University of Arkansas] because there was certainly the interest in having African Americans come to the university. The University of Arkansas is really one of the first of the southern universities to admit Negroes [black students] at that time. Even though it was segregated, they admitted them. I was at Morehouse College and my father was a professor at the University of Arkansas at Pine Bluff, then known as Arkansas AM&N College at Pine Bluff. Well, we were talking about my going to Law School and he suggested, because of the possibilities of my getting into the university, that he thought it would be a good thing for me to do. And so based on the discussions I had with him and the president of Morehouse, Dr. Benjamin Elijah Mays, I decided that I would try to enter the University of Arkansas Law School.

I attended from 1949 until I graduated in 1952. But I came on the scene when it was, really, a very pioneering experience. It certainly was from my standpoint and the others who came just before and after. I came on the scene with, well, Jackie was there, Jackie Shropshire was already there and I recall stopping through Little Rock, Arkansas, which is where Jackie lived, to let him know that I was on my way up to the University of Arkansas. My father and I drove there. I guess it was July after I was accepted. And Jackie spoke to me like a brother. He was just so pleased that somebody was going because he was the only one up there at the time.

And we went, Dad and I went on up after listening a little bit to what Jackie said and had a meeting with the dean of the Law School, then Dean Robert Leflar. He and I talked about my coming, joining Jackie, and told me some of the things that would be expected or not expected of the black students. We had a separate study room. We were not to sit down in the library, which was two floors up from where we were and we would be set aside from the white students in two chairs right across from the professor, but away from the white students.

Now prior to my being there, Jackie had been moved from a separate study room from where Silas Hunt had been to the regular classroom, but to a chair apart from the other students. Really a rail was built between him and the students. But Wiley Davis, the criminal law professor, was the one who said that he and others could not accept that so he had them remove the rails that kept the chair apart from the other students. This is the condition that existed when CC [Chris Mercer] and I came in the fall of 1949 so that was one thing. Another, white students complained about our using the student restroom facility. So it was decided that we would use the dean's private restroom, which was inside his office, meaning that we had to request a key from his secretary/receptionist to get to the restroom. That didn't seem to work too well for other people. They seemed to complain about that and then we were moved from there to the faculty restroom, which was inside the regular student restroom, meaning we had to pass through the student restroom anyway to get there. So those were some of the types of things that happened to us in the early beginning stages. Many others, but those are the things that come to mind.

When I went to Judge Howard's funeral in 2007, I was asked to speak. And one of the things I said, and have said on many occasions, is that we came to be like brothers in supporting each other because all of us had to experience many of the things that I am telling you about. There were five of us there, in the year 1951, which is the year that Jackie [Shropshire] graduated. He became the first black to graduate from the university. By the year 1951, in addition to CC and me, George Howard and Wiley Branton were there. And so they had to take up the same kinds of things that we did.

Now, by 1951 some of the things had changed. The first case in Texas that was decided by the Supreme Court and the *McLauren* case in Oklahoma in 1950, had determined pretty much that you could not, I mean, separate Law Schools, which were not equal under the circumstances. So we used those, [laughing] by going into the main restrooms, and a few others things, but that in particular is one thing that sticks out in our mind that we were able to go use the regular restrooms. But I'm saying that because a few things were changing for the better by the time that George Howard and Wiley had gotten there.

We received no assistance from the university. No. We—Jackie, CC, and I—stayed in the community. In my family were Cashmere and Chrystal Funkhouser with their young daughter Carolyn, and so I stayed with them for two years. The third year I stayed in the dormitory in what they called the Quonset huts. Now George Howard, when he came, I think he was able to begin staying on the campus. Incidentally, as I said things, in some instances got better, he became president of his dormitory, Quonset hut.

To describe my feelings toward the university while there, well again, that is not an easy question. There were problems and great disappointments at times. By problems I mean situations. When you felt good about being able to make things better, there is no doubt that much of what we were doing was getting to know new experiences. The white students looked at us [laughs] sometimes as if they felt that we shouldn't be there. We could feel that. There's no doubt about that. The attitudes and situations were such that they looked on us as just not wanting us there. But it developed to the extent that some gained respect for us and we for them as we moved along. They saw that we had abilities that we could not only respond, but we sometimes made good grades. We were able to exchange as students to the professors and we came to have them respect us as students. Now, that is not with all. But some of them, of course, came to be friends.

It's difficult to say in a broad sense how I felt or we felt, but as we moved along we eventually felt comfortable in the Law School. I guess about the second year, I was invited to write on the *Law Review* staff. I don't know if it was a professor or not, and even the dean eventually discovered that I could write very well and I came to be a member of the *Law Review* staff, which of course is considered a great honor from the standpoint of what happens in Law School. There were, I think about eleven to twelve people on the *Law Review* staff. And eventually, I wrote five case notes and a comment, which is a longer legal article, and was named the comments editor in my senior year, my third year of Law School. So I'm saying that different kinds of things like that happened as we moved along as people discovered we had abilities [laughing]. We helped make the Law School what it was.

George Howard graduated in 1954. See, that's the reason I'm saying that he came the first of 1951; see, that's the year that Jackie graduated. So that's the reason I said I know all five of us were there at least for one year together. George did not respond very much to the university. I don't know what happened to him. He never said to me. [Ambassador Haley was asked about the alleged statement that was made by Judge Howard that if the Lord let him leave Fayetteville, he would never return.] Did you ask CC? I don't know what happened to

George Howard. I had not only heard it before, but I don't know that I ever asked him that question direct. Now, he was the only one who did not respond too much afterwards. I don't know whether he ever came back to the university. Someone said that he didn't.

You know, where George Howard and I are concerned, we got along as I said very well. A lot of us did at the university when the five of us were there. Of course, there were, I'd say, misunderstandings from you know who if he didn't like what somebody else was doing. Of course, in 1951, I was a second-year student, Jackie was a senior, and so George was a freshman. First year, I don't think he did what we said [laughing]. I don't mean that by any means negatively, but he kind of looked up to us to get support.

I have returned to the university on several occasions. I can't tell you how many times I have been to the university. At least, I've done two requested lectures at the Law School and to the university. In some other capacity, I would say that I have been there at least a half dozen times and maybe more.

The biggest highlight, quite frankly, of my being there, was being invited to do the commencement address. That would have been like maybe 2002, and I received an honorary doctorate. And that was just after I had been to Gambia. I was named by President Clinton as ambassador to Gambia in West Africa shortly thereafter. When I came back, the university invited me to come and do the commencement. I think that was 2002. I've been back twice since then to appear on the campus.

My present feelings are very good from this standpoint toward the university. I feel, quite frankly, that I was in a position to develop more respect of people in general and I say that about myself as well as all of the pioneers in our capacity. We were obligating the university to grow in what a university ought to do anyway intellectually, from the standpoint of, let's say, making things better for people's understanding. Just understanding is what I think education should be and is. The university is a lot better because of the experience that it had with our struggles and with some of the other young white males struggles in coming to know each other.

I remember one of my friends and I'll call his name, Bob Lowe. Bob Lowe came from Texarkana, Arkansas, and his father was a plantation owner. But as Bob and I got to know each other, he said, "George, I've never met a black man like you." I guess we'd say a Negro then. "I've never met a guy like you with the intelligence that you have," and he learned that I could play a little Chopin. And he says all of the blacks, then Negroes, that he had known were sharecroppers that his father had. I think his father then had about forty sharecroppers. He knew them and recognized that they were not such he could look at on the same intellectual level as I and the others were. He says it's just a change of mind, but acknowledges that there are people he can talk to, appreciate, and respect like me. And we have maintained a very, very good relationship through the years.

Now, it didn't just stop with the white students at the Law School. One of my finest friends is Miller Williams. He is an internationally known poet having done a lot of things there at the university. But Miller and I came to be friends to the extent he calls himself, I as his big brother and he as my little brother. And I am, at his request, the godfather of Lucinda: Lucinda Williams, who is a musician of some real renown. It's just a lot to say, but my experience at the university has been one that has been very, very meaningful, significant to me. Not only did I develop a lot of respect for people then, but I can say right now, Chancellor White and others certainly have done a lot to enhance where we are and our people are to make the university the kind of place that it is. I am very proud of it to be frank with you. We even have a very fine young dean there [Cynthia Nance]. And you know how proud we are that she is very, very able and don't you think that I don't talk about her and the university as to where it is now [both laughing].

The experiences at the university grew by getting to know and developing into a new environment. I had grown up in the south, as I said my dad taught at AM&N and prior to that, he was a college professor. We had lived all over—Langston in Oklahoma, Alabama A&M, Elizabeth City State Teachers in North Carolina, and other places. Then of course, my having gone to service, which was still in the segregated atmosphere, there's no doubt about that. The service was completely segregated when I was in the second war. I then went to Morehouse and then to the university, so you see the southern roots were there. There's no doubt about that. But I found a new stage where I could use those experiences to make things better, not only for ourselves but to have the experience with white students and to develop those things that were in sometimes a hostile atmosphere. To develop into an experience like that to make things better was not only my desire, but hopefully—hopefully—an ability to make things better and we did. Now, and I say I, but we because it was a collective black students' effort. It started first with Jackie. Incidentally, I don't know how I would have done had I been Jackie [only one]. But after Jackie, CC and I came and we developed as we moved along. We were able to talk to other white students and they became friends in some instances.

Let me say to you that all things were not that easy, but I want to share one thing about one class that we had. In Agency, for instance, every student had a number for exams. You know my number was two hundred and twelve in Agency. This was my second year. And the professor, who incidentally was a Jewish professor, Stan Leavy, never called on CC and me. We were taking the class together and when the grades came out they posted them on the bulletin board downstairs. We still had our separate study group. So the white students in the class came down, a lot of them, and they were saying, "Whose number two hundred and twelve?" Well, that was my number and we were far enough in our study room that we could listen, but we didn't go out there though. I said to CC that Leavy has flunked me. I was just so, so upset thinking he had flunked me. Well, after the grades were in, then you could go upstairs and see what the numbers mean relating to the names. And so after a while this guy, whose name was Roy Bray, "George," he says, "congratulations you made the highest 'A' in the class." I could not believe it. Certainly, I went out there afterwards and it said 212-A. and in parentheses, was "highest in the class." And later Roy Bray came back and said, "George, I want you to know that some of us demanded that we see your paper." So they went in and read my paper. And then he said, "I want you to know, you wrote a damn good paper. A damn good paper." Now, I'm saying that to say there were types of things that did happen, and Leavy, however, of all the reasons, was not a professor there the next year. They released him.

So it was not all just what we were doing, you understand. There was a process of people. Even some of the faculty were getting some problems. Those who were doing what's right sometimes suffered from it. I don't know whether Leavy actually wanted to leave or not, but he wasn't there the next year. And I'll give you another example of the kinds of things that happened along those lines with faculty. In my Contracts class, after the exam was taken, we had the books that we had to submit. After the exam was taken, you know how people in Law School and other places are when they start talking about how your exam was. We were in a room, they were talking, and the professor was in there, too. His name was Joe Covington. He's deceased and eventually he came to be dean of the Law School at Missouri University. But anyway, he said, "Mr. Haley, I don't know how you could have done so well on an exam." He said, "Because you had such an excellent book," that we had to present to him. He kept talking and said, but he hadn't graded my paper yet [laughing]. Well, when he said that, he hadn't thought about it because he was my professor. What my number was, to get my name and number together, but that, of course, nobody said anything, but we recognized and realized that was the kind of thing that happened. Just those two kinds of experiences are there with all kinds of things happening at the university. I made a "C." I was glad to make a "C" [laughing].

Black graduate students started coming in during those years. One certainly in particular was Peter Faison. We came to be good friends. Peter, I believe, started out on the campus in the Quonset hut. Peter was the one I knew and recognized best. We are still very much in contact. He was at George Howard's funeral, as was CC, of course.

But basically you asked me about my feelings about the university now. I really am very supportive. And I've said this before. When it comes to the education and the training in the broad sense that I received, and I say that pretty much for the others I can speak, as well, I hope, the pioneers, it was an experience that broadened all of us as well as the people with whom we dealt. From the standpoint of the legal training that we got, I have never felt that it was inferior by any means. In fact, I've been able to use my legal training and felt as comfortable with Harvard or Stanford or whoever else because I have had to deal with them as well. The university has certainly given us good legal training and the broader scope of what life is all about, and developing more the brotherhood of man. This is what I look at. And I use in my own philosophy the words from the Bible: "When a man say he loved God and hated his brother, he is a liar. So how can he love God whom he has not seen and hated his brother whom he has seen?" And I say the fatherhood of God presupposes that all men and women are brothers and sisters. And that of course enables me, not only then but now, to try to make more brotherhood and sisterhood for all of us.

■ Christopher C. Mercer Jr. (1949–1954), attorney

Interview by Lonnie R. Williams, August 6, 2007
Office of Attorney Christopher C. Mercer Jr. in Little Rock, Arkansas
For detailed biography, see Appendix A, page 285

I entered the University of Arkansas in September of 1949 to obtain the degree, at that time, the LLB. It was a law degree that was a bachelor of law. But since that time, they give persons a JD, doctorate of jurisprudence.

Why did I select the University of Arkansas? I'm an Arkansan is the primary reason. I wanted to go to Law School and maybe you need to go back to the beginning to see why I selected the University of Arkansas.

I had grown up in a little town of Pine Bluff. I had gone to AM&N College there. I ended up at AM&N College in 1942 and I finished in 1946. At the time that I finished college, there was a buzz going around in the black community wanting to test the University of Arkansas for admittance of blacks into the various departments. I was footloose, fancy-free, and kind of offered myself up to the group, but it never got off the thinking pad. The emphasis was in the parties trying to do something about integrating. Everybody had been operating under the separate but equal doctrine. Everyone knew separate was not equal.

For black students to get advanced schooling, the state had a program of paying your tuition to go to school in other states. But it was always treacherous going out of state to go to school. First of all, it took a lot more effort to go out of state to school than it would to go to school in state. And many times when you went out of state to go to school, your allegiance was to where you matriculated rather than back here. So I wanted to go to the university because it was my home university and I thought I was entitled to be able to go up there.

The Law School program was a three-year program. It took me several years to finish my three years because of financial reasons. I entered the university in September of 1949. I actually completed all my work in 1954 and marched in January of 1955. They were having mid-year convocations at that particular time. I finished in the summer of 1954 too late for marching with the class of 1954 and marched with what was called the first class of 1955. If I had gone straight through, I would've been in the class of 1952 because I started in 1949. But I dropped out a couple times for financial reasons because I didn't have money to go to school. Most people don't know anything about that [laughing].

Well, I don't know whether I got a role or whether I ended up having a role in the history of African Americans at the university. The first black was admitted to the University of Arkansas at Fayetteville in February of 1948. That was Silas Hunt. The second black was admitted to the university in September of 1948. That was Jackie Shropshire. Also in that same year, Edith Irby [now Edith Irby Jones] was admitted to the med school here in Little Rock. You didn't have quite the contention in the atmosphere of integrating the university going to school here in Little Rock that you did have with the student going to the flagship university up at Fayetteville.

February 1948 was Silas Hunt, which was the second semester of the school year of 1947 through 1948. September 1948 was Jackie Shropshire. September 1949 was George Haley and myself. February 1950 was Wiley Branton. In September of 1950 was George Howard. These six persons have been dubbed the Six Pioneers. There's a room up at the Law School now called the Pioneers' Room. They first had a classroom called the Pioneers' Room. Then, when they did some expansion in the Law School, they built a specific room for that purpose. It can be used as kind of a conference room, but it also stands as an exhibit hall when it's not in use. So when you say what my role was, I guess my role was what they have dubbed as one of the Six Pioneers. Of the Six Pioneers, only two of us are still living. That's George Haley and me. Of course, Silas Hunt died in 1948. He didn't get a chance to matriculate long. Jackie Shropshire and Wiley Branton have been dead for maybe fifteen years. George Howard died here this year, in 2007. George Haley lives in Silver Springs, Maryland, the DC area. I've been here the whole time.

I guess you could talk about those experiences up there, but it would take a lifetime trying to recount everything that happened. The things that I guess stands out the most are some of the hardships I experienced in trying to matriculate at the university. I was, first of all, without funds. I didn't have any scholarships. I was trying to go on my own and that made it very difficult. The reception was hot and cold. There were some that were very, very extending in their attitude and in their outreach and there were some that were cynical and menacing. I never personally had any physical encounters, but sometimes ignoring a person and staring through them like they are not even there was more hurtful than if they would hit you in the head with a brick. That's the way I would say, 80 to 90 percent of the students acted. They just acted as if we were not even there. Didn't even see us! We had a small group that did react negatively, but they were not overt. They would do it in subtle ways. There was a small group, though, that was very extending, tried to sympathize with us, and make life a little better. I always identified a name of one person who was somewhat the epitome of that group and he's still at the university and that's Miller Williams. Miller Williams is a world-renowned poet, but when I first knew him he was a struggling student. He was in school working on his master's in zoology and it's almost ironic that his fame has come as a writer, as a poet. Even though he was majoring in zoology when we were in school, he published his first little book of poems.

Miller was the subject of a lot of ridicule. He was called "nigga lover" so many times, I don't guess you can count them all. He was unwavering in his allegiance and there was one professor that taught sociology, I believe. He really didn't have any relationship with us except that he was sympathetic to our plight. His name was Stephan Stephan. His first name and his last name were spelled and pronounced the same S-T-E-P-H-A-N, S-T-E-P-H-A-N. Dr. Stephan was very extending to us and was very comforting. Except for the reassurance and the outreach that persons like them extended to us, it would have been so unbearable. I don't know that we would've been able to take it.

When the university admitted us, they didn't admit us with open arms. It was a gradual process. Ironically, some sixty years later, I hear rumblings from some students saying that it is no better now. I can't believe that. I know it's a whole lot better with as many students as there are today. The black alumni association has about seven hundred to eight hundred members. Well, we went from one to two to three. Then you talk about the six pioneers and you can multiply that one hundred- or two hundred-fold. There has to be some good things.

The thing that is significant, more than anything else, is that I did receive a legal education and there were times when they tried to make it a little tough on me. They tried to flunk me out. The knowledge that I received, they can't take away. That was the attitude I took when I was up there. I received some scores that I didn't think were fair. I was put on probation and I told them, you can put whatever you want to down on that paper for a mark, but I know I got the information up here in my head and you can't take that away from me. Though you can take that score away from me.

The same thing happened to me on the bar. The first time I took the bar, I flunked it. Now that was in the summer of 1953. I took the bar again in March of 1954, at which time I was very dejected. I was not nearly as mentally prepared to take it as I was the first time. I had the attitude, well, if I don't pass it, I might as well be digging a ditch. Not that I had sour grapes, but I went in there the next time and in my heart I know I didn't do as well on the exam in 1954 as I did in 1953. I made the highest score! It's on record that I made the highest score on the exam in March of 1954, but I don't flaunt that around as much.

But I've had many a moments to reflect on my experience at the university. And I'm convinced that the quality of the instruction that I got there is comparable to what I could've gotten anywhere else. I've tried cases all over the country. I've met lawyers from the prestigious schools. I ain't worried about none of them. They don't bother me.

One thing that I've always had a thrill out of is seeing my name in Senior Walk [laughing]. I don't know of any other institution that does that. I've never heard of one. That's extremely unique.

In all fairness, when you go back to the question of why you go there, I'm by incident of birth, I was born in Arkansas. And if I'm going to improve anything, I would want to improve Arkansas. I'm not going to live in Arkansas and berate it and be pulling for Texas. I use Texas as an example. I ain't going to be pulling for Missouri or Kansas. And though Arkansas is not a utopia, it's not a perfect place. I've gone a lot of places that I think are much worse off than Arkansas.

Well, the accommodations in the classroom room. When they first admitted Silas, he had all of his classes separate. He was at the Law School, but the professor taught him one-on-one in the basement. He had none of his classes with the other students. And, of course, he only went one semester and part of a summer. He got sick that summer and died that August. Everybody think white people—or try to say—must've done something to him up there. "Ya'll better watch out!" is what they would say to us. But it's my firm conviction that he succumbed to something he caught in the battle of North Africa when he was in the service. I think it was something he caught over there that caused his early demise.

Jackie Shropshire, who was the second one, went in September of 1948 and in the first semester of 1948. He had his classes by himself, all of his classes. Then they moved him into the classroom, in one or two classes as an experiment to see how it would work. That is how it was done and that's where the infamous rail came into play. You may have heard about the rail, the infamous rail. They built a little rail about ten to twelve inches high. Just like if you take an iron pipe and you go to the wall and come out, maybe three feet to a point, put a pipe here and then go over here and put a pipe over here. Just something symbolic and then you put a chair right in there as if to say, symbolically, you were segregated in the classroom. Of course, ironically a picture of that got out, and of course pictures were being taken of blacks that were trying to integrate other southern schools at that time. The most classic one that I recall during that particular time was Ed McLauren, who was supposed to be integrating the University of Oklahoma. He was in education and they actually built a wall, a partition, put it in the corner. And for him to participate in the classroom, he had to look around the wall and there was a picture of his head looking around the wall [laughing]. There was no wall up here, but there was this symbolic thing.

And, of course, after all this adverse publicity, the thing that caused it to be taken down was the faculty itself. The person that led the faculty brigade was the most unlikely person you could think of. He had the most profound southern drawl that I've ever heard. His name was Wiley Davis, professor of law. Wiley Davis's southern drawl was so profound it dragged the ground. And they went in one evening to Dean Leflar, who was dean at the time. The center is named after him now, Leflar Law Center. They went in to him to say, you know, it was an insult to their integrity. What they were all talking about was for the symbolic rail to be up there. That if it wasn't down by the time classes started the next morning, all their resignations would be on his desk en masse the next morning. The entire faculty was threatening to resign. Dean Leflar supposedly said to them, "Gentleman, at this hour of the evening, who could I get to get that rail down by in the morning?" They left the ultimatum with him, "That's your problem." As history records itself, the rail was down by the next morning [laughing]. But

Jackie did not get moved into all of the classes. He was in one or two of the classes. The rest of his classes he had by himself in the basement for the whole year.

In September 1949, they called themselves, quote "integrating the classes in full." That was the year I was a freshman, George Haley and I. And we never had separate classes. We were in the classrooms with all the rest of the students and so was Jackie. There were three of us there by this time. Silas was there by himself, Jackie was there by himself for the whole year. Then the next year, George and I came. In actuality, George and I gravitated toward each other. Two little black freshmen there. We studied together. We walked together. When we got in class, we sat together. That was by choice, wasn't by force.

Now, they didn't have accommodations for us on the campus. When Silas was there, they made arrangements for him to stay with a black family out in the community. He stayed with Mrs. Joiner. Mr. and Mrs. Joiner. When Jackie came, he stayed with Mr. and Mrs. Joiner. When I came, I stayed with Mr. and Mrs. Joiner. But George, and I don't know how he found them, he stayed with the Funkhousers. Now, Funkhouser might sound like German, but they were black. And Carolyn, their daughter, is still up there in Fayetteville. [Ms. Carolyn Funkhouser Bradford is married to J. D. Bradford and is a retired employee of Standard Register Company.]

George Haley stayed with the Funkhousers our freshman year. Then the second year, I didn't go back school year 1950 through 1951, because I didn't have the money. But it is my understanding that they still stayed in private homes, the second year. The third year I came back they [university administrators] called themselves making room for us on the campus, but we didn't stay in one of the traditional dormitories. We stayed in what was dubbed Lloyd Hall. Lloyd Hall was a series of army barracks that that they had. There are dormitories over there now, but all of that area over there was where they had maybe about eight to ten of these army barracks. These army barracks were designed to house graduate students and foreign students.

I don't know what caused us to run George Howard for president of Lloyd Hall, but we did. I don't think they realized who he was. He won [laughing]. It wasn't just our one barrack that he was president. They called themselves an organized entity for the students who lived over there. He won the thing and that was what caused the Penix—spelled P-E-N-I-X—the Penix to write him congratulations. That was in, maybe, 1952.

During my time of my study, I felt like every other student. I'm assuming every other student thinks the work is too hard. No time to do anything. You are going under adverse circumstances. You don't have any money. I didn't have any real deep-seeded animosity toward the university. I guess it was best to let people hopefully interact and become acclimated to each other. But with the cold feeling I felt, cold shoulder everybody was giving you, I kept thinking I'll be glad when I get it over with and get out of here. One of those kinds of things, when you look back over it, I guess it was an awkward situation for everybody.

Many persons, well, not many, had ever experienced anything like this. Not knowing how anybody knew how to act, but thankfully, most people took it in stride. I don't know that every student up there was trying to extend a long arm of friendliness to every other student. Not people running in cliques anyway. I don't think we were treated necessarily any different than any other student. I don't know that I have any impressionable recollections one way or another. I know we were bent on staying there, trying to get a good education, and all of us were very conscious of the fact that if we flunked out we'd let everybody down. We didn't have the access to camaraderie and communication even with people right within the Law School. It was a small little circle.

Some people were treating us right, but we were having to fight to integrate the Law School, the Law School organizations, and the student bar. We were not members of the student bar. We didn't attend the beer busts and Gaebale. I remember when we had to vote for that purpose. We had a big meeting in the old student union about whether or not blacks would attend the beer bust or whether we would attend the banquet. Our attending the banquet was supposed to be, wasn't any qualms about it. But the dance was a different thing. There were girls there in evening gowns and dancing. Of course, we had to approach girls from out of town. I approached a girl from Fort Smith. She wasn't my real patooty, but she was a fox [laughing]. She was glad to come up there to be with me. Her name was June Scott. Dean Leflar opened up things about the second or third song. Old dean came over and asked me if he could dance with that girl. The fellow that got up and spoke against it the hardest—this was one of the reasons he was speaking against it—he said, "It ain't me, but my fiancée. If her daddy knew I was carrying her to a dance with blacks, he would disown her." As fate would have it at the time of the banquet, he was down sick in the infirmary on the campus and couldn't attend. His fiancée was there dancing and she had more fun than anybody [laughing].

I have returned up there many a time. I returned for the fortieth anniversary [of Silas Hunt enrolling] in 1988. I returned for the fiftieth anniversary in
1998. I've been up there for the dedication, ribbon dedication of the Six Pioneers Room, and made a little old dedicatory speech. I'm supposed to be going back in September [2007] for something they call themselves doing. It's something involving integration of the university. They are having a series of seminars and speeches.

I'm a died-in-the-wool, true and blue Razorhawg [laughing]. I live and die with all their aspirations. When the university is down, I'm down. When the university is up, I'm up. I think there ought to be more. Sometimes I think they are doing good. Sometimes I think they are doing bad. I was familiar with the exposé that Wendell Griffen had. I know about how mad a lot of folks were about how they treated you [Lonnie R. Williams]. I know about all that. I feel about them like I'm a member of the family. I feel that I'm qualified to compliment them and I'm qualified to criticize them. I don't think they are as good as they ought to be, but I don't think they are as bad as a whole lot of folks are claiming them to be. I think some people sincerely are concerned about the image and want to do right. The old adage that it takes a while to get things done and I think some people are working on it. I don't believe it's going to get worse, but it's going to get better. It's a matter of one step back, two steps back, and one step forward.

There's a whole lot of difference than it was originally. You've got not only lots more matriculation by students. When I was there, it was just basically on the graduate level. You've got all the undergraduate students there now. I've only had one of my nine children to matriculate there and she didn't go but one semester. She went school year 1966–1967.

But you have people on the faculty. I was up there when they installed Cynthia Nance as dean of the Law School. I know that isn't a permanent thing. They cycle that around, don't they? I think they cycle it around. I thought that was significant. I was up there for that dedication. I'm anticipatory when you ask me how I feel. I want it to do good. I'm disappointed when I see negative things about it. I want it to succeed in everything and that includes football and basketball [laughing]. I don't know if they are at the top of the list for me. But every time they lose, I suffer.

I think I've discussed all of it one way or another. Some of it may be repetitive. I'm very appreciative of the experience I had and I think maybe the adversity I endured, maybe, made me a better person, made me a stronger person. When you immunize someone against something, then they can repel it. In order to immunize you against that disease, they give you a small dose of it [laughing]. So the small dose of the various things they gave us at the university meant we were able to endure that. It makes you a stronger person. You're not susceptible to those things. If you can overcome one obstacle, you learn how to overcome obstacles and you learn how to roll with the punches in life. I'm happy with that. There may be others who had worse experiences or there may be others who had better experiences, but I just happened to be born at a time when we were initially doing it.

I'm happy that we overcame some of the obstacles and that things are still moving forward. I don't know that people of color find that we are conspicuous by virtue of our color. That means we stand out in talking about experiences. The same sort of opposition that I hear about students experiencing at the University of Arkansas now, the complaints that the students of color complain about, the students at Amherst in Massachusetts where my son is, same complaints. I dare say that if you are a person of color, that you won't experience some obstacles wherever you go. What I would encourage all people, who are in similar situations like I am, let's find a way to break up this mess and overcome it. It takes all of us to do it.

I'm hoping that somewhere down the line, my progeny, my grandchildren, great-grandchildren will find it within their province to go to the University of Arkansas. By that time, it will be a lot better. If not my direct progeny, then my heritage and other black students. Of course, things are a whole lot better up there now than they were initially. Not a utopia, but maybe never will be. You get people who say they want to do right and people don't look on them with favor if they don't do right. Even if they are doing wrong, they are not going to admit that they are doing wrong. It ain't popular. Not only is it not legal, it ain't popular. Even when it first became illegal, after *Brown v. Board of Education,* it was popular to resist. That is not popular any more. Nobody wants to be identified in that vein.

Chapter 2

Taking the Moderate Path

Desegregation in the 1950s

> I am fully aware of the tenseness and delicacies in this present climate and deeply believe that moderation is of tremendous present importance. I also believe that moderation as a concept is not enough—that the moral imperative is that we make much more rapid progress toward real equality of opportunity and status.
>
> —John T. Caldwell, 1956

John T. Caldwell, president of the University of Arkansas from 1952 to 1959, wrote the above comments to a friend, Ervin Canham, the editor of the *Christian Science Monitor,* in April 1956 after Canham solicited statements from Caldwell about his thoughts on desegregation.[1] In keeping with the university's policy toward public remarks on desegregation, Caldwell asked not to be quoted. Caldwell explained that any words attributed to him could be used "by malefactors to the disadvantage of the institution." However, Caldwell made clear his unequivocal, heartfelt support for desegregation. In a multi-page letter, Caldwell, a native of Yazoo City, Mississippi, declared desegregation a "moral imperative," and saw schools as important instruments "that reduce the disadvantages of inferior circumstances at home." Caldwell expressed no patience for white southerners who opposed desegregation nor for those who endorsed gradualism, the idea that blacks must give society more time before civil rights changes could be implemented. For Caldwell, opposition to desegregation simply served as continued attempts by whites to deny the personhood and citizenship of people of color. In Caldwell's view, southern whites needed to be admonished to do better and to move with "'deliberate speed'" toward the goal of "full realization of equality of opportunity for the Negro."[2]

Caldwell's comments revealed his personal feelings about the need for desegregation in schools and other public areas. Throughout his letter, Caldwell consistently advocated racial inclusion as a "legally and morally correct and practically sound course" that the nation should follow.[3] However, one should not interpret Caldwell's passion on the subject as an indication that he implemented sweeping changes at the university during his tenure. To the contrary, as president, Caldwell initiated few modifications to improve educational oppor-tunity or to enhance the social experiences of black students on the Fayetteville campus. Largely, Caldwell maintained the institution's slow, cautious, and responsive approach toward desegregation.

Throughout the 1950s, civil rights became an increasing part of the national conversation. The NAACP continued its assault on de jure segregation while other groups such as the Montgomery Improvement Association took the fight for equal opportunity for blacks to the streets. The university kept a close watch on national developments, especially those involving education. University officials seemed bent on anticipating potential legal problems and developing solutions that would upset the status quo as little as possible. Five months before the famous *Brown v. Board of Education of Topeka, Kansas* decision, the civil rights case in which the Supreme Court declared segregation in public schools unconstitutional, Caldwell presented a report to the board of trustees about the admission of black students to the newly formed School of Nursing. Caldwell considered it "inevitable" that the university would receive formal applications from black students for admission to the Nursing School within the next few months and wanted to get some direction from the board on the matter. Citing both the legal and social fallout that would accompany denying qualified black students access to the Nursing School, the report favored accepting qualified black nursing applicants. Although nursing students would technically be undergraduates (the university only accepted black graduates at the time), the course of study was specialized and exclusive to the University of Arkansas. Furthermore, the state of Arkansas faced a desperate shortage of black nurses. The report suggested that the failure to admit blacks might trigger events that would leave the university "in a vulnerable position—possibly in a court of law and undoubtedly before the bar of public opinion."[4]

Despite endorsing admitting blacks, the report argued that the acceptance of blacks to the Nursing School, particularly on the Fayetteville campus, had to be monitored and controlled. Black students would be carefully screened in order to ensure that their numbers fit within the capacity of the university to house them. Also, black students would be encouraged to take their first year of work at another accredited institution in order to complete a basic core and then transfer to the university.[5]

In March 1954, the board considered the report on black nursing students. However, instead of voting on the recommendations, board members decided to table further discussion until the Supreme Court had ruled on the *Brown* case. By delaying a decision, the board hoped "to be in better rapport with public opinion" in its future deliberations on the nursing issue.[6]

The *Brown* decision sent shockwaves throughout the South as the Supreme Court invalidated the power of states to deny black students access to state-supported white schools. Some schools immediately complied with the ruling. Others tried to ignore it, while still others created devices with the purpose of circumventing the decision. On March 12, 1956, ninety-six southern congressmen expressed their displeasure with *Brown* in an unprecedented fashion by issuing the "Southern Manifesto." In this statement, southern lawmakers declared *Brown* an "unwarranted exercise of power by the court," and voiced their determination to preserve segregation and the southern way of life.[7]

The University of Arkansas's immediate response to *Brown* was to do nothing. University officials seemed bent on allowing some of the uproar to pass before taking any steps in the spirit of the ruling. Furthermore, officials were unclear on what if any legal implications the decision had on university desegregation policy. It was not until January 25, 1955, that Caldwell revisited the question about blacks in the Nursing School with the board of trustees. Caldwell sent them a message marked "confidential," informing the board that the university had several applications from black students for admission and one from "a highly qualified young woman." He urged the board to quickly make a decision formally or to simply allow the university "to work through these [applicant] cases selectively and quietly." The board allowed the university to do the latter.[8]

It would not be until after the second *Brown* ruling that the university would take another important desegregation step. *Brown II* established the process by which segregation would be dismantled. Litigants would have to bring lawsuits against individual school districts in order to force desegregation. The Supreme Court ordered these actions to begin with "all deliberate speed."[9] In August 1955, Arkansas attorney general Tom Gentry, responding to a joint request by presidents of all state supported universities, issued a statement on the effects of the *Brown* rulings on the desegregation policies at public institutions of higher learning. Gentry opined that the *Brown* decision would apply if a lawsuit was made against a public university for the admission of a black undergraduate student.[10] Shortly after receiving Gentry's comments, university officials circulated an official procedure with regard to enrolling black undergraduates. Similar to the methods developed for screening black applicants to the School of Nursing, the university required potential black undergraduates to be interviewed by a university official "to determine the seriousness of the purpose" of the student and "to evaluate the applicants personal habits of cleanliness." Another reason for the interview was to apprise the students of the conditions of the university campus and "nature of the challenge" that lay ahead.[11]

The university now admitted black undergraduates, and university officials had a process that enabled them to control the number and type of student allowed into the institution. The university wanted to ensure that blacks accepted by the school understood the social rules and would comply. When potential black undergraduates raised questions that challenged the status quo, university officials sometimes discouraged them from attending. Such was the case of Joe Louis Flowers, a black graduate of Richard B. Harrison High School in Blytheville, Arkansas. In October 1955, Flowers sent a letter to President Caldwell expressing his interest to attend the university and inquiring about educational and social opportunities available to him. Not only did Flowers mention his interest in the study of medicine, law, and engineering, he also wanted to know if he would be able to play intercollegiate athletics and be allowed to enjoy student parties and dances.[12]

William J. Good, now the assistant to the president, responded to Flowers in Caldwell's absence. In a letter that would dampen the excitement of just about any student considering a college home, Good informed Flowers that it was very unlikely that he would be allowed to play on any of the school's athletics teams and that there would be few if any opportunities for him to attend dances and parties. Good explained that although the university had no official policy banning black athletes, many of the schools in the Southwest Conference refused to play integrated teams and that the university did not believe that the time was right to "press that issue." With regard to student social outings, Good warned Flowers against "crashing" parties. Good made plain that the university did not force student groups to accept all students at their sponsored parties and dances. Good asserted that the admission of students to such social events was a "privilege, not a right conferred upon them by the mere fact that they are students at the university."[13]

Good directly suggested to Flowers that because of his desire for "social leadership and social prestige" he would be better served seeking admission to "Arkansas AM&N College, or some other accredited institution for Negroes" for the three years and then applying for admission to the University of Arkansas. Good did not promise him that the social setting at the university would be different by then but intimated that Flowers might mature enough to make those things less important. In concluding his letter, Good advised Flowers to contact Oscar Fendler, a Blytheville attorney and chairman of the county alumni committee, to get more information on the university.[14]

The effect of the university's more rigid admission policy for blacks resulted quite naturally in few blacks enrolling on the Fayetteville campus. A study conducted by the university in the fall of 1956 revealed sixteen students, with only eight of them being undergraduates. Many more black students made it to the campus during the summers to fulfill graduate residency requirements. During the two summer terms of 1956, the university estimated that over one hundred and fifty black students studied on the Fayetteville campus.[15]

The dearth of black students attending the Fayetteville campus during the regular terms also meant that little would be done to enhance diversity on the main campus. Over the course of the decade, student groups and the university's central administration sponsored only a few events that involved African American speakers or entertainers.[16] This combination of small numbers and limited social opportunities forced black students to endure an isolation that greatly affected their perception of the university. In this section, we hear from some of these students and gain a better understanding of how they managed the university's policies and campus environment.

■ Waldo Bronson (1958–1960), educator

Telephone interview by Lonnie R. Williams, September 4, 2007
For detailed biography, see Appendix A, page 286

My name is Waldo Bronson and I entered the University of Arkansas in Fayetteville in September of 1958. I went in as an electrical engineering major. In my senior year in high school, I applied to several colleges and universities including the University of Arkansas. I don't even know why I applied there. I knew they had a good electrical engineering school. In June, I got a letter from them saying I had been admitted to the University of Arkansas. I had my room assignments and everything. I just couldn't believe it for one thing, but it was true. And then in July of 1958, I got a registered letter from the university saying that the governor had decided they would no longer have integrated housing and my parents and I needed to come up there. They would help me find housing in the community. We drove up there and searched in the community where we found a place for me to stay since I couldn't stay in the dorm, governor's orders.

I was at the university for two years. When I was at the university as an eighteen-year-old, I wasn't even looking at being the first or anything like that. I was there trying to get a degree. I didn't realize I was the first of anything. I do know that my roommate, Dave Lawson, I'd like to believe he may have been the first African American in the engineering department. Quite possibly, I was the second. I don't have any statistics on that. One of the things I do know was when I was registering as a freshman, they asked me if I played an instrument and I said I played drums in high school. This guy in the ROTC said, "Would you like to play drums?" I think I was the first [black] musician at the University of Arkansas. I played drums in the ROTC band and I have pictures of that in the yearbooks and all that kind of stuff.

David [Lawson] was like a junior. He was a couple of, three years ahead of me? David . . . I don't know how long he'd been up there and all I do know was my freshman year was his last year there. He left after that and I never heard from him again. I think somebody told me he enrolled in Purdue and pursued a degree there. I can't substantiate that in any way. This young man that I mentioned earlier, Marian Greene, from St. Louis, I think that's the Marian Greene that was David Lawson's cousin.

At the university, it was interesting. I never ran into outright hostility where I was afraid, physically afraid. Students there formed study groups, stayed up all night, spoke and didn't go out of their way to do anything more than that. I remember one white guy who was in a class with me. He had me come over to the married housing once a week to study for one of the math classes we were taking. His wife would make cookies. That was all new because I had never been around any white people before. I don't know. I'm trying to think. I remember Lance Alsworth was on the football team. He was a star and I do remember him. Every time he would see you on campus, he would always speak to you, which was something most of the other people wouldn't do. Most of them would duck their head or turn their head the other way. I remember him. He always spoke to me.

I have the utmost respect for the university for having the whatever it took to even go through with integration in 1948. Even when they admitted me, I thought they were waaaay ahead of their time. None of the other universities in the south had even given a thought to that, but the University of Arkansas did it in 1948 and was doing it quite successfully until the governor came along and said some things had to stop. So I have the utmost respect for the University of Arkansas. I always felt the university was light years ahead of the general population of Arkansas.

I left the university in June of 1960, and in 1996 my son and I stayed in a timeshare in Eureka Springs, about sixty miles from Fayetteville. And so one of the days we were there, I told him we were going to Fayetteville. I wanted him to see the University of Arkansas where I told him I had gone to school. We drove to Fayetteville and I showed him where my house used to be. Showed him the campus and so forth, but that was the only time I had ever been back to the university. I still have the greatest respect for the University of Arkansas.

My roommate, Dave Lawson, had a 1949 Ford, light blue. We would drive it to and from campus to our housing. I don't remember walking to school, but maybe once or twice. I pretty much drove Dave's old car to class. I did walk one morning. Somehow, Bill [Morgan]—and whomever—gave me the grief for having dust on my shiny shoes. I said I walked three miles to get here, but that didn't make any difference [laughing]. You got to remember I was eighteen years old, no bills, no anything. Just a kid.

I don't know what George [Mays] told you, but [laughing] I think there were nineteen blacks when we were there and maybe five thousand or so whites. I know the numbers aren't correct, but we used to joke that "when I get through beating up my three hundred, I'll help you with yours" [laughing]! I don't know if George told you about that.

But you know, everybody remembers something particular to them. I remember one night it was snowing and George and I were headed back home. But we passed the frat houses right in front of Old Main. The white boys were having snowball fights. The non-Greeks were fighting with the frat boys. It was dark. They couldn't tell who we were and so we were in the group with the non-Greeks. We were throwing snowballs like crazy. I said, "George, we better get out of here before they realize who we are."

I don't know if this is going to come up, but academics. There was nothing in place to help me academically. I had a counselor, but maybe I should've gone to him more. But back then, you didn't go to the counselors. You just didn't go. He was pretty nice, but they didn't go out of their way to help you or anything like that. I still remember some of them and remember their names. I don't remember any outright hostility or prejudice.

Two years. Why did I stay just two years? Very simple. I was in electrical engineering. The first year I got my grade point I went to summer school and hung out with a guy from Little Rock who was getting his master's. I wasn't studying. I messed up those two classes and then came September. I moved into a house with George Mays and this guy Marian. I just didn't take my work seriously, so I ended up flunking out. That's basically what it was. But that engineering school, it was too tough. I wasn't the only one. Half the white boys had to go home.

What happened? The good thing about mine was my first year. The president of the University of Arkansas at Pine Bluff, Dr. Davis, and his son lived right next door to us and Dr. Davis was working on his PhD. His son was working on his master's. When I flunked out, I went back to Little Rock, stayed out a semester and then I went to Pine Bluff. I talked to Dr. Davis and he said, "Hey, you can come down here. It's the best place for you." I went to the University of Arkansas, Pine Bluff. It was AM&N then and Dr. Davis Jr. was the physics teacher. He told me, "Look, I've got some smart guys in here and they are waiting on you to get here because they want to test you to see how good you are." I didn't know it, but he told those guys he had a guy coming from the University of Arkansas and he was sharp. The first test we had in physics, I made an eighty-seven and the next score was fifty. I think they knew then who I was [laughing].

Another piece from the University of Arkansas, I learned what studying was about—how to set goals and stuff like that, even though I didn't follow through when I was up there for all kinds of reasons. People tell me now, "Well, it was because you were black. You had all these pressures on you and all that kind of stuff." Well, those were excuses. I say if I had put my nose to the grindstone like I should have, maybe I would've gone much further. I'm not regretting what happened. I went to the University of Arkansas in Pine Bluff. I found a whole new social life, which we didn't have at the University of Arkansas in Fayetteville. I found a major, made good grades, and graduated with a degree in math. I had a successful career in the educational system, principal of one of the high schools here in Flint, and don't even look back at it.

I'm not bitter about anything. One of the things instilled in me as a kid was, even though you failed, you didn't give up on life. One of the funny things about it, I was a little disgusted when I was told I couldn't come back. I had a job that summer. George Mays and I worked at the Cadillac Company. I was washing cars. When school started, my mother said, "What are you going to do? Are you going back to school?" I said, "No, I'm going to stay here and work for the Cadillac Company." In November, I raised the door on that carwash rack and that cold air hit me. I think it was that same week I went down to Pine Bluff to talk to the president about getting back into school. From there, I stayed two years and graduated.

The University of Arkansas gave me a good foundation. The University of Arkansas at Pine Bluff gave me a good foundation with a social life and a place to study. I have no hard feelings about the University of Arkansas. In fact, I'm proud to have attended there. I was interviewed about four years ago because it was the anniversary of the *Brown versus the Board of Education* and someone told them I was from Little Rock. The newspaper came to talk to me, took pictures, and I showed them my yearbook from the University of Arkansas. The photographer opened it to my picture in the yearbook and put that on the front page of the newspaper along with a [more recent] picture of me, of course. I get a lot of questions. You went to the University of Arkansas? That kind of started that ball rolling.

I retired in 2000. I taught three years in Little Rock, came here and taught here three and half years, and was promoted to administration in 1969. I have been in administration for most of my career.

Glad to have had you call me and talk about this! That was a good part of my life. I met a lot of people and enjoyed that experience. I'm sure it's a much different place now. A guy named E. Lynn Harris from Little Rock—I don't know if you read about him or knew him—he talked about his experience at the University of Arkansas and all I could think about, Lord have mercy. How different they are now than when I was there!! He was the editor of the *Razorback?* We were doing good just to get a picture in the *Razorback*.

■ Melvin Eugene Dowell (1959–1963)

Interview by Charles Robinson and Lonnie R. Williams, July 7, 2007
Interviewed in the St. James United Methodist Church basement, Fayetteville, Arkansas
No detailed biography available

I am Melvin Eugene Dowell. I entered the university in 1959 after graduation from Fayetteville High School. I was a business administration major with a specialty in insurance and real estate. I was the first person born and raised in Fayetteville to attend the University of Arkansas, Fayetteville.

I selected the university because of finances. We're talking about 1959. During that time, I did have a white benefactor, a local businessman, by the name of Hugh Scarborough. He paid my tuition and any other incidentals that I required. My involvement with the Scarboroughs was because he used to be a member of this church. I used to clean up for the Scarboroughs and he had an accounting office down on Block, straight down from the square. I used to walk to school by Scarborough's office.

I was at the university for a little longer than four years. I became an academician [laughing]. I did finish, which God blessed, put my mom's mind to rest. I know the Whitfields were here at that time and you may have heard about Sherman's. [Sherman's was a small black-owned tavern in the black community located where the Yvonne Richardson Center now stands.] Bob [Whitfield] and Bill [Whitfield] lived next door to Sherman's. I'm sure they can attest to this. Those were some troubling times.

Racism abounded. This was my encounter with racism on the campus. These two white boys always had some snide remarks to make. There were Greek houses as you come across at Dickson. These two white guys always had snide remarks to make under their breath.

I would describe my present feeling toward the university as disdain. That's personal. I can remember this one instructor and he had a strong southern accent. Ainsworth was his name. I don't know what his last name was. I was taking a class from him. I don't care what it was that I took. I took it personally and I'm sure he didn't. To him, I was just a black spot, a nonexistent black spot. I subsequently took that same course from . . . I think it was a marketing course . . . from . . . what was his name? E. J. Ball. The same course that I had taken from Ainsworth could never get even a "D" from him. I re-took the course from Dr. Ball, you know this was several years later, and I was just about to drop out of school had it not been for the financial assistance that I received from Mr. Scarborough. At any rate, I did not drop out of school. I can't put my finger on it, but my walls seemed to have turned around. Yes, in fact, I got an "A–" or something like that under Ball.

Describe my present feelings toward the university? After graduation, I did manage to get my name inscribed on the walk. At the time, it was in front of Old Main. Aside from the few instances of out and out racism, I did manage to graduate and get my name inscribed on the walk in front of Old Main.

Do I think much of the U of A and that experience today? I try not to.

George Mays . . . and I'm sure the Whitfields remember . . . I think George had transferred from AM&N. There were some graduate students. I don't recall all their names. Of course, the dorms were not even integrated at the time. Bob and Bill lived in a house next to Sherman's. Their older brother, George, was instrumental in breaking down the segregation of the movies here. He was very articulate and did not back down from anybody.

There was no integration at all in athletics. The coach at that time, Frank Broyles, said there wouldn't be, if he had anything to do with it. I don't have anything else to add. That's basically what I have to say.

■ Peter G. Faison (1951–1952), county agricultural agent

Interview by Lonnie R. Williams, September 27, 2007
Interviewed in the home of Peter G. Faison
For detailed biography, see Appendix A, page 286

My name is Peter G. Faison and I enrolled in the University of Arkansas's Graduate School in the fall of 1951 with a major in agricultural economics. The name of the course of study for that time was rural economics and sociology.

Two of my professors at Arkansas AM&N College, now UAPB, encouraged me to go to the University of Arkansas and help pave the way for others to follow. That reason, and the fact that I wanted to find a place for graduate study within the state, is why I chose the University of Arkansas, Fayetteville.

Five other black students were on the Fayetteville campus while I attended the school term of 1951–1952 plus the summer session of 1952; they were Wiley Branton, Christopher C. Mercer, George Haley, and George Howard Jr., all in the university's Law School, and Harvey Daniels in the Graduate School studying agricultural education.

No particular role was played by me in the history of African Americans at the University of Arkansas. I simply was trying to obtain a quality education without leaving the state of Arkansas. However, I was credited by the Black Alumni Association of assisting in the integration of the UA Graduate School. Also, I participated in the annual Aggies versus Engineers "Tug of War." We, the Aggies, won the match by pulling the Engineers through the flood of water. I was very glad to be on the winning team and remained dry.

The experiences I had while on the UA, Fayetteville, campus often referred to as upon "the Hill," were varied. Some of the white students were polite, friendly, and many were not friendly at all. One white couple, who were students there, invited us to their table at meal time or one would come and join our table. There were times when a white student would call the blacks "niggers," but this was done behind our backs. Water was thrown out of upstairs windows at times and there was the time that a bottle of ink was thrown out of a dormitory window that broke just behind my heel. Some of the ink did splatter on my trouser leg. A few rocks were thrown in our direction; however, we were not really in danger of being injured.

Five blacks—Christopher C. Mercer, George Haley, George Howard Jr., Harvey Daniels, and I—were living in Lloyd Hall "F." This was the only one of the six converted army barracks that was integrated while I was there. Wiley Branton built a house in the predominantly black neighborhood which was a few blocks down behind the county courthouse. Going to school and living on the Fayetteville campus did not always leave me with a comfortable feeling. We went ahead with our everyday task, business as usual.

With a few exceptions, I felt okay about attending the University of Arkansas in the early fifties. There were two teachers whom I thought used whatever grade I made to establish the curve for class. In one class, farm finance, I had a "B" average on our weekly quiz. When the final exam was given, I made the score of eighty-three. I got a "C" for the course because a "B" grade was eighty-five to ninety-four. On one occasion, I knew that I would make an "A" for the course; however, when the grades were passed out, I got a "B." My previous quiz scores were always in the mid-nineties and my final grade was ninety-two. To get an "A," the score had to be ninety-five to one hundred. All of this took place during the time when teacher tests were being passed around in a closed circle, which helped to set the curve high. Unfortunately, I did not belong to that circle.

Yes, I did return to the University of Arkansas, Fayetteville, campus on many occasions after I left in the summer of 1952. After I was employed as an extension specialist—Farm Records and Tax Management with the University of Arkansas Cooperative Extension Service —I made numerous trips to Fayetteville each year. While I was working out of the state extension office in Little Rock, I coordinated ten Farm Income Tax Schools over the state of Arkansas and one of those schools was conducted at the Hilton Hotel in Fayetteville. During the period of April 18, 1978, until August 29, 1990, I made an annual trip to the UA, Fayetteville, campus to attend an economic conference. The fiftieth anniversary of the Black Alumni Association was held in Fayetteville in April of 1998 and I was invited to attend. An award was presented to me at that meeting for assisting in the integration of the University of Arkansas Graduate School.

The conditions have changed considerably in recent years in contrast to what it was in the fifties. [Enrollment exceeded 1,000 black students in 2009; see Appendix B.] There are more than one hundred black students attending the University of Arkansas and living on the Fayetteville campus. I know that it is a great school and that an excellent education can be received while attending there. I would perhaps be an all "A" student if I had the opportunity to attend classes there now. While attending classes at the University of Arizona in 1978, I took six hours of credits and made all "A's." The black students on the University of Arkansas, Fayetteville, campus are living in integrated dormitories on the undergraduate level. Some of the black students are making lasting friendships with white students on campus.

Before I left the University of Arkansas in 1952, I was told that I needed to take six additional hours of credits and maintain an "A" average to obtain a master's degree in agricultural economics. In the summer of 1954, I did go back to take those hours; however, my advisor assigned me one more class that the professor had given me a "C" in the first time I was there. I was further assigned to a visiting professor from the University of Georgia. After that, I returned home and decided that a master's was not all that important anymore.

In the summer of 1961, I decided to change my major to school supervision and administration so that I could get a better-paying job. The school that I chose was Tennessee A&I State University, now the University of Tennessee-Nashville. The school in Tennessee was actually my second choice because I thought that by changing my major, I could return to the University of Arkansas and pursue the master's in supervision and administration. The reply that I received back was that I could no longer obtain a master's in any field at the University of Arkansas. My grades at the Tennessee A&I State University were mostly "A's" with a small number of "B's."

One of my daughters attended the University of Arkansas, Fayetteville, for one year on scholarship. This was the school term 1972–1973. After a year upon "the Hill," she was allowed to transfer her scholarship to the University of Arkansas, Little Rock. She completed her degree in music with a minor in drama at UALR and was able to live at home while doing so. Our daughter is now teaching elementary education in Alexandria, Virginia, after changing her major and receiving a master's degree from the University of Maryland.

The experiences that I gained while attending the University of Arkansas have benefited me in charting a path in my life's work. However, I would not like having to do it all over again.

■ George Mays (1958–1961), real estate

Telephone interview by Lonnie R. Williams, August 27, 2007
For detailed biography, see Appendix A, page 287

I'm George Mays. I entered the University of Arkansas in 1958 to obtain a BSBA. I graduated from the university in 1961. I made great friends while in Fayetteville, but at the same time was glad to get away when I received my degree. I remember Dr. Payton, professor of industrial psychology at the time, told me the best black student was no better than the average white student. My time in Fayetteville helped me understand people at a young age, at a difficult time, and my dealing with change. During the time I was there, Governor Faubus required the faculty to sign loyalty agreements.

My grandmother, Bessie Mays, had gone to the University of Arkansas under the graduate program. She passed while I was in high school. I just felt that I owed it to her to attend there because she wanted me to go to the University of Arkansas. And first of all, I didn't know whether I could go to the university [laughing]. I went to AM&N my first year on a football scholarship. I got a call from a guy named Jack Mitchell, who was then a coach at the University of Arkansas, and he suggested I try out for the football team. Well, I did and I made a commitment. I wrote to the university and they accepted my transcript to go into the business school. Dean Milam, who was then the administrator/director of the business administration area, made me bring my father up there before he would let me in because I was the first black to enter the University of Arkansas business school. And he made me bring my father up there so that he could tell my father he wasn't going to be responsible for me if something happened [laughing] to me while I was up there. I decided to go really as a result of the fact that my grandmother talked about it, and at that point in time, I thought it would be a unique education for me, if I got in. I wasn't planning on staying in the state so it would be one that nobody would believe.

My grandmother received her master's there in the early 1950s. My grandmother was a teacher. She went there for a summer program for teachers. They let black teachers use that program.

I guess they fired Jack Mitchell. While I was in the process of signing up, Jack Mitchell got fired and Frank Broyles came in as coach of the football team. I didn't have a chance to play football. That invitation to play definitely wasn't extended. It really wasn't extended to anybody until the Southwest Conference started playing black players. He told me specifically when I talked to him about that [laughing]. He told me that was his first year and he wasn't going to rock the boat. He basically told me, "I ain't about to play you. You can come out and run around with the team, but I ain't about to play you. I'm not going to do that." He also told me since I had played with AM&N, I had to sit out two years. Which I could've corrected, but there was no point in correcting.

I think the University of Arkansas at that point in time was as good as or better than the University of Mississippi. You had silent opposition at the University of Arkansas, both in the professorial area and some of the student body. The student body was cordial, except when it snowed and you were walking. They would target you for ice balls [laughing]. They were good at that. I can remember two basic incidences at the University of Arkansas. They had one professor up there named Payton and I was doing very well in his class for half a semester. Then we had this talk. He indicated to me that the best black student was only as good as the average white. I took exception to that and went to Dean Milam. Dean Milam said that was his opinion. At that point in time under the way he was grading, I had an "A." He changed his grading to an essay-type concept. That meant that he was the man that made the rules. That was the golden rule, so he gave me a "C."

I remember my speech teacher because she said I had a real southern accent, meaning that I talked funny, and I could never give good speeches. That's because she had a real southern twang. But most of the good teachers that I had were there my first year. Even in my first year, the University of Arkansas had assigned us a dorm until Faubus came up. I guess I started there in 1957 because I started there the year that Central was integrated. Faubus came up and basically apologized for the fact that we were there and they lost our rooms in the dorm. So we had to stay in the city. And as you know, Fayetteville, as a city, integrated the high school, junior high schools, and the elementary schools a lot earlier than many in the state.

We never did live in the residence hall. Holcombe Hall was the residence for men at that time. They were dealing with putting us in Holcombe Hall, but for some reason that just slipped by the wayside. They didn't have any rooms in Holcombe Hall.

I played intramurals sports up there. My time at the university really wasn't extremely bad. I made some good friends. Although I ran into some degrees of prejudice, I just figured it like my father had told me—white people are going to be white people. So when they acted like white people, I just ignored them and did what I had to do [laughing]. That sort of carried me through.

I had this friend, Bobby Morgan, a cook at the Ag house, the agricultural house. And not only did I get good food, but the Ag guys were very good. I didn't get any prejudice from what I thought were the real rednecks of the campus. They were great people. All in all, I'd say that my relationships were fairly good. I just had to hitchhike to come home. I didn't have a car. My father didn't let me take my car until my second year. I would just hitchhike. I would just go out on the highway, stick my thumb out, and hitchhike back to North Little Rock. I remember hitchhiking one time. I was with a fairly young group of guys, three of them. I was sitting in the back seat and this guy says, "You know, I have never been this close to a nigger before." And I told him, "Look, I don't particularly like that word." He said, "What do you want to be called?" I said, "I'd like to be called either George or black." And he said, "OK, I'll call you George because you ain't black." We had a lot of those.

I had a job working at a club that's no longer there. I only worked for this club for a year. That was an interesting experience. I was a big guy, so I didn't have that much trouble. The only real trouble I ever really had was in the weight room. A guy wanted the weights, so I gave them to him. I mean I just handed it to him. It slid down his chest and hit the floor. They treated me fairly in that incident because I told them he called me a nigger and I thought I had a right to retaliate. Dean Stillwater obviously agreed with me—not the business school, but the whole school. All in all, there were some facilities I couldn't use, but nothing I couldn't do at the University of Arkansas. As long as I wasn't expecting a rose garden, which I wasn't, everything was all right. I think black kids there now have a harder time than I did because they are expecting something that I never did expect.

I've returned to see some people—Bill Morgan before he died. I have a friend, Edith, who was in nursing when I was in school. I haven't really participated with the University of Arkansas a lot because even though I could do anything, there were a lot of things that I couldn't join and could not participate. I didn't really get close to the University of Arkansas from a social standpoint. My social life was either at the Wesley House or the Garland House where the ladies stayed. All the black ladies stayed on campus at a place called the Garland House. They were either graduate students that were there full-time or undergraduates there in nursing.

I think presently the University of Arkansas is a fairly good institution. It has gotten a reputation as a partying school, which I wouldn't know anything about. One of the things I remember is there used to be a singing team called Shirley and Lee. They brought them up there to sing. Waldo [Brunson] and I were sitting out there on the step. Everybody came up and thought we were Shirley and Lee. Obviously, I made him Shirley and I became Lee. We signed autographs [laughing]. But when they had a real black blues guy there to visit, they wanted us to take him out. The only place we could take him was to the "hole." The black community was in the hole! But all in all, I don't feel any difference from the University of Arkansas.

I feel better about the University of Arkansas than I felt about UCLA. I went to UCLA when I was working. I used to go there at night and I feel about the same. I didn't have a chance to participate in UCLA's social activities because I was either working during the daytime or going to school at night. UCLA was so big I had to get a bicycle to get to school. Now, I enjoy the football team and I enjoy the basketball team. I think they were really unfair to Nolan Richardson. I knew Broyles, and I know Broyles from a long time ago, so I know what Broyles really thinks and so does Darrell Brown. I wanted my son to go to the University of Arkansas, so obviously I don't dislike the University of Arkansas. He chose to go to UCA.

I go up there now because I enjoy that part of the country. I enjoy the wintertime. I enjoyed going up the back side of the hill, racing, when I had my car. Trying to avoid the sheriff of Ozark and trying to get through Conway without getting a ticket. So there were several things about the University of Arkansas that I remember and remember very well. I guess I just don't want to carry around the bad things about the university, but I can't forget what Payton said. That has inspired me for a very long time. It was a really good statement to carry with you and Payton left that year for the University of Mississippi.

One of my classmates at that time was Lance Alsworth. I got Gene Dowell to come to the business school because I didn't want to be the only black in the business school. Gene Dowell was born in Fayetteville. I used to talk to him and tell him to come on to the university. He did. He came to the university and I think he was the second black in the University of Arkansas business school. Andriana, Barbara, I forget Barbara's last name. Marion Greene, who was in pharmacy school up there, and he graduated. Waldo Brunson. Lawrence Davis Sr. Lawrence Davis Jr. There weren't that many of us. I'm forgetting Ms. Wilson, who I used to ride with when I didn't have a car, and a girl from Fort Smith. There weren't but about twelve to thirteen of us total.

My biggest experience with the University of Arkansas was riding up there with my father [laughing]. My father had to take off work to take me up there to meet with Dean Milam and while on the way up there, my father was telling me how stupid I was for wanting to go up to the school with all these white people. I was going to get killed. They were going to hang me because there were all these white girls up there. After I lived through my first year, I don't think he thought I was going to get hung any more. Every time I said something, he was telling me how those white people messed up my thinking.

At the University of Arkansas from an overall standpoint, I thought I had some good instructors. I can remember at least four of them that didn't leave, but most of my real good instructors left the first year. That was when they had to sign the loyalty agreement. Those that wouldn't sign the loyalty agreement left. Those that did sign the loyalty agreement were the older guys that needed the job. I had two of those as instructors. I remember they kept apologizing to me for signing that agreement. I remember that very well.

Dell said it was a good thing I was there. Dell was an older guy that taught retail management. He used to say black people need to start their own community business base, go into retail, and have their own operations. He kept pushing me. I told him that my father had a restaurant business and I was going into it. It was retail operations. He finally stopped and just dealt with me on markdowns, markups, and stuff like that. I think all in all, it was a good experience for me at that point of time in my life. It really prepared me for the life that I was going to have to deal with after I left the University of Arkansas. I didn't plan to deal with that life here, but I did deal with it in California. It worked out because the only thing people knew about Arkansas at the time was the Beverly Hillbillies or Central High School. I had to show my transcript [laughing]. I had to show I went to the University of Arkansas. I had to write back for a transcript to show that I had graduated. I had to start carrying my degree because they didn't believe it was easy to get a degree. I had to carry my stuff.

I didn't make a lot of problems for myself. One of the experiences I had was at a place called George's. It was right next to the movies. They didn't let black people in. What we did was put a turban on our head, put a black dot in the middle, and went in. We had beer and pickled eggs. Acting like we couldn't speak English, those white people just looked at us, [laughing] talked to us, and we drank a lot of beer.

Just as long as you weren't a black American, you were welcome. We could've been Japanese, but we couldn't pull off the Japanese [laughing]. We looked like we were from India. We made sure we had the dot. We probably had a bigger dot than we needed.

The city itself was a good city for blacks because there weren't that many of them up there. The blacks that were there excelled in high school sports such as football and basketball. They just couldn't go to the University of Arkansas. We participated in the community, the black community. All in all, I got nothing really negative to say about the University of Arkansas. "Best of times, worst of times."

■ Gordon D. Morgan (1955–1956, 1969 to present), university professor

Interview by Charles Robinson, Summer 2008
Office of Dr. Gordon Morgan at University of Arkansas, Fayetteville, campus
For detailed biography, see Appendix A, page 287

I began seeking a master's degree in sociology in the spring of 1955. The *Brown* decision was in 1954 and a semester or so after that decision the university started admitting black undergraduate students. There must have been one or two such undergraduate students admitted in the fall of 1954, but most of them came in the fall of 1955.

When I completed AM&N College (now UAPB), the John Rust Foundation was developing a mechanical cotton picker. They saw that it was going to displace many people in eastern Arkansas in the cotton-growing territory. They offered me a scholarship to study rural sociology at the University of Arkansas. They knew there would be a problem with the changing labor force in the region. The Korean War was underway and I did not take the scholarship, but went to serve in that war. Upon leaving Korea, I enrolled in the University of Arkansas mainly because it was more economically feasible for me. The Rust scholarship was not held for me.

I was aware of the university's integration. The school had been integrated and there were a handful of African Americans on the campus. I knew most of them personally, including some of the ones at the medical school. The others I knew from different connections at AM&N College. I started at the university in the spring of 1955 and by the summer of 1956 I had completed my master's degree.

As a student, how would I describe my experience? About the only thing I remember was being in classes with some later very noted people; most of them were football stars like Pat Summerall and Billy Ray Smith.

One of the mistakes I made was when the chair of the Department of Sociology asked me to be a teaching assistant, which I turned down. That was a mistake because I could have gotten a little extra money to go along with my GI Bill. I didn't take it because I was a little bit afraid that I could not measure up to the responsibility of teaching and grading "whites." I had no real understanding of the role of a teaching assistant.

I didn't have any trouble with anyone. Nobody ever said anything negative or did anything out of the ordinary. By this time, a very small number of African American students were living in what they called the "Hutch," an old army barracks. Foreign students and veterans mostly lived there. We all got along well. I didn't have any trouble with anybody on campus nor did I have any problems with faculty members.

We didn't consider our social life to be that negative. As I said, there ended up being about five graduate students and about three undergraduate students, three girls. So we had kind of a social life among ourselves. When we weren't studying, we could go to the dances making sure that we danced amongst ourselves. There were several other activities. Some of the guys were in plays and you could participate in anything practically that you qualified for.

Dr. Martin Luther King Jr. was killed in 1968 and by the beginning of the next school year they had kind of worried me about coming here. I joined the faculty as an associate professor in the fall of 1969. I guess they could have found somebody else. Since the chairman of the department had been one of my professors, he knew me very well and thought I could be a person that could fill the bill.

Did I feel respected by black and white students alike? I might have had a little more trouble with some of the black students because they expected me to be on the frontlines and defending them in any kind of activities in which they were involved. One Afro student leader, in the early days that I was here, called me into the office set aside for student leaders. Before his group, he demanded to know why I was not doing more. Why I had nerve enough to give a black student a low grade or something like that. We had that kind of problem. As far as the white students were concerned, they never went to any dean on me and if they did, it never got back to me. I understand there were some people out in the state that did not think it was a good idea to have an African American professor. They were always writing the president [David W. Mullins] demanding I be fired. I'm sure it happened under some other presidents, but according to people who worked for Mullins, whenever those notices came, they were thrown into the wastebasket. I was granted tenure after one year. I didn't learn of having been granted tenure until about ten years afterwards. There was just too much to do to be worried about something like that. A few other midwestern schools were asking for me to join their faculties. I was promoted to full professor in 1974.

Did I have any interaction with Black Americans for Democracy? Yes I did. Plenty. I advised them and helped get their newspaper together. I had lots of activities with them. When I came, there were no other black faculty members. There was a young man in the area of student relations. We came together. They called him an assistant dean. There was only one instructor, Dr. Margaret Clark, in foreign languages. A black faculty member or two were added each year thereafter, though the number remained small for years. It was not easy to get activities for black students. I started writing plays and I would have them enact these on the campus, on the stage. One of the persons involved later became a judge, Wendell Griffen. I encouraged other students to write their own plays, including Patricia Young, our first black Miss University of Arkansas. She was quite active on campus and later became a lawyer after working a few years for Jesse Jackson in Washington.

I think most of the students felt pretty good about the campus and were not having any real problems, other than academic. When they decided to establish their separate societies, part of this was based upon tradition. For instance, we brought the Greeks on campus in 1974. The reason for that was not so much because we were rejected by the Anglos societies, but we had that kind of tradition in our own families for these were a part of the separate schools most of us attended. We had traditions we did not wish to see deemphasized.

We did have a couple of guys who would really challenge the system. It seems mostly when African Americans challenged the system they got more points than when they did not. For instance, R. D. Rucker was a very favorite challenger. Everybody loved Rucker. If the campus sponsored an outstanding speaker, Rucker would rise up, stop the speaker in the middle of his speech and clarify some statement the speaker had made. He would often take twenty-one hours and said he was not being challenged. He would go in classes, even though he didn't major in some field, let's say chemistry, for example. He would audit the chemistry class and straighten that professor out. He was very well read. He eventually got a PhD at the University of Iowa, interning in Russia for a degree in that field. He finished with a law degree at the University of Texas. He died about three or four years ago.

The main thing that I have a little misgiving about the University of Arkansas is I don't feel that they really challenged me. I was never really smart in classes. I think there may have been some racism going on then because people were a little bit unsure about whether we should have black people living up to their dreams and potential. Thus they seldom pushed, encouraged, or stretched us to our limits. The best example is that I wrote a paper in sociology on which I made a "B–". By the way, if I had gotten one more "C," I would not have gotten out with my degree. That paper that I got a "B–" on when I got to Washington State University about three or four years later, I used for a kind of preparation for publishing. I had to do something because a student in the department so washed my face with a publication he had done in the *Journal of Marriage and Family*. I thought we might fight. Washington State encouraged students to publish. I dug out that paper—published it in one of the very respected journals. The first offering in the journal was the president, a man who was just going out as president of Harvard. I was number two. That paper made the *Journal of Crime and Delinquency*.

I wanted to be a criminologist at that time, but was being rejected. I barely passed at the University of Arkansas. I had interned in parole and probation at the Federal Correctional Institution, Englewood, Colorado, in the summer of 1955. I think I was among the very first to participate in that internship program.

Success at Washington State was kind of eye opening to me. Why was I no good at the U of A and was, quote, "some good" at other places? As a faculty member, the question still bothers me. I did try to do my best. I was asked to be a Visiting Distinguished Professor at Washington State University around 1992. When I came back to the university, I thought I had enough papers and books to go up for university professor, but I got knocked down. This must have been around 1993. I forgot about it and did not apply again. I got university professor several years ago.

Black studies program? There were several of us, including Nudie Williams, involved in black studies. In fact, it was going on before you, Dr. Robinson, came. We had "black studies." Adolph Reed started it. Students demanded different kinds of courses. They were demanding to have a black studies focus. People in the sociology department supported it. Dr. Elaine McNeil was a big supporter of the program. It has had a history that goes back several years.

■ Helen Maxine Sutton Cannon (1955–1958), clinical nurse

Telephone interview by Lonnie R. Williams, September 12, 2007
For detailed biography, see Appendix A, page 287

My first name is Helen, middle name is Maxine. I'm known by Maxine Sutton, my maiden name. Cannon is my married name.

During my early years, I regularly attended Mt. Zion Baptist Church. It was because of my religious background that I became interested in becoming a missionary. Rather than choose the far-reaching mission of teaching the masses, I decided to focus on family and community. It was during my mother's hospitalization at Baptist Hospital that I became interested in the nursing phase of her treatment. I entered the University of Arkansas bachelor's degree nursing program in the fall of 1955. My goal was to become a registered nurse after graduating from high school and completing two years at Arkansas AM&N College in Pine Bluff, Arkansas. While attending AM&N College, I wrote to the University of Arkansas at Fayetteville twice seeking information and never received an answer. A complaint was made by the Urban League and NAACP. Still no response was received.

I later discovered the University of Arkansas had been requesting information and test results about me from faculty at AM&N. I eventually received an application packet. There were sick people, a nursing shortage, and one couldn't even attend school to be a registered nurse in one's own state. There was no logical explanation. I chose the University of Arkansas. I spent one year at the University of Arkansas at Fayetteville and two years at the University of Arkansas Medical Center in Little Rock.

As far as I know, Billie Rose, Marjorie, and I were the first three blacks to enroll at the undergraduate level at the University of Arkansas. Blacks at the graduate level enrolled earlier [mostly medical and law students].

My experiences varied; there were some nice people and some who weren't. We had to be flexible. That's all I can say. We were unable to live in the dorms. I was first to arrive on campus after being driven through the beautiful Ozark Mountains. I didn't know of Billie Rose and Marjorie's interest in entering the program. I had applied for campus housing. Holcombe Hall was the only dormitory on the assigned street. On arrival, I presumed I would reside there. After surveying the unoccupied rooms, I chose a nice corner one on the second floor. I waited several hours before being told that the place for me to live was next door. I took a quick glance and stated "that is not a dormitory, it's a house." It was called Garland House Apartments. Of course, I was real disappointed because I couldn't live in the dorms. Marjorie and Billie Rose came later and lived at the same place.

Curious about laundry facilities, we were told that we could wash our clothes in the dorm, but couldn't when the others washed theirs. Because they resided there, they would get first choice. We laundered our clothes and linens in the bathtub and hung them to dry. We couldn't live or eat in the dorm. Most of the time, we prepared our own meals. We would occasionally eat some place (I can't remember where) but couldn't really afford expensive foods. There was a store next door with a deli counter; delis were expensive, too. We had a full schedule and did not have time to prepare lengthy meals. We often prepared meals at night for reheating at a later time.

So "what was it like being three young ladies up there on our own?" It was so different than attending a black college. When I went to AM&N, I was part of campus life. I felt I could participate in anything if I wanted. I could place a flower on a homecoming float or even be a participant. I felt loved and thrived on it. At the University of Arkansas, life was totally different. I just felt like a speck on a page, very insignificant. I shutter to think of our fate when in the middle of the night an angry mob attempted to break down our solid-core kitchen door with a heavy object. Screaming and very frightened, one of the girls enlisted the help of our off-campus friends. Standing in the middle of the living room, I envisioned being protected by the full armor of GOD. Two of the friends who came to our aid were Mr. E. K. Blakely and Dr. Gordon D. Morgan, who later coauthored a book, *The Edge of Campus*.

The classrooms weren't bad. My sociology teacher was super. I was very familiar with that subject because I had taken social sciences at AM&N and knew some of the subject matter. The instructor was from Austria, I think. He tutored us at his home. I was quite a class participant. One of the students predicted that someday racial barriers would be a thing of the past. I was too choked up by his comment to say "thank you."

We had not exchanged conversation during our bacteriology class. Billie Rose was very pretty and fine featured. We decided to play a trick on the students to get them to talk to us. "Billie, where are you from," we asked. "England," she replied. Heads turned and some of the students said, "Really, is she?" We laughed and answered, "England, Arkansas." She, of course, was from Little Rock, but we wanted to break the ice and show the students that we didn't like being ignored. Thereafter, we had no problems conversing. The nursing classes were okay. We got along well with our nursing classmates.

The three of us joined the band and were told by the band director we couldn't march in parades or participate in activities out of town. We weren't issued band suits, which precluded us from participating in campus concerts. I really wanted to because of my previous band experiences in high school and at AM&N College. It was obvious that the director wasn't pleased with our presence. We only practiced with the group. Some of the students were real nice, and others were indifferent. The guy who sat next to me was really friendly. The guy who played first chair was a French horn major, blonde guy. During practice, he'd give me those awful go-to-hell looks. He never said a word, just glared. I couldn't excuse his behavior—too bad, really too bad. I was told the interim director was substituting for the director who was on sabbatical leave. We received a letter from someone in the department asking us to return. We decided to concentrate on our nursing courses and declined.

I stayed in the Garland House one year and attended one summer session. Black teachers would also attend summer school to work on their master's. We were allowed to live in Cornell Hall. It was necessary to attend summer school because I lacked some requirements. I could have made better choices at AM&N had I been issued a catalog from the University of Arkansas. I met some classy people during that time. Daily, I was awakened to the sound of opera, sung by an attractive photographer's wife. She had such a beautiful voice and I enjoyed listening to her warm up. Living at Cornell Hall reminded me of an earlier visit to another place on campus, a sorority house where one of my friends (or friends) resided. It was such a beautiful place with red, plush carpeting. We had group study prior to attending a particular class. My initial attempt to visit was unsuccessful because the matron, sitting at her desk, informed me that I "couldn't go up there" [second floor]. I called Sara and informed her of the same. She kept a watchful eye and had me return when the coast was clear. Although my next attempt was successful, I did not enter those doors again.

In describing my feelings toward the university, I felt that I received a good education. The university provided each student with their own equipment. At AM&N, we had to share equipment with each other. This experience enabled me to work in a multiracial environment.

I visited the campus when I attended the Living Legacy Awards in 1998. I saw more black students and hope they are participating in campus life. I noticed that blacks were now living in the dorms. WOW, I'm glad I lived long enough to see this!

Entertainment? We just found entertainment. We proudly learned the alma mater during our orientation week and to "call the Hogs." Across the street from the Garland House was a tennis court. We waited our turn until the white students finished their game. I developed a love for tennis because of those experiences.

Marjorie, "the baby," was the youngest of the three. Some students would ask, "What do you do for entertainment?" We attended a place on Saturday nights called the "hole in the wall." It was really a lady's house [Ms. Naomi Smith Parker, grandmother to Danny Carr, Sarah Carr Thrower, Leona Carr, Glenda Carr, Carlos Carr Jr., and Sandra Carr Taylor]. The basement was converted to an entertainment area for some of the local young people. We saved our nickels to play our favorite songs in the jukebox. Marjorie decided that we were to tell others that we went to Club Holé [jokingly pronounced Ho-lay]. It sounded a little classier than "the hole in the wall" [laughing]. I learned to dance the jitterbug there. We also enjoyed playing the stereo while harmonizing our songs. We attended some of the campus affairs, dances, basketball games, et cetera. We threw our football tickets on the ground after comparing seat assignments and discovering that we had to sit in the end zone. I sometimes visited the students at Holcombe Hall to wet set some of the girls' hair. Three to five days weekly, we attended vesper services at various denominational gatherings. We also took a bus trip to a Methodist retreat and joined in the singing of folk songs. We worshiped in the black community and were sometimes invited to delicious dinners at the homes of some of the parishioners.

Sleeping soundly, I was awakened from a nap one afternoon by the smell of smoke from an unwatched, overheated pot. A student from another building alerted us after seeing the smoke. The fire was quickly extinguished by Marjorie and Billie, who hosed down the place. I don't recall having a fire extinguisher. We were not provided with any type of emergency contact information.

I've had some interesting experiences in Little Rock. The director of nurses had warned me that I would have no social life; I didn't ask her to clarify that statement, but I presume she referred to interracial dating. I assured her that my only goal was to become a nurse. A pharmacy student sometimes escorted me home, walking a few steps behind. We talked very little, but he seemed to be quite a gentleman. I panicked when he found my phone number and called my home. Remembering the dean's strict warning, I exclaimed, "I will be kicked out of school—not you!! They will allow you to finish, not me." I later dated a handsome, black medical student—problem solved.

Lisa, an honor student, recalled the class walking out of a restaurant when I was refused service because I was black. Later, we did our pediatric rotation at an office across the street from the state capitol building. We were easily identified because we wore our beautiful student uniforms. At the lunch break, we discussed the possibility of eating where the former group had. I was hesitant and suggested lunch at Whit's Café that served all races, but separated them by partition. My classmate said, "No, we can't do that. You're as good as we are; you can eat where we eat." I responded, "There is the part of life you have never seen; I'm going to show you what life is really like. I'm going to eat with you, but there will be problems."

The employees behind the steam table were black and served us without hesitation. There had been some dignitaries from Africa in Little Rock who had recently visited and were treated with royalty. I thought, if I didn't speak, they wouldn't know my identity. When making my selection—roast beef, gravy and potatoes, et cetera—I just pointed instead of speaking. Sitting at the end of the counter was the cashier, who was white. When she tabulated my bill, I shrugged my shoulders as if I didn't understand her, and then opened my hand from where she removed the correct amount of money. Immediately after we were seated, a waitress informed Nora that the manager wanted to speak to her. At that moment I asked, "What does he want?" She responded, "He wants to talk to her [Nora] right now.", I told her, "No, he's not going to talk to her right now. We bought this food and we're going to eat it because we paid for it." "He wants to talk to her now," she insisted. And I repeated my objection. "I'm going with her because I want to hear what he's going to say." After a speedy lunch, we were ushered to a room where a young man appeared who asked, "What are you?" I asked him, "What do you mean, what am I?" "You know what I am," I said. He laughed nervously. "They were going to riot out there." "The only reason they didn't riot is because I told them you were Puerto Rican—they were OK with that." I decided I would not to return.

I was advised to live at home since I was from Little Rock. Although I lived at home, I frequently visited the nursing students living quarters at the medical center. There was no evidence of discrimination by the students. They were a fun-loving group who like to sing on the elevators and sunbathe on the roof. Someone reported this activity. I am sure the medical students who lived above were sorry. I attended some of the medical school dances; interesting how sociable some of the students were when under the influence of alcohol there seemed to be no racial barriers on the dance floor.

On graduation day one instructor had broken all the rules and insisted that I had not completed my last project. When, in cap and gown, and in the long procession line, I was quietly reminded that it had not been submitted. This was incorrect. I retyped a paper in triplicate until 4:00 A.M. After retyping it, I advised her that I had slid it under her office door. Tired and sleep deprived, I accepted my diploma proudly because of my parents presence, but I really didn't care if I graduated or not. It was the applause of the audience that snapped me out of my state of bewilderment.

My public health instructor, who I believe was from Michigan, had encouraged me to leave the South. Beaming, she exclaimed, "You didn't break down. You never cried, you never cried." It was my faith in God almighty that kept me strong. I also remember the words of Reverend Jesse Jackson—"Don't let 'em break your spirit."

■ Sanford Tollette III (1951–1954), educator and minister

Interview by Lonnie R. Williams, September 27, 2007
Interviewed in the home of the Reverend Sanford Tollette III
For detailed biography, see Appendix A, page 288

I entered the University of Arkansas in 1950 or 1949. I did not go to the campus in 1949, but I took courses from the University of Arkansas in 1949 in Pine Bluff, extension courses. I went on the campus in 1951.

I was there as a graduate student for a master of science in education. However, they changed it before I graduated and it became a master of education. I had no particular reason for selecting the University of Arkansas. It was convenient and I was sort of in a hurry. I had four years in the service. I call it losing four years. I am eighty-two going on eighty-three.

I attended for about three summers, only during the summers. No, I wasn't a first. Really, my attendance was a minor role. I went to get a degree or two.

My mother's first visit to the university was around 1920 or 1921 with her father who was a teacher for the black school there. She visited the campus and her father said to her, "One day, you'll be coming to this school." That was in the 1920s, early 1920s. She finally got her master's in 1956.

My experience was mixed. There were some good, some bad. I don't remember names very well. I do remember a Dr. Bent. Dr. Bent was very liberal. Rosenberg was my major professor, but actually my advisor, unofficially was Dr. Bent. He really gave me a lot of guidance.

I do not remember the people's names, but I stayed down behind the courthouse in "the can." That's what they called it. There weren't any black neighborhoods except for "the can."

We are used to working through disadvantages (walking back and forth from where I lived to campus). The only bitterness that I had was I had one course where the professor did not call my name. He did not recognize my hand when it was raised. I approached him about allowing me to answer questions. He said to me, "You will pass the test negra because negras have good memory." I think that is what they called us. I guess like animals.

The dormitories were not really open. They had special dormitories for blacks. I didn't try to stay on campus. I wasn't welcome.

You might want to interview Peter Faison. He was one of the first, very first African Americans up there. There were several of us there for several summers.

Socialize? Well, had I been an undergraduate, it would have been necessary. As a graduate student, we were a bit more mature. But we did. We socialized with each other on a social aspect.

I am reluctant to say what I want to say. The truth is I was just there. I wasn't excited about being there. I went there for a degree, period. It was just easier to go there than it was to go out of state because they had just opened up. They used to give blacks out-of-state scholarship money to go somewhere else to do graduate work. They had just opened up after my frat brother, [Silas] Hunt, went there. Hunt and Shropshire. One or two others I think might have been ahead of me.

Silas Hunt. We went to undergraduate together at UAPB. He was an Alpha.

You know Alphas, "First of all. We transcend all." There was no fraternity on campus, no black fraternity. He was a member of a black fraternity, but he was an Alpha from Pine Bluff. Gamma Delta Chapter. He graduated ahead of me.

What kind of man was Silas? Likeable person. He was pretty smart academically. Sometimes you don't know really what's in people until later. I had no idea that he was going to the university until he went. We communicated very little. He didn't get back often and he was stressed out from my understanding. You might have been told the story that he was taught one-on-one in the basement. I understand after awhile several white students went down there and took advantage of it.

I have returned to the campus. I've been to two homecomings. I visited the university several times when my sons were there. I walked the walk, saw my name and my mother's name. That was a dream of her father's in the early 1920s. I remember even then after I was born, as early as the early 1930s as my grandfather used to put us on his knee. He'd say, "This boy is going to be a doctor. This boy's going to be a teacher. That boy's going to take care of Pa-pa when he gets old." That was his dream for his grandchildren.

My brother was really, technically, the second graduate of the University of Arkansas Medical School. We got some history of our own up here this week at Central High School. We lived history, got involved. Edith Jones. Edith Irby Jones entered, but she got married, had a baby, and took leave. My brother, Truman Tollette, and Dr. Jackson, M. A. Jackson, were in school behind her. Actually, Jackson went across the stage technically before Edith. Edith came back and graduated. But she was the first to matriculate. That is the true history. I guess he'd be the third black graduate, technically. He was the third to enroll, but they both really marched before Edith marched.

Sometimes I don't have as positive a feeling as I should have about the university. I saw the university as almost an alien country for blacks. I grew accustomed to small colleges that cared about students. I got the feeling the university was just a machine. If you made it—you made it. If you didn't, all right, you go on. It was not warm, if you want to ask that. I had the feeling we were tolerated, barely tolerated. Even the professors were hostile. Hostile!

One more thing I'd like to say. I had some hostile professors, but I had some that were liberal for an easier term, so it wasn't all bad. Every crisis, help is somewhere. So being a minister, I still have faith. There is always help. There is somebody there now willing to help students more than there are systems. We can be just so systematized that we forget the human element. That's what really happens to large universities, they get to be institutions. I'm not being critical because you got to have large institutions. You were up there a long time, what do you think [laughing]? You were up there long enough for it to come apart.

The only thing is, I am really happy to see the changes that have come. You had no black professors when I was there. Now you have black professors and black staff members. I'm glad to see the change. That gives me hope. I would like us to be more a part of it, aside from just athletics. I see athletics wag the dog instead of the dog wagging the tail. What's the name of the president? How many people know that? They know the coaches. They know Frank Broyles. You ask a guy on the street if they know the president. Ask ten people. They don't know.

You didn't ask me that, though. I think many athletes have been used. Use their talents and sometimes they don't get a fair break afterwards because actually it is a whole lot of money. Those folks make millions of dollars a year and the athletes can't even take a gift. To me, something is wrong with that. Of course, I'm a minister. I don't think like other folks, but I'm glad to see the changes that have come about. You were there almost thirty years? I want to congratulate you.

■ George L. Wesley (1954–1955), university professor

Self-recorded interview, October 29, 2007
For detailed biography, see Appendix A, page 288

This is George Wesley and before getting started I want to commend Dr. Williams and Dr. Robinson for taking on this project. It is a significant reflection of where we were, where we were going, and where we are as far as the University of Arkansas is concerned. I entered the

University of Arkansas in September 1954. I was in pursuit of a master of arts degree in speech and theater. Of course, the University of Arkansas was at that time the obvious graduate effort because it was the state university and most of us didn't have funds to go beyond the state or really it was difficult to go just within the state.

At the time I entered, there were six or seven of us [blacks] in the graduate programs. I completed my degree in the summer of 1955 and the degree was conferred December of 1955.

My role there was varied. John Marshall Robinson Stevenson was there at the time and we were the first black theater majors. I had a role in, I think, two plays. I did Caesar and Cleopatra early on and by God, I can't remember what the other one was. Certainly it was a minor role because I was first of all not known as a great actor and then, of course, the limitations of roles and casting in the productions. I did the technical aspect of theater because my emphasis was technical theater. In terms of building the sets, working with crews, and that sort of thing, I was very active in that. I was active in the efforts in broadcasting. Now there was not a significant broadcasting program, but it had always been an interest of mine as an undergraduate.

By today's standards, the equipment was not a live broadcast facility. But it was beneficial because I later went to the University of Michigan and it had its own really commercial facilities. I was not out of place. I would say the training was significant.

There were other things. I think we did a thing in the spring called "Gaebale." I believe that is what it was called. I worked on a crew with that. John Marshall and I were inducted into the National Collegiate Players, which was unique because at that time there were not many blacks who were members of the National Collegiate Players. We felt that pretty much an honor.

There were interesting moments on campus. We didn't really find real segregation or discrimination as such. Not many racial instances. I do recall there were a couple of minor ones and these I can look at as just typical collegiate bs, you know. I can remember we were in the little amphitheater attachment to the theater and it was below one of the dormitories. We were out there going through the paces for some production and somebody said, "Hey, boy! Get your hands off that white woman!" We didn't get excited about that. It didn't really rattle anybody.

Most of us, well, all of us lived over in what was called at that time Lloyd Hall F, which is over the hill by where the Law School stands. That was housing for graduate men. There weren't that many of us in there. It was an integrated situation. Those of us who were black did live in that area. But we had to go across to Holcombe Hall's dining hall. I remember we would usually go as a group because they opened at a certain time and we'd take off across campus to eat. One day we were walking into the dining hall and some of the football players were in there. I remember specifically, somebody said, "Well, I see a dark cloud descending upon us." Naturally, we kept on; there were never really any major conflicts while we were there. I guess we can appreciate that.

We felt comfortable, especially in theater, which is a much more liberal discipline. We would walk across campus together. I remember one night, I became aware of myself as one of the young ladies in the drama department lived in one of the sorority houses just before you get to Lloyd Hall. We were just walking along. We were talking about the show we were getting ready for and that sort of thing. All of a sudden, I thought, maybe it was eleven o'clock at night walking down a dark street with this young white female. I thought it was looking like it was a date. We walked on up to the intersection and there was a traffic light. I became very aware of people stopping at the light and looking over in our direction. Nothing was ever said, nothing was done. We weren't trying to do anything different or anything like that. But it was one of those things. It was a breaking of a new dawn in terms of relationships. There was no relationship between us. This young lady and I were leaving about the same time and we knew each other, of course. Nothing really happened.

One other thing I forgot about that happened at one of the football games. At games, there was no discriminatory seating or anything like that. We would go wherever our assigned tickets were. I think at the time you had an activity fee and you'd just go where that ticket led you. On this particular Saturday, my seat put me in the midst of the card section. That's okay, that's cool. I've had that experience before. So you know what card to put up when and that sort of thing. On the signal, you'd put that particular card up. I remember one of my cards slipped down under the grandstand. I often wondered what that hole looked like when they held up that card, probably a dark hole.

Later, during the time of outbreaks of different politics and different political student voices, we got a little involved in that. That sort of gave us a feeling of you can get some things done if you group together. In the student union, there was a barbershop. We decided to protest that the black students couldn't use the barbershop. I remember we went all the way up to the chancellor and finally they declared that the barbershop had to be opened to all students. Later on, we decided, "Man I'm not letting any white folks mess up my hair." I don't know if any of us got our hair cut there. We would go down to the village and get haircuts.

Overall, my feeling about the university was good. It was what you might consider normal. Certainly we had been preceded by Hunt and Branton, people who had gone on ahead of us, primarily in Law School. I think the university was ready for the interracial student body per se. There were also teachers, black teachers around the state, who would attend during the summer working on graduate degrees. So they were ready for us that came up there as full-time students. There were no great problems, really felt like regular students. We got involved as much as we could in terms of the time we had.

I have been back several times. I guess my earliest return was maybe when I was teaching at the Arkansas AM&N. At the time, I was coach of the debate team. We went up to the university to a debate, which was interesting. Another time, my family and I were in the general area and decided let's go on up to the campus to find my name in the sidewalk. That was always a very unique concept. I looked, looked some more, and finally over in an area where they were doing some building. I looked down and my name was not there until I removed the soil. I could show my daughter my name on the sidewalk. A couple of other times I went up. I attended the black student reunion program a few years ago [1998]. I think that's a great idea you guys have come up with and I hope it continues to grow.

My feelings toward the university today have not really changed. I haven't been as active as the university would like me to do based on the request for funds and that sort of thing. I'm a proud Razorback and every now and then, I'll see somebody, realize they are a Razorback, put forth my recognition, and let them know I'm a graduate of the University of Arkansas.

I guess that's about it. It was a great experience because you expand your awareness of different people, people from different places who carry into, especially in our graduate situation, great experiences that we had. You find yourself trying to catch up and at the same time, look like you are right in step. We did get the degree. The experience that had been afforded through all students in their undergraduate schools or through their summer workshop experiences, and that sort of thing, certainly got them off to a running start as far as fulfilling the promise. But we didn't think of it in terms of making history. We were thinking in terms of try-ing to get those hours so we could get out of there and finally make some money, to pay back loans or whatever.

Overall, it was a very good experience. I'm proud of the progress that the university has made. Having on several occasions had black student leadership, people like yourself [Lonnie Williams] who have gone through there and kept the pride and proven the worth of black aca-demicians. And certainly my old buddy who is up there, Gordon Morgan, who is a stellar pro-fessor that everybody recognizes and appreciates at the University of Arkansas. I'm proud of you guys and I look forward to the final product of this effort. Thanks a lot.

■ Billie Rose Whitfield Jacobs (1955–1956), educator

Written response to interview questions, September 14, 2007
For detailed biography, see Appendix A, page 289

I attended the University of Arkansas, school year 1955–1956, to pursue a BS degree in nursing. I selected the University of Arkansas because: (1) the university offered a program leading to a BS degree in nursing; (2) the university opened its doors to black undergraduate students for the first time in 1955; and (3) the cost of tuition and fees were factors. In order to attain a BS degree in nursing at that time, my choices were to either attend the University of Arkansas or travel to another state. I am the second child in a six-sibling family. My oldest brother was already enrolled at AM&N College in Pine Bluff, Arkansas. My parents expected all six of us to get a college education. Therefore, it would have been a financial burden, if not impossible, for them to pay college tuition and travel for their children, plus out-of-state fees, had I enrolled in a college or university in another state.

I attended the university for one year, 1955–1956. In 1955, along with two other young women, I was one of the first black students admitted as undergraduate students at the University of Arkansas, Fayetteville.

My experience at the university was a disappointing one. I had been excited about going away to college and becoming a nurse. Whereas, the other two young women and I were allowed to enroll in the university, I learned very quickly that that was the extent of our priv-ileges. We were not permitted to live in the dormitories and take advantage of the amenities offered to our fellow Caucasian students. We were housed in a small frame building on the edge of campus next to the beautiful red-brick Holcombe Hall. At that time, it was freshman women's dormitory. We were responsible for our own safety, our own meals, and found it nec-essary to travel off campus to do our washing, purchase food items, and take care of other needs. These things were available on campus to the young women living in the dormitories. Our mode of transportation was to walk to a bus stop where we rode public transportation to different parts of the city to get the supplies we needed. I was eighteen years of age when I enrolled in the university. It was my first time away from home and this unsupervised experi-ence caused me to be anxious and, at times, fearful for my safety.

I don't recall outward resistance to our enrollment and attendance; however, we very strongly felt the university's lack of concern for our well-being and interest in our education. One example I will cite was that the three of us played musical instruments (flute, French horn, and trombone). We auditioned for the band and fulfilled the requirements. We attended rehearsals, and I played well, alongside my fellow flutists. Early in the fall semester, we were called aside by the director and were told that we could only play with the band while at the university, but would be unable to travel and perform at events held off campus. The decision, he said, was made on behalf of our safety. Because we were consistent in attendance and performed well, it was difficult to accept that reasoning. We felt discouraged. We gradually stopped attending band rehearsals. At no time did either the band director, members of the staff, or fellow students question our decision to drop out. No one ever invited us to return to band classes. That nonchalant attitude suggested that we were not important, that it was probably a relief for the director that we were no longer of concern to him, and that no one really cared or valued our skills and participation. It was as if we had never existed. That lack of concern may have been more devastating than had we been openly harassed.

I had been an honor student in high school and had attended junior college two years, 1953–1955. I graduated with honors from both high school and junior college. During my first two years of college, I took courses to prepare for a science-related career, specifically nursing. Two of the courses (chemistry and biology) were not offered at my junior college, so it was necessary for me to leave campus and take those courses at Philander Smith College. My grades were good at Philander Smith College, as well. At the university, though, my achievement level did not measure up to that of my prior educational experiences. The courses at the university were not too difficult. I had the ability to master them. But, the overall negative atmosphere and the feelings of omission were distracting and contributed to my lack of interest in doing my best.

I don't recall having any positive experiences at the University of Arkansas. It was a year of disappointment, struggle, and feelings of rejection. At the end of that year, I was ready to leave. My parents gave me permission to do so and I promised them that I would continue to pursue my education until they and I were satisfied. I fulfilled my promise to them and met my own higher education expectations. I was married after leaving the University of Arkansas. When I resumed my college education, I changed my major and attended Harris Teachers College in St. Louis, Missouri, where I received a BA degree. I went on to acquire an MA degree from Washington University and received an advanced degree from the University of Missouri.

In general, during my time of study at the university, I felt as though the university did only what was legally necessary regarding allowing black undergraduates to enroll. Neither prior to nor during my attendance, do I recall the university recruiting or making available brochures or providing information at our high school or junior college. We initiated our own enrollment at the university. Although the three of us attended the same high school, where two of us graduated in the same class, we were unaware of the others' enrollment until we arrived at the little house on the edge of campus. There were thousands of capable black students across the state of Arkansas whom I believe would have been eager to have had the opportunity to attend the university. But, the university had not reached out to us or to them. That was clearly obvious based on the fact that only three of us were enrolled that year.

Yes, I have returned to the university several times since my departure, but it took forty-two years and a very, very special invitation, and occasion for me to do so. In 1998, Dr. Lonnie Ray Williams, assistant vice chancellor for Student Affairs, and the university's Black Alumni Society (BAS) invited me to participate in the fourth Black Alumni Reunion. This was a celebration of the fiftieth anniversary of the enrollment of Silas Hunt (1948). Alumni, including the first three black undergraduate students and some of the first black graduate students, were involved in a "whirlwind" of exciting, memorable, and enjoyable activities. We were considered "early pioneers" by the BAS, which was quite an honor for someone like me who had attended the university for just one year. I had done so not with the intention of integrating the undergraduate school, but solely for the purpose of getting a nursing degree. During the reunion there were seminars, lectures, press conferences, symposia, a picnic, informal chats with students and staff, and an awards banquet, to name a few. We were honored by the BAS and by the School of Nursing. Everything was well planned and ran smoothly. I gained a totally different glimpse of the university in 1998 than I had in 1955–1956. The reunion was a joyful occasion and the number of black students and black alumni on the campus that week was phenomenal. In 1955–1956, I never dreamed that the university would embrace black students and employ black staff in responsible high-level positions.

My husband, Ernest Jacobs, joined me for this very fine event. We were so impressed with the positive changes at the university that we joined the BAS and made a contribution to the Alumni Association. We returned to the university to participate in the next BAS reunion where we were again warmly received. We continued to contribute to the Alumni Association. We were so enthusiastic because we believed, at last, the university was making an effort to embrace diversity among students and staff. In addition to participating in the BAS reunions, when Dr. Williams received his doctorate, we traveled back to Fayetteville to surprise him. On that occasion, we had opportunities to become reacquainted with persons we had met in 1998, and chat with other staff, students, and alumni. We felt very welcome and proud to be part of history being made.

We have continued our communication and developed a friendship with Dr. Williams and his lovely wife, Mary. He kept us informed about events at the university through his ongoing correspondence via U.S. mail, e-mail, phone calls, and our occasional visits. He also kept us up-to-date on special events held at the university and the progress that was being made. He was proud to share the university's growth, and we were very pleased to get the information. As contributors to the Alumni Association, we also received the university's alumni magazine, *Arkansas,* a viable publication featuring a wide variety of staff, students, and activities. As we read the articles, we were pleased with how the university had changed for the better, and planned to continue our contributions and to visit the university when special activities were held.

My feelings toward the university at this point are like those I believed the university held for me when I was a student there—indifference. The university did not treat me in an overt, harsh manner in which I was openly harassed. Instead, my existence was literally ignored and there was no attempt to meet my needs. It was as if the university, by denying my existence, did not have to acknowledge that it was "integrated." From the time I left in 1956 (and for the next forty-two years), I had not thought too often about the university. Then in 1998, I had the opportunity to see the university in a more positive light. It seemed to nurture black students and there appeared to be an openness and communication among administration, staff, and students.

I acquired positive feelings about the university. I was warmly received and I observed what appeared to be tremendous progress being made in regards to an acknowledgement, acceptance, and promotion of racial diversity. The honor that was bestowed upon my fellow classmates and me that year, the overwhelming welcome extended by Lonnie Ray Williams, the BAS, black staff, and students, and by Mike Macechko, executive director of the Arkansas Alumni Association, contributed to those good feelings. It was obvious that Dr. Williams's hard and brilliant efforts and accomplishments were paying off on behalf of the university's goal towards the end of diversity. He was the university's champion!

Then, there was a turn of events during which Dr. Williams was treated extremely unfairly by the university. He was in the prime position to fill the opening of vice chancellor. He had done the work, he had fulfilled the qualifications, and he was well known throughout the university, Alumni Association, staff, and community for his effectiveness. Instead of being promoted to vice chancellor, Dr. Williams was being demoted. Despite the efforts of the BAS, some members of the university's staff, and others, the issue was not resolved to everyone's satisfaction. I openly expressed my thoughts and made a plea to Chancellor White on Dr. Williams's behalf. Dr. Williams eventually left the university. My connection to the university was lost, so I severed my relationship with the university. It was as if it was 1955–1956 again. On the surface, things looked better and more promising than in 1955–1956, but this act proved that racism was "alive and well" at the university. I realize that organizations must make decisions regarding staff assignments based upon performance, need, and other factors; however, promotions are many times made for the wrong reasons. In my humble opinion, politics and racism were the factors that propelled the negative actions taken toward Dr. Williams.

Now, I only think of the university when I look at the beautiful mementos from 1998 (plaques, pictures, newspaper articles, copies of the *Arkansas* magazine, etc.), or when I recall or share the positive experiences I had at the university during the period of 1998–2002.

One of the things I vividly recall from 1955 to 1956 was that as I walked across the campus, from day to day, I observed the various sorority and fraternity houses, and the dormitories. They were big and beautiful, but unapproachable for me. We resided next door to Holcombe Hall and from our little house I could see the young women coming and going. They seemed to be happy and carefree. Some of the young women who lived in the sorority houses, those from Holcombe Hall, and the other dormitories were in my classes. I would overhear their animated and happy discussions about the activities at their dorms or their sorority houses. Going to the homecoming game, football and basketball games, dances, and other events seemed to be such fun for them. That, it seemed to me, was what college life was all about. Only vicariously did I get a feeling for how enjoyable it must have been to be a full-fledged college student, to belong. We were allowed to enroll in the university, attend classes, but were not actually a part of the university.

As I draw this to a close, I would like to add that the positive, memorable experiences that I had at the 1998 BAS reunion put everything from 1955 to 1956 into perspective and helped make what had happened in those earlier days all worthwhile. The event in 1998 is what I choose to remember. Those experiences left me with warm and uplifting thoughts, true and long-lasting friendships, and a better understanding of why all of this happened. Those will forever be in my heart. For these reasons, I am thankful. There is nothing more that I choose to do on behalf of the university. I only pray that somehow, in some small way, a life was improved because of the sacrifices that were made by those of us who were there "first."

■ Marjorie Wilkins Williams (1955–1959), professor of nursing

Written response to interview questions, July 20, 2007
For detailed biography, see Appendix A, page 289

I came to the university in 1955 at the age of seventeen. I enrolled in the College of Nursing. I selected the university because it was the only way for me to become a registered nurse without leaving Arkansas. I came from a large family and could not afford to go out of state. When I heard the university would have to accept African Americans to their new nursing program, I took advantage of the opportunity. A bachelor's degree in nursing was relatively new at that time. Most nurses attended hospital-based diploma schools.

I attended the university for four years. I was one of the three undergraduates to integrate the UA. We were all from Little Rock, knew each other, and enrolled in the nursing program.

In describing my experiences at the university, just getting to campus was an ordeal. I left Little Rock by bus, which made a change in Fort Smith. Because I sat in the "Colored" waiting room, a bench in the back of the station, the intercom system never reached back there, so I missed the first bus to Fayetteville. I finally got brave enough to enter the main terminal and inquire about the schedule, only to learn I would have to wait several more hours for the next bus. I made sure I didn't miss the next one.

We were unsupervised young girls, and apparently the white students knew it. Late one night a group of white boys banged on our door. We were absolutely panic stricken because we felt they were there to do us harm. All we knew to do was to call the few black graduate male students we had met (including Gordon Morgan). They came immediately, defused the situation, and suggested that the guys return during daylight hours, if they wished to visit us. They never returned.

The three of us attempted to join the band since we all played instruments well and were bored. After passing the audition, we were told that we could play at campus activities. We decided it wasn't worth our time and never returned to practice sessions. Of course, no one called to encourage our return.

Another unforgettable experience took place in Little Rock. Football games were divided between Fayetteville and Little Rock. By 1957, I had clinical rotations at the university medical center there. Since students received free tickets to the game, I secured an extra ticket for my fiancé. As soon as we sat in the student section, we were told we would have to leave. It was humiliating to be escorted out of the War Memorial Stadium while other students looked on.

While traveling to various clinical sites and rural health departments, I lived with black families while my classmates were put up in dorms or hotels. When we stopped for meals during travel, I stayed on the bus while they went in to eat. I would insist I wasn't hungry or didn't need to use the restroom.

One experience I will never forget took place at the State Mental Hospital. The black ward was so deteriorated that my instructors refused to put me there, so all of our students were placed on a male ward that housed youth. I was assigned a patient who was about my age and we got along well. Every so often the ward would have "Socials" and young ladies from their ward were invited over for snacks, to dance, and socialize. During my first social, my patient asked me to dance with him. I was doing so when the music was abruptly stopped.

The nursing supervisor came to me and stated that they wouldn't tolerate integrated dancing. I had no choice but to leave and return to campus. By the time I arrived, my instructors, who were not at the hospital with us, had already been notified. I never returned, never completed that rotation, but received a "B" in the course. I was delighted to receive the grade.

The university did nothing to make our stay on the campus safe and/or comfortable. We were mostly ignored, but at times were humiliated and rejected (previous statements). We were left to fend for ourselves and we did. A few instructors were nice to us and one even offered extra tutoring, but I remember one instructor who refused to give me the good grade I had earned.

In April 1998, the UA Black Alumni Society invited the three undergraduates who first integrated the campus to receive the "Living Legacy Pioneer Award." The three of us—Maxine Sutton Cannon, Billie Rose Whitfield Jacobs, and myself—were also given a reception by the Department of Nursing. The nursing department gave us a belated welcome and a lovely plaque.

I know that our students are now able to enjoy campus life and are active participants in all aspects of campus life. I was thrilled when I heard that black students could live in campus housing and not subjected to isolation and overt discrimination as we were. So yes, my feelings have changed. We had no black professors or staff, no one with our interest in mind. I only hope that current students appreciate what they have.

There were times when I felt so wronged and/or ignored. On the campus, the three of us—Billie Rose Whitfield Jacobs, Maxine Sutton Cannon, and myself—supported each other. We were mostly left alone and offered little if any assistance. For example, we lived in a house next to the freshman ladies' dorm, but had no access to the facilities there. We had to buy and cook our own meals and even though the dorm was next door, washed our clothes in the bathtub. We had no chaperone during our first semester there and no protection. No one so much as gave us a number for the campus police if we needed them. We were completely on our own.

Having said all this, I will also say that the university prepared me well for the career I have chosen. I learned a lot about people and about myself. It taught me perseverance, tolerance, and I have done well in my profession.

Chapter 3

To Prevent "Irreparable Harm"

Desegregation and the 1960s

The University's stance, philosophy or guiding principle in response to race relations should be providing every student opportunity to work towards his goals at the university.
—David W. Mullins

President David Wiley Mullins made the above statement in an interview on November 4, 1968, when asked about the university's policy on civil rights.[1] Mullins avowed that the university embraced the idea of providing all students regardless of color every opportunity "to work towards his goals," and he intimated that the university treated all students the same. Although Mullins's statement accurately reflected official university policy, his remarks failed to fairly capture the profound differences in the experiences of black and white students on the Fayetteville campus in the 1960s and the role that the university played in perpetuating these differences. During the 1960s, the administration at the University of Arkansas continued treating black students in many ways as unwelcome outsiders. In fact, the university slowed the tide of change that had been occurring since the late 1940s and appeared determined at times to bring some aspects of desegregation to a complete halt. Over the course of the 1960s in order to gain greater access to university auxiliaries and facilities, black students and their white allies had to compel the university to accept further civil rights reforms.

The University of Arkansas entered the 1960s responding to indirect assaults made on its desegregation efforts made by state officials. Governor Orval Faubus, known nationally for his resistance to a federal mandate to desegregate Central High School in Little Rock in 1957, encouraged the state legislature to pass two laws designed to intimidate and punish state employees who supported civil rights. Act 10 of 1958 required all public schoolteachers to file an affidavit listing every organization to which they belonged or supported financially over the past five years.[2] Act 115 of 1959 prohibited the employment of any person who was a member of the National Association for the Advancement of Colored People.[3] These edicts along with the increasing interests of state officials in learning about the university's desegregation practices in the late 1950s motivated the university to adjust its policy involving the housing of black male students. Although black male students had been previously placed on a separate floor of Lloyd Hall, by 1959, the university abandoned this housing arrangement and reserved the dorm once again for whites only. Black men would have to find housing off campus. Black women would continue to occupy two off-campus segregated houses purchased for them by the university.[4]

In the early 1960s, black and white students eager to see civil rights reforms at the university began to pressure the administration. The desegregation of university dormitories and athletics were the usual targets. In December 1962, a group of black and white students calling themselves "Students for Freedom" picketed the campus main library for an hour in a quiet demonstration against racial discrimination in university housing.[5] In several articles in the *Arkansas Traveler,* the campus student newspaper, students openly challenged the university's refusal to integrate its athletic teams. These condemnations became even more common after a chief sports rival, the University of Texas, officially modified its policy in 1963 to allow for black students to participate in sporting events.[6]

The national growth of the civil rights movement served as one of the main factors that stimulated greater on-campus activism in the 1960s. During this decade, the movement reached its high point. Major civil rights personalities such as Martin Luther King Jr., Malcolm X, and James Farmer held rallies and organized marches throughout the nation. The most noted of these demonstrations was the famed March on Washington in August 1963. At this event, over 250,000 people gathered at the Lincoln Memorial to express their support for a new, stronger civil rights bill. King delivered what was arguably the greatest public address of his life, the famous "I Have a Dream." As a result of the efforts of the civil rights proponents, the following year Congress passed the Civil Rights Act of 1964. The law banned discrimination in places of public accommodations, including public schools. Any institution of learning guilty of violating the act ran the risk of losing federal funds. The statute also forbade institutions and private businesses from discriminating in the hiring, dismissing, and promoting of workers.[7]

In 1964, emboldened by actions at the national level, black students on the Fayetteville campus launched an assault against university practices they deemed discriminatory. In January 1964, Raymond Carter, a black sophomore, formally complained before the Arkansas Advisory Committee to the United States Commission on Civil Rights about the university's treatment of blacks. Carter called for an end to the segregated dorms and athletic programs, and he drew attention to the university's policy of interviewing black student applicants before accepting them for admission. Carter described how he had traveled over two hundred miles for his interview only to be asked by the interviewer if he had any questions. For Carter the interview requirement was not only a "waste of time," but also unfair, for it required only blacks to be interviewed.[8]

On August 17, 1964, two black students, Robert Whitfield and Joanna Edwards, filed suit in the federal district court at Little Rock alleging discrimination by the university. Although housing became the principal issue tackled by the court in addressing the suit, Whitfield and Edwards petitioned the court to remove racial barriers "in the fields of varsity athletics, hiring of instructors, social organizations, recruitment of high school students and all other activities coupled with a racial policy." The hearing took place in September of that same year. During the proceedings, Whitfield, Edwards, and their attorney, George Howard, president of the Arkansas chapter of the NAACP and former university Law School graduate, argued that the university's exclusionary policy would subject the students to "irreparable harm," if it was not changed immediately. The plaintiffs testified that the housing practices were racially discriminatory and that they would make better grades if they had access to university housing. On September 5, the court ordered the university to allow Whitfield and Edwards into the dorms. Basing its ruling largely on *McLaurin v. Oklahoma* (1950), the court argued that the law required black students to be treated in the same fashion as whites at integrated schools. Although the court did not issue relief to blacks as a class for the fall 1964 or rule specifically on the other areas mentioned in the suit, university officials could read the handwriting on the wall. After the suit, the university would allow blacks to use the dorms and establish an official policy endorsing the equal treatment of students at the university.[9]

Despite the change in housing and its assertions of equal treatment, the university still received criticism from students about its failure to fully embrace integration. In a letter published in the *Arkansas Traveler* in October 1966, Paris Sabbs lamented the fact that the university had no black faculty. Sabbs also chastised the university officials for failing to recruit black athletes. With regard to the dorms, Sabbs criticized the university's practice of pairing students on racial grounds. Black students were housed with black students; otherwise, they lived alone. According to Sabbs, "The University goes out of its way to make sure that black and white students will not have a chance to know one another under any of its social conditions."[10] In February 1967, after receiving other public complaints about its housing policy, the administration removed race-listing on applications for housing.[11]

In March 1968, seventy-five black students met with President Mullins to express their grievances with certain university practices. Among them included the failure of the university to recruit black students or a sufficient number of black student-athletes and the playing of the song "Dixie" at university-sponsored functions. Also, the students stated their desire to have black instructors. There were no black instructors employed by the university on the Fayetteville campus at that time. After the meeting, the students marched silently around the university's administration building to continue their protest.[12]

The assassination of Dr. King in April 1968 shocked and dismayed the students, faculty, and staff on the Fayetteville campus in much the same way that it affected people all over the nation. Four days after King's murder, students held a memorial on university grounds to commemorate his life. On the following day, the university canceled morning classes in honor of King's funeral. Many people wrote letters to the editor of the *Traveler* expressing condolences to the King family and support for King's mission and legacy. Some of the letters went even further, criticizing the university's civil rights' shortcomings and offering proposals for ameliorative improvements. However, not all of the letters to editors agreed with the general sentiment of appreciating and recognizing King's significance. One student letter complained that King's death had been given too much publicity. When John Rowe, a black student, wrote a response to this letter, the school paper failed to print it. This omission triggered the Black Americans for Democracy (BAD), a new student organization, to barricade the journalism building to shut down the publication of the paper for a day in protest.[13]

Race relations on the Fayetteville campus were further frayed by the growing controversy over the playing of "Dixie" at university-sponsored events. In the fall 1968, a campus-wide controversy arose over the playing of the song. Although black students had registered their opposition to the practice earlier in the year, by November they had been joined by a white student group called the Southern Student Organizing Committee (SSOC). The SSOC appealed to the student senate to ban the playing of the song in December 1968 because of its offensive meaning to black students. The senate, however, could only agree to table a decision to a later time because of the strong support that many white students gave for the continuation of the practice.[14]

By 1969, civil rights activism on campus had begun to reflect the impact of the "black power" phase of the civil rights movement. Across the nation, black students had taken charge of civil rights efforts and demanded more profound and immediate changes to the environments in which they studied, worked, and lived. The "Dixie" controversy had not yet been resolved, but black students, now led by BAD, became even more determined to see the song banned at university-sponsored functions. On November 25, 1969, members of BAD disrupted a pep rally, preventing the band from mounting the stage in order to play "Dixie." The following day, BAD leaders led a delegation of sixty students into Mullins's office, left a list of grievances, and walked out without having any discussion with the university president. A week later after a rancorous and tedious debate, the student senate voted to recommend that "Dixie" not be played at any university events. However, the vote was nonbinding. That same week during a pep rally held in downtown Fayetteville tied to the famous football contest between the Razorbacks and the Longhorns scheduled for December 6, students waved Confederate flags. Also, a local radio station continued its game-week tradition of playing "Dixie" every twenty minutes. Although the band director, Dr. Richard A. Worthington, promised to comply with the student senate vote and not play the song at the game, members of BAD made plans to occupy the field if the band failed to live up to Worthington's pledge. Worthington kept his word so no protest occurred at the big game.[15]

In the following oral histories, we gain further insight into the lives of black students on the Fayetteville campus during the 1960s.

■ Sharon E. Bernard (1966–1969), banker

Telephone interview by Lonnie R. Williams, September 17, 2008
For detailed biography, see Appendix A, page 290

My name is Sharon Elaine Bernard (Miller). I entered the University of Arkansas in 1966 to obtain a BSL and a JD.

Why did I select the University of Arkansas? Actually I didn't select the University of Arkansas. My husband, George B. Miller Jr., did and I was following him. He selected the university because we wanted to stay in Arkansas and be able to go home to Helena once in a while to check on our businesses. We had two daughters, and we sent them to Detroit, Michigan, to live with my dad and grandmother, who took care of them while we were in school. We spent most of the summers in Detroit with them and worked as law clerks there the summer of the 1967 riots.

I was the first black female to attend the University of Arkansas Law School. I entered under a special program as a junior in college, and was the last person who entered the Law School under that program. I was a 4.0 student from Arkansas AM&N College with a sufficient LSAT score. Therefore, I graduated Law School with BSL and JD degrees. I was the first black female to graduate from the University of Arkansas Law School as well as the first black female licensed attorney in the state.

During the three years I was there, there were three women, including me. The other two were white women. I do not know when the next black females came and, according to Dean Nance, the school records don't reflect when the next black female came.

I always said that when I left the university in 1969, I promised myself, my family, and my God that I would never return to that "hell hole." It was a very long, tedious, trying, and negative experience for me and my husband. It started with we could not rent a place to live—a decent place. So we bought a brand-new mobile home. Although we had no children or pets, no one would rent us a space to park our mobile home. After going to all the mobile home parks and being denied, we finally found a Jewish owner who was willing to rent us a space. However, by the end of our first year, almost everybody else had moved out, and they had to close the mobile home park.

We had to find a new place to move our mobile home, which necessitated a wild goose chase all over town to all the mobile home parks once again. This time we only found one because I went by myself, signed the rental contract, and then George showed up after we moved in. The owners had the nerve to come over and ask me why I had not told them I was married to a Negro, at which point I told them I was a Negro, with a legal rental contract, we were two law students, and would they please vacate our property and leave us alone. They did leave because we were law students and because the wife had shared some very personal and embarrassing information about her relationship with her husband when I went in to sign the contract. Apparently, out of fear that we would sue or that I would disclose the information, she quickly encouraged her husband to leave us alone. It was a nightmare, even outside of Law School, just to live and there was no one . . . other than the two of us, and we stayed at the Law School most of the time.

When we went to class, we were treated like lepers in the large auditorium where we had most of our classes. We would sit in the front row because I had been raised by my grandmother and she had taught me that I was not a "back of the bus" person. Consequently, I had always sat at the front of the class.

As a result of our sitting up front, in the big lecture hall at school, there would be ten empty rows behind us. The other students acted as if they would somehow contract a disease if they sat near us! It was very difficult for me because I was from Michigan and had only been in Arkansas since 1961. I am not saying that racism did not exist in Michigan because I know it did and still does, but it is different, not as outward. I became far more aware of it as I lived in Arkansas and even more so at the university. I know that I would have left the university my first year if George had not been with me, because I just thought the way we were being treated was outrageous, intolerable, and for no reason, as far as I was concerned.

My husband was treated worse than I, I think, just because he was with me. He was "downgraded" in his grades. I think both of us were ultimately, but for him it was far worse. We had each other and that is what got both of us through that time. It was a very difficult experience and I just did not appreciate it. Consequently, I complained about it far more than George; I think because he was from Arkansas, and more accustomed to this level of racism than me. I was constantly identifying discrimination and haranguing George about it.

There was very little about the school that I appreciated. I only had three professors who helped, not by anything that they specifically said or did much more than saying, "hello" and "how are you," which was more than any other staff person said, including the dean. The three professors were Dr. Leflar, Professor Guzman, and Professor Gittelman.

Our freshman year, there was only one other married couple in Law School, and they were seniors, Susan and Jim Norland from Oregon. There were two women other than myself in Law School after Susan graduated. I decided we would start a chapter of the oldest and largest sorority in the nation. I was the founding president of Kappa Beta Phi Sorority, one of the other women was the vice president, and the final woman was the secretary/treasurer. I understand that it is no longer on campus and that's unfortunate, but we did it just to say, "We are here," and to show that there is power, even where there are only three women. The sexism at the Law School was "alive and well" just as the racism, and this was really a new thing for me as well.

As for the black people, Richard Mays was a senior and graduated, which left just Perlesta Hollingsworth, George, and me. So it was very, very tough. Extremely few people were friendly and that is a difficult life, all just because of your color—one of the blessings God gave you that you cannot change. Race does not define who you are or how you should be treated, just as gender should not, but both did at the U of A Law School from 1966 through 1969. But we were determined, we were not quitters, and we intended to succeed no matter how difficult or lonely it was.

To compound matters further, in our senior year we had a car accident and my neck and back were injured. My doctor said to me that I had to stop. He told me that I had to drop out of school and I said there was no way. There was just no way. When I told him, "I cannot," he replied, "Well, then your husband will have to carry all your books. He will have to carry yours and his." We said, "That is just what will have to happen," and so George did exactly that!

I just caught hell my senior year. That year, Professor Guzman designed an externship-type class, at my request, and George took it with me. I was extremely interested in criminal law. I did extensive, in-depth case studies of the discrimination in the criminal justice system, focusing on the segregated juvenile justice system, as well as the death-row cases.

In addition, during the last semester of my senior year I was told that my English Proficiency Test from Arkansas AM&N College was not acceptable and I would have to take the exam again or I would not graduate or get my BSL. I was like, "Pardon me?" I had been writing more than adequately for two and a half years in Law School. At that time, we had to write essay answers to all Law School exam questions, not multiple choice like now! Furthermore, I was an assistant instructor in legal bibliography, the research and writing class, in my freshman year! I did not understand this at all. Needless to say, I know if you do not use it, you lose it, and all those little idiosyncrasies in the English language that you have to know, I might have forgotten. Further, as this just appeared to be a "designed" roadblock, I felt I needed to be fully on my "Ps and Qs." Therefore, I got a tutor, quickly took a refresher course for the English Proficiency Test, and then passed it again!

It seemed that they were doing anything and everything to try to stop me from graduating. I had a calendar that I marked off every day of our senior year—we were very tired, we missed our children terribly, and we were ready to go. At that time, the Temptations had a song, "You Can't Stop Me Now." It became my theme song for my senior year when it seemed everything was against me. I was in pain, constant pain from my neck, and everything was going wrong. George was hauling all of our books everyday. He was tired and irritable, and I felt like, "Oh my God, can I just get out of this hell hole, get my children, and go home!" It was awful. I just cannot tell you. There was nowhere to go and there was nothing to do. You do not have any time to do anything anyway while in Law School. We had little or no time, but sometimes to relax, George would try to swim at our mobile home park, but when he got in the pool everybody else would get out. So I guess you could say we had our own big swimming pool!

In Law School, it's not like you really worry about interacting with anybody, just because you really do not have time. We did not have time to eat. We did not have time to do anything, really! In addition, we had children in Michigan we had to communicate with every break we had. They were just two and three years old when we left them. We had to go to Detroit to spend some time with them on our Christmas breaks. I spent summers with them. I missed my children so much during my years in school. Their absence added tremendously to the solitude and misery we suffered during our Law School years.

My husband felt because we were not working, we needed to find a way to bring in a little money. You could not work. I mean you cannot work when you're in Law School. I tremendously admire people who do. George decided that he would work the football games to earn a little extra money and somehow he managed.

We would actually pull against the university at the games because they were so dirty. It was my understanding that Coach Frank Broyles had said that he was never going to have any black people playing for him on that field. The university itself obviously agreed and did not want any black people playing. However, I remember when a young black man came from another school, Jerry LeVias, on their football team, and he was exceptional. Someone stole his uniform, his cleats, and everything else. When they put him on the field, the uniform was hanging off of him because it was not his. However, he took the field and he killed U of A. We were so happy. We were screaming. We just could not pull for the university; it was just far too racist.

Oh, it was so racist everywhere there. I just cannot describe to you everything. Even when we graduated and my family was coming down, we reserved twenty rooms, so we integrated a hotel there. I can't remember the name of the hotel chain. But whatever the hotel was, they did not want to give us those rooms when they saw that they were for black people. Once again, I had made the reservations, and they had made the assumption that I was some race other than black. They were horrified, but stuck since I had guaranteed all the rooms and was a Law School student. Again, I could not believe the level of racism, but I knew I would be happily leaving in a few days.

Just about everybody who was nice to us from the beginning to the end was Jewish. The one student at the school that was friendly and studied with us, Alan Nussbaum, was Jewish. Other than the couple from Oregon and my two white female sorority members, I cannot tell you anybody else who was non-Jewish and friendly. The other two female law students and I got along well because there were just three of us and nobody wanted to be bothered with any of us. I think they were friendly because they were just as lost and lonely as I was. At least I had my husband. They didn't have anybody. So it was a very difficult time and I did not have any positive feelings towards the university.

The combination of racism and sexism together was too much, especially for a person like me who was not accustomed to being quiet. In fact, when I got married in 1961, my father did not want me to move to the South. My father and mother were from Mississippi. He was very, very against me going to Arkansas because he said, "Sharon, your mouth will get you killed. You are not going to shut up." So my father's advice was to "establish myself as a crazy black person because then white folks will leave you alone and you won't be killed."

My father was so glad to see me finish with the university. Every time I called to check on my children and told him about school and what was going on, he would say "Oh my God, this girl is going to get killed." I would tell Daddy I really was in a place where I just said to myself, daily, "I am not going to quit. I am not going to let them just dog me out. I do not care what they say. I do not care what they do. I am going to finish this. This is something that I am going to do. They might as well get it through their heads. They might as well leave me alone, and they might as well accept it. I am going to finish." And that we did together!

But it is as I said in my 2008 speech at the university, racism is today, and was then, certainly alive and well. I mean one week the headline was "First black couple finishes Law School." The next week the headline was "First black couple can't park trailer in Little Rock." So not only could we not park it in Fayetteville three years earlier, but we couldn't park it in Little Rock, the state capitol, three years later.

I am happy to be back in Michigan, my birthplace and where all of my family resides. However, I love Arkansas and would take nothing for my experiences there, for they made me a much better and more sensitive person. The first time I came back to the University of Arkansas Law School to give a speech was in 1989 to speak to the Black Law Students Association. When I was invited by a black female law student, I told her, "I do not want to come back to that hell hole and relive the many deeply painful memories of my three years there." I really did not want to go down there, but she was so insistent, and the black students really wanted me to come. There were about seventeen black law students at that time. It was my pleasure to meet the students, and share my life experiences during and since Law School. For that reason alone, I was glad I returned.

Dr. Leflar and some other professors came to hear me speak and I said to them, "Your affirmative action program must be a program just written on paper because if I have been gone twenty years and you do not even have twenty black students, it is obviously a total failure." Dr. Leflar said, "Sharon, you were always such a fighter and I see you still are," and I replied, "I always have been and always will be."

After that, I never heard from the Law School again until 2007, when Dean Cynthia Nance was appointed. I understand that after seeing the Pioneers Room with the first six black male graduates, she asked, "Well, who was the first black woman?" Nobody knew the answer. She said, "I want to know who the first black woman was and get her down here. Further, how is it that you cannot identify the first black woman graduate?" They found me, and I went down in 2007 to give a speech, which was sponsored by not only the Black Law Students Association, but also the Hart Society and the Women Law Students Organization.

On that occasion, in 2007, Professor Guzman had left a note for me because he was unable to attend stating he was so happy that I came back. The note was read to the audience before I spoke. It was an apology for not being sensitive to the issues that attenuated my being the first black female. He apologized for not reaching out to me or recognizing that I might have needed his attention or assistance. It was a very sensitive, warm, kind, well-written, and well-received note.

His note did, however, raise the issue, in my mind, of whether they even knew I was black and perhaps that had led to some of the issues that they took out on my husband and me. It was certainly not something that we hid; I think that it was just the way that I look. Many people mistake me for Greek or Arab, and back then, in addition to being fair-skinned, I also had blonde hair. Now, as well as then, people choose to identify me as almost any race other than black. But I was the first black female and I did not deny that nor ever try to be anything else at the Law School. Moreover, George is of a darker, more Mexican-looking or caramel-colored skin tone and we were always together.

Professor Guzman also stated in his note to me that he recognized my abilities and that he just had faith in me. He said I always walked with my head up and I never reached out for anybody to do anything to help me. Further, he said I never said, "I am the first black female and why don't you help me?" That is, however, something I never would have done. For most of my life I had been the first black in all of my schools. I was used to that. I was used to racism just not at the level at U of A Law School. I was certainly not used to sexism combined with racism and I think that is what made it even more difficult.

Now for me to be a happy person who has the university alumni sticker on my car, I have come a long way from the person who was "never going to return to that hell hole." I have come a long way, a very long way. This is all because of Dean Cindy Nance, my driving down and being in a hotel on Martin Luther King Drive, entering the Law School and seeing all races and sexes sitting next to each other, and that there are black professors at the Law School! Oh my God, never in my lifetime did I think that this would be the Fayetteville that I would see. Never! Ever! I told them just that in my speeches.

In February 2008, when the Law School recognized Silas Hunt they brought graduates down from each decade since Silas. I represented the sixties. During the program, George Haley represented the fifties and talked about how wonderful the school was when he attended it. When I spoke, I adamantly disagreed with several of his points. One of the things I said was, "George, they must have been kind to you because you were a Republican or something because they were not kind to me at all, a decade later." Another was, "George, all that nice-ness you're talking about just was not happening here in sixty-six. That was a long time after you were here. Maybe it was because I am a woman, I do not know. But my husband was here and they were not nice to him, either!"

In addition, when I gave my speech in 2008, I took my noose. It is a real noose, which was hung over my head while I was attending an Arkansas Institute of Politics lecture in 1970 as a practicing attorney. The white male attorney who did it said it cost him fourteen dollars to make. He was very disturbed because I was in a rape trial in Fort Smith in the courtroom of the famed "hanging judge" for a young black basketball star with a white married woman as the alleged victim. My co-counsel was Jimmy Meyerson, a Jewish New York NAACP Legal Defense Fund attorney and the Honorable George Howard; the inmates called us the Mod Squad. That speech took place during the time when during the Mercedes-Benz Golf Championship banter about how the young players could catch Tiger Woods it had been suggested that they "lynch him in a back alley." This exchange resulted in a *Golf Week* magazine cover depicting a noose and entitled "Caught In A Noose." Tiger Wood's agent described the incident as a "complete non issue." My point in taking my noose was that it wasn't a "non issue" for me in 1970 and has never been a "non issue" for black folks in general. I hung it up in my home so my children understood that it was not a "non issue," and have showed it to my grandsons and taught them that it is not a "non issue" today.

My noose no longer hangs up in my home, but is prominently displayed because I will never forget the fear I had in driving back to Fort Smith alone that night. Moreover, the man who made the noose was also going where I was going and I did not know what he was driving. This was particularly important given the fact that, in self-defense, I had beaten him up with the desks, chairs, and anything else I could find in the lecture hall. As I was the only black in the lecture and no one, including the lecturer, came to my defense, I had fought him all by myself.

In 2008, I thought I was only speaking to students, professors, and staff. However, the chancellor of the university was there, but I didn't know him. He came up after the speech and he said, "I want a few words with you." He took my hand and did not turn it loose. He then said, "You are the real deal and such a fighter." I said, "I say what I mean and I mean what I say. I have had to fight all my life and I got a degree at this university."

They still have the Pioneers Room and they still only have the six black male Law School graduates on display. They still do not have me there so I guess, to them, I am not a pioneer, at least not a recognized U of A Law School pioneer. I told Dean Nance that I find that very insulting. But, I believe if anyone can make it right, it is her. That is probably my only negative feeling toward the university now, and it is not the university, it is toward the Law School specifically.

I have no lasting negative feelings towards the university now. I proudly display a Razorback sign in the window of my car. I drink from my big Razorback mug that I bought when I was down in February 2008. What does that tell you? That I have positive feelings! Okay. I do. I really do. I do not have any problems. I actually got a little bit frustrated when the black coach, Nolan Richardson, was down there and then they got rid of him. I got mad again. But I am really all right now.

What made my feelings change? Well, it was really Dean Nance. When I went down and saw the number of students, the black students, and the changes at the Law School, I was impressed. To tell you really, when I spoke to the staff in 2007, I gave the speech the first time to just an open room of guests, students, and professors from all over the university. The second day, I spoke to the Law School and other university staff. I really enjoyed that presentation. I believe real and lasting changes can be made at the faculty and staff level, as there are so many "Sharons" even though there will not be another Sharon Bernard. Thankfully, there will never be another "first" from a black perspective, but there are students who will attend the Law School and need help and will not ask for it, will not know how or whom to ask for help. Staff needs to reach out to them, sometimes just to explain how to study, or brief, or research, or what electives to take, or how to manage time. They may never reach out to the professors because they are uncomfortable and may not know how to approach the faculty. The staff needs to reach out to the students because they are in foreign territory, afraid of failure, do not ever have enough time, have no personal time, and are always in a hurry to run home and start reading and briefing again.

I also told them, to know that the university did a national search and then hired Dean Nance from within says that there is a major change in the university's ethos. When I met her, I said, "Oh my God, what amazing thing has happened here in Fayetteville?" It has truly changed dramatically.

I believe Dean Nance is a real change agent. When I saw her office, it reminded me of my home, which is also filled with African American art. I first met and shook her hand as I was walking in to give my speech. I said, "I prayed all the way down that you were not Condi, like Condoleezza Rice, because if you were, you were getting ready to go on a rough ride with this speech of mine." And she said, "Oh no, I can tell I like you already."

What really changed my mind was Dean Nance. I mean in terms of the Law School the fact that the Law School or the university, and whoever chooses the dean of the Law School, chose her in the first place shows that they have come a long, long way. In addition, Professor Guzman's warm apology tore at my heart. I always knew he was special as a professor, but now I know he is a special caring man who was willing to reach out even after thirty-eight years in a very warm, public apology.

During our three years of school, there was just no peace unless we stayed unto ourselves. There was a peace that we had when we drove to Michigan to see our children. In Fayetteville, it was just hell to pay! That's why I called it a hell hole for us. Period! At the school, at our home, even at the Catholic Church people looked at us like we were crazy. I mean even when I was admitted to the Catholic hospital in Fort Smith the nun told George, "Now boy, just sit her bags down, you leave Miss Miller, and just tell Mr. Miller we're going to take good care of her." The racism was just so blatant everywhere; it was just horrifying to me.

I am just glad we survived. That is all I can say, because I know we were truly blessed. Poor Silas Hunt did not have a prayer. They needed to name the new Law School after him. Not the building down the street, around the corner, or whatever that is they have named after him. That is not enough. Because of segregation and hatred he was required to attend Law School alone in the basement boiler room. He was not even permitted to use the toilet facilities. They killed him. They should not have done that. It was wrong, and it was pure, unadulterated racism.

They should have asked some of us who suffered down there at that hell hole as pioneers after him, the original pioneer, what we thought they should have named after him in order to honor him appropriately. In my view, he deserves the highest recognition possible by the University of Arkansas, the Law School, and by state and local government officials.

■ Harold B. Betton (1965–1971), medical doctor and minister

Written response to interview questions, July 14, 2007
For detailed biography, see Appendix A, page 290

I entered the University of Arkansas as a freshman student, at the age of seventeen in 1965, and graduated with a bachelor of science degree in agriculture in spring of 1969. Upon graduation, I immediately entered graduate school and graduated with a master of science in natural sciences in 1971.

I selected the University of Arkansas because my brother, one year my senior, enrolled as a freshman in 1964. By the way my brother, Farrish Earl Betton, was the first black graduate in electrical engineering in the school's history.

I was the first black graduate in the School of Agriculture with a BS degree in agriculture (I think). As a black student, I was the only black student in the College of Agriculture for the full four years and the first black undergraduate student working in research at the college.

My time at the University of Arkansas was inaugurated with devout racism. My first class ever in college was a 7:30 A.M. MWF English class. The first day of class I, and another black student, sat on the front row and all of the white students sat in the back of the class. The teacher, a graduate assistant, said nothing. Each of my classes remained a chore, but I had to develop an attitude to deal with the racism. That attitude was to study, study, and study! I developed an attitude that I had to be superior to everyone in the class and make an "A." It did not always happen, but my heart worked toward that end.

I must admit that there were a few professors that will always stand out in my mind; these were not racist and treated me as a college student. Dr. Lowell F. Bailey, chairman of the Department of Botany, Dr. Paulissen (Bacteriology), Dr. Slack (Plant Pathology), Dr. Wickliff (Department of Botany). In general, the Department of Botany and Bacteriology were excellent. The professors in the Department of Plant Pathology were exceptional as well. All in all, the University of Arkansas prepared me for what was ahead, graduate study at the University of Arkansas for Medical Sciences School of Medicine and medical school at the University of Washington. By then, I was so used to being the only black student that it was no longer enigmatic—it was an accepted norm. This characteristic worked to my advantage because I had developed an attitude of the necessity for superiority that it persists today (thirty years into medical practice).

The sad part about being a college student during this time was the extracurricular. There was nothing for a black student! During this time, no black student would have ever been able to play athletics. Going to a game, of any type, was more threatening than ever. Upon admission to the school, it was the first year black students were allowed to move into the dormitory. I did not because my brother stayed off campus and I elected to not be that sort of trail-blazer.

There were only twenty black students on campus, spread so widely that you seldom came into contact with any. As a student, I forged friends among a nucleus of black students because the attrition rate was high. Many could not take the pressure, racism, ostracism, and rejection. To this end, as a student I am sure that I became somewhat introverted, studying all of the time in order to prove superiority. This was in retrospect unhealthy.

By the time I reached graduate school, more black students were on campus and at least we had parties that represented an outlet for downloading pressure!

At the time of this study, I must admit that I have difficulty considering myself as an alumnus of the school. Yes, I graduated with two degrees, but the feeling is mixed. When I applied to medical school, I asked three former professors of the school to write letters of recommendations. Those letters were so negative that the psychiatrist on the Admissions Committee, University of Washington School of Medicine, Seattle, Washington, phoned them and after his interview concluded that racism was at the root of their letters. At their request, I asked a new set of professors, Dr. Wickliff from Botany, Dr. Lowell F. Bailey from Botany and one other that I can't remember. Their letters were the opposite of those previously sent. As an aside, I want to add that I graduated from medical school in three years, not the customary four; therefore, academic ability was certainly not the problem.

In addition, upon graduating with my BS degree in agriculture, I distinctly remember asking the dean whether I would graduate with honors—since my GPA was very good. His reply was, "Other students studied also!" This was a no and I did not; that was the final slap in the face for me that has carried a bad taste for going on forty or more years.

I have only returned to the university twice since my leaving, once with my son because I gave a talk in Fayetteville to a group of doctors and secondly after my first semester of medical school. I had to fly from Seattle, Washington, and stopped in Fayetteville to make a personal visit to one of the professors who was the chief proponent of a bad recommendation letter. I wanted to tell him, and I did, that it was his letter that made the school accept me! I have no desire to visit the school.

My feelings toward the university have certainly cooled some; they have made positive strides and are trying to correct past diseases. I admit that my tenure was more pioneering and as a pioneer such treatment was expected. I am not bitter, but when I talk to my contemporaries about college life they often have such positive experiences compared to my negative ones. I certainly missed something that can never be regained.

I have vented quite a bit and have never put much of this down on paper in my life. You may use whatever is appropriate in your paper because it is real. Each student's experience differs. Contact James Haymon—the first black member of the Razorback band. Contact my brother, Farrish Earl Betton, the first black graduate of the Department of Electrical Engineering.

I certainly forgot to include the true story behind the first Ms. BAD (Black Americans for Democracy) pageant. It was the brainchild of two people, Harold Betton and James Haymon. We ostensibly wanted to get the best-looking women on campus to highlight and also have a good time; therefore, we thought of the Ms. Black Collegiate of Arkansas and invited the best contestants from each school in the state. The winner would have a meeting with the governor of the state, Dale Bumpers, to discuss the problems of black students across the state of Arkansas. The winner of that first pageant was from Arkansas AM&N College, Pine Bluff, Arkansas.

The meeting was indeed held at Hanks Doghouse, Little Rock, Arkansas. The then president of the University of Arkansas, Dr. Mullins, called the governor's office and actually helped us secure an audience with Governor Bumpers. What began as a party idea turned out to become a tradition. We had no budget for the first affair. The decorations came from leftovers from a student union affair the night before, flowers. We had a weekend of activities that started with a Black Americans for Democracy (BAD) gospel choir concert on Friday night. It was very well attended by faculty, staff, students, and community people. Black students from the University of Arkansas and community made up the choir. The next night was the pageant,

Saturday. The judges were William Betton, James Haymon, and a few others. The weekend proved to be one of the first and best black-sponsored affairs in the school's history.

Lonnie, you must remember—this affair was held in 1970 on the heels of a much turbulent time in our nation's civil rights history and many university faculty/staff had become more sensitive to the needs of the student. Just one year previous to this, the spring of 1969, black students protested against the school newspaper and blockaded the door, preventing the publication of the newspaper for a day. This was met with much press and negative attitudes among the students of the day. Just as students around the nation protested conditions and college campuses saw a rise in black student organizations, the University of Arkansas was no exception. In 1969, Richard Nixon attended one of the university football games and black students organized and wanted to protest during half-time, but this was aborted out of fear of the Secret Service.

■ Darrell Brown Sr. (1965–1972), attorney

Telephone interview by Lonnie R. Williams, January 9, 2010
No detailed biography available

In 1965, I entered the University of Arkansas with the intention of majoring in pre-med and subsequently changed the degree to sociology and psychology. I attended seven years—four years as an undergrad and three years in Law School.

Why did I select the University of Arkansas? To make a long story short, back in 1964, Sevier County training schools were on the verge of integrating with the school district here in Horatio, Arkansas. I wanted to be a part of a school system that was integrated and would give me an opportunity to experience some of the same opportunities that other non-African Americans had experienced in schools at that time. I chose the University of Arkansas because it represented an opportunity to be involved in an integrated setting of kind presenting academic opportunities, at least potentially, that were available to others.

While at the University of Arkansas, I was the first to play football at the University of Arkansas and among the first group of blacks to reside in the previously all-white dormitories, Humphreys Hall, specifically in 1965.

Speak about my experience at the U of A? Well, first I think that I'd like to focus on the social experience of being among the first group of blacks of any significant numbers to attend. The social experience was really challenging. That is to say, that while we were a part of an academic community at the university, it appeared we didn't have any social interactions and did not have significant social interactions with the other facets of the university. We didn't have active participation in the government of the university, the student body government. At that time, we had absolutely no social activities going on at the university, but basically we were involved in or lent ourselves to going down to the black community, which was then called the "can." If we went to church, we went to the "can." If we went to a social function, party or something, we went to the "can." If we had any other social functions, it was simply by ourselves in a separate situation. We were similarly isolated, should I say, like an island within the university system.

As far as the athletic aspect is concerned, needless to say, it was a trying experience for me. I was a little country boy from Horatio, Arkansas, having had an optimistic attitude about society, how great integration was going to be, and how many opportunities would be out there—until I walked into Wilson-Sharp . . . and walked into the athletic training department and indicated I wanted to play football. It was like a refrigerator—cold. In the sense that I felt that it was obvious that I was not wanted. I was not needed and that by being there or stating that I was wanting to play football, it was sort of like a forced situation they had to deal with one way or another. I didn't know any other football players who were playing. I really had never played football before in an organized fashion. I really wanted to play football.

I felt discouraged a lot of times, on and off the football field, from participating in football. An example would have been I was not allowed to eat in Wilson-Sharp with the other athletes. I had to eat at Brough Commons most of the time after practice ended at six P.M. or later. Brough Commons had closed. There were many days I didn't have an opportunity to eat because I had to run from the football field all the way up to Brough Commons to try to see if I could get any food to eat to tide me over for the night. I can say that the lack of food left a bad taste in my mouth when I left practice and trying to make a point.

I'll say this. I wanted to be the first black football player at the University of Arkansas. I wanted to open up a door. I wanted to be among that first group who went to the University of Arkansas because I wanted to open up a door—very significant in my life at that time, while being aware of Martin Luther King's objectives, goals, and other black leaders to try to make a difference and try to make a change. That was foremost in my mind. I thought I only wanted to make a difference. I not only wanted to make a change, but I wanted to be successful in doing that. Therein lies the frustration. The goal of wanting to make a change, to be a part of the change, and to be successful, but at the same time meeting insurmountable odds and facing very difficult obstacles such as racial attitudes that existed among maybe the student body and the university at that time. But I was not going to be deterred. My mother encouraged me not to give up, but to continue to attend. Because I can tell you there were many nights that I wanted to get on the bus and come back to Horatio, Arkansas, or go to the University of Arkansas Pine Bluff, which was then AM&N College.

I would always ask myself the question, what impact could I make in the civil rights movement and what would be the nature of that impact? If I left the university, what would that say about my participation in the civil rights movement? All of the students there probably experienced a great deal of frustration in the community, in the school, in the academic setting, and in our academic endeavors. I can recall Harold Betton and I being in a class, in this particular class, we were told we would never get an "A" in the class, no matter what. Even though our test papers were comparable to some of the best papers that were actually written or results that were turned in, and that was frustrating.

I remember the biggest number of people came from Little Rock, sprinklings from Pine Bluff, and other places. And because of our limited numbers, we just had a little clique, and that little clique was all we had. I dare say that every student in that first group suffered emotionally because of the experience of being the first. So if I had to characterize it so you can get to your next question, we experienced a lot of joy for being able to be at the institution. We were proud because we were proud to be at the institution when we went there. We became frustrated for the experiences that we had. Needless to say, those experiences made some of us stronger, but it also tore down the psyche of a lot of others that were in those small numbers to the point where they left or their frustrations manifested in other ways that certainly would not have been intended before we started to attend the university.

Being the first football player at the university was probably the best and worst thing that has ever, ever happened in my life. It might have been bad for me, but at least it opened the door for others. I thought I was out there getting ready to go out and play football, and be treated like the other football players. I was terribly mistaken. I remember one time I was basically kicked the football for a return. I happened to be the only player on my side of the field, playing against eleven others coming after me for the purpose of tackling me or whatever they were going to do. I considered myself to be a tackling dummy. Later on in my stay at the university, I felt like if that was the case, I just gotta do what I gotta do.

When we came to what we called fourth quarter, I had a chance. To describe it to you, fourth quarter was the time when the football players carried into the indoor facility to work even harder at the end of practice so that when we played football, if we got tired, it did not diminish our ability to participate at a higher level. Basically, what would happen is that running backs would be paired with running backs, quarterbacks would be paired with quarterbacks and some running backs as well. I was paired with linemen a lot of the time. In terms of wrestling or something like that where you need not just speed but physical endurance and strength. Looking back on that, [laughing] it might have helped me, but it certainly didn't help me at the time because it was continuously frustrating. Me weighing one hundred eighty-five pounds trying to wrestle someone at two hundred sixty pounds. That was one aspect.

The other aspect that was extremely frustrating was while I was out there practicing, I'd hear words like "Hurt that nigga. Tackle that nigga." Those kinds of derogatory terms, that was frustrating. There were a few of the players and a coach who would say, "Hey, keep your head up, keep on doing what you are doing, and don't worry about that." There were not great numbers of those who did that. But by and large, if I had to talk about friends that I had at the university, a significant number of them would have come from the football team. There were others I had forged friendships with in the academic world. I remember names that I'm not calling at this time, but that was good.

But my frustration grew and grew everyday. You can't imagine how it feels to want to do something so bad and to be discouraged every step of the way. I was so anxious to play football at the university. Somebody had told me one time that if you really want to play, make yourself available to that coach. I remember we were playing North Texas State. Mean Joe Green [future NFL Hall of Fame] was on the other side of the line at the time. The coach yelled down the decks if there was anybody who had played guard. I hadn't played guard at all. I'd practiced guard. I just wanted to go in. He didn't let me go in, but he did let me go in as halfback at the time and I had the pleasure of being tackled by Mean Joe Green. I guess that's my claim to fame . . . playing in that game. Other games, basically just playing whenever, wherever they wanted to put me, I was ready to go. I didn't want to give up.

I played a lot of basketball in high school. I had some feelers from John Brown University and actually had an offer to play at the University of Arkansas, Pine Bluff, AM&N. I can tell you in the middle of the season for football, I was seriously considering going to John Brown University or to AM&N. At that time, John Brown University was all white, too, and I would have been the first black basketball player there, but I decided to stay no matter what, especially with my mother saying this was what I needed to do. My mother was a teacher and retired after some thirty-eight years in the teaching profession. My daddy was a janitor who cleaned up, worked hard all his life to try to get his four kids in school, and all that played a part.

I guess another one of those frustrating things, during my entire tenure as a football player at the University of Arkansas, I never had a playbook. I remember once I was in the huddle. I think John Eichler may have been the quarterback at the time. He called white thirty-two or whatever the play would have been. The other players backed away from the huddle and I whispered into his ear, what was I supposed to do? He was going to give me the ball! I said, "Oh, OK." I said, "Which side?" [Laughing] That's how bad it was. I never saw a playbook.

Then after all that, being called names, things like that, and having to run up the hill to Brough Commons, which was not a short distance and required extra conditioning to get there to the dining room to be told that it just closed, that taught me another lesson, too. I had to be kind of ingenious. So after about a week or two it was clear, I'm not going to make it to the dining room on time. So instead of me running to the dining room, I got to know some of the people in the kitchen. I would knock on the door and ask them, "Can ya'll save me a plate because I'm not going to get here in time?" Those guys did. That was the only way I had a chance to eat after practice. I think I might have eaten at Wilson-Sharp one time, one day. Boy, I tell you, the food was good [laughing]. I'm still struggling with it. Why can't I eat like these guys, eating all the steaks you want, all the eggs you want, and just thinking that opportunities and situations that were afforded to other people that I was deprived of?

You have got to understand my background. I came from a small town, may have been seven hundred at the time. The one thing, regardless of your color, if a person didn't like you, they simply did not like you. Skin color in Horatio was not the primary controlling factor as to whether a person liked or disliked you. I am sure that there were some people that hated you or treated you differently just because of the color of your skin. It might have been something you did or something like that. So when I went to the university, I kind of thought that it might be something like I had already experienced. I was a bit naïve. I was sort of walking blindly into the situation. In high school, I was a track star as well. We didn't have a track. I never had training on how to throw the discus, how to run hurdles, how to throw the shot-put, et cetera. We didn't have uniforms or anything. We had to wear a white shirt, white gym shorts, and whatever shoes we had. I remember I ran track barefoot on a cement track at the Peach Blossom Relays they used to have.

Going back to my point about Horatio. These guys had read or heard that I was running track. I went up to Horatio, which was an all-white school at the time; I told them what I was doing. And I said, "Can any of ya'll help me?" All of the athletes came to me and gave me a shot-put, instead of the rock I was heaving. They gave me a discus to throw and showed me how to throw it, instead of a flat rock that I was trying to throw. They gave me hurdles instead of saw horses that I was using and if I ran into one of those, I wouldn't be able to walk at all. But it taught me how to clear hurdles!! [Laughing.] The lesson I got from that, as a person running track, looking at a saw horse as a hurdle, in life it's the same thing. You'll run into all kinds of hurdles, small or tall, and you have to make up your mind to clear the hurdles. Those guys helped me. Each one of them told me in 1964 . . . I can't say each and everyone . . . they all told me, "I wish you could be here playing football and track all of the time." That's what they said.

With all of that backdrop and them saying what they said, I asked my mother, could I just stay here one more year, so that I could enjoy this and there in the motivation to go to the

University of Arkansas. My brother was already at AM&N at the time. I could've been up there with my big brother. But in any event, all that kind of got me going along with the fact that we had an environment of the civil rights movement. Sit-ins and demonstrations had been taking place all across the country. All that was a backdrop; it made me a different kind of person that had all these dreams. Crazy? I don't know. When Martin Luther King said he had a dream, I had a dream! And it was really and truly a dream, which did not come true all the way, but which did in many respects.

But the one thing that I can say that I learned about that experience is that all people are not bad, but of those that are bad, they stuck out like a sore thumb! They were more visible. They were a constant reminder of who I was and what my place was. That was a constant struggle for me not to resign myself to staying in that place. I wanted to move, do something, and make a difference.

Another frustrating thing occurred at the university when I was up there playing football; there was a time that Jerry LeVias from SMU was down there playing football. There were other players being recruited across the country, USC obviously and others. I think OJ Simpson was playing at that time. The words spoken to me at that time, "We don't need one now." If you don't think that in the midst of running up against eleven people, carrying the football, acting like a football dummy, a tackling dummy, not being able to eat when I finished practice, and being called a nigga, don't you think that frustrated me? It made me angry! And even to this day when I see . . . I shouldn't say to this day, which is true . . . but when I decided to get out of football and do something else, I would watch TV, see a black athlete running that football, and cry like a baby. It hurt me that much [crying/pause].

This is a lot during an interview [crying]. It rekindled a lot of my frustrations that I relive, when I'm dealing with some of the things that happened, how things could've been different had people accepted that we were equal, and there were differences because of the color of our skin, but anyway I'm over it. I'm over it. Let's move on.

I played in the 1965 season. I went out for spring football in 1966. In 1966, I was injured. I had a thumb injury and a knee injury. Of course, that was something else that I didn't need at that point in time. I think Hiram may have come up at that time, but I decided that, well, I've paid my debt. It's time to move on. I want to make a change. That's when I started focusing on law. I played in 1965, throughout the spring football, got injured, and left the football program.

Describe my feelings toward the university while I was there? I was frustrated and disappointed. My bubble burst when I came to the University of Arkansas and experienced what I experienced. But I think it made me stronger. It reinforced in my mind that if there was going to be a change, then we had to be determined to make a change, to stay with it, and not just give it up. That was the only way the difference was going to come about. And so it was a learning experience. It was a bitter experience and it was a bittersweet experience because to this day I can still say there are still two or three people that I consider to be my friends because of that experience. I thank them for that. It was a football group and it was different in a way because we did share one common goal—it was to play football. But even though we shared that common goal, a lot of people's background came in to make that experience not so delightful and to make it hard, but I wouldn't give. I'd do it all over again because I think it was worth it for me as an individual and the others willing to follow me.

I have returned to the university and it had to be . . . it might have been fifteen years . . . maybe 1980 or later that I actually returned to the university. On that first trip to the university, I just went through the campus. I didn't even stop. The next trip to the university was when I was a lawyer, practicing law. That would've been in the 1980s and then after that, I went up after my daughter was a student and running track. I've been going ever since. And my son, who graduated from Law School, gave me a reason to go. I didn't try to deter my children from going. I have two now who are going to the university. All of my children went to the university despite my experience. I've never one day tried to discourage them from going because I thought that was a decision they had to make. They knew the history. I think each of them were determined to move forward and carry on whatever little legacy I may have had by attending the university.

I feel that in a lot of areas, the university has taken steps . . . I should say . . . to bring about a change in the perception that we have or that I had about the university and the university community. I think that the university has at least, during the period of time of my graduation until the 1990s, I guess, they made some strides, but not enough. I see more black professors, not enough. I saw more students at one time than I see now. Not enough. But there is, and always will be, room for improvement of race relations and an environment of equality at the university, just as it would be at any other university.

As a result of my experience and what I have seen, the university has stated and committed itself to make some strides toward diversity and equality. They have to continue. It's an ongoing thing. I'm never going to be satisfied completely. I think it's a higher institution of learning that should not only be made available to students who are willing to go, but also for those professionals who want to teach and become a part of that system in order to effect real change. There has to be constant dialogue. I saw at some point in time . . . I saw complacency. When Nolan was employed, "Oh, we got a black coach." That wasn't good enough for me. I know Nolan and I know what he went through as evidenced by conversations and events that happened. The university has made strides, but there are still strides to be made. And I think that this administration, especially, should and it appears to be making a concerted effort to keep moving. It can't happen overnight, but we cannot be satisfied by having one, two, or three or any number associated with diversity, but deal with competent minorities being involved in that institution whether it's academically or administratively and to make sure that each and every representative of that institution understands what the commitment of the University of Arkansas should be. It is not a university of just those who want to go up there. It's a university which should represent this entire state that is composed of minorities, and otherwise, males, females, blacks, Hispanics, Asians, whatever the case should be— and not just be lip service to it.

I have seen many frustrated professionals who would have enjoyed going to the University of Arkansas who didn't. I have seen many athletes during the period of time from then until now who wanted to attend the University of Arkansas but didn't want to because other universities were reaching out. There was a time when the administration, and I won't say all the people in the administration, but there were those that demonstrated their opposition to . . . I'd say, and I don't like to use this term . . . but to fully integrating the university community, giving everybody a fair shot and a fair choice. That's the most political statement I can give.

During that period of time (while I was there), we were demonstrating. We had an organization called Black Americans for Democracy, which was . . . I think Gene Hunt was president at that time. There were a lot of other things going on in the state at that time, too. I think about that time there might have even been a group that went to the capitol. But anyway, that was the atmosphere. It was a tense atmosphere. We wanted to make change. We didn't want them to play "Dixie" anymore. We had pep rallies where we were confronted. As a matter of fact, we took over the pep rally. There may have been fifteen others maybe, went down in front of a Razorback rally, and said it is going to stop. You will not do it again. You will not play it again. Our intentions were to demonstrate at the Texas-Arkansas game. We had a meeting that was planned that particular night. I used to jog and all that kind of stuff. Prior to the meeting, I had been jogging and a car of guys came by, yelled out some obscenities and derogatory remarks. I heard a "Pow!" I thought it was just a firecracker or something and kept running until I reached down and got a . . . felt a little pain in my knee. And at that time, Jimmie Wilson and some other people came and got me. I didn't even go to the hospital at that particular time. Eventually I did go to the hospital, but I guess at that point in time, it also caused other people to rally around the sincerity that we had about achieving the goal of having a democratic system that would incorporate us into it and not disrespect us.

One of the things, and I know you know, when you're playing "Dixie," it might mean something to someone else, but it meant nothing to me except in a racist attitude. I was hurt, but that's probably because I was still there, but then when I go, I go away. And then there were rumors going around saying that it was all staged and that kind of stuff, but the bottom line is I let other people know exactly what happened that night and it didn't surprise me that nobody would accept credit for doing it. So we just kept moving along. I could walk. I could breathe. I could talk and I could breathe, so let's go after it. Let's keep on going. It was real tense before that time and after that time at the University of Arkansas. Racial tension was at its highest. There were certain members of the Black Panther party around in that area—Kansas City, visiting the university, et cetera, and the university community. There were a lot of things going up. One thing about that group and BAD, they were determined to make a change or did not give up trying to make a change. This was in 1969.

My experience at the university was mixed with . . . as I said before . . . joy, frustration, anger, and the development of a determination to make a difference. The fact that Martin Luther King gave his life while I was attending the University of Arkansas—the fact that I was aware of what was going on at the University of Arkansas—redefined and strengthened my commitment not only to make a change, but to be a part of that change. Being called a "nigga" was obviously more offensive to me at that time and at that place because I was slowly, slowly beginning to believe that a change was going to come and that people's attitudes were changing. I remember living in Holcombe Hall, and I was very active in Holcombe Hall. That was more or less the athletic dorm for intramurals really. It was stacked with athletes. And during the SMU "game of all games," members of the university community, students, tried to attack me in front of Holcombe Hall and started calling me "nigga" and about four or five of them started approaching me. At that time, I was not one to run. But I also knew that the odds were not too good. The only thing I had was fast feet—I wasn't going to run. So I grabbed a chair and as I grabbed the chair, some of the white residents of Holcombe Hall came out and heard these guys calling me all these names, joined in behind me, and said you are not going to touch him. Now, I don't know whether that means I was their "nigga" or what, but the bottom line is I accepted that as some solidarity at least among some of those people who were willing to stand up and resist some of the racism that had already been demonstrated.

And again, if you listen to my story, the theme of it is that there were so many mixed emotions and there were some people that were at the university who could never deal with those mixed emotions. There were some people that were at the university when I went up there that left that university ragged in terms of their mindset. I mean completely and mentally broken. And it was because of their experiences. You know the social life, zero. Academics frustrating and you felt like you were an outcast, but you shouldn't have been. But I can say this one thing, everybody that went up there, I gotta take my hats off to them. They helped make a difference and they helped make a change. The frustrating part right now is that when I look around and I see young black athletes involved in the program and having problems, I just get frustrated because there needs to be an intensive program there to make sure that we're not slipping back into the 1950s and 1960s in terms of how black athletes are perceived and not only as athletes but as citizens and people that are equal. That frustrates me. I wish there was some way we could help the young black athletes at the university, not just physically. They really need somebody to walk with them at the university, to constantly remind them of what their goals and missions are and that is to get an education, develop athletically, and stay out of trouble. There is a need for counseling from someone who understands the many pitfalls that they face. There is a need for these young men and women to know that if they need help or advice, it can be obtained. The bottom line is that we must have concerned professionals readily available and involved in the lives of these young people on a daily and weekly basis. Many are immature in a lot of ways and unfortunately have no realistic concept of what the future holds and what to do now to positively affect the future. Inclusion. Inclusion to me is still a part of every aspect of the university.

I was so proud when Gene McKissic became president of the student body. I kind of smiled and said, "You know, who would've thought it?" And how I felt that same emotion January when Obama became the President of the United States. Regardless of whether Gene McKissic was the president of the student body, regardless of whether Obama is the president of these United States, the one thing I can tell you from my experience that I understand is this—don't you ever forget, don't you ever forget that the color of your skin to a significant number of people still makes a difference. If our attitudes are controlled because of the perception of somebody's pigmentation, then we are still in need of change. And we might not change everybody's attitude, but I want to change how people can segregate or put obstacles in front of you to keep you from becoming part of this society as an equal participant with an equal opportunity to succeed and to have a chance in these United States and in this world.

I know that because of the university, I think I have developed an attitude that I don't ever want to hurt anybody. I don't want to see anybody get hurt. I don't want to see gangs of blacks fighting against each other at a time when we need to be together. As a result of my experience at the university, it is clear to me that if you are divided, you will fall, and there was division at the university, even among the blacks, but certainly among the student body at times. And because of that, it has taken so long for any significant change to occur. It is frustrating when I see our young professionals still hesitant to speak out, to make a difference. But it is equally satisfying to see those who are willing to do it. And another thing that my experience at the university and in life has taught me is that we cannot have people who rise to the top, who are professional blacks and forget who they were, forget about those others who are still striving and struggling, not just to get to the top, but to survive. I can tell you I saw that at the university. Our black community and the university were a microcosm and a reflection of society. Everything that was happening in society was happening at the university. And if we know that it's a microcosm of society, then not only do we need to start changing these attitudes at the family level, but we need to continue with great energy at the university level.

At any academic institution, whether it is high school or the university, we've gotta make sure the clouds and the smoke are removed to see things as they are, call them what they are, and don't become complacent. I've learned that if you become complacent, you forget, you lose focus. And other people are still left behind. I've never been one to fly under the radar. And when I attended the university, it was not my intention to fly under the radar. I wanted to make a difference, I wanted to make a change, and I was committed that if making that difference, making that change, meant that I would have to sacrifice something, then I was willing to do that. I'm not going to tell you that I was willing to die. But I can tell you that death did not scare me. I knew there were times when I was in the eye of someone who had evil intentions, but I also knew that I believed my mother's faith and my dad's faith in God, even though I did not profess it at that time, served as my backbone to do whatever I was going to do. And to remember that golden rule about doing unto others as you'd have them do unto you and because of that rule, if I have ever hurt anybody, if I caused any harm to anybody, you can rest assured that it was not by design and not intended. If everybody has that attitude, this would be a better world. That's it. I finished my bachelor's in 1969 and Law School in 1972. One day I hope to write a book about all of my life experiences, from the hills of Horatio to the hills of Fayetteville and back.

■ Margaret Clark (1967–1968, 1969–1998), university professor

Written response to interview questions, September 12, 2007
For detailed biography, see Appendix A, page 291

I received an MA in French in 1968 and an EdD in 1969 from the University of Arkansas, Fayetteville. As a member of the Arkansas Foreign Language Council, which was organized in 1965 by the Arkansas State Foreign Language Specialist, Miss Wilma Jimerson, I served along with Dr. Lawrence Guinn, the chair of the foreign language at the University of Arkansas. Miss Jimerson had been largely responsible for encouraging me to apply for the two National Defense Education Act (NDEA) scholarship grants I had received. Dr. Guinn informed me of an Elementary and Secondary Education Act (ESEA) master's degree scholarship grant program that the foreign language department had received and urged me to consider applying for one of the scholarships. I received the scholarship grant and therefore entered the UAF in the fall of 1967.

After receiving my master's degree, I returned to Merrill High School and continued to teach French and Spanish. I also continued to serve on the Arkansas Foreign Language Council. One of the things that the council was suggesting as a means of improving the quality of foreign language education in Arkansas was to get people who teach foreign languages, the practitioners, to become qualified to be professors in colleges of education. Again, I was encouraged to consider enrolling in a doctoral program for this purpose. When Dr. Guinn offered me a part-time instructorship for the fall of 1969, as a follow-up to the visiting instructorship I had already received from the foreign language department at the University of Arkansas for a 1969 summer program for training high school foreign language teachers, I accepted and then proceeded to enroll in a foreign language education doctoral program in the College of Education.

It took one year to complete the master's degree. I finished my doctoral studies in three years, and then it took me about three years to get into the "jargonese" of education before I was able to concentrate on the doctoral dissertation. After all, during this time, I was teaching two classes in French and two classes in education, advising foreign language majors in the College of Education and those majors in the College of Arts and Sciences who wanted to become foreign language teachers, supervising foreign language students teachers in area schools, supervising graduate assistants who were teaching the basic elementary French courses, attending meetings and serving on committees at the departmental, college, and university levels, along with endeavoring to complete the dissertation.

I believe I was one of the first African American faculty members inasmuch as I was hired as a part-time instructor in the foreign language department in 1969 (coupled with the visiting instructorship for a special SNEA 1969 summer program sponsored by the foreign language department). I was the first African American hired as an assistant professor to teach in the College of Education. (Another African American woman was hired at the same time to work in the dean's office.) I co-sponsored the chartering of the campus chapter, Kappa Iota, of the Alpha Kappa Alpha Sorority, Inc. and served as its graduate advisor for twenty-two years and also as its faculty advisor for most of those years. Through my encouragement and support, two members of the chapter agreed to be the first African Americans to serve as secretary and president (not at the same time) of the Pan-Hellenic Council. This kind of service, seemingly, is no longer possible inasmuch as the National Panhellenic Council was established and it sends representatives to the Pan-Hellenic Council. The latter is still the organization, I think, that grants permission for sororities to be on campus.

Given the fact that I am a retired associate professor emerita in addition to having been a student, I must say that my experience overall has been mostly positive. During my year as a master's degree-seeking student, I truly enjoyed being a student at the university. There were six of us who were high school teachers in French and six in Spanish. In the special ESEA program, we all became friends and those of us in French truly bonded. We had our own study sessions, pizza parties, and outings. One of the two who were French teachers living in Fayetteville often had the group over to her house. The professors were very kind, also. We were often included in departmental activities, including parties at the home of the chair and other faculty members.

During my doctoral years, I was a part of the French faculty, and as such, I was included in all of the departmental social activities. This included parties at the chairs' homes (there were four different chairs) faculty members' homes, at restaurants, pizza parlors, and some at the office that also included graduate students. I had started a special friendship with the wife of one of my professors from the master's degree program. Her name was Carolyn Locke and she became my best friend. Four other members of the department also became colleagues with whom I worked closely on both departmental and externally funded projects as well as close friends: Professor Mark Doyle, Dr. Irene Bergal, Dr. Rita Falke, and Professor Marjorie Rudolph. After I passed my doctoral exams and was offered an assistant professorship by the dean of the College of Education, Dr. Fred Vescolani, I began to develop friendships with faculty members in the College of Education, including Dr. Don Miller, Dr. Martin Schoppmeyer, Dr. Sallie Lee Hines, Dr. Gary Taylor, and Dr. Phillip Besonen. Dean Vescolani had an open-door policy and I always felt comfortable being able to go in and talk with him about any academic problems or concerns. Several of my fellow doctoral classmates also became good acquaintances to whom I could go over the years for assistance due to the kinds of positions they held: principals, administrators in university programs, and area businessmen.

As a professor, I have had some wonderful highlights that I have planned that have given me many good feelings of satisfaction and gratification: three externally funded foreign language conferences for area practitioners and three externally funded English as a Second Language conferences for area practitioners. As the faculty member responsible for the chartering of the Pi Delta Phi, the French national honorary society, I was pleased at the types of activities we sponsored, including bringing in representatives from the French and Canadian consulates.

As the advisor of the undergraduate Alpha Kappa Alpha Sorority chapter, I was pleased with the fashion show in the early 1980s that included participation by most of the Greek sororities and fraternities (both African American and Caucasian), the roundtables having different perspectives on issues presented by UAF faculty members, the sponsoring of a series of lectures by Dr. Daniel Littlefield (a professor from the University of Arkansas at Little Rock) on slavery as practiced by the five civilized Indian tribes, by the initiation of the Equity Step Show that includes ALL Greeks, and by the initiation of Asians (and later on Caucasians) into the chapter as members, During the year in which I was also serving as the sponsor of the African Student Union, I facilitated the scheduling of activities at which both the chapter members and other Greeks interacted in social activities with the African students.

It was a surprise and a delight to have the organizers of the Ira Aldridge Players ask me to serve as their faculty sponsor. It was an even greater surprise to be asked to perform on their readers' theater program.

I had good feelings toward the university during my study times. This is what I have tried to describe or relate in the above answers. I had core groups that made my stay here very wholesome and productive, satisfying, and gratifying. First, there was my community of French and Spanish teachers in the special ESEA program; secondly, there was the foreign language faculty; thirdly, there was the group of women in civic organizations that befriended me and asked me to join their different organizations. Mrs. Othelia Paul, who worked in the dean's office in the College of Education, was a dear friend and mentor for me in this respect. Fourthly, there was the African American community, especially those I call my Fayetteville family: Sherman and Minerva Hoover Morgan, and Minerva's two daughters, Patricia Polk and Melba Smith.

I never left after my return in 1969. Basically, I still have many very good feelings about the university. However, when I reflect back over the years, there were some areas of concern . . . overall expectations, a diminishing of collegiality among some colleagues, some differences in the granting of promotions and tenure, some inequities in the workloads and the salaries; however, I recognize that this is what research universities are all about.

The university has been a place where I have been able to grow professionally and personally. I was able to teach in Athens, Greece, for one summer in the Arkansas-in Athens program sponsored by the College of Education. I have so many good acquaintances across departmental and college lines. I have lifelong friends from my master's degree, doctoral, and professional work days. I have seen some of my advisees be able to obtain doctoral degrees. I worked to get Latinos included in the Holmes Scholars program (Dr. Natalia Salazar was the first). I have been able to capitalize on collaborations with several of my colleagues, especially my dear friend Dr. Annette Digby, who is now the provost and vice president of Academic Affairs at Lincoln University in Jefferson City, Missouri. I have been able to make presentations at numerous state and national professional meetings and international meetings in such places as Mexico City, Mexico; Toronto and Ottawa, Canada; Muscat, Oman; Rio de Janeiro, Brazil; Singapore; Santiago, Chile; Darussallam, Brunei, and including one professional meeting on a cruise liner in the Caribbean to and from Nassau, Bahamas . . . and most of all, I have enjoyed the yearly anticipation of meeting new students, many of whom have become good friends and acquaintances, . . . plus I truly loved teaching.

■ Viralene J. Coleman (1957–1959, 1966–1969), university professor

Written response to interview questions, September 2007
For detailed biography, see Appendix A, page 291

I entered the University of Arkansas, Fayetteville, in the summer of 1957 and returned the summer of 1959, receiving the MA degree in English. I returned to the UAF in 1966 and remained for three years, earning the doctorate degree in English in 1969.

I selected UAF because I was somewhat familiar with the campus; it provided housing (I had two children with me), and it was not too far from my home in Pine Bluff. I spent three years and two summers at UAF. I think I am listed as being the first African American to receive the PhD degree from UAF.

I have only pleasant memories of my tenure at UAF. I was there as a thirty six year old married mother of two, working toward an advanced degree. I was an instructor in English at UAPB on sabbatical the first year and on Title III the last two. I found the professors and students to be cordial. After I graduated, I would encounter many of them at statewide English meetings. I still exchange Christmas cards with one family, every year. I felt more comfortable during the 1966 through 1969 periods. While the students were always polite, the acceptance and warmth were more apparent during the later period.

I have not returned to the campus. I am glad whenever I read about a minority student enrolling at UAF. I notice it as well as its increasing the number of black faculty members. The movement toward diversity on campus is upward. A bit slow, but upward, nevertheless.

I retired from the University of Arkansas at Pine Bluff in 1999. I am now professor emeriti of English and a former chair of the Department of English, Theatre and Mass Communications. Occasionally, I serve as adjunct professor of English and teach an evening class in literature or freshman composition.

■ Alice Davis Butler (1965–1969), administrator

Interview by Charles Robinson, March 5, 2008
Interviewed at the Arkansas Alumni Association on the University of Arkansas campus
For detailed biography, see Appendix A, page 292

My freshman year was 1965–1966. I lived in Hotz Hall. For the first semester, I had no roommate and I knew absolutely no one else in the nine-story building. There was a name of another girl on the door to the room I was assigned, but she never showed. I went from living with my parents and four sisters in a segregated small-town environment to a forced integrated environment. I remember when I applied for dormitory housing I was required to submit a picture with the application. As I recall, the university had just been ordered by the federal government to tear down the segregated Scotts Hall that was for black students and to integrate the university housing systems. I am certain the requirement to send a picture was to make sure there were no roommates of different races.

I was assigned a mentor by the university and she met me in my room at the dormitory. She was Caucasian and she was a sophomore. She met with me many times throughout my freshman year. She gave me advice, tips on living in a dormitory, and registering for classes. But she did not live in Hotz Hall and even if she had, she would not have been able to give me advice on how to handle isolation and racism. I had a horrible first semester living alone. This was all new to me and I had no one else with whom to share my fears and tears. The girls living on either side of my room did not speak to me, they did not include me in gatherings; the counselor on my floor was overwhelmed. I slept, ate, studied, and lived alone.

While many of my dorm mates would not socialize with me, they were curious, critical, and condescending. For example, when I needed to straighten my hair after my swim sessions, many girls would come from their rooms, stand in the hallway, and ask, "What is that horrible burning smell?" I would close my door to keep from answering their questions. Eventually two girls came to my room and asked me what I was doing to my hair. Embarrassed, I explained. But later I decided either because I did not want the attention or because I wanted to assimilate, I would wash my hair, set it on rollers, and set under a hair dryer. This was the custom of the majority of the white girls. I had to buy the dryer, rollers, and my hair looked more like an Afro than the other black girls. At least I did not draw attention to myself; interestingly, my hair began to grow thicker and longer since I was not using hot combs on it every other day.

As to academics, the first standardized test I took was at the university. My academic counselor met with me to go over my results. My scores in every area were tremendously embarrassing for me. I realized while taking the test that there were many questions about many different subjects, the majority about which I had no knowledge. I had thought I was smart; afterall, I had graduated number three in my class of fifty-plus students. But the conclusions were that I needed to take remedial English, math, and reading. I cried for days. It was not until I saw other black and white students in my remedial classes who lived in my dormitory, and some had graduated from Central High in Little Rock, that I begin to realize I was not alone in my need for remedial education.

In retrospect, I should not have been surprised because I knew that our high school textbooks, laboratory equipment, and materials were all used and passed on to us from the white school in our town. They (the white students) received new books, and equipment and we received their leftovers with missing pages, markings, and drawings in them. Separate was not equal.

I did not know how to swim so I decided to take Beginner's Swimming. This was a mistake because the pool was being renovated for the first nine weeks of the semester. The first day in the new swimming pool building, the swim instructor came in class and ordered all of us to jump in the pool and swim a lap. Every student except me jumped in the pool and started swimming. I did not know what to do and the instructor stared at me, but said nothing. So I started at the shallow end and using the steps I slowly stepped into the pool as tears of fear began to stream down my face. At that point, every one seemed to be looking at me. The instructor came over to me and in what sounded like a loud voice said, "You do know how to swim, don't you?" I replied, "No, this is a beginner's swimming class, right?' and she countered with, "Yes, but most people already know how to swim." The instructor never entered the pool to help me; she bellowed commands to me from the deck and because everyone else knew how to swim and was taking the course for an easy "A," she clearly resented having to teach a true beginner. I made a "D" in the course, in great part because I practiced every chance I could. The instructor was little help, but kind students who were in the pool on my practice days were more helpful and they were white.

Another racist incident happened in my French class. I had never studied another language and knew no French at all, not even the most common expressions. I had never even heard the language spoken. Of course the professor spoke French from the beginning; he asked questions and many students raised their hands to answer. I was the only black student in the class and I was sitting in the first seat of one of the rows. The professor came to within a few feet of me and asked several questions of me in French. He kept repeating them over and over as though I was going to get the language just by him repeating the questions several times. I said to him, "I don't know French. I don't understand what you're saying." Some of the students began to laugh. I began to cry and when he saw I was upset, he stopped, started speaking English, and began to teach the class. I believe, but for my race, he would have picked on just me to focus his questions after he knew clearly I did not understand a word he was saying. Another racist incident happened to me during the summer of my junior year while taking another French class.

In summary, I spent a lot of time in my room alone studying. I called my parents frequently, sometimes twice a day. I felt so lonely and isolated. I had no boyfriend, but I did have classmates from my high school that lived in a nearby dormitory. But it was not until I met two black girls from Little Rock who lived in my dorm on the same floor as I did that I began to feel more comfortable. I became good friends with one of them and we would later become roommates for our sophomore year. I also had a roommate for the second semester of my freshman year; she, too, was black.

My sophomore year, 1966–1967, I lived in Carnall Hall. I had a roommate who was black. Life was different and easier. I do think it was during my sophomore year that race became less of a factor for me. That is, I thought less about what race a person was when I talked to them or socialized with them.

My roommate and I became really close friends with two white girls who lived on our floor. One of them had a car; we studied, played cards, and socialized together daily. I even carpooled from Little Rock with the white girl that had the car. I remember fondly my year in Carnall Hall, my friendship with my roommate, and the other two girls whose names I still remember, but will not mention them here.

During the summer of my junior year (1967–1968), I lived in a dormitory; the name of which I cannot remember. My next-door neighbor was a young white woman whose major was French. How fortunate for me. She and I were also in the same French class. So we sat next to each other in class and we studied together in the dormitory and in the library. With her help, I learned to read and speak the language really well. When it was time to take the final class exam, we went to our usual seats. But before the professor passed out the test, he told me to move my desk to the front of the class and to turn my desk so that I sat with my back to the rest of the class. I asked him why, but he did not answer me. So I quipped, "Oh, I know; you just want me to stand out even more than I already do." My classmates all laughed. I was the only black student in the class. He made no comment to my quip and after I moved my desk as he had instructed, he began to pass out the test. There had never been any incident between my friend and me in class, so we were totally baffled as to why he singled out me. I can only conclude he did this because of my race. This happened to me almost forty years ago, but I remember it as though it happened yesterday. Nonetheless, I made a "B" in the class.

During my junior and senior years, the country was in turmoil and change in racist practices was underway. MLK [Dr. Martin Luther King Jr.] and RFK [Robert F. Kennedy] had been assassinated; these assassinations spurred many of us to speak out about how we felt and how we were being treated on and off campus. The "Black and Proud Movement" and the "Afro" hairstyle became popular among the black students on campus as well. I cannot tell you how many of my white friends asked me how I got my hair to "stand up like that." It was so very empowering; I no longer felt I had to assimilate. Wearing the afro was a confidence booster.

As black students, we also began to speak out about racial injustice where we saw it. We started with the football team. Football was extremely popular during this time. The team was number one in its conference. The coach, Frank Broyles, was outspoken about not wanting any black players on his team. I remember him being quoted as saying the team made number one without them [black players] and so he did not need them. So many of us would go to the home football games and sit among the university crowd. We would cheer for the visiting team, if they had black players on their team; for example, LSU. These practices angered every one around us and could have been dangerous for us, but we did it. During this period of time, the basketball team did have black players; so we attended all the home games we could to cheer on the U of A team because it was integrated.

Also during these years, there were at least two campus demonstrations in front of the university president's office. We were protesting racial practices on and off campus. In the city of Fayetteville, there were many restaurants and businesses that did not allow black students. Our demonstrations were peaceful, and there were both white and black students in the crowd.

During my senior year (1968–1969), the student council invited a number of prominent speakers to address the student body on various issues. I remember with great clarity and disappointment the night Muhammad Ali came to speak. I was excited and proud to attend the session with Muhammad Ali. But my pride and excitement turned to horror and dejection, when Mr. Ali began to share his views on the need for racial segregation. For example, he spoke about how he felt black students should go to all-black colleges and should support "black-only" businesses and should live in "black-only" areas of a city. I remember him saying that he could not understand why any black student would want to attend the U of A.

Needless to say, I was—and I know I speak for my friends who were sitting with me on the first few rows in front—in total disbelief and really angry. What is he saying? Can he really be saying this in this mixed crowd at this time? Is he serious? These were all questions that were being whispered around as we listened incredulously. I left without benefit of hearing his entire speech. I had enough.

Before he left campus that night, word got out that Mr. Ali was inviting black students to his hotel room. I went in spite of my anger. I wanted to ask him why? We also knew that at the time, Mr. Ali lived in an exclusive area of an east coast state (the name of which escapes me), but the area in which he lived and was raising his children was not all black.

When we arrived in his room, Mr. Ali jumped up from the couch where he was sitting and said, "Women," and began to approach me hurriedly; I was the first woman to enter the room. The young man who was my date for the evening, jumped back when Mr. Ali approached. I remember saying to my date, "Some date you are." And, he quipped, "If he wants you he can have you." Nothing happened. Mr. Ali said he was only joking. But with body guards stationed all over the suite holding loaded guns, my nerve to take him on about his segregationist views was lost. Instead, we listened to him talk about his life and watched as the student body representative came to the room to pay him in cash. He spread all of the money out on the table for us to see. The whole scene was so unreal and yet it did happen. I have never forgotten it.

How do I view the university now? I came into my own while at the university and the experiences helped prepare me for the real world. I really do believe I was better prepared after graduation than were my high school classmates who attended an all-black college. Mainly because I had to learn how to live, study, and socialize in a forced integrated environment. The only missing component of my university experience was not being allowed to "Rush" to be a member of a sorority. In hindsight, it would likely have been an unpleasant experience for me being a "token" in a sorority house. I would have liked to have been able to compete, however, and then decline the offer. But I was not allowed simply because I was black. During my junior year, one sorority, whose name I cannot remember, invited me to a formal dinner one night. I cannot remember if this was their way of evaluating me to decide if I should be allowed to "Rush" or what. But the sorority never contacted me again. Nonetheless, all of these experiences prepared me for the real world, and I learned from each and every challenging and racist experience I had. I contribute my ability to interact comfortably with a variety of people to my university experiences. I am pleased I attended the U of A at the time that I did. I am also proud that I paved the way for a number of my family members and other black students from my hometown to attend the University of Arkansas.

■ Joanna P. Edwards (1963–1965), university professor and minister

Written response to interview questions, August 5, 2009
For detailed biography, see Appendix A, page 292

I entered the University of Arkansas, Fayetteville, at the beginning of the 1963–1964 school year, transferring from Arkansas AM&N College, Pine Bluff, where I had been the recipient of the L. A. Davis Scholarship pursuing a double major in art and mathematics. With no financial support at the U of A, I decided to focus on the major in Art so I could complete my degree program. At one point, I wanted to change my major to architecture, but since jobs were not available for us either on campus or off campus, I could not change. Architecture would have taken me five years instead of four. I attended the University of Arkansas, Fayetteville, from 1963 to 1965.

As a result of my participation in the Pine Bluff Movement, I was "automatically and indefinitely suspended" from Arkansas AM&N College. Dr. Lawrence A. Davis Sr., then president of AM&N College, had told us that he would not re-admit us until we wrote letters apologizing for participating in the sit-ins. I did not feel that I had done anything to apologize for; therefore, I decided to transfer to Fayetteville. However, even after transferring to Fayetteville, it took Bob [Robert Whitfield], Bill [William Whitfield], and I over one month to get admitted to classes. The claim was that since we left a state-supported school in bad standing, we could not be admitted to another state-supported school until that had been resolved.

As a student, along with Robert Whitfield, I filed a class action suit against the university, which resulted in the desegregation of the dormitories, extracurricular activities (football, basketball, et cetera), and all other aspects of university life. When we matriculated to the university, we were basically only allowed to take classes. The university had a rule that single women under the age of twenty-three years had to live in university housing; but we could not live in the dormitories. Each African American student had to make a special trip up to Fayetteville for a pre-admission interview with either the dean of men or the dean of women. At this interview, they told us that we were not allowed to live in university housing. I was surprised at this because I had already sent my housing application along with the required deposit.

At my interview with the dean of women, I was informed I would be assigned to Scott House. Scott House was a wood-framed two-story house purchased by the university especially to house single African American women. No provision was made at all for the young men. They had to locate housing as best they could. It did not matter if they were handicapped and without transportation.

The experience of African American students at the University of Arkansas during the time we were there was quite different from Caucasian students. We were basically isolated unto ourselves. We did attend the pep rallies at the outdoor theatre, and spent time in the student union, but generally we had no white friends. One student sat beside me in my History of Art class, copied from me on examinations, but would not acknowledge me on the campus sidewalks. There were just a few African American students attending the U of A at that time; twenty-six the first year and thirty-six the second year. Of course, there were others who came up during summers to work on their master's degrees. As far as undergraduates were concerned, each school year a bunch of students were flunked out, mostly in nursing. Some of that still goes on I understand.

As far as school events were concerned, for me, the pep rallies were it, until they waved the Confederate flag, and started to sing "Dixie." At that point, we left. In 1963–1964, we still understood what the singing and playing of "Dixie" meant.

During the summer of 1964, Bob Whitfield joined me to file a lawsuit against the University of Arkansas. The hearing date was set in Federal District Court for August 1964, the judge who heard the case placed Bob and I in the dormitories for one semester as a test before other students were allowed to move into various dormitories on campus. Bob represented the men as a class, and I represented the women. Even though we had filed the lawsuit, I personally did not expect a decision so quickly, so right at the beginning of the semester we had to prepare ourselves mentally and emotionally to be in dorms where we were the only African Americans. I was assigned Carnall Hall, the oldest dorm on campus. Living in the dorm that semester was quite an experience. We ate formal family-styled meals in the dormitory dining room. Few people wanted to sit at the table where I ate, but it worked out OK.

While everyone avoided me like a plague, one student, Kay Turner, was determined to treat me with respect and to forge a friendship with me. She even went, without my knowledge and/or permission, to the dean of women to request that she be assigned to be my roommate. Of course, the dean told her no. I was happy, because even though I liked Kay as a person, I was enjoying my room with two beds, but paying for only one.

After a few of the other students got to know me, they told how they had planned to burn a cross under my door when I first moved. I really thought that was crazy and told them so, because first of all, there were lots of old wooden floors and trimmings in Carnall Hall; it would have gone up in flames immediately, and second, my room was by the fire escape. I probably would have been able to get out unharmed, they would not have.

One student told me that her daddy would have had a fit if he knew that she was living in the dorm with a "Negra" girl. Since the story had run for days in all of the state newspapers, including the *Arkansas Gazette* and the *Arkansas Democrat*, I asked her where her daddy was that he had not heard. She said that he was dead; before I knew it, I said, "Good."

During the spring semester of 1965, I met the first person that I had ever seen that had never learned racism. It was so obvious that she had not. Believe it or not, she was from the hills. Her name was Diana Smith. We became friends and still are today. She was from the Green Forest area, Alpena to be exact. No African Americans lived there, where her father was the school principal, and her parents had not seen the need to teach her to hate black people.

Being a very small, relatively isolated minority on campus, we mostly interacted among ourselves. We felt pretty protective of each other. Those of us who had been in the trenches of the Pine Bluff Movement had already bonded like sisters and brothers. Bob and Bill Whitfield and I were pretty protective of each other since we had been suspended, sat-in, and arrested together.

Many of the faculty members at that time were racist and did not mind showing it. Different from AM&N College, where the faculty nurtured and encouraged their students to be the best that they could be, and ensured that if you were a good student, you would go on to graduate school with some sort of fellowship, faculty at Fayetteville did none of this for their black students. By my senior year, I already knew that I wanted to study the history of art and discussed it with my professor who had just graduated with a PhD from Indiana University. He just sat there, listened to me (his B+ student), and offered no suggestions or advice on what I should do to get admitted to graduate school. Exactly twenty years later, I earned a PhD in the history of art, with an outside minor in African studies from Indiana University.

My drawing and painting professor was considered the most liberal professor on campus. He was a member on the board of the Arkansas Council on Human Relations, but he graded me down, telling me that I had to be much better than the white students to make it. That was probably true, but I still wanted a fair grade for the work that I had done reflecting tremendous improvement from the beginning to the end of the semester.

Other professors did the same thing. A "C" was supposed to be a good grade if you were African American. For some reason, they usually flunked students in English and Western Civilization; and the nursing students, in zoology. It was disheartening to see those students work so hard only to have to go home at the end of the semester. Many of them had their self-esteem so damaged that they never pursued the completion of their degrees elsewhere. I don't know if the students were better, or if the lawsuit began to tear down the barriers, but I think that most of the students who entered during the 1964–1965 school year were able to brave the storm and graduate.

As I have said earlier, we had almost no white classmate friends. Except for the nursing students, most of us were in different majors; therefore, we could not work in study groups. Out of class, we were our own friends. We usually ate together in the snack bar of the student union on weekends. Even with meal tickets, we had no access to cafeteria food on weekends. Other activities included going to the movies; a couple of times we even loaded into the three cars (Bob's, Gene's, and Carolyn's) and went night fishing. Even though most of us have not seen each other since we left Fayetteville, I believe that our common plight forged friendships that will always last.

There were two groups of people who really tried to make us feel welcome in Fayetteville; they were the African American community and the directors of the campus ministries. I particularly remember Jim Loudermilk at the Methodist Center, who planned programs et cetera, including all of the students. During the 1964–1965 school year, he even invited William Hansen, a SNCC (Student Non-Violent Coordinating Committee) organizer who had worked with us in the Pine Bluff Movement, up to speak. Occasionally, we played table tennis at the Presbyterian Center. I remember attending Bible study at the Episcopal Center and I sometimes attended the Episcopal Church.

The families of the African American community were wonderful. We ate as much at their homes as we did on campus. I particularly remember the Deffebaughs and the Funkhousers, but there were others. At that time, the African American population of Fayetteville was only about five hundred. Maybe they felt our pain.

During my first year there, the students in Scott House elected me president of the house. They placed me in a position of continually having to defend the rights of the students living there. I was always in the dean of women's office about one thing or another. One time, I almost got into trouble when my roommate talked me into going to Fort Smith, against school rules. Almost as soon as we arrived in Fort Smith the worst storm ever started, and we had to slowly return back to Fayetteville going about twenty miles per hour or less around those sharp mountains making us late for curfew. I never did that again! On Monday morning, we were in the dean's office with the guys implicated for trying to help us cover our misdeed.

The real problem living in Scott House was the fact that the university placed a house mother over us who constantly reported us—sometimes truth, sometimes not. We were not on the university switchboard; therefore, white guys would sometimes call in and curse us or call us names that I refuse to repeat. Late one night, someone called and said that they had a bomb planted and that they were going to "blow you black. . . . to pieces." We reported it to the house mother, who reported it to the university for safety's sake, but did not support us. The university moved us out of Scott House for the night. Instead of moving us to one of the new dorms that were almost empty at that time, they called and asked Mrs. Funkhouser if we could stay overnight at her house. That is where they placed us!

On another occasion, a cross was burned on the lawn of Scott House. During one period, the lock on the front door was faulty; therefore, we never knew when someone could just walk in on us. Ice, rain, or shine, we had to walk from Scott House to the student union for breakfast, lunch, and dinner.

Have I returned to the university since my departure? In fact, I was invited back to the university about three or four years ago to speak. While there, I visited and spoke in Dr. Charles Robinson's class. Unfortunately, my invitation to the campus was coupled with another event that overshadowed it, and participants did not have the opportunity they needed to discuss the history of my experience at Fayetteville.

To some extent the U of A has changed, but not enough. That feeling of elitism, where it is believed that African Americans just don't measure up, still prevails on the campus. Desegregation of the faculty could improve. Even those who apply do not get the feeling that their applications are seriously considered. I am not in Fayetteville now, but can still see and feel it where I am. Too many students have had their career goals destroyed by that university. When I visited the campus three or four years ago, I could feel the second-class treatment of some people on the campus.

After the lawsuit, things did seem a bit better. During the spring semester 1965, the judge allowed anyone who wanted to live in the dorms to be placed there. All of us applied to different dorms. There were three of us in Carnall Hall. The men could now live in the dorms. We could participate in athletics and on-campus organizations.

I need to correct a little history on how the lawsuit came about. One day when I entered the student union, a group of students had just about finished their lunch, and were still conversing. One student, Raymond Carpenter, was basically asking or challenging the others to go together with him to file a lawsuit against the university. Everyone got up and left, but I told him I would join him in a lawsuit. Well, after the semester was over, we returned to our respective homes, Raymond to Little Rock. As the summer passed, I heard nothing from Raymond and wondered if he was still going to file the suit. When I called him, he told me he could not file a suit because his mother (a teacher) might lose her job. At that time, this was quite possible. I decided to go on with the suit, and went to Attorney George Howard to see if he would handle my case. He said he would, but we should really file the suit as a class action suit. We needed a woman to represent female students as a class and a man to represent male students as a class. Bob Whitfield had been president of the Pine Bluff Movement and was like my brother. I knew he would be willing to join in the suit, so I called him. He said he would do it. His attorney was Mr. Harold (can't remember rest of name) from Little Rock. The suit was filed quickly, and the case was heard by the federal judge in August before school started. The idea to file the suit was Raymond Carpenter's, but it was Bob and I who actually filed it.

Wendell L. Griffen (1968–1973, 1976–1979), judge and minister

Written responses to interview questions, September 15, 2007
For detailed biography, see Appendix A, page 292

My experience with the University of Arkansas dates back forty-plus years to 1968, when I enrolled as a fifteen-year-old physics major. Twenty years and several months earlier, in February 1948, Silas Hunt became the first black student to enroll in the university during the twentieth century when he enrolled in the School of Law. Hunt's enrollment made Arkansas the first state institution of higher education below the Mason-Dixon line to enroll black students without litigation. One would have expected the university, our flagship institution of higher education, to have capitalized on its historic advantage. It has failed to do so.

The university did not permit black students to live on campus until 1965, a few years before I enrolled as a freshman. When I entered, the Marching Razorback Band played "Dixie" at all pep rallies and at football games. Black students were openly taunted and harassed, especially during the week of the Arkansas-Texas football game. Although black football athletes from Arkansas had been distinguishing themselves at other colleges and universities across the United States, they were barred from playing for the University of Arkansas.

Because of these and other inequities, black students formed Black Americans for Democracy (BAD) to challenge and attempt to change the unjust climate in which we were attempting to obtain a higher education. One of our major goals was to end the playing of "Dixie" at pep rallies and other sporting events by the Marching Razorback Band. After our polite requests were refused, we eventually decided to embrace the civil disobedience tactics employed by Dr. Martin Luther King and his followers.

In late November 1969, we took the stage of the Chi Omega Greek Theatre before the pep rally scheduled for the Arkansas-Texas football game and refused to leave, thereby preventing the band from performing. In doing so, we realized that our very lives were at risk. After all, we were a handful of black students who dared to confront thousands. After UA band director Richard Worthington courageously announced that the band would discontinue playing "Dixie," black students were targeted for even more hateful behavior. Darrell Brown was shot the night before the 1969 Arkansas-Texas football game. UA president David Mullins initially refused to visit Darrell in the hospital, but changed his position after Dr. Gordon Morgan begged him to visit Darrell.

I relate this history to remind readers about the callous disregard toward cultural diversity, and particularly the official mistreatment of black students, that was practiced by the UA at the highest leadership levels during my undergraduate years. Despite the historic enrollment of Silas Hunt in 1948, the UA was a very difficult place for black students. Some faculty members were openly hostile and dismissive. However, black students found solace with each other and were befriended by a number of open-minded white students, faculty, and staff members in ways that helped us survive. Black male students took pains to walk black coeds to study at the university library during evening hours to protect them. We helped each other register for classes, and warned each other about bigoted instructors to be avoided. Of course, we often commiserated together, as the opportunities for social interaction were very limited. We could not even obtain barber or beauty services on campus. We produced our own entertainment, attended to our own barber, beauty, and health services, and tried to help each other survive.

Meanwhile, the campus administration disregarded our predicament. After Jerry LeVias, a running back who played for the Southern Methodist University Mustangs, helped SMU embarrass Southwest Conference football teams, Frank Broyles of Arkansas began recruiting black football players, starting with Jon Richardson of Little Rock. The athletic department began recruiting other stalwart black Arkansas athletes such as Robert Palmer (then holder of the state high school 400-yard record), Vernon Hune (who was a champion hurdler and joined Palmer as the first black scholarship track athletes), Jerry Jennings (a Fort Smith football defensive standout), and Almer Lee (a Fort Smith basketball standout who had been considered by the Harlem Globetrotters). It was good to see them, and to see Hazel Shaw of Tulsa come to Fayetteville with her gymnastic skills.

Nevertheless, a glaring gap existed between the experience of white students at the university and that of black students. On one hand, black students saw evidence of slow improvement as black and white students worked together to help elect Gene McKissic as student body president in 1972. However, many black students experienced insults, abuse, and injuries that scarred them beyond repair. Those who survived cannot forget what we endured.

I graduated from the university in 1973 with a degree in political science and received a regular army commission on my graduation date. After my military service obligation ended, I returned to the university in 1976 with my wife so we could pursue our graduate and professional degrees. Patricia Greene and I married in December 1974, while she was enrolled as a graduate student in the UA Department of Psychology. In 1978, she completed the requirements for her PhD in clinical psychology and became the first black woman to attain that degree. In 1979, I completed the requirements for my JD at the School of Law. We each received our degrees during the 1979 commencement ceremony and promptly moved to Little Rock to begin our careers.

Between 1979 and 1990, I did not return to the University of Arkansas except by invitation of the School of Law. At the urging of Lonnie Williams, who was then a staff member in the Division of Student Services at the university, I reluctantly attended the first Black Alumni Reunion in 1990. It was a cathartic experience on several levels to see the black alumni with whom I had struggled to survive. For most of us, the decision to return had more to do with our affection for Lonnie Williams and our desire to reconnect with each other than any fondness for the university. The U of A was where we obtained our degrees, but it was not our alma mater ("benevolent mother").

Lonnie Williams eventually persuaded me (after many entreaties) to accept a position on the board of directors of the Arkansas Alumni Association. During much of the decade between 1990 and 2000, I worked with several efforts to address racial diversity shortcomings at the university. My principal concerns involved the glaring need for major improvements in recruiting, mentoring, promoting, and retaining black students, faculty, and staff members. I also drafted the initial by-laws for the Black Alumni Association and served as the initial president of that alumni constituency group from 1998 until 2000.

After the UA administration attempted to demote Lonnie Williams in June 2000, I discontinued my efforts to support UA diversity initiatives. When Nolan Richardson Jr. was fired as head basketball coach, I publicly criticized his firing. Reaction to my criticism in 2002 triggered the first of several efforts to punish me by the Arkansas Judicial Discipline and Disability Commission. Ultimately, I prevailed in each instance.

I am pleased by the progress demonstrated by the School of Law in racial diversity. I am thankful for many friendships that grew out of my experiences at the university and will forever cherish those ties with beloved former college and law students, and with some of the faculty and staff of the School of Law. I will always cherish the encouragement that I received from the cadre of the Army ROTC program during my undergraduate years, as well as the solace I obtained from members of the St. James Baptist and Methodist Churches of Fayetteville, and University Baptist Church.

However, the overall record of the university concerning racial diversity is unsatisfactory. Despite starting ahead of the rest of the South, the flagship institution of higher education in Arkansas has squandered countless opportunities to be a leader concerning social justice and racial diversity, particularly in the areas of recruiting, mentoring, promoting, and retaining black students, faculty, and staff. Regrettably, the University of Arkansas has not capitalized on the historic opportunity that Dean Robert A. Leflar of the School of Law, Silas Hunt, Wiley A. Branton, and W. Harold Flowers created when Hunt enrolled in the School of Law and Branton attempted to enroll in the Business School in 1948. For instance, when the Campaign for the Twenty-First Century completed its historic fundraising effort resulting in one billion dollars being pledged toward UA development, not even one percent of that amount was dedicated for diversity efforts.

The University of Arkansas could have been the undisputed leader concerning racial diversity for the South. It is not. Arkansans should view this reality with tremendous regret.

April 6, 1998

Dr. John A. White, Chancellor   **Hand-Delivered**
University of Arkansas
425 Administration Building
Fayetteville, Arkansas 72701

Dear Chancellor White:

Thank you for including me in your schedule on your trip to Little Rock today. I suppose that your schedule is quite busy, and understand that your decision to meet me was one of several choices about how to spend your time on this trip. I certainly want to honor that choice by using the time wisely, so I am giving you this letter to state two specific areas of concern that I hope we can discuss during our meeting and work on afterwards. They are: (1) Black student recruitment and retention; and (2) Black faculty recruitment, retention, and promotion.

Black Student Recruitment and Retention

Less than six years ago, the Arkansas Alumni Association urged the University to adopt specific goals and measurable objectives for recruiting Black students, faculty, and staff. Recruitment goals were finally set by Chancellor Ferritor, as University records no doubt indicate. I was on the Alumni Association Board of Directors when the recruitment goals and objectives were discussed and adopted, and remain concerned about whether the University is aggressively recruiting and retaining Black students. My strong concern in this area has heightened now that the Board of Trustees has adopted admission standards that place greater reliance on standardized test results.

I certainly endorse the laudable aim of attracting the best minds to the state's flagship institution of higher learning. However, appeals to "raise the standard" have often been used to exclude Black people. I would not have been admitted to the School of Law had the existing admission standards been in place in 1976, and I fear that there are many bright Black students who will be excluded from proving their abilities by the new admission standards.

I also fear that the goals and objectives for recruiting Black students will be compromised by the elevated admission requirements. Whatever merit there may be for limiting the talent pool of students to those who meet the new standards, the standards should not be used as excuses for failing to meet and exceed the recruitment goals and objectives that the University committed to six years ago. Therefore, I hope that your administration will keep Black Alumni informed about how the University is achieving its goals for recruiting, admitting, and retaining Black students. After striving so hard and against so many things to arrive at the recruitment and admission goals and objectives, we cannot afford retrenchment.

Black Faculty Recruitment, Retention, and Promotion

The University has a less than admirable record in this area based upon the information that the Alumni Association developed. I am well aware of the factors that have been cited for the low number of Black faculty on the main campus; however, none of the excuses are persuasive. Fayetteville, Arkansas, is not close to a sizeable community of Black professionals, but neither is Boulder, Colorado. Our geographic distance from large numbers of Black people does not prevent us from recruiting Black athletes from even the largest urban areas; it should not excuse failure to successfully recruit Black faculty. That U of A faculty are generally paid less than faculty at neighboring state major universities is no excuse; we somehow manage to pay coaches on par with what most other major college coaches earn.

For years I have urged the administration to include Black alumni in the effort to recruit Black faculty. I am unaware of any serious effort to do so. The Alumni Association urged the administration to establish goals and objectives for recruiting Black faculty. I have no information suggesting that they exist. Absent information to the contrary that demonstrates serious effort and the will to make changes, I find it hard to believe that the University has a genuine commitment to recruiting, retaining, and promoting Black faculty.

The failure to aggressively correct this glaring shortcoming places an inordinate burden upon the few Black faculty members at the University. They often find themselves mentoring students from a variety of disciplines because those students do not have Black role models and mentors within their academic departments. Given that most

Black professionals in Fayetteville and northwest Arkansas are likely to be affiliated with the University, the failure to recruit, retain, and promote Black faculty means that the families of Black faculty members will rarely be able to regularly interact with other Black people in meaningful ways. Absent clear evidence to the contrary, it appears that the University has committed to doing nothing, or little, to increase the number of Black faculty at the main campus or to ease some of the pressures that isolate them from meaningful contact with other Black professionals elsewhere in Arkansas.

I hope that you will persuade me during our meeting that my assessment is incorrect and that the University has made meaningful and sustainable advances in attracting Black faculty. I hope that you will show me that Black faculty members are attaining tenure status and advancing in rank in greater numbers. I hope that you will show me that improvement in this area is a significant part of the standard of assessing the effectiveness of the Vice-Chancellor for Academic Affairs and the academic deans. If so, then I will commend the University for this progress, and will discontinue my less than commendable conviction about the sincerity of the administration's commitment to make improvements.

I have been associated with the University since 1968 when I entered as a freshman. Society has changed in many ways over the past thirty years. While some change has occurred at the University, you have accepted the challenge of leading an institution that trails other leading state universities in recruiting and retaining Black students and in recruiting, retaining, and promoting Black faculty. I am willing to work with you in overcoming that challenge, provided that the administration is committed to doing so.

However, I will not mislead you. My wife received her doctorate in psychology and I received my law degree from the University in 1979. We continue our friendship with several members of the faculty and administrative staff, and we cherish our ties to other Black alumni. However, our assessment of the commitment to make significant changes in the areas that I have addressed is not favorable. As students and in our careers, we have been required to overachieve. Meanwhile, the University appears to lag behind concerning matters that mean a great deal to us. Now that we are at the mid-point of our careers and lives and must contemplate how to invest our time, financial resources, and direct the future education and commitments of our sons, we look with special concern for meaningful improvement at the flagship institution of our home state. Unless the University demonstrates the same kind of overachievement that its Black alumni have demonstrated in the matters that I have mentioned, we have no reason to invest our time and the fruit of our talents and labors in the University. Likewise, we have no reason to influence our children and their peers to consider the University for their higher education and to encourage Black scholars to invest their genius there. This is certainly true if the new reliance on standardized test scores results in fewer Black students being educated at an institution with few Black faculty members at the first state-supported institution of higher learning in the South to admit Black students without litigation.

Again, thank you for including me in your schedule today. I hope to see you when my family visits Fayetteville for the Black Alumni Reunion later this month.

Sincerely,

Wendell L. Griffen

▪ Eugene Hunt (1969–1972), attorney

Telephone interview by Lonnie R. Williams, October 30, 2007
For detailed biography, see Appendix A, page 293

I believe I entered in 1969. I say that because we had the last mid-year class going into Law School at the University of Arkansas, Fayetteville. I entered Law School for the purpose of getting a JD degree.

I had graduated from the AM&N College at Pine Bluff, a historically black college. I finished all coursework in 1967 except I failed French. I had to work a year and a half or so in order to save money to finish one course I owed at AM&N. I finished in 1969. My going to Fayetteville was purely an economic circumstance, where I took five hundred and fifty dollars with me to Fayetteville and when I finished registration I had twenty-five dollars left.

I attended the university three years. I finished in the winter of 1971. I obtained a law degree. At that point, I could not take the bar exam so I was hired to work a year as the assistant dean of students. I worked nine months on staff at the University of Arkansas, Fayetteville.

I can't see myself in that fashion [as an African American first]. I will say that as an upper class person, or a student at the graduate level, there were a few of us who were kind of looked up to for purposes of guidance and leadership and I was one of those individuals and to the extent the students had a certain level of concern. Keep in mind these were some of the brightest kids in the state of Arkansas who had gone to the university to get undergraduate degrees. They were sensitive, in the sense that one of the first things they were concerned about was the university did not have black faculty. I think we had two or three black faculty members on staff at the time. I think Dr. Gordon Morgan in sociology and Professor Adolph Reed in political science were on faculty. And there may have been one other individual on faculty. Their concerns were addressing the administration and asking why don't we have more black faculty persons, if you do indeed embrace us and want us to come here.

Another issue they were concerned about was what they perceived as being overt racism, in the most prominent fashion, I would say in the playing of "Dixie" at the ballgames. That was essentially received as being a fight song. The students were very offended by that. They were making their concerns known to the administration and asking that this kind of display be discontinued. I did not play any major role in any events at the university, in my opinion, I think. There was a black student organization called BAD [Black Americans for Democracy]. I think I probably served a year as its president, but in that regard they were just talented people who did things that needed to be done who raised concerns that needed to be raised. They were not innocuous. They were very respectful. It was quite a path. They all came from very good backgrounds. There was no real need for leadership in that regard other than if individuals had to look to a particular person for a clearinghouse in connection to the issues that would later be presented to those students. That's what the president did, but I was mostly involved with my law studies and also working a half-time job. I had to work through Law School for economic reasons even though the rule was as a freshman law student you were not supposed to work. They told me that and I made an inquiry as to who I was to live with and everyone was silent. It was quite apparent that I would have to work. So I worked the entire time that I was at the university, except one month when I drew food stamps.

The administration was very sensitive of the concerns that the black students articulated. But keep in mind, the administration, not trying to maintain the status quo necessarily, they were responding to a constituency even in connection with the playing of "Dixie," if you understand what I am saying. While they did that, they still actively let the black students know that they were welcome. But as we know, there was a perception, and unfortunately to a degree, there is still a perception that if you're black, you're just not quite good enough. I remember very specifically some of the young male students raising as issues their involvement in a creative writing class. The instructor in that particular class made a statement that we look at now and we would be agog at him having made that statement. But the statement was in this class, let's write about something. Let's write about the black community. Let's write about something vulgar, something dirty such as the black community. And the black students were very, very incensed about that. The furor in connection with that particular comment did not last for just a week or two.

There are many of them who still remember that type of comment and that kind of offense, the offense that was taken at that. It was very distressing for someone to tell me that someone else had said that. And of course the students were involved in some counter demonstrations with the rallies that were held on Friday night before the Saturday ballgame. At the Greek Theatre, there were some counter demonstrations and an expression of different opinions or opinions anti-"Dixie" as well at those who saw, the whites, who saw nothing wrong with "Dixie." Now there was not a single black person that understood or appreciated the culture that gave rise and that sustained the playing of "Dixie" at a state university. There was not a single one. So while there were differences of opinion, those opinions were reflected in terms of black—anti-"Dixie"; white—pro-"Dixie." Even though there were some white individuals that were sympathetic toward the issue, but please keep in mind they were in a minority. There were indeed counter demonstrations in connection with that and demonstrations that the black kids took very seriously because there was a level of uneasiness about personal safety presented in that fashion.

And 1969, I believe that was the year of the Arkansas-Texas game when the president and various other dignitaries came, and there were plans to go out on the field. My memory on that is rather vague because there are some venues that I don't revisit, if you understand what I am saying. But it was a very tense period of time, those two or three years. There were some instances where the students occupied some of the offices, but in a very orderly fashion.

I will say this, the administration was very very sympathetic. And the administration, to my knowledge, I'm very confident, never used force in connection with the demonstration of concerns. I'm very confident of that. I will say there were students, there were white students, who had a degree of hostility toward the black students. I'd hear that they're there, they're in the majority, and a small minority of individuals such as black individuals present themselves, and they'd raise the question "how dare you provoke or advocate changing some of the cultural things that have been in place for quite some time." These kinds of issues were raised and these individuals were equally as passionate as the black kids were on the other side of the issue. There were concerns in that regard. But throughout the entire experience, there were sympathetic individuals, white individuals. George Van Hook, he's down in El Dorado now as a district judge, lived in the dorms on campus so he would have been very familiar with what was going on. James Seawood was very, very bright, very, very active. He was one of the individuals, an undergraduate that could share some very detailed details of what went on and some very poignant circumstances that you would be concerned about. Natalie Dyer, another individual. Kathy Caruthers, who's married to Dewey Fitzhugh in Little Rock now. She is a lawyer, as well as her husband. Jimmie Wilson was very active. Jimmie is a very prominent attorney in Phillips County. His son Dion . . . Dion is also a lawyer and a graduate of the university. There were a number of individuals. Darrell Brown in Little Rock played a very prominent role in the evolution of and advocating, an advocate for change in the system.

In response to the kinds of concerns that the students were articulating, the university persistently was very well meaning, felt that we were at a point where the black faculty person and staff persons were hard to get because the change that was taking place in Fayetteville was the same that was taking place all across the country. The demand for the talented black individuals was very high and the demand probably at that point exceeded the number of available prominent persons to take the positions that needed to be taken. I worked as a student night manager in the student union. The law students were the only individuals initially entrusted to run the union, to open it up and to close it after hours. I'm recorded to be the only black person who was given that level of trust and developed some very, very close relationships with white counterparts by virtue of being in charge of the union for four or five hours a night as the work was apportioned out to the law students. Myself, Steve Clarke, he later became attorney general, Jim Darr, who was a lawyer. There were several others who participated in those kinds of activities. I think the social interaction, the black and the white students, initially I think had to do with, in my opinion, the white individual trying to overcome the idea that there was something intrinsically different about a black person. So having conversation with a person and realizing that there are so many things in common kind of moved part of that, that mystic and the shroud of mystery in connection with the personality, because it's very easy for me to feel that there is something different if we had been traditionally kept apart. If there has been segregation, there has to be, logically, some predicate for there being individuals treated differently and we all of course know that there are no differences as far, intrinsic differences, as far as race goes. Black, white, whatever, there are no differences.

But overcoming the perception, overcoming an institution that fostered separation, that fostered the kind of racism that goes along with treating one person less than, less than another person [that is the challenge].

I had some very intimate, pleasant experiences when I was in Law School; all of them were not. In 1980, I had been out of school for eighteen years. I was at a meeting and I was very surprised that one of my professors walked up and said, "Hi, Gene Hunt," and I said, "Hi, fine." And he commented to another person, "Gene Hunt made the highest score in my class." And that was the first time I had heard that. That was absolutely shocking. It was not chic, it was not *in*. When would he tell me, at the point that I was in school? Mort Gitelman, a Jewish professor, gave me the AM Jur Book Award for having written the highest paper in land use while I was in Law School. So that was kind of the exception. Mort retired as the professor emeritus just two or three years ago. A very, very fine gentleman. We had just a number of very fine individuals. I think that the single distinction that Mort Gitelman had, or a Ray Guzman, was that they were willing to take that step that maybe some of their counterparts were not accustomed to taking or were not brave enough to take. Mort gave me the book award and said, "Gene Hunt, for a good paper in land use, for one of the—or even *the*—highest paper in the Law School." An American juris prudence book award was given to the highest papers or one of the best papers in the Law School. I just point those two out and there were some other individuals who were very sensitive to the black students.

When I entered the Law School, there were four black individuals in the Law School at the time. There was George and Sharon Miller, Les Hollingsworth, and Jim Hamilton. They were the seniors. Those three graduated; Jim and I were there. Then Darrell Brown came in behind me. Those were the numbers. It was kind of a solitude in terms of any distance being there, but I realized that I went there for one thing and that was an education. I saw so many who flunked out and left and I was not deterred by that number because I did not go there to come back with less than what I went for. It was an instructional time. It was an informative time in the sense that you look at some experiences and understand them in retrospect, but not at the time that they were occurring. Because I could not understand a white person wanting to talk to me to reach the conclusion that there was a difference or that there were no differences. I considered that to be somewhat offensive, being perceived as a curio. And the black individuals were indeed that because while I consider the other black individuals strange in the sense I would go a day or two or three and wouldn't see anyone who was black, but then when I saw them it was necessary for me to walk a block or two out of my way with them just to have a conversation with them. A real conversation rather than my feeling that someone just wanted to check me out and see what was going on within the recesses of my mind. So it was different, it was quite different.

I lived in Lafayette House. I was there and I was the only African American in the house. After a semester, other residents came to me and told me that they had given the landowner permission for me to live there. That is, the landowner went to them and said, "The colored boy is going to come here and stay, if that is okay with the rest of you." They didn't say that to be disparaging. They said that, I think, out of anger. Keep in mind, all the black students had had, or did in fact have, experiences similar to mine, or experiences that were more striking than mine because I spent most of my time in my room working or on my job working on my lessons or at the library looking at my lesson. Most of the black kids were *crème de la crème*. Their parents owned funeral homes. Their parents were college or high school administrators or they were business people in their various communities. Those young people had a series of experiences that would dwarf the experience I had because I was not as exposed as they were to the campus life. There was a little area in Fayetteville that is still there now that was referred to as the, well in various manners, they called it "the can" and other individuals, white individuals, referred to it in a different fashion. But it was important that we connect with that particular black community, some three or four hundred people there, which made up about 85, 90 percent of all the blacks in northwest Arkansas. It was very interesting. It was extremely very interesting. It's no phenomenon that when I go back to Fayetteville, I do indeed go back there now. I have good friends that are there. There were some monumental, some disparities of racism, lack of equal opportunity, as there are in many other places.

It was an encouraging time in the sense that what drives people, typically something from inside. If you let something from outside drive you, it tends to turn and change you. But so as long as you can take what is out there that is positive with the right spirit about going forward, then of course you come through and you do okay. You don't let a series of negative experiences dictate or define who you are. We were quite fortunate that, in the main, the black student body did not let the circumstances, the experiences, or the comments define who they were. They knew who they were. It was . . . the best of times were when the black students got together and quite often the worst of times were when they were apart. Not being able to support each other. Not being able to . . . just have a level of commonality with each other. It was necessary. My wife had gone to nursing school even though she had a baccalaureate in business, and Fayetteville was so nice at that point to her. I suppose partly because of being a very small minority you don't threaten anyone. She wanted to stay. I wanted to come back to Pine Bluff. We did indeed return to Pine Bluff. It was a number of years before I had the desire to return to Fayetteville. I did indeed return.

We had individuals: George Van Hook, with the Law School; Edwin Keaton went to Law School; Gene McKissic, the first black president of the student body; Leon Jamison went on to be a judge; Jimmie Wilson, who served in the legislature, is a lawyer; and Darrell Brown was a lawyer. We had a tremendous number of black people who had a desire to achieve, the ability to excel, did in fact do that and they have had a disproportionate impact on Arkansas in the positive sense—on Arkansas as well as the other places they have gone. Look at it from the standpoint of it being a very worthwhile experience where the individuals went there to prove themselves, came out, and were much, much better off because of having had the experience, and still knew who they were when they went there and were still basically the same person, but still changed when they left and continue to be the same person also very much changed because of the social dynamics and interactions with the students and with the faculty at the university. It was a very good time and it was a very bad time.

I did nine months as the assistant dean of students. There was a contract period. I finished Law School and I was waiting to take the bar exam. Dr. Bill Denman was the vice chancellor in charge of student affairs and we had about six assistant deans and there had not been an assistant dean who was black prior to Joe Tave. Joe Tave was an assistant dean before me, but the assignment that Dr. Denman gave me was an advisor to the J board, the judiciary board at the university. I was an advisor to them because of my background, my legal background. I was also an advisor to the Pan-Hellenic Council, all of the Greeks on campus. I know Dr. Denman did that intentionally and for a purpose. There were no black fraternities on campus at that time. You had young, very wealthy, middle-class, white individuals who went to the university. Typically, the fraternities, we perceived them as being middle-class social institutions and upper class. I had the role, I suppose, of advising them. But in the midst of all that was a circumstance where I was constantly aware of, but it did not cause a level of discomfort, where they were looking me over.

The students and I got along very, very well. The male students as well as the female students, even to the point where the university wanted me to remain on staff when I decided to leave. But they did not convince me to stay. So between the judicial board and as the advisor to the Pan-Hellenic Council, it was quite an experience. The young men as well as the young women were always respectful. I never endured a single insult. I was always welcome in terms of giving advice or interacting with them.

Describe my feelings toward the university while I was studying? Those were the good times and those were the bad times. It was cold, the school was cold. I did develop very close relationships with some white individuals, but over all the school was cold and insensitive. Even if they were trying to do better there was such a distance that the school had to travel. Still right now, the distance the school has to travel, if it is going to be the kind of institution that it should be and God wants it to be. But I do see the school, as things have evolved, trying to be more sensitive and doing a better job. They're providing a level of equity in education and also a level of equity in treatment that it becomes, there is hope in that regard. When I left, I was kind of in a hurry to leave because I had that kind of experience in my life. You move in close and talk to individuals and what I considered to be somewhat offensive, if anyone talks to me and tells me you are not like other black people, and I don't know what they are talking about and that's a hard conversation to carry on. I'm looking at a Dr. Lonnie Williams or a Gene Hunt and implying or saying very directly, as had been said, that you are not like other black people. That's pretty strong. You've been there.

The university was . . . I considered it to be cold when I left, but things have warmed up. Things have warmed up some. But the question I think is whether or not it has come full circle to the point that the message gets around and it can do the level of good that it ought to be doing. I suppose I am looking at there being an optimum level of prominence, appreciation, and contribution to the blacks who have not had an opportunity. I say the blacks because the white individuals typically have not been the victim of the kinds of things that is causing you to write this book or to conduct these interviews.

I've been back a couple of times for the continuing legal education. I've been back just to see some friends at the university. I have quite a few friends in the community and all around Fayetteville. I've been back out of nostalgia. I've been back maybe a dozen times and I've missed . . . I have been to only one black alumni organization. I say that and I am very sensitive. There's some kinds of activities that I . . . it is very difficult for me to participate in . . . because I have to analyze and understand why it's going on. I think there are some things out there in society that we cope with because we have to. But as far as revisiting certain experiences, I don't do very good at that. I think it is too emotionally draining as an experience for me to get really, really worked up about it and wanting to go back to that as I would a good meal. Do you understand what I am saying?

I suppose that is my reasonable explanation for not making all the alumni, the Black Alumni Reunions. I think it is good for us to come together and so forth, but in the midst of those kinds of circumstances, I just don't do real good in that. That's kind of up close and personal there.

■ Jerry Leon Jennings (1969–1971), educator and minister

Telephone interview by Lonnie R. Williams, September 4, 2007
For detailed biography, see Appendix A, page 293

I arrived at the University of Arkansas in the fall of 1969. I was there to get a physical education degree. I selected the University of Arkansas because it was in my home state. It was at that time we had the integrating of the public school system, Northside High School. I was having a great high school career. There were plenty offers that I had from other major universities in the Big 8, Pac 10, or Pac 8 as they were at that time. I just felt I ought to go to the university. I always saw them on television. Jerry LeVias was a state player at SMU. I had some coaching from several people, et cetera, but for some reason I wanted to go to the University of Arkansas.

I got there in 1969. I played basketball my first year. There were a few games in 1971. We played the Liberty Bowl December 30. I played in the Liberty Bowl with the football team then never returned until 1973 when I finished my degree. I just didn't go back. I didn't flunk out. I just didn't go back.

I was actually recruited by coach Duddy Waller, the basketball coach, and Coach McKenzie, who left Arkansas and took a job at the University of Oklahoma as a football coach. There were some guys that came after that, but we had been invited to the university even before we signed a letter of intent. Coach Waller and Coach Linwood Cathy, his assistant, came down with my junior college coaches and took a picture with my mother, my father, and the coaches of Phillips County Community College when I signed my letter of intent. The picture was as if to say "you are signing with Phillips, but the underlying fact here is we want him to come to the university." And that was done to assure me that they were really interested in me coming to the university. It took a while. The head basketball coach from the university came down and took a picture of my mom in our living room with Fred Powers and Arch Jones, who were the coaches at Phillips College at that time. So my role was, I will let you and other historians decide that fact, I don't know of another scholarship athlete that was signed that was African American. Richardson was signed that next summer or maybe that spring. I really don't know when Jon Richardson was signed, but I know Almer and I were offered a scholarship prior to being academically ready to go to the university.

They were not ready for us socially at the university. I would go as far as to say a whole lot of things were not ready. In terms of athletic treatment, I can't think of anything other than being around guys who had never been around black athletes. The odd thing about athletics is you are kind of respected for what you can do as much or more than your pigmentation. I can't say that they never hung black cats or wrote anything on my doorknob or my door, never called me the N word to my face. We got along quite well. I made some lifelong friends at the U of A. One of my dearest friends, John Bozeman, who I was a high school teammate with in Fort Smith Northside, is now a congressman. I could go on and on.

There was not much to do socially. There were several of us on campus then, nothing like it is now. There was nothing African American friendly. The music. The settings. I know there were prejudices at the U of A and being an athlete my eyes were open to that. I'm not some brother that's trying to be something other than a brother, but I just didn't run into overt racism. I remember one time we went to see a movie with the football team. We were in Houston. We were going to play Rice University. Before the game, the coaches would take us out to see a movie. It was a modern show where these two, the black and the white guy, were con men. They walked into the town. The movie scene opens and he's got a rope around his neck and they are bringing him into town. Now this is in the early 1970s, so things are starting to change and be a little open, but it was such a demeaning role. I'm thinking, "How can they bring us to see this picture?" Well, I get up and I leave the movie. I go out and I stood out in the middle of the hall waiting on the rest of the team to come out. When they came out, the guys, the white guys and Richardson, were laughing and Jon told me it wasn't anything like it appeared, but Jon knew me and knew my thinking. My white friends, Mike Saint and those guys, were telling me this. It was just my interpretation of something I didn't think was right, but the movie wasn't near what I thought it was.

Coach Broyles . . . I know about all the prior things that have been associated with him. When I came back to the university to get my degree, I went by the athletic office. They extended a hand to me to help. I can go on and on, but they never treated me as anything other than a student athlete.

I went to the university on a basketball scholarship and they had some injuries. I had made All-State in football at Northside and I had made All-State in basketball. I talked to Coach Broyles from Arkansas about football. I talked to Coach Waller from the university about basketball. But I chose the basketball scholarship. I went to junior college to play basketball, so I went on the basketball scholarship. And they said come on, why don't you give it a try, full scholarship, et cetera, et cetera. There were some guys that were playing basketball at the time for the Razorbacks. Well, I didn't think they were as good as I was. He was going to throw in the juniors and seniors that he had been dealing with, so I went out and gave football a try and stayed with football until I left.

Other than being thrown into a big-time situation, with not having any prior knowledge of just how immense the whole situation was, football and academics combined. In high school, I didn't think I was prepared for the curriculum and the academic stuff. I had to dig down and get with it with the athletics to realize it was not as taxing as I thought. And I am sure they could have played me more. I know they could have played me more. But it was more of a big business. It was just because they were white guys and they didn't have time to wait on you to heal. I had a knee injury. They had to go with the next guy. After coming to that realization, it was all understandable.

Have I returned to the university since my departure? Oh, they have an alumni deal up there and I go to watch ball games. I go to see my children there as well. I go by the athletic department and it is changing to the point that there are just a few guys that I know. I think after the next regime that comes in, it'll be almost the end. The access that I have right now, I probably won't have. I can get in at about any level I want to at the university. I can go to Coach Horton; I can see Coach Broyles, Lewis Campbell, or Coach Nutt. Residuals of being a Razorback have been real well. I go up and support the Hogs. I'm a Hog fan.

I don't try to sugar coat anything because I know I've heard things that were said prior to my arrival about giving preference to players, other than black players. He'd rather have this kind, a black snake rather than . . . I've heard all of that, but I didn't encounter it. I was angry when I heard about it, but I never encountered it. I try to dispel any crap that I hear. I know

Coach Nutt is a fine man. I know him to give a brother a second and third chance. Looking on the field today and I see several guys back out on the field, both white and black. There are a lot of positives. I know Coach Lewis Campbell. I know the kind of gentleman he is. Lewis Campbell's wife, he was dating her when I was in college. Lewis's wife had a brand-new automobile. I drove Lewis's brand-new Monte Carlo four or five nights a week. I mean Lewis, Mike Saint, and Gordon McNolte. I would go to the AM&N College to watch the homecoming and ride with Gordon McNolte's sister all the way to Pine Bluff. She would pick me up and bring me back. I just don't have any bad reports.

Lloyd Phillips was an Outland trophy winner at the University of Arkansas in 1964. He had quit playing with the Chicago Bears, came back, and was coaching at the time when I was playing. I got angry one day at practice and left the field. I'd had a belly full of playing football. Lloyd left the practice field, came in, and persuaded me to come back. He said, "Don't ruin your scholarship over being a little bit angry." He's the vice principal in Rogers now. I see him all the time. We talk for hours. Jon Richardson, myself, Almer Lee, Vernon Murphy, nothing that wasn't self induced, nothing we had to be punished for. The only resentment I have about the University of Arkansas, and it's not a full resentment on my part, Dennis Winston, a great friend of mine. I think Dennis should still be coaching up there, but I just don't know the ends and outs. Dennis Winston is like a brother to me. He is younger than me, but as much as he loves the university and the state of Arkansas . . . . That's the only thing that is distasteful to me about the University of Arkansas.

Your opening statement about being a part of the history at the University of Arkansas, that includes my name on the sidewalk, my daughter's name on the sidewalk, my experiences with traveling, and running through that "A." The airport at Drake Field was under construction one time and we had to fly out of Fort Smith, so we rode a bus down to Fort Smith and flew out of Fort Smith. We saw the people that I had known all my life, saw me grow up, see me walk through that terminal with my Razorback attire on and say, "Hey, Jerry, how you doing?" My wife, that I'm married to now and that I dated when we were in junior high, moved to Indianapolis. She was watching the Liberty Bowl game. She saw me on the sidelines, saw my face and knew who I was. My mother, the pride my mother, father, and my little brother had—it's one of those personal private things, but my pride of being there and seeing all these guys that are there now.

You can't get on the sidelines anymore, but I used to be a guest on the sidelines and there were those kids who didn't know me from Hogan's goat. Just to see them and see so many of them and to see people in different capacities. When you see just a regular student at the university when times weren't so great, and now you are affiliated at a high level with the University of Arkansas. It's personal, but it's a glowing ember that I treasure.

My daughter is a Razorback fan because her dad played at the university. My wife takes great pride in that. It is just something that I did. I want the Razorbacks to win every game. I'm a part of that. I don't shout that from the rooftops. It is just a prideful thing that I am affiliated forever with the university.

■ Gerald Jordan (1966–1970, 1995–present), university professor

Written response to interview questions, October 29, 2008
For detailed biography, see Appendix A, page 294

I enrolled in the U of A in the fall semester of 1966 to earn a BA in journalism. I chose the U of A because the school had the best journalism program in the state. I spent four years at the U of A and graduated with a BA in journalism in May 1970. Although I cannot document this, I believe that I'm the first black journalism student, therefore j-grad at the U of A.

My U of A experience was generally positive. I enrolled in a small department and the faculty took an interest in my involvement. I was active on the *Arkansas Traveler* staff, the student newspaper, and the *Razorback* staff, the yearbook nearly from the beginning. I got on the paper staff during the spring semester of my freshman year. I joined the yearbook staff during the spring semester of my sophomore year. I worked on both staffs through graduation.

I think that our freshman class might have been the first group of black students to live in the newer dorms—Humphreys and Yocum for the men. I'm told that those halls were desegregated in January of 1966 [1965], but that could be verified through records of the court order to open all U of A residence halls.

I remember that housing applications included the requirement for photographs. As you might well imagine, black students were paired with black students, with only limited exceptions. I can remember stories of angry white parents storming out of the halls during move-in day upon discovering that their son had been assigned a black roommate. The housing policy then allowed roommates to transfer at semester if they found they weren't compatible. We cooked up a scheme to notify housing that we didn't get along with our roommates, knowing full well that no white kids wanted to room with us. The upshot is that most of the black students in Humphreys ended up with de facto private rooms. And we didn't have to pay because we didn't ask for private rooms. No whites wanted to bunk with us.

We turned those things into jokes. Even the affronts in Brough Commons, when a black student would sit at one end of a long dining table, whites would get up. At first it was offensive and hurtful, but most of the black students were determined not to let the whites know they were getting to us, so we turned it into a game. Whoever was headed for a meal early was designated to reserve a table—usually a pretty good one—simply by sitting wherever he wanted and emptying the table of white students. That didn't last long, though. Many whites saw the folly of it and quit moving. A few even saw the cruelty and joined us and became friends— some to this day. We did the same table scheme in the student union.

Tables and roommates soon fell by the wayside. My roommate during my sophomore year was by choice—Tommy Love. He went on to become a residence hall counselor and that meant that he got a private room in his junior and senior years.

My roommate for the first semester of my junior year was a white kid who had graduated from Little Rock Central. He was a party animal and an absolute hoot. He stayed out all the time and consumed massive quantities of beer, which led to his academic demise in the spring semester. I had a private room again.

I thought that journalism, ahead of targeted programs for minority students, did an OK job of helping and directing my career. I won department scholarships and internships two summers in Little Rock (with the *Arkansas Democrat*). As I progressed in the business, I realized that a lot of help came from outside the department, notably Robert S. McCord, who by the way was the *Traveler* photographer who got the historic shot of Silas Hunt enrolling at the U of A. The managing editor of the *Traveler* then was Robert Douglas, who later became a legendary managing editor of the *Arkansas Gazette*. Douglas and I became friends by the 1980s. He told me the story of how the administration wanted to downplay the arrival of Silas Hunt and how he ordered an extra edition of the *Traveler* that day. It's in Special Collections at Mullins Library.

I heard stories of faculty who were hostile toward black students' aspirations. I don't recall encountering any. By the time we arrived in 1966, many of the upperclassmen had a pretty good book on whom to take and whom to avoid. We flocked to classes taught by outspoken liberals—Louise Cramer, Roberta Julian, Otto Zinke, Mary Parlor. And, while they didn't give grades in sympathy, they seemed to understand that our matriculation at the U of A might include some hurdles not faced by the full student body. Anyway, they were good to talk to and understanding in times of difficulty. The journalism department, as I said earlier, made sure that I didn't get lost in the shuffle and Ernie Deane, who became a lifelong mentor, planted the seed for me to get serious about my studies and seek a graduate degree at Northwestern. I did, and essentially mirrored his career path: UA undergrad, Northwestern grad school, work in the newspaper business, and return to the U of A on the journalism faculty.

From the standpoint of covering the U of A administration and observing things as a journalist, I think the administration—then president David Mullins—could have done lots more to make black students welcome and a part of the university. Maybe I'm remembering what wasn't by thinking too much of what I've seen since then. I just remember that there seemed to be a lot of sink or swim and that made me even more grateful to the relatively small size and welcoming atmosphere in journalism.

I returned in the fall semester 1995 to join the journalism faculty after working twenty-five years in the newspaper business: *Kansas City Star, Boston Globe, Philadelphia Inquirer*. I had visited the department frequently for J-Days programs and other visits. Harry Marsh, who succeeded Jess Covington as department chairman, worked the *Kansas City Star* copy desk, where he got to know Bob Pearman, then managing editor of the *Kansas City Times* (morning edition of the *Star*). Pearman was an Arkansas grad and told Marsh there was another Arkansas grad on staff. Marsh and I became friends and he encouraged me to visit more often. That's how I met Roy Reed, who had retired from the *New York Times* and was on the journalism faculty. When Roy retired, I got a call asking me to apply for the job.

I have seen measurable progress at the U of A, notably in programming and black administrators here. That said, I believe that lots more can be done.

■ Jackie "Jack" Ray Kearney (1970–1974), attorney

Telephone interview by Lonnie R. Williams, November 14, 2007
For detailed biography, see Appendix A, page 294

I entered the University of Arkansas in 1970. I came with the intent of getting my political science degree. I graduated in 1974. Quite frankly, I never got my degree. I was one hour short because I dropped a course. I had already been admitted to Law School at Syracuse University so there was no necessity in getting the degree and to this day, I'm still one hour short.

There were many reasons for selecting the University of Arkansas to continue my education. I had gone through high school during the 1960s, which is very central to my decision on where to attend college. The 1960s, to me, opened up a myriad of avenues for all young people, but particularly for black people.

Because I had grown up in the Delta, I saw the expanding horizons everywhere I looked. Everything that was happening in the late 1960s and early 1970s was new. I wanted to be sure that I went to what I considered to be the best and most progressive school, to get the best education I could. I guess there was political motivation to me wanting to attend the university because I saw it as having fewer than it should have of minorities. And I had the confidence coming out of high school to believe I could compete anywhere I wanted to. I thought the university was the best you could go to in Arkansas and that's why I chose it.

I later had several other family members to attend the U of A as well. My older brother, Jesse, was already a student there when I enrolled. And that helped a great deal because we were a farm family and had not experienced the world that much. I would've still gone to the university, but I would've been much more nervous about having gone there if Jesse had not gone there and blazed a trail and made things a lot easier. There were several other family members who followed in time, but Jesse was the first one to attend. Jesse and I were very close in high school and have always been very close all our lives and remain that way. I visited with him and talked with him about what it was like to attend the university. John [brother] came shortly after I did. He went to the Law School. John, Jesse, Janis, Julius, Joann, and myself. That's five siblings and then both of my sons and most of my nephews are attending or have attended there.

I was an athlete in high school and considered a very good athlete even though I was from a very small school. I can remember if I can go back with you a little bit. Frank Broyles used to have an extremely popular show on Sundays talking about that past weekend's football game. Because it was the 1960s, he would answer questions on this TV show. Because it was the 1960s and there had started to be black athletes at some of the southern schools, one of the questions asked to him at one time was why he had no black athletes. I think Arkansas had played Tulsa and a particularly black athlete there had out-shown Arkansas and beat them. I think it was a set-up question, although I didn't understand it at the time. He answered that he could not find in Arkansas an athlete with the ability to play football at the University of Arkansas and with the intelligence to be admitted there. And I was very offended by that. I think I may have been a junior in high school at the time. But I was offended by that answer, so I wrote to Frank Broyles and told him that when I finish school, I'm going to show you that there is someone in Arkansas who can both play at the University of Arkansas and get admitted into college. But Jon Richardson was recruited that same year, the year before I went.

I still played football. I was active in student life. I also did very well academically. I was elected to the judiciary board and I was the first black person, I think, to be elected. The judiciary board ruled on cases involving university students.

My eyes were wide open to everything when I first arrived at the University of Arkansas. Some of the things I remember most are that there was liberalness about all students at the University of Arkansas, but I was particularly interested in black students. I remember the pride blacks from eastern and northeastern Arkansas seemed to have in their being black. I hadn't seen a lot of that growing up. I don't know if I tried to pick up on it, but I just picked up on it. I also liked the university because I had grown up in a small town where everyone knew you and noticed everything you did, but on this huge campus, I could go there, get lost, and be myself. I found other people with whom I shared a lot of interest. There was a lot of camaraderie because the number of black students was small enough that people generally knew each other. And the times were social enough that if you knew each other, you got socially involved with each other. We had parties all the time. We had gatherings. We had meetings where people would argue and exchange ideas. And so it was an invigorating time for me and I enjoyed my stay there throughout all the years I was there.

As to football, at the time the freshmen couldn't play on the varsity. Jon had come there the year before I did. He was already making himself a star. He was on the varsity and I of course was a freshman. I went out for the team and I played. I can remember that I never talked to Mr. Broyles enough to know if he remembered my letter. Though, someone else told me he mentioned once that he did recall the letter. But I can remember he was coming out and watching me play and telling me he was amazed at my ability. Unfortunately, I got injured the next to last game of my freshmen year, got my leg injured fairly badly, and was never able to play football again.

I was the only black on the freshmen team at the time and that was an odd experience for me. It was just strange to be the only black person and travel. We were expected to be dressed in suit and ties when we traveled. I didn't get along with anyone well enough to feel very comfortable when we traveled. We traveled to say Texas. I think we went to SMU, and we played a game at Texarkana. I'm not sure who we played at Texarkana, but we traveled to these places on a bus and I was the only black on the bus. It was not a very pleasant thing to be traveling with the team and not feel particularly friendly with anyone. Playing in a game, once I started playing, I would forget about these things.

As far as encouragement from the rest of the student body, I didn't [receive any]. The black people, who were attending school, probably didn't even know I was on the freshmen team because freshmen were not that well publicized. And I had not been highly recruited. I had just come out and decided I was going to make the team. I knew Hiram McBeth was trying to make the varsity, and I was getting to know him. I knew he had gone out. I think Darrell Brown, who I later heard had also gone out for the team, was enough older than me that I didn't even know him. And I'm not sure that I knew while I was playing that he had even gone out for the team. And that was one of the reasons that, when I got injured, that it was so easy for me to drift away from football all together because I don't know that very many people even recognized me as a football player.

While I was there, I quite frankly know there was a school of thought that the university had a racist element to it. That it was foreign to the culture of black people. But frankly, I never felt that way. I felt fairly comfortable on campus all the time. I was aware that most of the people attending the university were white. Most of them were not simply white, they were foreign to black people in terms they appeared to have had no cultural interaction with black people at all. I just simply did not let that bother me. And I enjoyed my time with the university and I thought the university was pretty progressive. I think there are people at the university now who are trying to keep that progressiveness going.

I've always felt an affinity to the university since I first attended school there. I return there often. I have kept in constant contact with the university and I go there for all sorts of reasons, to enjoy myself, and to support the university. The university, about the time that I was graduating, started finding black people and putting them in positions. One of them was a young man named Lonnie Williams. And there were others that they had there who gave black people a source of pride and were very, very essential to the black people coming in. I thought that was an extremely progressive step for the university to take and has helped their image immensely. But yes, I've always supported them and I've always enjoyed the things that I go back for—football games, seminars, lectures, and to visit with the university Law School faculty and things of that sort.

The reason that I think the university is trying to improve its diversity is that, I think that Dr. White, who is there now, I believe he has a genuine interest in moving the university forward in a way that I agree with. I think he has a genuine interest in seeing diversity and growth in the university, and so that makes me proud of the university. There are things that I wish the university would move faster on, but generally I feel very favorable and I want to see things keep progressing the way they are.

I do believe the university is a source of pride for the state. I don't know if it's always been the best university for academics in Arkansas, as I believed when I first went there out of high school, but it's moving toward that. I am proud of the university. I am satisfied with what it did for me.

■ Almer Lee (1969–1972), manager

Telephone interview by Lonnie R. Williams, October 29, 2007
For detailed biography, see Appendix A, page 294

I entered the University of Arkansas in 1969 as a physical education major. I was there from 1969 to 1972.

I was there on a basketball scholarship. I guess I was actually the third black picked. Thomas Johnson was the first, but he transferred out his freshman year. Vernon Murphy came. I went to junior college for a year and I came in 1969 as a sophomore.

My experience there was great. It wasn't hard to adjust to because I had already attended a high school that was white and had no problems. The athletic department, racially, everybody was treated the same. Now, I am sure there was prejudice on campus, but I did not run into anything, especially with the athletes. It was like everybody was the same.

Jon Richardson, Jerry Jennings, and I think John Sales came in as a freshman. We had other black athletes in track and we had some walk-ons. They lived in Razorback Hall. I think there were only three or four of us that lived in Wilson Sharpe Hall.

Being there wasn't a problem to me because I was there for a purpose. What they did, they did. What we did, we did. It wasn't like they intimidated us or anything of that nature. It was different. There were not a whole lot of black students there. Whatever we did socially, the community interacted with us.

I was respected everywhere I went, both in the classroom and on the streets. I had to get used to the atmosphere where I was. Blacks had no places to go, but other than that it wasn't a bad experience.

Since I left, I have always kept up with the athletic department. I will always be a Razorback. I go back all the time. When Coach Sutton took over, we had a good relationship.

Coach Richardson . . . I don't know Coach Richardson that well. The little bit I knew of him was good. When Houston Nutt was hired, he called me, and invited me back because he felt like I should be recognized. I never did stay away, but these last ten years I have been going quite frequently especially during football season.

I'll tell you what I would like. I would like for the university, and the athletic department, to recognize all the athletes' accomplishments from the earlier years that you don't hear about. You don't hear about the 1960s, the 1970s, and the players that were there in football and basketball. One would think we did not have good players back then. People like Martin Terry, Dean Tolson, and Vernon Murphy—those guys were outstanding. We had real talented players. Vernon Murphy played professionally in Mexico. Martin Terry and Dean Tolson were drafted into the NBA. When you start talking about good players, great players that played here, you don't start with Sidney Moncrief. There were great players there before him and they should be recognized.

Basketball was not a favorite sport at the time. We brought interest in basketball up. We brought it out to where people started getting interested in it. People should go back, really study it, and review the history. They would know that we were pro players. We got drafted and all that. It is a shame the abilities those players had like Martin Terry, unstoppable! Dean Tolson–rebounding, scoring, and running the floor at six feet nine inches or six feet ten inches. You don't hear anything about that. That's what I want. I wish people would shed a little light on that because if you are winning, it is awesome. The thing about it is, they've always been winning. I wish these people would be more recognized.

■ Hiram McBeth III (1968–1977), attorney

Written response to interview questions, August 2, 2007
For detailed biography, see Appendix A, page 295

I am pleased to provide my contribution to the subject project with personal reflections and documentation. What you will find in the following pages is documented in the 2003 book entitled *Horns, Hogs, & Nixon Coming*, by Terry Frei and published by Simon & Schuster.

The book details the underlying stories of the most famous football game ever played at the University of Arkansas, The Big Shootout of 1969, attended by Billy Graham, President Nixon, George Bush Sr. and George Bush Jr., Bill Clinton, Winthrop Rockefeller, J. William Fulbright, G. Gordon Liddy (and other Watergate notables), and it also tells the story of an African American student at the University of Arkansas, Hiram McBeth III (me), who was attempting to integrate the University of Arkansas Razorback football team. It goes on to tell how I became the second African American to play in a varsity football game for the Razorbacks.

I entered the University of Arkansas at Fayetteville in September 1968 as a pre-med major. The University of Arkansas was selected by my parents, Hiram McBeth Jr. and Mary P. McBeth because they wanted my sister, Barbara McBeth Lewis, and me to graduate from the best college in the state of Arkansas. In their minds, the University of Arkansas was the place to be educated.

I earned a bachelor of arts (BA) degree in political science in May 1972; a master of arts degree in May 1974; and a juris doctor (JD) degree in December 1977.

In January 1969, I began my athletic endeavors as a walk-on (nonscholarship) athlete competing to play football as the first African American to do so with the UA Razorbacks football team. My goal was to be the first African American to play on the varsity squad. The team was lily-white at the time.

Darrell Brown was the first African American to play on the Shoats (the freshman football team); however, he blew out his knee that first year (1966) and was unable to continue to play varsity (NCAA). I was encouraged by Darrell Brown and some of the upperclassmen who knew I was a starter in high school with the Townsend Park Eagles, Pine Bluff, Arkansas, and that because of my size, speed, and strength at that time thought I might have the best chance of any black student to compete for a spot on the team. I agreed and I showed up at Barnhill Fieldhouse for spring training 1969 and let the coaches know that I was going out for the team.

The mission of the African American students was to integrate EVERYTHING that was segregated at the University of Arkansas, including the mighty Arkansas Razorbacks. In the year 1969, the Razorbacks were a powerhouse football team which was expected to contend for the national championship, which they did . . . later in the year 1969 at the Big Shootout. The rest is history. The University of Texas, which defeated Arkansas on the way to the national championship (defeating Notre Dame in the Cotton Bowl), was the LAST ALL-WHITE COLLEGIATE FOOTBALL TEAM IN THE UNITED STATES.

In April 1969, on the way toward my goal of integrating the University of Arkansas Razorback football team, I became the first African American to play in the Red-White Game (the spring intra-squad game) in the history of the University of Arkansas, held in Little Rock. As I remember, there were more than 12,000 spectators at that game and the *Arkansas Democrat* and the *Arkansas Gazette* both had big write-ups in the paper about how the team was about to be integrated by me and my participation in that game.

In the Big Shootout game on December 6, 1969, when President Nixon attended the game between Arkansas and Texas (and declared the Texas Longhorns national champions after their 15–14 victory over the Razorbacks), my picture was included in the game program. I was the only African American to be pictured in the programs of Arkansas and Texas. At that time, I was the only African American member of the Razorback B-team practice squad. I was the first African American ever to be pictured in a varsity football program.

In September 1970, Jon Richardson became the first African American to suit up and play in a varsity (NCAA) football game for the University of Arkansas Razorback football team when he played against the Stanford Indians in Little Rock.

October 1970 was a milestone for me and for African American students at the UA. Against the Wichita State Wheat Shockers, I became the second African American to suit up for a varsity game. Notably, the game was played less than two weeks after most of the Wichita State football team members were killed in a plane crash on the way to an NCAA game. I did not play in that game, although we won something like 69–0. Jon ran for at least one touchdown (punt return) and I am told that archival footage show me greeting him after he scored.

In the 1971 season against the Tulsa Hurricanes, only Jon Richardson and I suited up for that game. This was to be a monumental event because I was scheduled to play and become the second African American to play in a varsity game for the Razorbacks. I was scheduled to make my home-field debut in that game (the coaches were preparing me for it), but we were upset 21–20 by Tulsa and I didn't play in that game.

In October of 1971, I later played in several more games including the Razorbacks upset of the national champion Texas Longhorns in Little Rock at the game called "Revenge at the Rock." Arkansas won something like 31–7.

After the 1971 season, I still had one more year of eligibility under NCAA rules for the University of Arkansas Razorbacks for the upcoming 1972 season. By 1972, Arkansas had a big influx of African American players such as Jerry Eckwood, Ivan Jordan, and Roland Smith, to name a few. I was eligible to graduate already (could have dropped several course hours and maintained NCAA eligibility), but I had achieved my goal . . . to help integrate the Arkansas Razorbacks football team. So I went on to graduate in May 1972 with a BA degree in political science and headed for graduate school.

The foregoing chronicles my role in the athletic history of the University of Arkansas as a young African American student.

As I have written, the mission I was charged with was to integrate the Arkansas Razorbacks football team. I was consumed by that. I was incensed and insulted that I was bigger, stronger, faster, and smarter than my counterparts (and they knew that by direct competition with me on the field), yet I wasn't getting a fair opportunity to play.

I will say this: On the 1971 team, I was a senior and good enough to have started at defensive halfback (cornerback, these days). I was head and shoulders better than any reserve (second-string player) on that 1971 team. I will always feel that way. I am on record as having caused season-ending injuries to two (white) scholarship athletes, who to my recollection, never again played football for the Razorbacks. Although I did play on special teams, I deserved a more prominent role. I believe the reasons are two-fold: First, to allow a walk-on African American to compete and excel on the field would have demonstrated a flaw in the system. The question would then have been asked, "If this guy can walk-on and out-perform our scholarship white players, why wasn't he and others like him recruited in the first place?" This would have been an embarrassment to the University of Arkansas Razorbacks and their system of recruiting at that time. Secondly, because I was a year older than Jon Richardson, the same question would have been asked: "Why hasn't the University of Arkansas Razorbacks recruited African Americans like Hiram McBeth III already?" Additionally, for me to have performed well would have diminished the impact of Jon Richardson as the first scholarship African American player.

I was fortunate to be attending the U of A because my parents told me so. At sixteen and seventeen years old, I wasn't really thinking about the future. As with others of my era, I was thinking about the racial problems at hand, having fun, and avoiding Vietnam (although my father would not permit me to have a deferment . . . he thought it was cowardly). In retrospect, however, attending the University of Arkansas was the best thing that could have happened for me.

The African American alumni have been holding reunions since 1990. I attended the first several reunions and I have attended the last three, including this year, 2007. I attended the Silas Hunt Awards to honor my good friend (and trainer while I was going out for the football team), Gerald Alley of Pine Bluff, my neighbor, and high school (and college) classmate who received a Silas Hunt Award.

I am truly grateful to the University of Arkansas and proud to be an Arkansas Razorback. I have always thought Fayetteville was a great town and the university a great place to receive an education.

▦ George McGill (1964–1969), insurance

Telephone interview by Lonnie Williams, October 31, 2007
For detailed biography, see Appendix A, page 295

I enrolled in the University of Arkansas in the fall of 1964. My goal was to earn a degree in pre-med and go to medical school. I instead earned a degree in education. I had a brother who attended the University of Arkansas prior to my arrival. He was an outstanding athlete and wanted to play football at the university, but at the time the university was not integrated. He was denied the opportunity to play football because of his race. Yet he enrolled and obtained a pre-med degree. He graduated in 1959. Attending the University of Arkansas was something special for me because I had a lot of respect for my brother Donald and I wanted to follow in his footsteps by attending the University of Arkansas.

Don never talked much about the social environment on the Fayetteville campus. Therefore I had no idea what to expect when I hit the U of A campus in the fall of 1964. I discovered I was not allowed to live in on-campus housing. The dorms were not integrated at that time. The dorms were not opened to black students until the spring of 1965.

My first semester on campus was traumatic, to say the least. In most classes, I was the only black person. I was not required to take remedial courses because I had outstanding teachers in my high school, Lincoln High. Being the only black in most of my classes did not bother me very much. I did feel isolated, but this did not bother me much at all. The feeling of isolation was something I learned to deal with. There were maybe forty to fifty black students in the entire student body. We were very close and had a strong bond. The classroom situations were not good, the extracurricular activities were not good, but on the other hand we made the best of our situation. I made lasting friendships.

The things that I do remember that will always stay with me that were harsh often occurred in the classroom. I remember a professor asking me why I had enrolled in his microbiology class. After I explained my desire to go to med school, he suggested that I change my major and that I really should not consider becoming a doctor. I was shocked that the professor would literally tell me I should pursue another profession. There were occasions when I heard racial slurs yelled across the campus as I went to class. I was not distracted or never did I feel threatened. I simply kept aware and was prepared to defend myself if necessary.

My undergraduate years were in time of protests and the era of black identity. This was the time era of the black power movement. I recall the time we protested the publication of an article that appeared in the campus newspaper, the *Traveler*. The black students felt the article was racist and we demanded the newspaper print a response that was written by Gerald Jordan. The newspaper refused to print the response and we held a protest march that ended on the steps of the chancellor's office where our response was read in public. We threatened to stop the presses, if the letter was not printed in the *Traveler*. We actually marched to the *Traveler's* office with the intentions of taking over the presses. There were several blacks from the Fayetteville community that marched with us. We got word that some of the Razorback football players were coming to stop our protest. They never arrived. At one point, we demanded President Mullins meet with us to address our concerns. We were told he was out of his office. We were determined to see him. So we held a sit-in until he came out to speak to us. The university printed a publication on the black student history at the university. It was a nice publication chronicling the black American experiences at the university. We also demanded the band stop playing "Dixie" at athletic events. We threatened to interrupt any athletic events where "Dixie" would be played. The racially charged events did not discourage any of the black students. We bonded closer together and acted as a support base for each other. We all had a drive to succeed and excel.

I would think anyone who has attended a college or university would say that the educational experience probably was of some benefit. My education at the University of Arkansas was a benefit for me, particularly residing in the state of Arkansas. People in Arkansas take a lot of pride in their flagship university. When I returned home from the university with a degree, particularly my MBA, many opportunities were available to me. Life is full of challenges and when I attended the University of Arkansas there were many, academically, racially, and socially. Other than attending class, most of my time was spent in the black community where housing was available and affordable. Many of my meals were provided by the kind, generous families that made up the black community, especially on weekends.

During my undergraduate years, there were no more than four or five black students that owned a vehicle. These were a special group of students that shared their vehicles with the other black students. If someone needed to make an emergency trip, someone would make a vehicle available for them. If we went somewhere, for example a party or go to Lake Wedington for a picnic, it would be amusing because we would make four or five trips to make sure everyone got there. I do recall that the guys had this thing, it was never spoken, but when we had a dance, none of the girls would leave without dancing with one of the brothers. In other words, there was nothing about the girls that would keep us from dancing with them. You know how young boys are today. The girls have to be cute or pretty to get a chance to get on the dance floor. We made sure all of the girls had fun. It was sort of an unwritten rule to make sure everyone had a good time.

There are so many things that flash across my mind. Some of them traumatic, some of them fun. Attending the University of Arkansas in the mid-1960s was a very special time in my life. Being young and excited about our futures, most of the black students did not dwell on the negative aspects of campus life. We stepped up and met the challenges that came with demanding equal access and treatment. We were few in number, yet we were very close. I would even go as far as saying we were a family of students committed to getting an education first. We had made the decision nothing was going to keep us from getting our degrees from the University of Arkansas. Certainly, some students transferred after a year or two, but there was a core group of black students that stayed and completed the course.

▇ George B. Miller Jr. (1966–1969), real estate

Interview by Lonnie R. Williams, March 17, 2009
Interviewed at the Holiday Inn in West Memphis, Arkansas
For detailed biography, see Appendix A, page 295

I entered the University of Arkansas in 1966 to obtain the degree of doctorate of jurisprudence from the Law School. Describe my experience at the University of Arkansas? It was hell! But I expected it. The hell I caught at the University of Arkansas was different from what my wife, Sharon Elaine Bernard (Miller), experienced because being from the north she did not expect the racism and sexism to be as difficult as it was. But having grown up in the South and gone to school—through high school in Helena, Arkansas—there was nothing they threw at me that I did not expect.

When I started trying to find a place to live in Fayetteville, Arkansas, I looked around and checked places for two days and still could not find a place to live. I searched the surrounding area, what would have been a close drive three to ten miles from the Law School, but I could not find anyone who was willing to rent to us. It was then that I went to the Law School dean and said admission is not going to mean a lot if we do not have a place to stay. He said, "Let me see what I can do."

In the meantime, I went back home to Helena and bought a new mobile home. I told Sharon we were going to have to live in a trailer because nobody would rent to us even though we did not have our children or pets with us. The only places that were available were in run-down properties in an impoverished area and I just could not see putting my wife in any of it.

I loaded the trailer with the things that I thought were essential from our home. I parked the trailer on the shoulder of the road in Fayetteville and went from trailer court to trailer court and after no one had admitted me, I remembered when I had brought it to the dean's attention, and he said, "We'll work on it." I went back over there. That's when I found out that our future governor, Jim Guy Tucker, also resided in a trailer court! Apparently the dean knew Tucker. I do not know what happened behind closed doors, but I know when I got there, Jim Guy Tucker greeted me and Sharon. He was the only friend that we had outside of Richard Mays, whom we met shortly after that and who was a black man from Little Rock, Arkansas. Richard turned out to be one of my closest friends.

Now those three years were hell! There is no other way to describe it. I have not been back to the University of Arkansas. I have no desire to go back. Things were just ridiculously racist while we were there, and as a result, we had little interaction with any of the other students. Out of my schoolmates, the only friends we felt like we had were Jim Guy Tucker, who was white, Richard Mays, who was black, and Allen Nussbaum, who was Jewish. We also met and became friends with a white married couple from Oregon, Jim and Susan Norland. They caught hell just like us because they were "Yankees from Oregon." They really caught hell, but they were funny and took it in stride, for the most part.

One of my most memorable classroom experiences occurred during my first year in contracts class. There was this guy from Georgia or Alabama who kept kicking the back of my seat. He kicked the back of my seat during every freaking class. My wife and I sat next to each other, on the front row. No one sat on the same row as us, and initially, no one sat behind us for several rows. But, this guy decided he would come down and sit behind me, cross and re-cross his legs constantly, thereby kicking my chair incessantly. During every class session, and class met three times a week, he would kick my chair or me. I prayed on it, trying to figure out what I was going to do. Finally, after about three days of having my butt and seat kicked, the situation got the best of me one day when Sharon turned to me, looked me in the face, and said, point blank, "How long are you going to let this white boy kick your ass?" Well, that did it. Without a thought of anything at that point, I grabbed him and told him what I would do if he ever touched my seat again. After that, he never did it again. He moved back up a few rows with the other racists and we never spoke again, but I never got my seat or butt kicked again, either. Most amazing of all, when it happened, the professor did not say one word to either of us about the situation, but when it came to receiving our grades, it became clear that was how he would handle it. Consequently, I got a "D." I did not get kicked out of school, but I got a "D." I do not think the guy who had been kicking me received a "D." I think he got his regular "A" or "B" because he was a pretty decent, albeit immoral, student. Sharon got a "C" and she and I were pretty equal in our ability. Both of us should have received higher grades in that class, but at least I did not get kicked out of school and I did not get a written reprimand.

There were other things like that. At the little coffee stand they had, there was an honor system where you were supposed to put your money in the box in exchange for a cup of coffee. I got accused a couple of times of not putting my money in the box when I had, in fact, done so. I was buying coffee for Richard Mays. He acted like he did not want to buy coffee in order to keep down the controversy. Quite often, we drank coffee out of the same coffee cup. That might have been where the confusion came in. No white person ever offered me a cup of coffee. They never offered to treat me to a cup of coffee. I was not invited to participate in anything that the school had going on in regard to anything.

In desperation, I did somehow, someway, manage to get a little job working at the football games for the Razorbacks because I owned a movie theater, had business experience, and was older than most of the other kids. As a result, I was able to make money during football season for those four or five games that they played in Fayetteville. I was allowed to work the gates and made pretty good money doing that.

We also got followed by the police all the time. As for parking, I got tickets no matter where or how I parked my car. I just accepted the fact that I would get tickets. I even went to the student court with Richard Mays as my attorney. He was one year ahead of us, and we won on some of the traffic tickets that I had gotten. Even something as simple as just trying to park was a challenge at that time!

Just about every other aspect was made intentionally worse and more difficult than it should have been. I do not harbor any bitterness about it. But for those people who do not know what it was like, I thank God they never have to know or experience it. If I had not received that assurance on the front end—do not worry; it is going to be okay—I probably would have given up. There was another black guy from Pine Bluff and they flunked him out, although he was a very smart man. He came in the same year as Sharon and I did, but he only lasted until Thanksgiving, without even completing the rest of that first semester.

The black undergraduate students appealed to us, as black law students, to help them with their problems. We were constantly in a situation where, if we did anything, we would get kicked out of school. On the other hand, if we did not do anything, the black kids would think we were cowards or something like that. And one time, I remember specifically, the black student body wanted us to do a sit-in at the football game on Razorback field in Fayetteville. And I said, well, we will go down in history because no one will see or hear from us again in front of 60,000 white people after we walk out on that field and stop the game! That will be that on that! Needless to say, we did not do that.

There were things going on constantly. We managed to make it in the trailer park from the summer of 1966 to the end of the school year in 1967. They came to us and said we better find somewhere else to live for the next year because we were not going to be allowed to come back to the trailer park and, if we did, they would tear it down before they would allow us to continue to live there! I thought they were joking and I did not take them seriously at first. But, then I got a call that I needed to move the trailer or they were going to tow it to the police repo lot or something. They had decided if we were going to live there, there would be no trailer park. They kicked out sixty trailers in order to get rid of me and Sharon. Once again, my trailer sat on the side of the road in Fayetteville while I came from Detroit back to Arkansas during the summer to find another trailer park that we could put the trailer in. Bear in mind this was a brand-new trailer. This was not a raggedy one. But I could not find anywhere to put the trailer.

At that time, I told Sharon, this is going to call for some very creative thinking when we get back so we will have to go into Fayetteville about two weeks early. I called Richard Mays over in Little Rock and he said he would come and help us. So the three of us—Richard, Sharon, and I—went to this brand-new trailer court in August of 1967. I told Richard, "You drive and I'll sneak Sharon out of the car, she is real fair-skinned." I told her not to go in there and say she was black. Instead, I told her to just go up to the door like a white woman and talk like a white person. Finally, I told her I had her back and that Richard was going to drive the getaway car if I had to come in to rescue her. She was uncomfortable, but she did it anyway.

Sharon was so convincing. Again, God works in strange ways. The woman who was there managing the trailer park confessed to Sharon all the negative things that were happening to her with her husband and various other problems. She talked to her for thirty minutes. We were sitting outside and did not now know what was going on in there until I peeked into the window and made sure I did not need to bust in with my only weapon—a baseball bat! I saw them sitting there and they were conversing back and forth with each other. Finally, after about forty-five minutes, Sharon came out with a signed two-year lease. When we brought the trailer in, the woman came over. She tried to have me arrested. I told her I am married to that woman that you keep referring to as "the lady." She said that could not be and I said, "Yes, ma'am, it is." I was setting the trailer up with the trailer moving company personnel. She did not want me to do that. I had to convince her. I pulled the paper out and showed her the contract signed by Sharon and her. I also hinted to her that my wife had told me quite a few things about her and her marriage. She just hung her head at that point and walked away. We stayed there for two years until we graduated in 1969.

It was tough. It was not impossible. Sharon and I took the bar together in 1969. We know we both passed, in reality, but they claimed that we had failed. I raised hell about that. They said, "Well, it was not that bad, you scored 74½ and she scored a 74¾." We asked ourselves how that could be if 75 was passing and the test was 100 percent subjective? At that time, there was not one question that was multiple choice or true/false. All of the questions on the bar exam were subjective, just as Law School itself had been. A 74½ and a 74¾—both of us were somehow less than one point away from becoming licensed attorneys? It was absurd!

Sharon took the exam again in 1970 and flunked it by herself, again, according to them. This time, her score was even closer, but still not a passing 75 percent. In the summer of 1970, she took the bar exam a third time. For that sitting in the summer of 1970, she was pregnant, her stomach was sticking out two feet, it was hot, and she was extremely angry and frustrated. She would tell you herself that her performance on that exam was her worst performance by far and yet, according to the bar examiners, that was the bar exam she passed out of the three that she took. By that time, I believe they had accepted the fact that I had taken a job in Memphis, Tennessee, with the Equal Employment Opportunity Commission and that I was not going to practice law. They thought I was just going to be a businessman and that is exactly what I kept telling them. I made it clear that they were not going to put me through it ever again. I told them: "I've been doing all I can do on this. I've done my part. I've carried this thing. I did it! And I do not feel any shame about it." Consequently, Sharon got her license in the fall of 1970, a year after we had graduated, and became the first black woman to be licensed as an attorney in the state of Arkansas's history.

I, on the other hand, never went back and took the bar exam again. I have refused to submit myself to the whim and fancy of the "powers that be" ever again. However, as a trained Law School graduate, I have utilized my legal education to represent myself and my business interests, *in pro per,* in a variety of legal matters, successfully. These matters have involved cases as diverse and sundried as antitrust and unfair competition; breach of contracts; eminent domain; landlord tenant law; domestic matters, and even simple traffic cases, among others. My legal education has therefore been very helpful and saved me literally hundreds of thousands of dollars in legal fees. I am extremely proud of both Sharon and myself for surviving Law School and becoming great role models for our children, Cylenthia LaToye Miller, who is now a judge, and Sharon Miller, who is an obstetrician/gynecologist.

I have never been back to the Law School and I do not have any intention of ever going back. But I am very pleased about the Law School's selection of Dean Cynthia Nance. Although I have not met her personally, I strongly support her and her efforts to increase diversity in the student body and among the faculty. I am especially thrilled that the dean is a black woman.

■ Gene E. McKissic Sr. (1969–1976), attorney

Interview by Lonnie R. Williams, September 23, 2007
Interviewed at McKissic's office in Pine Bluff, Arkansas
No detailed biography available

I entered the University of Arkansas as a freshman in 1969. My declared major was political science.

Why did I select the University of Arkansas? I didn't. My parents did. That was in 1969 after the Civil Rights Act of 1964, Voting Rights Act of 1965, and it was in the middle of the civil rights movement. My parents thought that the world I lived in was not going to be segregated like the world they had grown up in and spent most of their adult lives. They told all of their children to prepare to live in the world as it is going to be when we were adults. I was in Fayetteville for seven years; four years to get an undergrad degree, a BA in political science, and three years to attend Law School.

If I am not mistaken, there were fewer than one hundred black students, undergrad and graduate in the fall of 1969. As a freshman, I started to participate in the Residence Hall Association, which was already changing student dorm life. In my freshman year, Gary McDonald was president of the Residence Hall Association. I met him and we became very good friends. I was a student representative from Yocum Hall. At the time, I think there was only one other black female who was representative for her particular dormitory. I was elected to the student senate as a sophomore. Then in 1972, which was my junior year, I ran for student body president and became the first elected black student body president at the U of A. Now, I have not actually confirmed this, but there was a book printed that listed me as the first Afro-American president of a predominantly white university in the south. I had some of that information and unfortunately it was accidentally destroyed.

In 1969, there wasn't blatant racism to the degree that Silas Hunt experienced such as being segregated in a basement or not being able to go to the restroom with white law students or having to live in segregated housing. That ended I believe in 1964 with a lawsuit by a gentleman named Whitfield. When I enrolled, there were blacks in the dormitory, but in all of Yocum Hall there were only eight black males. The university had just moved females into Humphreys Hall, which was next to Yocum Hall. I guess there were . . . may have been eight or ten black females in Humphreys Hall. There were so few of us when you consider Yocum Hall had probably seven or eight hundred students and Humphreys had about the same. We represented less than one percent of the population in these dormitories. I don't know the exact number, certainly we did not represent more than one percent. So black students became very close knit and we hung together. We still were not accepted as being legitimate college students who had the intellect and the sophistication to be accepted as equals. We had a lot of conversations in the dormitory with our white counterparts about why this or why that. Why would we not go to a black school? Why would we want to attend college where we were unwanted? There were those kinds of dialogues in the dormitory. Black students weren't accepted by many white students, but there were white students who displayed no prejudice and still others who became lifelong friends.

Now, I will say this about the faculty, for the most part with a couple of exceptions, I was treated well by the faculty. I believe I received the grades I deserved and did not experience racism in the classroom.

In 1969, there were lots of racial conflicts in Fayetteville, depending on where you were. Let me give you some specifics. We knew as black students that if you walked by the Kappa Sig House on Dickson Street, particularly at night, that was hazardous. Kappa Sigs were known to throw things, shout things, shoot BB guns and pellet guns at black students. Instead of walking in front of Kappa Sigs house at night, I would walk on the sidewalk in front of the engineering building, which ends at the intersection of Dickson and Arkansas, which places you just past the Kappa Sigs' house. I had been called things and had beer bottles thrown out of windows that would shatter on the sidewalks as I walked by. I never ran. I was never going to run from them. As a matter of fact, I probably would have confronted them, but I took precautions to avoid being hurt by them as some other black students had been.

There was more than one incident my freshman year where black women were walking across campus had been followed, verbally assaulted, inappropriate verbal propositions made to them to the degree that a couple of black women left school because they became terrified. So black males started the "Soul Patrol." We had a rule. Black males would not allow a black female to walk alone at night on or off campus. Females were to notify a black male in the dorm next to her or some black male on campus. We would escort them because black females didn't experience the same problems when they were in the company of a black male. So the welcome mat was not out. Dr. Martin L. King Jr. had been killed in April of 1968; the Vietnam War was raging almost on a daily basis; there would be a confab of students protesting something. A lot of it was stimulating and discussions would be about race, school integration, busing, as all of those were hot-button topics.

The first week of December 1969 was probably the most intense week of my life and probably a defining moment in my life in some ways. The reason is it happened early in my freshman year, the week of the Big Shootout. The University of Arkansas was number two in the country and the Texas Longhorns number one and you have this fever-pitch Razorback atmosphere all over the state that is magnified on campus. President Nixon was coming to the football game, and at the same time we have this issue of the Razorback Band playing "Dixie." Black Americans for Democracy (BAD) was the black student organization on campus, and I believe Gene Hunt was president. BAD made a decision that we would not allow the band to continue to play "Dixie."

We considered "Dixie" then, and I still do despite some of the new-wave thinking, an insult. BAD went to a band meeting trying to raise the racial questions; our efforts were unsuccessful. We then made a decision to protest the playing of "Dixie" during the shootout weekend to focus public attention on the issue. So you had this Razorback fervor and nine thousand plus students in support of that fervor. And you had this handful of black students, and I do mean handful, who were saying, "You shouldn't be able to play 'Dixie.'" The fabric of that is much bigger than the song. The fabric of that is the will of the majority coming in conflict with the black minority that in the world of Fayetteville was a gnat on the elephant's butt. Blacks were irrelevant. I think, looking back on it, a lot of it had to do with respect as individuals and collectively. We were no longer going to be invisible in Fayetteville. I don't know that I thought about that at the time, but reflecting on it, I am sure respect had a lot to do with it. The University of Arkansas was no longer going to ignore the fact that black students were a reality and were going to be respected. We were going to be treated with dignity. The band director at the time didn't have a problem not playing "Dixie," but the song was popular with the fans. The majority of fans wanted it and the majority of the band wanted to play it, so they decided to play it.

On December fifth, the night before the game, there was a pep rally in the Greek Theatre located in the center of the campus. BAD made a decision we would take over the stage, if the band attempted to play "Dixie." I will never forget. I was eighteen years old. This was my first extended time away from home, and we take this vote in a BAD meeting to protest. We know that it is a very dangerous situation; people could get hurt. The Greek Theater is packed, just absolutely packed, standing-room only, with everybody from this state that had game tickets. The national media was on the campus. Gene Hunt went on the stage to try and make a statement—I believe to the effect that if the band didn't play "Dixie," BAD wouldn't protest. And the crowd started cat calling and shouting him down. Some of the black students went to the aisles to the steps descending into the Greek Theater and began to block the band running down the steps to get on stage. Gene Hunt said there wasn't going to be a pep rally unless the statement was read. Can you visualize a few black students telling several thousand white fans attending the most important pep rally in Razorback history that the statement was going to be read or the pep rally would be disrupted!

I was on the stage at the rear. I don't remember how many black students went with us, but there were maybe twenty of us down there. Bottles and rocks were being thrown like missiles fired out of the audience, just raining on the stage. We knew that in a physical confrontation a fight wouldn't last long. I was standing at the back of the stage in the center. This is one of those times I have to go back to my mama and daddy saying, "Maybe God takes care of babies and fools," or He just blessed us. There were beer bottles exploding on the stage and sizable rocks landing all around us. I can remember rocks hitting in front of me and beside me, and I could see beer bottles landing on the stage and the only person hit was a white cheerleader when the glass from a beer bottle shattered and cut her on the thigh. Nobody else was hit or injured in any significant degree. I don't know why not. It was like raindrops missing us. The tension was so thick you could feel it and see it on the faces of everyone. We didn't know what would happen. We didn't know if the crowd would storm the stage. We didn't have weapons. We were just there saying we were going to stand up for ourselves. I learned during that week that the greatest fear really is fear itself and if you are fearful, you are already defeated.

I've said before, I enjoyed my time at the U of A. But I think it had to do with the times. I think it was a much different time than say in 1948 and 1955 when there was no Vietnam War, no civil rights movement to the degree we are talking about, no women's liberation movement. There was a confab of social change, ideas, events, movements, whatever you want to call it, that were going on at the same time. People were questioning conventional wisdom, conventional roles, and conventional conduct. Societal rules were changing and fast. Couple that with a college environment where you could have intellectual debate, true intellectual debate, without people thinking you were ignorant, or a pointy head, or racist just by virtue of fact that you thought differently. For the first time, white people were asked to consider what it was like to be educated in segregated schools as opposed to assuming blacks are supposed to be in a separate place. Whites had to start taking a look at things that were happening and not from a white superiority viewpoint. The gay liberation movement was sort of bubbling to the top. All of those issues generated debates and forums that students could participate in, different ideas and speakers coming to the campus. It was a time of great intellectual curiosity, growth, eye-openings, and having lived in a small town that was totally segregated, totally controlled by the white power structure where a black person's ideas didn't matter. It was my first experience with freedom. Nobody back home was going to ask you what your ideas were, not only because you're black, but because you were young, so your ideas didn't matter a lot of the times even within the black community. To be in an environment where you could express an idea or have an intellectual conversation and challenge yourself was a breath of fresh air for me.

Describe my feelings toward the University of Arkansas during my time there? Two things: A time of great freedom and, yet, a time of great pressure. This pressure was created by the fact that you're black at a university where you're such a minority. At that time, there was no BET, no black radio stations. You couldn't get a haircut because there were no black barbers. No places that you could go and buy clothing that would suit you. Fayetteville was not at all geared to accommodate you, to make you comfortable. No black church that was immediately accessible. No black faculty or staff. I believe Dr. Gordon Morgan was just joining the faculty as its first black professor. So we were basically always living in a white man's world, expected to perform or leave. We knew if we failed we were going back home to a segregated world we were all trying to escape. The pressure was for us to go there and to succeed so that we had a chance for a better life somewhere.

As a college experience, it left a lot to be desired in terms of you being socially comfortable. For instance, the first time I attended a Razorback football game, and I think the Hogs opened the season against Tulsa, we were pelted by white fans. Our seats were right down in front and the fraternities and sororities were seated above us. The whole game we got pelted with ice, cups, paper wads, and spit balls. The whole game! And when we would stand up and look around, you're looking in the faces of thousands of people who could have done it and all of them are sitting there as though "it wasn't me." We would sit back down and immediately something else would strike us in the back of the head or it would fly past you and hit somebody else. That's one of the reasons, for a while, black girls wouldn't go to Razorback games because white fans would throw things that would get in their hair. Fans would douse us with beer and it would get all over their clothes and in their hair. Even if there wasn't any rain, when black girls attended games, they would take umbrellas. That was the only way they could protect themselves. We finally learned to arrive for games early in time enough to occupy seats on the top row. We went up to the top seats and therefore in order for someone to throw at us, they had to turn around to face us. And we could also throw something down on them. It changed everything, but that is what we had to do.

What being pelted did to us inside . . . we came to see a football game . . . and instead we had the rednecks throwing ice on us and our dates. Those things cut pretty deeply. A lot of black students would refuse to go to the games not because they didn't support the Razorbacks, but they didn't want to deal with the fans, the humiliation, and the risk. And they didn't want to sit there while people yelled, "Sit down, nigger," and called your girlfriend names. You didn't know who did it. People around them wouldn't stop them and wouldn't support us, even if they didn't agree with what was said. But some of us kept attending games and then those things stopped.

Have I returned to the university since my departure? Many times. So many I couldn't even tell you. I bought season football and basketball tickets shortly after I graduated from Law School and I have gone back many, many, many times to Fayetteville. I have also been back just for events including the black reunions. I served on several committees, UA Alumni Association Board of Directors and the Black Alumni Society Board of Directors in years past and have tried to stay involved with the university.

[**Williams:** "People often credit me for the Black Alumni Reunions, but I tell them that was actually your idea. In 1984 when we did the tenth anniversary of Omega Psi Phi, we invited friends of the fraternity back. You, the Kearneys, and others were our mentors at the time, came back, and I remember what you said. You said, 'Lonnie, this is good; it needs to be done on a bigger scale.' That's what you said in 1984, and that was the impetus for me doing the Black Alumni Reunion in 1990."]

Actually, I know we had that conversation and I know I said those things. But really, if you're credited, that is fine with me. We had an unofficial reunion in Little Rock in 1976.

When I say unofficial, there was no organization sponsoring a reunion. There wasn't even a fraternity at that time, just a group of us who were friends getting together. We just called other black students who attended UA and we got together in Little Rock. I can't tell you the name now of the night spot . . . but on a Saturday night, we got together in Little Rock in the spring of the year. We probably had thirty people there, maybe more. We just got a bunch of tables together and had a party one night, just to see each other. We had another one in Little Rock around somebody's wedding. Your [Lonnie Williams's] being on campus facilitated organization and continuity. You took the ball and ran with it. The rest is history. It was just a natural outgrowth of a real desire of black kids who attended U of A over the years not to lose touch.

Talk about my advocacy for getting African Americans in administration in the athletic department? I can tell you what my thinking was then and is now. An athletic department is usually the face, and in some ways maybe not the soul, but certainly the spirit of a university. And if black people are ever going to be fully accepted as part of a university, the easiest route to me is to be significantly represented in the most visible university department. People in South Bend and at Southern Cal in Los Angeles know the Razorbacks, but they don't know about the university. And to a lesser degree the same thing is true for many people in Arkansas. If the administration is fully diversified, I think it levels the field because blacks become part of the university's fabric. You influence the thinking. You influence the decision making, you influence the policy making, and such influence should then bleed down to the rest of the university and the state. There can be an all-black team, but if all of the policy making, all of the decision making, and all of the money is controlled by the white power structure as it is now, then diversity is stifled. I've said it long before it happened, and tried to tell people in the administration, you don't need to have Nolan Richardson isolated. He needs a contact person(s) within the administration who looks like him and whom he can trust who has some real authority, who is a decision maker so that he can trust the lines of communication. When the whole administration is white, that automatically creates some doubt and issues, especially given that he was the first and only black head coach and administrator at the time. Given the time he was born and given the history of the University of Arkansas, there had to be some built-in mistrust.

I went to Frank [Broyles] and that was early, and to the chancellor, saying, "You can't have a lily-white athletic administration." I think what happened to Stan Heath, what happened to Nolan Richardson, what happened to Robert Johnson, what happened to Tavaris Jackson, who is now the quarterback of the Minnesota Vikings, resulted from this failure. A lot of it comes from the fact that you have basically a lily-white administration and a lily-white coaching staff. I think there would have been some different approaches, different line of communication, and different comfort levels if black people occupied some administrative positions. I think there would have been different awareness, which could have avoided the meltdown of the whole athletic department. And maybe, because I knew Nolan and Stan, I believe both of them were somewhat uncomfortable in their situations, sometimes because of the lack of communication with the administration and the boosters who influenced the administration.

To my knowledge, there has never been a black person on the Razorback Foundation board. That is the money that controls athletics. You have a limited number of black people in the administration other than in student affairs. So I don't know how a black person could be in a top administrative position without having some suspicions toward the administration and the athletic administration. I thought to remove doubt . . . the way to do it . . . is for the UA administration to take the lead, integrate at the highest level. Have black associate and assistant athletic directors and not just black people in student affairs. Student affairs people don't make policies and they don't make money decisions.

In 1998, the resolution adopted by BAS addressed this issue. I wanted the university administration at the time, and I wanted the alumni association at the time, to support the resolution passed by the Black Alumni Society that called specifically for the hiring of blacks within the athletic administration. And this was before Nolan was fired. If the UA had voluntarily integrated at the administrative level in athletics, the public would have accepted it. The athletic department could have done it, and the public would have accepted their decision. I think the university sends a subconscious message that blacks are not competent to manage the affairs of the athletic department, to occupy policy-making positions and to be decision makers about the Razorback Nation's business by keeping it lily white.

Most Razorback football teams are 65 percent black or greater. The Razorback basketball team has generally been 90 percent black or greater. Those are the two major revenue-producing sports that help support all Razorback team sports. Yet, the policy-making positions are still virtually lily white. Now, I think the message that sends to players is you can play at the University of Arkansas; you can be great at the University of Arkansas; you can make All-American; you can make All-Conference; you can make All-Pro; you can win bowls; you can win national championships, but you are not smart enough to come back and be in sports information, in administration, you're not smart enough to come back and make decisions. Only former white players are smart enough. That's really what it looks like because many former white players have been hired within the athletic department. There was not one black former Razorback until Marvin Caston, that I am aware of, who was ever hired by the athletic department. That to me is the university having a slave master's mentality toward its own black products. It is insulting and disrespectful. That was my position long before 1998 and that is my position today. The university system's office, the chancellor's office, the athletic department, and the athletic directors—they are directly responsible because they have the power to change it and they haven't.

Presently, I think it is better at the university for the black students because the times have changed. Most black and white kids now have grown up going to school together. They listen to the same music. They watch the same television shows. They wear a lot of the same dress styles. These are commonalities within the society that exist now, and there are fewer unknowns than there used to be. But when I walk into university administrative offices, the system administrative offices, I don't see black people there occupying decision-making positions. When I go into the athletic department, and we pushed to have the one assistant athletic director that was there and has now graduated to become a full time athletic director, I still don't see black people in charge of any decision-making positions or controlling any of the monies or controlling anything other than some assistant coaches. Still, Arkansas has never had a black offensive or defensive coordinator in football and not a black head coach in any sport, except basketball. Again, all of the people who are in decision-making positions are white. So to me the University of Arkansas administratively is still living in the 1950s. They need black folk to pick the cotton and produce the profit, and otherwise they don't need input from blacks. They don't need or desire to have discourse with blacks. They certainly don't need them making management decisions.

I am disappointed when you look across the landscape of America that my alma mater still doesn't see fit to hire individuals on merit and to treat them equally. Now, I know they would disagree with me about these things, but let's look at the numbers. The numbers don't lie. I have been asked repeatedly by some of the individuals in high positions, "Well, where do we find black people to do those things?" I say you find them in the same place you find black people to play football and basketball. You go looking for them and recruit them just like you do everybody else. But you can't be afraid of them and you can't just hire people to do only what you want them to do or to think only what the university tells them to think. You have to hire blacks and let them direct their own programs and do what they think is best within the framework of the university. And I don't think the university really wants or likes black people who think for themselves. I think they want black people who will obey orders and stay in their roles as black people who work for a major university. I don't think the atmosphere there is conducive for intelligent black people to go there and expect to rise to top administrative roles. I don't think we are there yet. That is a big disappointment with me and the University of Arkansas.

I think the University of Arkansas is behind the times and behind the general population as far as where it stands with regards to its relationship with black people. I think in 1969 it was ahead in some way because of the experience with Silas Hunt and the young black ladies in nursing. I think they were ahead of the state of Arkansas. I now think the state is ahead of the university. I believe the majority of the fans would have been more forgiving with Nolan, and was in favor of recognizing his accomplishments, recognizing the accomplishment of the 1994 and 1995 Razorback team. I have heard that from many, many white Razorback fans and even just fans in general. There was a fight and it is over with for the fans, but it is not over with for the administration.

I think too many high officials at UA still believe black people to be intellectually inferior. We're incapable of being independent. That is why when you have board [Board of Trustees] members who admit under oath that they openly used the term "nigger" and tell racist jokes, the administration never stepped forward to offer one word of criticism or ask board members to apologize. It shows a lack of moral courage by the administration and really it says to me that at the UA, "We acquiesce in board members or people in policy-making positions calling black folks nigger." Does the university's silence give consent? So my feeling is UA is behind the state. I don't think the public would have supported that at this point in time. UA needs to change its attitude and thinking.

But I don't confuse administration with being the University of Arkansas. I am proud to have graduated from Arkansas with two degrees. I love the university. I support them as you know with my time, whatever meager talents I have, and whatever few dollars I have. And I will continue to do that because there is no perfect situation. I just believe that part of what we do as humans is try to make it better for the human beings who follow us. I don't think that means that we have to march in lock step with policies and positions that are disrespectful to us as human beings. That is why my problem is with the system administration, university administration, and athletic administration. I have not seen from them, collectively or as individuals, any significant degree of respect for black people as humans. Therefore I support the university, but I disagree with those individuals occupying leadership positions.

Attachment 3

RESOLUTION
OF THE UNIVERSITY OF ARKANSAS BLACK ALUMNI SOCIETY
CALLING FOR INTEGRATION OF
UNIVERSITY OF ARKANSAS ATHLETIC DEPARTMENT ADMINISTRATION

WHEREAS, the mission of the University of Arkansas Black Alumni Society is to promote communication and friendship among Black Alumni, faculty, and friends of the University of Arkansas by providing a forum for exchanging information and organized activities, including information about conditions at and policies and practices of the University of Arkansas that affect racial justice, and

WHEREAS, the Black Alumni Society takes pride in extolling the positive accomplishments of the University of Arkansas regarding academic excellence, intercollegiate athletics, and the accomplishments of faculty, staff, and alumni because those positive accomplishments advance the image of the University, and

WHEREAS, the concern of the Black Alumni Society for racial justice arises from the unique pilgrimage that Black students, faculty, and staff members have experienced at the University and the Society's awareness that this experience includes significant instances of exclusion and insensitivity on the part of the University community as well as steps to correct the effects of historical injuries and discrimination, and

WHEREAS, one of the areas of historical discrimination at the University of Arkansas is the administration of the University of Arkansas Athletic Department and its auxiliary entities: although the Athletic Department has been led by Coach Frank Broyles for most, if not all of the time that persons of color have participated in varsity athletics at the University, persons of color have continually been excluded from administration of the Department and its auxiliary entities such as the Razorback Foundation: although athletes of color have excelled on the courts and fields of competition at the collegiate and professional level, including outstanding performance on championship professional teams in the National Football League, the National Basketball Association, the Athletic Department presently has no person of color in its administration and persons of color continue to be severely under-represented at the coaching rank so as to perpetuate a regrettable history of race discrimination that harms the image of the University and all alumni, and

WHEREAS, the Black Alumni Society believes that persons of color are capable, given equal opportunity for inclusion and fair treatment after being hired, of serving effectively and successfully at all levels within the Athletic Department including administration as well as coaching, but that their absence from the administration and under-representation as coaches is due to hiring practices and actions that wrongfully perpetuate their exclusion and under-representation,

THEREFORE, BE IT HEREBY RESOLVED, that the University of Arkansas Black Alumni Society hereby calls upon Chancellor John White and the Trustees of the University of Arkansas to direct Coach Frank Broyles to immediately present a plan of action for correcting the exclusion and under-representation of persons of color from the administration and coaching ranks within the University of Arkansas Department of Athletics, and its auxiliary entities such as the Letterman's Club and Razorback Foundation.

BE IT FURTHER RESOLVED, that the Black Alumni Society calls upon Chancellor White and the Board of Trustees of the University to direct Coach Broyles to give first consideration to Razorback alumni of color in hiring administrative management for the Athletic Department so that past acts whereby those alumni of color have been wrongfully excluded or under-represented will not continue to perpetrated.

BE IT FURTHER RESOLVED, that the Black Alumni Society calls upon the Arkansas Alumni Association Board of Directors to include the subject of this resolution at its next regularly scheduled meeting and adopt a companion resolution calling for similar action, and that a representative of the Black Alumni Society be permitted to address the Alumni Association Board of Directors at that meeting so that a plan of cooperative effort can be developed and put into action as soon as possible.

ADOPTED this 18th day of April, 1998, at Fayetteville, Arkansas, by vote of the Black Alumni Society.

_____

Wendell L. Griffen, President

_____

Patsy Lowe Gatson, Secretary-Treasurer

■ Ray E. McKissic (1967–1971), minister

Telephone interview by Dr. Lonnie R. Williams, April 21, 2009
For detailed biography, see Appendix A, page 296

I entered the University of Arkansas in 1967 in pre-medicine. I graduated with a zoology degree in 1971. I went to the university because I was from Pine Bluff and did not want to go to school at home. We have a historically black college at home in Pine Bluff, but I didn't want to go to school at home. I wanted to go into medicine and by matriculating at the university my chances of going into medical school would be enhanced since the university had a medical school in Little Rock.

I wanted to make a difference on campus. I didn't want to just go through and not have any type of wholesome affect on the student body or my peers. I wanted to make a real difference, a positive difference while I was there at the university.

I actually followed my sister, Freda McKissic Bush. She went to the university four years before I did. She was a nursing major. I did major in medicine and we were going to have a clinic together in Pine Bluff, but it didn't quite work out that way because I went into the ministry my last semester. I was one of the first students in the black gospel choir that we organized back in 1971.

The choir was the brainchild of Tony Wright, who was from Las Vegas, Nevada. He did his bachelor's degree at AM&N College in Pine Bluff, Arkansas. He came up to the university to work on a master's in English. Tony and I would sing in Missouri where his fiancée lived. We would sing at the University Baptist Church in Fayetteville, the Baptist Student Union, and in other places. He said, "Why don't we start a gospel choir?" We started a gospel choir because there wasn't a whole lot that black students could do on campus. Back then, there were no black fraternities or sororities and only a few were in athletics. So Tony Wright was the first director and pianist. I was one of the soloists in the choir, and that was a first experience, being a founding member of that group.

I think it was called the Black Gospel Choir. Black was beautiful back then and it still is. I was also one of the first founders, first organizers of Black Americans for Democracy on campus, which I think we first organized either the first or second semester I was there, back in the spring of 1968. There was a lot of unrest; racial tension was very high on campus at that time. The campus really was not prepared to receive blacks. We were only about 1 percent of the student body. There were about ten thousand students overall and only one hundred and thirty-three blacks. They just weren't ready for us. We had to do things that made the campus more conducive for black students. So we organized Black Americans for Democracy. There were no black professors and only a few in sports and we had to do something to make life more conducive.

BAD was the hub of the activities for the black students. There was not much else that we could participate in. We were sort of a close-knit group from all over Arkansas. I was involved in the Baptist Student Union, which none of the other black students felt free to participate in, but being a minister's son, being very religiously oriented, I joined the Baptist Student Union and was very active in that. I was also an active member in University Baptist Church located right off campus and so I was one of the leaders in that aspect of student life. Wendell Griffen, from Little Rock, and I sang in the singing group for college students at University Baptist Church. I think it was called The New Creations. We just sort of tried to stick together because we knew things were kind of difficult for racial minorities on a predominately white campus. It was survival really. Things actually boiled down to trying to survive in everyday life. It was kind of difficult for the average black student.

Well, like I said there were no black professors. So we had to push for the first black professor that came to the university. I think it was Dr. Morgan. He was in the sociology department. There were no black studies courses, so we had to push for that. There was one black basketball player, Thomas Johnson, who was from Menifee, Arkansas. After the first semester, I think because things were so difficult for him, he transferred to Hendrix in Conway. There were no black football players, so we had to march, demonstrate, and everything to make the changes that you see today. So, of course, you now have plenty of black football players even black coaches. Nolan Richardson, we just recognized in 2009 by the Black Alumni Society and the championship basketball team of 1994. All of those changes that were reaped later on, we started back when I was in school in 1967–1968. So I'm very happy to see these changes take place.

But of course, it all goes back further than that to Silas Hunt—I think the first black student who matriculated at the university back in 1948. Like I said, my sister Freda back in the 1960s, 1966 and 1964 and other students were just a small minority. And so we set the ball rolling to get it where it is today. I was so happy to come back to the campus this year. Of course, a lot of changes have been made since I was here thirty-eight years ago, since I graduated. But I'm glad to come back to the campus and see these changes. I did get up and sing with the choir when they invited me to come along with the alumni and be a part of the last two numbers at the 2009 reunion. They call it the Inspirational Singers Choir now, but I think when it first originally started it was the Black Gospel Choir. Of course, Edwin Hawkins, the Edwin Hawkins Singers of the Northern California Community Choir, they were just coming into national prominence and we did a lot of Edwin Hawkins's numbers. "Oh Happy Day" was one of our favorites led by Gladys Faye Edwards of Lake Village. I led a song by the O'Neal Twins out of St. Louis called, "I'd Trade a Lifetime (For Just One Day in Paradise)." And we were very well received. The very first black gospel choir concert was very successful. There were about forty to fifty students in the choir.

Describe my feelings toward the university during my time of study? Well, I guess it was mixed. I was glad to be there because I felt like I was getting some of the best education Arkansas could offer. But there was so much prejudice, racial prejudice, and antagonism toward black students when I first went there that it was almost unbearable. The spring of my freshman year, 1968, on April 4 I was coming back to the dorm. I heard this loud roar, this loud cheer. When I got into the dorm, I asked the RA, one of the black RAs, Nathaniel Thomas, the only one in the dorm at that time. I went to the door where the cheer was coming from and I heard someone say, "Oh man, they got him in the head, I hope he dies." I didn't know who they were talking about. So I went to the black RA and I asked, "What is going on?" He said, "Haven't you heard? Martin Luther King just got shot." That's just how prejudice the campus was at that particular time. As black students, we felt like we were under siege. It was very difficult. Those days were very difficult, but I'm glad to see the changes that have taken place since that time and I just hope the students, especially the black students on campus, appreciate those that came before them and the sacrifices that were made so they can enjoy the privileges that they have today.

Have I returned to the university since I graduated? I was at the second Black Alumni Reunion back in 1993, about sixteen years ago. I returned this time in 2009 and would like to say the campus has made a lot of changes as far as growth and involvement of the black student body. I went to seminary in Texas and I came back in the spring of either 1970 or 1971 when my brother, Gene McKissic, was elected the first black student body president (Associated Student Government). I've been back about three times. I also recall returning for Gene's graduation from Law School. Gene paved the way for a lot of the advances that black students have made and continue to make at the university.

I still have mixed feelings about the university today. Like I say, I'm proud to be an alumnus of the university. A Razorback, if you will. But I still feel like my experience at the university could have been much more enjoyable had the university been prepared to receive the black students that matriculated during the time that I was there. My feelings are still mixed, but I'm just happy about some advances being made today. I do feel a whole lot more could be done, and with the passage of time, more will be done. But change is slow. I think you know it took them all this time to recognize Nolan Richardson and the contributions he made with the 1994 basketball team, some fifteen years later. That's just too long. They should have been recognized much sooner than that. So I think there's still a double-standard for blacks and the way blacks and whites are treated on campus.

I just feel like my experience at the university prepared me in a sense for what I'm doing now. That is, I'm a minister and it helps me to know that I have to love everybody regardless of who they are, or what they've done, forget about the hurts of the past, still love people in spite of what may have happened, and then move on. And it's strengthening because trials, tribulations, and hardships help to make a person stronger when they depend upon the Almighty God to see them through. That's the only way I made it through the university. I think many other black students would be able to say the same thing. Had it not been for the Lord on our side, where would we be? It also gives recognition to the university. I'm proud to be a graduate of the University of Arkansas because hardly anywhere you go in the United States, people have not heard about the university. When I went to Texas to Southwestern Baptist Theological Seminary, the University of Arkansas was a well-known and well-respected school. So I'm proud to be an alumnus of the University of Arkansas, Fayetteville.

I appreciate your taking time to have this interview with me and I hope it will help to encourage someone else along the way, those who will later be coming along to the university, and those that are reading may get some insight from the African American perspective. I would also like to say not all of it was prejudice against us. Because me personally, and also my sister, Freda, went to school on loans. There weren't many scholarships for black students at that time. Sometimes, we would fall a little short of the grade requirements for a particular loan and the loan officer at the school would say, "Hey, I know you didn't quite make the grade point, but we got a little extra money to help you. I'm sure you can get your grade average up." So it wasn't all prejudice, there was some grace involved in helping me, my sister, and I'm sure perhaps other black students as well. She is now a medical doctor in Jackson, Mississippi, and I am a doctor of ministry. I have a doctor of ministry degree from Howard University School of Divinity in Washington, D.C., where I presently reside. For me, the university was an interesting but mixed experience. But all in all, I guess it balanced out in the end.

■ Vernon Murphy (1968–1972), minister

Interview by Dr. Lonnie R. Williams, November 17, 2007
Interviewed at hotel in Texarkana, Arkansas
For detailed biography, see Appendix A, page 296

I entered the university in the year of 1968 when I started as a freshman on a basketball scholarship there, a four-year scholarship at the University of Arkansas. I was very excited to go there. Many people from the Texarkana area, where I am from, really encouraged me to go because they felt there was not enough black cooperation or black players at that time at the University of Arkansas. In fact, they had one gentleman who had just started in basketball and there were none in football. If you were on scholarship, you stayed in Wilson Sharp, the athletic dorm.

I had about eighty-two scholarship offers from all over the nation, Villanova, Drake, University of Houston, University of Colorado, Wichita State, Oklahoma Sooners, Rice, TCU, SMU, and many others. As I said, many people here in Texarkana wanted to help integrate the University of Arkansas. They were lawyers and state representatives, and they gave a big banquet with townspeople there, the mayor, and everybody expressed how they wanted me to go to the University of Arkansas. Eventually, I did narrow it down to Wichita State, University of Oklahoma Sooners, and the University of Arkansas. And they did convince me to go to the University of Arkansas.

I attended from 1968 to 1972. I did not get drafted because I believe the coach at that time, Lanny van Eman, had put me to an inside position and I told him that that would probably ruin my chances for professional basketball, but he didn't seem to care. That year I got out, in 1972, I did not get drafted. The Dallas Cowboys called me and asked me about coming out as a free agent. I accepted their offer, went down, and would eventually get cut later on.

In my very last game at the University of Arkansas against Baylor, we scored about one hundred thirty points. That particular afternoon I realized that I owed the Arkansas fans the best of me because this coach had not allowed me to do that. He had not allowed me to play the best game that I knew how to play because I broke all freshman records and at this time he would not let me play. I went to his office. The last game with Baylor, which we did win, I literally talked to him. I told him that I owe the fans of Arkansas my best play and I owe myself to play my best tonight. I really told him that he better not stop me and that I was going to play this game tonight the way I know I can play to the best of my ability. I walked out and I slammed his door. That night we played and I started the game, jumped center, and I actually took over the guard position for the first time in my life there at Arkansas. We whipped Baylor. I think it was somewhere around one hundred thirty to eighty-five or something like that. That wasn't really such a good experience for me right then, but those are the things that happened while I was there.

What was my role in the history of African Americans at the U of A? Yes, a scholarship. There was one black gentleman . . . I believe his name was T. J. Johnson. He quit and that left me there. I graduated. When I did graduate from there, it made me the first black to start, continue, and graduate with a bachelor's of science degree in education. When I did leave in 1972, I lacked nine hours. I went to try out for the Dallas Cowboys. I then went to Mexico and played professional basketball there, won a championship, and tried out for the Atlanta Hawks coming back to the United States. That failed. Then San Antonio Spurs. Then I went to Israel and tried to get a chance to play European ball. The war continued in Israel and that canceled those games. I came back to school in 1973 or 1974. Frank Broyles was nice enough to continue my education so that I could finish my degree. I thank God for him for that. I finished my degree and left in 1975. My father had gotten sick here in Texarkana and I had to come back here to help him.

T. J. got there in 1967 on scholarship. He had come in and we would often talk. There was just too much pressure on him from the things around, and things not going right with black and white relationships. He didn't feel he was being treated right and so he said he was just going to get out.

I think they treated us a little bit better, athletes, when I say us. There was another guy came the next year named John Seers and I recruited a guy named Almer Lee. Actually, I later recruited Ron Brewer and Marvin Delph. Those were the times that we—Johnson, Seers, and

I—there still was some tension. But as I said, I believe the athletes were treated a little bit better than other blacks that were on campus. Some talk, run-ins, and some things that were happening there. I noticed with the athletes and games, the blacks would go to their parties and the whites would go to their parties, and it wasn't such a big deal with me.

One time after season, we were playing some basketball on our own about twelve o'clock or something and there was a guy named Terry Don Phillips—he played football. I think they said he had a brother that played with the Chicago Bears. I believe they were from Long View. We were out playing ball there, and we had done some bets, or something in biology class, about the atrium and auricle of the heart. We were out playing ball and were still talking about it and I said, "Well, man, the bet's off because it is basically the same thing." I walked away and he called me a bastard. He's a big football lineman. I turned, walked away, and he hit me behind my head. I stumbled and I immediately turned around. He charged at me, put his head in my stomach, which I began to beat his head, and he finally let go, hit the floor, and stood up again. And I slapped him several times before he could even turn around good. He backed on away and said, "Your arms are too long." From that incident, people kind of got respect because everybody thought he was so bad and that I had stood up against him. Those kinds of things happened, but we made up later. I was in Wilson Sharp looking at television at one end, the east end I believe. I saw him walking in the back of me. I just watched. He just came up to me and literally apologized for hitting me, doing what he did, saying what he said, and all that. We became friends and from then on we had no problems.

Basically, on campus I didn't have too many other problems besides just with the coach. I know one year, actually, from my freshman year to my sophomore year when I came back. People don't know that I was the only person in the dorm with a mustache, but that was my agreement for signing the scholarship. I had just a small mustache, but I did not want to shave it. And I would have gone somewhere else because I did not want to put a razor on my face and they agreed that I would not have to shave, and so I signed contracts with them. But my sophomore year, when I drove up in the car, Lon Ferrell, the man over the dorm at Wilson Sharp at the time, met me getting out of my car and told me right away, he didn't even hardly say hello, he just told me, "You had better shave that mustache off. Now! Or you can get back in your car and you can go back to Texarkana with your scholarship!" I thought what a cruel thing to do. So I had to go shave my mustache off. That really burned me up on the inside! I felt smaller than an ant behind that.

We really had no problems when we'd travel. We didn't get treated any worse than anybody else wherever we went, the hotels or anything. Everyone was friendly. One thing that was real funny in the dorm where we lived. Danny Keater, lived up at Mountain Home, used to ask me about going home; he was my first roommate. One of the first things he said was, "We don't have any blacks in our hometown." I told him, "Well, I'm not going up there." But anyway, he said, "I don't know how to treat you? I've never been around black people before." I told him to just treat me like you would any other white person or any person period on the whole earth and said that would be fine. He said, "I'll do it." He got to be one of my best friends, just from behind that. That was something.

One night, I believe a guy named Grisham became my roommate. He tried to make me feel at home. I was lying on my bed. We were in my room. Keater and I were in there and Grisham was telling us about how he had been in the hospital and had to put some pins in his knee or his foot. It was very interesting. They were trying to make me feel good. Letting me know that blacks are okay with him, I guess, and he let me know there was a black nurse and the way he said it was, "You know, I had the nicest little nigger nurse that was helping me." And I just turned my head over on the pillow and I really was smiling. It isn't going to bother me a lot, but I didn't want them to see me laughing so I turned my head on the pillow. Then turned back around and we kept on talking like nothing had ever happened. I was understanding that when people that are in different parts of cities wherever they come from, up in the northern part of Arkansas, or wherever, that they were getting used to integrated schools.

That period was a big adjustment time for racial understanding. Other than that, and playing basketball, everything was fine. The other coaches treated me fine. The dorm was fine. Everything was good there and that's basically where I spent a lot of my time. Sometimes we would go out to places, party and things, and other than that I didn't have a real hard time. I do remember one time, Martin Terry and I went out about eleven or twelve o'clock on a Friday night to get something to eat, not far from the airport, Drake Field, in Fayetteville. We were starting out of the car and saw some people who had been drinking. One man came out, saw us out there, and he called us "Niggers." My friend Martin grabbed a Coke bottle in the car and started to open the door. He was going to hit him with it and I reminded him of who we were, and if we got in a fight that we would be in the newspaper, on the television. I said, "It is not even worth it. The man has been drinking. He doesn't know what he is doing. And that's okay with me." As I have said, I've learned to adjust myself to people and things around me. But those are some of the circumstances we had to go through while we were up there. I am just trying to think . . . that's probably about some of the worst times. Other than that, my whole deal was just to try to play basketball and try to play professional.

Dean Tolson was my roommate one year. I think he was all-time rebounder, even still today. Moncrief and I are still tied for second place in history there. Almer Lee, Martin Terry, and I drove a convertible Pontiac all the way to Shreveport to try to recruit Robert Parrish. While we were there, I believe Bobby Knight called from Indiana. But anyway, we rode around with him, brought him something to eat, and just tried to recruit him generally. He finally decided he was going to stay at Centenary and later went on to the Celtics.

I believe maybe I was treated a little bit better than other students. We were in the newspaper and on television all the time. I had no problem with classes. If I did have problems, all I had to do is tell the coaching staff, and they would get us a tutor. Bring them down and pay for them to help us get through school. And education was more important to me along with basketball than any other type of thing. So basically, I just really believe the athletes were treated fairly decently.

One of the things that happened that many people do not know about was around 1969 that we had a hard time with things. Some of the black students there did not like the playing of the song "Dixie" and they wanted them to stop playing that song. About that time, President Nixon was going to fly to a Texas-Arkansas game, which he did, and all the black students were going to march and protest at half-time about the playing of "Dixie." And so that word got around. They let the president of the university know that this was what was coming down, that the blacks were going to march. They had contacted me and wanted me to march with them. I was thinking seriously about it, whether I wanted to or not. What happened was at the last moment before halftime, the president of the University of Arkansas called the band director, and told him that they were not to play "Dixie" anymore. I can tell you that the song "Dixie" stopped at the game when President Nixon came to the Texas-Arkansas game in 1969.

I had not been up actually in twenty years. I still felt bad about the basketball situation because the coach did not care enough to allow me to play to a point where I could go pro. And that hurt me for years, for thirty years. This last year I started going to some games. I had become a pilot and I could get there a little quicker ,also. I got to meet Coach Heath. That is the time and era when I started going back. I went to talk to Frank Broyles. Frank Broyles got with some of the staff about looking into the record books. They said they hadn't really thought about it, but I told them it was important to me. We looked at the record books and ended up with the conclusion that Vernon Murphy—me—I am the first black basketball player, or athlete, period, to go to the University of Arkansas and to graduate at the University of Arkansas.

Now, I came up in 1968. In 1969, there was a gentleman named Jon Richardson being the first black football player on scholarship. In 1969, I believe Joe Ferguson, a quarterback, came up in that year. One of the things we did notice as black people is that Jon Richardson would run the ball down to the five-yard line. They would run it down with a black player and they would give the ball to the white player at the five-yard line. They would let the white player continue on and get glory for finishing the touchdown. Someone said his name was Dickey Morton. People were happy with that.

I do have another experience. I believe it was the Texas-Arkansas game. Instead of watching it on television, I'm right there at the stadium so I just went down. They probably always waved the rebel flag and I didn't have a complaint. Sometimes people laugh about it now, but I was way up in the top watching Jon Richardson, the black football player run. He was a good runner for the Razorbacks. He would run the ball hard. This was just before they stopped playing "Dixie," and they were playing "Dixie," waving the rebel flags, having a great time. I am sitting up in the middle with my little face, up in the middle of everybody just trying to do my little part for integration in the United States and Jon was doing good. I was proud of him and people were clapping their hands for him. Low and behold, Jon fumbled the football and somebody said, "Get that nigger out of there." Right in my area! I just politely got up, walked down the stairs, because I didn't I know what I am in the middle of now, and walked back to Wilson Sharp dorm where all the athletes live, and finished watching the game on television. I have been adjusting myself that way until things get better.

Describe my present feelings toward the university? They have changed. I have become a minister now and I realize you have to forgive and try to put things behind you. And I think it hurt me. First, because the coach didn't care enough to help me get to play pro and play me in the right position. I'm getting to be more forgiving. I get back more now as a regular alumnus and enjoy football, basketball, and all the sports that the university has. I get a chance to see a few games every year. So my feelings have changed in that direction. But that is where I went to school. I am an alumnus there and I am supporting it.

That is basically it. I've hit most of the things that I thought about. We went to classes. The teachers didn't show us any favors. We could get our own tutors. All they expected of me was just to keep my grade-point up so I could continue to play sports. That was most important. I'm not sure whether I looked into the depth of black activities on campus. It didn't have my attention at that time the way it may have had other people. I was comfortable being an athlete there, except for the little coach problem, and all the other situations were just regular living life, just fine with me.

■ Deborah Hill Thompson (1966–1980), university staff

Interview conducted by Lonnie R. Williams, July 7, 2007
Interviewed in the Yvonne Richardson Center, Fayetteville, Arkansas
For detailed biography, see Appendix A, page 297

My name is Deborah Hill Thompson; I went to the University of Arkansas in 1966 to pursue a bachelor's degree in elementary education. I wanted to attend an institution away from home, Little Rock, Arkansas, but still remain within the state. My parents had always told me I could attend school anywhere in the state. Both my parents, and my middle sister, had attended this university. My father, Jethro A. Hill, received a master's of science and my mother, Barbara L. Hill, received a master's in elementary education. My middle sister, Geneva Hill, was entering her junior year during my freshman year. I had been on campus several times and was somewhat familiar with the university and the black community. Consequently, I chose the University of Arkansas.

I was with the university for approximately fourteen and a half years as a student and employee. My undergraduate degree was completed in 1970 with a BSE in elementary education and graduate degree in 1973 with a MEd in counseling. I felt compelled to continue with my master's because my parents and both sisters—Jacquelyn Hill, University of Toledo, MEd counseling, 1968, and Geneva Hill, University of Illinois, MSW, 1971—had received their master's degrees.

Upon completing graduate school, I started my counseling career in the financial aid office. My first position was financial aid officer, assistant director, for the three years. In that position, I counseled students, parents, and administered federal, state, and local funds to undergraduate and graduate students.

After working in the financial aid office, I worked in the newly opened counseling center as a staff counselor (coordinator of career development). I was the first African American to work in the counseling center in this capacity. This position allowed me to use my counseling skills with individual and group sessions. I specialized in career counseling and organized and developed the career component of the counseling center. This enabled me to teach a one-hour noncredit career development course, design and develop a career library. I worked under the supervision of Dr. Joe DeOrdio for four years before being transferred to the Career Planning and Placement Office.

As a counselor (assistant director of Career Planning and Placement) in the Career Planning and Placement Office for two years, I continued to coordinate the career development services and was responsible for coordinating all on-campus recruiting for two hundred fifty company representatives. I briefly served as interim director for approximately six months. When I first started working in Career Planning and Placement, Lawrence Crockett, an African American, was interim director.

Overall, I had a positive experience at the university. This was due to my familiarity with the campus, the black community, and my sister's presence on campus for two years. When I arrived on campus, I knew that my number-one goal was to get an education. I didn't really have any academic problem. The only problem I had in the classroom was myself. My grades reflected the effort I exerted. The Little Rock Public School System provided me with a strong academic background. We had some excellent black teachers; in fact, some were superb teachers.

They prepared us to go any place and excel. I attended all-black schools and am sure that excellent teachers existed throughout the system.

There were some times when I felt the university had different standards for black students. When you looked around and saw blacks paying for an education and not able to fully enjoy and participate in everything they had a right as a student, I felt rejected. I felt I was accepted only because of the law rather than a potentially good student from Horace Mann High School. However, I had a mission to get my education and I did not allow ignorance to prevail. You can not fight every battle nor can you ignore every battle. You have to decide which ones are relevant and approach the battlefield with winning on your mind. I saw BSE and MEd on my battlefield and chose to get them. However, there were some institutional distractions that I chose to fight along with determined black students and faculty. I can't recall having a single one-on-one confrontation with a white student during my entire fourteen and a half years with the university. All of the racial injustices I experienced resulted from institutional ignorance!

As far as the social aspects, when I first came to campus, I knew most of the black personalities on campus. My sister knew all the ropes and had paved the way for me. It was through her that I learned about the campus and community social networking. The black church played an integral role in accommodating the religious, social needs, and concerns of black students. On Sundays after church, many of the black families would make their homes available to us and prepare some of the most delicious meals. Others would provide transportation during the week to those who needed to conduct business off campus. Moreover, my very first week on campus, I met my husband-to-be, Semon F. Thompson. We started dating shortly thereafter.

However, there were some social organizations on campus that I wanted to become affiliated with but I couldn't because of my race. It was very exciting to me during the first week of school to see the sororities and fraternities get together and go through rush. I knew that I could never become a part of that. I would have loved to have been featured as a Razorback Beauty or cheerleader. Here again, my race prevents me from becoming completely immersed in campus life. I didn't dare try to be a part of those social organizations because I didn't want to subject myself to disappointment. In other words, I wanted to be in a situation where I had some degree of control which allowed me to keep my focus.

I was heavily involved in black activism. There was an organization on campus called Black Americans for Democracy (BAD). This group served as a sounding board for many of the blacks on campus. It was a means of addressing some urgent needs, concerns, and issues of black students. Oftentimes, these concerns resulted in peaceful black demonstrations and sit-ins. Black students felt that if things were going to change, we had to take the appropriate action and do it for ourselves because if left to the administration, we didn't feel concerns would be addressed. So with that in mind, we were trying to make an effective change. It is interesting to note that my sister, Geneva, came up with the name BAD. A group of black students had gathered to form a black student organization. Geneva stood up and said, "We are all black Americans for democracy." Thus the name Black Americans for Democracy emerged.

Here are some of the demonstrations I remember. Hill Hall [Journalism Building] incident: the *Arkansas Traveler* had printed a letter submitted by a white student making derogatory remarks about blacks in general. A black student submitted an article refuting those racist comments, but the *Traveler* refused to print the letter. The black students got together and barricaded all entrances to Hill Hall, preventing the production of the *Traveler* and classes for an entire day.

Pep Rally incident: black students had tried to get the administration to stop the Razorback band from playing "Dixie" at pep rallies and football games. Without any success with the administration, black students prevented the band from entering the stage of the Greek amphitheatre for the pep rally. The band members and rally participants moved to another location without incident with the black students.

March around the administration building: black students were demanding black football players, cheerleaders, scholarships, and black faculty and staff. Several demonstrations were held on various locations on campus. Because of the frequency of demonstrations, the administration decided to call a noted black consultant to campus. The consultant arrived on campus and met with BAD. He was so moved with our concerns that he led a protest march around campus beginning with the administration building. All of the demonstrations and protests were well organized and peaceful without any confrontations.

In view of the institutional racism, I did not have a lot of bad experiences on campus. Because of prayers, a close-knit black social networking on campus, and the black community, I was able to achieve my goal of getting an education in a timely manner. I would strongly encourage blacks to attend the university today. Their number-one mission is to get an education. They do not have the barriers and distractions today that existed during the last forty years and earlier. Many or all of those barriers are a thing of the past. However, blacks should not take anything for granted. They should realize the sacrifices of those before them that make their existence possible. Knowing about the injustices that once graced that campus should make blacks more determined to achieve their goals. Black students should realize that systems are in place to address all of their needs and concerns.

Forty-plus years after my first encounter with the university as a student, I think that time has brought about a positive change for the better. First of all, the physical surroundings are unbelievable. I didn't recognize Razorback Road and the main entrance to the campus. The university had always been a sprawling spectacular campus and all the new physical facilities have enhanced the grandeur of campus. The black student population has grown from fewer than one hundred to almost one thousand. I can remember going for several days at a time without seeing other blacks on campus. It's a good feeling knowing that many of the blacks are reaping the benefits of some of your personal efforts and struggles. My assumption is that black students have become fully immersed in every aspect of university life. Again, I would encourage prospective black students to attend this institution. As parents, my husband and I strongly recommended that our daughter, Chioma, attend the university. She chose to attend UALR, which is a part of the university system. I wish all the students success at the university.

■ Semon Frank Thompson Jr. (1961–1982), prison superintendent

Interview by Charles Robinson and Lonnie R. Williams, July 7, 2007
Interviewed in St. James United Methodist Church basement, Fayetteville, Arkansas
For detailed biography, see Appendix A, page 297

Semon Frank Thompson Jr. is my name and I entered in 1961. I came as a pre-med student.

Why did I select the University of Arkansas? I've asked myself that question a lot of times since then. I came up at a time when the nation was caught up in the civil rights movement and I was trying to find my own place in the civil rights movement. People all around Little Rock, like the Whitfields, there were all personalities involved in the struggle. There was a lot of activity from a Little Rock environment. That was a little part of it because I knew of the integration issues at the University of Arkansas. I guess the thing that sort of tilted it in that direction was as a black high school graduate you couldn't get a pre-med education anywhere else in the state. And I sincerely, at that time, wanted to become a doctor. But that dream ended after the first semester when I made an "F" in chemistry. I had to change my major [all laughing]. I got a degree in social work.

Off and on from 1961 through 1982 I was at the University of Arkansas. There were three years of military service in between entering as a freshman, leaving for service, and coming back. When I came back, I made up my mind I was going to finish at the University of Arkansas because I had flunked out the first two years. It was something that I had to do for myself. I had to get my degree from the institution where I had experienced this academic failure. I owed it to my own self-confidence and self-ego to go back and get that degree.

What positions did I hold while at the U of A? I served as graduate resident of Hotz Hall. Deborah and I married in 1970. I became a graduate assistant in September of 1970. I served as patrolman with the Department of Public Safety [now UAPD]—served as a criminal investigator. When they appointed me to criminal investigator, I became the first armed officer on campus in the history of the University of Arkansas, which met with a limited amount of controversy. I became assistant dean of minority affairs and became associate dean of students during those years.

As a student . . . and I think my brother-in-law (Eugene) Dowell was quite modest in relating his history here . . . Gene and his family, among some others in the community, were quite instrumental in giving many black students who came into this isolated environment a sense of home. Even during those days, there were student demonstrations under the leadership of George Whitfield, Melvin Dowell, myself, Carolyn Funkhouser, and a couple of other students. We did some sit-ins to help integrate the movie theaters, particularly a place right there by the Kappa Sigma Fraternity house [UArk Bowl on Dickson] and then the one right downtown by the courthouse [Ozark Theater]. We did some sit-ins in some restaurants and theaters here. They were eventually integrated.

Later on I served as assistant dean for student affairs. I was involved with providing faculty supervision to the black student organizations. The first activist student organization started out as being called Black Americans for Democracy, BAD. There were a number of demonstrations the students were involved in and I served as intermediary between black student interest and faculty. There were some student demonstrations where the black students blocked the entrance to the journalism building because the student newspaper presented a biased reflection of black student interests. There were concerns about full integration of the athletic opportunities not being made available. There were a couple of young cheerleaders, I'm forgetting their names so forgive me for that, who were very wonderful students who wanted to be cheerleaders. There was resistance in allowing them to get on the cheerleading team and the black students wanted to stage a demonstration in support of them. There were a lot of intermediary functions that I provided in that capacity. There was once a program called the Graduate Information Bank that was started during my administration where we collected information on students who had graduated from college from across the country, had earned master's degrees, and were looking for employment. Our office would make those names available to various positions that were coming up through the recruitment process. Three or four people were hired as a result of the Graduate Information Bank into the University of Arkansas staff.

When I came up in 1961, I knew what neck of the woods I was hunting in. I knew of the legacy of George Haley, the Whitfields, and what they had to go through up here. This environment didn't let me down in terms of what I anticipated. Racism abounded, though I lived in the basement of a white family's home because, at the time, blacks were not allowed to live in the dorms. George Whitfield was a roommate of mine. A few blacks were graduate students. A number of us lived in the basement there.

I came prepared to be involved in those integration-desegregation issues. I take responsibility of not making the kinds of grades I should've made, but I chose to become quite involved in the civil rights efforts. The first civil rights demonstration on campus I was involved in was a march that was right in front of the library and had to do with integration of the dorms because the dorms didn't get integrated until after 1963. George Whitfield and I were the only blacks in this demonstration. Those were the beginning stages of campus activism and the Whitfields carried through with the lawsuits, et cetera, that ultimately got the dorms integrated. So my feeling about it is it was a fight. Not a fight unlike the fight that was being fought across the country. I didn't ever have my personal ego damaged by it because I knew what came with the turf. I think getting involved in civil rights gets you labeled. Willingness to demonstrate and take on the administration doesn't make your path any easier. I did, with some degree of bitterness . . . didn't like the part of history that was being reflected. I failed academically, so like I said earlier, I came back to get my degree from here. When I look back over it, it was a chapter that was character building for me. I ain't mad at nobody, but I know that I dealt with it.

If I have been remiss at all in not going back and shaking someone's hand or giving them a hug, it would be a gentleman by the name of Lyle Thompson. Lyle Thompson was always there in some kind of capacity. He and his involvement with the Unitarian group and his connection to progressive-minded people who primarily were associated with the Unitarian organization were a constant source of support for the civil rights effort. Were it not for those people at the times when I really felt down, there were a couple of times that I would've just bailed. They were providing comfort, counseling, a good meal and place to stay, financial resources, advocacy for you among the faculty. Lyle Thompson and a couple of other people, in a unique way, stood out among all of them as far as I'm concerned.

Some of the details are a little fuzzy. In 1969, there were articles that the black students were interested in getting published in the students' newspaper called the *Arkansas Traveler.* The article was so edited that it was not accurate at all. Black students were not able to get our information fairly published and the students were really concerned about it. The reason for the demonstration in front of the journalism building had to do with the fact that the student newspaper did not have any black students on the editing staff. If I remember correctly, over time, we were successful in getting students on the editing staff.

I think our demonstration, student demonstration, in getting cheerleaders was ultimately successful. There were a couple of young white students by the name of Johansen (Johansen twins) who were cheerleaders, who really fought existing culture here as students. They were successful and very popular. From the inside, they were advocates of trying to get the young black cheerleaders on and that was a success.

I did mention earlier that we were successful in integrating some of the public accommodations. I think being the first black criminal investigator was a part of the history. Being the first one, I'm not sure that much about being armed, but I made my career in law enforcement so I know what being armed is all about, but being the first person to be armed, either black or white, said something in terms of the campus beginning to turn in what it was willing to do. It would be the year about 1975.

Having become associate dean of students (1978), that's a positive. I'm really proud among the number of things that black students did here. I think they had been aware of a lot of sacrifices that a number of personalities had gone through up until my time and I was only symbolic of that at this particular time. When the position was advertised for the associate dean of students, they did not want to hire me because I did not have a graduate degree, but the black students knew of my involvement and they knew they didn't want anybody else to be in that position but myself. I just stood back and those young people went over to the administration building and just sort of said to the administration, it's going to be Semon Thompson or anybody else you bring in here will catch hell. So they had me. I like that kind of cohesiveness and identification of focus of purpose for a cause and that's how the student organization was mature in some ways.

BAD became STAND after I left. I left in 1980. It would've been 1977 and I left in 1980 and became executive director of Economic Opportunities.

I'm just overwhelmed at the statistics in terms of the number of students that are on campus. Whether or not it should be many, many more students, I don't know. I'm locked into comparing it to when I was here. It's just so many more. Having you sitting here interviewing me is an impressive experience. There are, comparatively speaking, so many more faculty and staff members as I understand it. I don't know what the exact numbers are. Sometimes, I make the mistake of comparing progress by looking at where we are now to where we were. That could be a mistake. In fact, the comparison ought to be where we ought to be. If I would compare today to those times, there is just a significant difference by leaps and bounds.

The U of A experience for me? Looking back, I was a fairly gifted person, if you would allow me to say that. Fairly unfocused and full of confidence, but I didn't know exactly where I wanted to go over the long run in life. I think the University of Arkansas experience built character because it tested me in a lot of different ways. I don't think every bad experience in life is necessarily a bad one, if you learn to profit from it, if it builds character. The University of Arkansas was a character-building experience. I know what it is to go into Brough Commons and sit down to a table and all of the students get up and leave. I could eat in the cafeteria, but couldn't live in the residence hall. I know what it's like to go into Brough Commons and the students at the top of the stairway as you're going to get a meal will let all the white people get in front. I know what it's like to be real hungry after walking from the basement, walking a mile to eat, and the line getting longer. One day, I was just too hungry to let that happen again. We fought and nobody broke in front of me again. You just don't want to break in line of a hungry man, a hungry black man, and I didn't have that problem anymore. I have a friend, he was a friend of Gene's, Gene Witty, he decided to go to Brough Commons with me to sort of sit and demonstrate. There were those that were okay at sitting at the table. That was the day following the fight. So the next day I went to eat and five other white students came over and in a symbolic demonstration of support for the fact that I had a right to eat there. We could eat in the cafeteria, but we could not live in the residence halls.

To answer your question, it was a character-building experience. Ever since then, I've been much more focused about what I want in life. I've had the self-confidence, if I put myself to it. And without the University of Arkansas experience, I think it may have been more of a painless way, but it built character.

▪ Earnestine Banks Walton Russell (1965–1968), educator

Written response to interview questions, April 6, 2009
For detailed biography, see Appendix A, page 297

I attended the University of Arkansas in the summer of 1965 and the spring of 1968. The university was the only institution offering a master's degree in home economics (consumer science).

I was the only black student in all of my classes. There was some fear. Blacks were not allowed to get off the bus in Rogers, Arkansas. There were some fields of study that blacks had very difficult times in trying to complete the requirements for a degree. Some areas of study blacks just were not encouraged to enter (English). There were very limited, or none at all, opportunities for blacks to participate in campus activities. There were no black professors, black office workers, and no black common labor workers. All of the black women were housed in one living quarter. There was only one television in the building. The television was in the lounge. Rabbit ears were the only thing one could use, if she had her own TV. The radio stations only played country and western music. There were no black barbershops or beauty shops. When blacks would go down town to the Square, the white children would just stare.

I was a student when Muhammad Ali came to the university to speak. His coming caused a great deal of controversy at the university. There were a large number of individuals around the state of Arkansas who spoke against Ali being allowed to speak. Muhammad Ali refused to serve his country in the military. The university did not cancel his appearance. I went to the program. I heard Ali speak. He had so much courage and did not appear to be afraid. Of course, I had fears that something bad might take place. I can still remember Muhammad Ali saying, "Everything that is bad is always black! In the books that little children read, it was the old black cow that would not do right. The black cat crossing in front of a car bringing bad luck."

During my time of study, I felt proud to be enrolled at the university. However, I was happy to have completed my study. I have returned several times. I was studying to receive a specialist degree in vocational education. I may have completed fifteen or eighteen hours on a specialist degree. I have attended the Black Alumni Reunions. I also had two children to graduate from the University of Arkansas, Trent A. Walton Sr., with BS and MS degrees in chemical engineering and Sheila Walton with a BS degree in accounting. Many trips were made during those years.

The university has changed its attitude toward blacks. I know that there are more blacks attending the university. Blacks are allowed to seek degrees in most of the high-paying careers. There are black professors on the university staff now.

■ George W. Whitfield (1962–1964), university professor

Written response to interview questions, July 31, 2007
No detailed biography available

This tells of "my life and times at the University of Arkansas and AM&N College, 1962–1964 in Fayetteville, Arkansas." I was born in Scottsboro, Alabama, in my great-grandfather's and grandfather's home, but my family moved to Little Rock, my father's home before I started elementary school. I graduated from Dunbar High School in Little Rock in 1952 and began work on my baccalaureate degree that fall at Arkansas AM&N College. Following a year in college and a three-year stint in the U.S. Army, I graduated with a bachelor of arts, *magna cum laude* in May 1958. My major was English, speech, and drama. I was a three-year letterman in football and captain of the debate team. That fall, I took a job at Merrill High School (Pine Bluff) as a teacher of English, speech, and drama, assistant football coach, and junior varsity basketball coach. I also served as drama and debate coach, and with two other English teachers started a weekly school paper.

Professor Oliver T. Shannon, chair, Department of Mathematics, at Arkansas AM&N College, had harangued me from graduation to go to graduate school. My rationalization was I couldn't afford it. He challenged me by saying, "If I get you some money, will you go?" I reluctantly said yes. He nominated me for and I won a Woodrow Wilson National Fellowship (WW). One of the members of the Fellowship selection committee was a U of A English professor. The Fellowship, which paid all tuition and fees and provided a small "tax exempt" stipend, enabled me to start work on the master of arts degree in rhetoric and public address at the U of A. It also helped substantially with financial demands of a family. When I received the WW Fellowship, I had been working, married three and a half years, and was the father of two young children. With few financial resources, I was unable to take my young family to northern universities that accepted Negroes. Fayetteville obviously was closer to my young family and less expensive both to travel and to live. The Department of Speech and Drama at U of A had a solid regional reputation and had several prominent scholars in the department. These combined circumstances led me to opt for the U of A. I enrolled in the master's program in the summer of 1961 and received the MA in speech at the spring 1962 commencement.

I was nominated for and received a joint Woodrow Wilson Dissertation-Southern Education Foundation Fellowship enabling me to work on my doctorate. In the fall semester 1963, I satisfactorily completed requirements for the degree, which was awarded on January 24, 1964. The day *after* I learned degree requirements were completed, November 23, 1963, was the day that President John F. Kennedy was assassinated!

When I began at the university, there were about twenty-five black students enrolled. The majority of them were undergraduates. Their choice of majors resulted in this handful of students being scattered into several departments with diverse schedules. In spite of the small enrollment overall, the small number of blacks meant you rarely saw anyone of color. There was an effort to get black undergraduates enrolled in programs in which no or few black students had previously enrolled. The program was not apparently successful. These students were "hand picked" based on high school grade-point averages and test scores. What had NOT been tested was "academic sophistication." White students had access to stockpiles of course information and test files. These data were the exclusive property of Greek letter and other student organizations. The black students were not aware that one could drop a course in which he was either failing or not doing well up to the point of taking final examinations. White students used this tactic to protect their academic status. They would drop courses *after* hearing all the lectures and having completed all the assignments *except* the final. They would retake the course under the *same* instructor repeatedly, if required, until they felt they would get the desired grade. The black students either were not aware of this tactic, or could not afford an extended stay because of economic circumstances. Attrition was high.

There were no blacks in my department except Julia Smith, from Grambling, who started after I completed my master's program. Her husband was enrolled in the Law School. The two of them left for Chicago at the end of the next year. I frequently studied in the Law School library. The students there were serious and there were few interruptions. The law faculty was tough but amiable and supportive. I fondly remember Professor Lawrence Spies, who debated William F. Buckley, a guest lecturer, to a standstill during a public forum.

Preston Torrence of Little Rock began the doctoral program as I was finishing mine. We took two classes together. He left to earn a doctorate at Atlanta University.

Among the unique experiences I encountered, was teaching a section of the general education speech course. The semester I enrolled in the graduate program, the speech and drama department had its largest and most-diverse enrollment ever. At least one student from Louisiana, Connecticut, Rhode Island, Texas, Oklahoma, Missouri, and others were enrolled in the master's program. There were twenty-eight in all, the largest and most-diverse group in the department's history! Most of these were employed as graduate teaching assistants (TAs) with each assigned two sections of the general speech course. A couple of them worked in either the scene or costume shop. One other worked as an assistant to the professor of dance, mime, and movement. After several weeks, one young lady unfortunately died from a case of "walking" pneumonia. Since the loads and schedules of the TAs and faculty would not allow them to take an additional class, I was asked to take it. Of all the students in the master's program that year, I was the ONLY one qualified and available. I am not certain, but *I may have been the first black person* to teach a class on the regular schedule on the main campus. There was some *administrative* hullabaloo from the president (Dr. William "Moon" Mullins), but there was little choice. I was not paid, principally because the WW Fellowship wouldn't allow it. The others received tuition credits and out-of-state fee waivers. It was a good experience for all. The students had never had a black professor/teacher. The department and the university had never had a black teacher as far as I know. I was well qualified, did a good job, and both students and university officials acknowledged it.

During that period, I had upset the establishment by organizing and leading protests about the unavailability of housing for black undergraduates. After several weeks of protest, the "administration" relented. The administration hastily renovated an old off-campus sorority house for black women students. The graduate women served unofficially as "house mothers," waiving university housing policy. Mesdames Carter, Greenhouse, and Wiley, all doctoral students, served informally and unofficially as "house mothers" for the young women. The university did not provide housing for graduate students regardless of race or gender. Word came to me, through the graduate dean to my department chair, that the president wanted to know whether I had missed any classes during the protests—the classes he didn't want me to teach in the first place! ALL dorms were white only. The exception was during the summer when a substantial number of black in-service teachers were provided with a black-only dormitory. Black males were provided with a floor usually in a vacant dorm during the summers only.

During regular semesters, there were a number of untoward incidents involving "ride by" white males shouting out racial epithets, sexual slurs, and profanities at the women in the off-campus home. These threats to the safety and well-being of the women gave urgency to the protests mentioned above. Private housing, with families or in apartments, was severely restricted. The indigenous black community was some distance from the campus and had limited housing. One older white couple, who had retired to the area, had a basement arrangement to house three black males. Their house was within easy walking or biking distance from the classrooms and libraries. I lived there for a year and a half. One of two younger faculty with a few or no children opened their homes nearby. Dr. Bob Shurfranz, assistant professor of agriculture, and his wife, Marilee, had a basement "apartment" they rented to John Stevenson. When he graduated, I was fortunate to get the site. It was uphill from the football stadium, hence a bit farther but with more privacy and commodious arrangements. I had a bicycle and could pedal down one hill and up another passing the fine arts building to go to Old Main. My department, classes, and professors' offices were located in Old Main. Several students, black and white, lived on Markham Hill in an abandoned Boy Scout camp owned by the widow Markham. (She was owner of several service stations in Oklahoma and Arkansas. She owned a Rolls Royce, which she kept in an air-conditioned carpeted garage!)

Dr. George R. Kernodle, an outstanding theater professor with an international reputation, selected me to perform in several short plays. These led him to cast me in the role of "God" (a leading role, playing against "Satan") in the Broadway award-winning play, *JB*. *JB* is based on the book of Job in the Christian Bible. This was a main stage production, open to the public, and a part of the department's regular theater season bill. Interestingly, a reporter from Minnesota happened to be passing through and attended one of the performances. He wrote an article in his hometown paper, which not only commended me for my performance, but commented on the irony of finding a black student/actor playing God in a production at an "all-white" university in a segregated part of country.

I reference dorms above. Some of the facts are: the university did NOT provide housing for graduate students except for those who served as head residents; the university did not provide housing for any black students except during summer terms; with the able assistance of attorneys Wiley Branton and George Howard, we were able to get commitments from the administration to provide housing for undergraduate minority students on the same basis as for whites.

A number of white students had joined the protest efforts to desegregate the dorms. Our motto was "Open minds, Open dorms." Savoring an apparent victory, many of them were eager to expand the effort. (ONLY two black students participated, Semon Thompson, a freshman from Little Rock, and Gene Dowell from Fayetteville. There were two Gene Dowells involved, one black, one white, both Fayetteville High alumni.) Many of the participants were the offspring of faculty, but the larger portion were regular undergraduates with many associated with the student religious centers. The exception was the Baptist Student Union. No one openly acknowledged belonging to the BSU.

During the 1961–1964 period, a substantial number of young "intern" ministers were enrolled at the university. They were attached to sundry student religious centers, the Wesley Foundation, the Newman Center, and Hillel House, among others. Students associated with Disciples of Christ, Presbyterians, Episcopalians, and others were actively involved. The Wesley Foundation center was across the street from the Union and a handy place to gather and plan. We were allowed to use office equipment for nominal correspondence and duplication. The minister in charge (I hope he forgives me for forgetting his name, but he was very supportive) had retirement plans. An intern United Methodist minister, Jim Loudermilk, was assigned to assist with a rather large population of Methodist students. The plan was to have Loudermilk succeed the retiring pastor/director. Because of his activism, the church fathers were NOT going to allow Loudermilk to succeed him. The retiring pastor decided to stay on. His seniority made it his option! So he stayed until the church fathers relented.

We were not formally organized, had no officers, no regular meeting times. We ultimately called ourselves, at the insistence of the press, Students For Freedom, acronym SFF. This was done tongue in cheek and for the press who had to identify the effort somehow. A part of the name business related to two of my brothers, Robert and William, who were vigorously active in the SEAM, Southeast Arkansas Movement, in and around Pine Bluff and into the rural areas. Their activism led to expulsion. Both came to Fayetteville and enrolled. They lived with Mrs. Lodene Deffebaugh. Years later, my youngest brother Bill married Mrs. Deffebaugh's daughter, Jimmye.

SFF (pronounced "Siff"), with vigorous encouragement from Professor Howard Whitlach, the university's sculptor and art professor, began a strong movement to open the city park pool and swimming program to ALL children. Spring weather had begun to break; many youngsters took to the lakes and ponds to swim. Many of the black youngsters did not know how to swim and knew little about water safety. Two of them drowned.

I had earned the Water Safety Instructors badge (WSI) through segregated Boy Scouts of America. I knew what it was to go to swimming holes, unhealthy, unsafe, and unsupervised locations to swim. That's where I had learned to swim before entering the Scout program. Professor Whitlach was a WSI certified instructor and had initiated the swimming program at the city park pool years prior. I went to the pool each morning seeking admission. When it was learned I had been denied admission, several SFF members joined and their numbers grew every day until the city closed the pool to EVERYONE. A member of the chamber and owner of one of the largest poultry processing plants in Fayetteville promised that if I and my organization backed off, they would keep the pool closed for a cooling-off period and then reopen it, including the swimming safety programs to ALL children and people. I agreed under the condition that he would hire a substantial number of blacks at his segregated job site. The pool would open without restrictions, he would hire the employees, but if NOT, we would return to the pool entrance and picket his business establishment. Attorneys Branton and Howard agreed to hold off legal action until the matter was resolved. The pool was opened without restriction. I was the first black person known to swim in the city park pool. We did experience difficulty in getting black residents to apply for the jobs!

I often wondered about the "supporters" of segregation and discrimination. Many of the people with whom I interacted as student, instructor, fellow class member, church member, and the many roles I played while at the U of A were essentially open minded and thought the system unfair. Many risked the derision of parents and peers to work in the efforts to make things better.

Mrs. Essie Carter of Pine Bluff and now Dr. Carter, was one of the few black persons on campus with a car. She was beginning her doctoral program; I was in my second year. She offered me a deal that any time I could get away she'd go home, if I would drive. I could ill afford a car, so that was good news for me. On weekends, holidays, and other occasions, she, Mrs. Electa Wiley, the Mrs. Phyllis Greenhouse, and I would head for Pine Bluff.

The week I was notified I had satisfactorily completed all requirements for the EdD we had just cleared the mountains when the music playing in the background stopped. I was driving and tried to find a station that played "adult" music, but all were "talking." I thought I heard "Kennedy" and shushed everyone. That's when we heard that JFK had been shot in Dallas!

I mentioned Dr. Kernodle, and his wife, Portia, earlier, but there were several professors who were helpful, patient, and influential. In "my" department, there was Dr. John "Jack" Murphy, Dr. (Moses) Blair Hart, Dr. Raul Pizer, Professors Mary Davis, Don Besinger, and Norm DeMarco. Dr. Murphy was my major professor in the speech program and gave outstanding advice and support through my doctoral dissertation. I had done a major research project about black orators and orations. I focused on Frederick Douglass in Dr. Murphy's History of American Public Address class. I did a major paper that he thought worthy of publication. At his insistence with his support, the paper/article "Frederick Douglass: Negro Abolitionist" was published in *Today's Speech, The Journal of the Eastern States Speech Association*. During the semester, I had introduced historically significant black orators since the textbook did not include them and the course syllabus did not acknowledge them.

Dr. Rudyard Kipling Bent was my major professor in the College of Education. Never have I met a kinder and gentler person. He was scholarly, the author of several books, one of which was the standard in departments of pedagogy across the country. He also demanded quality performance. Dr. Henry Kronenberg, dean of the college, took me under his wing when Dr. Bent was away on a visiting professorship. There were others not associated with my academic program who were substantial morale boosters, sage strategists regarding internal and off-campus politics. Among the many of those is Dr. John Pine, history, who happened to be blind, but was the warmest and most helpful human I've met. The same is true for Dr. Phil Himmelstine, philosophy, Dr. Bud Zinke, physics, and Dr. Roberts, music and choir director.

All in all, I had a good experience during my stay. I made some wonderful friends, many of whom touched me and left impressions even though I lost contact. As referenced above, some took what were risks at the time in the face of reprobation and in some cases the likelihood of reprisals. I made some good friends, several of whom have passed through town, stopped over for a visit, come by my office or home as they hurried about their business. Dr. Don Wilmuth, a classmate and Texan, offered me a job at Brown University where he had earned a professorship. The combination of financial concerns and my determination to be successful restricted my socializing to coffee between classes, an occasional beer after rehearsals, or with some of my young minister buddies, or class-related study groups. I operated in a virtual cocoon, to class, to rehearsals and performances, to the library, to study session, and to bed. This limited my circle to contacts in which it was unlikely that anyone would either say or do anything hostile or hateful. If any one in that circle was inclined differently, he kept it to himself. After the first summer, my neighbor, former professor, and friend John

Marshall Stevenson moved exclusively into the doctoral program. That left me as the lone black graduate student in speech and drama. I had NO "racial" frictions from any of my professors and only one of my classmates, whom I ignored. He was chastised by other students and later apologized for untoward remarks. Ironically, he was from Louisiana, which ultimately became my home. Fortunately, he was not aggressive and our professors and peers were intolerant of *his* intolerance. We were all graduate students older and more mature than the undergraduate crowd. We worked together in the theater and had coffee together, studied together. In many ways, I was insulated from any hubbub that might have occurred on campus. During our protests at the president's office, which was in the main library, some of the jocks jeered and hissed, et cetera. One of the few who didn't was Lance Alworth, a Mississippian who went on to star in the AFL/NFL. On one occasion, when the jeering became most boisterous, Dr. Kernodle came out of the library, announced "I'm from Alabama, I guess I'd better join this picket line," and he did.

The one professor, who even my white peers advised me was pure racist and to avoid his class, gave me credit for everything I earned including a final "A." One evening on my way to a class, unaware I was behind him, he said to a colleague, referring to me, "He's a smart assed nigger." I made no comment nor made my presence known. In his class the next day, he was the same curmudgeon as always. I never mentioned it; he never mentioned it. The other professor I didn't know.

I had interesting conversations with some students. Some were "on my side," who had honest questions, curiosity. Some didn't really understand what life in southern America was all about, only what *they* had experienced. For many, I was the first Negro they had ever known as a peer. Some were opposed to desegregation and tried to convince me of the correctness. The most common excuse for opposing desegregation was "miscegenation." Some of the excuses were funny on their face, but bespoke of deep-seated feelings that belied the intellectual opposition to segregation and discrimination. Most weren't malicious, just uninformed, or misguided. I only had one physical threat. It came from a fair-skinned, blond-haired *Panamanian* who stuck a loaded revolver in my face as I was walking home alone after leaving a discussion on civil rights one evening . . . Scared me to death! Seems he felt I had more than a professional relationship with a young woman with whom I had appeared on stage. I reported it to university police, but never heard more about it, nor saw him again.

I was frequently invited to the homes of faculty and middle-class locals for dialogues on civil rights. Many of these were supporters of the "cause." Opposition was based on concern with miscegenation. My response was consistently harsh. These affairs usually included a meal, or refreshments, good news to a starving grad student.

Winter commencement was held on January 24, 1964. The Christmas holidays came between the end of classes/examinations and commencement. During the ceremonies, my family sat next to Governor Orval Faubus, whose son Farrell was receiving a law degree. My father reported after the commencement exercises that the governor asked about me and congratulated my folks and, to my father's surprise, shook his hand! Typical of my father's generation, it was difficult for him to recognize the use of racism as a political ploy. Similarly [there was] George Wallace, who said after losing an election several years later, "I'll never be out *niggered* again," and he wasn't!

In my mind, there are far more positives to my experience at the university than negatives. I worked hard, earned two degrees, and generally had a pleasant experience. I learned far more than was taught in classes, even though I learned plenty there.

■ Robert Whitfield (1963–1965), educator

Interview conducted by Charles Robinson and Lonnie R. Williams, July 7, 2007
Interviewed in St. James United Methodist Church basement, Fayetteville, Arkansas
For detailed biography, see Appendix A, page 298

My name is Robert Lorenzo Whitfield. I started at the University of Arkansas, at that time, it was Arkansas AM&N College in Pine Bluff and we were booted out after being involved in the civil rights movement there, Pine Bluff Movement. We came here [University of Arkansas, Fayetteville].

We wrote letters to the University of Arkansas when we were kicked out of AM&N in 1963 and we asked for literature and information so we could apply for enrollment. When I say we, I speak of my brother, myself, and two or three others that were also booted out of AM&N. We received a huge packet from the University of Arkansas that included booklets, enrollment forms for several other colleges in Little Rock and surrounding areas, all the way up to Conway. The packet came with a nice letter suggesting that Fayetteville was a difficult route from Little Rock and we might want to consider some of the other institutions that were closer, more convenient for us.

When we got here, it was clear we were not welcome here. We stayed in the "can" as it was called [African American neighborhood]. There were no facilities for black students here. We lived several different places after we got here until we finally decided that we needed to stay in the dormitories. This was a real concern of mine. We had some discussions and all we were told was, "This is not the right time." And we were just trying to be pushy.

We decided we needed to get into the dormitories. We protested. Several students came together and to no avail. So we approached our attorney and went to court (1964). The females had a house a couple of blocks down from the campus that they stayed in. At least they were convenient to campus. We [males] had to walk a mile to get to the school and classes. Sometimes we'd be late and we received abuse for being a little tardy. That was really the real purpose behind getting into the dorms—so we could have that access. At any rate, our lawyers took us to court. Bottom line, the judge said, "Whitfield, I'll just tell you the truth, when I was a student at the University of Arkansas the kids ran up and down the hallway at night, drank, noisy, et cetera, et cetera, loud, and all that." I said, "Well, Your Honor, I would at least like to have that opportunity." The lawyer said that was the nail. We won that case.

Also Mr. [Semon] Thompson mentioned the food situation, eating in the cafeteria. This was like years later. I was reflecting on that as I was listening to him. When we went to the cafeteria to eat, we were able to eat in the kitchen area and not in the cafeteria area. We got concerned about that and we wanted to sit outside the kitchen in the cafeteria area. I was surprised years later they were still having that problem. In the suit process that came up, we had access to the cafeteria where all the other kids sat and ate. Again, at that time in 1963, when we would sit down at a table, if there was anyone there, they would immediately remove themselves and relocate. There were a few students that would show a little support, but they would be harassed. But we found out later, they would be harassed so another time they would look at us and give us smiles—but at a distance. They would not take that risk.

Another experience I had coming through the University of Arkansas, I was not [sharp], but my brother that preceded me was very sharp. I was one of those students that followed him. In high school, even when George would have a test, he would have fun and go in the next day and ace the test. He put a lot of pressure on me. I had to do a lot of bookwork and studying at home. I wasn't going out enjoying myself when I had a test. I'd get in those books and get a decent grade because of that. Same thing happened when I got here. Again, I went into that classroom and knew what was expected of me. I knew my older brother had preceded me here.

My baby brother, Bill, and I were here at the same time. We would get together and some of the courses we had, he'd help me check my work and vice versa. We'd work that system. When I'd get in class and get finished with an exam, I said, "How'd I do, professor?" And he'd say, "Oh, you did real well." Then when I got my grade, it would be a "D" or "C" and I'm thinking I know I busted this out. I know I did much better than this. They were just professors. I didn't know their names. I couldn't call their name right now if you pulled a gun to me. But I knew they were not being fair to me.

After a period of time, I decided to go on and get my degree. I went back to Little Rock, went to Philander Smith College, and did real well by the way. I received my BA in elementary education.

But I remember leaving the "cup" [another name used to refer to the African American neighborhood] and coming up, passing all these [white] churches. We attended churches in the community. It's interesting. I said, now that I'm staying in the dormitories, I'm leaving the dormitory now going back down there a mile to church and all of a sudden, it was late! By the time I get there, church is almost done! I walked up on the [white] church step, it was like, bam! All of a sudden five or six folks, "What do you want? Do you know Jesus?" I'm just confused. This is just church! This is where all people go to worship! We all worship God! I was totally confused. I never thought about it until after the experience. Just wait a minute. They went back inside and came back out. Some stayed out, standing like guards. It was really a shocking experience for me. I was that naïve. The school was one thing, then the community. This is church! I've been brought up in the church and that was one place you could go for solace, speak to your Lord, and that sort of thing. That really was a shocker. I really was almost heartbroken. I couldn't believe that happened and I experienced that.

Let me back up. My twin sister was here at the time, Roberta. She'd been staying in the dormitory. She'd been here for summer school in the women's facility for blacks. We had a professor and I can't think of his name, but he was very supportive. He tried to do things that others wouldn't do. I think it was the same name, Thompson. At times you just felt like, wow, what's happened? Why? When somebody of the opposite race came in, it would give you a better perspective and a little belief there were human beings despite the experiences we underwent. He was kind of a buffer. When I would tell him about my grades and the situation, he would let me know. By the way, I was told at the time the "C" was a black "A." So you are doing good. Somehow that didn't sit right with me. I couldn't accept that.

We, my sister and I, drove into a service station one time to buy gas and generally we would pay cash. This time I wrote a check. The owner of the station looked at the check and said, "Whitfield. My wife is a Whitfield. And what is your name?" "Robert and Roberta." We had a discussion and all. He said, "Ya'll might be related," in a joking way. "I'll tell my wife about it," and I gave him my number. They called and invited us over for dinner. We were so impressed. Things like that made you believe people were human and they were real and genuine. We got to meet and talk. They found out their relatives originated in Lonoke where our father's family came from and we decided there was a bond, a relationship.

We had some good times and some bad times. I felt like it was something that had to be done. The time was just right. The doors should be open and totally open to all the public, anyone. And we brought with us our experiences from Pine Bluff. James, my brother Bill, I can't think of all of the names of the brothers that came up with us. Joanna Edwards was involved in the suit with the dormitories. The girls weren't in the dormitories they were in a house. It was open for everyone at that time, both the men and the women. We had a good bond and all. God works in wondrous ways. We cannot forget that. As I looked back over the experience, we were just instruments for God. We give Him the credit and He was opening the doors. Unfortunately, it was a slow process. As I listened to [Semon] Thompson, they experienced the same kind of prejudices that we experienced early on and it still hasn't happened. These prejudices will never end and they never have. They continue as we look at the situation on campus.

I think some progress has been made, but I think it's been awful slow. After all of the experiences from day one, chains and ropes around chairs, and calling coons, et cetera, et cetera, it is just a more subtle racism as I sense it now. I just don't understand how and why people don't just become loving and caring for each other. I have no animosity, no hostility, or hate, or anything. The only thing I regret is that somehow, some way, those attitudes and beliefs have not changed. I think about Coach Richardson. I think about the black teachers that have come through here now and their walk is all good, but yet I don't believe they have the openness, or the support that should be afforded to any and all persons, regardless of race, creed, color, et cetera, et cetera. I think the progress has just been too slow. Again, I don't know who, no hate, no hard feelings. I'm concerned about the big picture.

The lawsuit to move into the dorms was in 1964. We went in that year. I was the first black in the dorm. I had applied to get in. So after the suit was won, the dorms were open to all. They opened the dorms and the cafeteria.

I can't think of anything else right now to say. I have kind of shared some of those experiences with you. But again, after hours and after school is over and stuff like that, those students that had the right heart, but didn't feel as threatened by their peers, would show some kindness—we would have a little fellowship and friendship. But we knew when we got back on the campus and classroom, that we wouldn't have the same relationship. That was encouraging on the one hand, but discouraging on the other hand. Why couldn't we have that solidarity throughout rather than just at those times? But we understood at the time because of the impact of racism—because it was so prevalent here. When you had those experiences, where people became just people, it is always a rare occasion. It was a heart feeling always warm.

■ Robert Whitfield, Melvin Eugene Dowell, and Semon F. Thompson Jr.

Interview conducted by Charles Robinson and Lonnie R. Williams, July 7, 2008
Interviewed in St. James United Methodist Church basement, Fayetteville, Arkansas

Thompson: Referring to a classmate, George Whitfield, being involved at the swimming pool [Fayetteville pool integration] and at the time George was a close friend with Curtis

Larson, who Gene [Eugene Dowell] knows quite well. And Curtis had just staged a march from Fayetteville to Alma with a paratrooper partner of his in support of integrating public facilities. Curtis felt the integration efforts, on our part by sitting in, were too slow. And Curtis wanted to move forward with integration now—"Don't give me a slice of bread. Give me the loaf," kind of attitude.

They marched to Alma and George [Whitfield] was in support of him. In the meantime, George had been going to the swimming pool attempting to purchase tickets for admission. On three occasions, he was refused. So George and, I think it was Curtis, one other person, they went to the side of the swimming pool and frightened the folks in the pool because they stood up and started taking their pants off. Well, they had their swimming trunks on under their pants and they started taking their pants off. The white folks inside the pool thought these black men were getting naked outside the swimming pool. Actually, they took their pants off with their swim trunks on, went over the fence into the pool. White folks emptied the swimming pool. Cops came and ushered George and the others out. And for the sake of keeping the process of integrating the pool from being too sensational, pool administrators went into negotiations and ultimately opened the pool without there being a formal protest or any legal actions.

I do think that my giving this information does bear some checking out in terms of minute details. But it was George who staged the demonstration by going into the pool without admission. And they got it ultimately integrated. A little bit earlier you were observing that you weren't aware that there was still an issue about how black students ate in the cafeteria. I think the part I was describing was when I was having trouble on campus the year before you came up here, Bob [speaking to Robert Whitfield, who came in 1963]. I came in 1961 through 1963 and so those issues were occurring during those times. When you were here, fall 1963–spring 1965, it was a little bit later. I'm just attempting to put events and dates into perspective, with no intent to differ with you.

Williams: Mr. Dowell, you mentioned earlier in your conversation about Wiley Branton, Jackie Schropshire, and others living in the community in the early 1950s. How much did you all rely upon and what was the impact of the black community while you were here in those early years.

Whitfield: We were very, very, very well received by the black community. We just felt comfortably at home. We didn't feel like we were away from home, almost. We were just totally received by the black community. That made a great impact on us and relief for us to have at least that kind of support there. It was like we were not sure whether to expect it or not. But we assumed that it would be that way. It was and it made a difference in our lives.

Williams: Can you describe some of the things the black community did specifically to welcome you?

Whitfield: They prepared food for us. They provided transportation for us. They gave us a little money on the side when we didn't have to ask for it. They would know when we were struggling, and they would give a little money on the side. Of course, they would open their doors, let us stay there. It was just like being at home.

Thompson: Absolutely. Here are some of the names worth mentioning, if I may: Lodene Deffebaugh, Rose Dowell, Minerva Hoover, Ms. Funkhouser. Forgive me if I am leaving any names out, but those were the ones.

Whitfield: Lalamae Morgan. Those were outstanding personalities in making students feel accepted and supported. And I think if you continue interviewing about the history, you will find that either of us, and not my name necessarily would be included, either of those that you are looking for that may have made some contributions along those lines, you will find they all had some kind of root in the community. Almost all of them had grounding or a base of support in the community. Without that, I think the efforts would just have sort of petered out.

Dowell: I don't know. Did we mention before, George Mays? He was like George Whitfield. Everybody knew him. He had no ifs, ands, or buts about him. He was straightforward.

Thompson: Two of the other names of the students that were involved in sit-ins and the efforts to integrate public accommodations were Ora Godfrey and Carolyn Funkhouser. Ms. Funkhouser is a resident of the community.

Williams: Approximately how many students of color at the time, in the early 1960s, were here at the university?

Thompson: Gene Dowell, Carolyn Funkhouser, George Whitfield, Connie Dawson, Preston Torrence, Dean Johnson, George Mayes, Bob Whitfield, Bill Whitfield, Roberta Whitfield. Did I say George Fisher? Ed Haynie, Reuben Blake, Columbus McCall. This is spanning at least a four-year period, from about 1959 to 1963. Columbus McCall, Bernice Baker, Diane Eubanks, Barbara Enock Lackey.

Whitfield: There was Joanna Edwards, who came from the Pine Bluff movement with Bill Whitfield and me. James Jones, James Oscar Jones, Pat Jones.

Whitfield: It was not salt and pepper then. It was more like salt. There were so few of us that whenever there was a big crowd and we were in it, it was just one little spot.

Whitfield: There were a lot of summer students, too. A lot of teachers would come up during the summer and take courses and stuff. We stayed over in the summer and they were more mature. We were working in the field sometime, and they were a real support, an encouraging factor, when they would come up.

Robinson: In the classroom, you mentioned on campus the white students tended to keep their distance. But in the classroom, was there any type of studious exchange?

Whitfield: When I went to class, I would try to be there on time, and most of the time I was there on time. I sat on the front row because I wanted to get all that I could get and give all that I could give. A lot of times, I was on the front row by myself when I got there real early.

Thompson: In most organizations or groupings that I have had association with, over a year's time you eventually find personality conflicts or clashes that take place from time to time. To this day, back during those times, among the undergraduate black students and graduate students alike, I can't remember a single ill word uttered on one person's part toward another. There was a bond that was just absolutely unbelievable. There was a love. There was support. There was empathy. Students understood what we were going through and the challenges being faced. A similar phenomenon happens in the military. You'll get GIs of different races fighting each other here stateside, but once you pick them up and put them on foreign soil, racial distinctions disappear and they tend to bond. I think we sensed, even though we weren't very good at articulating it, we sensed a common bond and circumstance. I learned to appreciate relationships probably in a more profound way in those days than I have since (my family being the exception). As a friend, I've known this gentleman [Eugene Dowell] and now he is my in-law, longer than I have any other person. And those kinds of relationships were developed during those years.

It is an honor for me [addressing Bob Whitfield], Bob, to really be in a situation being interviewed like this. I've not heard you tell your story before. I've heard about it. I'd heard about the Whitfields, but to sit at an exercise like this and listen to you personally tell your story is very rewarding and validating to me. You and I have exchanged bits and pieces of our past experiences here in Fayetteville. There are parts of his story that are just sort of good for me. I appreciate what you have done just that much more.

Whitfield: I don't know how to say it, but what I did was God centered. What I did was not to get a name for myself or any publicity or whatever. People have frequently told me, "You ought to write a book." I don't feel compelled to write a book. The Lord works wondrously. Just praise Him all the time. We're not angry. We're not mad. We don't hate anybody. We love everybody. God commands we do something. We didn't have any problems, but it was a preparation for us.

Thompson: Earlier you asked me about some of the student activities, activism among students. I guess one that comes to mind that was probably the most frightening was a demonstration of the black student body behind getting black cheerleaders on the team. This was taking place during the time President Nixon was supposed to come to campus. The black students felt like, if we want to make a statement, this would be a good time to do it. So the night prior to the game, this is the 1969 Shootout, one of the students said, "Let's stop the band." I mean the pep rally is a big deal. The band gets to march and students get all in a fervor. It's primarily a fraternity/sorority thing, but a lot of the other students are all frothing.

The decision was, as we heard the band strike up, the students were going to run down and take the Greek Amphitheatre stage. The band struck up the marching music and the black students went right down the middle of the Greek Amphitheatre, blocked the aisles full of white students, and took the stage. The band is thumping and approaching. That bass drum is just booming. They come to the top of the stairs with plans to march down the aisle, look down, and there all of us were. The band stopped, but they continued playing. One of the players ran around to the back of the amphitheatre because the black student leader had grabbed the microphone and was going to address the crowd on the behalf of the reason that we were there. One of the bandleaders ran and pulled the microphones so you couldn't hear. About that time, there was a helplessness that came across all of the students. We saw then that we couldn't get our message out because no one could hear us. We were going to have to be brief, and we needed to get out of there. But now it seemed like we were going to be made a mockery of the whole thing.

There was a tremendous and unnerving moment of indecisiveness. There we—the black students—were. The band was at the top paused for a moment, and then the band started coming down steps so some of the black students left the amphitheatre stage and ran up the steps to stop the band. Then rocks started coming onto the stage. One of the brothers on the stage took a big rock and threw it right back out into the middle of the crowd of white students. So the white students realized that this was getting serious, and some of the band members put their instruments down and started motioning to the crowd to leave and we were able to exit the Greek Amphitheatre.

The next day there had been a plan to go down onto the Astroturf while President Nixon was at the football game. There seemed to be quite a bit of momentum to do that, right up until the day of the game. And as the game took place, no students showed up. I stated earlier that I hadn't heard much of a difference of opinion among students, but there wasn't much debate about taking the Greek Amphitheatre. But there was a fervent debate about the risk of going down on the Astroturf enraged because of the playing of "Dixie." As it turned out, nobody went down on the turf the next day. Following all of that, like I said, cheerleaders were eventually let on the cheerleading team.

Williams: I have a question for you. Silas Hunt came in 1948. The first undergraduates came to campus, Ms. Whitfield, Ms. Williams, and Ms. Sutton, in 1955. You came in as an undergraduate in 1959 [Dowell]. Why did it take so long for a resident of Fayetteville to come to the University of Arkansas?

Dowell: I had mentioned earlier my presence as a student was largely because of the donation of Hugh Scarborough. If not for him, I would probably have ended up on the street because I certainly did not have the wherewithal to go to Pine Bluff.

Thompson: I do think that between 1959 and today there are a number of black students who have been victims of systemic racism that is born out of a process. A number of students, who were really, really bright students in their home environment, would come up here, and because they were not fortunate enough to get some of the connections that I might have had, which gave me the strength to come back as did maybe the Whitfields, they would come into this environment being accustomed to going to that board where grades were posted and looking for their grades somewhere near the top, but ultimately realizing that their grades were at the bottom. Something happened to them psychologically. Lonnie can remember, even as late as your years up here, bright students who went through essentially integrated environments came up to this college and they were just slain emotionally. Some of them developed lasting mental health issues. There were students dropping out of this environment up here who would not have dropped out of many other institutions. That's another story. And how you can get to the root of that, I'm not really sure. But that's a part of the story that we are telling here today. If you are going to deal with who we are and where we've been—we have to acknowledge that there were some victims. You're talking to some gentlemen today [those being interviewed] who grabbed on to some semblance of purpose and goals in life. There are some young people who came here and were completely knocked off track. That's part of this legacy here.

Chapter 4

BAD Challenges Desegregation in the 1970s

If you read closely and use your head for once, you can see a general pattern—2 black administrators, 1 black faculty member, 1 black starting football player and a few black basketball players—just enough to pacify H.E.W. but not enough to pacify the black students. We want more black faces in high places.
—Harold Betton, BAD Member, December 9, 1970

A report issued in February 1969 by the Department of Health, Education and Welfare provided a snapshot of the University of Arkansas and its desegregation efforts.[1] The agency offered ten "recommendations" intended to help the institution comply with the Civil Rights Act of 1964. The first six suggestions involved recruitment. The report encouraged university officials to visit predominately black high schools with information regarding financial assistance, to actively seek out qualified black faculty and staff, and to recruit black athletes to the same degree as white athletes. At that time, there were no more than one hundred and fifty black students out of a general student population of nine thousand on the Fayetteville campus. Also, there were only three black scholarship athletes and one black faculty member. The last four points dealt with discrimination on campus. The agency advised the university to prohibit the racially exclusionary practices of sororities and fraternities and to assign dorms without regard to race. Although university officials responded to the report by intimating that the institution was progressing in these areas, the report made it clear that much more needed to be done in the 1970s in order for the university to fully desegregate and to create a campus atmosphere that fostered equal opportunity for African Americans.[2]

The desegregation assessment done by the Department of Health, Education and Welfare in 1969 was followed by another in December 1970. Though the federal agency "complimented" the university for several programs, which included tutoring for disadvantaged students, a black culture center, and its efforts to recruit more international students, this second report once again criticized the university for failing to attract more black students, administrators, faculty, and athletes. The report noted that black undergraduates comprised only 1.7 percent of a student body of 9,653, and that the university had one black professor out of 506 faculty and only two black administrators. In the agency's estimation, the university needed "stepped-up recruiting programs" in order to increase the numbers of blacks in these essential areas. With regard to athletics, the desegregation assessment pointed to the seven black scholarship players that university athletics had out of two hundred and twenty-three also as an issue of concern. The report intimated that this imbalance could be rectified if the university conducted its recruitment of black athletes in the same way that it did for white athletes.[3]

University officials responded to the second report much like they had done the first. President Mullins issued a statement of support for the idea of desegregation, declaring that the university would continue its "diligent efforts" to recruit black students, faculty, and athletes. Mullins explained that he had "advised" deans and department heads of the policy of nondiscrimination in employment and "of the need to develop a more equitable racial balance in our academic departments." For athletics, Mullins stipulated no official change in policy or practices. In his opinion, the fact that black athletes had achieved starting positions in both football and basketball would serve to naturally increase the number of black scholarship athletes over time. Apparently, these limited measures by the university in response to the two federal reports did not satisfy officials of the Department of Health, Education and Welfare, for in November 1971 the agency formally requested that the University of Arkansas submit a plan to correct "deficiencies" in the employment of blacks and women.[4]

The black power movement continued guiding the efforts of black students nationally and at the University of Arkansas to create institutions of higher learning that catered to the educational and social needs of blacks. During the better part of the 1970s at the university, Black Americans for Democracy spoke to the issues that mattered most to students of color on the Fayetteville campus. Untrusting of the campus newspaper, the *Traveler,* because of questions of fair coverage, and desirous to more fully express the concerns of black students, BAD started its own campus paper, *BAD Times.* In its monthly editions, students in the organization wrote about national, state, and campus-wide problems that they believed affected their lives. BAD consistently challenged the university to expand its desegregation efforts. In November 1972, Jack Kearney, the assistant sports editor for the organization's newspaper, wrote an article urging the university to recruit more black football players. Kearney noted that the Razorbacks struggled that year against teams that had an abundance of black players.[5] In April 1973, *BAD Times* editors complained about racist professors and demanded that the administration hire black faculty. The article decried the abysmal state of the black studies program, urging the university to make it more than just a single course.[6]

Also in November 1975, *BAD Times* articles complained about the ineffectiveness of the university's Affirmative Action policy and the lack of "black entertainment" on campus.[7]

In addition to making demands for inclusion, BAD started programs that expanded the social opportunities of black students. Many of these initiatives focused on black life and community service. BAD developed both a choir and a drama club. It sponsored a beauty pageant and held dances in conjunction with homecoming. BAD also began Project Contact, a tutorial program for black students in the Fayetteville School District and initiated a fund-raising drive to help Bruce Mitchell, a black football player diagnosed with leukemia.[8]

One of the organization's most important contributions with regard to desegregation was the creation of the Black Emphasis Week. Begun in 1970, each spring, BAD held a week-long celebration of black culture. The events scheduled for the week included speakers; art, fashion, and talent shows; soul food dinners; films, plays, dances, and choir concerts.[9]

The 1970s witnessed a precipitous increase in the numbers of black students at the University of Arkansas. By January 1978, the university had almost six hundred black students, a total that accounted for 4 percent of the total student population.[10] Although the efforts of BAD to make the campus more attractive to black students had some effect on the increase, the major impetus for the change came from federal and state actions. In 1974, after receiving pressure from HEW, the state developed a desegregation plan. The plan had several provisions designed to encourage black students to attend predominately white schools. One of its more interesting features was a policy that allowed tuition waivers to a limited number of blacks attending the University of Arkansas at Pine Bluff, a historically black college, if they transferred to a school "where their race will be in the minority."[11]

In 1976, the NAACP successfully sued HEW, forcing the agency to require desegregation plans from states "with more specific" guidelines on how and when they intended to achieve full desegregation. As a result, Arkansas along with several other states had to adopt new desegregation plans. The new plan required the University of Arkansas to increase its black student population from 4 percent to between 9 and 13 percent by 1983. Because of the pressure coming from both federal and state governments, the university more aggressively sought out black students.[12] By the end of the decade, the university would also experience slight increases in the numbers of black faculty and administrators.[13]

The desegregation successes made by blacks in the 1970s did not mean that all white students welcomed these changes. To the contrary, throughout the decade some white students conspicuously challenged what they viewed as "Liberals elements" taking over the campus. Many white students opposed the ban on the playing of "Dixie" at university-sponsored events and heavily criticized Eldon Janzen, the band director, for recommending that the song not be played.[14] In 1971, the White Youth Corps, a student organization, passed out leaflets at the university, announcing its existence. This group called for white students to promote the rights of white students and to protect themselves against the "anti-American protesters and Liberal Scum," that had come to the campus. The leaflets went on to advise white students on how best to defend themselves against blacks.[15] Also in 1974, a student group called White Americans for Democracy petitioned for funding as a registered student organization. The group argued for the establishment of a White Studies Program and a White Awareness Week. In addition, its members wanted to raise four hundred thousand dollars in scholarships that helped disadvantaged whites. Furthermore, the group offered to finance loans for blacks interested in one-way tickets to Africa.[16]

Despite the opposition of some white students on the Fayetteville campus to the furtherance of desegregation, the 1970s proved to be a ripe period of the expansion of opportunities of blacks at the university campus. By the end of the decade, blacks could be found in many of the important areas related to student life. Now, the university had black athletes, cheerleaders, and sororities and fraternities. In the following oral histories, we are given a glimpse of how these changes affected the individual experiences of African Americans on the Fayetteville campus.

■ Lenthon B. Clark (1977–1995), university administrator

Interview by Lonnie R. Williams, March 8, 2009
Interviewed in the home of the Clarks
For detailed biography, see Appendix A, page 298

I joined the staff at the university on May 1, 1977. That was my first official day of work as director of financial aid. I was there eighteen years and two months.

How did I select the University of Arkansas? Quite honestly, the university sort of selected me. David Cooksey was the financial aid director before me. When David got his doctorate, he went to the Office of Educational Endowment. I was sitting in the office one morning, I wasn't even thinking about a job, and Bill Denman called. I was pretty happy at TSU (Texas Southern University). Denman and I talked awhile. He said, "Well, let's just cut through all the chat. We got a position of director of financial aid here at the university."

Honest to goodness, I wasn't interested in coming to the university because I didn't know anybody here. I'm going to be director of financial aid. I'm going to be completely in charge of financial aid. I'm going to run my own shop. And that, well, you know how the university goes. You are never completely your own boss. There's always somewhere down the line that you'd have to answer to somebody. But I can honestly say, I didn't have any problems with my work there and doing the job that I had to do.

I knew quite a few people in the profession. And the first thing I did was to make application for aid. Back in those days, you had to make application for federal funds. I talked to a guy in the head office in Dallas. He talked me into coming here. Now he has got to help take care of me. I was just that blunt with him. During that time, we increased our SEOG's (Supplemental Education Opportunity Grants) by like 150 percent. That was big. I would say a big star in my crown. But they never knew how it happened. You knew people and people do what they say they are going to do. From then on, it was almost pretty good sailing.

We had some ups and downs. Bill [Denman] got fired, left, or whatever. Merlin [Augustine] was the interim and we worked OK, never did have any problems. I was always aware that there were some pitfalls out there that you could step in. I had a lady that worked in the office, but I won't call her name. She took Shirley to lunch when we first got here. She came in one day. "I need to talk to you," she said. "There's a lot of racist folks up here and I want to talk to you about the things that may happen. I want you to be aware." I wondered what she was talking about and I found out later. She ended up being a good friend. Someone you'd almost go to battle with. She said, "There are some things here that have never been right. You're a young man and I just want to tell you where the rocks are so when you're walking across the water, you know where to step." Anyway, that was some help I had. Not that I wasn't aware of some things she was telling me, but it was so nice to hear it coming from her.

Describe my feelings when I was there? I can sum it up in two or three words. They had a glass ceiling. Okay! I was never going to be anything higher than director of financial aid. I wasn't going to be dean of students. I had talked to my immediate boss, the chancellor at the time, he said, "Well, you are too good at the financial aid stuff." So, I took that as a code word. I took that and I did mine. I had been there for ten years and the attitude was not going to change. But I think that would add to . . . what they call a glass ceiling . . . and when you reach a point. I'm saying it was nothing that anyone was doing to me, but just the realization that this is where you're going to be. I realized that it was where I was going to be and I had been there ten years. I'm fifty-five years old and I'm pretty happy. I've got fairly decent raises and on par with other directors in the division, Bob Barnes, et cetera. I said, "Well, I'm not necessarily satisfied and I'm not necessarily dissatisfied." Bob Barnes and some of the others could have said the same thing, but I had those feelings.

If it were up to me, I'd go back [visit campus] every two or three weeks!! [All laughing.] I don't have any bitter feelings, but I don't have a whole lot of love. It was just a job and I was able to hire staff that I wanted. Some staff I liked. Some staff I didn't like. When you do that and nobody dictates stuff that you should do . . . full-time staff . . . in other words, I ran the office and what else could you expect? Somebody had to approve when you hire staff, but nobody did. When Terry [Finney] came, that was the first true associate director and nobody had any agenda. I was just there and doing decent. Working like hell dealing with my TIAA-CREF so I could get out of here! [Laughing.] When I retired, I always said, "No looking back." So I don't look back at the negative stuff.

■ Shirley Clark (1977–1997), secretary

Interview by Lonnie R. Williams, March 8, 2009
Interviewed in the home of the Clarks
For detailed biography, see Appendix A, page 299

I started August 1, 1977, as a secretary in Career Planning and Placement and retired after twenty years. In fact, we had never heard of Fayetteville. Never! We heard of Little Rock, but never heard of Fayetteville. I didn't want to come, not at all. Lent [Lenthon Clark] said, "I think this is an advancement, or a step up, or whatever." I was offered a job at the university before we left Houston. We maintained our home in Houston and Lent said, "If you still want to leave, we'll go after a year." I said, "Okay." We came and during that time, I guess, it just kind of slipped up on me. The only thing that I was a little hesitant about was leaving family, church, and friends.

I just didn't think we should move. I took three months to find out how to get to the grocery store, find doctors, and things that we needed. Marge [Pomfret] was awesome. She helped me find the drugstore, grocery, and all the shopping outlets. She was a genuine good person to both of us. That helped.

It just kind of slipped up on me [the year] and I said, "Well, we'd been gone a year and I don't know whether I want to go back or not," and we didn't. By that time, the Texas family enjoyed coming to Fayetteville and coming over the mountains or whatever. That helped a lot. But job wise, a secretary is a secretary and I was good at my job at Texas Southern. I was forty years old when we moved to Fayetteville. I had twenty years of experience. I did not have a whole lot of problems. I brought a lot of the things that we did at Texas Southern with me and I thought I had a pretty good idea of what to do. My position at the University of Arkansas was fairly knew when I started.

I had five directors during my twenty years at the U of A, but I made the best of it. I have to be honest with you, Lonnie. I got disgusted with some of the people. I figured I could go somewhere and do something else. That's been my philosophy. If you give me a lot of grief or there are a lot of problems, then I'll leave, but I didn't. It got better and we moved to better facilities. I didn't want to change jobs at that point. I was getting older and I was comfortable.

I enjoyed the later years. The first few years, I didn't. It was pretty lonesome and I mostly went to work and came home. I didn't make friends. We had our friends in Texas. We kept separate lives from work and private lives. I was comfortable. I never had a great love for the university. I enjoyed some years and some I did not. Now to answer the second part, I've not been back to the university since I retired. I don't have any interest.

There was one director, Nola Royster, I actually respected. That was part of my job that I really liked. That was one of my hang-ups. I didn't have anybody that I really respected as a director. I didn't until Nola came on and I was getting ready to leave. Well, she did a great job, but to do what she really wanted to do . . . She passed away before she reached her full potential.

To me it was just a job, but I must say I enjoyed working with the students, recruiters, and getting to help the students get interviews and starting new careers. Like I said, it was a job. Some parts I enjoyed. Some I did not. I'm glad we came. I had never been to Fayetteville. It's a more comfortable style of living than Houston. I would do it again.

■ John L Colbert (1973–1976), educator

Written response to interview questions, September 13, 2008
For detailed biography, see Appendix A, page 299

I am John L Colbert originally from Rondo, Arkansas; a 1973 graduate from Barton High School in Barton, Arkansas. As a high school senior, I was recruited by Mr. O. C. Duffy, a recruiter from the U of A who happened to be African American. Mr. Duffy spoke highly of the university, and he felt it would be a good university for me to attend. After he had convinced my parents and me, I applied and was accepted as a freshman at the university in the summer of 1973 in pursuit of a degree in education.

Upon my arrival to the university in June of 1973, it was evident there were only a few African Americans on campus. I became friends with two of the other African American students. The three of us had to create our own entertainment, which often included the other few African Americans. The environment wasn't conducive and didn't cater to our wants and needs as far as any aspect of entertainment. Our social life was sometimes confined to our dorm rooms, especially during what was known on the U of A campus as "Texas Week." African American students were told to stay in their dorm rooms and off the streets because there was the possibility of being harassed by the white students.

With no social life for African Americans, it was necessary to create our own fraternities: The Omega Psi Phi fraternity was chartered in 1974 and I became a chartered member of Alpha Phi Alpha Fraternity, Inc., in the spring of 1975. Other black Greek-letter organizations ensued. As a means to provide a social outlet, Alpha and the other black Greek-letter organizations filled a huge void by creating a venue for socialization in the form of off-campus parties, scholarship balls, academic forums, and pageants, et cetera. I felt that my fraternity, and then later on, the local African American Baptist church [St. James Baptist Church] filled this void that was missing in the on-campus environment. The church and its surrounding black community stood as a refuge for me. I felt most comfortable when I attended the church and/or visited the homes of some local families.

Thankful for these outlets, since the university only served as an educational backdrop for me, I felt at ease in my pursuits. Because of the "incompleteness" that was a common thread among the African American students during that time, a bond of dependency developed: we learned to rely on each other. I was able to sustain the environment and complete my course-work in three years of attending the University of Arkansas. In 1976, with a BSE in special education and a minor in elementary education, I embarked upon my chosen career. I can also say that I was blessed to have met my future wife at the University of Arkansas. In August of 1975, the start of my senior year, I married the former Cheryl A. Jumper.

Having remained in Fayetteville as an educator, I savored the opportunity to return to the University of Arkansas in continued pursuit of my dreams: I earned a master's degree in education with emphasis in learning disabilities in 1981, and in 1982, I attained my Public School Administration Certification. I have maintained a constant relationship with the U of A by serving as the chapter advisor to our under-graduate chapter of Alpha Phi Alpha Fraternity, Inc., Kappa Kappa. In this capacity, I was instrumental in helping to secure the first black Greek-letter fraternity house, bestowed upon this undergraduate chapter in 1976. Though we've relocated, the Kappa Kappa Chapter continues to maintain a fraternity house at 1324 Markham Road.

As Fayetteville's first African American public school principal and formerly one of two African American principals in Fayetteville, I sat at the helm of Holcombe Elementary School where the University of Arkansas retains a classroom for the purpose of training future teach-ers. Joining Marie Parker of Great Expectations of Arkansas, I also stay connected to the U of A through its Excellence in Education initiative, as well as its commitment to holding fast the memory of the late Dr. Martin Luther King Jr. As chairman, and one of the founders of the Northwest Arkansas Dr. Martin Luther King Jr. Commission, I act as a liaison between our organization and the chancellor's office.

In reflecting upon the university, I readily agree there has been a great influx to recruit African American staff as well as students. However, through this influx, there still lies a need to address the social penury of the African American. These needs continue to be fulfilled off campus. I see that students still rely upon the local black Greek-letter organizations to provide venues and releases for their social life and entertainment. More African American faculty/staff are needed to address the African American students' basic need to visually experience same-race role models.

■ Edward Duffy (1972–1974), college professor

Telephone interview by Charles Robinson and Lonnie R. Williams, July 5, 2007
For detailed biography, see Appendix A, page 299

I came to the University of Arkansas basically to major, as a graduate student, in educa-tion. I had just recently been released from the military and I came there to continue my edu-cation. I had a brother and a sister there already at the University of Arkansas. My brother had asked me to come up for a visit. I came there to visit and while I was there I toured the university, the School of Education, met a few people, and they seemed interesting in having me. I went on, did the paperwork, got accepted, and that is how it got started. I was there from 1972 through 1974.

How would I describe my role in the history of African Americans at the University of Arkansas? I felt it was pretty oppressive. When I got there, basically there was a lot of . . . still . . . resentment of black students. I remember my first day there. I had parked my car. I was assigned to the Buchanan-Droke dormitory and there was no parking at the dormitory. There was a frat house there across from it and not understanding how it worked, I parked my car over there. The next morning I got up and the tires were cut, the windshield wiper was broken, and the "N" word was written on the windshield. And that sort of gave me a perspective of what I would have to deal with at the University of Arkansas. It's the one right across from Buchanan-Droke. I don't know what fraternity it is, but I saw the lot was full of cars and the next closest place was Harp's and I put my car in that lot and parked it.

I was assigned to Buchanan-Droke and I had a roommate. I walked in, spoke with him, and I put my stuff away. After I put my stuff away, he started packing his stuff and started leaving. As I moved in, he moved out. It was a nightmare experience in terms it was obvious that white students at that time were not comfortable with black roommates because mine left the day that I moved in. I remember the first week there were white students walking up and down the halls with Confederate flags. There were three blacks in that dorm at that particular time, and we confronted them about it because we saw it as an insult. They got a little hostile. We were sharing words, and we finally were making the point that we wouldn't allow them to walk around with the Confederate flag while we were there. They could do it in their room, but we didn't think they could walk up and down the hall with it.

My brother was very involved in the political scene on the campus and he sort of introduced me to some of the members of the organization called the Black Americans for Democracy. I met with some of the members, started going to the meetings, got interested in the organization, and ran for president the first year I was there. At the time, the organization was sort of weak and had quite a bit of corruption. There was a young man there on the campus that everybody said to be afraid of, and he had been using all the organization's, from my understanding, funds financing dances, shows, and he would take the money for himself. He had intimidated everybody and basically he was sort of taking it from the organization from a financial point. So when I ran, people were telling me, "Yes, be careful, he's been doing this all this time and he's going to try it again." My position was when I became elected, I met with the administration and let them know that no one other than the executive people could sign any work orders and things and so any events that we sponsored, I had to sign. I was never going to sign anything where the money of the organization could be manipulated and taken advantage of.

The young man was an older student, about my age. I had been in the military and was about twenty-four or twenty-five, and he was an older guy, too. He was basically, sort of a big guy, physically imposing, about six feet two inches, about maybe about two hundred fifty pounds or something. Everybody was physically scared of him, but being me, I had been in Vietnam. I wasn't scared of him. I wasn't thinking about upsetting him. I would just let him know he could be a part of this organization, but he would not be using our organization financially for his own personal needs. Once I got that straight, the organization began to build membership, began to be active, a lot of students got involved, graduate students and undergrad students.

I tried to lead an organization that would have relationships with other organizations at the University of Arkansas at Pine Bluff, the one in Monticello, the one also in Little Rock. At that time, other presidents in Arkansas were in conditions that were deplorable . . . mainly at the dormitories, always at Fayetteville. I tried to get the students at the University of Arkansas universities to have some impact to stop the building at the University of Arkansas, Fayetteville, until they fix some of the problems at the University of Arkansas in Pine Bluff. We did, to the board meeting at the University of Arkansas at Pine Bluff and the one at Fayetteville. I think we did have some impact on them basically doing a pretty good job at the University of Arkansas at Pine Bluff.

One of the most drastic things that happened while I was there, I was away from campus at one point. When I got back I found that a black young lady, who was an RA, had been slapped by a white student. The dormitory she was an RA in, all the males were supposed to leave at nine o'clock. She had instructed this male white student to leave at nine. He basically, to my understanding, slapped her and called her the "B" word. When I got back, I was told what had happened. I went to the administration and tried to get the administration to deal with it and they did nothing. We filed a suit in the local court and tried to get the local government to do something. They did nothing. We called a meeting of Black Americans for Democracy, and we decided that we would take action ourselves. This young man we learned ate in the cafeteria everyday at a particular time, so we got about thirty to forty students together. We decided when he goes to the dormitory that we would take justice ourselves and do what the school should have done, or the courts should have done. I maybe felt that when I was with him, I didn't want guys to rough up the young ladies. So five young ladies and about forty young men went to the cafeteria to wait for this guy to come. When he came in, we had someone to sort of bump into him with a tray. He hit the person and that gave the opportunity. We basically started a fight with him, beat him up very, very badly. About five of the other white students tried to jump in, and we were able to beat them up very badly, also. Basically a big fight broke out in the cafeteria, and they ended up calling the state police.

When the state police came to the campus, we had already left the cafeteria and went back to our dorms. But the school put out an arrest warrant for me. The young ladies from the Black Americans for Democracy hid me out in the dormitory for two days while the state police were looking for me. At that point, the sponsor and the financial aid director, I think his name was Mr. Cooksey, basically intervened with the administration. If I would agree to stop some of the political activities, the school would drop charges against me. So they called a meeting with the organization. We met and talked about it. We agreed to basically stop the things we were doing. They dropped the charges against me. As long as I was there, I don't remember another black lady, a black young lady being hit by a white student. I think it taught them that we have some respect. If we were in a position of authority, they had to respect our authority. I think it was the beginning of a new respect for black students and the campus. If something happened to one of us, if the school wouldn't do anything or if the county government wouldn't do anything, then the students outside would take action and do what they have to do to make it right.

I was shot at once. I was actually told that I should leave the University of Arkansas. I got a lot of threatening phone calls, notes, and stuff about I should leave the University of Arkansas. But I, somebody in the military from the Vietnam Infantry Rangers, I was really not afraid of what they could do to me up there. I just happened to be there at a time that there were a lot of things going on. And to somebody that just came out of a war, and saying they are going to do something . . . I was in Vietnam being shot at many times, hell. I still don't like to be shot at. That didn't really frighten me to the point where I was going to go off and hide.

There was a young man there who had some very serious connections. Actually he came to me and said there were some guns and things that I could have made available to the students there, but I chose not to do that because I believe that if we had a straight-up type of situation that many students would probably end up being kicked out of school, hurt. People could have gotten killed. I know in Fayetteville, if we had to go to court, we probably would end up being victims of the court because they had a very small black population and their county system, the government system, is very one-sided, also. But I was really tested at one point after they were threatening to shoot me. They would offer to me, from other groups, they would come to Fayetteville, and they were really ready to go into a real gorilla kind of thing, shooting at them at night or whatever. But if you need an answer at this particular time, at some point I was really tempted to get involved in that type activity. Most of the time before I would act, I would bring the things to some of the advisors. We had students from the Law School, from medical school, from undergraduate school. We were all very close together. There are a lot of people of goodwill and level-headedness that kept us sort of on the right path. Maybe from getting involved in some of the things that could have escalated out of control and got somebody from the dorms killed, or somebody kicked out of school. So it worked out pretty well.

I asked myself if I wanted to come back? I came back once since I graduated. The university leaves a bad taste in my mouth. I saw many black students that were taken advantage of there because there were so few of us and we could not fully protect each other. We did the best we could, but a lot of students were taken advantage of. A lot of students' instructors gave them such difficult times that they left. Very capable students did not get the opportunity to finish their education because of the harassing and difficult environment that they would face. And girls who were not prepared psychologically to deal with that type environment, they were not successful even though academically they had very good skills. It was a hostile environment for black students during the 1970s. You had to really . . . not only be academically . . . but you also had to have that mental attitude that you were not going to let the environment cause you not to be successful and to continue on the program that you started on.

One time since I left, I came back once and Black Americans Week held something. They wrote me and they asked me to come back. I came back . . . now this was about two years after I graduated . . . and a lot of the same kinds of things that I saw when I was there were still evident. And the student body seemed to be a lot more apathetic at that point. More of the same stuff. I was so disappointed that the students were not a little more proactive and doing things for themselves or dealing with the administration to make things better because evidently we had made some steps forward while I was there. But when I went back, it seemed like we had taken a step backward in terms of our resolve to deal with problems at the university rather than to confront them. It looked like the students were sort of accepting the status quo without actually challenging the status quo.

What are my current feelings toward the university? They have not changed a lot since then. I think as you get older you do tend to become more, I guess, understanding of things. I'm not as hostile now as I was right after I left because I realize that basically hostility is not good for me and it doesn't solve problems. But the university still is not . . . I don't hold the university as my alma mater. You know how people think of their alma mater, or as people sing the alma mater, as they wear the sweaters, the caps, and stuff like that. I don't wear those things from the University of Arkansas because I actually still feel that they basically . . . they went out of their way to make the black students feel unwelcome. I think that was totally unnecessary and I think the administration did not do enough to try to counteract that. They saw it, they knew it existed, but they actually didn't do anything to try to significantly change the atmosphere for black students. It did change, but I think it changed basically over time, as students came and went, our mindset, conditions and things have changed somewhat, but I think the university actively didn't do anything to try and change the situation and make the campus welcome for all students.

The only thing I can say is the students . . . when I was there . . . they were very, very committed to trying to change the university and make it better for the students who came after them. And the students in the organization made a commitment that students who follow us would not have to go through the same type of humiliation and the same type of environment that we found there. We made a conscious effort to try to change the environment so the students who came after us, the environment would be more conducive so they could basically come, get a good skill, get a good education, and not be confronted with intimidation, racism, and those kinds of negative things that made . . . caused . . . the environment to be hostile to students and make the environment almost intolerable for someone to learn in.

I would think that one of the things the university might want to do is to have students at some point to come back and speak to black students, not just black students but ethnic students, and make them understand some of the struggles of the students who went before them. Basically make them understand that they have an obligation to make the university better and more conducive to black students. You just don't go there and get your education. You should also have some commitment to make that school better, make the environment more conducive, and I think by having students who have gone through some of the trials and tribulations there talk to some of the students, might help them to make some type of commitment other than just getting my paper and leaving. A lot of students just want to get their degree. That's really fine, but I think they all should have some type of commitment to make the university better. And I think what you are doing and having students understand what has happened, I think that might help this process evolve.

I'm glad to have gotten the opportunity and I feel it's something that certainly can help the university to become a university for all students to feel at ease and welcome. And that's the way it should be because anybody, to learn, you need an environment that's conducive to learning. And when I was there, it was not. For black students, it was a very difficult environment for learning. We had to try to survive and learn when you could because there were a lot of distractions going on. I think this process will help.

■ Dinah Gail Gant (1971–1977), engineer

Written response to interview questions, September 5, 2007
For detailed biography, see Appendix A, page 300

I entered the U of A in the fall of 1971 to obtain a degree in civil engineering. As valedictorian of my Augusta, Arkansas, High School class, I automatically received a scholarship. Hence, that is why I selected the U of A. My first college choice never even responded to my application. I graduated in August of 1977 with a BS degree in civil engineering.

I was the first black female to receive a degree in civil engineering from the University of Arkansas. I also was a charter member Lambda Theta chapter of Delta Sigma Theta Sorority, Inc., and served as its first president. I also won the title of Ms. BAD (Black Americans for Democracy) and went on to serve as president of the organization.

After accepting the fact I would not be able to obtain "that" engineering degree in four years, I came to enjoy and now cherish the experiences at the U of A. I made lifelong friends there—Jennifer Hopkins, Gwen Bullard, Lydia Cannon Kearney, Beverly Hicks, Janis Kearney, O. C. Duffy, Chris Hinton, Wanda Smith, E. Lynn Harris, Pamela Croston, Joyce Taylor, et cetera (apologies to those I missed).

The academic experience and environment, though sometimes challenging in both instances, more than prepared me for the professional environment in which I now work. Though attempts are often made to make me feel guilty about not having attended an HBCU ([historically black colleges and universities] one of which never responded to my application), I am confident that my racial identity and experiences did not suffer from my attending the U of A. As a matter of fact, one of my twin daughters has the U of A as her first choice for college.

At the onset of my study, continuing students in engineering, O. C. Duffy Jr., Edward Bailey, and another whose name escapes me at this writing, were my guardian angels. They tutored, encouraged, and mentored me throughout my engineering studies. They constantly reminded me that not one of the students in my classes had any more capabilities than I. I simply had not been exposed to a lot of the prep classes and that they would be there to help me get over that. And, when as a freshman, another classmate refused to work on a survey team with me, the dean of engineering stepped in to take care of the situation. Also as a freshman and sophomore, my grade-point was established such that I was never in danger academically as the coursework became increasingly harder.

I have returned to the campus on numerous occasions. The first time was for the Jennifer Hopkins career day. I've attended at least four of the Black Alumni Reunions. In 1999, I returned as the speaker for the twenty-fifth anniversary of the Lambda Theta Chapter of Delta Sigma Theta Sorority, Inc. Also I was inducted into the Arkansas Academy of Civil Engineers and typically return annually for meetings.

I still feel that it (the U of A) is a great value for the educational and cultural experiences. I also have two biological sisters with degrees from the U of A. They also happen to be sorority sisters as well. At one time or another, four of my siblings and I were enrolled at the U of A.

I don't recall any formal "diversity" programs for students of color when I entered the U of A. However, the support I received from other students while at the U of A is something now duplicated in various diversity programs. I believe that they will always be needed. Coming from a legally segregated rural public school system in Arkansas meant that I had not even been exposed to classes such as trigonometry or physics. These courses would have "softened" my introduction to engineering coursework. My many mentors continued in their encouragement to me. Our high school students need exposure to as challenging a curriculum as possible.

I often tell my daughters that I loved being in college. It was the first time, on a routine basis, that I experienced "indoor" plumbing. I am proud to say I grew up as one of ten children to the late Floyd and Theressa Gant, sharecroppers on a farm "outside" of Tupelo, Arkansas. There were times when we only went to school when it rained and/or on test days as it was the entire family's responsibility to bring in the cotton crop. Neither of my parents finished high school, but they insisted that all of their children do so. We all did and eventually, the six youngest of the ten went on to college. Five of the six were once students at the U of A. I hope that says a lot about the opportunities I feel are within reach of students of color with limited resources.

The U of A, as life in general, presents both challenges and opportunities. I feel that it would serve an aspiring student well to embrace both the challenges and opportunities. (And, no I am not a recruiter for the U of A!)

▪ Patricia L. Greene Griffen (1972–1974, 1976–1978), psychologist

Written response to interview questions, October 14, 2008
For detailed biography, see Appendix A, page 300

I enrolled at the University of Arkansas in August 1972 because it offered the degree plan I wanted in clinical psychology. At that time, the psychology department actively recruited black graduate students as a result of the work of the National Association of Black Psychologists. There were three black graduate students admitted that year, Daphne Morris, Natalie Dyer, and myself. The following semester, spring 1973, the university hired the first black faculty member in the Department of Psychology, Dr. Brenda Mobley.

I attended the university from August 1972 through December 1974 and September 1976 to 1978. To my knowledge, I was the first black student to complete the PhD in clinical psychology. Before, there had been one black male to complete the master's degree.

Having grown up in central Arkansas and completed my undergraduate degree in the same area, I was initially confronted with culture shock. The department was supportive, yet struggled with understanding and relating to students of color. This was true for both faculty and students. Efforts were made through social events to reduce those barriers. Because I was in graduate school, most of my activities involved academic affairs and departmental interactions. There were opportunities to interact with black students, both graduate and undergraduate from other areas. The black students were very progressive minded, bright, and visionary. Interactions with the black students were very stimulating intellectually. I made friends that have lasted a lifetime from the time spent at the University of Arkansas.

During my time of study, I had mixed emotions due to the lack of racial progress at the university. There was an obvious cultural/racial/ethnic divide combined with insensitivity to closing the gap. Furthermore, there was a blatant lack of knowledge about blacks on the part of whites. There were instances when I witnessed blacks being treated as an anomaly at the graduate level. I also realized that this was the first time most Caucasians had close interactions with blacks.

I returned to the university to serve as a panelist when the psychology department celebrated its silver anniversary. I have also attended a few of the black student reunions as well as other events on campus. I have not been on campus recently.

I have been disappointed that the gains made during the 1970s have not lasted within the Department of Psychology. To my knowledge, there are no black faculty members nor black students currently in the department. Cultural incompetence continues to exist in a field of study designed to address the psychological/emotional needs of all individuals. With Arkansas becoming more racially and culturally diverse, it is disappointing that the institution for higher education in Arkansas is not more instrumental in equipping professionals to meet the needs of its diverse citizenry. It seems as if the department has regressed.

The area of clinical psychology has always been highly competitive to enter at the graduate level. As a result of the National Association of Black Psychologists, a door was opened for black students to enter graduate school during the 1970s. During that era, the psychology department made strides toward closing the racial/cultural/ethnic gap at the graduate level by providing opportunities for professionals to make significant contributions in the field of psychology. Unfortunately, this is not the situation today.

■ E. Lynn Harris (1973–1977), author

Interview by Lonnie R. Williams, September 25, 2007
Interviewed at Ella's Restaurant on the University of Arkansas, Fayetteville, campus
For detailed biography, see Appendix A, page 301

I entered the university in the fall of 1973 to obtain a degree in journalism. I wanted to go to the University of Michigan. Even though I was born in Michigan, had gone to high school there one semester, the University of Michigan was requiring me to pay out-of-state tuition. My mom basically couldn't afford it. So I decided on the university because I knew that I wanted the full college experience, even though I had never been here until the first time I came here to go to school.

I attended the university for four years. I was the first black in Cardinal 20, which was the outstanding twenty sophomore men. I was the first African American to edit the *Razorback*. I was the first African American male cheerleader for the Razorbacks. And almost every organization that I got in, with the exception of my fraternity, I was either the first black or one of the very first ones.

Talk about my experience being the first black cheerleader? Actually, I had tried out when I was a freshman, but none of the black girls that tried out that year made it to the finals and I knew that pretty well sealed my fate, so I kind of dropped out. When I was a junior going into my senior year that was one of the things I regretted, that looked like I wasn't going to have the opportunity to do because I was going to graduate. I didn't try out my junior year because I was real busy with the yearbook and I was real busy with my fraternity. That fall, for whatever reason, the black athletes went to Coach Broyles at the beginning of the season and said they wanted black cheerleaders. They threatened to boycott unless they basically got black cheerleaders. So Coach Broyles went to whoever was the sponsor at the time and told them that they needed to add two black cheerleaders. They had tryouts for just black kids. It was maybe fifteen girls and maybe four guys that tried out.

The interesting thing about it was the cheerleaders that year were not happy about this. They made it be known. They were very nasty during the tryouts. They made comments and what have you. I was a senior and I basically wasn't taking that crap. They didn't like me because I would talk up for the black girls and I would talk up to everybody else. You can't talk to me like that and you can't do this. When the tryouts came along, everybody assumed I would be the one to make it. And I did, too. And when the tryouts were over, they had some cheerleaders from OU and some cheerleaders from Arkansas to judge. The cheerleaders that had been teaching us were not judging. They chose this guy, Billy Lewis, and they chose Kim Nichols. Kim had been on the drill team at Jacksonville, but everybody thought that Dionne Harold, who had been a cheerleader at Brinkley, and myself, should have been the ones that were chosen, but we were chosen as alternates.

And the funny thing that happened, I remember being so disappointed and dejected because as an alternate I was only to get to cheer if Billy didn't cheer. I was walking back to wherever I lived, I don't remember where I lived at the time, but I walked through Wilson-Sharp and I saw Bruce Mitchell. Bruce was a Razorback football player at the time and one of the leaders of the team. He said to me, "Congratulations, man," and I said, "Congratulations for what?" He said, "On making cheerleading." And I said, "Oh, I didn't make it, Bruce. I got alternate." He was like, "There's no way you couldn't have made it." I said, "What do you mean?" He said, "I saw ya'll. I was up there watching. You were by far the best one." I said, "Well, I didn't make it." So Bruce went back and told some of the other football players and they called me and said, "Do you think you were cheated?" I said, "Well, I don't know." Lynda Jackson at the time was assistant dean of student affairs. She called me in the next day. She said, "Do you think you were cheated?" And I said, "I don't know. I don't have any way of knowing. I didn't see the scores." Lynda called Coach Broyles and they got the scores. What they found was that all of the out-of-town judges had given me perfect scores, but all the judges from Arkansas had given me zeros. Lynda said, "How do you get a perfect score and a zero?" It showed that they had in fact cheated. And so Coach Broyles called me in his office and he asked me did I feel like I deserved it. I said, "Coach Broyles, I've been a Razorback fan since I was a little boy and I'm really, really hurt by this." Coach Broyles went and told the cheerleading sponsor that instead of two, you're going to have four. And so Dionne and I were added to the squad.

The funny thing is that Billy did not return after that semester and they had to come back and ask me to cheer with both of the black girls because the other guy that had tried out just wasn't capable. But what was really interesting about it is that the guys were okay with it, the guys on the squad. But the girls were really, really mean. They did a lot of mean things to Dionne. I remember the first game we played, we went away to Baylor, and they told her they were wearing one uniform and we got to the game and they had on another one. I remember the first time we went away, them picking beds. We rented a room with two double beds and maybe it was five or six of us or whatever and there was a cot. They all rushed to get into a bed with each other and so the cot would be left for me. And so there were things like that. Dionne was a freshman and her feelings were easily hurt. She had come from a high school where she had been captain of the cheerleaders and everything. I basically had to take a tough stance kind of thing.

It was funny that when the year ended, the sponsor chose me to do what they call demos. Demos is a senior guy and girl who they think are the best ones to show the new judges what to look for in the Hog call and everything. That really pissed them off. I almost started to stay another year because I was twenty and I had just turned twenty that summer. I had kind of rushed through college. I had so much fun cheering. What was interesting is that the next year, all the girls who had caused all that trouble, none of them made it and none of the guys tried out, so I would've been captain. It would've been a different year.

I remember that was maybe the first year we really had a good basketball team and we were playing down in the Summit. We were playing U of H for the championship. I drove down from Dallas to Houston, but I couldn't get a ticket because it was sold out. One of the male cheerleaders had an extra uniform. He said, "Just put the uniform on and come in with us." So I ended up cheering that day. Interestingly enough, Lonnie, I wrote, when I wrote my memoirs, I put all that stuff in it, but I took it out and I took it out because since then Ms. Jean has welcomed me back into the family. I've gotten so involved in it and I would never want to do anything to embarrass them. So I took it out and I don't really even tell a lot of people that story anymore because it was a period in time.

Interestingly enough, the girl who was captain, who really did cause me a lot of grief, now she and I are pretty good friends. Her daughter is a student up here and I see her at football games. It's kind of like water under the bridge. Interestingly enough, her daughter tried out. Her daughter missed it by one vote and I was judging that year, but I had no idea it was her daughter until afterwards because they didn't look anything alike. I felt bad and I wondered if I had known that was her daughter, would I have voted differently? Always when I judge, I always tend to judge the black kids harder because I want them to be the best. I donate fifteen thousand dollars a year in Dionne's name because Dionne died shortly after she left here, she graduated here. She went on to become a pom girl, captain of the pom squad, homecoming and all that stuff, but she died of a heart defect shortly after she left here. We now have the Dionne Harold Spirit Scholarships that any of the kids on the squad are eligible for and all of them get at least two hundred dollars of that money. And so her memory kind of lives on. But it was a good time for me in the sense that I just totally ignored them. I think I was stronger than the girls were.

I think after that, the next year, Arthur Prewitt was on the squad and then Larry Butler. So there's been a long line of them. But it's one of the things that I'm most proud of, but one of those things that also caused me . . . I wouldn't say a great deal of pain because it was kind of like this is just the way kids are. I remember my mom being real nervous for me that first time we played in Little Rock. She just thought someone was going to shoot me from the stands. But it was a wonderful experience and I think God, in His wisdom, makes up for times like that in your life. When I came back up here to teach . . . how I got involved with cheerleaders . . . was their coach quit the day that I came up here. He quit and went to Mississippi State and Derrick Gragg, who was the associate athletic director at the time, asked me would I come down just for a couple of weeks and help Ms. Jean out. That was four or five years ago and I've never left. It's like I've gotten the full experience of what it's like to be a Razorback cheerleader as a coach. I've gotten to go to all of the games with them. The way the kids get along now, it's not a black and white thing. It's more of a personality thing, certain girls. It has nothing to do with race. It's been kind of heartwarming to me to see the program in the state that it's in now.

Talk about my experience as editor of the *Razorback* yearbook? It's like you didn't have a sponsor. It was okay, but I remember hiring Butch as my business manager because I knew what kind of person he was. Yeah, Butch Carroll, and that he was going to go by the book. I figured the only problem I was going to have is that they would be watching the money. I think our budget was like three hundred thousand dollars, and as editor, I was in charge of the budget and everything. The only person I had to answer to was the board of publication. That was something that the first week I was up here as a student, as a freshman, that I knew I wanted to do. I basically figured out what I had to do to get it.

Talk about my experience with Alpha Phi Alpha? Alpha charter was in 1975. We started with fourteen guys and we initiated thirteen. The interesting thing about that is that I got a lot of ribbing during pledging because of everybody from other Alpha chapters around the state. The word was out that they thought I was gay. Which I was, but I was not out and so I took a lot of additional treatment because they were trying to get me to quit. One of my best memories at the U of A is after we were initiated. I was secretary of my pledge class. After we were initiated, maybe two Sundays later, we elected our first officers and it was a brother up here who had transferred from UCA who had basically taken us over. His name was placed in the nomination for president and everybody assumed he would be president because he had been an Alpha for a couple of years. Much to my surprise, one of my line brothers nominated me. I thought, oh boy, this is going to be embarrassing. And it turned out it was embarrassing. It was embarrassing for him because I won. Sixteen to two was the vote. I think it was because my brothers knew how bad I wanted it and there were so many opportunities to quit. I was just a sophomore at the time and I was the first president of the Alphas here, which was a tough job, but all of those experiences have prepared me for my career when I went to work for IBM and my career now as an author.

It says a lot about what black fraternities do for people. For me, it was the kind of experience that I thought really did turn me into a man, so to speak. You know as well as I do those were the old school days when they really did pledge. Even though we were the charter line, there were brothers coming up here! We had to go to Tahlequah every week because they basically made us.

My experience here was a good one. There were some times when as a black student, there were difficult times. At the time, Texas was a big rival. And "Beat Texas Week," also . . . they used to call it "Beat Nigger Week," too. Even though I was never physically harmed or called any names, as a black student you were aware of what could in fact happen. So those were difficult times. I remember the first pep rally I cheered. A lot of black students came and they said that the last time any black students had gone to a pep rally was when they were burning the Confederate flag and trying to get the band. I remember being on stage, being so nervous, and like why are they here? Because I had gone to pep rallies before and I would be one of the only black faces there. They had basically come to cheer Dionne and me on. So when we were introduced, we got one of the loudest ovations that night. Of course, people from the different sororities and stuff. When those girls were introduced, they always got loud cheers, but the black students really did, in effect, support us. And this came across all lines. It didn't matter what fraternity you were in, they were very proud. I remember Sidney Moncrief telling us after one basketball game, "Ya'll make us proud seeing ya'll out there" and how much that meant to me. I had a fully fledged college experience. I made a lot of friends, both black and white students. Some that I'm still very, very close with to this day, but also when I came back to teach, the things that were missing from my experience were replaced. I mean the buildings still looked the same, but I came back with a new awareness of myself because the difficulties that I experienced were self-induced by the fact of being a closeted gay man. Because it was just really, really frowned upon and I knew that I had to act like everyone else. Sometimes that's difficult, but that was my choice that I made.

Describe my feelings toward the university during my time of study? Well, there was definitely some discrimination. I kind of took it upon myself to make sure that everybody was getting something. I remember I would encourage black girls to try out for Razorback Beauty and Ms. U of A and all that stuff, because to me, they should have every opportunity. But a lot of times, you find yourself knocking your head against the wall because they weren't ready to fully accept it. Janis Kearney always tells the story how she would never have been a Razorback Beauty had it not been for me because I was on her everyday to "submit your picture, submit your picture." But I also had people like Overtis Hicks (OV), who were ahead of me, who encouraged me and looked after me. Randall Ferguson, who I didn't really know, African American students who had gone to the university looked out for me and encouraged me. I felt I needed to do that same thing, but like everyone else I knew there was a whole big old world out there besides Fayetteville. I was anxious to taste it and I was anxious to get away. I remember graduating on a Saturday, that morning and that afternoon being on my way to Dallas with the thought that I would never, ever come back here again. But I didn't experience anything in the town itself. There were some. I remember getting into something with the black kids from the community because they looked at us differently. I sometimes tell my students today and sometimes when I talk, I talk about the experience. I think that I was involved in a lot of stuff because I thought it would help me, but I was also trying to keep busy to avoid dealing with myself. I often say my high school experience was one where I always won "friendly as this" or "class favorite," but I really didn't have any friends and I was afraid to form close friendships. But when you pledge a fraternity, you can't do that anymore. That's what the fraternity means. And that was the first time that I really had close, male black friends was when I pledged Alpha.

First time I came up (back) was when you first started the alumni reunions. I came up and Alphas were maybe having their ten-year anniversary or what have you. I came up and it was still rather painful. It wasn't a good experience. I was in . . . I wouldn't say kind of a rocky place in my life, so this was not the place for me to come. Even though I had a good time seeing people, it was just not a good experience and I wanted to get away from here. I felt even stronger that I would never come back up here again because it was all those memories that were not public memories.

There was a period in my life when I didn't even follow the Razorbacks. Interesting. That was a really, really difficult period in my life when I started to lose a lot of friends. I was drinking heavily and I was in a really, really bad place. That was prior to me starting my career as a writer. And again, it was going on doing things that I thought people expected me to do instead of doing what I wanted to do. I do think one of the things that I thought I had a more difficult time because I was African American in the journalism department. I was never, never encouraged to pursue a career in journalism. I didn't have a lot of advice. I knew who Gerald Jordan was, but I had never met him. You know, he was in Kansas City. O V was really, really good about . . . she was majoring in journalism, so was Janis Kearney. But there wasn't a lot of support for us as African American students. As always, why don't you major in political science or something like that? I think that if I had pursued a career in journalism, I don't know how successful I would've been. Even though one of the TV stations here wanted to hire me, they wanted me to go up north, get rid of my southern accent, and then come back to work for them.

I came in the fall of 2003 as a visiting professor. I've taught six semesters. I don't teach every semester. I'm not teaching this semester. That whole experience has been so different and so rewarding. I feel a part of this community and I feel a part of Fayetteville. But I do remember the day I came up here. I had never been on Interstate 540. It was the first time I had driven it because I knew the old pig trail. I remember just saying to myself, what in the hell are you doing, because I had left New York City. I was living in an apartment building where Janet Jackson lived and lived right across the street from Central Park. I was living the life of a celebrity writer. I got invited to parties. I got introduced to people I never thought I would meet. I was having a really, really good time. The chancellor had invited me back when the stadium was redone. He invited me to be his guest at the Boise State game. Florida A&M had done *Invisible Life*, the play; they were the first ones to do it. They invited me down and asked me to come down to speak to students. They treated me like I was royalty. One of the professors down there said, "Have you ever considered teaching?" And I said, "No, I haven't." He said, "Well, you need to have an academic home. And we'd like for you to come down here and teach in Tallahassee." I thought that would be exciting to do for a semester. So at the Boise State game I was talking to the chancellor. I said next spring I'm going to go down to Florida A&M and I'm going to be a visiting professor. I remember him putting his arms on my shoulder and he said, "You know, Lynn, that would be a great thing. You would be an excellent teacher." He said, "But do you know what would make it better?" And I said, "What's that?" He said, "If you could come here first." He said, "After you've done it here for a semester. This is your home and we'd like for you to come here first." I said, "Well, let me think about it." He had Bob Smith, one of his guys, to contact me.

This was around the time Nolan had just happened because they—Dave Gearhart—flew to New York to meet with me after the Nolan thing and showed me things that the public wasn't privy to. They were reaching out, they said, to some of the African American alumni to let them know what was really going on. I remember meeting him at the Sheraton, which was a couple blocks from my home. Dave was involved with recruiting me here, putting me in contact with Dean Bobbitt, and we talked about what it is I would do. It was only supposed to be for a semester. I remember the first day, being so scared, being like a student again and worried about what I was going to wear, what I was going to say. I remember going in reading something from my memoir and talking with my students. What ended up happening was there were a lot of football players in my class. And I was like, "Oh, can I have an autograph?" Or what have you because I was excited. Just the way they responded to me was so heartwarming, so heartfelt, and it made me feel so good. I remember the dean saying on evaluations he had never seen any professor get the kind of evaluations that I got from students. They kind of wanted me to continue to do it. So I taught the spring semester. Then I taught the fall semester and then the next semester I finally took off because I was getting behind in my work. But I found that I really, really enjoyed teaching, not only the literature part of it, but the writing part of it as well. My classes were demographically, black, white, and athletes to non-athletes to students who were serious about writing. It was just a wonderful experience. I thought that I would come up here, rent a hotel room, and catch the first thing out smoking every Thursday to Atlanta. That was the plan. I came up here and just got involved in the community.

There were articles and there were a lot of social things. White folks up here knew who I was and knew what I had done. So I was getting invited to a lot of things. I was just amazed at how comfortable and happy I was here. I regretted having to go back to Atlanta or wherever because it was taking away from what I was enjoying here. I became really good friends with Derrick and Sonja Gragg. There was finally an adult community of African Americans, people doing things. And so it was really a great place to be. That's kind of why I went ahead and bought a house here. Now I'm at a point in my life when I will always come back. I'm just that comfortable here. I've met some wonderful people and I've had some wonderful students.

Being cheer coach, it's helped my experience of what I feel about the program. I'm still doing that this semester even though I'm not teaching. When I leave you, I'll go home, put my warmups on, and get ready to go down there. Last year, as a matter of fact, I got certified because now you can't be a cheer coach unless you're certified. I had to go to cheer camp with the kids.

I would say my current feelings are of great warmth and love for this university and for this state. I don't think the university and the state changed as much as I changed. That has allowed me to enjoy a wonderful second half of my life. I'm sitting here thinking about it, interviewing and remembering. I don't think you and I ever had conflicts, but since we were in different fraternities, it's not like we were best of friends. Now, as you become an adult, you are one of these people I consider a really, really good friend.

Had I not come to the university, I never would have known that friendship. I would've never met people like you. I would've never met people like Derrick or Charles Robinson, who I have great admiration for, or Gerald Jordan, people who came from this state or people who migrated to this state. Because for a long time, I felt like I was embarrassed of this state. But what I find is that I was embarrassed of the way that I looked at this state of not giving them the opportunity to fully embrace me. It didn't take New York City or Atlanta or Chicago to make me who I am. All of who I am came from what I learned here.

[**Williams:** There were a small number of black students when you came. Describe how you saw the black student network during that time frame and compare that to the black students that you see today.]

I think we would've come to the aid of each other at the time of crisis. It wouldn't matter if you were an Alpha or I was an Omega. We liked seeing each other. We didn't have the pressure of the gangs and the pressures that some kids have today. I thank God for that. I always liked seeing other black students. I always liked the fact that I was considered one of those people who had an equal number of black friends and white friends. The way I think they are today is I think there are more of them so they have more outlets. I think it's kind of cliquish in a way; Alphas hang with Alphas; Omegas; and football players hang with the football players. But I think like us, I think they would come to the aid of each other. That's the thing that cements black students here and I think would always. I know the chancellor has plans to increase the enrollment by 2010, but people have to come up here and experience it to know what they can have here. I still think this is a tough sell in terms of coming to school. I don't know how many of us who have had children would send their kids to school here. We still have to overcome that.

I think the kids have changed. They are more fearless. We always had this fear that being black would keep us from having to do something. I don't see these kids as having that fear. They don't look at being black. I remember two black girl cheerleaders that I had. I used to say, sometimes their parents gave them too much confidence. I liked it. I admired them. They didn't think anything—you know—white folks! Kids don't look at it as much as we did. I don't think the white kids do either. There are still some that are raised that way, but for the most part, if they don't like somebody, it's usually not because they're black. It's usually because they bring up some fear. The white girls on the squad who had a problem with Kelly was because there were only a few of them. It was because she was so confident and confidence causes fear in people who are not secure with themselves. But they are fearless. Yeah, that's the thing about them. They are fearless.

One of the things that I do think, our generation never really got the opportunity to show courage because we were at the end of the civil rights movement and at the end of the Vietnam War. All of these major things that were happening in our lives, we weren't either old enough or [were] too old. I don't know what this generation of kids will do? How will they feel about their stay at the University of Arkansas? But I don't hear some of the things that I used to write, all of the teachers are prejudice or I'm being graded down. I think they accept their fate, so to speak. That maybe I'm not the "A" student in this class and I'm going to have to take a "C" and I'm going to have to work harder. I don't know if you feel this way, but I don't think they ever use the fact that they are black as much as they are not being prepared. I don't know if you see that at A State.

I'm glad I came here. This is where I was supposed to be. I can't imagine having a college experience anywhere else. Now, I can't imagine teaching anywhere else even though I'm entertaining teaching at Georgia because I want to be around for Brea's first semester. It's funny, Butch so enjoyed this child. She is the most loving little girl I've ever known and she loves me. And so I'm thinking about it just because I want to be around her at that time.

When you think about it, with the exception of the Little Rock Nine, our history is better than Mississippi and Alabama. When I think about this school, letting black students in without any kind of civil disobedience, so to speak. They had civil disobedience at Alabama and Ole Miss. But no, this has been a wonderful experience. There have been hard times, but for the most part, it is a part of my life that I always look fondly upon.

■ Karen Harris Tate (1978–1983), television and radio personality

Written response to interview questions, July 13, 2007
For detailed biography, see Appendix A, page 301

I entered the University of Arkansas in the fall of 1978. I was enrolled in the College of Arts and Sciences to pursue a degree in music. After one year, I changed my major to industrial engineering under the College of Engineering.

An opportunity was put before me by my high school principal, Mr. Gene Hooks, to apply for a scholarship where only Central High graduates who were going to the University of Arkansas, Fayetteville, were eligible. The scholarship was named for Captain Seymour Terry, who was killed in action in Okinawa, Japan. The year I was chosen as a recipient, a previous recipient had dropped out of the program making two Seymour Terry Foundation scholarships available where there would have been one.

I attended the university from the fall of 1978 to the spring of 1983. I completed correspondence classes from Fayetteville and from the University of Arkansas at Little Rock. I completed my degree requirement in January 1985. During that period, I was Miss Washington County 1982. The following year, the pageant was renamed Miss Northwest Arkansas. I was also a Razorback Beauty, 1978–1979.

I graduated in 1978 from Little Rock Central High School third out of a class of a little more than six hundred and sixty. My goal was to attend a college out of state, but I had no idea how to pay for it. Thanks to my principal, Mr. Hooks, I received a full four-year private academic and need-based scholarship to the University of Arkansas. I also received a freshman academic, music, and pageant scholarships to the school.

Many of my high school African American classmates also went to the university including my childhood friend and new college roommate. We were full of excitement and anticipation. I immediately pledged to study hard and to graduate someday.

Music had been a part of my life for many years, so I chose to pursue it as a career. However, I didn't want to teach, so after a year of study, I changed my major to engineering. I had been an honor society student of math, and it seemed to be a promising career for minorities. However, I didn't abandon music altogether. I continued to play my flute throughout college.

My first fall semester was great. In addition to making an honor society, I was chosen one of four or five Razorback Beauties by a panel of judges who interviewed us on current events and other special interests. At the time, I didn't realize how significant being selected was. But after winning, I became aware that it meant a great deal to a number of people, both black and white.

In the spring of my senior year in high school, I entered the Miss Black Teenage World of Little Rock pageant and to my surprise I won. Winning Miss Black Teenage World of Little Rock led to a state win and my first plane trip, an out-of-state experience, and my first scholarship prize. Most importantly, winning boosted my self-confidence. These were positive experiences. The next year as a music education student, I competed and won the Miss Black U of A pageant.

I decided to enter the Miss America pageant system with the encouragement of Jose Sanders, who had emceed the Miss Black Teenage of Arkansas pageant. It would turn out to be the beginning of a series of pageant entries that would become a type of summer hobby.

I started with the Miss Little Rock pageant in the summer after my freshman year. This would be the first of three times I would compete in this pageant. Over the next couple of years, I began to make some valuable friendships within the "pageant" community. Through Jose, I was introduced to Lynn Harris and Lencola Sullivan, Miss Arkansas 1980 and the first black winner. Another person, a former Miss Washington County and pageant insider, encouraged me to try out for the Uarkettes and later to enter the Miss Washington County pageant, one I hadn't heard of. Competing takes up time, something I had very little of while studying. Therefore, entering the Miss Washington County pageant would be only the second and the last pageant I would compete in during a school year.

Another official Miss America system pageant was the Miss University of Arkansas. I don't remember entering that competition, which, at the time, was sponsored by a fraternity on campus. For the first time I allowed race and class to prohibit my ambition. My thoughts were that I wouldn't expect to place simply because nonacademic fraternities and sororities were clearly racially separate, and I believed the winner would most likely be one known to them.

In the spring of 1982, I registered for the Miss Washington County pageant with a flute solo as my talent. There were about nine contestants. The audience included a small group of supporters including my roommate and best friend Sheila Rutledge. In the end, the judges selected me as Miss Washington County 1982, apparently amid some hushed controversy. I chose to disregard any negative rumors and to turn my attention to school.

The following spring, I crowned the new Miss Washington County—now under the title of Miss Northwest Arkansas. The sponsors had changed the name of the pageant. The person I crowned would later become Miss Arkansas.

The Little Rock pageant was held in the summer—one of the last local pageants to be held before the Miss Arkansas pageant. I gave it my best shot. I remember standing on stage for an unusually long time before the winner was announced. I was chosen first runner up. (Later, I learned from several reliable sources that I had won, but the sponsors of the pageant persuaded one of the judges to change their vote—the reason for the long delay in announcing the winner. I was told that the sponsors indicated they didn't know what to do with "black" hair. They ran a hair salon and the winner had made appearances with the salon as their official hair stylist. It took a lawsuit threat to collect just one hundred dollars of my winnings as first runner up. There were other prizes, but I never saw any of it.)

Instant gratification in the College of Engineering was few and far between. The courses weren't as stimulating as those in music. The studying environment in the School of Engineering seemed clannish. Students would often gather around several tables and chairs in a room and study together, establishing connections that would continue throughout their education. I very rarely joined in. Sitting with mostly white male students who seemed to be well acquainted with one another somehow didn't move me. In simple terms, I felt quite out of place. There weren't very many African Americans in the College of Engineering. With so few of us, we usually had different class schedules or traveled in different circles. I worked as hard as I could studying in the library, picking up a few summer courses at UALR, and by spending some summers studying in school at Fayetteville.

Participating in the community was part of my college experience. It helped me to survive and it made me grow as an individual. Living in Fayetteville as a student wasn't enough for me. I learned I needed to be around a variety of people. Over the years, I began to feel extremely isolated. It was difficult to see the light at the end of the tunnel. Not having personal transportation was a problem, too. It meant I was often stuck there over brief holidays and extended weekends. Towards the end of my education, I felt a strong urge to be in a different environment.

There was one incident involving a professor, who among the minority community was thought to be biased. Because this professor—Professor A (he is now deceased)—would routinely hold class over after dismissal, it would throw me late for my next class. That made not only his class difficult, but I was late for a subsequent class. Other students knew of the reputation Professor A, but because I wasn't tapped into the "network," I wasn't aware of how very difficult this was until I was knee deep into it. To make matters worse, I needed this class to graduate and he was the only one teaching it at the time. I was warned later by Professor B that my grade would be dropped one letter if I showed up late again. After being late for a class twice, I decided to leave Professor A's class at dismissal. As I was leaving, I heard him tell the entire dumb-stricken class that I didn't care about his class. At the risk of a failing grade from him, and a lower grade from Professor B, I decided to make my feelings known. After the students were dismissed, I firmly stated that his remarks were not fair and that I had been threatened with a lower grade because of his routine of holding class beyond its period. This professor was not pleased with my stand, wouldn't allow me to drop the class, and ultimately failed me. I also received a lower grade and an unfavorable opinion from Professor B in the other class as well.

However, I can tell you Professor A was unique. Overall, my experiences with teachers were good. Two individuals in the college helped me tremendously in my struggle to navigate the course requirements and to help me complete my degree. One was Dr. Taha, who allowed me to drop his much-needed class and to replace it with another course in the business school. Another person, Mr. Davis, helped me to gain credits by allowing my engineering classes from the University of Arkansas at Little Rock to transfer. Without them, I would probably have taken much longer to complete my degree requirements—if at all.

I have returned to the school on at least two occasions. Once during a business trip that brought me near the school. Another time was at the first or second Black Alumni Reunion.

■ Kenneth "Muskie" Harris (1973–1978), community relations

Telephone interview by Lonnie R. Williams, September 2, 2007
For detailed biography, see Appendix A, page 301

It was 1973, and business education was my major when I entered. I really didn't select the University of Arkansas. It was an opportunity given to me from a scholarship to play football at the University of Arkansas, being one of the first African Americans from Little Rock Central High to receive a scholarship to play football. I attended from 1973 until 1978.

I was the first from my family to attend the University of Arkansas. First from Little Rock Central High, noted for integration, so any students who come through those doors carry that tradition from the opportunity those Nine opened for us. After leaving the university, I had the opportunity to be the first black on the Alumni Association Board of Directors and while participating on the Alumni Association for three terms, I made the motion at the board meeting to institute a Black Alumni Association.

My experience at the university is still rewarding in my life. It went so fast. Everything was what I expected. It just went so fast. I played hard. I was involved. It's like I am still in it. Those times on campus, I'm not on campus but I am still participating because it meant so much to me. I put so much into being successful on the field and in the classroom. I'm still working to obtain my undergraduate degree. That is still a goal for me. My job and obligations prevent me from doing it, but now with computer on-line access, that is still a goal that I hope to accomplish in the next few years. The rewarding times of participating as an athlete, winning, and leaving the university with one of the best records as an athletic team is still a very rewarding experience.

I think there were a small number of black families in the whole Washington County, similar to the small number of blacks on campus. Just being at the doors of being one of the pioneers of it, from athletics and academics, is just a rewarding time that you still treasure. Doors you went through with others, similar, loved ones there to carry on that new tradition that is very young. I mean we don't have old traditions there, but that's what's exciting just to know that you're part of that pioneer effort for blacks.

I look at the era that I came through. I look at the motivation from my mom and dad. They were teaching us that this was an opportunity to go forth, forget the past. You can't change the past. This is a chance to improve the tradition and then I was a part of that integration. I was there for a reason. I didn't have the mentality of going up there trying to change anything. I was more or less involved in seeing how the whole operation worked. And that perspective has been very rewarding for me that by looking and seeing how things were running behind the scenes of the academic world and the athletic world, I am a businessman, your independent contractor. That's the rewarding doors that I looked at that I felt where some of the others were having rougher times because they were trying to change things instead of to blend in.

Did the athletic department do anything special to help the black athlete acclimate to the campus? They kind of did it in a way. I think it hurt us in a way because they sheltered us. Some being sheltered too long didn't allow them to step away and be as independent. It didn't take me, but maybe one semester, and I wanted to be as independent as possible, even though I had to adhere to the rules of the athletic department. And what Coach Broyles, Coach Matthews, and the alumni did for our parents, it's just too emotional almost to try to put it into words.

If you put it (my feelings toward the university) on a scale from one to ten, I never moved off of ten. Because of the environment that I grew up in and the friends I grew up with, everyone wanted to be a part of the university, but they didn't get the opportunity. I did.

Have I returned to the university? In returning to some of the alumni events, the Athletic Letterman's Club, we have a lot of social events. Then business, through my criminal justice work, allows me to continue to come back and travel through the state and through northwest Arkansas.

My feelings haven't changed. If anything I'm a little bit more involved now because the kids entering the university really need our perspective and our guidance. They need to see former athletes from the university who would help them see the prospects of their endeavors. I'm probably more involved than my teammates.

The questions that were asked, I don't think were very thoughtful and insightful. The person is only going to share their perspective about the university and their feelings and mine, like I said, were all good. What I would like to say is we are black Americans. Even when I made the proposal for the Black Alumni Association, to me it was in respect of what our families have done that we wanted to be identified with mainstream America involvement. And seeing it, to say "black" on one end and "African" on the other end, I just have trouble with that. I would think that we should be one and carry that tradition on. As a black American, as a third-generation American of African descent, I really don't think we need to use the words "African descent" with this new generation. I think that it's confusing to them. To me, that has been a sore that has hindered our cultural identification from "black" to "Colored" to "Negro" to "African American." I think we should really get locked in that we are proud black Americans carrying on this tradition. And I feel, Lonnie, right now that's the only personal feelings that I would like to express to my alumni friends, to carry on this tradition, and scores of opportunities that are going to come for the next generation.

■ Rhonda Bell Holmes (1975–1979), author

Written response to interview questions, July 18, 2007
For detailed biography, see Appendix A, page 302

I entered the University of Arkansas, Fayetteville, in 1975 for four years pursuing a bachelor of science in business administration with a major of data processing and quantitative analysis (computer information systems). I've been told that I was the first African American to graduate majoring in DPQA; however, I have not checked out the validity of that info.

During our time at the U of A, overt and subtle racial incidents were still taking place—not only at the university, but also in the northwest Arkansas area. We were told that there was a sign in Springdale that basically said "No Blacks After Dark." I don't know the exact reading of the sign because I never saw it; however, I do know that Tracy and another black student received a police escort out of Springdale every night on their way home from work during the summer. So just hearing about the sign and Tracy's experience had a definite effect on my actions. I only went to Springdale one time while I was in school—and that time was not really by choice.

Shortly after coming to the university, we began hearing of incidents that had occurred in the not-too-distant past, like what sounded like a riot in Brough Commons and a black student being shot during "Texas Week"—both of which were racially motivated. So we received and adhered to a variety of warnings. We were warned not to go out at night during "Texas Week," not to be in Springdale at night, and I even received a warning from one of my sisters who hadn't even attended the university. She told me that when I spoke with my advisor, do not let them put me in remedial math and English. I wondered why would they even suggest it, since I made "A" and "B" grades in math and English—but guess what . . . they tried. I declined their offer. I shared this same warning with one of the African Americans students coming behind me who also always made "A" and "B" grades in math and English. Unfortunately, she did not adhere to the warning and ended up in one of the remedial classes.

Getting past that—most of my professors were pretty good. They taught well, had good attitudes, and coped with my nonchalant behavior towards class. (I must be honest and say that I did not always put forth my best effort—but praise God, I've learned better.) I personally experienced only a couple of strange incidents that, I later surmised, were due to racism. One was with an English professor who always, always alternated between a "C" and "C+" when grading my and the one other black student's essays. Either I made a "C" and she made the "C+" or she made a "C" and I made the "C+"—*every single time*. Initially, I just thought, "ok—this is strange," again, since I've always made mostly "A" grades in English. Then, just how strange this was, was confirmed when I took another essay writing course and guess what—made "A" grades.

The other incident was near graduation, getting that final signature from my advisor who suggested that I may not do well in the computer field and should consider changing my major. Again, I declined the offer, continued in that field and did well. I later found out that I should have shared that experience with the African American student coming behind me—because the same man did the same thing to her. This really, really upset her and she has not been able to come back to the campus since that time. Fortunately, she did ignore him enough to graduate as scheduled and continue in that field—doing extremely well.

▪ Tracy Holmes Sr. (1975–1975), sales

Written response to interview questions, July 18, 2007
For detailed biography, see Appendix A, page 302

I entered the University of Arkansas in 1975. I received a bachelor of science degree in business administration in 1979 with a major in administrative management.

Why did I select the University of Arkansas? I was told by counselors that within the state of Arkansas, the university was the best school for those majoring in accounting—which initially was my major. For both of us (Rhonda and myself), this was also the furthest point in the state away from home—which made us feel more grown up.

I have been told I was the first black undergrad (and possibly first undergrad—black or white) to hold the position of assistant head resident. A graduate student normally held this position. This was the 1978–1979 school year in Hotz Hall.

As a minority assistant in Yocum Hall during my sophomore year, I had an opportunity to focus on helping other African American students (mainly freshmen) in transitioning into the university environment. I was able to mentor them as they shared and worked through their frustrations and concerns regarding academic and social life. A not so positive point is—there was nothing on campus at that time to address African American concerns and interest—for example, no black barbers, hair care products, radio stations, nothing geared to the black experience. Our social life consisted of weekend parties held by fraternities, sororities, movies during Black History week or month and BAD (Black Americans for Democracy) events.

I felt the racial tension between blacks and whites in the dorm, as well as the classroom, seemed to be caused by no understanding of each other's culture and backgrounds. As a resident assistant for one year, I had an opportunity to talk to both groups. These conversations informed me of the vast ignorance that fed this tension. Each group was very distrustful of the other. This segregation continued into the dining areas. One of the ways this tension culminated was another huge fight. I don't know all the details; however, I was told some white male students harassed/picked on/messed with a black male student. Shortly after that, his brother came to campus and all "h—l" broke loose. I heard and witnessed part of the fight in Yocum Hall—trash cans being thrown, bodies running and falling down stairs and the blood left behind. Unfortunately, one of the white guys, who got caught in this retaliation, was one of the "good guys." He was hurt very badly and I don't think he returned to school.

Academically, I never felt like anyone expressed an interest or cared. We both felt pretty isolated in most of our classes—being the only black in most classes. We were each other's main support—since we were dating and were both business majors. So we were very encouraged to see persons like Barbara Lofton in the Walton School of Business.

During my time at the U of A, I had a chance to practice and develop leadership and managerial skills by being a member, treasurer, vice president, then president of Alpha Phi Alpha Fraternity. I learned some of these skills in the variety of management courses I took; however, I also learned some from my father, Morris Holmes—who graduated from the university with his EdD the same year I got my bachelor's.

Rhonda and Tracy

Another more public event was the process of getting black cheerleaders and blacks on the pom squad. I'm sure we never knew all the details; however, what we do remember is that the black athletes had to threaten to boycott in order to ensure that we could have black cheer-leaders. I remember being in a BAD meeting hearing a representative of the black athletes say-ing how we, the black students, had to really back them up in their decision to boycott. I don't think they had to go through with the boycott. It seems that the threat was enough. The uni-versity/athletic department agreed to two sets of black cheerleaders (two males and two females) and (I think) two on the pom squad. I haven't really been keeping up—but I still don't think I've seen more than those same two.

The thought of coming back to the university did not cross our minds until the Black Alumni Reunions, as well as sorority and fraternity reunions, began. We currently live in Fay-etteville and these reunions, especially the BAS reunions, helped with that transition. The receptions held during the reunion, sponsored by the various colleges, contributed to us feeling much more welcome on campus than we had during our college days.

Thanks, Lonnie Ray, for helping us with that transition of feeling better about the univer-sity as a whole. If we had not experienced the reunions, the initial thought of moving to Fayetteville would have been very traumatic.

Seeing more African American faculty continually encourages us. We are also encouraged by knowing the university employs persons like Barbara Batson, with the Career Development Center. She sees the importance of inclusion and acts on that realization. It's not just talk for her. However, based on the percentage of African American students, it still seems that the leadership is slow in recognizing the value of diversity. Our feelings regarding this situation have changed because we've matured and because of our relationship with Christ. This enables us to view it differently. We've chosen to ignore the negative appearance and stay encouraged, expecting continued improvement. Due to the economic growth in northwest Arkansas, which seems to include recognition and value placed on diversity by businesses, this area has vastly improved for black folk and we believe the university is continually motivated to catch up. We are not to the point where we can encourage or recommend that young African American stu-dents come to school here yet; however, we would definitely not discourage them and we con-tinue to counsel and encourage those who have made that decision and with whom we come in contact. Our son initially considered the U of A, and we felt fine with it because Lonnie Ray was there and we had also met Thomas "TC" Carter and felt comfortable with him. We've also been told of many other parents feeling comfortable sending their child to the U of A after meeting or being told about Lonnie as well.

We must also add that we don't know of any school for which we would give a blanket recommendation. While going through the college selection process with our children, we learned that what is most important are the academic, emotional, social, and spiritual needs of the student, which is why they (our children) attended two different colleges and two dif-ferent graduate schools. It is a very individual thing.

We developed close, strong, lasting relationships while at the U of A—for which we are very grateful. Pledging, sorority and fraternity participation, and dorm life definitely con-tributed to some of our close relationships, but it went past that. It seems like the black stu-dents looked for ways to get together, have fun, and develop friendships. Since there were so few of us, there was a natural tendency to stick together, to expect help and support from each other. From time to time, there was some bickering/gossiping—but not so much to completely make people fall out with each other (I don't think). When things did get a little too tense, BAD would call a meeting to discuss it and clear it up if possible. I [Rhonda] remember a meeting in which we discussed black students not speaking to each other and improving our relationship with blacks who were from Fayetteville. We also remember having to coordinate parties/events on the BAD calendar so sororities and fraternities wouldn't step on each other's toes. Relationships were important.

■ Lynda Jackson Browne (1975–1982), educator

Telephone interview by Charles Robinson, March 2009
For detailed biography, see Appendix A, page 302

Before I begin, I would be remiss if I did not extend my personal expression of appreciation to Dr. Charles F. Robinson and Dr. Lonnie R. Williams, the editors of the *Remembrances in Black: Personal Perspectives of the African American Experience at the University of Arkansas, 1940s–2000s*. For those of us who have walked and shared this very special journey, this historical memoir will link our lives together forever at the University of Arkansas, Fayetteville.

Approximately two years after graduating with my bachelor's of science degree, I was approached by several of my college professors regarding a graduate course that was to be offered on the University of Arkansas, Pine Bluff, campus. A professor, Dr. Reba Davis, from the U of A, Fayetteville, was going to teach the class. Since graduation, I had been working full time with Arkansas Power and Light Company, so this opportunity seemed ideal to me.

During the course of the class, Dr. Davis asked me if I had ever considered obtaining a master's degree. After discussing all of my pros and cons regarding the subject, she asked me if she could provide a way for me to earn my degree, and allay my concerns, would I consider the possibility. My answer was absolutely!

Several weeks before I completed the class with Dr. Davis, she offered me the chance of a lifetime, a graduate assistant's position, a full scholarship to pay for my master's degree, and a part-time job, which would cover my remaining expenses. This was a tremendous blessing and set me on an unexpected path with the University of Arkansas, Fayetteville. Dr. Davis took a chance on me, and I will be forever grateful for her kindness, generosity, and faith in me.

On May 15, 1976, I graduated with my master's in education from the University of Arkansas, Fayetteville. Shortly thereafter, I accepted the position of admissions counselor, a newly created recruiting position in the admissions department. This position would afford me the opportunity to travel around the state of Arkansas while encouraging young high school students to consider continuing their education at the U of A, Fayetteville, campus.

Another person who was instrumental in forwarding my career at the U of A was Dr. Charles E. Bishop, a former U of A president. My first personal encounter with Dr. Bishop was on May 15, 1976, when he congratulated me as I walked across the stage to shake his hand as I received my master's degree. As Dr. Bishop shook my hand to congratulate me, he queried me as to what I was going to be doing after graduation. It was small talk, but my family certainly wondered what had sparked such a lengthy conversation between the president of the university and me.

Later that day after graduation, I was leaving the administration building and encountered Dr. Bishop and his family in a limousine. He rolled his window down to talk to me. Again he asked me what I was going to be doing and if I had a job. It was during that brief conversation that I learned about the position in the admissions office. It was President Bishop who said, "You'd be great at this job and I'd like to see you interview for it," . . . so . . . I did. When I was selected for the position, I could not have been more overjoyed.

Frankly, as a young person, I could not have asked for a better position. As I traveled around the state, I was supported financially and otherwise. I WAS IN HOG HEAVEN!

The director of the admissions office was encouraging, supportive, and created an atmosphere that was pleasant to work in every day. Shortly after I was hired, two additional staff joined us, one white female and one African American male.

As a minority, I knew (even though it was never identified as the mandate) that I was to encourage and recruit more minority students to the university. Throughout the state of Arkansas, I was received extremely well. Most high school career counselors were delighted that we were finally officially recruiting like so many other colleges and universities in the state.

Let me say this, although the reception to me was always great, there were times that I would go to "certain" schools and I could tell that they were surprised to see "me." On several occasions after I arrived, they would respectfully ask, "just to make sure," if I was indeed from the Fayetteville campus and not the Pine Bluff campus. Once in the door, all I needed was the opportunity to speak to the students who had expressed an interest in the U of A.

During my years in the admissions office, I was very successful in recruiting young people of all races to the university. In most cases, not only would I get to know the students, but their parents as well. For some parents, the last thing they said to their child was, "Stay in touch with Ms. Jackson (my maiden name). If you have any problems or concerns, she's going to be there for you." The kids I recruited were important to me, some remain friends today. I always felt an obligation to the students and their parents to ensure that once they were on our campus, they would be safe, and continue to strive hard to reach their personal goals.

On occasion, I would chat with Dr. Bishop and tell him how things were going. After about two years in the admissions department, another opportunity came along. This was the assistant dean of students position in student services. I was really intrigued with this position because I knew it would afford me the chance to spend more time working with the students on campus.

As information became available about the assistant dean of students position, it was my understanding that they were looking for someone with a doctorate. I spoke to Dr. Bishop about the position and mentioned about the educational requirement. Dr. Bishop said that if I wanted to apply for the position, I certainly could. He also said that if after going through the interview process, I was the candidate of choice, he would approve my appointment.

After many interviews with faculty, staff, and students, including the leadership of the organization Black Americans for Democracy (BAD), what I really remember most about the entire process was being nervous and excited all at the same time.

To make a long story short, my name was ultimately turned in as the candidate of choice to Dr. Bishop for approval and he approved me. To my knowledge, I became the first and youngest black female assistant dean of students. So for the second time in less than three years, I would hold two positions within the U of A, admissions counselor and assistant dean of students.

When I became assistant dean of students, one of my major responsibilities was serving as director of New and Returning Student Orientation. I worked very closely with the administration, financial aid, housing, and food service, along with other student services departments to create a wonderful orientation experience for our new students and their parents.

Prior to the new student orientation, I was allowed to interview and hire a number of students to assist me for the summer. It was actually my involvement with these wonderful students that ultimately prompted the creation of an organization called Big Brothers/Big Sisters.

Something that I really cherish, even in my work today as the owner of a Christian Leadership Academy for at-risk youth, I have a heart and passion for kids that are struggling. Many of the kids that I recruited were plucked from their small schools where they were stars, "A" and "B" students. Once they arrived at our campus of 16,000 students, they were lost. Often for our minority students, that challenge was even greater.

Many of the minority students would begin their college experience with wonderful credentials. They had fabulous ACT/SAT test scores and after arriving on campus would really start to decline. It was hard for them to acclimate to college life. There were a lot of black students who were doing well and making the transition. I thought perhaps if these students would serve as mentors to the incoming freshman students, take them under their wing, be a friend, perhaps their transition from high school to college would be easier. This concept was the beginning of the Big Brother/Big Sister program, which had its inception in 1979.

Successful upper-class students were interviewed and selected to mentor incoming freshmen. Their job was to answer their questions, introduce them around the campus, and be someone they could call on at any time. Although most incoming freshmen could have benefited from this program, it was for the black students only. (Some faculty/staff were concerned that the program did not include all students.)

At that time, my primary focus was to retain the minority students that we had worked so hard to recruit to our campus. With the support of Dr. Merlin J. Augustine, who at that time was the assistant to the president, Lenthon Clark, director of financial aid, and Dr. Bishop, I was not only able to create an outstanding Big Brother/Big Sister program, but recruit the brightest and best black students to serve as mentors. Ultimately, I was able to offer work-study positions for their valuable services.

The Big Brother/Big Sister program became Students Making It Lighter Everyday (SMILE) after a contest was held to re-name the organization. The STAND leadership assisted with the contest.

Recently, I was thrilled to learn that now, over thirty years later, the SMILE organization still exists on the campus. The name of the organization is now "Connections," and is housed in the Multicultural Center. The mentoring component, which was the foundation of the SMILE program, still remains. "Connections" is now an officially registered student organization with officers and a BUDGET!

I am confident that SMILE and now Connections have over the years helped to convert many scared high school students to confident college students. With the help of mentors, incoming black students are receiving the helping hand they need to get over those initial hurdles of feeling lonely and insecure, not having a friend, and being away from home. Just having that special "SMILE" helps them make the "Connections" that make all the difference in the world.

Another project that I was honored to assist in developing was the Inspirational Singers, the vision of Dr. Augustine. If I recall, this group was founded in 1977. While most of the fraternal organizations were represented on the U of A campus, we did not have many other outlets for the black students. Dr. Augustine and I wanted the students to have the opportunity to showcase their many talents, and we thought that a school choir would be a great outlet. Other colleges had traveling choirs; we believed a traveling gospel choir, much like the singers at Oral Roberts University, would be a wonderful addition to our campus. So once again, with the support and financial blessing from Dr. Bishop, the U of A Inspirational Singers were born.

As a faculty sponsor, I was privileged to travel the state with the choir, under the direction of Mr. David Lawrence, an Oral Roberts University graduate and a member of the famed ORU Souls Afire. Today, the Inspirational Singers remain on the campus, thrilling audiences with their illustrious voices.

So, how do I feel about my experiences at the University of Arkansas? Over the years my feelings have remained the same. At the university, I completed my master's degree. I also held two positions that I dearly loved, which allowed me to develop my passion of working with young people, something that I still do.

For six years, I served as the faculty advisor for the undergraduate chapter of my sorority, Delta Sigma Theta. As a single person then, I poured my entire self into the students and their special projects.

There is a story, the particulars of which I have never shared until now. Actually, I am grateful for the opportunity to set the record straight, especially regarding this truly historical event at the U of A.

Sadly, at one time, while our talented young black men were allowed to play for the U of A Razorback football team and other sports, we had no black cheerleaders. I was so proud of our black players when they staged a type of revolt and presented an ultimatum to the athletic department. They wanted black cheerleaders and had no intention of playing football until they had black cheerleaders.

Word of this reached President Bishop's office, and immediately the administration and athletic departments started the ball rolling. Dr. Augustine called me to his office, briefed me on the facts, and asked that I take the lead in securing two black cheerleaders (one male and one female). The black football players were thrilled. Once the flyers were distributed and the school newspaper broke the story, a number of students stepped forward to participate in the tryouts.

The process began with training and practice for all interested parties. Certainly, there was going to be an official tryout, but it was important to me that the students have an opportunity to learn the required routines. A schedule was prepared, and the all-white cheerleading squad started the training process. I NEVER MISSED A PRACTICE OR TRAINING! This charge was given to me and I was determined to see to it that everything was carried out fairly and according to plan. While I made sure to keep Dr. Augustine abreast of our progress, on occasion he attended the rehearsals personally.

Frankly, I don't remember the exact time frame that we were given to select the black cheerleaders. Seems that it was just a few weeks. What I do know is that the students who were interested worked very hard to be selected for this monumental first at the university.

From my perspective, the cream of the crop quickly rose to the top. Having witnessed the entire processes, it was easy see who had mastered the routines quickly. I am confident that the students trying out knew as well.

This story now takes an interesting twist and there is only one way to explain. The complexions or skin colors of our hopefuls spanned from one end of the spectrum to the other.

While subtle, it was obvious that the candidates with the fair complexions were favored by the white cheerleaders. Having observed their "preference," I kept a watchful eye on the situation.

On the night of the finals, everything went very well, or so I thought. Certainly, all of the students had worked hard and were excellent. In my opinion, there was a male and female who were outstanding, both just happened to be darker in complexion. When the names of the winners were announced, I was stunned! I am confident that most of the people observing and the contestants were as well. While taken aback, we were all willing to accept the decision that had been made.

What happened next was allowed only by the grace of God. While the final ballots were being quickly gathered, I casually glanced at them and just happened to see the scores that had been given to one of the students that I had deemed the most outstanding. The scores were so low. It did not make sense. I knew right away that something was terribly wrong! Then I thought, if one or more of the judges intentionally lowered the scores of the best candidates, there was no way that they could win. Had the tryouts been fixed? Had they cheated? If my suspicions were correct, all I needed was the chance to prove it!

Thankfully, that night at the finals, Dr. Augustine was in attendance. I immediately approached him and shared my suspicions. He asked if I was absolutely sure and if I could prove it. I told him yes, I could. While things were handled professionally, there was a lot of tension in the stadium that night. Frankly, I have no idea to this day just how much the participants were aware of, but they had to know that something was wrong.

That night, the ballots were impounded; it was agreed that they would be locked up in President Bishop's office safe overnight and would be removed the next morning prior to an agreed-upon meeting of all involved parties.

This incident did not make me a favorite in the athletic department and with the cheerleading staff. According to them, they had followed the process and now they were being accused of cheating. This certainly was not an easy time for them. They were already feeling the pressure, having just responded to the demands of the black players in the first place.

The cheerleaders felt they had been forced to teach these black kids the cheers. They were also upset that their stunts, designed for a certain number of people, now had to be revamped. And now, I had the nerve to accuse them of cheating. Dr. Augustine stood behind me completely and I greatly appreciate him for doing so. Frankly, I knew that this could possibly be a career decision on my part, but it was a chance that I willingly took.

The next morning, we all met in Dr. Bishop's boardroom. The cheerleaders, their sponsors, and a representative from the athletic department were all present. This was huge, a very big deal. Dr. Augustine convened the meeting, recapped the events, and accusations that had been made the night before. He once again asked me if I could prove my allegations. I was confident all I needed were the ballots to do so.

The impounded ballots were removed from Dr. Bishop's safe. Dr. Augustine assured everyone that no one had tampered with or had access to the ballots overnight. At this point, Dr. Augustine handed me the ballots.

Almost immediately, and in front of all who were seated around the table, I was able to separate the ballots into the required piles that proved beyond a doubt that voting irregularities had taken place. Unquestionably, the scores of the two outstanding candidates had been lowered by most of the cheerleader judges, thus making it impossible for them to win. I will never forget the looks on the faces of the athletic department's representative, cheerleader staff, but most of all the embarrassed and humiliated cheerleaders. Frankly, Dr. Augustine and I were just relieved that it was over.

As far as I know, nothing was ever done to reprimand the cheerleaders for cheating; they all remained members of the squad. Perhaps the greatest consequence was that instead of admitting only two black cheerleaders, they now had to accept the two whose scores had been altered. It certainly would not have been fair to penalize the students who had originally been selected; the only logical thing was have all four students serve as cheerleaders.

After the revelation, the meeting was short! We never discussed their motives and the color issue was not discussed. They cheated, they got caught, and we ended up with two male and two female black cheerleaders.

At that time, we thought it best not to let the general student population know what had taken place. They all needed to be able to work together as members of the squad. I agreed. Perhaps one day I will learn for certain, despite our efforts to spare them all the drama, if they found out anyway.

Two awards that I received from STAND meant a great deal to me. The black student government selected me Outstanding Faculty/Staff twice, once in the spring of 1980 and also in the spring of 1982. For six years, I held the position of assistant dean of students and was also staff advisor to the STAND organization. It was a privilege to serve in both of these positions.

Before I close, I must share one more experience that happened during my tenure in the admissions department. While on the road recruiting, I discovered that a recruiting tool, a brochure specifically geared towards the black students, would be a great resource. Permission was granted for me to design the publication. I entitled it "Reflections of You at the University of Arkansas."

The brochure highlighted college life from the black student perspective and provided an overview of the different services provided on campus. Also featured throughout the brochure were pictures of beautiful African artifacts that were housed in the U of A library.

I selected two of the top students on campus to pose on the cover. My vision was to find a place where I could take a picture with a mirror reflection to support the title of the brochure. The perfect location was found on the bank of a pond close to a friend's home. The brochure was so beautiful and I was extremely proud that I had accomplished exactly what I had wanted to do.

The incident that I want to share with you begins now. For weeks, I had worked extremely hard on this project. One afternoon, I announced I would be taking the brochure to the printer the next day. That evening I worked late at the office. I proofread the brochure several times because I wanted everything in the book to be perfect. Before leaving that night, I threw away all of the drafts, extra documents, unneeded scraps of paper, and left the finished brochure on my desk. My trash bag was so full that I tied it up. This simple act would later prove to be a blessing in disguise.

The next morning when I arrived, the brochure was gone! I have my suspicions as to what happened to it, but frankly, that is another story. The director of admissions was very upset and troubled about the situation. He asked would it be possible to reconstruct the booklet. It was possible, but I would need to find the notes and documents that I had thrown away the night before; otherwise, l was going to have to start all over.

Because I often worked late at the office, I had developed a great relationship with the night clean-up crew. Several of them were still there the next morning when I realized that the document was missing. When I ran down to the basement, very upset, I let the cleaning staff know what had happened and that I needed to find the bag of trash I had thrown away. I could not believe it—they stopped everything and made it their priority to help me find my discarded trash.

Fortunately, the garbage truck had not yet picked up the trash from the administration building, so at least I knew my bag was still in the building.

Have you ever dug through three floors of wet, stinky, nasty trash? The cleaning crew refused to let me help; one by one they opened the large bags of trash, determined to help me find the small bag I had thankfully tied up the night before.

The trash bags were clear plastic, so it was possible to see every disgusting thing inside of them. We had opened and searched so many of the bags, I frankly thought it was a lost cause, but . . . God had another plan. One of the bags seemed familiar, as I looked closer, I felt tears well up in my eyes. There was my trash bag, still tied up, with everything dry inside.

Bottom line— in several days, I recreated the brochure, we sent it to the printer, and it became a wonderful resource that was enjoyed by many of our incoming African American students.

Thank God for the black custodial workers (males and females) who rallied behind me that day. Sadly, I do not remember their names and it is likely that they will not contribute to this venture, but in my last thoughts, I honor them for the sacrifice they all selflessly made for me that morning.

In closing, I acknowledge and express heartfelt thanks to everyone who supported and encouraged me throughout my tenure as a graduate student and staff member at the University of Arkansas, Fayetteville.

■ Hannibal B. Johnson (1978–1981), attorney and author

Written response to interview questions, November 16, 2007
For detailed biography, see Appendix A, page 303

I entered the University of Arkansas, Fayetteville, in the fall of 1978. I graduated in the spring of 1981 with a double major in economics and sociology. I chose to attend the University of Arkansas because I wanted to stay close to my hometown of Fort Smith, Arkansas, for undergraduate studies. I figured that, as the state's flagship public university, I could not go too far astray choosing the U of A.

I entered the university at a time of swelling African American enrollment. I was not a "first" of any particular note. I believe, however, that I was the first (or perhaps among the first) recipient of the Dr. Martin Luther King Jr. Scholar's Award.

I entered the University of Arkansas during a period of substantial growth in African American enrollment. At the time, African Americans constituted about 10 percent of the student body. This critical mass of African American students made for a dynamic experience. In fact, in terms of absolute numbers, the African American student body at the University of

Arkansas seemed, based on my limited experience, huge. I had never been around so many other African American students.

Greek life flourished. The Alphas. The Kappas. The Qs. The Sigmas. The Deltas. The AKAs. The Zetas. Oh, and there were auxiliary groups: The Alpha Angels. The Kappa Sweethearts. With it came outstanding step shows and do-not-miss parties (both in the student union and off campus). Though I did not pledge as an undergraduate, many of my friends did. I was, in effect, Greek by association.

Sometimes, Greek life created divisions. The leader of the African American student association, STAND (Students Taking A New Dimension), reminded us that before any of us were Greek, we were all black.

STAND played an active role in campus life. As a new student, I recall the visionary leadership of Lloyd Meyers, STAND president. Lloyd seemed to always be on top of his game—knowledgeable of the issues and pressing for proactive and progressive action. I enjoyed working with STAND on student concerns as well as on events. Among others, Julian Bond and Coretta Scott King spoke on campus. Lionel Richie and the white-hot Commodores serenaded us.

As serenades go, it was hard to top the beautiful voices of the black-clad Inspirational Singers. They were perfect ambassadors for the university and impressive representatives of its African American student constituency.

Other informal ambassadors come to mind. Certain upperclassmen made an indelible impression, not because we were close friends, but because of their uniqueness of character and charm: Dionne Harold, vivacious and spirited; Deborah Cooper, "down home" and super sweet; Lloyd Meyers, charismatic and culturally astute; Trent Walton, singularly focused and studious; and Isabella Wofford, beautiful and brainy. These are but a few examples.

Back then, Lou Holtz and Eddie Sutton ruled the football and basketball roosts, respectively. Going to a Razorback football practice proved more than a bit interesting. Coach Holtz ran a no-holds-barred session. He used some "colorful" language to get his messages across.

Razorback athletes lived somewhat privileged lives, segregated from the rest of us in Wilson-Sharp dormitory. We knew, or at least we sensed, that they received preferential treatment at almost every turn—more and better parties, bigger and newer cars, plenty of money. The list goes on and on. While ordinary students seemed aware of this double standard, they seemed resigned to it. Athletes, after all, were practically demigods. Among the pantheon of my day were: U. S. Reed and Sidney Moncrief (basketball); Gary Anderson and Bobby Duckworth (football); and Johnny Ray (baseball).

I lived among the masses in the largest dormitory on campus. Pomfret, then a sprawling, co-ed dormitory down in the valley, boasted some of the best grub on campus. That explains the "freshman fifteen" that more than a few of my "dormies" and I packed on during the early months on campus.

As an upperclassman, I served as a minority assistant (MA) in Pomfret. I also worked the occasional weekend as a dormitory security guard. My task was to keep all those hormonal males off the women's floors during curfew hours. What a job!

As an upperclassman, I served as a SMILE (Students Making It Lighter Every Day), a freshmen advisor/mentor. SMILE allowed me a formal opportunity to help other African American students the way others had informally assisted me.

Overall, I recall my University of Arkansas days fondly. I thrived academically. With two majors, I took twenty-one hours one semester. (This is not advisable!) The campus was beautiful then, and it is even more beautiful now. I do recall a paucity of African American professors and administrators during my tenure. Drs. (Nudie) Williams, Clark, Morgan, and Reed —those are the African American professors whom I recall. Of those, Dr. Reed was the only one with whom I had a class (political science).

I have returned to the University of Arkansas on a few occasions since my graduation. For the most part, these visits were by invitation. They were speaking engagements connected to my books about the Greenwood District in Tulsa and the 1921 Tulsa Race Riot, on the one hand, or the all-black towns in Oklahoma, on the other.

I still have positive feelings toward the University of Arkansas. I hope that the school understands, appreciates, and embraces diversity to a far greater degree than it did in my day.

Like most things in life, you get out what you put in. If a student seeks educational access and opportunity, it is available at the University of Arkansas. Collegiate rankings of various sorts, while useful, are not the be all and end all of institutional analysis. In the end, we choose which courses to take. We choose how hard to study. We choose how much of ourselves to invest in education. The University of Arkansas offers a quality education to those who choose to avail themselves of it.

■ Janis F. Kearney (1971–1977), author

Written response to interview questions, October 25, 2007
For detailed biography, see Appendix A, page 303

I entered the UA in fall 1971. I changed majors a couple of times before settling on a BA in journalism. One reason I selected the University of Arkansas was that two of my older brothers were already students at the UA, and they would come home on weekends talking nonstop about their experiences there. It sounded really exciting to me and my sister Jo Ann, who was a classmate. We decided that was where we would go.

We also were lucky enough to visit the school during our senior year. We actually spent the weekend, stayed in the dorms, and met some of the upperclassmen who shared their own experiences on the campus. They all enjoyed being there. We were sold. Even if we hadn't been, our parents would have insisted that we go there—given the fact that they could rely on our brothers to monitor our actions, leaving less worry for my parents.

I was a five-year undergraduate student, given the fact that I changed my major more than once. After undergrad, I spent another year in graduate school, in pursuit of my master's of public administration. However, before completing that degree, my family (I was married by then) moved from Fayetteville to Little Rock in 1977. I spent a little over six years in Fayetteville.

I was one of the first black journalism graduates from the university. The two years I was in the program, there were a total of four black journalism majors—E. Lynn Harris, Mellonee Carrigan, Overtis Hicks, and myself. Before that, there had been two graduates—the late Jennifer Hopkins and Gerald Jordan, now a UA faculty member. In 1975, I became the first married student who was also a mother, selected as a Razorback Beauty.

Describe my experiences at the UA? I was seventeen years old, almost eighteen; when I left my home on Varner Road in Gould, Arkansas, enroute to the University of Arkansas. It was late August, a week before regular students would arrive at the school. As a freshman, I had to go through the few days of orientation.

My father drove me to Pine Bluff in his station wagon, and deposited me at the Greyhound bus station. It was my first bus ride and the first time I'd ever ventured into the small towns of north and northwest Arkansas. I arrived in Fayetteville late afternoon. The small bus depot was virtually empty. I had expected to be met by my younger sister Jo Ann, who had arrived on campus for the second summer session. But, she wasn't there. Luckily, there was one lone cabdriver who obviously knew the bus schedule. I knew I was in a different part of the state when I noticed the cab driver's long ponytail and "hippy" way of talking. He also seemed to know where all the dorms were located. I expect he made a pretty good salary during this time of the year.

Pomfret Hall was the university's first coed dorm. I remembered my brothers telling me how both boys and girls lived in the same dorm, and I just couldn't imagine that being true. But, it was . . . except that the boys lived on one side of the large dorm and girls on the other. The sexes were separated by a huge lobby and cafeteria.

I'm convinced that my eyes must have been huge and my mouth stood open in awe during the first hour of my time on campus. Gould, Arkansas, my hometown, was a tiny, rural town and my parents were strict church-goers. I had been socially sheltered all of the seventeen years leading up to this experience. Everything I saw was new. Interracial friendships were obviously pretty common on campus from the look of things. I was also struck by the number of foreign students on campus.

The lobby that separated the girls from the boys was easily the size of our entire house on Varner road. A couple sat at the cherry wood piano, playing lively tunes; guys strolled from one side of the dorm to the other, talking loudly and laughing, and a couple sat on one of the over-sized couches smooching in broad daylight!

While my friends and other students would complain regularly about cafeteria food, I never understood what the complaints were about. But, once I thought about it . . . most of them didn't come from the impoverished environment my siblings and I did. I was overwhelmed by the offerings—the variety of breakfast, lunch, and dinner food, and the fact that we could eat as much as we wanted. It didn't take me long to understand what the "First fifteen" meant. I gained the first fifteen, probably within my first few weeks there. Gratefully, I was able to get rid of the weight without trying too hard, since walking from Pomfret up the hills to my classes took a lot of calories each day.

During my first hour at Pomfret, a friendly student showed me around the building, especially the TV room; the laundry room, where I could buy detergent and get change; and even the door that students came in at night, if they were later than nine P.M. She warned me, however, that staying out past midnight would result in a talk with the head resident. I was only called in once during my tenure at the university, and that was after an attempt to impress an upperclassman by staying at a house party longer than I should. We thought we'd successfully snuck in right around one A.M., but were caught.

Another student took me up to my room, and though it was hardly a large room, and certainly a sparse one . . . I was pleased because it was *my* room. I had grown up in a household of seventeen children. While not all seventeen were home at the same time, there were at least seven or eight of us at home at one time, sometimes as many as ten. I never had a room to myself . . . and, for many years, not a bed to myself. My sister Jo Ann and I shared a bed for far too long.

There was no one else in the room when I arrived, but it was clear that I would have a roommate, based on the initial housing application. Later that evening my roommate, who happened to be white, would come in. She looked at me, then completely ignored me. She went to bed without speaking a word to me. I was taken aback, because of the interaction between blacks and whites I'd seen earlier. While I didn't run into a great deal of racial confrontations "on the hill," this was my first introduction to the fact that it certainly existed there.

For the next weeks, my roommate pretended I didn't exist and didn't make any attempt to hide her disdain for my presence there. She was very open about her unhappiness on her phone calls with her parents and bluntly asked if she could move. She moved out within a few weeks, to another dorm. We spoke less than five words to each other during our short cohabitation. Luckily, after the silent roommate left, I wasn't assigned another one. I actually had a room to myself for the rest of the year.

It was a great comfort to have older brothers already at the school when I arrived. Jesse was a junior, and Jack a sophomore. Later that year, another brother would enter the Law School at the university. This gave my sister Jo Ann and me a sense of security. But it also assured us that few boys would be brave enough to talk to us.

Jo Ann had come to the school during the summer, so she was one semester ahead of me. She took the time during my first week to tell me what she knew about the college experience, and we visited back and forth between dorms. She lived in a girls' dorm up the hill from me, Humphrey Hall. It was comforting to have my sister there on campus with me, though our relationship had drifted some since our childhood. There were times that we reverted back to the sisterly relationship we'd known so many years. We became friends with two girls—Beverly, from Augusta, Arkansas, and another Joann, from Pine Bluff. The four of us spent a lot of time together—playing cards when we should have been studying, discussing guys, and going to weekend parties.

While I greatly enjoyed most of my classes–especially American literature, world literature, anything related to writing—I didn't do well in those classes I didn't like. I also realized that because I hadn't had to study in high school to get good grades, I didn't really know how to study. Nor did I feel comfortable asking for help. So for two years, the most critical part of my college experience suffered. I also began a serious relationship during the spring of my first year . . . that didn't help my grades at all. I began spending much of my spare time with my future husband, Darryl Lunon, a young business major from North Little Rock.

My first two years of college life were exciting and enjoyable. I loved the idea of being a college girl, meeting new friends from different parts of Arkansas and the country, and learning new things about myself. It was abundantly clear to me and my parents, however, that my grades were far from what they should have been. For one thing, I had to finally settle on a major rather than shuffle from one to the next. I knew I wanted to be a writer, but felt I needed to find something more stable than writing as a major. Besides, I'd checked, and the school didn't offer a writing degree. I took loads of literature classes and creative writing. I started out with an education major, then changed to sociology, and finally settled on the closest thing to a writing degree, journalism. I had finally found the area that was right for me. My grades improved overnight.

In January of 1973, I discovered I was pregnant with Darryl's child. I had no desire to have a child at that point in my life or to get married. But, given the times and my parents' strict religious outlook on pregnancy and marriage, I did get married in June 1973 and our son was born in October 1973. Darryl II was born at Washington Regional Hospital in Fayetteville. Two weeks later, I was back in class. There was much more of a reason, now, for me to do well. I'd gone through the "wild" phase of my college life in just two years and was now ready to buckle down and become an adult. We were both very young for the kind of responsibility early marriage and parenting demands, but we vowed to make it work. Darryl was working hard to finish up his degree in business and working at night so that we could make ends meet. It was a real financial and time-management struggle and one that I wouldn't wish on any young student . . . but, we got through it.

It turned out that having my son was the best thing that could have possibly happened for me. He changed my outlook on all aspects of my life. I became a serious student, vowed to be a good wife and mother. My grades, from that point on, were better than even I would have expected. Choosing journalism was the best decision I'd made since arriving on the UA campus in 1971. It was the obvious answer, but one that I'd overlooked for the last two years. There were four African American journalism majors during the two years I was in the program. Two had graduated before. So in a way the university was opening up for history to be made, and E. Lynn Harris, Mellonee Carrigan, Overtis Hicks, and I were part of that.

My last two years as a journalism student were wonderful, though busy. I enjoyed most of my professors. During my six years on campus, I only had two African American professors —Professor Adolph Reed and Dr. Gordon Morgan. I enjoyed both of their classes very much. Dr. Morgan made us think outside the box—beyond the theory of sociology; and Professor Reed made us question the politics of America—to analyze more closely what we had been taught and told throughout our lives.

In 1975, I made history in a different way—thanks to the recommendation of my good friend, E. Lynn Harris, I was selected the first Razorback Beauty, who happened to be both married and a mother. I was also invited to try out for the Razorback cheerleaders, but that would have been pushing things a little too far. I thanked the caller and said I simply didn't have the time. Though neither of these are viewed as very substantive events to some, it did make a statement in light of the history of race and the barriers that were still falling away.

I am documented as a 1977 graduate of the university's School of Journalism, but in fact I completed my degree requirements in May 1976. I returned to the graduate school in January 1977 and took courses toward a master's of public administration. I only attended one semester and one summer session. Darryl and I moved to Little Rock, July 1977, after he graduated from the School of Business. Our son, Darryl II, was three years old by then.

In describing my feelings toward the university during my time there, I would say, overall, being a student at the University of Arkansas rates up there with the five best experiences in my life. It was a great training ground for dealing with the world, in large.

I grew up on that campus. I learned that few people in this world "give" you anything . . . you have to earn it. Though that may not be true for everyone, it is true for most people I know. I thank the UA for that lesson—no matter what their reason for teaching it.

I learned the vast diversity of our own culture—that there is as much diversity within our own race as there is between the races. I had never really given that much thought. But I also believed that it was a good thing. The other side of that is that the predominantly white student population gave me a bird's eye view of how the other half (or three-fourths) live. That experience gave me a better appreciation for being exactly what I am. I saw firsthand that, though we might not be better, we most certainly were no worse or less than any other race or culture. The television and magazine propaganda about the races just simply wasn't true.

I immensely enjoyed the beauty of the campus and the surrounding area. For me, personally, that means a great deal toward whether I can thrive mentally and emotionally in a place or not. I still think northwest Arkansas and the UA campus are some of the most beautiful sites in the country. Most of the people in Fayetteville were not consumed by race, which was a welcoming aspect of the area. I'm afraid, like most places, there were racists and there were instilled racist attitudes in at least one or two instructors I had, but I think it is saying a lot that I can remember only one or two with such attitudes.

I did feel that the class of 1971 was arriving on campus as the university's history was in the midst of change. Jon Richardson had been added to the segregated Razorback football team just two years earlier, and the basketball team was busy recruiting outstanding players from around the country. Black sororities and fraternities were being accredited on campus; blacks were being selected onto homecoming courts, to be cheerleaders and beauty queens, and slowly more black professors were being added. It was good to be a part of the positive racial progress taking place on the campus.

There was also a sense of family and security I felt in the black community on campus. We all knew each other, met, and partied together like family. There weren't enough of us, yet, to have a great number of cliques. For the most part, we were a cohesive group.

I have returned to the university quite often. I love going back to the campus. I enjoy seeing so many black faces that I certainly don't know them all, but I'm guessing they don't all know each other. That's progress and growth. It made me proud to be part of the early planning for a black alumni organization and even prouder when Dr. Lonnie Williams grew the black alumni organization to unbelievable membership. It's great to go back and talk to the new students and faculty. Each time I go, I look for progress . . . and I usually find it.

My present feelings toward the university are of gratitude and awe in the progress. I pray that it will continue to grow and progress and not get to a point where the leaders are "satisfied" with their progress. There is still so much to do—especially when it comes to our youth. The university has a ways to go to open itself up completely to diversity. There is a lot of growing room, but I can't help but see the unbelievable progress.

Thanks to the UA I made lifelong friends. I am so impressed, too, when I return and learn the amazing accomplishments of so many colleagues who went to the school. That says something about the school, yes . . . but it also says a lot about the character and integrity of the African Americans who chose the school. It was not a one-way street—just as we gained from the UA, the UA gained a great deal from bringing in outstanding young people from around this state.

■ Terry G. Lee (1973–1979), attorney

Telephone interview by Charles Robinson, August 16, 2007
For detailed biography, see Appendix A, page 304

I graduated high school from Holly Grove High in Arkansas in May of 1973 and I entered the university in September 1973. I had always inspired to pursue a law career or degree, so I majored in political science. I left there in 1979. I was finishing things up and I remained at the university, but I actually had finished.

Why did I select the University of Arkansas? Well, simply put, it was the best at the time in the state. I'm from a family of ten, seven boys and three girls. I'm number five. I'm in the middle and I am the first one in my family to attend college.

What was my role in African American history at UA? I did obtain a political science degree and then I left the university, went to St. Louis, then came back and entered Law School. I was first basically there to obtain the bachelor's degree in political science and by then quite a few firsts had been accomplished at that particular time. The only thing that I could say that I played a role in was as far as being the first would be during my stay at the university to supplement my financial situation, I became a resident assistant at Pomfret Hall, which was a relatively new dorm that had just been completed, a co-ed dorm there. And so after my freshman year through my sophomore year I became a resident assistant and remained the resident assistant throughout my stay at the university. But towards my senior year . . . junior and senior year . . . I also became president of the black student organization at the university and at the time it was called BAD, Black Americans for Democracy.

I was not the first president of that organization, but during my term as president of that organization there were racial tensions concerning blacks and whites, especially in athletics. Basically the football and basketball teams were majority, if not mostly, black and the cheerleaders were all white. And so one of the things we fought for and were able to obtain was to get the first black cheerleaders at the University of Arkansas through our efforts in BAD, the Black Americans for Democracy student organization.

I remember at the time that if we ever won a game, we were elated. The athletes and the young ladies would embrace each other and do all these other things. The officials, the athletic director, and coaches were always upset about that particular issue. This is aside from having the white females up at the athletic dorm, having instances of accused rape and things of that nature. We approached the establishment with an idea to alleviate some of that frustration by saying that it was high time for us to have black cheerleaders. In other words, I saw a negative situation and decided that it could be a positive to achieve a first. And that was since I know you don't like it, then one way to solve the problem will be to get some black cheerleaders.

Well, that didn't go over well at the time with the establishment because being African American we have heard too many times—"yeah, that's a good idea, but not now. And I have the alumni." They gave me several reasons. At the time, Frank Broyles was the athletic director and we dealt with two coaches—one with the basketball and one for the football team. I can't recall their names at this particular point, but I was dealing with Frank Broyles because he was their boss and he was the athletic director. There was an assistant athletic director also in the meeting, and they indicated that the time was not right and that that was OK.

Well, I did not take that very well because I thought it was a good idea and I understood they were very frustrated with it. They liked the idea, but they tended to be more concerned with what the establishment at the university and their alumni, which were majority white, would say at breaking new ground in a particular area. I never understood the dynamics of why it wasn't a good time. They just said it wasn't.

I did not accept this as being the last word and accept their position that any other time. I guess they never said when it would be the right time, or when I needed to get back with them. We thought about it and we (BAD) had a newspaper. We wrote about it. We had spirited meetings about it and met with various staff people and including the establishment, the president's office. I remember at that time the president of the university was a Mr. Bishop. He was also being considered for a cabinet-level position in the United States Government for I believe either commerce secretary or agriculture secretary. He went out of town and was returning to the university. He landed at the airport and so we had people to let us know that he was on his way to the university. I organized a group to surround the administration building holding hands and did not allow him to enter the building without breaking through our ranks. And so to say the least, he was very upset.

I asked him if he was going to talk to me. It created a big thing mainly because my office was right next to the Associated Student Government office, which was the larger white organization. They knew we were upset about it and so they watched my moves. . . . my every move, I should say. When we organized and got the group together, word spread, and they weren't there necessarily to assist us, they were coming to see what was going on. It drew a larger crowd than expected.

When the president was confronted with that particular situation, which he was informed of before he arrived, he agreed to talk with me and a select group of people of my choosing. He was going to have his people there, if we would disband the crowd and talk about it. I think this may have been 1975, 1976.

After that, it took us some time to submit names and individuals who were going to be trying out. After the training, the tryouts, and all of that, then they were selected the following season. I think that they actually took to the field in 1977.

My vice president at the time was E. Lynn Harris, the author. At that same time, Mr. Harris displayed his writing abilities and spent more time as the editor of the *Razorback* than as vice president of Black Americans for Democracy. Although it may have been more blacks attending the university back then than it is now, we were somewhat cohesive.

I need to give you a little bit more information on the individuals that were involved and Mr. Harris, also, to show you how he was involved in a whole lot of things. He became one of the males, but if he was going to be there they didn't want him lifting up white girls. So he had black girls.

To understand the dynamics of the political atmosphere at that time, just us being there brought tension, forced integration, and all of those other things will allow you a seat on the bus or a place in the classroom. But that does not necessarily mean that the place where you're sitting or seated has to welcome you being there. That was tense within itself. Then when you have athletes and they were the first ones that I would say raised the specter of race to a precedence of biased level in that here athletics is the moneymaker of the institution of most colleges and universities and essentially in Arkansas where there are no per se pro teams. The University of Arkansas Razorbacks had a reputation as being very good and it continues to this day as evidenced. Nolan Richardson and all . . . winning an NCAA title, so forth and so on. So they get a lot of press time and they get a lot of time on TV that normally you would not. They were somewhat glorified in a sense and so it attracted not only white females, but black females to these guys who are champions and titans, so to speak. They had a visibility and therefore with the victories go the spoils. They also had a lot of advances made to them by both black and white women.

There were several incidences of alleged rape or actual rape of people being prosecuted. I can't think of one case where there was a rape of a black female. The rape always involved white females or this girl wants to get next to you, a black athlete, so she thinks he loves her. He gets her up to the athletic dorm, has sex with her, and then turns her around to his friends. Then . . . or if he gets caught in the act or something, that which would have been consensual all of a sudden turns to rape.

So those things were going on and it was only evident in the public eye. Here's an all-black or majority-black team and the cheerleaders are white and that gets them closer to these guys than anybody else. I tried to find an opening to get something that was much needed. And it was an unwritten code that black men or women need not try out because . . . they didn't know not to try out because it was an unwritten code that you're not going to be selected.

I just wanted to clarify that it wasn't because of a specific incident that I said we got to fix this by going in and getting black cheerleaders. It was an ongoing thing that they did not necessarily like or want. One of my concerns was not to give justice to things that may not have gained notoriety that were all the more important as well. And I think one word of advice to you and Dr. Williams is that this is like a quilt, what you guys are doing. I believe that it is long overdue and it needs to be done. The story needs to be told, but it needs to be interwoven into the fabric of . . . everything is interconnected and so basically a seemingly insignificant incident between four or five people in the basement of a dorm maybe had led to a very significant incident, but no one is able to connect the dots.

I intentionally wanted to weave in other people in some notoriety and others that are not known. Author E. Lynn Harris can give you his version because he was not only an observer, he was also a participant. There were a whole lot of things that went on there . . . racial tension, fighting, expulsions, suspensions, criminal prosecutions of various things, and so forth.

Describe my feelings towards the university during my time of study at the university? That's a good question. It also conflicts. I think it needs to be answered from a perspective of where we came from, how we saw the world, our understanding and what we were exposed to once we got there. So take an eighteen-year-old from Holly Grove, Arkansas, near Stuttgart, Clarendon, Brinkley, somewhere in between Memphis and Little Rock. A farming community, a small town of less than a thousand people, majority black, forced to integrate in 1967. There is a white school on this side of town and the black school on the other side of town and then all of a sudden in the ninth grade, we are all together. Most of the white's ended up going to private schools because they could afford it. You had a farming community in workers, field hands, and the only elite in the community were teachers that taught at the black school. But I chose to go there because my mother told me that I could do anything I wanted to if I got a good education. She failed to tell me that there would be constraints on it because I was black. But that's good. Going to the university, I got to see firsthand racism and overt racism. I felt that it was an uncomfortable situation that they were doing what the law said they had to do, but it did not change people's attitudes. It was sort of like you can tell someone, it's illegal to discriminate against people and people that intend to do it will either remove themselves from the situation so that they don't have to follow the rules or they find another way to do it in a less offensive way.

I found everything that we did had to be earned, that we were even graded differently because if you have a view that I am inferior, even if my work is superior, your view of me will make you look at my work differently. Unfortunately, I didn't mind approaching or challenging [racism] because I gained a reputation early in high school after integration. I had a nickname of Nat Toon. So basically I was willing to do it, but we had the challenges.

They challenged me at every turn. They did not want me to be a resident assistant and president of a student organization. I challenged that and refused to say OK. I mean if there is no rule, the housing director just said, "You can't do it. You have to choose one or the other," and so I appealed his decision and the president of the university over-rode the housing director. I was the byproduct of a feud between them so anything that one was for, the other one was against. I was the beneficiary of it, but I can't say that he necessarily believes that they were doing it for my good. You get too involved and your grades are going to suffer, but I saw it as you just don't have the ability to do both—to do a good job in both and so I'm going to make you. But he couldn't tell me anything that prohibited it and when I appealed it, I won and remained the president of the black student organization as well as a resident assistant in Pomfret.

There were things of that nature that we continually had to prove ourselves. We had to always show that we were as good. We could never be better. We always had to prove that we were and we didn't have the full commitment from the university at that time. Anything we wanted, we either had to fight for it or demand it, and hopefully that has changed, but I don't think it has been totally eliminated.

I have attended two or three of the Black Alumni Reunions. I believe Lonnie Williams was instrumental in getting that started and bringing back the old heads, so to speak. The first two or three I attended. We would come back, some famous, and some not so famous. . . . tell the younger ones what we did and what the conditions were when we were there. As time went on, I've been back several times throughout the years to attend those reunions. And it's only, I'd say, during the last ten years that I have not been back.

Well, the feelings at this point are somewhat mixed in that now I pay my dues and I am a member of the Alumni Association as an entity with the Black Alumni Association. Once you join one you belong to the other. There's a chapter here I stay in contact with. I mean not the black one, but the white one. They e-mail us. They have tailgate parties if Arkansas is playing here or nearby, and host regular meetings. I said we need to have black chapters not only just the overall organization, but have chapters in the various cities where blacks have gone to work, so forth and so on. Lonnie attended one before he left the university or left Fayetteville to go to Jonesboro. We had a gathering here. He was going to be in town, we e-mailed everybody, and looked up a member list, got a pretty good turnout. We met at Dave's and Buster's, which is a popular place here that actually started in Arkansas.

But anyway, we met there and in recent years there has been a push for the more recent graduates to help boost enrollment and some of them that have done TV ads and so forth. They had us doing ads and commercials and I wasn't sure of all the details, but it appears that for some reason the university was being criticized for not having as much or a larger percentage of African Americans.

Now, we had that same situation when we were there. We're going back twenty-five or thirty years and it's the same deal, which shows me that there has not been a true commitment to recruiting blacks or retaining them there. Retention is a big problem. If you can get them there, but a lot of the athletes were playing ball, winning championships, and leaving without degrees.

I think my opinion is sort of the same as it was there before. It is unsettling to continue to hear the same problems and situations that I've encountered twenty-five, thirty years ago. I have an eighteen-year-old daughter. She graduated high school and started college last year. She is now in her sophomore year in a college here in Georgia. Her mother and father both attended and graduated from the University of Arkansas. My wife graduated with an engineering degree, industrial engineering, and I graduated with a political science degree. She obtained a full scholarship at a school here. Well, there were several schools that offered it to her, but she wanted to go somewhere near us.

We would have been able to get that same scholarship and financing at the university where it wouldn't have cost her anything. We did discuss it with her, but from what she knows and from our experiences, it was not one of the schools on her list.

▪ Charles Magee (1979–1984), university professor

Written response to interview questions, July 25, 2007
For detailed biography, see Appendix A, page 304

I worked at the University of Arkansas from November 1979 to May 1984. The university contacted me in the fall of 1979, when I was completing my PhD program in agricultural and biological engineering at Cornell University. They invited me to apply for an assistant professor position in the Department of Agricultural Engineering. I applied and accepted an offer for an interview. During the interview, the university's representatives convinced me the University of Arkansas would be a good place to work. I agreed and accepted the position in November 1979.

I worked at the university from November 1979 through May 1984 as an assistant professor of agricultural engineering in the Department of Agricultural Engineering. I was the first African American assistant professor employed in the Department of Agricultural Engineering and probably the first in the College of Agriculture.

Overall, my experience at the University of Arkansas was positive. I met and made some lifelong friends and colleagues, both black and white. However, there were a few incidents and occasions where I was being used just to satisfy racial diversity. One event in particular that I remember was the annual banquet that used to be held by the College of Agriculture for the agricultural students from the University of Arkansas, Pine Bluff. All of these students were African American. Supposedly, the purpose of this banquet was to recruit African Americans into the college. However, at the time, I felt the only real purpose was to put it in the civil rights report. One year after my arrival at the University of Arkansas, the assistant dean for the ag college insisted that I be the keynote speaker for this banquet, and I reluctantly accepted. He expected me to spout the company line; that is, how badly they wanted these students in the College of Agriculture. When my speech was contrary to what they expected, the assistant dean probably did not speak to me for the next six months.

When I joined the faculty in 1979, I felt the university was mainly trying to satisfy a federal civil rights mandate. Even though I have not been back to the campus since 1984, I have kept track of the university's efforts to diversify through friends, colleagues, and newsletters. The university has made considerable progress in diversifying its faculty, staff, administration, and student body. It has done a fairly good job in recruiting and graduating minority graduate students. Thus, I would like to commend the university for its success in this area. The University of Arkansas turned out to be a good steppingstone for my professional career.

Having grown up in Mississippi in the 1950s and 1960s, I never thought I would be teaching at the University of Arkansas, Fayetteville, just thirteen years after graduating from high school in 1966. As a nation, we have made considerable progress, but still have a long way to go before the playing field is level. My most vivid memory at the University of Arkansas is the concern and trepidation some of my white male colleagues had about me teaching two classes with mostly white females and a fairly attractive white teaching assistant (TA). I was assigned to teach two sections of a house design course for interior design majors. This course consisted of about 90 percent white females. Almost every time I would see one of my colleagues he would always highlight the make-up of my course and how pretty my TA was. I knew he was trying to feel me out to determine if I had an interest in my TA or one of the students. This was of great concern to him, since I was a young, single, PhD out of Cornell. He strongly believed the stereotype that every black man would want to have an intimate relationship with a white female. This colleague's concern and trepidation was ameliorated when I got married eight months after my arrival at the University of Arkansas, Fayetteville. From that point on, he very seldom mentioned my TA or the class.

■ Angela Mosley Monts (1976–1980, 2003–present), university administrator and minister

Written response to interview questions, November 27, 2007
For detailed biography, see Appendix A, page 304

I entered the UA in fall 1976. I majored in broadcast journalism and received a BA degree in 1980. I was young, crazy, naïve, and in love with my high school sweetheart. His name was Kevin Evans. He had received a football scholarship. My second reason (for attending UA), my father, mother, and grandmother thought it would be awesome for me to attend the school where blacks were not wanted. My great-grandmother was ten years old when slavery was abolished. My grandmother felt by me attending the UA, this was an opportunity for me to be the first one in my family to graduate from an institution that gave the appearance of not wanting African Americans. I attended three and a half years. I graduated a semester early.

Describe my experience at the UA? I was with a group of first African Americans, led by the late Bruce Mitchell, to stand up and say we needed African American cheerleaders. Although I tried out, I did not become a cheerleader, but my roommate, the late Dionne Harold, and E. Lynn Harris were the first African American Cheerleaders.

I felt very alone many times in the classroom. I was 95 percent of the time the only African American in my class. As a freshman, I would walk into one of the auditoriums and look around to see if there were other African Americans. The answer would be no. As a sophomore, junior, and senior, I became insensitive to checking to see if there was someone else there that looked like me. I learned to go to the front of the class, never the back, because I realized people had died and been killed for me to sit at the front of the class. But it was a lonely time.

It was very rare to have an African American professor. The African American students (the small number that existed, but compared to today it was a great number) would take certain courses as an elective to have an opportunity to interact with Dr. Margaret Clark, Dr. Gordon Morgan, the late Dr. Harry Budd, and Professor Adolph Reed. The African American staff also provided a "safe haven." I remember a Mr. Clark, Semon and Deborah Thompson, and a young lady in the financial aid office who were a tremendous help for securing funds for tuition.

Every African American on campus, regardless if you were an undergrad, graduate, or law student, we knew each other. We spoke and talked to each other. We were involved with organizations to bring us together for unity. During class time, we rarely saw another African American unless we were passing them on our way to class. I can remember walking down Dickson Street to go to the physics building and I saw this African American female. Excited, we crossed the street and began to talk to each other. She introduced herself as Isabella Wofford from Stuttgart, Arkansas. I later learned she was from Casco. This is how relationships began. Isabella and I later became roommates and sorority sisters.

The ever-evolving BAD (Black Students for Democracy) and then STAND (Students Taking A New Dimension) were the African American organizations and forums for students. We discussed issues facing students on campus; we relaxed, networked, and shared ideas. This group also was instrumental in bringing black artists and speakers to campus. The organization was a place you could go and everyone in the room looked like you. Whew! Thank you, Jesus. I also served on many organizations' boards. One board in particular was the judicial board. The late Gary Roper, an African American, was always before the judiciary board. I applaud the brother. He made sure the UA did what it was suppose to do from the administration down to the students.

We all got along. There was no way the Deltas could have a party without the AKAs, Alphas, Kappas, Sigmas, Zetas, and the Omegas. We got along. Every now and then, the Kappas would do something to make everyone mad, but we had a wonderful time as Greeks at the UA. We not only had fun with other Greeks, but with all students. I am a member of the Kappa Iota (KI) Chapter of Alpha Kappa Alpha Sorority, Inc. I had a wonderful time with my sorority sisters. I had so much fun; I wanted to pass this legacy down to my children. One of my daughters currently is a member in the KI Chapter. I guess what stuck with me was that this is a lifelong commitment. Building a legacy in my family was important. I remember on game days when the white fraternities and sororities would have mom and dad day. I remember generations coming back to the UA to participate in the celebration. I thought to myself that someday black Greeks will return to the university with their families as well.

My feelings were determination, an increased drive to excel and accomplish my goals and objectives. My goal was to leave the UA with a degree. I was not going to accept "no" from anyone that I could not achieve my goal. My goal was not a goal set only for me, but it was a goal set by my great-grandmother, who was ten years old when slavery was abolished. It was a goal set by a grandmother who had an eighth-grade education, but was a real estate entrepreneur. It was a goal set by my mother and father, who sacrificed everything to put four children through college, although my father never attended college and my mother attended two years of college.

I also knew I didn't want to stay for an additional semester. I studied hard and I played hard. I had good instructors. I did hear horror stories from students in the business college. I don't think the professors and advisors there (Business) were as helpful as the professors were in the journalism department and the Fulbright College.

I returned to the U of A a couple of times in the 1980s to attend Kappa Iota events for Alpha Kappa Alpha Sorority, Inc. But I really started coming back for the BAS reunions. We would have so much fun. Because of my involvement with the reunions, I became a member of the BAS board. My membership on the board eventually led me to a staff position with the Arkansas Alumni Association. I became the "Lonnie Williams" for the reunions. Only kidding, Lonnie. No one can replace the infamous Lonnie. Lonnie is a legacy who can't be replaced. The reunions are described as the largest event on campus that is not an athletic event. The reunions also gave some African Americans a reason to return to campus. But many still elect not to come back based on the treatment they received when they were here.

As the coordinator for the Black Alumni Society, many alumni tell their stories of why they have elected not to return for the reunion. Some of their past experiences are mind boggling, hurtful, and depressing. I've also had an opportunity to speak to other alumni who simply had a wonderful time at the university. Those alumni feel they had a great experience on campus, student life, and with the colleges and professors. They acknowledge their success because of the university.

I feel the university has come a long way since the 1970s. But I also feel the university has a long way to go. Diversity has to be a mindset that is woven into the fabric of the university's foundation. Diversity can no longer be the red-haired stepchild. Diversity is a reality that will not go away. The university has to seriously deal with diversity or stop saying it is a vital part of its spine. Diversity cannot be achieved by eliminating segments of the population by using ACT scores, grade points, or by not meeting need-based financial challenges. Diversity must be achieved by all means necessary. We must provide diverse students, faculty, and staff at the university, if the university truly wants to become "a nationally competitive student-centered research university serving Arkansas and the world."

I truly love the institution from which I received my undergraduate degree. I loved the institution so much, I sent my daughters here. My older daughter will receive her BS in 2008. My second daughter will receive her BS in 2010. My younger daughter will enroll in the university in 2010.

Is the university perfect? The university is far from being perfect, but I also believe it is not the worst experience an eighteen-year-old can encounter. My experiences at the UA prepared me for life. I received an on-the-job training for how I would encompass life. I had hard times. I remember when I took twenty-one hours and had a 3.5 that semester. I remember being the only black face in corporate America's boardrooms. I remember being the only black face in Kimpel Auditorium. I walked to the front, took my seat, took out my paper, and proceeded to learn. I walked over, sat by the regional president, took out my note pad, and proceeded to learn in the boardroom. The university helped to provide me with courage, security, assertiveness, and aggressiveness.

I remember crying tears of frustration, disgust, anguish, and wondering why I chose to get an education at a university that only wanted black football players and other black students were a byproduct that happened to come for an education. I remember crying those same tears of frustration, disgust, and anguish in corporate America. The eighties were a time when the word diversity was starting to surface. Corporate America realized the minority population made up a large number of its market share. No longer could product or market promotions look like the paper it was written on. Corporate America brought minorities into the board-room, but made sure a glass ceiling existed. The university brought minorities to the university, but made sure a class ceiling existed. Ceilings are made to be shattered and renovated. Corporate America and the university taught me to shatter and renovate ceilings in my life, whether they were personal or professional.

The university provided me with a stage to begin production on my life goals, aspirations, dreams, and principles. The lessons taught by the university were not only in academia, but also socially. At the time, I sometimes could not appreciate what was happening in my life, but now I look back, and I applaud myself with the help of God, Jesus, and the Holy Spirit direct-ing my life to have come to the university, sought and conquered my fears in and out of the classroom, and then onto the boardroom.

When I no longer felt corporate America was where the Lord wanted me to remain, the university became my source of employment. But just like I learned from corporate America, I have put those principles into place every day. I also learned from the university. I can do all things through Christ, who strengthens me, whether that is obtaining an education, applying for a job, or interacting with lifelong friends. I can make it because I made it at the University of Arkansas, Fayetteville. The curtains fall and the performance ends with a standing ovation because the stage at the UA was a perfect backdrop for my life.

■ Lloyd A. Myers (1976–1981), architect

Written response to interview questions, March 12, 2009
For detailed biography, see Appendix A, page 305

My experience as an African American student at the University of Arkansas was from 1976 through 1981. My arrival to the University of Arkansas followed an exciting and per-sonally fulfilling senior year at Little Rock Central High. Upon arrival at the University of Arkansas with my parents in the fall of 1976, I was pumped full of enthusiasm and high expectations set for myself. I was consumed by the challenge ahead to be accepted into the School of Architecture.

It didn't take long after my freshman year for the enticement to serve to re-surface. Several upperclassmen and fellow classmates who knew me from Little Rock encouraged me to become active with student politics on campus. Most were Alpha Phi Alpha fraternity mem-bers who knew my father, the Reverend Lloyd H. Myers, a lifetime member and former A Phi A national secretary, first in his class from Philander Smith College. I was soon disenchanted, though, with the Greek organizations as their agendas appeared then shallow and self-serving. Nor was I at all interested in anyone "paddling" or hazing me in any other way. My then-hardened view now toward Greeks is much more tepid now; I see the good they do and respect that. There are many times now that I wish I were an Alpha, like Dad. I'm not sure how, but almost immediately, I was chosen to represent our co-ed dorm on the Student Government Association. Immediately, running for president of the SGA was in my scope.

More eminent, however, were the conditions of student life for the African American student. There was a void with black student leaders and I had natural leadership skills. In the years since, I am grateful to other student leaders about campus, especially E. Lynn Harris, for nominating me to several campus-wide committees, which led to my voice soon being heard in many symposiums, panels, workshops, and dorm meetings all over campus. I was asked to emcee the Miss Black U of A pageant and soon after was scorned by some of my professors for having too many "irons in the fire." Not to be discouraged, I was totally enthralled by my ability to lead and with a vision that I felt I must share in some way, shape, or form. There were other student leaders like pre-law student Rodney Slater, student pastor Ron Lee, and Beverly Norwood who were leaders in their own right and great allies.

Black Americans for Democracy was the current black student organization. I believe it had been around for ten years or so. Although it was in capable hands, I saw a tendency for the black students to not engage in BAD and for the vast majority to take a very apathetic position on campus and reinforce divisiveness among ourselves. Clearly fraternities and sororities had much to do with this and I refused to accept that the few of us could not benefit from one another's friendship and camaraderie. One's first inclination was not to join something that had a clenched fist as a symbol and who's acronym was BAD. It's time had passed; perhaps left over from a time of greater frustration following the assassinations of the 1960s. I'm sure the decade of BAD was warranted and necessary for the injustices of the times. It was time for a new dimension to the black student condition. It became my most pressing mission to get students to get along better and to show an allegiance to one another as fellow black students trying to better ourselves. To me, this came only after love of God and respect for fellow humans. Certainly, this was more important than any allegiance to a Greek fraternity or sorority! Right? Why assimilate? Couldn't we create our own African fraternities and sororities? Well, as you know, I wasn't going to win that one!

Back to the black student union, BAD. I saw a need to redefine our purpose on campus. This is THE formative time in our maturation to adults. I, and others agreed, that "BAD" was not the analogy that we wanted for ourselves. Besides, Michael Jackson had not yet made bad a good thing.

The stereotypes in northwest Arkansas were deeply ingrained in the city and racial tension was always high. We all knew there were boundaries after which we didn't feel safe, even as students. This virtual boundary wasn't very far off the campus. Many of us were even uncomfortable at the local mall where I worked my freshman year.

It didn't take long to realize that the "climate" in the Fayetteville area wasn't so liberal. This was the first encounter of "conservatism" in my lifetime. I couldn't help but wonder what it must have been like when my mother was at the U of A working on her master's in the mid-1960s.

Although the demographics at the UA were quite different from Little Rock Central, I somehow felt that a positive image of the black student organization required a new identity beginning with a new name. After an enthusiastic student competition, STAND—Students Taking A New Dimension—was selected by votes of BAD's members. What was this new dimension? Who knew, but it was positive, that's for sure. I suppose it meant different things to different people. To me it was about carrying yourself in a certain way, deserving and subsequently requiring respect from those you associated with. Stand up! This was STAND to me. I later drew the *now* embarrassing logo that sold hundreds of t-shirts around campus. We wore them proudly. The professors at Vol Walker thought of me as a radical. Some were supportive, but they urged me to stay focused on architecture, which I eventually did. Although I was a bit of a recluse, STAND demanded that I invest in me in other ways than the classroom.

What draws a group of students from varying backgrounds together for four years to become engaged in a student organization with a cause? That was our charge. We went about restructuring the organization—chart and all—which was to be grounded by standing committees that were the heart and soul of the organization and allowed anyone to play a role. We encouraged students to play to their strengths and to get involved. STAND should be the best of us collectively.

We fought for representation on all the president's student committees. I often spoke. Looking back, I was always so serious. Thank God I out-grew that! [Smile]. We produced a newsletter to make sure our VOICES were heard. We made issue of real problems facing us. We worked within the system. We were systematic and made good sense. We got attention and were respected; we stood up. Several law students, grad students, and professors got involved and offered their knowledge and advice. We later won a senatorial seat on the SGA. We solicited and politicked for more funds, which we attained. We reached out and honored the elders in the community. I seem to recall that we were about 5 percent of the total student population of 15,000. We became a bright light on campus and were invited to work alongside the university's administration in trying to increase the black student population up to 9 percent by 1985 or something like that. The president often acknowledged us, usually through a liaison (a black staffer). We made big plans, established a Cultural Awareness Week, produced the Miss Black UA pageant, booked activist Dick Gregory, Ebony Fashion Fair, Coretta Scott King, and others. Mostly, we went about trying to better communications and relations among black students and our fellow white students as well as from Africa, Iran, Asia, and other cultures.

At the year's end, we held an Honors Convocation and acknowledged outstanding students, faculty, and staff. It was a good year, but clearly there was much to do. STAND thrived and had good leadership in the years to follow. That was twenty eight years ago. I have no idea how STAND has done since. I doubt it still exists in its original form, but I do hope its spirit lives on the Fayetteville campus of the University of Arkansas.

■ C. Calvin Smith (1970–1978), university professor

Written response to interview questions, August 25, 2007
For detailed biography, see Appendix A, page 305

I was a graduate student in the doctoral program (PhD) at the U of A, summers 1970–1974; 1975–1976 academic year; PhD history, 1978. I always wanted to attend the university and it offered me the best financial program for graduate study.

I was one of the first blacks to earn a PhD in history at the university. The other was Dr. Bobby Lovett (Tennessee State University). We graduated the same year.

The vast majority of my time at the university was spent pursuing my degree program. I was on a one-year sabbatical from Arkansas State University and had little time for extracurricular activities. There were few graduate minority students on campus during that time at the university, but my time there as a full-time student was made less stressful because I had one fraternity brother on the U of A faculty (Dr. Gordon Morgan) and one former instructor (Adolph Reed) from my undergraduate years at AM&N College in Pine Bluff, Arkansas. There were also two professors in the Department of History with whom I developed close relationships, Drs. Timothy Donovan and Willard Gatewood. All of these people made my pursuit of the doctorate successful. Although my free time was limited, there is one event that stands out. I was one of the sponsors of the first black fraternity on the U of A campus, Omega Psi Phi, Inc., fall 1974.

Other than my fraternity association, my feeling toward the university was almost entirely academic related and remains so today.

■ Morris Sylvester (1971–1976), accountant

Written response to interview questions, September 13, 2007
No detailed biography available

I entered the University of Arkansas in 1971 to pursue a BSBA in accounting. My reasons for attending were the financial support through various programs and it was the number one college in the state of Arkansas. I attended from 1971 to 1976.

I was quite active on campus. I was the first black elected to the University of Arkansas Resident Hall Association—vice president. I was the first black voice on the campus radio, KUAF, with a special black program. I worked on campus for a while as the first black dispatcher for the University of Arkansas police department. I was a founding member of the first black fraternity to be chartered on the UAF campus, Omega Psi Phi Fraternity, Inc. I served as editor of *BAD Times* newspaper by Black Americans for Democracy, and I believe I was the first black member of the University of Arkansas ROTC Special Drill Team.

Looking back over my experiences at the university, one special event comes to mind: I was on the radio working the late-night shift (10 P.M.–2 A.M.) with a serious storm approaching. I read every fifteen minutes the weather update from the teletype and I received this crazy call that said "Nig—if it rains tonight, your ass is dead." I will never, ever forget that call.

My feelings toward the university at the time I attended were that I knew I was not welcomed or wanted and the university did not put any efforts into making any of us feel safe or comfortable. My first accounting class was a special occasion. I went to my accounting 1001 (Mrs. Reed) and I sat on the front row of her classroom. She stared me down and said, "I don't want no nigras ever sitting this close to me. Move to the back of the room." I moved and received a "D" in my first accounting class. And yes, I re-took the class the next semester and received a "B."

I have returned to the university on several occasions, including speaking engagements, fund-raisers, and alumni-sponsored events. I was also featured in the *College of Business Administration Magazine* in the fall of 1993 issue as one with "Perseverance." My feeling at the present time is that the university is a great place to get an education and that is a positive thing.

■ Frederick Tollette (1974–1979)

Interview by Lonnie R. Williams, September 27, 2007
Interviewed in home of Reverend Sanford Tollette III
No detailed biography available

My name is Frederick Tollette. I entered the University of Arkansas in fall 1974. My degree is a BA in chemistry.

The University of Arkansas . . . that's about all I knew growing up in Arkansas. I kind of wanted to go to Howard University, but my parents wouldn't let me go that far. But in the same breath, we had a family heritage. My father (Sanford Tollette III) and my brother (Sanford Tollette IV) both attended the University of Arkansas, Fayetteville. I was there five years.

What was my role in the history of African Americans at the UA? I was the first black chairman of the Arkansas Union Governing Board, Arkansas Student Union Governing Board. That had to be back in 1978, 1977.

The University of Arkansas was quite an interesting entity when I was there. My era followed suit from the ones that came before us. We helped solidify and get the black representation of the university more prevalent; for instance, having our first black cheerleader and having our first black campus beauties. We wanted to make sure we were well represented. And that was probably just because of our forefathers. I know they were trying to do some things also, but we were the young bucks that came up there and we were the radicals with sense. We just knew how far to go so the university would not send us away.

My experiences there were difficult, but enjoyable. I had experiences in the chemistry department. I had a couple of professors tell me that I couldn't pass their class no matter what I did. I was like, what do you mean? And they told me point blank that I would not pass their class. My only glory at this point came in the end when my best friend walked across the stage and they said valedictorian, BA in chemistry. The whole department stood up and clapped. I came right behind him, Frederick Tollette, BA in chemistry, and all their mouths dropped open and I went, "Gotcha!" [Laughing.]

But what happened with that is I learned to maneuver because back then there were difficulties for black people. I was fortunate to have a French last name. I learned to use that to my advantage. I didn't challenge all those things I probably would've challenged before because I wanted to make sure I got my degree, since my parents were paying for it. They told me it was time for me to come out of there, so I learned to use that French last name to my advantage. If they didn't see me, they didn't know what I was because of a French last name.

I have no regrets. If I had to do it over, I would do it again because it has made a difference for those that are coming behind me. They need to know that some of us did stand up for what we needed to do at that university. But that university needs to know what we can do as black Americans.

You know, describing my feelings about the university while there, that's a bittersweet question. Being as young as I was, it did not matter what the university said I couldn't do because I knew what I was going to do. But in retrospect, I did see so many people come and go, which gave me a level of understanding of what the university was about, if you did not have the stamina to stay and fight, because it was always a battle. We had to fight for what we deserved even when we should not have had to.

Of course I've returned. That's my alma mater. No matter what, I have my degree from there. So I will always go back because that is still a part of me. My major reason for returning was to be a part of the Black Alumni Association and that is what made me begin to go back to the university campus—because that association is something that is needed and that has been viable. That has made the University of Arkansas wake up, meaning, the white alumni association, which is supposed to be the alumni association not labeled white or black. So that's what really brought me back to the university.

I don't think my feelings for the university have changed, not that much. But if I understand correctly, our numbers (African Americans) are still very low as far as recruitment and retaining of African Americans at the university. They still have a way to go. Apparently they are trying to do their part, but it's not enough yet.

I would tell anyone from the state of Arkansas who wants to get a quality education, not slighting any other fine institutions of higher learning in the state of Arkansas, the University of Arkansas is our number-one calling card supposedly for the state of Arkansas. If you have the opportunity to go there, I would say go. Fight that battle and get that degree.

■ Charlie L. Tolliver (1976–1981), university professor

Telephone interview by Lonnie R. Williams, August 26, 2007
For detailed biography, see Appendix A, page 306

I went to the University of Arkansas in 1976 as a professor in electrical engineering. I came to recruit minority students for the College of Engineering. I was the first African American professor in the College of Engineering.

Why did I select the University of Arkansas? Well, when I was in graduate school, a white guy bet me that I couldn't get the job. I called the department head and he asked me down for an interview. We talked. I liked what he said and I decided to come.

I was there from 1976 to 1981.

I wrote a proposal to the Winthrop Rockefeller Foundation, in connection with changing the minority engineering program. My goal was to get 13 percent minorities in the school, which I finally got up to 9 percent.

I hate to say this, but it was pure hell being there. I worked through a lot of racial problems. I had things put on my door. I had professors trying to get the cops to get me a ticket. I had professors to try and set me up with other professors' wives and when it failed they came back and told me. It was rough.

I feel kind of bitter about it because people were attacking me from different angles. It was strictly a racial problem, which I hated to deal with in my department, the college, and the city. Some of the professors were nice. Some of them were pure racists.

I haven't been back to the University of Arkansas since I left there in 1981. I filed my lawsuit against the University of Arkansas for discrimination and after my lawsuit was over they didn't give me employment during the summer. I left the summer of 1981 and I haven't returned back there since. Discrimination and harassment in the Department of Electrical Engineering was the premise of my lawsuit.

When you get old, you learn to try to understand why people do what they do. I learned to get along better after I left and saw some of the racial problems there, and the racial problems here in Houston. It is racial wherever you go. I met a lot of different good people, including whites, there at Fayetteville. Some of them were real nice and some of them gave me some junk when I went to the country club. I went there and someone asked me, "Whose wife are you here with tonight?" I tried to joke with him. I said, "And I am here with your wife." And he didn't say anything else to me. I'm not bitter. I just resent some of the things that happened.

The behavior pattern, the way they treat blacks, that's the problem—the way they have professors treat blacks. If you're a black and try to get along, I guess that means you're good. If you're kind of hotheaded, outspoken, they will "fluck" you. I feel sorry for the black kids. When I came there, there were twenty-three in engineering. And nineteen of them were on probation. I decided to come there for one year, in the summer 1976 and I was going to leave in 1977, but I stayed until 1981. I was trying to help as many black and white students as possible.

The TRMEP (Transition Retention Minority Engineering Program) proved that blacks could learn just as equals or better than the whites, if given the opportunity. I remember the grades. I remember incoming freshman at the University of Arkansas were 2.6 overall and my TRMEP Program was 2.73. I had some good professors in mathematics who taught these students. We taught English, pre-calculus, college algebra, and trigonometry to these students. When I got the program through the Winthrop Rockefeller Foundation, Dean Halligan told me, "Don't start it until the next year." I said, "No, I wanted to start it the same year." I had visited practically all the high schools in the state of Arkansas, talked to principals about their students. I had a lot of students ready to come to the University of Arkansas. I got the program and sent out my advertising. I was advertising for thirty-seven and I believe I got fifty-seven students. We admitted thirty-seven students I recall for that first year. They were quite successful. And we gave them a scholarship in the fall.

By the time the grant had ended the enrollment of African Americans in engineering had more than quadrupled. We had less than 1 percent in engineering and I think it went up to about 9 percent, if I recall. Nine percent enrollment of the blacks in engineering was due to my TRMEP program.

My assistant was Lonnie Ray Williams, and he was good. We worked closely together recruiting minority students. We had cookouts at one of the instructor's home nearly every weekend. He was a superb professor [Bill Orton]. He wanted the blacks to succeed there at the University of Arkansas. There were about three or four of the white professors who really wanted them to succeed. Some of them taught free in the program.

The African American faculty and staff at that point in time were not that large. We gave parties at various faculty members home. We gave a big party all the time. John Mitchell [assistant head coach for Pittsburgh Steelers now] would throw a party at his house on Friday night, just to give the community a place to gather.

I hope the next professor that comes there in the College of Engineering will be successful. It's a problem if they don't know how to treat professors as equals, not as a second-class professor but an equal professor. When you think, though, when I was getting that program the department head wanted to put us in the basement. I raised some concern and they put us up on the second floor. They wanted us in the basement, so the blacks wouldn't be seen. Dean Halligan, who became interim president at the University of Arkansas, when I went to him about some of the problems that I had, he told me, "I am a southerner and I do everything right." That's about all I have to say about that.

I hope you have the best success in everything you are trying to do. I hope they have removed some of the negative things that were there when I was there. I hope they have gone.

■ Trent A. Walton (1977–1981), university administrator

Written response to interview questions, February 9, 2009
For detailed biography, see Appendix A, page 306

I entered the university in 1977. My degree major was chemical engineering. Dr. Loren Heiple recruited me in mid-August. I had no plans to attend the U of A at the time I received a cold call from him inviting me to come up to the campus from Forrest City, Arkansas. My mother, Earnestine Walton Russell (MS Ed., 1969), also encouraged me to go to Fayetteville and to hear what Dr. Heiple had to say. She agreed to accompany me. That day, I made a major career and life-path change.

I attended the University of Arkansas twice: BS studies from 1977 to 1981, and later returning from industry for my master's degree in chemical engineering, 1982–1983. I was the first black student (and only one to my knowledge) to be recruited away from MIT to attend Arkansas for the purpose of being a "role model." Dr. Heiple described to my mother and me that he envisioned my role was to specifically answer the challenge of "demonstrating to other students and to my faculty that a black student could come here from eastern Arkansas and do well in engineering." At that time, I had no real concept of what a role model was, but I liked the sound of the challenge, knowing that my mother had also walked these sands in Fayetteville some years before completing her master's as a returning nontypical student between 1968 and December 1969. I also was too young to really appreciate Dr. Heiple for his strength and visionary leadership, actively seeking to make a difference in both the makeup and the environment of the College of Engineering in the mid-1970s.

The first thing I noticed when I got there was the isolation, lack of support, and structure for new students. I witnessed a handicapped young man on crutches, who happened to be black, arrive by cab as a freshman. As I was busy unloading with my family, I noticed as he sought directions, help on where to go, and to with whom to check in. I stopped briefly to ask if he needed help, but he declined. Sometime during this process, someone took all the young man's belongings from the curbside where the cab had left them. I saw him crying openly. He later called another cab, never to return again. I witnessed others have their hopes dashed due to an absence of structured support for new students. Many of them were like me, from humble beginnings and small/rural towns.

Those of us who survived through the years learned quickly to lean on each other, as we were small in numbers. Many days I only saw one or two other African Americans in my classrooms. Sometimes it was the same one or two and sometimes no one else that looked like me. I learned that I had to also have an internal compass to keep me moving forward because cultural isolation was simply part of my reality.

As a member of BAD (Black Americans for Democracy) and STAND (Students Taking a

New Dimension), I worked with Dr. Martin (president of the university) and other administrators on several student issues such as the refusal of barbers to cut the hair of black students in the Student Union barbershop. This issue had several evolutions. First, a black barber was hired and it was proposed that he cut our (black students') hair. Later, the barbers told us that if others saw them put their clippers to our heads, they would not be able to keep their white customers. Later, if memory is correct, the Union closed the barbershop.

In a strange way, the university experience caused all sorts of personal growth and skill development that was not on the curriculum. We had to develop novel coping skills. Our way of coping was to go to Sears and J C Penney, buy our own clippers, and give each other "bootleg" haircuts, if you did not have a car or could not afford to wait in long lines at the few available barbers down in the "hollow" (another name referring to the black community). To this day, I have only paid for two haircuts since 1977, lest I forget that simple pleasures should not be taken for granted. I have also passed this skill down to my two sons, who have been cutting their own hair for about ten years.

I served as a national delegate to the NSBE (National Society of Black Engineers), traveling to national conventions in Ohio and Pennsylvania under the direction of Dr. Charles Tolliver, electrical engineering professor. We later attended a regional meeting here where a major corporate representative told the entire meeting that "finding an articulate black engineering student is as rare as finding a talking dog" to the utter shock and dismay of the audience of more than one hundred black engineering student members of NSBE. This made many of us even more determined to succeed.

I felt that the university was doubly challenging curriculum-wise and culturally. I served as an undergraduate student ambassador for the engineering college, encouraging other students from eastern Arkansas to come up to "the hill." Parents had to be convinced as well as the students to take that leap of faith. I also was named on the Bell Engineering Design Approval Committee, having only a minimal role to provide input on restroom accommodations in the building plan. I served as a hall senator and also on the RHA (Resident Housing Association) J-board (judiciary board) where I heard several cases involving student issues. I did what I could to make things better.

I actively supported the College of Engineering and the Black Alumni Association over the years. I also have coordinated a joint effort with the university's Multicultural Center, then under the direction of Dr. Lonnie Williams, and brought the P&G's Underground Railroad Freedom Center Road Show to the U of A campus.

I care deeply for the university. This feeling is unchanged. Home is home, whether a mansion or a cottage . . . whether neat or disorganized . . . whether peaceful or full of turmoil—it's still home and you will always love home. When I return to campus now and see the vast increase in diversity, including other races other than black, I am encouraged. There are still areas where significant challenges remain. I do things to make a difference whenever I can . . . I come and talk to students, I send my own children here, and I donate regularly to a freshman scholarship fund that my wife and I created with the help of the BAS and Mrs. Angela Monts.

The years have taught me that the lessons learned on this campus prepared us for the challenges of the world ahead. In recognition of the contrast to some who may see it differently, I feel that it was a good character-hardening, or toughening, experience that made us true survivors and underpins the subsequent successes we encountered later in life.

I will do all I can to see the university continue to improve its diversity and environment for historically underrepresented groups while they get an EXCELLENT education that the U of A is known for. Moving back to Fayetteville in 2001 with my professional career, I saw many things have changed significantly and a few have not. The university is still a place where one can get a top-notch education. The university is still a place where we are making positive progress.

There is one thing that has definitely changed. I now see a new generation of innocence walking around the campus with no knowledge or conscious thought of what challenges their African American predecessors experienced walking to and from on those same prestigious sidewalks. I believe it is a good thing they do not have the baggage; however, I believe it is a terrible thing if they do not have knowledge and appreciation for the past struggles of those who worked so hard to reach their goals. Many steps were made looking down—not to avoid tripping over some upcoming obstacle, but to affirm that one had a firm footing where they stood right then . . . right there. Many days' tomorrow had to take care of tomorrow. With God's help, we saw the next day . . . and with his continuing help we will see a much-better tomorrow.

■ Lonnie R. Williams (1972–2003), university administrator

Interview by Charles Robinson, January 31, 2009
Interviewed in office of Charles Robinson, University of Arkansas, Fayetteville campus
For detailed biography, see Appendix A, page 307

I entered the University of Arkansas in the fall of 1972. My goal was to obtain a degree in mechanical engineering. I came here with the valedictorian of my high school class from Stephens, Arkansas. We called him Bobby, William "Bobby" Hanson. We were the first two African Americans from Stephens High School to come here as undergraduates. We kind of started a little trail. From there, seventeen other African Americans from Stephens High School migrated to the University of Arkansas. That seventeen included my sister Kathy; first cousin Cedric Williams; cousins Karress Manning, Trudell, Margie Nell, and Jackie Jones; and neighbors Yolonda Joe, Tanisha Joe, Marcia Porchia, Jerry Brown, Catrelle Henderson, Darnell "Pop" Bell, Eli Charles, Jennifer Lamar, and Victor Ross and his sister Kim. Like I said, I came here to major in mechanical engineering. That was a little lopsided thinking on my part. I eventually got a degree in finance and banking. Over the years, I received four degrees from the U of A: bachelor's in finance and banking in December 1977, master's in higher education administration, an educational specialist's in higher education administration, and a doctorate in adult education. Prior to doing the master's, I also completed most of the coursework for the MBA (passed thirty out of thirty-three hours). I had a couple problems in that program, so didn't finish that one. Guess you can say I missed it by a grade.

Ironically, my decision to come to the University of Arkansas had nothing to do with the University of Arkansas itself. I had seen the football team play when they were big-time in 1969, watched the games, and all that. But the decision had little to do with that. I had worked pretty much from the time I was old enough to work doing part-time jobs around town and on the farm. My father had it in his mind I would go to, at that time, Southern State College (Southern Arkansas University) in Magnolia, just seventeen miles down the road. I would live at home and continue doing what I had done in high school and that was work before I go to class, go to class, come back home, and work some more. I thought I had enough of that. I decided I wanted to go as far as I could in the state of Arkansas and I felt the University of Arkansas was just a little bit farther away than Jonesboro.

I came to the University of Arkansas in 1972 as a student. I did not leave the University of Arkansas until 2003 as a professional. I became a full-time employee in 1976 and I had a string of employment opportunities during that twenty-seven years. My first job was as a university police officer. I worked that for two years and moved over to be the night manager in the student union from 1978 to 1984. But along that time frame in 1981, I had a good friend, Dr. Charles Tolliver, take a sabbatical from the College of Engineering. He was the lone black professor in engineering and he had written a grant called the Transition Retention Minority Engineering Program (TRMEP). He needed someone, while he was gone, minority representation-wise, to run the program to recruit engineering students to the College of Engineering. He submitted my name and the dean was okay with it. My supervisor, Nianzer Anderson, and the director of the student union, Bob Barnes, allowed me to split my appointment. It was 75 percent with the student union and 25 percent with engineering and I did that for three years from 1981 to 1984. In 1984, I was appointed full-time director of minority engineering programs. In 1986, the director of minority affairs in the division of student affairs came open. It was taking what I was doing in engineering and taking it campus-wide.

I served as director of minority affairs/assistant dean of students under Dr. Suzanne Gordon starting in 1986 and decided again in 1990 that I wanted to try to leave the university. After a couple of interviews, the vice chancellor of student affairs, Dr. Lyle Gohn and Dr. Suzanne Gordon, associate vice chancellor, promoted me to assistant vice chancellor. From 1991 until I left in 2003, I carried the title of assistant vice chancellor of student affairs.

The university, from the time I arrived in 1972 and the time I left in 2003, was two different worlds. Even to the point when I got here in 1972, it was a different world from the people who had come here in 1969. Some of my mentors, when my class arrived here in 1972, were people like Gene McKissic, who was the first African American president of the Associated Student Government, Raymond Bogart, Marcellus Nelson, Wendell Griffen, Sanford Tollette IV, Claude "Nick" Nicholas, and Alvin Philips. Sanford was the first black drum major for the marching band. My first two years at the university, I was in the marching band. There were about eight blacks in the marching band, Sanford's wife at the time, Joyce, the two Mims sisters, Charles Frost, Vandell Bland, Ron Jordan, Marcellus Nelson, Tighthead (can't recall actual name), Shelley Brittnum Williams, and myself. When I say mentor, I'm speaking in terms of people who were either in graduate school or were upper class who took it upon themselves, in an unofficial way, to mentor the freshman class.

We were real small in number. To say there were three hundred of us would probably be an exaggeration during that time frame. We were a close-knit group. If you didn't see each other in class, which you seldom would because you didn't take that many classes together, generally, you would see each other at meal times. We formed those close-knit bonds. Even in the residence halls, more than likely if you were African American, you most likely had an African American roommate. Bobby Hanson and I were roommates our freshman year. My second year I had a white roommate, Randy "Tex" Teusch (pronounced touch). My third and fourth year, I was an RA.

You had a mixture of racial climates. Like I said, Gene McKissic could not have become the first African American president of ASG solely with the black vote, similar to Obama now, but you had those that had their attitudes. Living in the residence halls, in Yocum that first year, 85 to 90 percent of the folks had welcomed us with open arms. But generally, it's not the majority that causes you the problems. It's that minority within that the majority that causes you the headaches and stuff.

Over the years, getting into that 1990 era when students are more accustomed to integration and having their own, they were not familiar enough with the struggle to be concerned about racial issues. They only became concerned with racial issues at the end of a semester with a bad grade or when they had a particular problem themselves. But if you tried to speak to them about it prior to that, there was no such thing as a racial problem in their mind.

A lot of our goals were to try to make the campus as open as possible to every individual, not just the majority of the individuals. In the earlier days, some things you just didn't want to do—like walking down Stadium Drive, as we call it frat row. You knew you were going to get some racial epitaphs, or some bottles, or something thrown out the window at you. You just knew it and you just avoided it. As for the white fraternities, sometimes some were open to you coming to the parties and some were not. There were some clubs in town that were generally open. There was a pattern. All of them were playing good R & B music because that's what the people wanted to hear. But once the club started receiving a large audience of African Americans, particularly African American males, someone would get afraid that someone would say something to a white woman, whether or not she was willing to engage in the conversation or whatever did not matter. Next time you went there, the format had changed. It had gone from R & B to country western or pop. Sometimes they would catch you at the door and say you needed a membership, or they were full, or something and wouldn't let you in. But otherwise, if they wanted to get rid of the masses, they would just temporarily change the format of the music and they don't have to say you're not welcome. The music told you.

When you're here, you are trying to make it through the next day. "I've got to get this class out of the way and make it toward graduation," and you don't necessarily pay attention to your surroundings as much as you pay attention to meeting this goal so you can get out of here (although I did not leave for thirty-one years). Some things, like the overtones on campus, became second nature and that's how you dealt with them. If you knew you were going into a class with an instructor who had a history of being hard on African Americans, you knew you were getting a "C" or a "D" because that's what everyone has gotten prior to you. And there were professors that we knew to avoid. What you would try to do would be to make sure to set your core schedule where he or she was not teaching that class the semester you needed to take it or you waited and tried to get someone else. But occasionally, there were those times when you had no choice and suffered through it. That is what happened with me in the MBA program. I could not get around Marketing Problems and Statistics. You tried to deal with those kinds of matters.

I came here majoring in engineering and I have one "F" on my undergraduate transcript. I got it my first semester here. I was in drafting, graphics as they called it at that point in time. As I stated previously, living in Yocum, 85 to 90 percent of the guys in there were pretty good to try to help you. Well, I had one guy, Winston, who was a white guy in a different section of the class. He was getting "A's" on his graphics work. I was in a different section and I was getting low grades under the same instructor. Some of the older white guys had Winston helping me with my homework. Needless to say, Winston got an "A" and I got an "F." That was my awakening to what I was going to be engaged in for the next four to five years here at the University of Arkansas as far as trying to get a degree in engineering.

With all of those things, it is that I'm just trying to make it. Look at the institution as a whole. You have your support system because most blacks are going through the same thing. We don't talk about it a whole lot, but we know it's there. We talk about stuff and do things to try to keep our spirits lifted. Whether that's going to the gym taking over a floor playing basketball, or playing music, or whatever, we do whatever we can to keep our spirits lifted. As small as the residence hall rooms were, we partied in them like they were a club. We knew the situation out there, but we'd try not to dwell on it to the point of dragging our spirits down because some things we know are not within our power to change. They are just there! There was nothing going on to necessarily change it per se. There was a director of minority affairs on campus at that time when I got here. And you had some programming that was being developed along the way because there were no other programs coming through the mainstream or very few coming through the mainstream that would be geared toward African American interest. While I was here, those feelings for the university were not necessarily things of pride. Everyone said Razorbacks this and Razorbacks that. We were cheering for the black players on the team. We weren't yelling Razorbacks. We were yelling "Razorblacks." We were cheering for the Razorblacks during that time frame.

We knew everyone on the team because we saw each other on the way to class and in our small social networks. You seldom saw people in the classes, you saw people on the corners going to class. You'd take time there to talk. The corner of Brough Commons was a meeting place or the student union game room for males. If you didn't have class for an hour, it was not uncommon for folks to gather on the corner of Brough Commons, between Brough Commons and Gibson Hall, or Razorback Hall as it was called or gather on the steps of Gregson, just talk there between classes and stay in touch with each other. It wasn't so much how we felt about the campus because we were getting our energy and our support from the small number of people who were here.

You did have your bitter feelings because you had to go through some stuff that the majority of folks were not going through and you knew it was strictly because of the pigmentation of your skin. Yes, it chapped your butt so to speak. But you have been doing it all along, up through the early part of integration or either segregated schools and so I think that helped to make people stronger. Then there was the fact that a lot of people refused to give in. You come up here with a three-point grade-point average in high school and many walk out of here barely graduating with a two-point in some cases. Needless to say, you looked the devil in the eye and said you won—for a moment.

I started working in 1976 and 1976 through 1978 was probably the earliest large migration at one time of African American faculty members. Charlie Tolliver came that year (1976) in engineering. Carlton and Alberta Bailey came in 1978 with Carlton in the Law School and Alberta in the library. And I think Sam Brookins may have come in 1978 over in the Law School. Nudie Williams came in 1976 in history. Charlene Sykes came in 1976 in arts and sciences as well. Those folks showed up between 1976 and 1978 and it was like, wow! Because prior to that we only had Dr. Morgan in sociology, Dr. Margaret Clark over in education and foreign languages, Dr. Brenda Mobley arrived in 1972 or 1973 in psychology, and Professor Adolph Reed was in political science in 1971. I can't think of Wallace's last name or his last name may have been Wallace [Johnson]. He was in the social sciences as an instructor as well. Those are the faculty members I can remember being here prior to 1976. There may have been others, but not many. I think Dr. Merlin Augustine arrived in 1975 as assistant to the president and he was the highest-level black administrator at that point in time and was for a long time outside of David Cooksey as director of financial aid. Dr. Harry Budd was here prior to 1976 in the TRIO programs.

And that was actually about the time we started the black, it wasn't called Black Faculty/ Staff Caucus at the time, but black faculty/staff started having regular meetings where we would discuss issues in the early years during the late 1970s and eventually it developed into the Black Faculty/Staff Caucus. And that group had an impact. They had an impact on some things going on, but it wasn't like they were bragging about it or putting it on public notice what was happening. So from 1978 on, it started to grow just a little bit. I don't think the number of tenure track African American faculty has reached forty at any time. It has reached into the high thirties. Folks come in, stay a time frame, and then they are gone. You probably have more that have stayed less than seven years than have stayed here past that mark. For the longest time, Gordon Morgan was the only black associate professor or higher on campus. Rod McDavis came in as the first black academic dean as dean of the College of Education with rank and tenure in 1989. But prior to that, the move from associate professor to full professor for the majority of folks didn't occur too fast and I'm going back with 1978 and we didn't get our first black endowed chairs until close to 2000. Lisa Williams being the first one. Rod McDavis served as the first dean and we did not have another dean of a college until Cynthia Nance in about 2004 or 2005, excluding the library. We've only had two black deans. Prior to that, Merlin Augustine was the assistant to the president, later executive assistant chancellor (I think), and assistant vice chancellor for finance, and he actually served as interim vice chancellor for student affairs prior to 1984 or 1983 when Dr. Lyle Gohn was appointed as vice chancellor. Merlin served as interim vice chancellor for Student Affairs for the better part of the year.

During the mid-nineties, Dr. Dan Ferritor was chancellor and he was trying to make some inroads into minority recruitment especially on the graduate level as well as retention on the undergraduate level. He wanted to institute a program he saw at Ole Miss where African Americans who wanted to go to grad school could get a tuition waiver, thus creating the Lever Fellowship. Along that same time frame, the black caucus asked for more minority affairs representatives. At that time, we had someone in the College of Engineering (Mr. Thomas Carter III) and someone in the College of Education (Dr. Naccaman Williams). We were asking for more representation. Chancellor Ferritor agreed and that is how we ended up with the assistant to the dean in the College of Arts and Sciences and the director of minority affairs in the School of Business. I think the chancellor funded the position fully the first year reducing his support by a third each year to allow the colleges to gradually absorb the funding. Carl Riley was hired as the assistant to the dean for the College of Arts and Sciences (1992) and Genette Seawood, now Genette Seawood Howard, was the first person hired as the director of minority affairs for the College of Business followed by Dr. Barbara Lofton.

I was so impressed with what Chancellor Ferritor had done and during that same time frame, we were having problems with our student athletes at parties the black Greeks or the student organizations were sponsoring. It was seldom a week passed at a party that nonathletes and athletes were not getting entangled. I went and spoke to Coach Richardson and to Coach

Jack Crowe, the head football coach at the time, and told them about the incidents, and they both came to a meeting with the leaders of the student organizations. I remember Coach Crowe sitting up in the meeting that night and saying, "Look here. Whatever I can do to remedy this situation, just tell me. I'm here to work with you. It's from a selfish standpoint, but the last thing I need is for my recruiting competition to find out we have problems up here and tell my recruits that black folks are fighting black folks." That's basically what he said with some paraphrasing. "You've got problems up there and you don't need to be there. So you just tell me whatever it is you need." We asked for a few other things from Crowe, and he gave them to us as well. Both he and Coach Richardson were very supportive. Now after he did that, which was the same year Chancellor Ferritor had done those other things and also said he wanted a black cultural center. Yes, the ideal of the cultural center came from Chancellor Ferritor after his visits to other campuses and saw similar centers on those campuses. We were getting ready to do the Dr. Martin Luther King Jr. awards, and as in many previous years, very few people were nominated. As a matter of fact, nobody was nominated for the faculty/staff portion of it for this particular year.

These were the King awards presented by the Office of Minority Affairs at the university. I was director of minority affairs at that time. So Coach Jack Crowe and Chancellor Dan Ferritor were nominated. They were the first two white men to get the Dr. Martin Luther King Jr. award during my era (I think). It was given as a co-award. I can't tell you how much hell I caught for giving two white men the Dr. Martin Luther King Jr. award. I caught it verbally and silently. In my opinion, those two had done something that year that really made a difference for retention and recruitment of minority students. I thought they were very deserving of the awards.

In 1994, I believe that is the year, Maya Angelou published her book *Our Grandmothers* with illustrations by John Biggers. Alberta Bailey brought the idea to the caucus to purchase a copy of the book from personal donations. If memory serves me correctly, there were four hundred books published and each at a cost of $1,500.00. We agreed and raised the funds. The book was donated to the Special Collections section of Mullins Library. In 1995, a special program was held for the opening of the Multicultural Center. Lenthon and Shirley Clark were personal friends with artist John Biggers. We were able to negotiate through them to have him come up for the opening with an exhibit of his work from Lenthon and Shirley's personal collection of his work. While on campus for the program, he autographed the book for the caucus. That was a special moment having him on campus to do that and the purchase of the book in itself.

In regards to the Black Alumni Society, in 1984 I worked to create a reunion to celebrate the tenth anniversary of Omega Psi Phi coming to campus. It was the first black fraternity to come as a charter group in 1974. I orchestrated a reunion in 1984, but we just didn't invite the members of Omega back for that ten-year anniversary. We invited friends who were here as well. Even though you had the black Greeks, the law students came up with their own mock fraternity and stuff so everyone were friends. Some folks came back and Gene McKissic said at that point in time that this is good, but it would be good if there was something for everybody. And there had been an unofficial Black Alumni Reunion in Little Rock, but nothing on this campus. I kept thinking about this for a while and had spoken with Dr. Nudie Williams about it because they had a very good reunion network going on at Oklahoma State. Dr. Nudie Williams had received his PhD from Oklahoma State, and we had talked numerous times about their reunions. In 1989, I approached Mike Macechko, the director of the Arkansas Alumni Association about it. He said, "Yeah, it's a fine idea, but it's about three years down the road." I said, "Will you support me in my endeavor as we go ahead and try to make something happen for 1990?" He said he would do what he could.

We had the first Black Alumni Reunion in 1990. We had about one hundred and thirty-eight folks at the banquet and everyone involved believed for the first event it was a success. It was an eye-opening experience for a lot of folks because you had people like Shirley Williams who came back for that reunion. During the business meeting that Saturday morning of the reunion, she made no bones about it that she had not been back in twenty years since she left the institution. She said she never had any desire to come back, but this kind of served as a way to come back and put some of those fears and bad feelings in check. Like I said, when you're here, you know what you're going through, but you don't dwell on it. You try to keep yourself motivated. Once you walk away from here, you still don't dwell on it because it can eat at you. She expressed those feelings along with several others who expressed similar feelings. We never built the reunion up as a regular U of A reunion. It was always built up as a chance to come back and be with old friends, people who went through things that you went through. Not coming back necessarily to support the University of Arkansas, we were coming back almost like a family reunion. That was the premise for those early reunions.

We did the first one in 1990, another 1993, and 1995. It was after the one in 1995 at the end of 1997 we talked about formalizing an organization. Dexter Howard, at that time, was the lone African American employee in the Alumni Association. As a result of those reunions, he worked with us to become the second constituency group with the alumni association. We called ourselves the Black Alumni Association, an unofficial term and recognition. We formed the Black Alumni Society in 1998. During that time frame as well, when we started talking about the reunions, I think there had only been one African American to serve on the Board of Directors of the Alumni Association. After that 1990 reunion, there were three members appointed to the Alumni Association board of directors: Wendell Griffen, Randall Ferguson, and Linda Caldwell Walker. Wendell chaired a subcommittee of the Alumni Association addressing issues of minority students.

At the business meeting of the reunion, we always allowed for a university update by officials. At the 1990 reunion, Mike Macechko was the lone university official there or I should say the only white university official. Mike listened to the concerns and expressions delivered that day. He felt as though he caught hell! And he was right. It was nothing directed at him personally; he was there as the lone representative from the university as black alumni expressed their true feelings about what they had endured and why they had not considered coming back or supporting the institution. He took those concerns back to the chancellor and other administrators. He also supported this subcommittee formed on the Alumni Association's board of directors to address the issues and concerns expressed in that 1990 reunion. You could say it was after those reunions started that the black alumni started to get involved in an official manner expressing their concerns about what was going on campus. That subcommittee wrote a letter on behalf of the Alumni Association's board, expressing those concerns to the chancellor. That's when we (black alumni) officially started having a voice.

After the 1995 reunion, there were some concerns expressed. We had all these black athletes and had no black administrators in the athletic department. Gene McKissic chaired a committee of the Black Alumni Society (we were just forming the Black Alumni Society in

1998) and drafted a memorandum to the university, basically condemning the athletic department for not having any African American leadership. The chore was to take it as it came from the black alumni group to the Alumni Association board in that same form for their support. Gene McKissic and I were on the Alumni Association board at the time, but the Alumni Association board did not endorse it in that format. They gutted it pretty much before they signed off on it, but it was basically a very strong condemnation of the athletic department from the black alumni group about the lack of administrators, black administrators there. (See it in its original form behind Gene's interview.) Shortly after that, Derrick Gragg was hired as the assistant or associate athletic director. The society started to have an impact through those reunions and I guess you could say that influence sparked the interest with Chancellor Dan Ferritor. It was after he started receiving information from the black members on the Alumni Association board that he performed that search on retention and recruitment efforts. So you could say the reunions had an indirect impact upon some of the things that were happening on campus and getting the two additional minority affairs representatives in business and arts and sciences. And those were some of the ways we got started and it's had a positive impact.

Prior to the Black Alumni Reunions, I think the only black scholarships we had on campus were the Sidney Moncrief Scholarship, the Bruce Mitchell Scholarship Fund, and Bryce Morgan Memorial Fund. Since the Black Alumni Reunions, I think there are more than seven black endowed scholarships and the Beverly Enterprise Yvonne Keaton Martin Scholarship. The Yvonne Keaton Martin Scholarship has put more than a half million dollars from a spark that came from the Black Alumni Reunions. This happened through George McGill's connection with the president of Beverly Enterprise supporting minority students from Fort Smith and their educational efforts. I guess you could say a byproduct of the reunions has been an increase in privately funded scholarships for African Americans. Not to mention that prior to 1990, it would be safe to say there were fewer than one hundred black financial members in the Arkansas Alumni Association. At the height of those reunions there were more than six hundred people at the banquets. So we went from fewer than two hundred in 1990 to more than six hundred at the banquets in 2000 and financial membership exceeding eight hundred in 2005 in the Alumni Association from fewer than one hundred in 1990. The Black Alumni Society model has been used in other reunions and gatherings because of its success.

I guess out of all my years here, 2000 would probably be one of the hardest. In 2000, we changed administration in student affairs after a change in the chancellorship about two years prior. In 2000, the Division of Student Affairs was going through reorganization. I was part of that restructuring. This is what I was told. I was directing a program at that point in time. One of the two or three I was directing was called Youth Opportunities Unlimited Program and a portion of my salary came from that budget. I was told, during this restructuring, that my responsibilities would shift and that they did not know what my title was going to be. But that said, it was pretty much not going to be assistant vice chancellor. And I said, well, what about that portion of my salary coming from the grant because that grant was moved away from me as well? The word was, so goes the grant, so goes the money. Some of the areas I supervised had been shifted. I went from supervising eleven budgetary units down to about three or four. I viewed it as a demotion. Well, some of my friends from the Black Alumni Society and students viewed it as a demotion as well. I, nor they, felt it was an appropriate thing to do for someone who had worked so hard to try to retain students, been supportive of the university's efforts, and had developed this Black Alumni Society into the organization that it was. That created a big firestorm.

I was humbled by the way friends, alumni, and colleagues stepped up on my behalf. The chancellor received numerous . . . when I say numerous, I mean he received *a lot* . . . of e-mails concerning this activity. The news actually made *The Chronicle of Higher Education and Black Issues of Higher Education (Diversity Inc.),* in addition to the local and state newspapers. At that time, Wendell Griffen and Randall Ferguson were on the largest fundraising board at the institution. Wendell Griffen resigned from the board and being one of the first African Americans on a board at this level and his stature as a judge, it received national attention. That's how it made *The Chronicle.* He resigned over the treatment of an African American administrator, his friend.

We went through that over a two- to three-week time frame of not knowing. I asked the question of my supervisor in the conversation when I was told that I was being made director of the Multicultural Center. I was definitely going to be made director of the Multicultural Center and work with the Black Alumni Society as well, but didn't exactly know the title. I remember asking the question about why am I being made director of the Multicultural Center? The response was that I had been asking for a director of the Multicultural Center. I remember thinking when I got that response, I'm glad I didn't ask for a custodian! The center was created in 1995, but there was no money for a full-time director. So along with my role as assistant vice chancellor, I also served as director of the Multicultural Center and director of Youth Opportunities Unlimited programs as well as supervised Upward Bound, Veterans Upward, Multicultural Student Affairs, Student Support Services, Testing Services, Educational Talent Search, and worked with the associate vice chancellor with the budgeting and personnel in the Dean of Students Office. I was asking for a full-time director to increase the attention to the center and students.

The situation went on for about two weeks. I can remember reading Psalm 37 daily and multiple times a day. We went back and forth trying to negotiate something out of this. The administration's word was, "He isn't being demoted." They were looking at it from this regard. Prior to this incident happening, I reported to the associate vice chancellor of student affairs. Now after this incident, I was going to report directly to the vice chancellor of student affairs. In the chancellor's eyes and words, it wasn't a demotion, it was a promotion, because one level of reporting was going to be removed. My contention and others was, whether it was a level of reporting being removed or whatever, if your responsibilities are being diminished, if your salary is being diminished, and your title has been changed—it's a demotion! And there was no increase in salary in the promotion version. So that was the key.

I remember being called over to the chancellor's office after he had received a call from *The Chronicle of Higher Education* for their article. I was told that if this hits *The Chronicle of Higher Education,* I would never find another job in higher education. I had received the call from *The Chronicle* prior to going to his office, but had not returned the call. After the meeting, I went back to my office and made the call. Whether or not that story making *The Chronicle* is the reason I later did not receive offers after interviewing for several positions—I may never know.

After about two weeks of negotiations, the chancellor put the money back on my salary and the title didn't change. The responsibilities remained as they had outlined. And that was the key thing. A few other things I lobbied for during that negotiation did not happen, either. For instance, the College of Education was losing a grant at the end of June. Dr. Erica Holiday was on that grant and was doing good work in the College of Education. During my negotiations with the chancellor, I lobbied for him to provide funding to keep her on campus in that position on hard money. That did not happen. All of this changed my way of how I approached things at the university.

I remember Dr. John Dominick, who was a well-known banking professor on campus, came to me after that ordeal and he said something to the effect, "We taught ya'll back in undergrad in the 1970s that you work for that gold watch, but there is no such thing as a gold watch these days. You just got to get what you can get and get out of there."

My whole attitude changed and I started looking at making a way out of here. It just wasn't the same. To me, regardless of how my peers or the students respected me in doing my work, if my supervisor or the chancellor didn't care for it, my time could be over within a day with Arkansas being an employ-at-will state. It didn't make any sense to live under this cloud, whether or not you know you have a job here or not. I got the motivation to finish my dissertation and started looking at opportunities to move on. You need to feel comfortable and I just wasn't feeling comfortable with the leadership I was working under at that point in time.

All of this happened in late May and early June. I remember because it happened after we had had a very successful Black Alumni Society reunion in 2000. In September of that year, Dr. Jaquator Hamer, director of multicultural student affairs, was dismayed with what had transpired and looked for employment at other institutions. She was offered a position at Bradley University. I remember asking her, when she told me of the offer, to hold off on accepting the offer. I notified the vice chancellor of her offer and asked for additional funds to make a counter offer. I received two responses. One was she applied so she must want to go and the second was there was no additional funding to make a counter offer. Less than six months later in the same budget year, the vice chancellor's administrative assistant received approximately $5,000 in a raise.

They fired Coach Richardson in 2002. Like so many other African Americans, I didn't agree with that. The institution was preaching diversity as one of our top-five goals, but yet and still there was a revolving door of faculty and staff members. I mean a revolving door. There was a newspaper article, I think it was in 2003, when they had a big article in the *Arkansas Democrat Gazette*, front page and back, the entire page as a matter of fact, where they talked about the number of black faculty/staff members, key administrators who were here. My numbers may be slightly off, if you go back and look at that page now and you look at those sixteen or eighteen people that they mention, there are fewer than five that are still at the university. So the retention of African American faculty and key administrators has been a problem. Those are some of the things that you wonder about.

As far as my work experience, it has paid off immeasurably. My work has been respected. I have been respected.

I left the university with some very memorable moments. We opened the Multicultural Center in the fall of 1995. An idea brought about by Kevin Dedner, president of the Black Students Association at the time, and his staff, was the BSA Living Legacy Award. This was to be presented to people from Arkansas who had gone on to distinguish themselves. The first recipient was Mrs. Daisy Gatson Bates. At the award program in 1996, we viewed a just-released video about Mrs. Bates and the Little Rock Nine. I remember President Suggs getting up for remarks after the award was presented with tears in his eyes, apologizing for "what my people" have done. It was a very moving evening. Mrs. Bates was just the beginning of those worthy recipients. I am proud to say I received that same honor in 2004. I also had the distinct pleasure of having an award named after me, the Lonnie R. Williams Bridging Excellence Award presented to me as the first recipient at a multicultural graduation ceremony in 2001.

I had the honor of being a charter member of the first black fraternity chartered on the campus, Omega Psi Phi. In 1973, eighteen of us, ranging from first-year students to juniors, formed a group called The Brotherhood. Towards the end of the fall semester of 1973, we talked about bringing a fraternity to campus and discussed which one to bring. We pretty much had one common factor and did not know it until that moment that most of us had been influenced by men of Omega. We contacted Dr. Gordon Morgan and he made the process happen for us. Delta Sigma Theta was the first sorority to charter and they came across the spring of 1974. In the fall of 1974, fifteen guys started the process of pledging Omega and ten finished on December 7: Lonnie R. Williams, Morris Sylvester, Donald Hatchett, Charles Frost, Ephron Robinson, Cliff Cain, Edward McKeel, Ronnie Thompson, Arthur Ezell, and Edward Garland.

In 2002, as a member of the Northwest Arkansas Dr. Martin L. King Jr. Planning Committee, I suggested to the committee we approach the city of Fayetteville about getting a street named after Dr. King. The committee accepted the idea and charged me with meeting the city officials in getting the process going. We had two city officials working on the U of A campus, Kevin Santos and Lionel Jordan. I spoke to them about the idea and they took it to the city board. We could not get full support, but garnered enough support to get the street named the "Honorary Dr. Martin L. King Jr. Blvd." with plans for a permanent name change a few years later to allow the businesses time to prepare for the permanent change. The honorary street designation ceremony happened on the Dr. King holiday in January 2003. The designation was removed and name changed permanently in January 2009.

Like many people interviewed for this project, my experience at the University of Arkansas, Fayetteville, although challenging, was an experience that paid off professionally and personally. Working with the black alumni and the Alumni Association in putting together the Black Alumni Reunions enabled me to stay in contact with friendships developed over the thirty-one years of association with the university and to develop friendships dating back to the early pioneers that were there as early as 1949 to the present day. To have a hand in the Black Alumni Reunions and to see the benefits (direct and indirect) of the reunions and the Black Alumni Society (BAS), does give me a sense of great pride. I realize those benefits would not have been possible without the participation of everyone who joined the BAS, attended the reunions, or supported those organizations, events, or me over the years. Even with the challenges, I have been blessed.

Chapter 5

"Making an Honest Effort"

Desegregation and the University of Arkansas in the 1980s

> We felt that the name BAD created a bad image. We wanted to be connected with something good . . . We want this to be a student government organization, not only a black organization.
>
> —Karen Harris, Public Relations director for STAND

By fall 1979, the members of Black Americans for Democracy had changed their student organization's name to STAND (Students Taking a New Dimension).[1] In addition, STAND announced that it had revised group goals to go along with its new name. These goals included gaining an appreciation for black heritage; improving interracial relationships; emphasizing education; and helping members develop leadership skills. These changes made by STAND signaled its desire to move away from the confrontational style of the organization's past and to embrace new methods of coalition building with other campus groups. STAND hoped that by making itself more attractive to nonwhites and working within the traditional structure of campus governance that it could more effectively further the cause of desegregation on the Fayetteville campus.[2]

The modifications made by the members of STAND mirrored national trends. By the 1980s, the nation had undergone a counterrevolution to many of the social changes made in the 1960s and 1970s. Americans had lost patience with the massive and often-disruptive methods used by civil rights groups in the previous decades. As a result, street protest largely ceased. Civil rights proponents across the nation seemed more inclined to use the courts, state, and federal legislatures to hammer out policy deals that afforded greater access for underrepresented groups.[3]

In step with its new direction, STAND formally requested representation in the Associated Student Government in April 1980. The leadership of the organization petitioned for two guaranteed senate seats. Lloyd Meyers, the president of the group, explained why STAND merited such an accommodation. First, Meyers pointed to what he called the "imminent need" for the participation of black students in "campus-wide government and policy making," and the fact that blacks were not being selected through the normal process. Meyers commented that the "mostly warped-sided population in the living areas" worked as a real barrier to black student political representation. Second, Meyers argued that STAND served as the "nucleus for black students." According to Meyers, no other campus organization could claim to be the voice of black students politically, socially, and culturally. Third, Meyers believed that STAND deserved automatic representation in the student government because it would help the university achieve its goal of growing its black student population to 9 percent. For Meyers, a fixed place for STAND made sense because "STAND tries to present a positive image [of the university] to attract students."[4] The arguments made by Meyers and STAND proved effective. After about a week of debate, ASG awarded the organization two permanent senate seats.[5]

Despite its name change and more conciliatory approach, STAND maintained many of the social activities of its organizational predecessor. Black Awareness Week, though sometimes referred to as Cultural Awareness Week, had similar events such as choir concerts, plays, soul-food feasts, and lectures on black life. STAND also retained the Miss Black University of Arkansas Pageant. The organization incorporated other black-oriented activities such as a program celebrating Martin Luther King Day and Senior Weekend—a recruiting event in which black seniors from around the state were brought to the Fayetteville campus for a weekend with the hope that they would choose to attend the university after graduation. Furthermore, STAND continued BAD's community service orientation by serving Thanksgiving dinners for seniors and taking area children trick-or-treating.[6]

STAND's presence in ASG and its growing support (STAND claimed to represent 750–800 students) were not the only indications of progress relative to desegregation process at the University of Arkansas during the 1980s. In 1982, Merike Ann Manley became the first black woman selected as homecoming queen. In the university administration, Dr. Merlin Augustine served in the important role of the executive assistant to the president while Delores Brookins held the position of assistant dean of students and minority advisor. In 1985, the university made Nolan Richardson the first black head coach of any athletic program in school history and the first black head basketball coach in the Southwest Conference. Also in 1988, the university formally recognized the importance of desegregation by commemorating the fortieth anniversary of the enrollment of Silas Hunt.[7]

Although the university made strides to enhance its image relative to desegregation, it did not eradicate one of its most serious and persistent problems—black student enrollment. Over the course of the decade, the black student population declined, falling from a high of 699 out of a total of 13,982 in 1984, to 673 out of 14,281 in 1989.[8]

University officials expressed concern about the declining numbers of black students. University chancellor Dan Ferritor stated that attracting and retaining more black students was the "top priority of his administration."[9] However, university leaders believed that the institution was making "an honest effort" to recruit black students. To them, the primary reasons for the declining numbers were tied to factors outside of the university's control—financial aid cutbacks, the location of the Fayetteville campus, and student failure to meet admission standards.[10]

Not everyone agreed that the fall in black student numbers lay largely outside of the university's influence. Gregory Pitts, the president of STAND in 1982, asserted that the university lacked a "plan of action" to grow the black student population. Furthermore, Pitts felt that the university had made no "real effort" to make the 9 percent goal a reality. Pitts also raised questions about the campus atmosphere. He contended that black and white students did not interact enough with each other and that white students did not always welcome diversity. Pitts pointed to the poor reception that Merike Manley, the first black homecoming queen, received during a pep rally in 1982 as evidence. Pitts recalled that "she was booed at the pep rally." Finally, Pitts held that black high school students refused to attend the university because of their perception of a paucity of social activities for black students.[11]

In the following testimonies, we gain a better understanding of the campus atmosphere and the conditions that affected the experiences of blacks at the University of Arkansas during the 1980s.

■ LaTonia Clark George (1988–1992), manager

Telephone interview by Lonnie R. Williams, October 14, 2007
For detailed biography, see Appendix A, page 307

In 1988, I came to the University of Arkansas, Fayetteville, to obtain a degree in public administration. I selected the University of Arkansas because my brother, Paul Clark, had come to the university in 1986 in the engineering program. I decided to go there because I thought I could stay in state and save some money.

I pledged Delta in fall 1989. My line sister and roommate, Kris Hunter, decided that we were going to get involved in the Black Student Association (BSA) in the fall of 1990 or spring of 1991. We ran against the "Helena" Valley boys, Andre and James Valley. James and I ran against each other for the Black Student Association president and Kris, I think, ran for the office of either secretary or vice president. Kris and I won.

During our tenure in the BSA, there were several basketball athletes accused of raping a nonstudent female. During this accusation, the city of Fayetteville was investigating the situation and the U of A was investigating the situation. When I was notified, I got a late-night call at my apartment telling me that four players had been arrested. That was how the story came to me. I got on the phone and started calling a couple of players, trying to understand what took place. They knew one player who was definitely involved, but was unclear on everybody else. When I finally spoke with this player, I believe he informed me that he had obtained legal counsel and that he really couldn't talk to me, but that he was being told by the U of A that he was not able to continue going to class until the investigation was complete. He had to stop attending classes and was suspended officially because of the charges that were pending against him from the city, the prosecuting attorney's office.

Kris Hunter and I put on our thinking hats together, and said, "If they will treat student athletes like this, how will they treat other students?" Kris and I started working on a plan of action of how we were going to combat this situation with these student-athletes. We recommended to the player to continue to go to class and to tell whoever else was involved in the investigation to continue to go school. We didn't care what else happened. Our thought was, until the charges were officially filed and they were prosecuted, that they should have the ability to still go to school unless the school says, "You have been banned from campus."

Kris Hunter and I also put together a speech, and we called a press conference on the bridge outside of the student union. At the press conference . . . and I'll never forget Lonnie Williams, our BSA faculty advisor, giving me his opinion that he did not think we should be having the press conference. We purposely did not inform Lonnie of the press conference to ensure his position in student affairs was not jeopardized. The press conference got attention in the city and state.

In addition to the press conference, we sent letters to Chancellor Dan Ferritor and U of A president Alan B. Suggs. We also asked to meet with them to talk through this situation with these student-athletes because we felt there had been an injustice done.

At some point, one player's name was removed from the allegations because later he reached some type of settlement with one of the local radio or television stations concerning the use of his name. It turns out there were only four student-athletes on the basketball team being connected to the investigation with possible charges of rape and/or suspension or expulsion from the university. It is my recollection at that point is when we decided to have that press conference.

Chancellor Ferritor's office called us, and we set up an appointment with him. We were able to meet with him and address our concerns; however, he really couldn't say anything but [could only] listen to us. We never were able to see Alan B. Suggs, but we did send him our letter detailing our concerns and what we felt were the injustices against these student-athletes. The main point from the Black Student Association and from our office was if student-athletes could be treated like this, what about other African American student-athletes and black students at large. What would happen if just we, just African American students, were treated like this? These concerns were the premise of everything. I remember Lonnie Williams questioning us on why we were doing all of this and we said at this point, "We got to do what we got to do."

I'll never forget Kris Hunter and I were at our apartment. We received on our answering machine many calls from nonblack people calling up and threatening our lives. I'll never forget that because my mom said it was on TV in Pine Bluff, and she asked me not to do it again. It was a few weeks later, I think, this player and the team went through some investigations with the student affairs office, or whatever office that handled the investigations. From my understanding from the investigation from the players . . . I don't want to call any names. They said the accusing woman was able to come and testify at the school hearing; that's what I was told. Now my understanding is that type of situation had never happened before, where an outside person was able to come into an investigation on the U of A campus and give her/his side of the story. I don't think the players were ever able to confront her with their story during the school hearing, but I can't remember all the facts at this point, and maybe the records from the U of A may reflect better, but the players from my understanding were never expelled from school and the charges from the city were either never officially filed or were dropped.

I recall the players being suspended for a few games by Coach Nolan Richardson. They were able to go back to class. I really was thankful that the relationship with the players and others developed during our years at the university. I was also grateful of how Coach Richardson fought for the players, even though it was behind closed doors. Those student-athletes were his players. My heart really went out to him because he was being tested just as much as we were on that campus. This overall situation taught me, as much as we were living in 1988 to 1992 at the U of A campus, that racism was still alive in northwest Arkansas. I know this ordeal is a time that I will never forget.

When I went to the U of A, I was determined to graduate in four years. I wanted to set and maintain a standard that you could make it and you could graduate in four years. I recall Kimbra Bell and I being two students that came to the U of A in 1988 and graduated in four years. I am sure there were others that I cannot recall. Many of the African American students had or decided to have five- to ten-year graduation plans This was concerning to me at that time, but after thinking back on the pressure of living and working in northwest Arkansas, I can understand their plans and appreciate and admire them just the same.

There were several other dark moments during my stay in NWA as a college student. One of my concerns was when I was preparing to graduate in May 1992, I was informed that I was not able to graduate in May because there was some paperwork that wasn't filled out or was somehow missing. I was told by the administration building staff that I could not walk at the May graduation because my paperwork reflected a December graduation. I used my resources and spoke with Chancellor Ferritor and obtained the ability to walk in May. It was so weird what happened. All of my coursework was completed before the May graduation. Later that summer when the 1992 seniors' names were being placed on the senior walk, my name was left off of the walk. All of the seniors' names were placed in alphabetical order by last name on the walk. I had to go back to Dan Ferritor in the fall of 1992 and explain this situation to him. Finally, I think after three or four months, they went back and added my name to the very end of the list of 1992 graduates. I saw this as one more way I was being shown that you can't mess with the U of A without some consequences and hurdles to climb.

All of my time at the U of A was not bad. As a Razorback Belle, a member of SMILE, Greek life, and other great campus organizations, I had a chance to interact and build lasting friendships with students, faculty, and administrators that were from every walk of life and ethnicity; some of these individuals are still my friends today. However, I was concerned that there were a lot of black individuals that were at the U of A with me that left my first year, my second year, my third year, and some people say they will never come back to the U of A because of the experiences they had as a student. Some of Delta line sisters have said they are not coming back to the U of A even in 2009 because of the things they experienced when they were on the campus.

In 2008, I was speaking during a U of A advisory board meeting with Dr. Johnetta Brazzell and Peggy Boyles and I told them that if it were not for Lonnie Ray Williams at the U of A during my era that I and many others would not have made it. I believe that I am one tough cookie and a lot people used to call me TC back in the day which stood for "Total Control" because I acted as if I was in total control of my life and everything else. But to be honest, if I had not had Lonnie Williams, Dr. JoAnna Newman, and Ann Henry on my side, I would have left, too. I thought I was on track to graduate in four years, but at times I questioned my ability to make it due to comments that were made as I walked down the classroom halls. The looks I received from people as though I did not deserve to be there. At times, it felt like I always had things against me. It was a constant battle against doing right and staying in an environment where you felt most times you were not welcome. However, when I walk the campus today and meet with my fellow alumni advisory board members, I feel a change has come.

With some of the programs for the students that Dr. Brazell has put in place, with the support of John White, the face of the campus has changed in many ways for me. I am appreciative of the new success in diversity and inclusion at the U of A, but I figure we did what we had to do during our time to survive. I did not feel the faculty and administrators during my era understood the need for these type programs that John White and Dr. Brazzell put in place. I appreciate both of these individuals more than I can put into words. But, I give utmost credit to Lonnie Ray Williams, a man that many of us African American students owe our education and sanity.

Another key component of me staying at the U of A was the Greek Life system. It helped many of us bond together as one no matter what organization we pledged. The Greek system was all some of us had to hold onto.

I have some sweet and sour feeling about the U of A. Some days it is really sweet because I received my degree there and I have some great memories with a lot of great people of all persuasions of life. However, I will tell you that at the end of the day there were some sour moments that I could have left in a blinking of an eye and not thought twice about the university.

For me, I sympathize and empathize with people that don't want to ever step foot at the U of A because there are some valid reasons.

I recall the first time I came back to the university after I transferred away from northwest Arkansas with State Farm Insurance. I came back in 1994 after Nolan Richardson's 1993–1994 team won the NCAA Championship. During my visit, the 1992 team played the 1994 championship team. Many of the African American students came back for this event. After this, the black alumni weekends began to really take a life of their own. We began to start inviting others to come back. When Lonnie left the U of Arkansas and moved to Arkansas State University, the attendance of the Black Alumni Weekend began to slow down. For me, it was bittersweet when Lonnie left. It was sweet because I finally felt Lonnie was being recognized for obtaining his doctorate degree and his years of service in student affairs. It was sour because I did not know if Chancellor John White was doing everything in his power to keep Lonnie on the campus in some capacity. I was highly disappointed in the U of A when this occurred

Some people ask, "How do I feel when I walk the campus today?" To be honest, it's an eerie feeling. There were plenty of great times, but the bad times were sprinkled in more than I would care to have as a young adult. At a recent alumni advisory board meeting, I was listening to my white alumni talk about all of their great experiences on the campus. As I looked over to my line sister, Peggy Boyles, now director of Development in Student Affairs at the U of A, I thought, we were such mature students for our time. We had to be mature. We only had the SMILE program (Students Making It Lighter Everyday), a peer counseling program for students of color previously operated out of the Office of Minority Affairs in student affairs. People like Tajuanna Byrd, Deon Wilson, Gary Moses, and Angela Seawood heading up this program with other upperclassmen, who made freshmen like me believe in ourselves and what we could achieve on the campus. Those upperclassmen stood with us and said we can take whatever comes our way. We can show you that graduation is a realistic goal.

My present feelings for the U of A are very favorable. Again, with the help of Dr. Brazzell and John White, they have done some great things for the students and the university. I don't give out praise lightly, but they have made big strides in the last ten years or more. I'm extremely glad that there are enough people here that understand the value of diversity, inclusion, and are willing to walk the walk. There is still room for improvement, but times have drastically changed. I believe the U of A is trying hard to retain and enhance the lives of all students. There are many apologies that the U of A owes to its former students, faculty, and staff for the way they were treated. Chancellor Dave Gearhart and athletic director, John Long made huge strides in welcoming back Nolan Richardson and the 1994 championship basketball team back to the campus and Bud Walton Arena in March 2009. I was fortunate enough to be bestowed with the honor to be present for this auspicious moment. However, this type of faction is just one of many that are needed to remove the hurt and pain from many others. There are a lot of people that are still hurt by the U of A's past treatment, so the past has to be dealt with before we can fully move forward to the present and the future.

If I can just interject a few closing thoughts. I attended the fiftieth anniversary of the Little Rock Nine on September 25, 2007. This memorable day of events really shed light on my time at the U of A. By no means do I want to contrast my experience at the U of A with the experience of Little Rock Central in 1957; however, I found some correlations in their fight for a quality education and against race discrimination. I felt that at the U of A we had to fight with emotional race discrimination. In 2007, this event made me think about my time from 1988 to 1992 and how far this world still has to go! The U of A has made some great strides, but the future still is unknown.

Lastly, I would like to close with my thoughts on how the U of A can continue to be successful in recruiting and retaining African American students in northwest Arkansas. It is the utilization of the black Greek-life system. I know the importance of Greek life. If it were not for the black Greek life at the U of A, my story may be quite different. Through this system, I gained some valuable friendships and enhanced my leadership and teamwork skills along the way. These key things helped me stay and graduate. Not that I wouldn't have had these things if I weren't Greek, but I just question if I would have. I believe the black Greek-life system is a huge plus for the U of A and I still do not think to this very day in 2009 that they are capitalizing on how important this system is to the retention of African American students. I would be surprised if the correlation is not high. I would challenge the university to look at the importance of the black Greek life on the campus in the midst African American students being at a nonblack school.

In summary, I believe the U of A is heading in the right direction and I am happy to live in northwest Arkansas whereby I have the pleasure of seeing it thrive.

■ Dexter L. Howard (1989–1994), minister

Interview by Charles Robinson, spring 2008
Interviewed in office of Charles Robinson, University of Arkansas, Fayetteville, campus
For detailed biography, see Appendix A, page 307

I entered the University of Arkansas in 1989 and I obtained a degree in communications in 1994. I selected the University of Arkansas, sad to say, mainly for athletic reasons. I really was not into whether or not this was a good academic institution. I was at that time being a young person and not being guided quite the way I needed to be guided academically. I really was not looking for a wonderful academic institution. Not that I wouldn't have considered the university, if I were looking for that, but I was mainly looking for an athletic institution that I could continue playing football and on to the next level.

I came from Little Rock, Arkansas. I went to Central High School and was a highly recruited player in the state of Arkansas. Actually, it came down to the University of Oklahoma and the University of Arkansas. And, of course, I chose the University of Arkansas, being a homeboy from the state and had a very interesting time, to say the least.

After I graduated, I left the University of Arkansas and moved to Fort Smith. When I got ready to move back to northwest Arkansas, Coach Broyles (athletic director at the time) played a major part in me getting a job or at least getting my foot in the door of the Arkansas Alumni Association. I actually ended up interviewing for that particular job, getting it, and working for the Alumni Association for a year and a half.

During my tenure at the Arkansas Alumni Association as an assistant director of on-campus programming, I worked with constituent groups—alumni societies. I played a very strategic part in helping to form the Black Alumni Society. I was actually one of the founding charter members of the Black Alumni Society along with Professor John Newman, Dr. Morgan, Professor John Newman, Lonnie Williams, Wendell Griffen, and others. Dr. John Newman and I actually designed the concept of the logo for the Black Alumni Society.

Describe my experience at the U of A? When I got here in 1989, it was a very small community. It wasn't that overwhelming of a transition from Little Rock to Fayetteville other than the dynamics and differences in culture in terms of not seeing that many African Americans here. There were not very many African Americans here at all in 1989.

We have come a long ways in a short, short amount of time thanks to the university, Walmart, and Tyson Foods. But you can only imagine coming from an inner city where every two or three persons you're going to see is a black person; whereas coming here, it is probably every fifteen. You might hope and pray to see a black person.

What stands out in my mind is when I first got here. Our head coach pulled all the freshmen to the side, mainly African American freshmen football players, and told us two very strategic things. That it would behoove us to remember and to take heed to and do not be caught in Springdale after dark. That still stands out in my mind when I can get in my car and at nine and ten o'clock at night and drive to the Walmart Super Center in Springdale today. Just not so many years ago when I was a student here at the university, I was told by a white person not to be in Springdale after dark and also not to be caught out period on Halloween night. There was a rare case of some guys going around looking for blacks to hurt. Now, this was just in the eighties. . . . the late eighties leading into the early nineties. So that is hard to fathom and that's hard to imagine, but it was. It was still there. I remember a teammate of mine and I . . . we were driving, I forget why we were in Springdale . . . but we were driving back to Fayetteville on Highway 71 Business and we were at a stoplight by I believe it was the Springdale Country Club, where it is today. A car pulled up beside us, and it was a white family. There was a little child sitting in the back seat. He rolled down the window and was pointing. I couldn't quite hear what the child was saying, but you could tell the child was noticeably disturbed because he had never seen someone like that before. And that was kind of unnerving. It was kind of crazy to be here.

I personally never received any direct racial attack or anything like that while I was at the university. Of course, there was an undercurrent. The undertone of why are you here and we are just tolerating you. Everybody loved the Razorbacks. That was always a plus that I played for the Razorbacks, but I could only imagine being a regular student here. If I got some of the looks or some of the stares, I got them from being a football player. I could only imagine what I would have gotten if I were just an average Joe Blow student here.

I do remember a particular event with Pastor Jackson Hawkins, who was my pastor in college. He was kind of the black activist here in northwest Arkansas at that time. Something was going on that had some racial overtone to it and I remember him gathering as many African American students together as he could possibly muster, which a lot of us went to St. James, and we marched from their church up to the courthouse. I can't recall what exactly it was all about, but that event sticks out in my mind that it must have been serious enough for him to go all out like that. That is something to be considered—just that little number of years ago we were still dealing with things such as racism and I know that there are probably still some overtones now to a certain degree. But that's still real scary just to know that back in 1989 through 1994 when I was there that we were still dealing with things like that.

Describe my relationship with other black students? We had to be close because there weren't that many of us. Everybody knew everybody. Really! Everybody knew everybody. The athletes went to students dorms. We were always over in Reid Hall playing cards, playing dominos, and they couldn't come to our dorm so we would always be at everybody else's door. We were very close because we had to be. We went a lot of places together. There were those who kept off to themselves and the football players were an entity unto ourselves. It was kind of like we had our own little fraternity and we pretty much had our own little world.

The people that I associated with were real, real close. Most of us went to the same church. Of course . . . Dr. Lonnie Williams . . . Lonnie was kind of like a motivating factor for us to get close, for us to have unity among ourselves. He was the guiding force behind it. If you were a black student on campus, I mean if you were truly black, you would have been in Lonnie Williams's office at some point and time. Some students use to go there and hang out. You didn't have to want anything. You just go and see Lonnie. We were just very, very close.

What are my feelings about the university today? I'll be quite honest with you, Dr. Robinson, I don't feel as close as I would like to feel. I was on the board of the Arkansas Alumni Association for a number of years. It was seven years, I think. A couple of years ago I just rolled off the board after I stopped working for the university and went into full-time ministry. They asked me to come on the board there. And of course I felt a whole lot closer when I was on the board because I was in the inner workings and decisions being made on behalf of the university for the Alumni Association . . . through the alumni or representing the alumni, and attending various events here and there. But to a certain degree, it really seems like I'm really not that close to my alma mater and that could be on me as well. Just my own personal involvement to the degree and level to which I choose to be involved, just because I am so terribly busy building a church, ministry, and all those various things.

I feel close to the people at the University of Arkansas and I was just talking to Willyerd Collier, director of affirmative action for the university. My sister-in-law still works for the university, Dr. Angela Williams. It's not like I am totally separated. When certain people wrote off Dr. Williams . . . when he moved on to Arkansas State in Jonesboro . . . Lonnie was like a galvanizing force. He really kept everybody where they needed to be. He let us know that we need to stay close because the other African Americans coming along, they need us. They're our legacy.

You really don't see that galvanizing force there anymore. Not that . . . simply because it's not Lonnie there. I don't think it necessarily has to be Lonnie. I think it just needs to be someone who alumni can relate to that they can respect and that person has this type of charisma, like Lonnie, where they can be a galvanizing force. I think there are some reasons why that connector is not there. Even though we have the Black Alumni Society and all that good stuff, and I'm a member of the Alumni Association, but I really don't get communication from the Black Alumni Society.

I attended the last reunion [2007]. I was one of the recipients of an award. I think they probably could be a little bit more thorough with their records and with their communication followup. Make sure the alumni on the outside, and I live here in Fayetteville, but think about the alumni who are down in Star City, Arkansas, or Michigan or Detroit, Michigan, or wherever they are . . . in Atlanta, Georgia, how alienated they could feel. Now, they may not feel that way, but I know if I feel the way and I am here in Fayetteville and the university is right up the street from my church, there probably are a few people that maybe feel that same way that are not even living in the state anymore.

Were there any times as a football player that I felt differently as a black football player? Now that's a good question. Good or bad, there was some semblance of division in the team.

When I say division, I don't mean in a negative way. I don't mean that we hated each other and we didn't get along. We all got along, but it was just an unwritten rule, kind of a silent segregation. You go your way and we go our way and that's just how we were. Now, some white football players, we hung out with or whatever, but really more than anything all the black athletes hung out together like the black baseball players, the black basketball players, and all those guys along with the football players. It wasn't just like the whole football team hung out together. It was all black athletes.

I had some pretty good relationship with my coaches. I came to Arkansas for the coach, specifically, not necessarily the university. But I came to Arkansas specifically for Coach Hatfield. I wanted to play for him. He was a good man. He had good morals, ethics, and I wanted to play for somebody like that. With my coaches, I never experienced any type of racial overtones. They wanted you to play football, go to school, and that was it. I never really experienced anything from any of my teammates. It was like I said, they went to their parties and we went to our parties. Then when it was time to come together on the football field and get the job done, we were ready to do that. You really never had an opportunity to see yourself in any other light because we were a segregated community within the university.

I will be honest. I didn't even know there was a Black Student Association. And that's sad, but I didn't. The office was very, very medial. I don't even think they had an office. I think they had a little cubicle. It was something that wasn't given a whole lot of thought, in my opinion. When I started working for the Alumni Association, I got into the inner workings of on-campus things. I worked with some of the student organizations here on campus, ASG and the Black Student Association, and I was actually able to see the Black Student Association become what it should have been when I was in school. It became viable and sad to say through selling their importance to the administration, they persevered and they were given their own spot back in the union. And that was just back in 1998.

I was, on a lower level, involved in student government as far as our dorm. I was the president of Walton Hall Student Government. Each dorm had their own government setup, and I was the president of our dorm student government. I would call meetings and had to report to bigwigs on the campus about what's going on in our dorm.

I really don't think the university has given proper priority. I think we've given lip service, but I don't think we've given action toward a true diverse community, campus community. I am not just talking about African American. Of course, I am biased because I'm African American, but for the most part, you see someone like yourself, Dr. Morgan, of course Dr. Williams, and before she passed away, Dr. Nola Royster with career services. All were a major part of my success here at the university when I was a student.

Entities like those, and I'm not as involved on campus now, but I just don't sense the university has a major push to even be able to identify the absolute criticality of bringing more, specifically black high-level professors like you here at the university. Not just for role models, but because I don't believe the culture outside of our culture understands that in the black culture leaders are our role models. They are our teachers and who we look up to. Just like a pastor is a major role model in the black community, always has been, and probably always will be. I would personally like to see a greater push towards it. I understand because I was here when Chancellor White got here. I was very excited about his initiatives pushed forth and just becoming a reality. But from what I understand, I don't think we are any closer to that becoming a reality than it was when I was here last.

I just heard some demographic statistics about the African American community here on campus and it has dropped since I was last here and that amazes me. And to me, it's just that we are not prioritized on the higher level to be the ones in administration who make those types of decisions. It's almost like we are saying one thing out the sides of our mouths and we are doing another thing. Or we're not putting our money behind what we are saying we want to see. I think that really damages the legacy relationship. I have six children and they are going to be going to college here real, real soon. I'd be honest with you, and I'm not to the point right now as a parent, that I will just all out push the University of Arkansas. I love this university. I'm very thankful that I was able to get a very good education here that has allowed me to experience some level of affluence in life. But I am just not to a point where I could just all out say . . . you need to go there.

I understand what the chancellor [White] is saying he wants to see. But you know we've got to start seeing it. I'm a leader myself. I understand all the intricacies, how intricate planning has to go into things, and things taking place. I understand that, but it has been since 1998 that this has been going on. That is what I want to get on the record that I think we are missing out on legacy opportunities. When I was working at the Alumni Association, you heard a lot talk of legacy, legacy, legacy, and I'm just wondering if we ever fit in that legacy, if we're ever taken into consideration? Man I set in those long drawn-out arguments over the Pan-Hellenic Council talking about not allowing alcohol in the frat houses and if they are going take out early rush . . . all the parents were so fretful over it. I didn't understand because I'm not in that culture. I was trying to be as understanding as possible because I would only want the same treatment in return. We're talking about all this, but I am never hearing anybody say anything about . . . we need to do this so that we can make sure that the black students have a good learning environment, a good opportunity that encourages learning. You have to feel comfortable in the environment in which you are learning in order to be successful in that learning environment.

We have history here, but you really only see preparations to make sure things are in place for the white legacy not necessarily the African American legacy. I'm not saying this because I am African American, but that could work the same way for Native Americans or people of Hispanic decent. I'm sure they would say the same thing.

■ Reena M. Jackson Holmes (1986–1990), auditor

Telephone interview by Lonnie R. Williams, October 14, 2007
For detailed biography, see Appendix A, page 308

I came to the University of Arkansas in the fall of 1986 after obtaining my high school diploma from the Turrell, Arkansas, public school system. When I enrolled, my major was undeclared. I had a love for writing and communications and thought initially I would pursue a course of study in either communications or journalism. However, after taking a few college courses in the fine arts college and in the business college, I found a new love—accounting. I majored in business administration with a concentration in accounting and obtained my bachelor of science degree in the spring of 1990.

I attended the University of Arkansas primarily because it was a great in-state institution with an outstanding reputation for being a good school. Additionally, I received a scholarship opportunity to attend there, which made the possibility of me obtaining a degree more of a reality. Lastly, my parents, especially my mother, thought it would be great place for me to attend because her mother, Clemmie Williams, lived in Fayetteville and she thought my grandmother would provide a great support system for me while I was there.

Honestly, I did not do a lot of research on colleges and universities before I made my decision to attend the university, primarily because I was not planning on going into a specialty area and because I had limited financial resources. At the time I enrolled in the University of Arkansas, I had an older brother attending college at the University of Central Arkansas in Conway and I had a set of twin brothers coming out of high school just one year behind me. That meant within two short years my parents would go from having one child in college to having four children attending major colleges/universities. My father, Marion Jackson Sr., was a self-employed generational family farmer who received meager compensation for his efforts and my mother, Delois Jackson, was not employed outside of the home. To say financial resources were limited was an understatement. The fact that the university was an in-state school, which meant no out-of-state tuition, and coupled with the fact that I had received an academic scholarship, my decision to attend the U of A was rational and practical. The love and support I would get from my grandmother also factored into my decision to attend the university.

I had both positive and negative experiences while attending the university. After enrolling in my first accounting class, I became passionate about that area of study. I thought I had finally found my niche in life. I enjoyed the challenge of the curriculum and I embraced the evolution of the learning processes I was experiencing. However, when I encountered difficult times along the way, I did not feel I garnered much support from the academia. At one point, I was encouraged to change my major. In spite of that recommendation, I persevered, and was eventually awarded my bachelor's degree. I also obtained a master's degree in business administration from Arkansas State University in Jonesboro and became a certified public accountant. Additionally, I have obtained gainful employment in the field of accounting.

I recall having a discussion with one of my professors after noticing a discrepancy in the manner in which she compiled our grade-point averages as compared to the way she outlined it on the course syllabus. While discussing my concerns with her, she forcibly pushed me out of her office. I was shoved and demanded to leave, to which I obliged.

I also recall a Dr. [Franklin] Williams, professor emeritus, whom I spent a lot of time visiting during his scheduled office hours. He taught me a lot about living and giving. He had a passion for lions and he made me an honorary member of his "Lions' Club." He awarded me a two-hundred-fifty-dollar scholarship, which helped me further my education. I am not sure why he selected me. Perhaps it was something he read in a class assignment or perhaps he may have gleaned something from one of the many thought-provoking conversations we had in his office. Whatever the reason, I was—and am—grateful.

While attending the university, I did not seem to garner that warm fuzzy feeling some alumni seem to have acquired. I was not thrilled to be there. Once I realized obtaining a degree from the U of A was a real possibility for me, I just wanted to get out as soon as possible. It was that desire that kept me focused.

Although I visit my grandmother, who still resides in Fayetteville, several times a year, I have had little desire to visit the campus. On one of those grandmotherly visits, I did take my mother and my children to tour the campus. In the past, I have not been compelled to attend a reunion or any other events affiliated with the university. My feelings for the university remain unchanged. I still have no real desire to go back to the campus. However, I am entertaining the thought of attending the next black alumni reunion. I developed some friendships and connections while I attended the university that I would like to rekindle and the black alumni reunion may be a great avenue for that.

The University of Arkansas gave me my start in life. I completed my undergraduate studies their and went on to achieve an MBA and the CPA designation. I work in my field of study and I am currently employed by the great state of Arkansas. I am extremely grateful for my life, my family, and for the great start I received at the university. Overall, I think I faired pretty well for a small-town girl from a small school studying at the big university.

I am grateful to Dr. Lonnie Williams for the outstanding services, personal support, and encouragement he provided me along the way, and I am also appreciative for the professional relationship we forged and continue to enjoy today. Regarding the time I spent at the university, I have no regrets. Our life experiences are not always going to be rosy. When life throws you lemons, make lemonade! I will close with a quote by Booker T. Washington that seems fitting: "I have learned that success is to be measured not so much by the position that one has reached in life, but by the obstacles which they have overcome while trying to succeed."

■ Merike Manley (1982), producer

Telephone interview by Lonnie R. Williams, November 29, 2007
For detailed biography, see Appendix A, page 308

I enrolled in 1982 the same semester I was homecoming queen. I began college in September 1979 at the University of Southern California in Los Angeles. When my mother became ill the following year, I moved back to Arkansas and attended UCA for a while, and then I transferred to Fayetteville. Because my sister, Ritchie, was in school there, I was kind of familiar with the school and it wasn't that far from Conway. That was the same semester that I became homecoming queen, during my first semester at the school.

I kind of got a bad taste in my mouth after that semester. I don't know, maybe it was because I had heard so much about how people, or the Razorbacks, other graduates, and alums really felt about there being a black homecoming queen. I had some sour grapes, so I was there just that semester. As a result of becoming homecoming queen that year, the following January, I was one of about six SEC homecoming queens that rode in the televised Cotton Bowl Parade. This was the same year that SMU played in the Cotton Bowl, and Eric Dickerson was a senior that played on that team during the bowl game.

Why did I select the University of Arkansas? My father, Dr. Joseph Manley, received his master's in psychology from there and Ritchie was actually enrolled in school there. She is a year younger than me. It was an easy transition. As I said earlier, my mother had become ill and I had relocated to Arkansas from Los Angeles for that reason.

I was very proud of that (first black homecoming queen). I was surprised that I was the first. I had no idea about that fact at all. How all that came to be is that I was dating a Razorback football player at the time by the name of Danny Walters. Since he was on the team, he, another friend Daryl Bowles, and Gary Anderson encouraged me to run. I thought, why would I want to do that? They said, "Oh come on, you're pretty, come on, come on, why not, why not?" And then, I found out that Ritche was also nominated and was running. So I was actually running alongside my sister and the other ladies who participated in the process. I kind of liked that.

It was a big deal at the time. I don't know if they still have this procedure, but the football players were all given three votes. The African American football players told the other football players that they should vote for me. And then they could choose from whomever for the other two votes. I remember asking Danny, "How did this come about that I ended up winning?" He said, "Well, we got together and said, 'hey ya'll put just one vote for Merike and do whatever for the other two votes.'" As a result, I won the majority of the votes. I was so excited that I won, and it was then that some of the guys told me that I was the first African American, the first black female to win.

And then they told me that the administrators were having a problem, and that they couldn't believe that I had won. They had all the guys to vote again. And I won for a second time and they couldn't believe it again. They voted for a third time. They actually had three times that they made those boys vote because they couldn't believe that I had won. They just knew there had to be something wrong. That's kind of how it all started out. After those three votes showing that I had won, they weren't too pleased.

In previous homecoming elections, they actually had a parade. But they canceled the parade because I had won. And on the day of the game, apparently, they have a processional on the field. And whoever volunteered to ride the homecoming queen around on the football field that day pulled their vehicle out at the last minute because they didn't want a black girl riding around in their car, much less being the homecoming queen. Someone, I don't know what his name is, but I have a picture and Ritche has a picture of it, came in at the last minute and volunteered to let me ride in his car. He had a convertible white Rolls Royce and it was just gorgeous! It was white on the outside, with red leather interior, and he came and actually led the processional with his car on the field for the game that day. Thanks to him, he made my day despite all the other things that had happened with the voting and the parade being canceled.

I don't remember anything about a reception. I guess I was just so busy at the time trying to find a suit to wear and having my grandfather to come up, the late Richard Manley Jr. It was the highlight of his life. He was from Conway, Arkansas. He had never attended college. He was so proud that his oldest granddaughter was the first African American homecoming queen at Fayetteville. So he was so proud to escort me onto the field. And when he came up, he said it was really a memorable time for him. I have no idea of whatever else was canceled or done. But I do have the write-up from the paper the next day. My mother had the little clips and a picture. She had it laminated. I have it here at my home right now. It was just a headshot of me. It wasn't even an article. It looks like a byline at the bottom of the page in the paper. It only said, "Homecoming Queen waves to the crowd." And it was under an article saying that Gary Anderson had won the Crip Award. So it wasn't even as if the picture was being published in the paper for me being the homecoming queen.

I was just surprised it was such a big deal to everybody because there were a large number of African American players on the football team. I just didn't grow up that way. My parents didn't raise us to distinguish between black and white or whatever. It just wasn't an issue for us. So that was a little culture shock to me. It really was!

Of course, I prayed about it, and I had my family. I had my sister Ritche, my mother, my grandmother, and my grandfather as well as my friends who are still friends of mine now. Like my mother used to say, "Do what you're supposed to do and everything will work out." I was really young at the time, and I was just enjoying life and worried about my hair and the typical things that a girl would worry about at the time. I didn't get all wrapped up in everything else that was going on.

How did the African American students take this? Some of them I had spoken with were kind of surprised that the school reacted that way. I guess it gave them a reality check as well as to where they were. You know how things change, but some things never change. They were really up-at-arms about it, but that's not how I am and I didn't take it that way. I got a lot of support. People really rallied around me and were mostly surprised that things were canceled or changed and that I wasn't supported like the previous white girls.

I don't remember if it was before homecoming or afterwards, but they contacted me. The athletic department said they had two tickets for me and a friend to attend the Fayetteville game that was actually being played in Little Rock this particular weekend. I asked the person, "Well, you know, do I need to come down at halftime to be introduced or whatever?" And the person said, "Oh no, no, no. We're not going to introduce you!" I said, "Well, then, how are they going to know I'm there?" The previous queens were all introduced at the game there. They said, "We'll just announce that you're in the stands and you can just wave your hands." I said, "Are you kidding me? That is not going to happen!!" I was furious!! I was just furious. I said, "Well, just calm down, Merike, just calm down." My girlfriend, Sandra McKeller, and I drove through the pig trail to Little Rock. When we got to the stadium, we saw two little black boys. I said, "Hey, have you guys ever been to a Razorback game? Would you like to go?" They said, "Yeah, we want to go!" None of the people knew they were cheering for two little black boys that were sitting in my seats. I was gone. We knew how to work it, since we weren't going to miss being on TV or anything like that. That was one other experience with all that.

I guess it was just that I was very surprised because I had never experienced blatant racism like that. I do know that probably seven years ago, during one of the Fayetteville games, they had all the living homecoming queens to come back. They sent me one of the little gold crown pendants, and they were going to introduce all of the surviving queens. I didn't go! I thought, if ya'll didn't think enough of me then to introduce me, and now you think I'm going to come back subsequently twenty years later, and you're going to introduce me along with an entourage and everyone else—no! I was just not all into the limelight thing. I was just much more laid back then and kind of reserved. I keep to myself, so I didn't have any interest in going to that, either. Needless to say, I didn't make that event. So that's the most recent remembrance of that. It was something. It really was something!

Describe my feelings toward the university during my time of study? I guess because my mom was an educator, her thought was that education was always the main focus for my sisters and me. It wasn't a question of whether we were going to college, but where we were going to college. I was the first and only one to go out of state. So when I came back after being at USC and coming to Fayetteville, I was excited thinking maybe this was where I needed to be. That situation quickly let me know that Fayetteville wasn't where I needed to be. With me being such an open-minded person and being a free spirit, I soon realized that being in Arkansas wasn't exactly what I needed to do or where I needed to be. I appreciated the experience, but I was there for the education. That homecoming experience was something that was a great part of my life that I'm very proud of and everything.

It left a little sour note in my experience. I have not been back to Fayetteville since I left. I haven't even thought about it or even had the interest to do it. Not at all!

Describe my present feelings toward the university? Well, I guess when you're older and wiser you don't hold any grudges or whatever. I would love to come back. I do know there have been quite a few African American homecoming queens since that day, which I'm very proud of, glad for, and everything. My girlfriends and I were talking about coming back in 2008 for the homecoming events. I think we'll come up and participate in the festivities, reminisce, and everything. It will be an emotional thing for me, I'm sure, just to come back and see the campus. I watch the games from time to time on television. We just beat LSU the other day! Those Razorbacks pulled out that win. I don't have any animosity about things. I hear things like the emotional and academic environments have changed and things of that nature. So I don't hold any grudges. Life's too short to do that—way too short.

My father died when I was just twelve years old. He was from Conway, Arkansas, also. He was also the first black to graduate from the University of Central Arkansas, and they established an endowment fund for him. I'm very proud to be a Manley and so very proud to have had all those experiences in my life. I'm very honored and happy. Don't let the crying fool you. I'm very proud, very honored, and I will cherish this for the rest of my life that you guys have given me this opportunity to discuss my experiences there. I love the Razorbacks and I will try and come back for the 2008 homecoming and make my presence known. I'd love to come back and visit and everything. I guess the one keepsake that I've kept for the last twenty something years is a football that was given to me right after the game. Lou Holtz was the coach at the time. He presented the football to me. So I've got to track him down one day and get him to sign it for me. And that would just be the ultimate then. And I'll get it in the glass case and everything. But, yeah, I'm so very honored. I appreciate ya'll contacting me and giving me this chance.

▓ Karen Mathis Mongo (1984–1988), university professor

Telephone interview by Lonnie R. Williams, March 24, 2007
For detailed biography, see Appendix A, page 308

I came to the University of Arkansas in the fall of 1984 and declared a major in communication, receiving a bachelor of arts in 1988. I went into the graduate program to pursue a master of arts and completed it in May 1990. I chose the University of Arkansas initially because I was thinking I would major in engineering and they had a really good engineering program, but I never actually pursued that major. It wasn't a passion for me.

I was one of the earlier African American homecoming queens. I was selected as homecoming queen in 1986. I wasn't the first. I believe I was the third. Also I worked with what was the Black Student Association. At that time, we started a petition to argue for more blacks on campus and within faculty roles. For example, on campus working with Anthony Moore, and having meetings with then-chancellor Dan Ferritor, who, of course, at that time didn't seem to agree with our thoughts or desires in that way. But it was really important for us to express that. With the Black Student Association, we started a newsletter called the *Ebony Forum*, and I was the first editor of that. I don't know how long that continued or what else came out of that. We also started a theater group, and we named it the Ira Aldridge Players. And I served as the president of that organization as well.

Ebony Forum . . . I know that was 1987–1988. The Ira Aldridge Players . . . we started that in 1986. We had initially started a minority theater company, Sepia. We wanted to take on the name of a great tragedian and we chose Ira Aldridge. I believe that was 1986.

Describe my experience at the university? I'll start with homecoming queen first. With that, I didn't have a desire to participate in pageants or anything of that nature. I had done it years ago growing up as a teenager. But the Black Student Association wanted representation, and they asked me to represent them in the homecoming queen contest and I agreed to do so. Initially, we just had to submit a picture. After the pictures were posted, we had to go down to the athletic complex, have dinner, and introduce ourselves. The athletes were to actually choose their homecoming queen. That was the process.

So we did that. I was then named a finalist. Once I was named a finalist, that's when things became a little more controversial. At that time, the university was still, although integrated on paper, still pretty much segregated in my opinion. There seemed to be an attitude where they wanted to make sure they preserved separateness. Certain things were specifically for whites and not for the rest of us, although we were students as well. And part of what happened is that they changed the competition from just more of a popularity contest where the guys voted for whom they wanted to represent them. They decided to make it an interview competition. We had to go over again for dinner and an interview. We were asked questions by a host; the players witnessed our answers and voted based on that. We went through that process. I wasn't uncomfortable with that at all because I had done pageants before, had been used to that type of format, had to respond to an audience, and was required to think on my feet. Ultimately, I think, most of the guys there, black and white alike, were very pleased with my responses and my answers. They chose to select me to represent them and that was the competition. I was officially named the homecoming queen for the University of Arkansas.

It didn't stop there because at that point the photos were taken and things were put in the papers. There was a local car dealer who usually donated cars for the queen and the court to actually ride upon. I believe his name was Hatfield. I don't remember the name of the dealership specifically. I remember him calling me, tracking me down on my job where I worked at the library on campus, actually. I worked on campus in the library at the time, and I got this call from this man I didn't know. What he said to me was, he knew I was the homecoming queen. He introduced himself as something Hatfield and he normally donates his cars for the person to ride upon in the parade. "I saw your photos in the paper and I wasn't real sure about who you were, can you tell me about yourself?" And I immediately knew where he was going with that and I didn't want to buy into it. I gave him an idea of who I was, in terms of where I was from and my major. I never actually identified myself as African American and once I did not do that, he proceeded to come right out and ask, "Well, I can't tell from the photo. Are you black?" I said, "Yes, I am." At that point, then he did not allow us to use his cars. He did not want a black person riding in his car for the homecoming ceremony for the parade.

Bill Gray was the assistant athletic director to Frank Broyles and Bill Gray had a meeting with the entire homecoming court. At that meeting, I proceeded to tell him about the phone call and what happened. He immediately wanted to minimize the fact that it happened and didn't want to talk about it at all. He did say to me that they had a doctor in town who was actually a collector and that particular doctor donated . . . actually volunteered . . . to drive me in his car. I don't remember his name or anything about him except that he was kind, considerate, and nice enough to let a black girl ride in his car. He drove the car himself. It was a convertible Excalibur, very nice car.

I went on to represent the university at the Cotton Bowl. That year, the team went to the Orange Bowl, not the Cotton Bowl. But I came down to Dallas to represent the University of Arkansas in the Cotton Bowl parade as well as other activities around the metroplex.

Generally, I don't have ill feelings toward the University of Arkansas. As a matter of fact, I have affection for the University of Arkansas. I'm proud to say I'm an alumna of the university. I earned my degrees. One of the first jobs I applied for . . . right after graduate school . . . I ran into a woman who had had one of my major professors years ago when he was a professor at the University of Southern California. The interview was very short. She said to me, "You know what? You studied under Tom Frentz. Then I know what you know." That was the end of the interview; she offered me a job based on the reputation of a faculty member who was a major professor for me. So the University of Arkansas has opened doors for me. I'm very proud of my degrees and proud of my institution.

However, at the time I was a student there, there was still a lot of racism. That racism was often overt. I remember as a student challenging one of my professors over a grade dispute. No matter what I did, or no matter how hard I worked, he would never see fit to give me an "A." I remember one time, I cried because he gave me a "B" plus plus on a speech. What is a "B" plus plus on something like a speech? It's like grading an essay. How do you give a "B" plus plus? How come it's never an "A" minus minus? No matter what I did, I was never able to earn an "A" from that professor. When I entered graduate school there, classical rhetoric was a required class, and he was the only person who taught it. I had to take that class so I had to go back to him again. It was the same thing. He gave me a "B." At the end of class, on the day of final exams, he said to me, "You are a very good student," and I said, "I know," but he still gave me a "B." And then when we were going to prepare for comprehensive exams, I was the only black person in my master's program. All the white kids would go to different professors and ask, "What should I know and how should I prepare for the comp questions?" I wouldn't go to him initially because I didn't feel like he would give me any guidance. A couple of my friends in the program said, "Go to him. Go to him. Go ask him. He's told us what to study. Go ask him." So I went to him and I said, "Dr. Bailey, I'm getting ready to go through comps and I understand you are providing guidance to students on how to prepare and how to study. What would you suggest I focus on for the comprehensive exams?" He said, "Know everything." He didn't narrow the field at all. Classical rhetoric covers, technically, you could argue thousands of years almost, but he wouldn't help me at all. But that's what I expected and that was OK. I sat for my comps and did not have to write twice for a single question. I'm very proud of what I learned at the University of Arkansas. I'm very proud of the experiences I had there. Generally, it made me a better person. I think it made me stronger because when you are the only one, you have to be strong.

This is something that I don't talk about on a daily basis, so I never really think about it. But yes, I guess I am still hurt, yet grateful. I made it and I'm still making it.

I think during that time I was somewhat angry because everything was a fight; it was a struggle. I didn't think that we had a lot of support. We had few black staff members, a few faculty members, who you could go to—Dr. Nudie Williams, Dr. Gordon Morgan, Dr. Margaret Clark, and Dr. Carlton Bailey, for example, in the Law School, even though I wasn't in Law School, but I talked to him sometimes. Those people were very supportive. They were very cognizant about what we had to deal with at the university. Having a small network of support in place helped. I will say this—there was one faculty member, Dr. Richard Ray in communications, who really reached out to me. I met him when I was a freshman. He was really very supportive of me as an undergraduate and encouraged me to stay for graduate school. Ultimately, with his support, I was awarded an assistantship as well as a fellowship to the graduate program.

I've gone back a few times. I went back for a homecoming activity. They had sent information out and asked people to return. I went back to that. Then I've gone to a couple of games. I think I attended one or two games since then and some of the games have been played here. I've attended a few games they've played here in the Dallas area.

Describe my present feelings toward the university? I think part of it is realizing my part in it . . . how it happened. Things happen for a reason. The other part of that is I think the controversy with Jeremiah Wright during the Obama run for president of the U.S. is an example. Most people really think racism is something in the past. They think the vestiges of slavery are really nonexistent and mostly present in the minds of black persons and we're keeping those things alive, but that's not true. I think that there are many people, particularly white America, who really don't know the kinds of things (events, ideas, et cetera) that are institutionalized and that are perpetuated year after year after year with very little thought in terms of their impact on people of color or any disenfranchised group. Generally, I think the University of Arkansas is a good place to earn a degree. I think students of color who choose to go there must honestly ask themselves if that's the place where you will be able to flourish. I don't think it's easy. You have to have the wherewithal within yourself to want to flourish. I do get some of the newsletters and looks like there is some change being made. I don't know what I really think about the University of Arkansas. I don't like to say I have hard feelings. I learned a lot there. I learned things I needed to know for my profession and like I said, it's opened some doors for me.

I can't think of anything at this time to add. Generally, I can say there are times now that I think about it in detail it can be very hurtful, but I think my experience was probably better than most.

■ Roderick J. McDavis (1989–1994), university president

Telephone interview by Lonnie R. Williams, September 11, 2007
For detailed biography, see Appendix A, page 309

I joined the faculty and staff in 1989 in the position of dean of the College of Education and professor of counselor education. It was a great opportunity. I was looking to become a dean of education after serving as a faculty member in education and as an associate dean of the Graduate School at the University of Florida. The University of Arkansas presented a great opportunity for me to further my career by serving in an administrative role. I thought it was a great university and a great location with great people. I stayed for five years serving in that capacity. It was five quick years, but they were five very, very good years in terms of the opportunity and what we were able to accomplish.

I think I was the first black dean of any of the academic units at the University of Arkansas and, hopefully, I paved the path that others have been able to follow. I certainly enjoyed my experience in that role. I don't know what other firsts I might have accomplished as the first black dean, but certainly know that in terms of the history of African Americans at the University of Arkansas that was certainly breaking some ground. The Holmes Scholarship Program was after we got there. I think that was one that we take some credit for starting from the standpoint of creating opportunities for African Americans to get some financial support and get a great education.

On the positive side, it really gave me an opportunity to sort of demonstrate my ability as a leader. I think I was able to do some things, create some innovative strategies in the College of Education. One that I remember quite well was changing the four-year teacher education program into a five-year teacher education program. I think that really broke some new ground. The people I worked with were really great people and that gave me an opportunity to sort of challenge myself to be even better with the kind of skills-set that I thought I brought and hopefully was able to develop. On the other side of that, it was the challenge of meeting expectations both of the majority that that were there as well as African Americans. I think being challenged to do some things and have some questions about my leadership come up because of the fact that I was African American, but we were able to withstand the challenges that were in existence at that time.

I think overall I was accepted. There were some individuals who questioned my ability to provide the appropriate leadership for the University of Arkansas College of Education and in that regard, I think that some challenges were put in my way, but overall I was well accepted by senior administrators, by most of the faculty, by certainly the students who were in the college. So it was a very, very positive experience overall from the standpoint of how I felt I was accepted and the opportunity that I was given to work with students, faculty, and staff. And certainly at the community level, I felt very accepted there as well.

I feel very positive about my experience. I think that the University of Arkansas really focuses on creating an environment that is conducive to individuals that come into that environment. I was a person who was from another state, had all kinds of experiences at other places, but entering into the community, I was very well accepted. My family was accepted. I was able to do some of the things that I wanted to do as a leader and as a faculty member. So I think I had a very, very positive experience at the University of Arkansas. And even to this day, as I reflect back on my experience at the University of Arkansas, I feel very, very good about it from the standpoint that it was the first major leadership opportunity that I was afforded and in that regard I have very, very fond memories of my time at the U of A.

I have returned on several occasions for football games, for sporting events, just to partake in watching football games as well as just visiting with friends and former colleagues. The latest time that I was there was probably about ten years ago. But several times since I left I have come back in order to renew acquaintance and see some old friends and colleagues.

When I reflect on the experience that I had, I was very young from the standpoint of being a dean. And I think the leadership, the chancellor, and the vice chancellor for Academic Affairs, really entrusted upon me a great deal of responsibility. I believe that given that opportunity, I met my part of the deal by providing the kind of leadership that they look for and I had a great time. I really enjoyed working with the students, faculty, and staff.

The thing I really reflect on the most was the experience that my family and I had in the community. We were very well received in the Fayetteville community. I think that made our stay there that much better because when your family is happy, you're happy. My sons had great experiences in the schools and my wife was also teaching at the university. She had a great experience. I think the fact that all of us really had great experiences while we were there simply made my professional experience that much better. The one lasting impression that I have of the U of A is the same impression that I have of the state of Arkansas. I met some of the best people that I have ever been able to work with at the U of A and certainly across the state of Arkansas.

■ Katina Revels (1990–1994), photojournalist/editor

Written response to interview questions, September 20, 2007
For detailed biography, see Appendix A, page 309

I'm a Dallas native, and I chose to attend the U of A, sight unseen, in the fall of 1990. It borders Texas, allowing me to be closer to my grandmother, an Arkansas native who didn't finish the eighth grade. In three and a half years I finished my bachelor's degree, becoming the first member of my family to graduate from college.

My time on the campus was rich with adventures of self-discovery that helped shape the person I am today. I challenged myself from the classroom to social settings, work-study jobs, and extracurricular activities, including the student newspaper, yearbook, and radio station. I was founding president of the University of Arkansas's Association of Black Journalists, a student chapter of the National Association of Black Journalists.

What helped me see things clearly, in addition to my family, was a special program called SMILE. It paired an incoming student [freshman] with an upperclassman who shared a lot of the in-and-outs of the campus and social know-how.

I had a lot to learn, and a professor told me he would get paid whether I learned or not. Point made. High school success didn't mean anything. College was up to me, no one else. So I changed my habits. I studied and prioritized my involvement in extracurricular activities. The U of A was my place to discover my true strengths and weaknesses.

My first feeling toward the university is fond memories. I saw young entertainers become stars, young ladies become empowered women, and gentle men evolve into gentle giants, and these relationships have endured and even strengthened in the years since—all because of our common journey on the "Hill."

Dr. Nola H. Royster was a noted alum and educator from Little Rock and I owe her. Her mantra was giving back. Her strength was undeniable. She died in May 2001, yet her persona, vision, and passion for education lives on with everyone she touched. I embrace her motto for life: "Do what you can, where you can, while you can, when you can."

Now Top Stories picture editor for the Associated Press, I give back by returning for every Black Alumni Society reunion for speaking engagements, career recruitment, and social functions. They always bring back memories—the good and the not so good, but each an experience that helped make me what I am today and whatever I will become. That's my way of repaying Nola Royster. It's a moral obligation. They blazed the trail. I merely followed it. And because of that, I can say proudly that I'll always be one thing: Katina Revels, bachelor of arts, Class of 1994, University of Arkansas.

■ Cedric E. Williams (1988–1993), insurance

Written response to interview questions, August 26, 2007
For detailed biography, see Appendix A, page 310

I attended the Minority Introduction to Engineering (MITE) program during the summer of 1987 and the Transition Retention Minority Engineering Program (TRMEP) during the summer of 1988. I completed my coursework in the fall of 1993 with a BSBA degree in CISQ.

My parents said I could go to any college as long as it was in Arkansas. So I went as far as possible to the U of A. I also wanted a degree in engineering and Fayetteville was the only school in Arkansas that offered a four-year degree in engineering. I also had relatives that had attended the U of A, a first cousin (Lonnie Ray Williams) that was employed in administration on campus.

I enjoyed my college experience at the U of A. I enjoyed the interaction among all the African American students. Greek life was something that I was heavily involved with (almost too heavily); I was on academic probation for approximately one year after going through the pledge process. Greek step shows and parties were the main source of interaction among the African American students.

I enjoyed the relationships among my fellow African American students. I felt the U of A, at the time, did not offer any activities geared toward minority students. The U of A did not offer many, if any, African American lectures. I only remember one musical concert (Jodeci) that was geared toward black students and they backed out at the last minute.

I have returned to campus for Black Alumni Society reunions. I also try to attend one or two basketball games a year.

My present feelings are lukewarm toward the U of A. I love the words that are spoken from head administration officials about increasing diversity, but I don't like some of the actual actions that have taken place. Number one was the firing of Nolan Richardson. The basketball team was the one rallying point for black students on campus. It was something we could identify with and it was a great recruiting tool for the campus. Number two was the reduction in administrative duties for Lonnie Williams. Lonnie was personally responsible for starting the BAS reunions and also recruiting and retaining a large majority of the African American students during his tenure.

My parents had a different opinion of the U of A when I first started. Actually, it was of Fayetteville in general. When they brought me to campus for my freshman year, they would not even spend the night in Fayetteville before driving back. They actually drove back to Fort Smith to spend the night because of the impression they had of "the Hill" in 1988. (It was too close to Harrison.)

Chapter 6

Desegregation Work Still in Progress
The University of Arkansas in the 1990s

> We have to do some homework as a university . . . We have to make our campuses a place where minorities feel comfortable when they visit. We have to become much more sensitive to people who are ethnically, racially and culturally different.
> —Roderick McDavis

In March 1994, Dean Roderick McDavis made the above statement in response to the state legislature approving of the hiring of an affirmative action director for the University of Arkansas.[1] McDavis, the first African American to hold the position of dean of a college in the university's history, heartedly endorsed the decision of the legislature and saw the position as crucial to the institution's desegregation efforts. The new affirmative action director would assist in developing policies for the recruitment and retention of minority faculty, staff, administrators, and students. The director would also assess the university's compliance with affirmative action regulations. McDavis considered the hiring "very timely" because he believed that the nation was becoming diversified. McDavis also asserted that the new director would help bring a positive consistency to the university's minority recruitment and retention efforts, which he described as "below average."[2] In October of that same year, the university announced that Willyerd Collier Sr., an African American attorney, had become the institution's first affirmative action director.[3]

During the 1990s, the university made other moves to improve its desegregation efforts. In 1994, the institution opened the Multicultural Center to enhance the academic experiences of all students and to provide a special place for minority students to gather for programs, meetings, and other social events. In that same year, the university officially recognized the month of February as "Cultural Awareness Month."[4] In 1997, led by Willyerd Collier, the university established the George Washington Carver Project, a program designed to increase the racial diversity of graduate students by enhancing the institution's relationship with historically black colleges and universities. The following year, Lonnie Williams, the black assistant vice chancellor of student services, spearheaded the establishment of the Black Alumni Association which was formally recognized by the university. Also in 1999, Johnetta Cross Brazzell became the first black vice chancellor, and Lisa Williams became the first black faculty member appointed to an endowed chair position.[5]

The efforts by the university to create a more inclusive atmosphere produced small but important increases in the numbers of African American students who attended the institution in the 1990s. At the beginning of the decade, black students comprised only 4.68 percent of the total student body (684 out of 14,600). By 1995, this percentage had increased to 5.40 percent (797 out of 14,756). By 1999, this percentage had grown slightly more to 5.88 percent (1,003 out of 17,043).[6] Black faculty numbers would also rise slightly, growing from 2.8

percent in 1998 to 3 percent in 1999 of the total number of full-time instructional faculty at the university.[7]

Student-sponsored programs and columns discussing race and inclusion appeared regularly in the *Traveler*. Often, these campus-wide discussions about diversity occurred during the Martin Luther King Day Celebration, "Cultural History Month," or after some national incident related to race had sent shockwaves throughout the campus community. For example, in April 1993, after the Los Angeles riots, an event sparked by the acquittal of four white police officers for the videotaped beating of Rodney King, an African American, Regina Miller, a guest columnist, wrote an article in which she urged the campus community to begin seriously dialoguing about racism and its negative influences.[8] In 1995, after O. J. Simpson was found not guilty of the murder of Nicole Simpson and Ron Goldman, the *Traveler* interviewed Patricia Koski, the chair of the sociology department, about the implications of the different reactions of blacks and whites to the verdict. Koski suggested that the divergent reactions of blacks and whites stemmed from life experiences that are shaped by racial realities in America.[9] Also during the 1990s, a number of high-profile people such as Dr. Benjamin Hooks, the executive director of the NAACP; William Gray, president of the United Negro College Fund; and Dr. Samuel D. Proctor, pastor emeritus of Abyssinian Baptist Church, came to the university to lecture about race and American society.[10]

Undoubtedly, the most conspicuous incident that involved race and the campus community occurred in August 1995. Carlton Bailey, an African American law professor, went to the Sigma Phi Epsilon Fraternity house to take photographs of a black statue, tagged "Sambo," that someone had placed at the front of the house. According to Bailey, while he was taking pictures on the front porch, people from the house began "yelling 'nigger' at him." Also Bailey contended that a chair was thrown in his direction from one of the upper-floor windows. Bailey reported the incident to the university police. The police in turn informed the university administration. The judicial affairs department for the university conducted an investigation. Members of the fraternity house stated that they did not know who had called out racial epitaphs at Bailey. Neither had anyone intentionally aimed a chair at the professor. According to the fraternity spokesman, "They had been throwing objects out the window all afternoon." When asked about the purpose of the black statute, the members of the fraternity claimed that they considered "Sambo" to be "a positive, uplifting thing for black people." Further, the group did not consider itself to be racist because it had a member who was "part black." After completing its investigation, the university suspended the fraternity from activity on the campus.[11]

■ Celia Anderson (1997–2001, 2002–2003), author

Written response to interview questions, March 17, 2009
For detailed biography, see Appendix A, page 310

I turned onto the rock-paved driveway and continued until finally parking in line behind my teammates' cars. I couldn't help but notice the Razorback license plates that graced the fronts of most of them. I made myself a mental note to make sure I got one for my own car—as a freshman, I wanted the world to know I was officially a Lady Razorback basketball player.

In my neighborhood, that meant something—didn't mean very much to the older people who only heard horror stories about being black on the hill, but to my peers it meant I had made it. My name on the back of a Razorback jersey on ESPN brought pride to many: first, my immediate maternal family who had only one college degree before me, which belonged to a male. Second, to my friends from my neighborhood who had given me the nickname "college girl" and shielded me from the many pitfalls that were at my fingertips. And lastly, to Tommy, the elderly gas station attendant who clipped every article that had been written about me since junior high school and hung them proudly on the wall. I thought about them all as I walked through the door of my assistant coach's home for my first team cookout.

"Celia," my coach said, "I want you to meet my wife." I extended my hand to a middle-aged woman with a big southern accent and even bigger hair. "Nice to meet you," I replied. From there I was introduced to several other people, whose names I don't remember. After all of the formal hellos had passed, I found myself face to face with my coach again, "My wife collects Aunt Jemima's," he said, "She has everything, but the napkin holder!"

My heart dropped. I stood staring at the proud Caucasian man, confused as to whether I should smile or puke. Didn't he understand that Aunt Jemima is the image of the black woman who was forced to take care of white families better than she did her own? Did he not know that I was a child who was raised in Mississippi and had experienced what it was like for my grandmother to cook in a restaurant that we were not allowed to eat in? Didn't somebody tell him that I watched my great aunts rise early to clean houses across the river for the whites, while their grandchildren cleaned their own? Feelings stirred in me that I had never experienced before.

He continued to show me her collection. I said nothing. Instead, I smiled on the outside while my insides bubbled over like shaken coke in a can. I prayed no one would pop my top because the end result would likely splatter my true feelings all over her collection. I felt mocked and ridiculed. The same way I imagine the Native American feels whenever the Atlanta Braves or Cleveland Indians proudly display their logos. Luckily for everyone, my cap stayed sealed. After a complete rundown of each "keepsake," finally he moved on to the next player, taking her through the same racially insensitive routine that I had just been released from.

I sat down at the table where the Aunt Jemima salt and pepper shakers stared me right in the face, seemingly laughing at my cowardness. Why didn't I say something? Anything. It was my silence that allowed the showcase to continue. I fought back tears, somehow, making it through the party with my true feelings undetected. Two hours later, I was back in my dorm room hiding my face in shame.

I have to speak about my University of Arkansas experience in two separate categories: the athletic world and the student world. Contrary to popular belief, the two did not coincide for me. If my experience were a chemistry course, then the student world was the lecture and the athletic world was the lab.

"Come on, Celia! You can do it!" they yelled at me while my lungs were about to burst. I was on minute nine of the Blair Mile that all women basketball players had to run before the season.

I'm doing the best I can, I thought, wishing everyone would just disappear. I started pretty strong, right on pace with everyone else. But as we finished the first lap, the gap widened and I became the lonely tortoise, being lapped by a team full of swift hares. As they each passed by me, I wondered if I had made the right college choice. Could the first African American female player from Little Rock to sign on the hill in over a decade, fit into a system that would soon expect her to change everything about herself if she wanted to succeed? I had never run a mile straight in my life. Now, I was expected to run one in seven minutes or less. Well . . .

Twelve minutes later, I crossed the finish line feeling like the beauty queen who had never placed in a single pageant. My point guard gave me words of support, telling me it was good that I didn't quit, but her words offered me no comfort. Why didn't they understand that I had just been reduced from MVP of the state tournament, in which my team won, to last place? Why wasn't I good enough anymore? What I didn't know as I walked off of the track that day in 1997, is that I would ask that question for years to come—why am I not good enough? Not only was my physical condition poor, I would soon learn that according to the system that I had become a part of, nothing about me was quite right. There was an image of the "model" athlete, and quite frankly, I didn't fit the mode. I was a young girl starving for knowledge, never afraid to examine situations or question the status quo. I was truly malnourished in my mind. What I needed was outside of the realm of the "do as I say" philosophy that athletics offered. I needed to be a part of a world that encouraged diverse thinking and did not judge my worth based on whether or not my personal beliefs were in line with the people who made the decisions. I wanted to be taught *how* to think, not told *what* to think. Naturally, I fell into the arms of academia, which fed my mental [needs] and shaped me into the woman I am today.

Like many freshman, when I entered the student world I moved around campus like a snail, interested only in how I could pass a test without having to actually study and how I could spend more time on Dickson than I did on campus. Well, it was the college professor who showed me that both tasks were impossible. But they didn't pull me to the side and have a long talk—no, they allowed me to carry on as I wished until midterm. I will never forget those first grades; I had more flags than an Olympic stadium. I got the message. I heard it loud and clear. And that message still holds true in my life today. Because of one midterm grade report, I now know that you cannot get something for nothing—a lesson taught to me by my very first college professors.

It was this attitude that made me strive to succeed in the classroom. You see, there, I was always good enough, but somehow still pushed to be better. After finishing my BA, I returned to the university after spending a year playing basketball overseas to earn a master's in communication. This was one of the best decisions I made in my life.

One of the first courses I took was Writing the New Ethnography. Sitting there in the conference room of Kimpel Hall I heard a quote that has become a lifelong model for me, "I've spent a lifetime making of my life to be, more than the measure that others can see." I'm not sure who the originator of that quote is, but I heard it from one of my graduate professors who listed it as his life motto. What I didn't know then, is that that quote would become a change agent in my life.

In 2008, I was about to make the critical mistake of chasing the visible things, which I thought could measure my success, without ever developing those things which others cannot see. I just so happened to revisit that quote. After typing it up and putting it on my bathroom mirror, one morning between a brush and a floss, it all made sense to me. I thank that graduate professor for refocusing my attention on the development of character as the single most important measurement of success. What is talent without character's presence?

At the University of Arkansas, I fell in love with education. The world of academia made me truly believe that my birth situation did not determine my destination. After living in several cities since earning my MA in 2003, something keeps bringing me back to the hill. Perhaps it's the same voice I heard on the steps of Holcombe Hall the night after the party at my coach's house, which told me I was exactly where I needed to be. I thank the athletic world for introducing me to the student world. It was the University of Arkansas college professor that helped me find my own voice—but not just any voice—one that no longer sits in silence when racial insensitivity is staring me in the face.

When I sit at the football games immersed in a sea of red, my hog call is for more than just the players on the field. I raise my hands in praise for a university that encouraged me to show the world the greatness that my ancestors and college professors instilled in me. Go Hogs!

■ Eddie Armstrong (1997–2001), consulting

Telephone interview by Lonnie R. Williams, August 12, 2007
For detailed biography, see Appendix A, page 310

I entered the university to obtain a degree in political science in 1997. It was really my second choice next to a small college in New Orleans. I selected the U of A primarily because some of my high school friends and older friends that graduated a year before me at my high school selected the U of A. They played a strong part in convincing me, partially recruited, when they came home during the summer. I attended four and a half years from 1997 to 2001.

My role in black history at UA? There were a couple different things. ASG president 2000–2001 . . . being the second black was pretty historic to me. Around that time, they created another award. And I'm curious to know how many minorities, blacks, have won since? The Henry Woods Leadership Award is granted each year by Fulbright Arts and Sciences. I was one of the second recipients of that and the first African American recipient of that award. The Arkansas Alumni Association offers up an award each year called For Whom the Bell Peals or it had just begun or I'm not sure if it's an ongoing award and I'm not sure how many African Americans have received it; however, I'm sure the numbers of brothers are few who got those honors. So I guess that's a few marks on the history of the U of A. Another one is simply being a part of the class, late 1990s, 1997, maybe around 1999, when the influx of recruiting had made a change, started going up, as far as black kids being recruited as a chain in the university. Our class was one of the largest minority recruited, specifically African Americans.

The overall experience was something that can't really be matched. In some ways, it was a good experience because there were a lot of things that you had to overcome as far as hurdles, and nothing defines you better than overcoming hard work and hurdles in life. Learning how to work with people or work with students that you might not have been used to working with and vice-versa. They might not be used to working with you as far as the race lines are drawn. I came from a pretty mixed high school where blacks and whites got along fairly well. We all, like I said, decided to go to the U of A together, but one of the things that we experienced immediately, as friends from high school going to college, is that everybody didn't necessarily interact that same way. It was an interesting dynamic trying to get our old friends and new friends to get to the table together and just have a good time together.

When I think back on it, I give a lot of good praise to the fact that I did get an experience to be part of the minority numbers, part of a small group of African American students that were going to school there. Probably, a lot larger than it had been and coming through that with the kind of education, not just in the classroom education, but the education of life with all types of people and learning how to sit down in corporate America, or in the business community, to work with all kinds of races of people, and different ages of people.

One of the cool things about the university, as far as my experience that I'll never forget, is the fact that there still was a tight-knit family for the black community in small pockets and places in the community. Places like St. James' Church, the Multicultural Center, of course, in our dorms, and the student union, along with various other clubs and organizations such as the Black Students Association. All of these made for a good mix of being able to have a good base of family support from your own people that were at school with you. I had the opportunity to mix and mingle and learn how to work with all other races and cultures, how they got along, and how some of them didn't really know how to get along with others. We had a good time and made it a success.

I think there's a lot of that coming from the middle 1990s group of kids coming from high school to college. There weren't really a lot of those kids really messed up, or beat down from race, or a lot of oppression, or barriers that people from the 1960s and 1970s had to go through. This made for more common times, a lot of love, and support from many different areas. I remember Dr. Royster, Dean Cash, Dr. Williams, tons of people, Gerald Jordan . . . not only were there deans and teachers, but Jaquator Hamer . . . they were all friends and family—kind of like aunties and uncles around there trying to make sure that we got through this college experience. I give a lot of credit to having that whole mix of things making my college experience what it was.

All that to be said, my feelings toward the university are endearing because I'd like to see more black kids take advantage of the opportunity to experience the U of A. When I graduated college, left, and went to Washington, D.C., like a lot of my other peers, I didn't really want to come back to Fayetteville. I really didn't want to do much more than get my degree and be on my way. After what I'd been through in student government, talking to you, and talking about those people that I mentioned that were such a strong support, it gave me a drive to give it a second shot. I moved back to Fayetteville and contributed in a lot of different ways. I believe in giving back and this is why I created a scholarship foundation to hopefully plant a seed so more black kids can go to that college, go with a substantial amount of funding and support so they can get through college, but more importantly have the experience, access, and opportunities that I had, other kids had, and being able to break through boundaries.

Fayetteville is a real different place. I guess I mention Fayetteville versus the university because the city of Fayetteville has a lot to do with the reflection of how the university is as it relates to the campus, as it relates to an open environment, and welcoming community. When I speak about Fayetteville, I think about what that experience had to do with my experience on campus and I have to say that I was kind of torn because what the city of Fayetteville offered and what that campus offered were two different kinds of mixes in some cases. I came back to see if we can't break down some barriers and forge some new ground with getting more black kids to go to college up there, take full advantage of the education, and also take advantage of the environment that surrounds them. The hurdles and struggles that are going to come with it and the environment. You've got a lot of different odds against you in Fayetteville and most people don't know how to frame it right. They are good odds depending on how you take them. They are good odds and can turn into great opportunity.

I'm proud to have a degree from there, but really wished there was more in and around the community, the city at large, that could really speak to embracing the college experience for students that come to the university. That's probably where my change of heart came in. And still to this day, I have that change of heart because the working world of Fayetteville and the student world of Fayetteville are two different places. There are some things that both can do together to make it a little bit better in giving people an opportunity to know the environment that they are operating in before they walk into it.

I am proud alum. I won't be a lazy one. I'm one that believes that you get a good education, which leads to access, and then you get the opportunity you take advantage of it. And if there's an opportunity for you to give back and contribute to the cause in a greater way, you should. Each individual, if they'd like to take it on, should take on the responsibility to give back. Really, one of my reasons for going back and being involved with the university now is just so I can give my just dues back. Hopefully, more importantly, plant the seeds so that other kids can do the same. They can have a better feeling and state of mind about the university once they leave, once they graduate. I enjoy going back now. I also enjoy still watching it grow. It's still small in numbers as far as minorities. I think somehow, some way, if they can lock down that void and find some other challenge to overcome because that is one they shouldn't have to deal with too much more in the state of Arkansas or across the country for that matter.

There is an advantage to the discovery of what being in the minority can really mean. I'm really grateful for a lot of what people say about the struggles of those before us, from Mr. Hunt, Silas Hunt Hall named after him, and his integration of the college and the many, many others that came after him that were part of the smaller minority and prevailed to do great things. They really became a part . . . ambassadors for people like me to come along and being able to do what I did while there. I'm really more focused on making sure kids can know about the university in a positive light. There's so much you can learn in an environment that you may not have thought you could've survived and or thrived in. I think the university has all the tools in place in order for you to succeed and they can provide that. But I also think every student needs some support along the way. I'm grateful for my experience and hopeful that we can get more people to contribute together for future students along the way.

■ Johnetta Cross Brazzell (1999–2009), university administrator

Interview by Charles Robinson, spring 2008
Interviewed in Brazzell's office, University of Arkansas, Fayetteville, campus
For detailed biography, see Appendix A, page 311

I began my career at the University of Arkansas on January 19, 1999. I came here from Atlanta, Georgia, where I had been working five years prior at Spelman College. I was moving on from Spelman and looking for another opportunity within my field. My first impression had to be my flying here in August 1998. I left Atlanta and I landed in St. Louis. When I got to St. Louis, I got on this small plane and I quickly made the decision that this is not for me. When I got to Fayetteville, the person who met me at the airport said, "And by the way we're getting a new airport, with jets." Okay, I thought. We can have a conversation now.

Everybody I met seemed to be very warm and friendly. Dr. White and I spent a great deal of time talking about what was really important: where the university wanted to go, how he wanted to transform it and take it to national prominence. As I look back, compared to other opportunities I was looking at, this was very appealing to me. I could be a part of that transformative process. One of the things I kept saying over and over again in my full interview was that if you want to maintain the status quo, I am not the person for you. I have no interest in the status quo. I have other ideas about what we can do and how we can move. I did not get the job at Dartmouth and so that's when the University of Arkansas opened up as a strong possibility. And mind you, I had some offers at other places but the U of A meant the most to me and that is why I accepted the job.

As the vice chancellor for student affairs, I am responsible for campus life and obviously we are focused on the students here. Not that everyone else is not focused on that, too, but we are focused on certain aspects for students. I've worked in higher education now for thirty-five years. Where I was born, I went to a segregated school. I'm a child of the 1960s so I have a consciousness about the quality of public life. My level of consciousness is formed in terms of how I was born and how I was treated. With the exception of the five years that I worked at Spelman College, all my professional experience has been in predominately white institutions and so I have always had this idea in these institutions about equity, fairness, and how one creates an environment where all students can have access.

At those other institutions, however, I was not in the same position of authority that I have with Arkansas. And by virtue of the fact that I am the vice chancellor of student affairs means I have a special interest in the success of all my students. But I understand that students come from different backgrounds and experiences, in particularly African American students or students of color on a predominately white campus. We must make sure that we cover their needs as we create this environment for all students. I've also recognized that black students will look at me in a very different way than other students on this campus. I understand that it adds another element to my being here at the University of Arkansas.

When I got here, the university was just in the first year of developing a diversity plan. Committees had been formed and all the vice chancellors were a part of that process. The committee had started its work in September and so there was a commitment on the university's part to begin thinking about this concept. It was really important that I be a part of that process. But while that was being developed, I also knew that I wanted commitment on the part of my division about diversity. And so what I did was to designate the dean of students as the point person for diversity in student affairs. The university as a whole was still working out a plan and still figuring out what it was going to do. Within student affairs, we made that decision very, very early that someone would be responsible for diversity across the division.

Everybody had to have some responsibility for every student's success on this campus. Early on in that conversation we needed to figure out what that meant. It had to be a very clear message that everybody is responsible for all students not just black folks responsible for black folks.

How do we work with our student organizations and how do we encourage them to work with each other when it comes to diversity issues? How do we create forums to be able to facilitate conversations? Very early work that we put together was critical in how we were going to integrate students into this university. We wanted to ensure that every department in the university had a responsibility for diversity.

The other thing that we started doing was to change some of the faces within the division because when I got here there were very few black people working here and still very few today. When you look at where those numbers were when I came and where we are now, in terms of our ability to hire, there's been a dramatic change. My position was that if you have a good program with good ideas, you have ideas of where you want to go, and what you want to do, you can attract people. But you have also got to go out and find people.

Well, I would say that ten years later [it was ten years in January 2009] that this was the best decision I could have made. Timing is everything because I came at a time when the university was in the transformative process. The ideas and principles that are important to me professionally were embraced at this time. My ability and desire to work collaboratively across the campus may not have been embraced five years before or ten years before. But there was the opportunity to do so when I arrived. I kept saying from the very beginning that this is about forming partnerships. This is about collaboration. I had no desire or intent to create a division that is insular. I couldn't do that.

When I was at Spelman, I had a fabulous experience. It is a small institution for African American women. But it was a professional challenge for me to see if we could create the same sense of community at a larger institution. I had a strong working relationship with various folks on this campus and I am not going to sit here and tell you that everything has been perfect. More has happened than hasn't happened. I believe that our students are both better for it because that is the whole point of it—the students. Every student should be transformed by this experience. That was the other element of diversity, to create a community in which this should not be a conversation just about black people or just people of color. You must transform the white students that come here around the whole notion of what diversity is in their lives and what their responsibilities and opportunities are. Every student that comes here has to understand what this means to their own lives.

What do I think we can do to raise the numbers of black students or students of color? I think it's multifaceted. I find that Arkansas is a state that holds on to history longer than other places. And you know as well as I do, that there are a lot of black alums and people who are not alums who are not connected to this institution because of the historical past.

I am still struck by the fact that when I travel to other areas of the state and have conversations with different people, they say Fayetteville is so far away in their eyes. Given the geographic location of the institution from the base of where the black people are in the state, one can understand this. If you think about it historically, it is hard to get to this place. I am still amazed that this place flourished and that anybody could get here. I-540 opened up two weeks before I moved here so I never knew U.S. 71.

Arkansas strikes me as a state where people are just home bodies. They are home bound. I don't think that is just black folks. It is a statewide thing. For many of these families, as I talk to them, you could be asking them to send their kid to the moon, or California, or to New York, or to some other remote place. Fayetteville is just too far.

Another thing that I continue to hear is the perception of the whiteness of the place. And the kids don't want to be in a place where there are all these white people and not enough black people. They are not willing to come to an environment that looks very different from the environment of where they are. But I think that all of those things play in the mix. You have the historical and you have some people who remember what it was like in the sixties when blacks first came in here. You have a more recent example with the whole Nolan Richardson thing. We see minority enrollment dropping off as a result of that because I think that reinforced some of the historical stuff that people were remembering. This is a predominately white community. That's a reality. But some folks don't want to be engaged in that kind of community. You will find that this looks very different from what they're accustomed to. They are going to go to Memphis, or go to Jonesboro, and be near their home. So I think it is all of those things.

I think that if you can show individuals that they can have professional growth and a wonderful positive experience, they will go where they need to be. People will go to Iowa. Now I would never go to Iowa, but there are a lot of black folks that go to Iowa. Iowa has been very aggressive about creating an environment where people can come and be successful. I have found that to be the case as I've recruited African Americans to come and be here. If they ever come and see the area, then it's OK. Then you find folks who have been in other communities. I've found some black folks that lived in Iowa. Fayetteville looked pretty good after that. If you lived in Chicago, or you lived in Boston, maybe it is more difficult to leave. But I think professionals will come to a place that they feel they can make a difference. If people feel successful, they are going to be better from the experience.

What do I think diversity will look like at the University of Arkansas ten years from now? I think it is going to be longer than that. I think that's the reality of where we are. The area is becoming more diverse and that's going to make for some very interesting demanding interactions. I think the African American community across the state still will see that it has a higher invested interest and higher expectation of what the university is going to do for it. The demographics of the state and this I think will make a big difference. The local Hispanic population here is going to make a difference. It is one thing to sit around and bemoan the fact that black people aren't showing up, and it is a whole another thing to say, "OK, what are the plans to put recruitment in place?" We have done some of those in the most recent years. But we are slow. This is a state where you have the black folks, but white folks, too. The college population is not growing in this state. That's a reality. Now in the future, I think, we will have more and more kids of color here; there will be more and more kids coming and that could be a reality.

I just want anyone who listens to know that for me personally this has been a great experience. I understand that part of how my experience flows from my position. I understand that if I were a secretary here then I might have a different experience than I would in my current position. But I also know that being black, no matter what your position, doesn't always insulate you from unpleasant experiences. I have not had any of those experiences. But that doesn't define anybody else's experience, just mine. I will not deny anybody else's experiences, whatever it has been, and they can't deny mine. And so this has been a professionally good experience for me and I enjoyed being here.

■ Kevin Dedner (1995–1999), public health

Telephone interview by Lonnie R. Williams, September 5, 2007
For detailed biography, see Appendix A, page 311

I came to the University of Arkansas in the fall of 1995 and I set out to get a bachelor's in political science. I grew up in Little Rock and although I had been exposed to some historically black colleges and universities [HBCUs], had been on HBCU youth tours and whatnot, I never had anyone actively suggest that I go anywhere but the U of A. I was at the U of A from 1995 until the winter of 1999. I actually walked that spring.

I don't think my role was unique at the U of A. I don't think I played a first at anything, but I did try to play my part in making a difference. I was always conscious of trying to do something meaningful while I was there. I was active in student government and I was active in the Black Students Association, active in annual events like the Dr. Martin Luther King holiday and different things that were going on.

I actually served as president of the Black Students Association [BSA] for two school years, and I think the way it worked . . . we were elected the spring for the upcoming year. So the first year I was president of the BSA must have been from 1996 to 1997. Then the school year of 1997–1998. I think I served a consecutive term. I was elected . . . actually elected as a freshman and served two terms as president.

The Black Student Association's Living Legacy Award? I think that event was probably not the first time that something like that had been done, but the thing that I will tell you my first semester at school I was miserable. I did not enjoy the U of A at all. I came home over the Christmas break and decided that I was going to go back and give it another try—try to find my niche at the U of A. At that time, I had been flirting with getting involved with the BSA and I think I met Dr. Williams at that time, Dr. Nola Royster, and we started trying to pull it together. I think we started out working on the King holiday, trying to do something commemorative for the King holiday. That grew into a committee in the Black Student Association putting together a Black History Month celebration.

I had a very good relationship at that time with Mrs. Daisy Bates, who incidentally had asked me to help her go through some boxes and some things in her home that she wanted to donate to the university. We were trying to think of something significant to do for Black History Month, and I think that is how, in a nutshell, that was sort of born. We went to Mr. Williams and he helped provide the resources to get Mrs. Bates there. We ended up having . . . . I want to say it was like a three- or four-day event . . . that Mrs. Bates actually came on the campus, met with students, and there was a banquet on campus that Reverend Samuel Billy Kyles of Memphis, Tennessee, spoke. I can remember at that time the chancellor was Dr. Dan

Ferritor, and Dr. Ferritor said publicly that night that in all of his years as chancellor that was the best event that he had ever been to at the U of A. I think from there the Living Legacy Award just sort of flowed. It was ideal. The next year when I was president of BSA we honored Mr. Ozell Sutton, and it just sort of took off from there.

My experience is much different from those who are, say, maybe twenty to thirty years my senior. I am very thankful for my experience at the U of A. The best things and I have said this a lot, the best things I have in life, I owe to the U of A: my best friends, my wife, whom I met at the U of A when I was eighteen years old, and I am thirty years old now. We haven't been married a long time and that shows you the longevity of our relationship. So I really appreciate the interaction I had. For me, particularly for the work I do today, being at the U of A taught me how to work within systems, within a structure, within a process, a very structured way of getting things done and of getting things accomplished. Although we were the minority at the U of A, we still had a very rich, cultured experience. I don't know that that experience is the same for students there today. But we were fortunate that we had black administrators, black professors there who saw to it that we had a rich, fulfilling experience. I am very appreciative of that experience, but the thing I will say is that I saw a lot of young folk who were the cream of the crop from their hometown come to the U of A and the U of A chewed them up and spit them back out. Some of those folk never recovered.

I always wondered what it is that allows a minority to succeed at the U of A and some not to succeed. Frankly, if I had not made that decision when I went home at Christmas that I was going to go back and find my niche, I could have very well been one of those that the U of A chewed up and spit back out, and I would not be where I am today. In a nutshell, I am very appreciative of the experience. I have so many stories of how we learned to deal with institutional racism and tried to address them through a structured process. I think that has really made me who I am today because I learned to address problems in a structured way.

I'll never forget . . . I will share just one story with you. I had a good friend. He and I are still friends today. He was president of something, Residence Interhall Congress, and we commonly refer to it on campus as RIC. RIC is the governing body for the dorms on campus. I will never forget, one night I was walking across campus and I saw all of my good white friends coming in and out of what we affectionately call Brough, it was Brough Commons. So I saw all these white kids coming in and out of Brough Commons having a good time. I asked somebody and he said, "Well, we have coffee night every Tuesday night. We get free coffee, RIC pays for a band for us, we have free refreshments, a band performs," and I was thinking this is something. I went in and, sure enough, all my white friends were in there having a ball. But there were no black students there. The next day, just more intrigued by it, I called my friend who was president of RIC and asked him about it, and he said, "Yes, we pay for it; it is paid for with the student fee." I was thinking the black folk don't know anything about this. To make a long story short, we ended up integrating a little coffee night. But not only that, we started getting the black DJs to play there on certain evenings. In short, I think what the story tells us is that we learned to deal with processes, systems, and sort of tried to address our concerns through a systematic way. I think that the experience frankly may be unique to an African American's experience at a predominately white institution [PWI] in that you actually have to find a systematic way of addressing your concerns.

I can think of one other story. One time we were working on orientation and new students were coming. This young African American lady from Little Rock pulls up to the side. I had some kind of responsibility at orientation . . . I can't remember. She had received a RUSH booklet, and there were not any black fraternities and sororities, maybe the AKAs were in it. I can't completely say there weren't any, but the majority of the black fraternities and sororities were not in this RUSH booklet. She asked why there were not any black sororities in there and I said, "Well, let me check into it." At that time, I think they had Greek Services, Ms. Deb Euculano was head of it, and I called her and said, "I've got this publication that I believe your office produced it. It is really disappointing." I think by the end of that night we had called all the presidents of the fraternities and sororities and we had all agreed to write a letter. Now what we found out, like a couple of meetings later, is that the white fraternities and sororities were paying like fifteen hundred dollars a page to be a part of this publication. They were buying the space. Obviously, our organizations didn't have that kind of money. But moving forward to the next year, that booklet became a complete representation of the U of A Greek life, black fraternities and sororities were included. I think that was the unique thing about my experience there, that we learned to address things. I appreciate everything I learned in the class, particularly learning to write. I certainly appreciate that these days, but when I think about real life that's the thing I think has been most useful for me.

I had a great time at the U of A. I had the best time and what I did learn to do—my mother may have not thought so then—but I learned the careful balance of having a good time and trying to get your lesson at the same time. I will say this, although I was having a good time and it was a very rich experience, I never really considered myself a Razorback until it was almost time to go. Then it's sort of like I realized how fast those days had passed and I was trying to savor that moment. It was a very rich experience. I enjoyed every bit of it. I can't think of too many things that were frustrating other than when I was in a difficult class, but I never had any problems that were sort of unordinary for a college experience. I really valued the experience.

I have been to several Black Alumni Reunions. I have been to the Dr. King holiday programs. I will say one of the compelling things that draws me back always is among those who were there at the same time I was there; we know there is a Black Alumni Reunion. We are typically on the phone and we are trying to take a poll of who is coming and who is not. That is always the big influence of whether or not I show up because it's sort of like we know the days will never be the same, but it is something special to be able to get back with all those folk, to reminisce, to see people raising their families and into their careers now.

I think the U of A seems to be in spirit headed in the right direction. I will say what's frustrating to me; I just read in the paper yesterday that the U of A is opening a recruitment office here in Little Rock. Not to take anything away from the young man who is director of this office they are opening in Little Rock, but I noticed he did his undergrad at UAPB and he did his graduate work at Webster. It may sound a bit arrogant, but there is something unique about an African American who matriculated at the U of A. I think the only way you can really communicate that experience at the U of A for an African American is if you have experienced it yourself. I know that sounds very, very biased, but I really do believe that. So in a nutshell, one of the things that is somewhat frustrating to me today is I see the U of A contracting out things that even as a student I heard the alumni saying to them, "Help us help you do this." Today, instead what they are doing is contracting those opportunities out to firms and whatnot. I heard this conversation ten years ago from alumni who were committed to ensuring that minorities had a very rich experience there saying, "Help us help you do this." It's sort of like, I want to say bittersweet, but I don't know if that is the best way to describe it because I think that is one of the things that sometimes people, the administration at the U of A miss. The best advocates and the best salespersons you have for the U of A are those who matriculated there.

Instead of putting all these massive dollars into trying to create an image of the U of A that really is not so anyway, I think the better use of the dollars is to engage former students who have good things to say about the U of A.

I just want to say, I appreciate what you all are doing with this work and I respect the integrity of the intent because I think there is something unique for those who have . . . the minorities, the African Americans . . . who have matriculated at the U of A. It is a unique experience. I think the thing I would stress, just sort of random thoughts from my mind, if it were not for the black administrators and professors who were on the campus, Dr. Royster, Dr. Williams, Dr. Gordon Morgan, and Dr. Nudie Williams I am thinking of. It sort of says, although we were at a PWI, in some ways it felt like we were also at a small black school in the sense that Dr. Royster—I will never forget when I was president of the BSA—she called me by the name Mr. President—and that made me try and carry myself as a president. I think that those experiences just really help shape who I am today. I am very grateful for my experience there. I don't regret having been there. I don't regret having made that choice and, like I said early on, the best things I have in my life I owe to the U of A.

■ William Jeffrey "Giovanni" Flanigan (1995–2000), educator

Written response to interview questions, September 4, 2007
For detailed biography, see Appendix A, page 312

I came to the University of Arkansas in the fall of 1995, originally majoring in pre-med biology. All of my life, my mother had planned for me to go to Morehouse. At the beginning of my senior year in high school, I was accepted and awarded a full scholarship. I never even applied to any other college or university. Beginning my junior year, I attended the Multicultural Day at the University of Arkansas. I realized that there were more than just black athletes, but black students, who went to school there. The black faculty and staff were all very inviting, it was the top-ranked school in the state, and, to top it all off, the ladies were gorgeous (especially the Deltas at that time)! I decided that if I stayed in state, then Fayetteville would be the place. Harvard had offered me a full scholarship that I had turned down. So against my mother's wish, and to my grandmother's delight, it was the U of A. I attended the university from fall 1995 to spring 2000 (BSE Kinesiology in 1999, MAT in 2000).

My rap group, *Wishful Thinking* (featuring singer Dahlia Evans, DJ Derrick Dansby, and myself), became the first group to represent the university at the national level of the MasterCard American College Talent Search (ACTS) in Philadelphia, Pennsylvania, in February of 1997. After winning the MasterCard ACTS show at the university in November of 1996, we won the regional show at Southern Methodist University in January of 1997. The song that I wrote for the competition, "Stand On Your Own Two," also won the Chancellor's Award for Performing Arts in that year as well. We appeared on *Good Morning Fort Worth!*, and had mentions in *USA Today*, *Rolling Stone*, *Spin Magazine*, and on the *Today Show*.

My freshman year, first semester coincided with the Sigma Phi Epsilon incident involving Professor Carlton Bailey. Having your school make national headlines, *Ebony* and *Jet* magazines, among others, for all the wrong reasons was an inauspicious way to begin my college career. It was also the first time in my life that I witnessed first hand, blatant racism. All of the racism that I had encountered to that point was very subliminal and covert. I remember Kevin Dedner, former BSA president and fellow freshman at the time, and I being outraged at this incident. We went to speak with Dr. Nola Holt Royster and she allowed us to vent our frustrations on the mall of the student union. It was at this point that I knew why God had sent me to Fayetteville: to show the world that change hadn't come as swiftly as people would like you to believe. Kevin and I worked together as he spearheaded the move to celebrate Mrs. Daisy Bates for her lifelong body of work. Getting to meet Mrs. Bates is, to this day, one of the greatest joys of my life.

In the fall of my sophomore year, 1996, I joined the greatest organization in the world, Alpha Phi Alpha Fraternity, Inc. I became an ASG senator and a member of the B-funds committee. I was integral in the fight to maintain BSA's funding level after white students complained that we were getting too much funding and attempted to fight the movement to change the homecoming queen selection process after black women had won five in a row. I also was an RIC senator and the 1997 to 1998 RIC Senator of the Year. I served on the university judicial board for two years where I saw, first hand, the difference in treatment of black students compared to our white counterparts.

Having made the university look good in its dealings with minority students, I had gained great favor with Chancellor John White. I was invited to numerous chancellor's cabinet meetings and received numerous private scholarships. When the issue concerning moving football games from Little Rock to Fayetteville arose, he called on me to speak out in favor of the move. At the time, Eddie Armstrong, who would become the second black ASG president, spoke out against it. Not only was Eddie a friend of mine, he was a fellow black student. The statement the chancellor made to me was, "I hope Eddie's stance doesn't affect his candidacy for ASG president." I declined the offer and I immediately offered my full support to Eddie Armstrong and his candidacy.

I also was in the middle of a group of white students' bid to strip Courtney Tate of the RIC presidency he won, making him the first black president of that organization. They accused me of campaigning too close to a poll site, by saying, "Yo, vote for my boy Courtney," outside of Brough Commons. Then, the people who accused me were the same people who sat on the committee that initially ruled on the allegations. They were also the same people who worked for the person whom Courtney defeated in the initial and runoff elections. Needless to say, they ruled against Courtney and stripped him of his win. We ended up going through a protracted fight that lasted from the middle of the spring 1998 semester through the summer and into the middle of the fall 1998 semester. Finally, a special board was created and given the authority to have final say. This board included Dr. Lonnie Ray Williams, and they upheld the initial election. The white students wanted to protest because Dr. Lonnie Williams was black, failing to mention that he was the first black on any of the previous boards/committees throughout the entire ridiculous ordeal.

Witnessing all of this as a college student prepared me for the "Real World." I faced the "white is right" mentality multiple times during my time at the UA, and I am greatly appreciative of what it taught me. It was like on-the-job training.

I was always aware of the fact that the university and I had a symbiotic relationship. I made them look good in their quest to show sensitivity to minority students; and they gave me an all-expense-paid education that would be the foundation on which my adult life would be built. In my opinion, it was nothing more and nothing less than that.

I have been back to all but the most recent Black Alumni Reunions since I graduated in 2000, and I have been back for my fraternity's anniversary program and scholarship banquet. I also have been back at least once a year for a football game.

There was one reason and one reason only that I stayed at the University of Arkansas. That reason was Dr. Lonnie Ray Williams. I had many mentors during my time there. John L Colbert, Dr. Nola Holt Royster, Dr. Michael McFrazier, Dr. Jaquator Hamer, Dr. Charlene Johnson, Dr. Erica Holliday, and Drs. Karen and Reliford Sanders were all integral parts of my journey through the university. However, it was Dr. Williams who oversaw and guided my voyage from boy to man. My father died when I was ten and Dr. Williams filled a void for me at a time when I needed male direction. When the university allowed the vice chancellor to "restructure" Dr. Williams's entire department, subsequently forcing him to leave, my feelings toward the school were forever changed for the worse. I cannot, in good conscience, recommend any students to go to Fayetteville without the benefit of the mentors who saw me through. Not to slight those African American instructors, staff, et cetera, that are there now; however, there are hundreds of blacks who have attended the UA over the past twenty-five years and they all share a common link: Lonnie Williams. The fact that the Black Alumni Reunion is the largest reunion of students at the university speaks volumes about that common thread. When they wronged Lonnie, they wronged me, and I am not currently prepared to exonerate them for this transgression.

All in all, I know God intended for me to go to Fayetteville. I have met lifelong friends, a lifelong father figure, and lessons that will forever dictate the paths that I take in the future. I am appreciative for all that the UA taught me, the good, the bad, and the ugly.

■ Crystal D. Hendricks Green (1996–2001), engineer

Written response to interview questions, October 17, 2007
For detailed biography, see Appendix A, page 312

I enrolled at the University of Arkansas in the fall of 1996 to obtain a BS in chemical engineering. When I made the decision to stay in state for school, the U of A was my only choice. The university had a good engineering program and they appeared to be increasing their focus on diversity. I was the first recipient of the university's Coca-Cola Foundation scholarship.

My experience at the U of A was very rewarding. I not only earned a degree, I grew up, and learned a lot about myself. When I stumbled, as most college students do once or twice while during their years in school, there was always someone there to mentor me. I still keep in touch with college professors and university officials who took the time to relate to me and make me realize that I could have or do anything as long as I worked hard.

I tell people all of the time that I did whatever I wanted to in college. I took advantage of every opportunity I could. I participated in small group tutoring for classes, Greek life, leadership opportunities, and professional societies for students, one-on-one mentoring with faculty members, and interaction with university officials. By being involved in so many aspects of campus life, I received a well-rounded experience at the U of A. The university truly has a lot to offer to potential students.

I enjoyed my years at the U of A. I didn't always agree with university policy or changes that were made, but I always felt like I had a voice or that someone was representing my views. I wish there had been more diversity on campus while I attended the university. There were not many black students in my classes or in my dorm. There were hardly any black university officials. However, the few people in "positions of influence" were always accessible. They always made you feel like you were a part of the family and that you mattered. That always meant a lot to me.

I have returned to the university to attend two Black Alumni Society (BAS) reunions, one homecoming event, and an anniversary for my sorority's chapter on campus. Events that took place after I left the U of A (e.g., firing of Nolan Richardson, etc.) have soured my feelings toward the U of A somewhat. However, if you simply walk away without voicing your opinion or trying to develop a solution, I feel you are part of the problem. Thus, I still intend to be a member of the Alumni Association and support future BAS reunions/events.

■ Tanisha L. Joe-Conway (1991–1995), producer

Interview by Lonnie R. Williams, February 10, 2008
Interviewed in the home of Tanisha Joe-Conway
For detailed biography, see Appendix A, page 312

I entered the University of Arkansas in 1991 to obtain a degree in broadcast journalism. I selected the University of Arkansas because I had always wanted to go there first of all. Even when I was in high school, I just thought that was the place that I wanted to be. Having a local connection to home with Mr. Williams, Lonnie Williams helped with the recruiting process. I also had three close cousins who were already there at the U of A, so I got to come up and visit a few times, see the campus, talk to a few people, and I decided that was the place I wanted to go. I was there for four years from 1991 to 1995.

I guess my role was that I was the first Ferguson Scholar [Black Alumni prior to name change] at the U of A. I was very pleased and privileged to receive that honor.

I had a good experience at the University of Arkansas. I was a pretty quiet student so I don't think I took advantage of a lot of things that I probably could have. My professors were very good. They were excellent in the field and so I got a chance to take part in a lot of things related to my field to help me later on like internships, not only in TV but in radio. I met a lot of lifelong friends, a lot of friends who I still keep in contact with now. I think that was a great thing that came from having to be so close knit because there weren't so many of us there.

During my time of study, I really did love the university. I think I had a great opportunity and like I said, I had a great network. The African Americans there in the administration like Lonnie Williams and others . . . those kind of people who are dear to me and helped me a lot as I was making my way through the university. I think that those kinds of things really helped me a lot and helped to endear me to the university.

I've gone back a couple of times for reunions early on after I left. I have also gone back to do a couple of speeches as part of my job and other things done through my work with AETN. We've gone back several times and been taping at the university. So I've been back probably more times for work purposes than for anything else.

My feelings have changed some towards the university due to some of the things that have transpired such as with Mr. Williams leaving, the situation with Nolan Richardson, and Stan Heath. Some of those things really made me pay a little closer attention to some of the politics and dynamics of the university. So I would have to say that some of those feelings that I had when I was there have changed quite a bit.

I had a few instances when I was there in classrooms where people asked questions related to race and that kind of thing, but you kind of chop that up to different people and different experiences. I think after I left and some of those things that transpired really did put a small damper on some of my feelings towards the university.

My experiences at the university changed me coming from a small town. It opened up a lot of opportunities for me, introduced me to a lot of different kinds of people, and a lot of different things that I was able to do. I can say it was a wonderful experience for me to have and for me to be able to get into my career actually being directly linked to being affiliated with the University of Arkansas. One of my professors knew someone at AETN and wanted me to apply there. That was the way I was able to jump right into my field. I would say my time at the university was filled not only with a very good education, but also a great networking tool.

■ Monica M. Jones (1991–1995, 2008–present), university staff

Telephone interview by Lonnie R. Williams, March 5, 2008
For detailed biography, see Appendix A, page 313

I entered the University of Arkansas in the fall 1991 and pursued a bachelor of arts degree in psychology. One reason I selected the University of Arkansas was the great scholarship opportunity I received, or that I was awarded. I looked at several universities, not necessarily in the state of Arkansas, but all over the country. After I visited the campus and just got a feel for what was going on, it was for a weekend during my senior year—minority visitation weekend, it just felt like that's where I needed to be. The scholarship was offered later. I'd been to the campus previously several times because my cousin played football there. He entered the year before I did. It just felt like that's where I should be. I found a good community and good support system there. I graduated in 1995.

Was I an African American first? I was one of less than ten at that time, granted the honor of being selected as a homecoming queen. I believe it was 1993. That was really a combination of a lot other things that I did because I was really active on campus. That was monumental because it was kind of a confirmation of or recognition of work done. I was active with several organizations such as the Black Student Association, the STAR Program, my sorority Delta Sigma Theta, and so all of that kind of culminated into the homecoming honor.

My overall experience, when I reflect back, was primarily positive times. The positive interactions I had, most of those interactions, were within the African American community that existed on the campus. Most of my experiences had dealt with most people who looked like me, acted like me, and had a lot of similar beliefs. That was kind of my experience, not that I was sheltered because I knew all the things that were happening on campus. I knew of a lot of the issues that were going on when I was an undergraduate student there. There was a rally with the Klan in downtown Fayetteville. We didn't feel threatened so we understood historically how it has been in the city of Fayetteville and in northwest Arkansas. We learned through interactions we had with the faculty and staff, like Dr. Williams and Dr. Morgan, the history of the U of A. And knowing what the history was, we were able to deal with that somewhat uncomfortable situation. But it didn't directly impact us on campus because we kind of built a wall of security through our sense of our community. We were told these are the things that we are not going to do during that time and how we are going to protect ourselves, our psyches, and everything else to deal with an uncomfortable situation.

I did have other uncomfortable situations. For instance, when I was homecoming queen, traditionally, the queen's picture had been placed on the front of the program and the year I was queen that practice was stopped for some reason. And there was, I don't even remember what it was, but it was a like a character or cartoon or something of old-time Razorback times. Whatever! I don't even remember specifically what it was, but my picture wasn't on the front of the program nor was it on the ticket as it had been in the past. The only people who gave me a reception, who even celebrated really on the whole, were the Black Student Association and other minority organizations on campus. So that kind of left a little resentment and a little sting in what was supposed to be a very exciting time. From the support, as I mentioned before, from the black community on campus and even outside of the university—that support helped me through that situation.

Overall my experience was good, but it was only good because of the support system that I had and have. A lot of opportunities that I received were through the multicultural office and center. I worked in Dr. Williams's office, starting in the summer of 1995 with the "Youth Opportunities Unlimited Program." I interacted with SMILE when Dr. Jaquator Hamer was there. I worked with her on projects and was involved with the Inspirational Singers. Through those experiences—that is what kept me there. That's what kept me coming back year after year. And really having a passion and love for the university, it was all cast from those experiences. Had those not been there, or those individuals not been there, or had I not had those experiences, positive experiences, with that population of folks, I probably wouldn't have stayed at the university.

While I was an undergraduate there, I was really excited to be there, to be a part of the university, to be a Razorback because that was a tradition in my family. To be a Razorback and to really get into athletics, that part was exciting. On the flip side, some of the practices, realizing, and remembering back, I mean I was green. . . . very, very green. I was an inexperienced young woman learning the ways of the world and how people interact. How race, class, and gender interact and impact everything that you do and experience. There were eye-opening experiences when I started realizing some of the things that happened behind the scenes. And some of those happened while I was a student. Other revelations, I guess you could call them, came about when I was a graduate student at the university or/and when I started working at the university.

Primarily, I learned a lot when I was an undergraduate and graduate student there. Like I said, my support system made it positive and it helped to kind of push to the back corners of my mind the negative or uncomfortable experiences I had. I just try to reflect on the good things that happened there. Overall, I enjoyed being there and that is the way I remember the university. I remember most of the people in that institution.

On being a staff member—it was really an interesting transition because I felt like I had kind of a very interesting perspective. I knew what students felt from when students were supposed to go to this office, then go to this office, and they weren't getting the information they needed. I really knew how to navigate the system from the student's perspective, which helped me become, I think, a better staff member on campus because I knew how students would think about things or how they would operate. I was still connected to them because I worked with undergraduate students in the organization while I was a graduate student.

But it was really eye opening to see all the behind-the-scenes stuff that students didn't see. It really helped me to gain a better understanding of how universities operate and how things come about. Universities, especially state institutions that are relatively large, move very slowly. Change was slow. As a student, we wanted it right then, but as a staff member I gained a lot more perspective and understanding of the process. It was difficult as a staff member when you see so many marketing publications going out with we promote this, we support this, this is what we believe in, and then when you're sitting in meetings, or receiving e-mail, and that's completely the opposite. The message is opposite. So learning how to deal with double-talk and people really talking, as a lot of people would say, talking out the side of their necks because they would say one thing and really what they meant, or the intent, was not really genuine. It was interesting because when I started at the U of A as a student, I was under one chancellor who I considered my chancellor, Chancellor Ferritor. When I graduated as a graduate student, there was a different chancellor there, Chancellor White, and he was there when I started as a staff member. So the ideals of diversity, inclusion, and those type of things that were really a part of my undergraduate experience—that were taken through my different iterations on campus as a graduate student and then as a staff member—shifted because the public message was we promote diversity and we're giving money here and there. But what was going on was the reduction of funds for, say, programs on campus, or the displacement of responsibilities, or stripping of responsibilities.

So on a lot of levels it was very disheartening because the kind of shine, or the polish, was stripped away once I became a staff member. I saw what was going on behind the scenes. Day in, day out the staff members, minority staff members on campus, were the ones primarily fighting for diversity on the campus and not within the administration. The administration shouted that that's what they were doing, but that wasn't the case because they were the biggest obstacle from my perspective. That's part of the reason I left the University of Arkansas in 2002 because of a lot of changes that were happening that weren't positive and that were to the detriment of students and to the university overall. The overall reason I left was to pursue my doctorate.

I returned to the university . . . must have been three times since I left. I returned right after I graduated. I only left for six months between undergrad and grad so that really wasn't a departure, it really was a nice little sabbatical. From graduate school, I left for . . . I guess it was for another six months . . . and then ended up coming back to the university as a staff member in the College of Education as an advisor. I returned during those six months for graduation from my master's program for commencement.

After I left, I then went to another institution. I came back for Dr. Williams's retirement when he left the University of Arkansas and went to Arkansas State. I came back for that celebration. It was a huge wonderful celebration and I made a fool of myself because I was bawling and everything else, but he was a big part of that institution, part of my history, and I can't even say part—all of my history at the university was directly tied to him. I remember meeting Dr. Williams when I came in as an undergraduate from day one of orientation. He was like "come on . . . come in here, sit down, and talk to me." Those were the types of the relationships that you remember. People who actually reached out to you and you care for. I definitely couldn't miss when he was leaving the U of A.

And then I came back one additional time for a job interview with former basketball Coach Heath for a position as an athletic advisor. I ended up not taking that position. It was really interesting to come back as "an outsider" and to see some of the similar dynamics that were there when I was a graduate assistant. I was like, yeah! This is probably the best step for me considering my educational aspirations. So those were the last times . . . I think that was the last time I returned.

My present feelings for the U of A, in my heart of hearts, I still love my school, but that is tied to the people. It's hard for me to separate out because as I said before my memories of the U of A are the Black Alumni Reunions, when I helped that undergraduate student with that celebration, Delta weekend, or Kappa weekend, or homecoming, and primarily that was with the community of people I felt comfortable with. So my love for the institution is directly tied to those connections with those individuals. But in the same vein, it's kind of hard to articulate. I will say it like this. I see all the progress that was made in the interest of diversity, promoting students, and to see that go backwards, almost erasing everything that was done prior to me becoming a student, while I was there as a student and while I was a staff member . . . seeing a lot of that erased is very, very frustrating to me, and very disheartening.

I try to keep and stay abreast of what's going on, what changes are happening. Now it is changing, so only time will tell what pans out with the new chancellor and his administration coming onboard.

As far as information about me, you were asking indirectly. I think a lot of who I am and the belief I have, not fully, but some belief and a lot of my development as a student, as a budding scholar, and as a budding professional, I learned at the University of Arkansas. But the credit can't be given fully to the institution because my education didn't come from the mortar and brick there. It came from the individuals there and a lot of the individuals that I learned from are no longer at the institution. So it is kind of disheartening not to be able to go back because I know some people talk about, oh, I went back to my school and Dr. such and such was there and Mrs. such and such was there. That same connection is true only in part. Only a few people I knew as an undergraduate student are still there, Dr. Gordon Morgan, Dr. Barbara Lofton, and Dr. Fruend. I know it's hard for people to remain at the same institution forever, but it kind of saddens me a little bit because a lot of who I am, and a lot of who I became as a professional, I attribute directly to my interactions with the Minority Affairs Representation: Dr. Lofton, Dr. Lonnie Williams, who I stay in contact with, Dr. Karen Sanders, and others . . . all these people/professionals, but my connections to them is through the U of A and it continues beyond the U of A, but they help me day in, day out to continue to grow and to be better.

I have to say I'm glad this project is being done because I think it will provide the university, as well as the students who have matriculated through the university, a better understanding of where the U of A was and where it is going. Where it is right now, I really don't know because it's hard to really kind of say, because they're in a state of transition right now. But I think the project will provide great perspective and hopefully . . . hopefully and prayerfully really, people will take an honest look at what students are saying and what sentiments are being conveyed in order to make the institution a better place.

One of the things really impressed on me when I was there is that we need to stay connected to the institution in order to make it better for the students that follow us. I think about all those individuals that came back to the Black Alumni Reunions year after year, especially those early on when they said—talking to the older alumni saying that "I never stepped foot back on the campus" to hear them say "this is my first time back in forty years" . . . I don't know. Hopefully, someone will really pay attention to what people are saying, look at the time span, and understand what all that really means in the broader context and the historical context, not only of the institution and of the state and of the country because what happened on the hill is happening in other places. Good, bad, and ugly, but paying attention to the why and the what behind the scenes is a lot more important, in my estimation, than trying to just look at the number of black people who were there as this point and at that time. Those numbers represents lives, experiences, and I think this project will convey a lot of that and hopefully help the institution become better.

■ Trenia Miles (1990–2003), university administrator

Written response to interview questions, October 26, 2007
For detailed biography, see Appendix A, page 313

I enrolled at the U of A in fall of 1990. I earned a BA in psychology, 1994; MS in counseling, 1997.

Why did I select the University of Arkansas? I attended Minority Achievement Weekend when I was a senior in high school, had a great experience on campus, and decided this is where I wanted to attend school. The people that I had come in contact with were very positive and friendly. They made me feel welcome.

One of the things that stood out to me on the first day of class is a feeling of alienation. I recall instances where I was the only black person in a class of at least thirty-five students. I remember riding the bus back to my dorm the first week of school, where again, I was the only black person on it and thinking to myself, "What have I gotten myself into?" I later decided in my mind that I had just as much right to be there as anyone else. I was not going to allow anyone to make me feel inferior, or that I did not belong there, so I pushed forward with my eye on the prize—a degree.

Overall, my experience at the U of A was great. I had a strong support system of friends and staff. My friends and I have maintained a strong sisterhood of at least sixteen years. In addition, since I was a first-generation college student, I became a part of Student Support Services (SSS). Student Support Services is a program designed to assist first-generation college students in their transition into college. I was provided free tutorial services, counseling, and workshops designed to help me become successful in college. Dr. Lonnie Williams and the late Dr. Nola Royster were staff members who were great advocates, mentors, and supporters of me as well as other African American students.

One situation that I recall that took place at the U of A that seemed to unite African American students was an incident where a few prominent African American athletes were accused of raping a thirty-plus-year-old white woman. As African American students, we banned together and protested to the administration in their handling of the case. As a whole, we felt that it was racially motivated and decided to speak up against it.

Another negative event I recall is when members of a white fraternity threw a chair out the window of a fraternity house at a black law professor. The fraternity was reprimanded and suspended from the campus for a few years as a result. I will say that the U of A handled the situation swiftly and sent a message to everyone that this type of behavior will not be tolerated.

Although the following may pertain more to the city than the university, I believe that the university could have been more instrumental in helping minority students feel a part of the community by using their influence to help us push for things that were important for minority students in the early 1990s such as Black Entertainment Television (BET), a black radio station, and black hair and make-up products. As a black student, I felt cut off from the rest of the world, particularly the black community, due to the U of A's location. The U of A is located in Fayetteville, Arkansas, where Caucasians make up, at the time, about 90 percent of the population. There were very few black television shows shown on TV and no black radio stations. I remember feeling very disconnected to the black community, especially when I went back home to Pine Bluff, Arkansas, on the weekends or for a break. I was behind on the latest issues within the black community as well as the latest music. Having a black radio station or BET television would have made our stay in Fayetteville a lot more tolerable and might have helped the U of A's retention of minority students.

At first, my attending a historically white institution was challenging because I was not used to being the only minority in a room full of Caucasians. It was even worse outside the campus. I recall white people staring, some with disdain in their eyes, like I should not be there. I had made up my mind that I had just as much right to be there as they did. It was definitely an eye-opening experience. If I did not have the support of my friends and other staff members at the U of A, then it would have made completing college that more challenging. Overall, my feelings were those of determination and perseverance.

I have returned to the university on average about three to four times a year. I've gone for events such as homecoming and black alumni weekend. In addition, I have gone to visit family, friends, and former co-workers who still live in Fayetteville.

I appreciate my experience at the university. In my opinion, if I can survive at a historically white institution as a minority, I can survive almost anywhere. If I had to do it all over again, I would still choose the U of A because of the friendships I cultivated. Equally important is the fact that the curriculum prepared me to do graduate-level work at other institutions. The U of A was the real world for me.

For any minority student who plans to attend college at the University of Arkansas, I would strongly recommend that you develop a support network to assist you in completing your academic goals. A support network may come from friends, faculty and staff, a local church, or other students to name a few. Also a positive attitude and optimistic outlook will go a long way. At the end of the day, life is what you make of it. Moreover, you must believe in yourself. I believed that I could be successful, so I made choices that were consistent with my beliefs like attending class, maintaining good grades, and utilizing campus support systems, to name a few. More importantly, my faith was strong and I relied on it when things got tough.

There will be obstacles such as people and circumstances that will try to deter you from reaching your goals. However, you have to persevere even when you feel like giving up. The Bible teaches us that suffering produces perseverance and perseverance produces character and character produces hope. So we must continue striving toward our goals and claim what's rightfully ours.

■ Cynthia E. Nance (1994–present), university dean/professor

Interview by Lonnie R. Williams, April 17, 2009
Interviewed in Dean Nance's office, University of Arkansas, Fayetteville, campus
For detailed biography, see Appendix A, page 314

I joined the University of Arkansas faculty in the summer of 1994 as an assistant professor of law. I had two offers after the interviewing process, one at Pittsburgh and one at Arkansas. When I went to Pittsburgh, it was cold and people were getting carjacked in the parking lot, and the faculty members were just not as warm. So I came here, the flowers were up, and everybody was like, "We really want you to come" and they offered the same salary so it was really a no-brainer. It seemed like a much better place to begin a career.

What is my role in the history of African Americans at the U of A? I believe I am the first black professor to join the faculty at assistant professor and make it to full (excluding the library). That was in fall of 2006 for that and then the first black woman to head a college unit as dean.

Describe my experience at the university? I guess I would start back before I got here and talk about how proactive the dean and some of the faculty were in recruiting me to come. I was at Iowa at the time as a teaching fellow. I worked a lot of nights and I was trying to work on my dissertation. They would e-mail and send pictures of flowers. They were very active in making me feel welcome. So I guess I have to start with that. Early on, Chauncey Brummer was involved in gathering together a group of black professionals. He had a bunch of folks over to his house. That really made me feel welcome. So I really knew there was a black community that wanted me to be here.

I think being involved with the undergrads in the sorority [laughing] was a significant experience. I'm not really sure right now how that was a good thing. I'm just teasing. Seriously, it's been really fun to watch our young ladies grow up. I know Gwen is now an anesthesiologist and several are members of the bar. Many of them come back for these events (Black Alumni Reunion). They still e-mail, Facebook me, and that's a good feeling.

My promotion to associate professor signaled that I had a job because as you know when you're on a tenure track, you're always worried about that since until you get tenure you can be dismissed. That first significant vote was a real relief. It also brought a raise with it, so that was really nice as were the votes to become full professor and when my colleagues backed me in becoming the dean.

Talk about my experience as dean? Let me start with the good first. My fear was, and it turned out to be unfair, that a lot of the older members of the legal community and my alumni base would be skeptical about my appointment, but that just has not been true. Big love from the older folks. I get handwritten notes and cards saying keep doing a good job, and folks jockeying to have me when I'm in town. That's really been a blessing. It's taught me something about myself—about my expectations of other people, and not to put that on them because it may not necessarily be true. In fact, we have an alum [imitating in southern accent] who says, "I'll just call my friend and tell them. I'll just call my friends and tell them you don't have an African American dean. We have that at Arkansas!" The stories and cards have really been neat to see. And the bar has been wonderfully supportive.

I want to show you something that I got in the mail. I was keeping it on my desk to never forget. You know how people get too big for their britches? So this lovely little letter came to me and I want you to see it because sometimes people don't know. I have a much better appreciation for what a person who is first goes through and how gracious they are because you just never know what kinds of things are happening to them. What I should tell you is that they not only circulated it to me, but they gave it to some of my colleagues and they sent it, at least they said they did, to the provost and to the chancellor. It is five pages, single-spaced talking about everything that is wrong with me and how I do so much for black people and how I'm bringing the Law School down. I was keeping it right there so I would never forget because that is history. There are, though, people in the building who have expressed to me and to others doubt about whether I should have this position, whether I'm qualified for this position. My annual review last year had some noticeable feedback saying that while I'm a very nice person, I am not really qualified to do this job and similar comments.

I started July 1, 2006, as the dean. The other deans have been supportive. It also helped to have Johnetta [Cross Brazzell—vice chancellor for student affairs] and Carolyn [Allen—dean of the library] here to be able to have some conversations about the influence race and gender play on these roles. So I do miss Johnetta being here, but Carolyn and I still go to lunch every once in a while. One of the things that she said to me, this is Carolyn talking to me, "I think you take things too personally." And I said, "Well, that may be true, but it is to some extent." She's like, "Look, some of the things you get are just because you're in that role. Even if it's not, then you can't carry it around. Otherwise it will impact your success." That was a helpful conversation.

Describe my feelings toward the university? Well, I know the history of it and I watched what happened to other people. I didn't experience those negative things. The things that were hurtful to me or that were challenges to me happened in the micro-context of the Law School. But at the university level, I guess I have to say, I kind of feel spoiled because when they were recruiting me, Dan Ferritor was the chancellor, and he didn't meet with every candidate for a faculty position. We sat in his office and visited for an hour. I thought that was just what happened to everybody. I didn't know. He told me when I left his office, "If they're not good to you, you just let me know." And I just thought he just did that for every new junior faculty member. Then I found out. People were like, he didn't ask to see me. "Oh, I'm sorry! I didn't know." I was just telling the story because I thought it was cool. He was really, really supportive. With John White, although I did not initially have a personal relationship with him, after a while whenever I was at something where he was, he was gracious. I know there were a lot of things that went on, but I didn't experience any of that. Bob Smith as provost was very supportive of my career and of me. Quite frankly, I think he did a very brave thing in making the choice to support me for this position because there were some in the community (I mean I had been raising hell a little bit as a faculty member with some business interests) who gave a little push back. It was a brave thing to do because in a way the Law School signifies a lot of things so to make that decision is saying, "Yes, we really mean it in terms of diversity, opportunity, and that kind of thing." I've had a really good career here.

It wasn't always easy to be here. A lot of it is just being here, being black, a woman, and single. You still have to get your stuff done, manage your life, and it's not like you can call someone to say, "Would you pick up my laundry? Would you take the car in, or would you check on the cats?" You have to manage that and to some extent there is no recognition of the uniqueness of that. Here's what I mean. Most of our top administrators are married. The old model of a dean is a married guy and the wife gets the cocktail party ready or picks up the guests and meets you. When you don't have that, there is a significant additional amount of stuff to manage. I told to my friend Carolyn Jones (Iowa), who is running the Law School deans' workshop, I told her that you all gave us scenarios with an angry alumnus, a faculty member who is dissatisfied with a raise and a student who may have issues, but nowhere in the scenarios did you say things like your kid gets arrested, or you get a lump, or you have elder care issues. That's the real challenge, I think, in managing not only the professional responsibilities, but all the other stuff that makes you who you are.

I didn't realize how much I would have to give up. You know when you're a faculty member you can kind of say whatever you want. I do feel, and I did have this conversation with the provost, to some extent . . . silenced is too strong . . . muted maybe on some things. I had to quit the Democratic Central Committee because I have alumni who are of all political persuasion. This was the most exciting presidential election ever and I couldn't say what I really thought. There were a lot of people who, because there was a woman and a black guy running, wanted to hear what I thought. They wanted to talk about it. I was just not at liberty to do that because now it is not about just me, but there's an institutional interest in not alienating anyone. That kind of thing. The same is true of some of the organizations that I was involved with. I am not sure that until you get into this role, you really think about that. You just take that for granted.

The other thing and this is all of us whether you're a dean, or you're just a faculty member, or you're on staff. I guess I can't speak for all black folks. I'm just going say for me and I think a lot of other people feel this. There is an enormous pressure to get it right. Like you never, ever hear people say, "Well, we had a white guy as dean once and he really messed up so I don't know about that." But it will be said in the context of race and gender. In addition to which, because of the legacy of Silas Hunt in the Law School, when my appointment was announced, I mean before I was even dean, I had cards, letters, and e-mails from black folks I didn't even know. I went to Judge Humphreys' church and people were crying. That's enormous. It's wonderful, that kind of love, but also for me, it's like, "Oh Lord, don't let me mess up because all these people." Do you know what I mean? They have so much hope, pride, and all that and you're kind of carrying everyone with you everyday. That's kind of an emotional point, it's big. Being able to recognize Chris [Mercer], George [Haley], and knowing what this means to them. It's big and I don't think that anyone that hasn't been through this can understand. So I felt pretty proud about that.

I was just at a dinner. The Harold Flowers Association nominated me for an award at the King–Kennedy dinner in Little Rock. CC [Chris Mercer] was there and it is just, every time he's there, it is like, "Thanks. I'm going to make you proud." That's pretty big, Lonnie. And I really want to protect, preserve, and build on that legacy. That's really important to me.

People wouldn't know that. I guess I don't tell them because you can't walk around everyday and say, "I'm trying not to mess up Silas Hunt's legacy." It's just something really, really personal and intense that I just feel. But it's always there. I'm serious. That's real, something in my heart that I carry around everyday. And for the kids in the building, when they are being knuckleheads and not going to class, I think I can have a conversation with them in a way that no one else could.

The problem with a lot of people is they see you in the role when you're already in it. They don't know what you went through to get here. It's not like, oh, I was born into this rich family and they sent me to Harvard and Yale. It wasn't like that. And so it is important to go out talking to young people, too. "Now you see me in this and you see people giving me props, but you know I cleaned houses. Even in Law School, I cleaned houses." For them to understand, it's possible for you to get here, too, because you're not talking with someone who came from privilege and then had all these things happen. I think being a part of that legacy, advancing that, creating access, and opportunity for the next generation of people is critical. And quite frankly, and this may be controversial, but I feel very concerned about brown people, about Latino/Hispanic folk. I think sometimes their voices are not heard. I've been very disappointed about how divisive that issue has been among people of color. I say to people, "Fifty years ago we were them. So then how can you turn around and do that to somebody else?" So I work at being very visible in that community, going to the citizenship ceremony and swearing in, and going to the events put on by the Hispanic Women Organization. I get it. I really try putting my money where my mouth is, for those I see as the next wave of underrepresented people and work to create access, warmth, and making them feel welcome as well. I guess those are things you wouldn't know unless you asked me.

BLSA [Black Law Students Association] surprised me. In fact, the president of BLSA, Donnelle Walker, is my research assistant so I don't know how she was able to keep this from me. BLSA had its banquet last Saturday and it started at six. My mother is in the hospital and her visiting hours start at six. I called the president and I said I'm coming. I have my suit on, but I'm going to be late. It's very important for me to see Mom everyday so that she knows that she's not just locked up on the unit. So I go to see her. When I called Donnelle, she got real quiet. I said, "No, for real I'm coming." I just thought she thought I wasn't going to make it.

I missed the speaker, Carla Martin, our alumna. They gave awards out to all the different students, some wacky ones like the Betty Crocker award for the person who did the best cooking for the soul food supper and stuff like that. It was really fun. Then they got a little bit serious and said, "We've been going to these BLSA events around the country and we noticed that a lot of the BLSA chapters are named for the significant people in the life of the institution or who made a difference." I'm sitting there thinking, "This is so awesome, we're going to have the Silas Hunt BLSA chapter." And then she went on and said, "We've already talked to national BLSA and the executive committee has voted and the membership has voted to rename our BLSA chapter the Cynthia E. Nance BLSA, Black Law Students Association Chapter." I just looked at them. I was so shocked because nobody names anything after you, especially while you are alive. They had just really surprised me. I went up and they had a beautiful lucite plaque that they gave me. I started to say "wow" and I just started to cry because it was just so wonderful and so loving. I explained to them why I was late. So you're rushing around trying to get through life and then all of a sudden, something wonderful happens. We had that moment and took pictures, but it's a big honor. And then to really drill it home, they made me swear in next year's officers with the name of the chapter. That was kind of weird, but it was kind of fun. They got me good.

Well, here's what I'd like to say to young people who look and say they can never be me. That's not true. You just don't know where life is going to take you. I didn't come in a straight line. I went away to college, dropped out, worked as a security guard, worked in a drugstore, worked as a midnight computer operator, and it took me ten years to get my bachelor's degree between junior college and back to Chicago State, which is a historically black college. The way it's sometimes looked over by professional schools. So my point is that even if you haven't always done what you were supposed to do, or you've been a knucklehead, or you're starting over, or whatever, you just never know. Leave yourself open to possibilities. The other thing I would say is sometimes your mentors won't always look like you.

The other thing I'd say is be open. I think sometimes we are less than trustful about people. We think they won't get it or this and that, but you'd be surprised who your mentors would be. Provost Bob Smith . . . if you looked at him you'd never think that he would be someone who would target a woman of color for such an extraordinary role. But not only did he do that, he had my back. And he was there and I could talk to him. He coached me through difficult situations. He taught me a lot about being an administrator. Don't limit yourself to who you're open to and who might be able to guide your career and to help you move forward.

■ Ebony Oliver Wyatt (1999–2003), manager

Written response to interview questions, September 25, 2007
For detailed biography, see Appendix A, page 314

I attended the University of Arkansas from 1999 through 2003. I selected the University of Arkansas mainly due to my experiences in the ACAP (Accounting Careers Awareness Program) through the Sam M. Walton College of Business and partly due to my receiving a local scholarship, the Yvonne Keaton-Martin Scholarship, which financed half of my college education.

My role in history in regards to the University of Arkansas is multifaceted. For one, I was the first member of my immediate family to attend college and graduate with a four-year degree. Secondly, I helped change young African American's perspectives about the University of Arkansas, by serving as a "poster-child" of sorts by having my picture used in several U of A publications. I feel that this was vital in showcasing the fact that African American students are leaders at the U of A and by providing young African American students with a face/personality to which they could relate.

My participation in the 2006 U of A Minority Recruitment Ad Campaign consisted of a thirty-second television spot and radio advertisement. When I initially agreed to participate in the ad campaign, I didn't have any idea of the impact that it would have on the state's African American student population and minority recruitment. I remember hearing some recruitment figures during an alumni meeting and if I recall, minority enrollment increased by 30 percent the following year. In addition, I have received several calls and e-mails from students all over the state thanking me for motivating them to attend college and for being a positive role model.

My experiences at the University of Arkansas have been positive. I received a quality education at absolutely no cost (due to scholarships) and was exposed to university faculty and staff that had a vested interest in my success both as a student and as a young professional (Dr. Barbara Lofton, Dr. Lonnie Williams, Barbara Batson, Mike Morris, and M. Shernell Smith).

I thoroughly enjoyed the time I spent at the University of Arkansas. I was educated in a structured, high-quality environment that prepared me for my career. I have returned to the U of A's campus on several occasions to partake in events such as homecoming, the Black Alumni Reunion, and the Sam M. Walton "Business Alumni Advisory Council" meetings. I was invited to join the Business Alumni Advisory Committee in the fall of 2006, which has been critical in helping to provide the college of business administration with a fresh perspective on what is needed to equip students to be successful in their careers. In 2009, I joined the Black Alumni Society board to continue to do my part in serving the university as well as helping to support the Black Alumni Society's programs and initiatives.

I have positive feelings toward the university. I still would like to see more African American faculty and alumni contributing (volunteering with students, in class settings as speakers, actively participating in the alumni society, committees, etc.) so that the needs of our students as well as the needs of the university are better served and so that our viewpoints are communicated. I would like for the Black Alumni Society to take a more active role in helping to attract African American students to the University of Arkansas's campus, assisting in facilitating the growth and development of current U of A students, and to develop a strong partnership with the university administration. The Black Alumni Society has a significant opportunity to be an agent of change and advocacy for current and future students and for the University of Arkansas.

■ Terry N. Perkins Rolfe (1990–1994), forensic serologist

Written response to interview questions, November 11, 2008
For detailed biography, see Appendix A, page 315

I entered in 1990 to work on a degree in architecture, but completed my degree in microbiology. I attended from fall 1990 through summer 1994.

Why did I select the University of Arkansas? Actually, the U of A was my alternate choice in the event that I could not afford to attend the college of my choice. My plan was to attend Howard University. My family and I were packed up and ready to go when I received a phone call saying some mistake had occurred with my housing plans and I had no place to live! They told me to come on up anyway and that we could *try* to find a place for me to stay. Well, you know my mom wasn't hearing that and neither was I. I called the U of A and told them of my dilemma. They told me that they would gladly reinstate my scholarships and sign me up for new student orientation right away. Housing would be taken care of and so would my financial aid. Needless to say, I took the offer and moved up to the U of A the next week.

Overall, my experience at the U of A was very positive. I met some of my best friends at the university. In fact, my very best friend became my husband. I am a first- generation college student, so it was a big deal for me to leave home for four years to study and earn my degree. I learned a lot during my stay at the university, and grew up quite a bit. The black population in Fayetteville was very small and outside of the university and church, I really didn't interact with the "locals." But, the black faculty at the university helped to mold me and make my experience there such a positive one. I connected with so many other black students early on as well as with staff like Dr. Lonnie Williams, Dr. Nola Holt-Royster, and faculty member Dr. Eddie Jones, who made my stay positive and exciting.

I enjoyed my experience at the university. I was very proud to be a student there. The city of Fayetteville was quite the adjustment, but the university was a good fit for me. I grew up in schools that were predominantly white, so the racial imbalance at the U of A was familiar to me.

My husband and I always return for the Black Alumni Reunions. Occasionally, I work in the northwest Arkansas area and when I do, I try to stop by.

I have always been proud to be a graduate of the university. I feel like my own experiences were positive, but I do realize that others don't share these same feelings and with good reason. The university, in recent years, has made some questionable decisions that I must admit have influenced my opinion of the school. When the university allowed Dr. Lonnie Williams to resign his position, I was shocked. I still cannot believe that the treasure in Dr. Williams was overlooked so easily. Dr. Williams was the university's greatest connection to black students: past, present, and future. Looking at the university today, I can still see evidence of what the university lost when it lost Dr. Williams from the standpoint of student recruitment and retention all the way down to the Black Alumni Society. Dr. Williams's presence is greatly missed.

I must say that I have been disappointed in the university's recruitment efforts. I see other colleges and universities attempting to recruit minority students, and the U of A lagging far behind. It is my hope that the university will begin to show the minority community that they are interested in them and that the University of Arkansas has something to offer black students. That needs to be a priority.

▨ La Tina Watkins Washington (1989–1994), software developer

Written response to interview questions, December 12, 2007
For detailed biography, see Appendix A, page 315

I entered the University of Arkansas in the fall 1989. I initially majored in chemical engineering, but after the first semester, I changed my major to computer science engineering (which then changed its name to computer systems engineering).

I was somewhat familiar with the campus. I was selected as one of six minority high school students to participate in an internship that was held during the summer of 1989 on the campus. I was originally enrolled to attend college at Jackson State University on a full scholarship, but after having visited the JSU campus, I decided to enroll at the U of A. I attended from 1989 to 1994 and graduated! Seriously, when I attended my commencement in 1994, there were only three African American students walking away with a diploma: myself, Jacqueline, and Derrick.

As I think back on my experience with the U of A, I cannot think of any one event that stands out in my mind. From an educational standpoint, the university met a lot of needs of those who were there to pursue a degree. Although I do wonder why I never considered the university seriously, I wonder if it may have had something to do with minority recruitment. I remember TRMEP (Transition Retention Minority Engineering Program) being a big program during that time, but I don't recall any recruitment efforts at my high school for this program. I think because the black minority population was very small at the time, it allowed for us to have a tighter bond among ourselves; we were a community within the big community. I never had a problem with relating to any of my professors; I was blessed to have professors who were either accustomed to or expected diversity. If anything, the biggest task was to find black hair-care products in northwest Arkansas!

If I were to describe my feelings toward the university during my time of study, I would say none adverse. I was there to get an education and to get away. It was very helpful to have those people who had previously attended the U of A who were currently on staff to help with finding ways to accomplish things.

I have returned to the campus on several occasions to attend the BAS reunions. Outside of these reunions, I have not ventured back to the school. Not even for homecoming . . .

I think they (my feelings toward the university) have changed somewhat. Concerning the fallout of several prominent people at the U of A, it just kind of makes me wonder what sort of dirty laundry the school has been hiding. . . .

■ Lisa Williams (1999–2003), author/CEO

Telephone interview by Charles Robinson and Lonnie R. Williams, July 6, 2007
For detailed biography, see Appendix A, page 315

I believe I came in June 5, 1999, to the University of Arkansas, Fayetteville. I came to become the Oren Harris professor in logistics, Oren Harris chair in logistics. I was a full professor with an endowed chair. The second chair was the Garrison Chair of Supply Chain Management.

Why did I select the University of Arkansas? I did have other choices. Primarily, the most competing choice I had was my current position. I was a professor at Penn State University, very successful, extremely happy professor there. But what appealed to me about the University of Arkansas is that it had a youthful program in terms of it was pretty new and they had the desire to move to the next level. I thought they had the caliber of faculty to do that. They had the resources and they had a relationship with Walmart, which was and still is a premier user of logistics and logistical services. So I thought I had certain things in place and could really make a significant difference by coming to the University of Arkansas. I left in 2003, four years.

I was the first, to my knowledge, African American professor in the marketing and logistics department. I was the first African American to hold an endowed chair, actually in the country not just the U of A, but certainly it was the U of A.

There are many layers to that question (describe your experience at the U of A). Let me start with the first one that comes to mind and that is . . . Wow! . . . one is being a professor there and what I could do with the student body, student population. I was honored to be a professor at the University of Arkansas and have a great deal of contact and influence with the undergraduate, master's and PhD students. I think my presence there was able to heighten their awareness of the school because I was a nationally known professor. Of course, I became the first African American to hold the endowed chair position and actually hold two of them while at the University of Arkansas and brought a great deal of recognition to the school, both national and international.

So because of the recognition, there were a lot of students and professionals that came to the University of Arkansas because they had heard I was there. That was an honor to be able to have some influence over people and people's lives in a positive way. In terms of the historical significance, I'm going to be honest. I'm a Yankee, as they would say, I'm from the North. I had heard of the stories of my people and the struggles we've had in the South and certainly I know about the Little Rock Nine and et cetera. So there was a part of me that truly understood how significant of an appointment it was.

Once I came there, I started interacting with the students, with the culture, and within the community. I more deeply understood what a significant position it was for us as a people, for me personally, and then for the university and even the state on a larger level. That has a great deal of responsibility. I wanted to do something to leave a positive legacy long after I was physically no longer there. It gives me a great deal of pride to know, God knows, great deal of pride to know, there were so many people before me that lost their lives and lost their freedom so I could have the opportunity to be educated, let alone to have the opportunity to come into a predominately white university. When I heard about previous students before me, who had come and were not allowed to study in a classroom, not allowed to sleep in the same dormitory as the rest of the population because of their skin color, I was simply [whew] had an even greater deal of respect and honor for what they sacrificed so that I could be there. I didn't take it lightly.

Before I came, I didn't know how significant it was. After I got there and the more that I found out, wow! I'm just indebted to be who I am and for the people that laid the groundwork before me. In terms of my experience while I was there, there was a mixture. I met some very dear friends, both black and white, that were extremely helpful and have become lifelong friends. And then I met people who assumed I had the position purely because I was an African American. I think that was quickly dispelled as soon as I had a conversation with them [laughing] and pointed out some of the things that my record purely held. There was a mixture there, but all in all, the University of Arkansas, again because someone came before me and laid that path for me, my way in terms of race was not that difficult. People had traveled the path. It was paved full of blood, tears, and sacrifice. I got to walk on the path when it was pretty smooth. Yes, I bumped into a couple of people, but nothing that was life alternating or something that would've scared me in any way.

[**Williams:** Describe your feelings toward the university during your time here.] That was actually a question that was mixed, too. To be honest with you, there is a part of me that will be forever indebted to the University of Arkansas. My experience, I was the first African American to graduate from The Ohio State University and first one to get tenure at Penn State. Then I was the first one again to get the endowed chair and become a full professor at the

University of Arkansas. That was huge. And to my knowledge, this hasn't been done. There isn't an African American that has become a full professor or held the endowed chair in my field. The University of Arkansas allowed me to make a tremendous stride in my professional career, which I would not, wouldn't say would not have done, but it would've taken years to do so. For that reason, I am grateful and because of the position I was able to garner recognition for the university and for myself. I had a chance to meet people and represent the University of Arkansas in many arenas.

And whenever there is something new and different, people don't know how to react. I did have my share of challenges while I was there. I'm not . . . how can I say this? I'm not naïve enough to think that some of the challenges were because of my race. I think the fact that I was a novelty . . . I was so new . . . that many people didn't know how to interact, how to deal, how to make decisions where I was concerned. They felt some of it was due to newness. The University of Arkansas, because of a great deal of research and funding, was elevated to a very high status very quickly. And anytime you have . . . whether it's an individual or organization move up quickly in the ranks, there's this kind of balancing effect that has to take place. I think during my time there, there was a balancing that was happening with the U of A and the College of Business. Some of it was racial and gender bias as well.

There's a part of me that says [long pause], you know being an African American period in this country, being an African American female in this country, so much so, there are certain things you always deal with. You become numb. Meaning you don't see all of it, you just accept it as part of the playing field. You understand that you can expect certain things to happen or certain things not to happen because of who you are when you walk into the room. So I experienced a lot of challenges while at the University of Arkansas and think some because the University of Arkansas was new and trying to gain some of their balance from where they had to come. I think some because I was new to the system, culturally, and as an individual. Thirdly, I think I walked into an environment that, I don't want to use clichés, but it really was a "good old boys'" network when I walked into it. They were used to operating on one level and I was used to working on another level and that caused some conflict.

Have I returned to the university? No, I was in Fayetteville recently. I wanted to meet some friends at the U of A. I didn't get a chance to. It didn't fit into my schedule.

Describe my present feelings toward the university? Wow, that's a very good question. Let me first of all be as honest as I have been, but let me be a little more specific. When I left the University of Arkansas, it was not [long pause], gosh, how do I say this? It wasn't pleasant for me. I left the University of Arkansas because I thought there were things happening to me that shouldn't happen to an endowed chair or full professor. I've been around universities. I had seen how endowed chairs were treated and I thought I was being treated differently. And I didn't appreciate it. I made it very clear. I had made several statements to various administrators about how I was being treated. They were always very nice, very cordial, and I would always be given the same, "We'll handle it. We'll take care of it." But ultimately, nothing was done. And so in due time I became frustrated and said, [laughing] "There's more in life than being constantly frustrated every day." And as much as I love my colleagues and still do, as much as I enjoy being a professor and conducting research, I figured I could do it on my own and it probably took me . . . I've been out now four years. It probably took me a good year and half to two years before some of my frustration subsided. But some of my [long pause] before my being angry with them had subsided. So I left of free will and free choice because I was an endowed chair and had tenure. Certainly, 100 percent my choice. I just figured I wanted to have a different type of professional life.

I left angry, really, I did. I'll be honest. I left angry and looked forward to a new aspect of my life. Now, I can look back on it and I've been gone four years. I see that time was an incredible foundation for this life that I lead now. Without that difficulty, without those challenges, and without me standing out in my own anger, I would not have the opportunities that I have now. Now, looking back on it those people that I held anger towards that I thought didn't treat me fairly and I thought were undermining me, or demeaning me in some way, I am grateful to them. Had they not done that, I would've stayed in a situation that wasn't working for me. It is kind of like that old analogy of the frog and the pot of water that boils? If it boils slowly, the frog doesn't realize it. Well, thank goodness, the pot didn't boil slowly. It boiled very quickly, very hot. So I understood that I was in an environment that wasn't working for me, so I left.

If they had been more accommodating to some of my requests, and I'm not saying that they didn't accommodate any of my requests, that is certainly not true. They really tried to be accommodating. Plus, I had the second endowed chair (Garrison Chair of Supply Chain Management), so they really, really wanted to keep me. Basically, I didn't feel that I was really being treated like a full endowed chair. I thought that I was being treated very much [laughing] like you would treat a child and I didn't appreciate it. The water got hot very quickly, I left. If it had been more subtle and if it would have been more like subtle heat that was gradually increasing, I could've been there for years and that would've not been in my best interest because I would've been unhappy and subsequently it wouldn't have been in the best interest of the University of Arkansas. Ultimately, it worked out perfect for me and I believe for them, too.

Let me give you an example. And I think this sums up what I was saying about how I wasn't treated as I think an endowed chair should be treated. I was an endowed chair [laughing] and I had this research idea that needed to be tested in the corporate environment. I made arrangements to go away for a year and I'm trying to think, I was going away for a year and test this research philosophy within the environment of the corporation. And I did need someone to teach my courses. I was very fortunate that I had a vice president of, I don't know if I can mention the company, but I'll say two vice presidents of two different Fortune fifty, probably Fortune ten even, companies that would come in for the year and teach my courses. I was going to be actively involved, teach a lecture or two, and work very closely with these gentlemen. I wasn't going away out of the country. I would primarily be working with taking this research I do and combine with a corporation. I was told that my services were better used teaching the undergraduate classes and that I could not conduct these classes because I needed to be teaching undergraduates.

I love teaching undergraduates. I'm not making a statement about that, but what I am making a statement about is that an endowed chair, professor that has the resources to support her research, that has already lined up more than qualified people to come into the classroom and teach them an additional perspective than anyone else would have, and still be there hands-on, and teach the class to work with the executives. To say, oh no, you can't do that even if you have the funds as an endowed chair, you can't do it because we need you in the undergraduate environment when this research had never been done, and could've done some tremendous things in terms of logistics leadership. I didn't get it. I didn't understand it. I didn't think it was fair. I didn't think that any endowed chair around the country would have to deal with that decision. That was for me the straw that broke the camel's back. That does not work for me. That was the deciding factor. That's when I left. Three, two weeks later, I wrote my letter of resignation. Because again, the idea of an endowed chair is supposed to free you up to do research. And here I had, not only the money to do it, but the support of corporate, so many positive repercussions in that. These people could've hired the students because they were in the classroom. There were more money opportunities from these companies to be partners with the university. So there were so many different opportunities from what I was creating, but people couldn't see that. And I felt that instead of being supportive to grow and expand and become more of a greater professor that I was trying to be stifled and placed in a box. And that is what I rejected.

That situation is exactly what happened. Exactly the way I said. OK, I'm gone because I felt that it was a learning environment where I could grow and become as successful, happy, and productive as I should be. I thought an endowed chair was supposed to basically ensure that you could do that. You were no longer hampered by financial concerns or resources, that you had this freedom that you could do research unobstructed. And to find out that wasn't the case, then if I wanted to do my research that was very disheartening. That is why I decided to leave. That is a fact. Now, four years later, what I want to make really clear is that was the best thing that could've happened to me because what it required me to do was say, look, Lisa, you are looking at this incredible opportunity in the face. No one, as far as I know, on the planet has this incredible opportunity. Your brothers and sisters have died sacrificed, so you could have this opportunity. Now, they are saying you can't do this. You can't be all that you can be. You know you can be! Now this is the question. Who will have control over your life? Is it the university that says, no [laughing], or is it my own inner mind, my responsibility to my ancestors that came before me that says there is nothing or no one that can prevent you from becoming all you can be. That was really the choice. I chose to leave. I chose to move into a way to expand into a fuller person, fuller academics, and scholar. It has allowed me to grow and grow in business acumen that is self-knowing, confident, and enjoy in a way that I could never have expected or understood. It was a tremendous springboard for me living this incredible life that I do now. If you would've asked me a year ago, two years ago, I may have still been saying that they weren't right. They did this to me. It isn't right. It isn't fair. I wasn't arguing it wasn't true or not. I would certainly say that how I was treated isn't how an endowed chair should be treated.

However, that experience was invaluable to me and I appreciate every person I ran into that gave me a challenge as well as those people who were very appreciative. Because again, what I am creating now is literally just phenomenal and I would not have known I could do it had they not really put me to the test and said who defines your life? Is it external? This endowed chair? This six-figure salary? Or is it internal and who do you owe your life to? Are you responsible for your life or is it these external people that are saying what you can or cannot do. So all in all, I'm extremely appreciative to the University of Arkansas. In my heart of hearts, I am appreciative for every experience that I had there.

Really, I don't want you to think it was all negative. I really don't think Arkansas deserves a black mark. From me they don't. They did me a tremendous favor. They were new to the game and they didn't know.

Chapter 7

Destination

Diversity and Desegregation in the 2000s

> One of the things *Raising the Bar* stresses is the importance of diversity on campus, the university's top institutional goal. This means creating a campus community that mirrors not just our state, but our country as a whole. We're striving to enrich our learning environment by increasing the diversity of our students, our faculty and our staff. By doing so, we're creating that critical exchange of viewpoints, opinions and beliefs that foster innovation and understanding.
>
> —John White

Chancellor John White made the remarks above during one of his annual State of the University addresses in 2007.[1] As was the norm during his ten-year tenure, White emphasized the importance of diversity, referring to it as the institution's "top institutional priority." For White, enhancing the diversity of the campus encouraged "enlightened conversation" and pushed the university toward "inclusive (educational) excellence."[2] Based upon these public statements in support of diversity, White took steps to expand opportunities for African Americans at the university. In 1999, White named Dr. Johnetta Cross Brazzell as the vice chancellor of student affairs, making her the first African American to permanently hold that title in the university's history. In 2002, White supported the appointment of Dr. Carolyn Allen as the dean of the library. Four years later, the White administration named Cynthia Nance as the dean of the School of Law. Both Allen and Nance were the first African Americans to rise to the level of dean in each of those administrative units.[3]

White sought to demonstrate his support for African Americans and diversity in other ways. In 2002, White created a Diversity Task Force with the charge of creating a diversity plan for the institution. The group conducted a number of campus climate surveys and created a document with objectives and benchmarks for furthering diversity over a three-year period.[4] In 2005, the university created the office of the chief diversity officer and hired Carmen Coustaut, an African American woman, to head it.[5] In 2006, White authorized additional funding to go toward expanding the African American Studies Program in the Fulbright College. The extra funding led to dramatic increases in both the courses offered that focused on the black experience and in the students that formally aligned with the program. Also in 2006, the university established the Silas Hunt Awards to recognize the contributions of African American students, faculty, and staff to furthering the cause of inclusion on the Fayetteville campus.[6]

The growth of the African American student and faculty numbers during a portion of the White years suggests that more blacks (at least for a time) saw the university as a more inclusive campus. In the fall of 2000, 965 African American students were enrolled. By the fall

2002, this number had grown to 1,022.[7] Black teaching faculty witnessed a similar increase, going from 3.1 percent of the total instructional faculty on the campus in 2000 to 3.9 percent in 2002.[8]

Though significant, these changes did not suggest that race had ceased being a potentially explosive issue at the university. The dismissal of the men's basketball coach, Nolan Richardson, revealed this fact. In March 2002, the university fired Richardson for comments that he had made during a press conference. During the press conference, Richardson had complained that he was being treated unfairly because he was black, and he also asserted that the university could buy out his contract if it was dissatisfied with him. In December of that same year, Richardson sued the university, alleging racial discrimination.[9] The trial lasted for several months, and although Richardson ultimately lost his case, the university's diversity image was severely sullied. Nowhere was the negative impact of the Richardson case best demonstrated than the enrollment of African American students. In the fall 2003, the black student numbers fell from an all-time high of 1,022 to 1,005. Just one year later that number had further declined to 981, despite the fact that overall student numbers had increased. In terms of percentages in a period of three years, the African American student population had gone from 6.37 percent in 2002 to 5.68 percent in 2006. This percentage fell further in 2006 to 5.28 percent.[10]

The university's actions to effectively desegregate continue. Today, several of the colleges have written diversity plans that highlight the need to seek out African American students and staff. Also the position of chief diversity officer has been elevated to the status of a vice provost and given a seat on the chancellor's executive committee. These steps and many others suggest the University of Arkansas recognizes inclusion as an issue is still very much alive and must be addressed regularly. The voices of black students, faculty, and staff in this section reflect this ongoing engagement and intimate the university has much work relative to diversity in its future.

■ Randy Dorian Brown Jr. (2001–2005), university staff

Telephone interview by Lonnie R. Williams, August 27, 2007
For detailed biography, see Appendix A, page 315

I entered the University of Arkansas in the fall of 2001 and started as an undeclared business major. I later selected my major for small business entrepreneurship and graduated in the summer of 2005.

Why did I select the University of Arkansas? My family! My father attended the University of Arkansas, as did my mother and that was a very big deal to me. I attended the Accounting Career Awareness Program [ACAP], a summer enrichment program through the business school, and that got me interested. I also attended a multicultural leadership conference coordinated by Sonja Savage, a former employee, and although this program does not exist today, it formally introduced me to the U of A.

My role in the history of African Americans at the UA? I guess one is being an African American period! Definitely serving as SGA president in the 2004–2005 academic school year and as SGA treasurer in 2002–2003 and 2003–2004 terms.

I loved my time at the University of Arkansas. It was a great time. I was exposed to a lot of experiences that I don't think I would have gotten had I not gone to college, especially the University of Arkansas. I was exposed to a lot of opportunities at the University of Arkansas, especially with the Associated Student Government (ASG). It was sometimes difficult because I remember sitting around the room and being not only one of the very few people of color, but at times, the only African American in the room during senate meetings. As far as having people that looked like me, it was a very different experience for me coming in as a first-year student and being a senator within the ASG and not really having anybody that looked like me. But I guess the flip side of that is people used to tell me to be more active within ASG in hopes of getting more people that looked like me involved. By the time I was president, I think that was something that was beginning to happen. The senate was a lot more colorful at that time. There was definitely more people of color and with that more people of color able to get a support group and a network.

One of the most trying times happened when I was in ASG during the spring of 2004, right before I had run for president of ASG. I was the treasurer, and at that time there were members of the ASG senate that attempted to impeach me for not following my duties as treasurer. The allegations were completely fabricated and the impeachment was never followed through, but I still was left to defend my work and character. Additionally, I wanted the opportunity to review the allegations with the senate to see if the senate felt that I had done something wrong. The simple fact is that it was a select few individuals that were seeking my impeachment. After that very difficult time, I began to question if it had anything to do with me being black. The process of me questioning alone was rough on me. When I went through the issue of questioning, I wondered if racism was the reason they targeted me, or if they targeted me because of my position of treasurer. I was the one that was responsible in following through in my duties, yet I was the one questioning. I already questioned being in the organization altogether. I already questioned not ever being genuinely accepted. Even though I was an executive, very few knew me or even showed an interest in knowing me. I always felt like an outsider trying to fit in and then they questioned my job performance. I was held to a different standard than my counterparts, but I guess that's the life of a black man.

I was able to overcome it and I was elected ASG president. I knew the student body supported me through electing me as their president for the next year. Advocating support from other students of color ended up being my biggest aid because the students of color (especially African Americans) rallied around me and supported me. My primary focus was for people to know the facts, if they were going to support me. If they knew the charges and they knew my response, then they would know I did not fail to fulfill my responsibilities. It felt as though the black students on campus won the ASG election. I started to see more black students engaged with ASG after the election and that started to make me feel more comfortable at ASG.

Initially, I had some ill-will towards the university because I did not feel I was supported completely during that time. I believe that had I not been aware of what was happening, I could have easily been railroaded through the process, which was the goal of those that initiated the impeachment. The support I needed came from some of the staff in the Office of Student Affairs. They provided me with the support that the university did not provide. I love my experiences at the University of Arkansas and would not trade them for the world because I was able to learn a lot from them.

Since I graduated, I have returned for homecoming 2005 and fall 2005. I've returned periodically with my fraternity brothers and check in with a few administrators on campus. That was probably spring of 2006. In the fall of 2006, I went to the University of Arkansas for the USC game.

My present feelings about the University of Arkansas have not changed because the university still has a long way to go with regards to racial equality. There is a lot of institutionalized racism at the University of Arkansas and it is truly inherent within the university system throughout its traditions and its undertones. I would like to see racism addressed and removed from the institution, but I know it will require the dedication from people within the University of Arkansas community.

The University of Arkansas has gotten a bad rap, and it has had this rap for African Americans especially from my parents' era. Older generations speak negatively of the University of Arkansas because of its history around racism. I found it to be a great place. There were very rare instances or acts of being call the "N word" while walking across campus or during homecoming. For the most part, those isolated incidents were very few, and they did not encompass my entire experience. However, the university has a lot of work to do, but then again, I'm at my third institution. I went to the University of Vermont for graduate school, now I'm currently employed at Florida State University, and all institutions need work. It is definitely in need of growth and development on campus. Institutionalized racism still exists and it is still somewhat of a "good ole boy" system at the University of Arkansas. It needs to be addressed so that the University of Arkansas is welcoming and open to people of color.

Dr. Williams has had to call me numerous times to get me to edit my section and I recall wanting my section to be something profound and deep. I wanted it to be something scholarly. But I realized my story, just like those before me and after me, is deep, profound, and scholarly. The stories of the "Hill" both told and untold have much merit to them. The more I think back on my experiences, the more I wish I would have reflected in those moments. I am great at living and surviving the moments, which I think is inherent in me as a black man. But to survive is not enough. We must begin to thrive and that begins with us understanding our own stories and the stories of others.

■ Synetra Gilmer (1999–2004), manager

Written responses to interview questions, September 10, 2007
For detailed biography, see Appendix A, page 316

I entered the University of Arkansas in 1999. When I initially enrolled, I was undecided; however, I thought that I wanted to become a physical therapist. After I learned I would have to transfer to another school after a few years, I quickly changed my mind. I had taken some community college web building classes my last few years of high school, so I then decided that I would do something with computers and business would be the best way to go.

Why the University of Arkansas? The University of Arkansas provided me with the most financial assistance. Being raised in a single-parent home and knowing very little about college in its entirety, did not afford me the opportunity to attend school out of state or many other places *in* state. During high school, I was fortunate enough to have a homeroom teacher and also a principal whose son had attended the U of A. Tracy Hayes and Loutileous Holmes were very influential in my decision to attend the U of A. Hayes helped me enroll in classes to prepare for the ACT so that I would score high enough to get accepted and also to receive a few scholarships to attend. I am very grateful to them both because if it had not been for their encouragement along with my mother, I don't know that I would have made it.

I attended the university from 1999 to 2004. I finished my coursework to attain my degree in computer information systems in 2003 and decided to add another major shortly before the school year ended spring of 2003. Me, being an African American female, knowing how tough it would be to compete in my field and land that dream job that I had worked so hard for in college, I decided to further diversify by obtaining a degree in transportation and logistics. I completed that degree in May of 2004.

During my time at the university, I played a crucial part in getting the northwest Arkansas chapter of the NAACP established in the area. It was a very rewarding experience for me. I was still so young and to be a part of history at a predominantly white educational institution, that's something that I hope I live to tell my kids, nieces and nephews about when they embark upon deciding where to attend college.

My experience at the university was truly good, a very interesting experience, but yet sometimes troubling. I quickly learned a lot about life. Coming from the town of West Memphis where there was one high school that everyone in the city attended, everybody for the most part got along and we didn't really have race or prejudice issues. Then to Fayetteville, Arkansas, where I saw very few people that looked like me and in public, occasionally when I did see someone that looked like, it seemed that they did not see me. Moving to northwest Arkansas was definitely a culture SHOCK. I can still remember going to the mall alone for the first time after my mom had dropped me off for my first fall semester. It was like being in an old movie where African Americans were not highly favored in the communities and certain individuals felt they had no place there. A friend and I were shopping in one of the local department stores and we were literally stalked throughout the store and hunted as if we were dinner for the hungry lion pursuing us nearly twenty steps behind. I was so shocked, appalled, and disturbed that people actually behaved that way. I mean, no one had warned me that things like that would happen to me. I was literally ready to pack up my things and run the five-hour drive back to my hometown. But because I was determined not to become another statistic in the city of West Memphis, I toughed it out, gritted my teeth, and by the grace of God I prevailed.

During my time of study at the university, honestly I felt like just a number. I was just another little black face in the sea of Caucasians that also attended while I was there. It wasn't until I was introduced to Dr. Lonnie Williams that I actually felt like I belonged there. Dr. Williams was like a father to me. He was like that with everyone. Individuals like him, Monica Jones, Angela Monts, and Dr. Erica Holliday helped me to sustain throughout the tough classes and trials of being a broke college student. I owe them so much. They truly made my stay at the university worth it. The multicultural center gave us a place to go and be with people that looked like us, acted like us, and were experiencing the same problems as us. It also helped us to understand why so much ignorance existed in the area and empowered us to want to cause change. Thus, with their help we were able to form groups like the [local] NAACP and sustain others like the Black Student Association, Black Graduate Students Association, and Black Law Students Association. Without good people like them to guide me and help me along the way, I would not be the person that I am today.

I reside in northwest Arkansas and I am very involved with the Alumni Chapter of Alpha Kappa Alpha, which serves as advisor to the Kappa Iota undergraduate chapter at the U of A. I'm also a member of the board for the Black Alumni Society, so I return back to the yard quite often for various programs that the undergrads are hosting or programs that the Alumni Society is hosting. Every two years BAS hosts the Black Alumni Reunion and I have been involved with this project since I was an undergrad. So I've had the opportunity to see it grow and to meet some very interesting people that attended the university long before I did.

With all the events that have occurred in the past few years with the Nolan Richardson and Stan Heath incidents, I feel the university has improved but it certainly has a very long way to go. This year [2007] they named an African American female law professor, Cynthia Nance, dean of the Law School and that was a substantial stride in history for the university. However, it will take much more to make a true difference on that campus.

In my experience at the U of A, there was definitely more good than bad and if I had it to do all over again, I would. I learned a lot about life by attending the University of Arkansas. I don't believe I would value those lessons as much had I not gone through those trials, tribulations, and also joyous moments. I would like to thank you all for allowing me the opportunity to share this and also everyone that played a critical part in getting me to the university, through the university, and to where I am today. Words could never express my gratitude.

■ Quantrell Willis (1999–2005), PhD student

Written response to interview questions, January 10, 2008
For detailed biography, see Appendix A, page 316

I came to the University of Arkansas as an undergraduate student in August of 1999. I came with the intention of becoming a pediatrician someday, but I found myself passionate about education and later began heading in that direction in terms of my education at the University of Arkansas.

I actually didn't select the University of Arkansas. I was headed to a prominent HBCU for men, but two women were instrumental in convincing me that Arkansas was the place for me; my mother, Edna Hightower, and Sonja Savage. My mother wanted me to be close to home, being that I was the first person in my family to attend college. I had reservations about going to the University of Arkansas because I didn't know much about it and at that time there was a racist connation associated with the school. I didn't want to go through that experience. Sonja Savage was instrumental in helping to secure a scholarship through a program entitled "The African American Convocation" in which her office would seek out some of the best and brightest African American students in the state of Arkansas. She was very personal in her efforts. She called me often, spoke to my parents, wrote personal letters. She truly believed in my ability to succeed at the University of Arkansas, and she proved it with her actions.

Through all my ups and downs while at the University of Arkansas, I graduated in May of 2005 with my bachelor's degree in sociology/African American studies. I then began working with the University of Arkansas library in June of 2005. In the spring of 2006, I began taking classes towards my master's in higher education. I graduated in the summer of 2007 with that degree. And at the tender age of twenty-five, I am currently pursuing a PhD in higher education at Kansas State University (I am currently the youngest person enrolled in my doctoral program).

While at the University of Arkansas, I had several roles other than being a student. During my senior year as an undergraduate, I was the president of the Black Student Association. While at the U of A, I had the opportunity of being a part of a group of young black men that started the first-ever group at the U of A solely for the uplifting of young black males. The group is known as Student African American Brotherhood (SAAB) and was formed the summer of 2005. It is still growing strong to this day. It is a nationally recognized group and can be found on the Internet. After graduation, I served as co-adviser to SAAB and the Black Student Association and was also given an Excellence in Leadership Award. As a graduate student, I was also blessed to serve on various community and university communities (executive board member of the Black Alumni Society, president of Black Graduate Students Association, NWA MLK Committee, Phi Beta Sigma Graduate Chapter, et cetera) that addressed African American issues and events.

While working on these various committees, I began to realize how important it was to be around those that cared. Being a minority at this predominately white institution, I oftentimes felt alone, isolated. I had a rough undergraduate career at the University of Arkansas. Coming in as a first-generation college student was difficult. My mother and my stepfather were smart people, but had no idea what college life entailed being that they only attained high school diplomas. I have to say that God was always with me, and He is truly the reason why I have been able to sustain and persevere. My parents weren't able to provide me with all the information about the ins and outs of college, but they continued to provide me with spiritual insight. I never considered myself to be "dumb" or "stupid." I believe for a while I was sleepwalking as an undergraduate student, but a series of events caused me to awaken.

In addition to my many accolades, I was blessed with a son during my senior year of college. I wasn't sure what I was going to do, so I did what I knew best; I prayed and began moving towards God's promises. With the support of many people around me, I chose not to give up. When I had a hard time believing in myself, it was the people that I will mention later that helped to instill in me a burning desire to move forward; they believed in me when no one else did. During this time, I knew that I had to continue my education by getting my master's degree for the sake of my son. I wanted to be able to provide him with a better future, but I had one problem; I had an undergraduate grade-point average of 2.345. I needed at least a 3.0 grade-point average to be admitted into the master's program. I went on to apply to the program.

Of course I was met with some opposition. Some administrators/faculty felt that I shouldn't consider pursuing a master's degree with my academic background. They felt as if I wasn't capable of doing the work and said that my career goals of being a college president didn't fit the program. I do acknowledge that I had a low GPA, but I knew that it wasn't a true reflection of what I knew and what I was capable of knowing. I submitted my application materials and was told that I could enroll in two courses and then my application would be reviewed again. This was all done with the help and support of people at the University of Arkansas who believed in me when no one else did. I began taking courses on a conditional basis; meaning I needed to make a 3.0 grade-point average or above in the courses to have a chance in being fully admitted into the program.

I took the courses and passed. I met the 3.0 grade-point average for the classes. I soon began my master's degree in the summer of 2006 and graduated the following year in August of 2007. I graduated with a 3.5 grade-point average. This was substantially better than my undergraduate grade-point average. My experience taught me plenty. It taught me to take advantage of the opportunities that are present. I learned a great deal of patience and respect for wisdom and knowledge from those that had been through the same situations that I went through.

As a young black male at the University of Arkansas, it was important that I had a support network. I felt as if the institution in itself wasn't a welcoming environment. When I first stepped foot onto that campus as a student, I felt out of place, but there was one man who made it his goal to greet African American students with open arms. That man was Dr. Lonnie Williams. I remember Dr. Williams coming down from his office in the student union to talk to students and encourage them to find ways to make the most of their University of Arkansas experience. He would tell us we needed to affirm ourselves on this campus. He would not only talk to us, but he would provide us with the resources we needed to make this possible. Through all my ups and downs, his statements stayed in my head, "you deserve to be here," "this is your campus as much as it is anyone else's." In this day and age, it is still important for students to have this type of support in order for them to have a holistic college experience. I was by no way dumb or stupid as my GPA may have indicated in some people's eyes at the University of Arkansas, but I was just a young man in need of some support, a young man who had in him the desire and will to be successful, but just needed a hand to guide me. It truly took a village to raise this child while I was at the University of Arkansas. In closing, I would like to thank the following people below for my development as a person and scholar:

Special thanks to God, my mother and father (Edna and Jimmy Hightower), Courtney and Nathaniel Willis, Jaalon Willis, Lonnie Williams, Charles Robinson, Johnetta Cross Brazzell, Gordon Morgan, NWA Phi Beta Sigma Fraternity Graduate Chapter, Black Alumni Society, Angela Monts, Derrick Gragg, Aisha and Cedric Kenner, Elizabeth McKee, Alberta Bailey, Joe Seabrooks, Demetrius Richmond, Niya Blair, Adrain Smith, Malikah Nelson, Chris Medrano, Parice Bowser, Deborah Korth, Trakenya Gordon, Ernestine Gibson, St. James Missionary Baptist Church, Daniel Pugh, Andy Mauk, Gigi Secuban, Pleasant Hill Missionary

Baptist Church, and all those that helped make my dreams become reality. I apologize if I've failed to mention anyone. Thank you and God bless.

"It must be borne in mind that the tragedy of life doesn't lie in not reaching your goal. It lies in having no goal to reach. It is not a calamity to die with dreams unfulfilled, but it is a calamity not to dream. It is not a disgrace not to reach the stars, but it is a disgrace not to have any stars to reach. Not failure, but low aim, is the real sin."—Benjamin Mays

Afterword

Write This Down

> Then the Lord said to Moses, Write this on a scroll as something to be remembered and make sure that Joshua hears it, because I will completely blot out the memory of Amalek from under heaven.
>
> —Exodus 17:14

Write this down: In Exodus 17, following a major victory, God instructed Moses to record the momentous events that had occurred as testimonials and evidence of God's grace and goodness to his people for future generations to know. Rarely is the gift in what we write down for ourselves, but rather in what we write down for others.

Like the events in Exodus, the narratives of these black pioneers are victorious and important, and they need to be written down and remembered. Thus, with a divine sense of urgency and while those in this book yet live, Robinson and Williams felt called to write down the stories and journeys of blacks at the University of Arkansas as an important part of African Americans' legacy to be shared with others so that we won't forget the struggle for education and so that we will have something to refer to it in the future. These narratives are an expression of the African American community; they express a unique blend of amazing resiliency and African American spirituality, particularly in the face of racist discrimination.

As a proud native of Arkansas and a proud graduate of the University of Arkansas, I am humbled and honored to be a part of this piece of history in more ways than one. I entered the University of Arkansas in the fall of 1994 with no earthly idea that this would be a pivotal point in my life. Though a native of Arkansas (born and raised in Pine Bluff), I returned virtually as an outsider from Chicago after more than twenty years absence and was welcomed back into the fold.

In simple, straightforward narratives, *Remembrances in Black: Personal Perspectives of the African American Experience at the University of Arkansas, 1940s–2000* has managed to capture a dynamic history of black people through the stories they tell of their experiences as students, faculty, and staff at the University of Arkansas for more than a half a century. Through their lived experiences, their stories tell of the violent struggles and inhuman conditions the pioneer blacks at the University of Arkansas had to endure during the racial desegregation era in order to get a decent education.

In the words of U.S. ambassador George Haley, "The white students looked at us sometimes as if they felt that we shouldn't be there." And we could feel that. Sadly, these experiences and feelings of not being wanted that African Americans experienced at the University of Arkansas back then continues now, for African Americans, women, and other people of color, like myself, who work or attend schools at predominantly white institutions. It is what Turner and Myers (2000) refer to in their book, *Faculty of Color in Academe: Bittersweet Success,* as a "chilly and unwelcoming environment." The stories speak of horrors such as being made to sit in the hallways of classroom building so as not to integrate white classrooms. Yet, the same voices show pride, honor, and fidelity for the same institution that did not welcome them. Most of them have returned again and again with dignity and a genuine love for the University of Arkansas.

Some of the experiences of earlier black students at the University of Arkansas and other white colleges and universities were horrific at worst and inhumane at best. For example, United States ambassador George W. Haley, referring to his entrance into the University of Arkansas Law School in the fall of 1949 wrote, "White students complained about us using the student restroom facility. So it was decided that we would use the dean's private restroom, which was inside his office, meaning that we had to request a key from his secretary/receptionist to get to the restroom. That didn't seem to work too well for other people. They seemed to complain about that and then we were moved from there to the faculty restroom."

Despite the humiliations and the less-than-humane treatment recalled by these alumni, this book leaves the reader with a sense of spirituality and fortitude, healing, reconciliation, and pride, a belief in mankind's redemption, and a sense of hope. In their own words, these magnificent and proud students and graduates (both of old and the new) give us a glimpse of the importance of education. Like the book of Exodus, the stories of these brave individuals contain foundational truths about deliverance, human flaws, redemption, and the law.

According to oral accounts from other African Americans at the University of Arkansas and documents from my program area, I, too, was a pioneer. It is still hard for me to digest that in 1998, at the end of the twentieth century, I would be considered a pioneer in anything, let alone a first from a program area in an institution of higher education. It is still hard to believe that I was the first African American to graduate with a doctorate from the counselor education program.

Nonetheless, as I reflect back on my experience on the university campus, my cup runneth over. I am honored and humbled to add my voice to the chorus of the black men and women in this book who are much more deserving of that title of pioneer than I. As one of the pioneers so elegantly put it, "I, as all of the pioneers, was in a position to develop more respect for people in general. We were obligating the university to grow in what a university ought to do to make things better for people. The university is a lot better because of the experience that it had with our struggles."

I am proud to know that my name is carved into the sidewalk on the Fayetteville campus along with the all-white Class of 1905 who carved their names into a sidewalk. I am proud to know my name is carved into the sidewalk along with those African Americans who pioneered so that I and other blacks *could* have our names carved into a sidewalk on the campus. And thanks to the vision of Charles Robinson and Lonnie Williams, and their commitments to write this book, the stories of these individuals will be permanently engraved into the history of the University of Arkansas. The testimonials in this book will remain a written legacy as testimonials and evidence of God's grace and goodness for future generations of students of all colors, races, ethnicities, and nationalities.

—Aretha Marbley
University of Arkansas (1994–1997), PhD 1998
Associate professor, Counselor Education,
Texas Tech University

Epilogue

> We were proud to be at the institution when we went there. We became frustrated by
> the experiences that we had. Needless to say, those experiences made some of us
> stronger, but it also tore down the psyche of a lot of others that were in those small
> numbers to the point where they left or their frustrations manifested in other ways that
> certainly would not have been intended before we started to attend the university.
> —Darrell Brown Sr., January 9, 2010

This volume attempts to shed light on the experiences of African Americans who participated in the desegregation of the University of Arkansas from the late 1940s to the present. In it, we find stories of black faculty, students, and staff, making tremendous sacrifices in their efforts to create a more-inclusive campus environment. The importance of this work goes far beyond any emotional concern about the history of African Americans at the University of Arkansas. Instead, this oral history fills a sizable gap in the literature on desegregation in higher education. Much is already known about the lives of African Americans at southern institutions that directly and defiantly resisted the presence of blacks on campus. However, these stories derive from a southern institution that was viewed by civil rights proponents as progressive in regards to the desegregation process. By better understanding the struggles of African Americans at the University of Arkansas, historians gain valuable insight into what people of color at institutions with similar circumstances probably experienced.

These oral remembrances also provide us with a sense of the change and continuity over time that has accompanied the process of desegregation at the university. As we contemplate contemporary issues of diversity and inclusion, we come to realize that although the most glaring symbols of hostility to the presence of blacks on the Fayetteville campus have long been removed, the challenges to attracting larger numbers of African Americans still remain. From 1983 to 2009, African American student enrollment grew by only 302 students, while over this same span the overall student body increased by more than 5,300 students. The difference in the volume of growth suggests that despite the more than two decades of diversity-first rhetoric by university administrators and their concomitant attempts to create a more culturally friendly campus environment, most African Americans in the state view the University of Arkansas as something other than a school of choice.

It is fair to surmise that one of the current obstacles to growing a larger black student body today is community awareness of the harsh experiences that people of color faced at the university, especially in the earlier years of desegregation. Although this volume is the first to chronicle these remembrances, these stories have been passed from generation to generation in African American communities throughout the state of Arkansas and beyond. The effect of such dissemination has been to create among community members both a fascination and fear of the university. African Americans respect the university because of its size, resources, and state and national acclaim, but they also fear that it has not yet completely eradicated the vestiges of its nonwelcoming past. Today, many people of color stand waiting for the University of Arkansas to cogently demonstrate that diversity and inclusion are seminal strands of its institutional DNA.

This volume can be viewed as an important instrument in bridging the gap between the university and the African American community, for it clearly illustrates the centrality of African American pioneers to making the university sensitive to issues of diversity and inclusion. Through their sacrifice, these African Americans proved they have a connection to the university that is powerful, historic, and still relevant. Because of their past service, African Americans today have much less to fear about the university and much more to gain from experiencing it. By owning this history, the University of Arkansas signals that it accepts its past mistakes relative to desegregation and that it intends to actively foster greater opportunity for all of the state's citizens. Through their current efforts, university leaders must continuously demonstrate that although they cannot undo the past, they are using it to liberate minds and souls in order to create a more perfect university.

Appendix A

Biographies of the Interviewees

Chapter 1

George W. B. Haley

George Williford Boyce Haley was nominated U. S. ambassador to the Republic of Gambia by President William Jefferson Clinton, and sworn in by Vice President Al Gore at Howard University in Washington, D.C., in September 1998. He had come a long way since entering the University of Arkansas School of Law in 1949.

Drafted into the U.S. Air Corps shortly after his eighteenth birthday, Haley spent the next three years in military service. He was twenty-one years old when he entered Morehouse College in Atlanta. He had considered attending Harvard Law School, but a letter from his father persuaded him otherwise. "Segregation won't end until we open beachheads wherever it exists," his father wrote. "The governor of Arkansas and educational officials have decided upon a quiet tryout of university integration. You have the needed scholastic record and temperament, and I understand that Arkansas has one of the South's best Law Schools."

In 1952, George Haley opened a legal practice in Kansas City, Kansas, and served as a deputy city attorney for Kansas City. In 1964, George Haley, Republican, was one of the first two African Americans elected to the upper chamber of the state legislature of Kansas.

In 1969, Haley accepted an appointment as President Nixon's chief counsel to the Urban Mass Transportation Administration. In 1973, he joined the United States Information Agency (USIA) as the associate director for Equal Employment Opportunity and later became the agency's general counsel and congressional liaison. In 1977, he accepted a partnership in the Washington, D.C., firm of Obermayer, Rebman, Maxwell, and Hippel before establishing his own firm. In 1989, Haley was appointed by President Bush to serve as chair of the Postal Rate Commission. (Information obtained from Answers.com http://www.answers.com/topic/george-williford-boyce-haley.)

Christopher C. Mercer Jr.

Christopher C. Mercer Jr., an attorney for more than fifty-three years, was born in Pine Bluff, graduating from then-segregated Merrill High School in 1942. He received an AB degree from AM&N College in 1946. In 1955, he received his LLB degree from the University of Arkansas School of Law.

Mercer taught at the now-defunct Corbin High School on the AM&N College campus in 1945–1946. He served as principal of Conway County Training School at Menifee in 1946–1949. In 1949, Mercer entered the University of Arkansas School of Law at Fayetteville. In 1950–1951, Mercer taught at Carver High School, Marked Tree.

Mercer had already successfully passed the Arkansas Bar Examination in March 1954. Sixty-five individuals took the exam, including only two African Americans. Thirty-three passed it. Mercer's score was the highest. Mercer practiced law in Pine Bluff for one year with the late Wiley A. Branton Sr., former dean of Howard University Law School and a former Law School colleague.

Mercer served as the NAACP field secretary for the state of Arkansas in 1957–1958, during the Little Rock Central High School crisis. He served as aide-de-camp to Daisy Bates and counseled the Little Rock Nine and their parents, including taking five of them to and from school during the first semester of their enrollment.

In 1967, he was appointed the first black deputy prosecution attorney in the South, and he has served as a special judge in several of the municipal courts and circuit courts in Pulaski County. Mercer is the father of nine children, six grandchildren, and six great-grandchildren. He is married to Pamela Mercer.

Chapter 2

Waldo Bronson

Waldo Bronson was born and raised in Little Rock, Arkansas, and attended the Little Rock Public Schools, graduating from Horace Mann High in 1958. He was admitted into the electrical engineering program at the University of Arkansas, Fayetteville. He transferred to Arkansas AM&N College in Pine Bluff, Arkansas, after two years at the University of Arkansas.

Bronson graduated from AM&N in 1963 with a BS in mathematics and a minor in physical science. He started what was to become a career in education by teaching in Malvern, Arkansas, and after six weeks transferring to the Little Rock Public Schools, where he taught mathematics for three years.

Bronson moved to Flint, Michigan, in 1966 and taught mathematics at Whittier Middle School for three years, where he was selected to participate in an administrative training program for minority teachers. He was then promoted to assistant principal and later became a high school principal. Bronson retired in 2000 after a very rewarding career in education.

Bronson is an elder at Trinity United Presbyterian Church in Flint and an accomplished photographer. He is enjoying his second career as a financial advisor.

Peter G. Faison

Peter G. Faison was born on March 1, 1924, in El Dorado, Arkansas. He was an honor graduate of Booker T. Washington High School, class of 1942.

Faison spent three years in World War II. He enrolled at Arkansas AM&N College and received a bachelor of arts and science degree in agriculture in May 1951. That fall, he enrolled in the Graduate School of the University of Arkansas, Fayetteville, majoring in agricultural economics.

In 1952, Faison taught vocational agriculture at the Ouachita County Training School in Bearden. In 1953, he married Othello Evelyn Owington of Holly Grove. They have five children, all of whom are college graduates; two of the five also have master's degrees.

In 1966, Faison received the master of arts in education degree in supervision and school administration from Tennessee A&I State of Nashville. He also studied at the University of Central Arkansas; the University of Connecticut-Storrs; and the University of Arizona-Tucson. Faison served four years as principal of Carver Pine Elementary in North Little Rock; three years at Immanuel High in Almyra; three years at Central High in Lake Village; and four years as superintendent of the East Side Special School District of Menifee. He also worked as a county agricultural agent in Conway County. He worked for the UA Cooperative Extension State Office as an extension specialist in farm records and tax management. He planned, coordinated, and conducted the Farm Income Tax Schools in ten locations across Arkansas. He revised and prepared the *Arkansas Farm Account Book,* co-authored and published the first farm record book for small and part-time farmers, and published a quarterly leaflet, *Tax Tips.*

Faison attends Bullock Temple Christian Methodist Episcopal Church and serves as a steward. He is the statistician for the Arkansas Region Christian Methodist Episcopal Church. Faison became a Prince Hall Mason in 1961; he is now a 33rd degree Mason and Noble of the Mystic Shrine. He is a Past General Conference Grand Joshua of the Heroines of Jericho of the United States of America and Bahamas.

George Mays

George Mays transferred to the University of Arkansas, Fayetteville, as a sophomore from Arkansas AM&N College, where he had a full football scholarship. His grandmother (Mrs. Bessie Mays) took him to Fayetteville to see her name in the senior walk (1955 master's). She became the reason he transferred to the University of Arkansas, Fayetteville. He received a BS in business administration with majors in management and industrial psychology.

Upon graduation, Mays moved to California to work on the Hound Dog Program and the Apollo Program. He was later promoted, becoming one of the first major contract buyers for North American Rockwell. He then became director of administration for the Tyland Corporation in Torrence, California. He joined the Litton Corporation as a program management specialist. Litton transferred him to Pascagoula, Mississippi, and he moved to Arkansas at the invitation of then-governor Winthrop Rockefeller to manage the Economic Development Program, a black community development program. In Arkansas, he began publishing *The Southern Mediator Journal*. His career later took him back to California to work for the Byron Jackson Company, a company manufacturing nuclear pumps for power plants.

Mays returned to Arkansas to work with his father in developing BG Mays Realty and he manages this business today. Mays is a father and is married to Sherrie Snowden Mays. They live in Little Rock, Arkansas.

Gordon D. Morgan

Gordon D. Morgan received his postsecondary education from the following institutions (all degrees in sociology): BA, Arkansas AM&N College; MA, University of Arkansas, Fayetteville; PhD, Washington State University, 1963. He spent several summers at the University of Minnesota Graduate School and served in the U.S. Army in Korea and Japan during the Korean War. He is currently a full professor of sociology at the University of Arkansas, Fayetteville.

Dr. Morgan's teaching experience includes high school math and social sciences, 1956–1959; Arkansas AM&N College, 1959–1960; Washington State University, teaching and research assistant, 1960–1963; Lincoln University, Jefferson City, Missouri, 1965–1969; and the University of Arkansas, Fayetteville, 1969–present.

Other work experiences include parole and probation intern with the U.S. Bureau of Prisons, 1955 summer research assistant; Teachers for East Africa Project, 1963–1965, with duties in East Africa: Columbia University Study of Scandinavian Prisons, summer 1976; and extensive study of the Caribbean for the course, "The Contemporary Caribbean."

Dr. Morgan's writings include many articles in scholarly journals and local, state, and campus newspapers. He is the author of ten books. Among those are *Winners Never Quit: Marguerite Rogers Howie, African American Woman Sociologist*; *No Violence is Progress: Early Integration at a Southern University*; and Toward an American Sociology. His unpublished works include at least thirty-five manuscripts on sociological and general topics. He has also written many plays and several novels.

For the last five years, Dr. Morgan has taught the course, "Special Topics in Whiteness." He has received postdoctoral grants from the Ford Foundation, Russell Sage Foundation, the National Endowment for the Humanities, and the American College Testing Program.

Helen Maxine Sutton Cannon

Helen Maxine Sutton was born on June 20, 1936, in Lincoln County. At age three, she moved to Little Rock. She graduated from Paul Laurence Dunbar High School in 1953. She was awarded a band scholarship to Arkansas Agricultural, Mechanical and Normal (AM&N) College in Pine Bluff. She completed her freshman-year coursework in 1953–1954. She majored in music and biology and was initiated into Delta Sigma Theta Sorority.

In fall 1955, Cannon was accepted into a new training program for registered nurses, and was one of three black students to be officially admitted as undergraduates. Cannon spent one year at the

University of Arkansas, Fayetteville, and two years at the University of Arkansas for Medical Sciences (UAMS). As a graduation gift in 1958, she received a beautiful engagement ring from Jimmie Cannon.

Cannon began her nursing career at UAMS and later worked in a Kansas hospital. In Kansas, the Cannons' baby daughter was the first black child born in the county. In 1963, Cannon accepted an assignment at a county hospital in Nebraska. In July 1964, Cannon and family moved to the desert town of El Centro, California. Their third child, a son, was born in El Centro. Cannon worked for more than twenty years at El Centro Regional Medical Center, where she continues to work part-time as a clinic nurse. Cannon's nursing specialty areas have included obstetrics, neurology, psychiatry, medical nursing, surgical nursing, and pediatrics. She has worked as a school nurse, earning a Life Credential–General School Services (Health and Development), grades K–14. She has earned more than thirty hours of postgraduate work and facilitates a lupus support group. Awards include Nurse of the Month as well as special recognition by the Family Solutions Organization. Maxine and Jimmie Cannon celebrated their fiftieth wedding anniversary in November 2008.

Sanford Tollette III

Reverend Sanford Tollette was born in Hempstead County; however, his parents lived in Tollette. His father was a Methodist minister, and the family moved frequently as a result. He attended school in Tollette, at the Howard County Training School.

Reverend Tollette received his bachelor's degree in chemistry from Arkansas AM&N College in 1949. He is a member of Alpha Phi Alpha Fraternity. He received his master's degree in education administration from the University of Arkansas, Fayetteville, in 1954. He also earned a master's degree in vocational counseling from Arkansas Teachers College in 1959. He has served as an instructor with the U.S. Naval Reserve and was awarded special recognition by the Eighth Naval District. Reverend Tollette has also taught off-campus courses in life sciences for Arkansas State University, Beebe.

His professional career began as a science teacher and coach at Lafayette County Training School (now Stamps High School); principal of Guernsey High School in Hempstead County; principal of Townsend Park Dollarway District, Pine Bluff; and principal of Smackover Training School. He left teaching to become a counselor in rehabilitation services in Hot Springs, which later was absorbed into a social services program for the state of Arkansas. He later went back into the classroom as a science teacher in Pulaski County.

In 1960, Reverend Tollette became a Christian Methodist minister. He has pastored churches in Texarkana, Hope, and Pine Bluff. He is married to Sammie Nell Irving of Dallas. They have two sons: Sanford Tollette IV and Frederick Tollette. Both sons are graduates of the University of Arkansas.

George L. Wesley

George L. Wesley received his BA and BS degrees from Arkansas AM&N College in 1954 and his MA from the University of Arkansas in 1956. He has also done graduate work at the University of Michigan-Ann Arbor and the University of Oklahoma.

Wesley served as the executive director of the Metropolitan Fair Housing Council of Greater Oklahoma City (2001–2007). He has also served as interim professor of television production at Langston University; public relations officer for the Oklahoma Housing Finance Agency; community relations officer for KTVY Television, Channel 4 in Oklahoma City; assistant professor of speech and drama at Grambling State University; and instructor of speech and drama at Arkansas AM&N College.

Wesley has served as a member of the Oklahoma City Arts Commission; the board of directors of the Oklahoma City Arts Council; Langston University's public relations advisory board; the Oklahoma Human Rights Commission (appointed by Governor George Nigh); the board of directors of the Metropolitan Fair Housing Council of Oklahoma City; and the board of directors and regional vice president of the National Broadcast Association for Community Affairs. He is an active member of Omega Psi Phi Fraternity.

A partial listing of his awards includes National Academy of Television Arts and Sciences EMMY Award (1974); Resolutions of Achievements—Oklahoma City mayor, Oklahoma House and Senate

(1974); Distinguished Service Award—Langston University (1981); Ambassador of Goodwill—Oklahoma governor George Nigh (1982); Presidential Citation—National Association for Equal Opportunity in Higher Education (1985); Omega Man of the Year—Eta Iota Chapter, Omega Psi Phi Fraternity, Inc. (1985).

Wesley has written, produced, and directed a sensitivity film to aid employers in dealing effectively with the language and actions of minority employees. He has produced an antidrug film used in high schools for the Urban League crime task force. He was associate producer for the Emmy Award–winning documentary, *Through the Looking Glass Darkly*. He developed the mass media curriculum and degree program at Grambling State University, developed and built radio station KGRM-FM (the only radio station in Grambling) as a training facility, and wrote and narrated Grambling Band shows, including a show for the inauguration of President Tolbert in Liberia, West Africa. He is the founder-director of Black Liberated Arts Center, Inc., Community Theatre, as well as working as an acting coach for stage and film.

Billie Rose Whitfield Jacobs

Billie Rose Whitfield Jacobs grew up in Little Rock, where she attended the historical Dunbar High School and Dunbar Junior College. In 1955, Jacobs and two other Dunbar High School alumnae made history (unintentionally) when they were admitted to the University of Arkansas as the university's first black undergraduate students. Jacobs received a BA from Harris Teachers College in St. Louis, Missouri, an MA from Washington University, and completed advanced studies at the University of Missouri in St. Louis.

Her professional career began in St. Louis as a teacher and reading specialist at Henry Elementary School. She was employed by the school district of University City in 1969 and remained there until her retirement in 1993. She served as a reading specialist before becoming an assistant principal. In 1975, Jacobs began a thirteen-year career as an elementary school principal. She was promoted to assistant superintendent in 1988. Jacobs also served for several months as interim superintendent of schools in 1992. Jacobs has served as an adjunct professor, teaching reading education and volunteer teaching courses at Fontbonne University, Maryville University, and Forest Park Community College.

In 1998, the University of Arkansas honored Marjorie Wilkins Williams, Maxine Sutton Cannon, and Jacobs for their participation in integrating the university in 1955 as undergraduates. At this spectacular event, the three were reunited for the first time in forty-two years. They were recognized by the Black Alumni Society of the university for "Significant Contribution to the University of Arkansas," including the "Living Legacy Pioneer Award."

Jacobs was initiated into the Beta Delta Chapter of the Alpha Kappa Alpha Sorority in 1962. She and her husband, Ernest, have been married for fifty-two years and are the parents of two daughters, Cathy Yvonne Jacobs and Carol Sue Jacobs Allen, both school teachers in the Ladue School District. A son-in-law, Donovan Allen, is an engineer with the Eastman Kodak Company. Jacobs is the second oldest of six Whitfield siblings. Five of the six Whitfield siblings attended and/or received degrees from the University of Arkansas.

Marjorie Wilkins Williams

Marjorie Wilkins Williams worked as a professor of nursing for San Antonio College for thirty years, served on the School of Nursing faculty at Troy State University, and worked as a general staff and operating-room nurse.

Williams was one of the three black students first officially admitted as undergraduates at the University of Arkansas in 1955. She received her BS in nursing from the university in 1959 and an MS in guidance and counseling from Troy State University in 1972. In 1977, she earned an MS in nursing from the University of Texas Health Science Center.

Williams was a member of the Texas Black Professionals in Higher Education (TBPHE), Who's Who in Nursing, Who's Who in Nursing Education, and the Texas Black Nurses Association. She served as chairperson, Allied Health Division, Texas Community College Teachers Association. She has received the Nurse Educator of Texas Award and the Alamo Community College Service Award. She enjoys reading, bridge, league bowling, and traveling.

Williams is married to William Franklin Williams, also an alumnus of the University of Arkansas (MSE, 1956). They have two children and two grandchildren.

Chapter 3

Sharon E. Bernard

Sharon Elaine Bernard, Esq., first exhibited leadership, commitment, and chutzpah when she became the first black woman to graduate from the University of Arkansas Law School and to become a licensed lawyer in Arkansas in 1970. In Law School, she was the founding president of the Kappa Beta Pi Legal Sorority.

After practicing criminal and civil rights law in Arkansas, she returned to her birthplace, Detroit, Michigan. During her thirty-year career at Michigan National Bank (MNB), she was a powerful community leader. She served as the chairperson of the board of directors of numerous organizations, including the Michigan Children's Trust Fund, for which she was the founding chairperson; the Detroit Police Commission; and the Detroit Urban League, where she was the first female chairperson.

Bernard retired from MNB as a first vice president and the statewide director of CRA/Community Development. At her retirement, she also served as a board member for fifteen community organizations, which reflected her values and core principles. During her many years of service, Bernard has received numerous awards for her outstanding leadership and commitment including Michigan 150 First Lady; Humanitarian of the Year (Optimist Youth Foundation); Foster Care Board Member of the Year (Michigan Federation of Private Child and Family Agencies); Child In The Hand (Life Directions); Excellence Award—the Corporate Woman (Top Ladies of Distinction); and Outstanding Volunteer Services (Central Region, National Urban League). Recently, she has also received several awards from the University of Arkansas School of Law, recognizing her as their first African American female graduate and for her accomplishments throughout her career.

Divorced in 1975, Bernard has raised two successful daughters, Judge Cylenthia LaToye Miller and Dr. Sharon G. Miller, who share her commitment to community service. She is also the proud grandmother of Michael, Nicholas, and Jordan.

Harold B. Betton

Harold B. Betton, MD, PhD, MS, MA, ABFP, and FAAFP, has been the principal physician at the Betton Clinic in Little Rock since 1978. He has also been the pastor of New Light Baptist Church in Little Rock since 1993. And he has served as an instructor at Arkansas AM&N College (1969–1970).

His education includes a BS, agriculture, University of Arkansas, Fayetteville; MS, natural sciences, University of Arkansas, Fayetteville; MD, University of Washington School of Medicine, Seattle, Washington; Board Certification in Family Practice by the American Board of Family Practice; master's of arts in biblical sciences, Trinity College and Seminary in Newburgh, Indiana; and a PhD in biblical studies, Trinity College and Seminary, Newburgh, Indiana.

Dr. Betton is the former chief of family practice at Baptist Medical Center, Little Rock (1985–1986, and 1999–2000). He serves on the editorial board of the *Family Practice News* (1996–present). He is a member of the American Academy of Family Physicians (1975–present); Pulaski County Medical Society (1978–present); American Diabetes Association (1999–present); Arkansas Medical, Dental, and Pharmaceutical Association, and was president from 2005 to 2007; and the National Medical Association. He serves as an adjunct professor of religion at Arkansas Baptist College, Little Rock (2006–present) and is a reviewer for the *Journal of the National Medical Association* (2000–present).

Dr. Betton has served as a Scoutmaster for Boy Scouts of America and on the medical staff for National Boy Scouts of America Jamboree, Fort A. P. Hill, Virginia.

A partial listing of his publications includes: *Old Testament Biblical Studies for Preachers: Selected In-Depth Studies*; review of *Writing, Speaking, and Communication Skills for Health Professionals,* by the Health Care Communication Group, *Journal of the National Medical Association* 94 (July 2002); and coauthor of *Spirituality and Medicine: Can the Two Walk Together?*

Dr. Betton is married to Angela R. Betton. They have two children—Benecia M. Betton, BA, JD, Esq., attorney at law, associate at Quattlebaum, Grooms, Tull, and Burrow; and Alexander Julian Betton, BA, MA, JD, Esq., a probation officer for Judge Proctor.

Margaret Clark

Dr. Margaret Clark, a native of Dixie, Georgia, attended public schools in Dixie and New York City. She earned a BA in foreign languages from Arkansas AM&N College and an MA in French (1968) and a doctorate in foreign language education (1978) from the University of Arkansas, Fayetteville. Prior to studying at the University of Arkansas, she had two National Defense Education Act (NDEA) scholarships: French Level One (1962) to Rutgers University and French Level Two (1964) to the University of Massachusetts in Arcachon, France. She studied as a Fulbright-Hays Scholar at the University of Paris (Sorbonne), 1964–1965, and for a summer at the University of Besancon, France.

She was the first African American to teach in the Department of Foreign Languages at the University of Arkansas in 1969 and the first African American to teach in the College of Education. She taught French from 1969 to 1993 and Teacher Education from 1972 to 1998. She taught one summer in Athens, Greece. She retired in 1998 as an associate professor emerita.

In 2006, the University of Arkansas named her one of the first ten Silas Hunt Legacy awardees, and a scholarship was presented to an incoming freshman in her name. The Phi Alpha Omega graduate chapter of the Alpha Kappa Alpha Sorority, Inc., gave her its first "Hats Off" Award in 2006 for her achievements and community contributions. The undergraduate sorority chapter has established a scholarship in her name. Dr. Clark was primarily responsible for both the chartering of the campus chapter of Pi Delta Phi, the national French Honor Society, and of the Kappa Iota chapter of the Alpha Kappa Alpha Sorority, Inc. She was also instrumental in the chartering of the Phi Alpha Omega graduate chapter in northwest Arkansas and served as its first president.

Viralene J. Coleman

Viralene J. Coleman received her BA degree in English from Arkansas AM&N College and her MA (1959) and PhD (1969) degrees in English from the University of Arkansas, Fayetteville. She has done further study at the University of Illinois-Urbana, the University of Massachusetts-Amherst, and Hobart and William Smith College in Geneva, New York.

Dr. Coleman served the University of Arkansas at Pine Bluff for thirty-seven years as a teacher of English and literature. She currently serves as professor and chair of the Department of English, Theatre and Mass Communication. She is nationally recognized for her innovative approaches to teaching composition and literature. She has served as test developer and reader for Educational Testing Services (ETS) and CLEP (College Board), and as a test reviewer for the National Endowment for the Humanities.

Dr. Coleman has received numerous fellowships, including a Woodrow Wilson National Fellowship, several grants from the National Endowment for the Humanities, and a Rockefeller Grant. She has written and received funding for more than fifty proposals from such agencies as the Arkansas Humanities Council, the National Endowment for the Humanities, SYNERGY Forum, and other public and private agencies.

In 1984, she was named the Arkansas Humanist of the Year. In the same year, she received the Distinguished Faculty Award by the UAPB faculty. Prior to her appointment at AM&N, Dr. Coleman had taught in the public schools of Arkansas as an English teacher/librarian.

A native of Rosston, Arkansas, she is a member of Faith Presbyterian Church, Pine Bluff Alumnae Chapter of Delta Sigma Theta Sorority, and the AM&N/UAPB Alumni Association. The wife of the late Elijah Coleman, she is the mother of two children, Sandra and Ronald, and the grandmother of two grandchildren, Jamillah and Ronald Coleman Jr.

Alice Davis Butler

Alice Butler was born in Dermott, a small town about one hundred miles southeast of Little Rock. Her parents, Fletcher and Thelma Davis, raised their five daughters in a loving and disciplined home environment. She attended a segregated elementary and high school system, and all other facets of her life were segregated as well—church, recreational, and social. Butler entered the University of Arkansas as a freshman in September 1965 and graduated in 1969.

Butler's oldest sister and her husband, who lived in Richmond, California, had invited her to live with them. She met her husband-to-be the month she arrived in Richmond. They married after a one-year courtship and have been married almost forty years, with two children, a son and a daughter. Their son is a practicing physician and their daughter is beginning practice as an attorney.

Butler worked for the federal government for thirty-one years, beginning as a personnel intern for the navy. She served as the personnel officer for a naval weapons station and as the regional personnel officer for the Department of Health and Human Services. She ended her career as the regional human resources director for the Social Security Administration's San Francisco region.

Butler retired in 2005 and enjoys staying physically and politically active, studying Spanish, singing in her church choir, traveling, and volunteering.

Joanna P. Edwards

Joanna P. Edwards, PhD, was born in Sherrill, Arkansas, the youngest of ten children of James Wesley and Laura Freeman Edwards. Edwards is a professor emerita in humanities and art history, University of Arkansas at Pine Bluff, where she taught from 1994 to 2009. Prior to UAPB, she taught at Spelman College, Atlanta, Georgia, and the University of Wisconsin-Whitewater.

In June 1961, she enrolled as a freshman at AM&N College. In fall 1963, she transferred to the University of Arkansas, Fayetteville, where she graduated with a BA in 1965. She completed her AM in history of art (1976) from the University of Michigan, Ann Arbor, her PhD degree in history of art (Africa, Mesoamerica, and Oceania) at Indiana University, Bloomington.

At UAPB, Dr. Edwards developed several programs such as *Linkages: Exploring Socio-Cultural Affinities Between Africa and the African Diaspora;* Brown Bag Lunch and *Ralph Bunche* film with documentary filmmaker William Greaves; *Breaking the Cycle of Cultural Bondage Through Knowledge and Reconnection to the Past: African American Thinkers 1865–1950,* with historians Drs. Alan Colón, James Turner, Kenneth Hamilton, and Kevin Butler; and a program with nationally acclaimed storyteller Mitch "Gran'daddy Junebug" Capel, interpreter of the works of Paul Lawrence Dunbar. Between 2002 and 2005, as a research scholar and scriptwriter with the Arts and Science Center of Southeast Arkansas, Dr. Edwards collaborated in development of the documentary, *The History and Influence of African American Churches in Jefferson County, Arkansas, 1850–2004.*

Dr. Edwards is an ordained minister and from 2002 to 2007, she developed a radio Bible teaching ministry, *Core of Restoration,* and an inspirational program, *Woman to Woman.* Since returning to Arkansas, she has done biblical and Middle Eastern studies at the American Institute of Higher Biblical Studies/South Central Graduate College, Sherwood, and the Institute of Holy Land Studies (JUC), Jerusalem, Israel, where she studied geographical and historical settings of the Bible. In 1997, she returned to attend the Dead Sea Scrolls Congress. In 2006, she researched Ethiopian Jews at Israel' Ben Zvi Institute.

Wendell L. Griffen

Wendell Griffen is chief executive officer of Griffen Strategic Consulting and is an Arkansas lawyer, jurist, legal educator, religious leader, and public speaker. In 1974, Griffen, who is a 1975 graduate of the Department of Defense Race Relations Institute (DRRI), now known as the Defense Equal Opportunity Management Institute (DEOMI), began counseling mid-level military unit leaders and managers about cultural competency, cross-cultural relationships, conflict resolution, team-building, and morale as an officer in the United States Army. In 1976, Griffen received the Army Commendation

Medal for his work in those areas as leader of the Race Relations/Equal Opportunity Office of the 43rd General Support Group.

After graduating from the School of Law of the University of Arkansas in 1979, Griffen became the first person of color to join a major Arkansas law firm (Wright, Lindsey and Jennings of Little Rock), and became a litigation partner in 1983. In 1985, then Arkansas governor Bill Clinton named Griffen chairman of the Arkansas Workers' Compensation Commission, making Griffen the first person of color named to that state agency and the first to chair it.

In 1995, then Arkansas governor Jim Guy Tucker appointed Griffen to the Arkansas Court of Appeals. While on the Court of Appeals, Griffen also remained active in professional, civic, and religious life, including service as president of the Pulaski County Bar Association, president of the Judge William R. Overton Inn of Court, pastor of Emmanuel Baptist Church of Little Rock, and parliamentarian of the National Baptist Convention, USA, Inc. Griffen has also served on the Council for the American Bar Association Section of Science and Technology Law, co-moderating a 2001 ABA Annual Meeting Forum on envisioning the implication of science and technology on law.

Griffen concluded his tenure on the Arkansas Court of Appeals at the end of 2008. Beginning January 1, 2009, he joined the faculty of the University of Arkansas at Little Rock's William H. Bowen School of Law as a visiting professor of law, teaching pretrial criminal procedure and leading a seminar, "Cultural Competency, Inclusion, and Law."

Griffen is married to Dr. Patricia Griffen, a clinical psychologist in private practice. They are parents of two adult sons.

Eugene Hunt

Eugene Hunt has been in private law practice in Pine Bluff since 1972. He has served on the Arkansas Board of Law Examiners from 2000 to 2005. He has served as a special justice on the Arkansas Supreme Court, special judge for Jefferson County, and he has served on the Arkansas Court of Appeals (2008). He also served as assistant dean of students at the University of Arkansas, Fayetteville, from 1971 to 1972.

Hunt is and has been active in numerous church and civic organizations in Pine Bluff and Jefferson County. He is a deacon at Old St. James Missionary Baptist Church; a life member of the NAACP since 1996; a board member and chair of Pine Bluff Downtown Development, Inc.; and a member of the Jefferson County Board of Governors. He also served as a member of the Arkansas Criminal Code Revision Commission, the Arkansas Ethics Commission, and as co-manager of the Jefferson County Child Support Enforcement Unit from 1990 to 2000.

Two of Hunt's high-profile cases include (1) *Goldman, Powell and Olloway v. Marsh, Secretary of the U.S. Army,* P.B.C. 75–36, 441 F.3d 572 (8th cir. 200) (8th cir. 1983), a class action lawsuit settled in February 1995. The Court entered a memorandum opinion and found that the United States Army had engaged in a pattern and practice of discrimination based upon race in the promotion of black employees working in the wage grade and general schedule positions; (2) *Eugene Hunt, et al v. Clinton, et al* P.B. C-89–406, which sought to establish judicial districts where black voters select judicial candidates of their choice. The case was settled November 1991, via a consent decree, which created ten circuit judgeship positions with black voting-age majority districts where black voters have chosen to select ten black circuit judges, including two females.

Jerry Leon Jennings

Jerry Jennings is a native of Fort Smith, Arkansas, where he attended public schools. He was one of the first black athletes to attend Northside High School. He accepted a basketball scholarship to the University of Arkansas as one of its first black scholarship athletes.

Jennings was head football coach at Darby Junior High School for two years and then head basketball coach at that same school for the next thirty years. He retired in May 2009, having taught thirty-four years.

Called to the ministry in 1997, Reverend Jennings was pastor of Mount Calvary Missionary Baptist Church of Poteau, Oklahoma, for eight years and is currently pastor of the Mount Moriah Missionary Baptist Church of Fort Smith.

Reverend Jennings looks forward to entering seminary in the fall of 2009 and retirement with his wife, Terry, and their three daughters, Brandi, Alexis, and Whitney.

Gerald Jordan

Gerald B. Jordan is a native of Malvern and a 1966 graduate of the all-black Annie Agnes Wilson High School. He worked for metropolitan daily newspapers for twenty-five years before becoming associate professor in the Walter J. Lemke Department of Journalism at the University of Arkansas in 1995. His focus is print journalism. He has a BA in journalism from the University of Arkansas, 1970, and an MSJ from Northwestern University, 1971, and he is a Nieman Fellow, Harvard University, 1982.

Jordan joined the department from the *Philadelphia Inquirer*, where he was a reporter and a Washington correspondent. He became an assigning editor for the *Inquirer* in 1989 and worked in the suburbs and on the City Desk before he was named North Zone editor, with responsibility for a two-county edition reaching 110,000 readers. He began as a sports writer for the *Kansas City Star*, where he reported high school sports before he covered beats of the National Basketball Association and the National Football League. He was also an editorial writer at the *Star* and the *Boston Globe* before spending three years as a TV columnist for the *Star*.

Jackie "Jack" Ray Kearney

Born in Gould in 1951, Kearney attended Fields Elementary, Fields High, and Gould High (the "white" school in Gould), graduating in 1970 as class president and third academically in his class.

He enrolled in the University of Arkansas in September 1970, majoring in political science with a minor in economics, and completed course study in 1974. He enrolled in September 1974 at Syracuse University College of Law. He received his JD from Syracuse in 1977.

Kearney was sworn in as an attorney in September 1977 and began practice in Magnolia. In 1978, he moved to Little Rock and served as the attorney for the newly created Arkansas Crime Commission. As of 1979, he served in the Arkansas Appellate Public Defender Office. From 1981 to 1984, he was in private practice with James Smedley. In 1984, Kearney relocated to Tulsa, Oklahoma, where he is believed to be that city's first African American in the public defender's office. In 1988, he returned to Arkansas to serve as assistant attorney general, director of Arkansas's Consumer Protection division, and ethics attorney. In 1991, he was appointed Arkansas's first director of the newly created Ethics Commission.

In 1994, Kearney returned to private practice. He continues to serve on various charitable and government boards of directors. He married Sandra (Sandy) Hager in 1980 and they have two sons, Jackie Ray Jr. (who died in 2005) and Jason. Both sons attended the University of Arkansas, Fayetteville. Jason Kearney now practices law with his father and lives in Fayetteville, Arkansas.

Almer Lee

Lee is a 1968 graduate of Fort Smith's Northside High School. He attended Phillips Junior College in Helena for a year and was recruited to play basketball for the University of Arkansas, Fayetteville, from 1969 to 1972. He was the third African American scholarship basketball player after Thomas Johnson and Vernon Murphy.

After playing Razorback basketball, he played professional basketball in Europe with a team in Amsterdam, Holland, for two years. On returning to the states, he worked for Worthen Bank of Little Rock for seven years in the lending department and later for the Arkansas Department of Human Services, where he presently works in the medical assistance area with Medicaid. His community service has included working at the Dunbar Recreational facility in Little Rock for five summers conducting basketball clinics.

Hiram McBeth III

The Honorable Hiram McBeth III received his BA in political science, MA in political science, and JD degrees from the University of Arkansas, Fayetteville. He now resides in Dallas, Texas, where he has a private law practice, the McBeth Law Office.

McBeth has served in the following positions: administrative law judge I, Texas State Office of Administrative Hearings, Dallas, Texas; appeals hearing officer, Texas Workforce Commission, Dallas, Texas; manager of purchasing, the Associates Corporation of North America, Irving, Texas; attorney, Law Office of Hiram McBeth, Dallas, Texas; project manager, Memphis Housing Authority, LeMoyne Gardens Hope VI Urban Revitalization Plan, Memphis, Tennessee; senior litigation attorney, Federal Deposit Insurance Corporation (FDIC), Dallas, Texas; assistant public defender, Dallas County Office of the Public Defender, Dallas, Texas; and director of Procurement, Regional Transit Authority (RTA).

A short listing of voluntary and professional associations include the State Bar of Texas; the State Bar of Arkansas; J. L. Turner Legal Association; Dallas Black Criminal Lawyers Association; Texas Criminal Defense Lawyers Association; United States Court of Appeals, Fifth Circuit, New Orleans, Louisiana; and the United States Court of Appeals, Eight Circuit, St. Louis, Missouri.

George McGill

George McGill is the owner of McGill Insurance Agency, Inc., in Fort Smith, Arkansas. McGill also owns a consulting firm involved in diversity and political consulting, Eiffel Limited Co., and is co-founder of Cornerstone Community Development Corporation. Cornerstone has been recognized nationally for its innovative holistic approach to community development. The city of Fort Smith awarded McGill the Spirit of the Frontier Award for the preservation of the historic James K. Barnes home, located in the Fort Smith Historic District.

McGill was a student at UA Fort Smith (formerly WestArk Community College). He received bachelor and master's degrees from the University of Arkansas, Fayetteville. He is a U.S. Army veteran trained in artillery fire direction. McGill has worked on political campaigns for President Bill Clinton, U.S. senator Blanche Lincoln, and U.S. senator Mark Pryor.

He currently serves on the board of the Fort Smith Regional Chamber of Commerce, the Riverfront Development Task Force, the Bass Reeves Legacy Initiative, and the Fort Smith Round Table Civic Club.

McGill established the Elizabeth McGill Scholastic Awards program for elementary schools and founded the "Billy Boots" program, which provides shoes for children in need. He co-founded the Yvonne Keaton-Martin Scholarship program, which has provided almost one million dollars in awards to area students. He also founded the Martin Luther King Jr. Golden Hands Award, which goes to citizens who give freely to make a difference for others. He is a team sponsor and volunteer for the Stephens Boys and Girls Club.

McGill has previously served on the Arkansas Contractors Licensing Board with two terms as chair. He has served on the Arkansas Department of Labor's Prevailing Wage Commission and served as chair of the Fort Smith Planning Commission. He has served on the boards of Abilities Unlimited, the Salvation Army, the Fort Smith Girls Club, the First Tee of Fort Smith, and the Elizabeth McGill Senior Citizens Center.

George B. Miller Jr.

George Miller's mother pushed him to honor his father's life and legacy by excelling in school and in life. Every Miller since Reconstruction has earned a postgraduate degree. As a result of the untimely death of his father when George was only a baby, he was raised by his mother in a single-parent household. Ultimately, all the hard work and sacrifice paid off when he graduated as a National Honor Society student from segregated Eliza Miller High School, in Helena, which had been named in honor of his paternal grandmother.

Miller was admitted to Michigan State University at sixteen. He joined the Swim Team, joined Men's Glee Club, and pledged Alpha Phi Alpha Fraternity, Inc. Following his return to Michigan State in 1963, he graduated with a bachelor of science degree in pre-dentistry.

Miller and his wife of five years, Sharon Elaine Bernard Miller, enrolled in the University of Arkansas Law School, making them the school's first black couple. After graduation, Miller oversaw the family's business interests, which included the first African American–owned movie theater in the United States, other commercial rental property, and residential rental property. He also built and operated the first airport-based music store in the Nashville International Airport in Nashville, Tennessee; operated the first black-owned barge yard in Port Arthur, Texas; and began plans for revitalizing Beale Street, the "Home of the Blues" in Memphis, Tennessee. This latter endeavor led to the founding of the Beale Street Development Corporation and the creation of Miller Memphis, Inc. Miller also accepted a job with the Equal Employment Opportunity Commission where he worked from 1969 to 1972.

Today, Miller is president and CEO of Miller Memphis, Inc., which owns one of the largest and most attractive parcels of land on Beale Street. A premiere movie theater Miller built in 1974 is now a nightclub, but it still stands as one of the most architecturally interesting buildings in Memphis.

Divorced in 1975, Miller has four children—Judge Cylenthia LaToye Miller, Dr. Sharon G. Miller, George B. Miller III, and Syminee Cole Miller. He is also the proud grandfather of Michael, Nicholas, and Jordan.

Ray E. McKissic

The Reverend Dr. Ray McKissic is the minister of visitation for the Triumphant Baptist Church in Hyattsville, Maryland, where he serves individuals and groups in private homes, churches, nursing centers, rescue missions, hospitals, and jails. His lifetime experiences help him understand the relevance of and necessity for ministering to the whole person in body, mind, and spirit. He is a native of Pine Bluff, currently residing in Washington, D.C.

Reverend McKissic was a premedical graduate (BA) of the University of Arkansas, Fayetteville. He also earned the MDiv from Southwestern Baptist Theological Seminary, Fort Worth, Texas, and a doctor of ministry from Howard University School of Divinity, Washington, D.C. He is currently an instructor of biblical studies at the John Leland Center for Theological Studies in Arlington, Virginia.

Dr. McKissic is a teacher and scholar who has developed and instructed teaching programs in Arlington County middle and high schools, Arkansas Baptist College, Maple Spring Baptist Bible College and Seminary, Howard University School of Divinity, and area churches and correctional facilities.

He has served as the pastor of Union Baptist Church of Hot Springs and First Baptist Church of Smackover and as assistant pastor of churches in Texas, Arkansas, and Washington, D.C. His pastoral experience includes evangelism and outreach, teaching Bible study, and serving as a Scoutmaster. He is president and chief executive officer of Panoplia Ministries, a biblically based teaching, evangelizing, counseling, training, and writing organization specializing in equipping today's people to understand spiritual warfare in our twenty-first century world.

Vernon Murphy

Vernon Murphy received more than eighty scholarship offers coming out of all-black Dunbar High School in Texarkana, Texas, in 1968, including offers from places like UCLA, Villanova, Oklahoma, and Colorado. He chose to attend the University of Arkansas, becoming the second black scholarship basketball athlete. Freshmen did not play on the varsity squad at that time. Murphy averaged 24.9 points per game on the 1969–1970 freshman team.

After playing basketball for Arkansas, Murphy tried out for the Dallas Cowboys football team in 1972 as a receiver. After the tryout for the Cowboys, he played semi-professional basketball in Mexico, but returned to the United States and tried out for the NBA Atlanta Hawks and San Antonio Spurs. When he made neither team, he went to play basketball in Israel in 1973 and made the team, but did not get an opportunity to play because the Yom Kippur war broke out at the opening of the season.

In 1974, Murphy returned to the University of Arkansas to finish his degree. With that accomplished, he became the first black athlete to graduate from the University of Arkansas.

While in Bethlehem in 1973, Murphy accepted his call into the ministry. He is now the pastor of Freedom Fellowship Church on East Street in Texarkana.

Deborah Hill Thompson

Deborah Hill Thompson is a high school graduate of Horace Mann in Little Rock. She received her BSE in elementary education from the University of Arkansas, Fayetteville, in 1970, and her MEd in counseling from the University of Arkansas, Fayetteville, in 1973.

Her employment history includes terms at the University of Arkansas, Fayetteville, where she was assistant director of financial aid (1973–1975); coordinator of career development with Career Planning and Placement (1975–1979); and assistant director of Career Planning and Placement (1979–1981). She also worked at Philander Smith College as a counselor in Student Support Services (1981–1985 and 1996–1999); the University of Arkansas at Little Rock as a counselor in Testing and Student Life Research (1985–1990); and at Great Rivers Vocational Technical Institute in McGehee as a vocational counselor (1990–1992). She worked as a real estate broker and boutique owner (1992–1998) and returned to Philander Smith College as director of Student Support Services (1999–2000).

Semon Frank Thompson Jr.

Semon Frank Thompson Jr. is a 1969 graduate of the University of Arkansas with a BA in social welfare. He has completed graduate hours at the University of Arkansas School of Law and additional hours in the field of public administration. He is a graduate of the Arkansas Law Enforcement Training Academy, becoming one of the first armed police officers at the University of Arkansas.

Since 1994, he has been employed by the Oregon Department of Corrections as the superintendent of Santiam Correctional Institution and Mill Creek Correctional Facility (2003–present); superintendent of Columbia River Correctional Institution and South Fork Forest Camp (2001–2003); assistant director of Community Services (2000–2001); assistant director of Institutions division (1997–2000); and superintendent of Oregon State Penitentiary (1994–1997).

Prior to moving to Oregon, Thompson served with the Arkansas Department of Corrections as superintendent of the Wrightsville Unit (1993–1994); superintendent of the Delta Regional Unit (1989–1993); and personnel administrator in Human Resources, directing 1,500 employees. Other areas of employment have included Thompson-Nash, Inc., Realtors; grants officer, the Rockefeller Foundation; center director, Little Rock Job Corps Center; executive director, the Economic Opportunity Agency of Washington County; associate dean of students for the University of Arkansas (1976–1978); criminal investigator with the University of Arkansas Police Department (1975–1976); assistant dean of students for minority affairs for the University of Arkansas (1972–1973); graduate resident assistant (1970–1971); and instructor, the Job Corps Center of Fayetteville, Arkansas (1969–1972).

Thompson has received numerous hours of special training at the National Institute of Corrections, the Wiesenthal Museum's Tools for Tolerance, the Federal Bureau of Investigations training course in hostage negotiations; and training in bomb investigations. Some of the awards he has received include the Willamette University Law Students "Living Legend" award for contributions to the advancement of minority and human rights; and the Warden of the Year award, presented by the North American Association of Wardens and Superintendents in 1997.

Earnestine Banks Walton Russell

Earnestine Banks Walton Russell was born April 17, 1936, in Dansby, Arkansas, to James Oliver Banks and Emma Jean Johnson Banks. Walton Russell's high school years were spent at Lincoln High

School in Forrest City. The earning of a BS degree in home economics from Arkansas AM&N College was the fulfillment of one of her goals. Walton Russell enrolled in the College of Agriculture and Home Economics in 1966 at the University of Arkansas, Fayetteville. She completed all requirements for an MS in home economics (consumer science) in spring 1968.

She was a home economics teacher for several years, and she has worked for the Office of Economic Opportunity and the Office of Economic Opportunity of Eastern Arkansas. She worked for thirty-two years teaching vocational home economics (consumer science) in the Forrest City School District. Some achievements include service as department chairperson of the home economics department, Forrest City High School; honorary member of New Homemakers of America; president of Forrest City Arkansas Educational Association; and Gala Award Educator of the year, 2008. She retired from teaching in June 2001 and retired from Wal-Mart Stores, Inc., in June 2003 after twenty-seven years of service.

Walton Russell married Tommy L. Walton in 1958. The couple had two children, Trent Avery (T. A.) Walton Sr. and Sheila Renae Walton. Both children are graduates of the University of Arkansas, Fayetteville.

Walton Russell is a member of Prosperity Missionary Baptist Church, Forrest City; a member of Delta Sigma Theta Sorority, Inc.; a member of Semper Fidelity Women's Social Club; the Order of the Eastern Star; the Arkansas Educational Association; and the Northeast Arkansas Educational Association.

Robert Whitfield

Robert Whitfield was born January 1940 in Scottsboro, Alabama, but reared in Little Rock. Whitfield's public school experiences included attending Little Rock's Southend Elementary, Gibbs Elementary, and Dunbar Junior High and graduating from Horace Mann Senior High in 1957. After graduation, he joined the United States Air Force, served four years, and received an honorable discharge in January 1961. He then enrolled at Arkansas AM&N College. After a short stay at the college, he, his brother, and a group of friends were approached by a couple of civil rights activists. By February 1963, they had organized their first sit-in at Woolworth's in downtown Pine Bluff, and the group selected Whitfield chair of the Pine Bluff movement. They organized several mass meetings and invited many civil rights leaders to speak, including the Reverend Dr. Martin Luther King, John Lewis, and others. As a result of the stir they caused the school and the community, some were expelled from Arkansas AM&N College.

Whitfield enrolled at the University of Arkansas, Fayetteville. He quickly learned there was no housing for black students on campus. To that end, Joanna Edwards and Whitfield filed suit against the university and were instrumental in opening up the dormitories for black students.

Whitfield transferred to Philander Smith College and completed a BA degree in elementary education in 1967. He taught school in the Little Rock Public School system and was appointed by then governor Dale Bumpers as director of the Office of Economic Opportunity.

Whitfield has been married to the former Constance Elaine Clayborne for the past forty years. They have two children, Jawanza Robert, a high school counselor in Chester, Virginia, and Dr. Anika Tene Whitfield, a podiatrist in Little Rock. The couple has one grandchild, Maya Ashanti Whitfield, a high school senior in Chester, Virginia. Whitfield has three brothers, John, William, and George, and two sisters, Billie R. Jacobs and Roberta Kelley. He attends Union AME Church, serves as president of his neighborhood association, and is a member of Alpha Phi Alpha Fraternity.

Chapter 4

Lenthon B. Clark

Lenthon B. Clark was born in Marshall, Texas, the youngest of seventeen children. He graduated from Pemberton High School and Wiley College. He received an MBA from Texas Southern University, Houston, Texas.

Clark came to the University of Arkansas, Fayetteville, as director of financial aid in 1977 after leaving the same position at Texas Southern University. He retired from the University of Arkansas in 1995.

During his career, he has served as president, Fayetteville Chapter of Habitat for Humanity; member of the National Association of Student Financial Aid Administrators Twenty-fifth Anniversary task force; president, the Arkansas Association of Student Financial Aid Administrators; member, Committee on Governance and Membership, College Scholarship Service Council; chairman, the Executive Committee, Southwestern Region of the College Board; member of the Committee on Program Review and member, the National Council of the National Association of Student Financial Aid Administrators (NASFAA); regional vice president, NASFAA, member of the Selective Service System; president, the Texas Association of Student Financial Aid Administrators; and member of the College Scholarship Service Committee on Guidance and Publications.

Shirley Leffall Clark

Shirley Leffall Clark was born in Shreveport, Louisiana, to Houston and Addie Turner Leffall. She grew up in Marshall, Texas, and attended New Town Elementary and Pemberton High Schools. She graduated from Wiley College in 1956 and married Lenthon B. Clark in December of that year.

Shirley joined the staff at Texas Southern University as an administrative assistant for Lyceum and Culture, later working for twenty years as secretary for Career Services. In 1977, she and Lenthon B. Clark moved to Fayetteville. In August 1977, she began working in the Career Services and Placement Office at the University of Arkansas, until she retired as secretary emerita in 1997.

John L Colbert

John L Colbert, a native of Rondo, graduated from Barton High School in 1973 as the first African American valedictorian. Attending the University of Arkansas, Fayetteville, he received a BSE in education (1976) followed by an MSE in 1982.

In 1986, Colbert began his career in education as the first African American special education teacher at Bates Elementary in Fayetteville. He became the principal at Howard Elementary School in Fort Smith (1984) where he worked until returning to the Fayetteville district as the first African American principal in 1987, and Colbert also served as the principal of Jefferson Elementary School until 1995. In 1995, he was selected to serve at the helm of the newly constructed Holcombe Elementary. He was hired as the first African American associate superintendent of the Fayetteville School District on July 1, 2008.

His community service includes Kappa Kappa and Omicron Zeta Lambda Chapters of Alpha Phi Alpha Fraternity, Inc. (charter memberships in both chapters); chapter advisor to Kappa Kappa Chapter of Alpha Phi Alpha Fraternity, Inc.; past NPHC advisor, Yvonne Richardson Community Center Board of Directors; Fayetteville Community Foundation Board of Directors; and Prince Hall Mason (Royal Arch Mason, Knights of Templar, 32nd Degree Consistory, Order of the Eastern Star, Senior District Deputy Grand Master). Colbert has helped organize the Fayetteville's Martin Luther King Jr. "I Have A Dream" March for twenty-seven years and the MLK Celebration Banquet for eleven years. He is the advisor and founder of the Northwest Arkansas King Team. He is also a member of the St. James Missionary Baptist Church.

Colbert was the 2006 National Alumni Brother of the Year, Alpha Phi Alpha Fraternity; inducted into U of A Greek Hall of Fame; Outstanding Advisor of the Year Award; Kappa Kappa Seven Jewels Award Winner; Dr. Martin Luther King Jr. Community Award. Two awards have been named in his honor by the Kappa Kappa Chapter and Omicron Zeta Lambda Chapter. He is married to Cheryl, and they have two children, J'onnelle and Janneesa.

Edward Duffy

Edward Duffy is a professor of psychology in the Department of Social Sciences of the Miami-Dade College, North Campus. He has a bachelor's degree in sociology, a master's degree in counselor education from the University of Arkansas, and an EdD in counseling from the University of Miami. After graduating from the University of Arkansas in 1974, he moved to Washington, D.C., where he worked as a counselor at the University of Maryland, College Park, for four years.

In 1979, Duffy began his employment at Miami-Dade Community College, Wolfson Campus, as head of the Department of Counseling. He transferred to North Campus where his primary responsibility is teaching. He is also chairperson for the Department of Social Sciences Recruitment task force, which focuses on recruitment and retention of students in the social sciences.

His teaching style is student centered. He believes the classroom environment is critical to the learning process. He also believes students learn as much from each other as they do from their instructors.

Dinah Gail Gant

Dinah Gail Gant is one of ten children born to Floyd and Theresa Gant (deceased), former sharecroppers in Woodruff County. She is a 1971 graduate and valedictorian of Augusta High School in Augusta. Gant holds a degree in civil engineering from the University of Arkansas, Fayetteville, where she was inducted as a member of the Arkansas Academy of Civil Engineers.

Gant was a charter member of the Lambda Theta Chapter of Delta Sigma Theta Sorority, Inc., at the University of Arkansas in 1974. She is a Golden Life Member of the Milwaukee Alumnae Chapter Delta Sigma Theta Sorority, where she has served in numerous capacities, including president. She is a thirty-one-year active member of the sorority.

Gant is a founding member of the Delta Memorial Endowment Fund. She is a Girl Scouts of Milwaukee area troop leader and coordinator for seven years. She has served as a youth coordinator for both the Ebony Ice Ski Club and Badger Racquet Tennis Club. Gant is also a member of the Milwaukee Chapter of Jack & Jill of America, Inc.

Gant is currently employed as chief design engineer for Milwaukee Water Works. Most important, she is mother of twin daughters Deena and Theresa.

Patricia L. Greene Griffen

Patricia L. Griffen of Little Rock is a clinical psychologist in private practice with Clinical Psychology Services, Inc., an independent practice she established in 1983. Dr. Griffen also serves on the faculty of Philander Smith College in the Department of Psychology.

She is a native of Malvern, and she completed a BA in psychology from Ouachita Baptist University, Arkadelphia, graduating *magna cum laude*. After receiving the MA in clinical psychology from the University of Arkansas, Fayetteville, Dr. Griffen joined the staff of Pikes Peak Family Counseling and Mental Health Center in Colorado Springs, Colorado, as a psychologist. She was also an instructor in the Department of Psychology at El Paso Community College. In 1978, Dr. Griffen was the first African American to earn a PhD in clinical psychology from the University of Arkansas. Dr. Griffen then joined the faculty in the Department of Psychology at the University of Arkansas.

Dr. Griffen has held positions as director of Psychological Services for Adolescent Inpatient Treatment for the Arkansas Mental Health Services Division, director of South Pulaski Services for Central Arkansas Mental Health Services, and psychological consultant for the Restore Drug, Chemical Dependency, and Eating Disorder program at Riverview Hospital and St. Vincent Medical Infirmary. She has also been an adjunct professor in the psychology department at the University of Arkansas, Little Rock, and she was psychological consultant for the Southwest Employee Assistance Program.

Dr. Griffen has served on numerous charitable and professional boards. She was appointed to the Arkansas Board of Examiners in Psychology by former governor Bill Clinton and served as chairperson of that board. Currently, Dr. Griffen is on the staff of Baptist Medical Center and St. Vincent Medical Infirmary. She is a member of the American Psychological Association, and the National Register of Health Service Providers in Psychology and is past chairperson of Arkansas Commitment Parents Advisory Board.

Dr. Griffen is married to Reverend Wendell Griffen, a former judge on the Arkansas Court of Appeals. They are the parents of two sons, Martyn, a graduate of the University of Pennsylvania, and Elliott, an undergraduate at Henderson State University.

E. Lynn Harris

E. Lynn Harris, born in Flint, Michigan, grew up with three sisters in Little Rock. He attended the University of Arkansas, Fayetteville, where he was the school's first black yearbook editor, the first black male Razorback cheerleader, and the president of his fraternity. He was an honor graduate with a degree in journalism.

Harris sold computers for IBM, Hewlett-Packard, and AT&T for thirteen years. He quit his sales job to write his first novel, *Invisible Life*. Failing to find a publisher, he published it himself in 1991 and sold it at black-owned bookstores, beauty salons, and book clubs before he was discovered by Anchor Books. Anchor published *Invisible Life* as a trade paperback in 1994.

Invisible Life was followed by *Just As I Am* (1994), *And This Too Shall Pass* (1996), *If This World Were Mine* (1997), *Abide with Me* (1999), *Not A Day Goes By* (2000), *Any Way the Wind Blows* (2001), *A Love of My Own* (2002), *I Say A Little Prayer* (2006), *Just Too Good To Be True* (2008), *Basketball Jones* (2009), and *Mother Dearest* (released posthumously). Harris's novels have hit the *New York Times* bestseller list, and they have also appeared on the bestseller lists of the *Wall Street Journal, Publishers Weekly, USA Today, Entertainment Weekly, Washington Post,* and the *Los Angeles Times.* In 2003, Harris published his first work of nonfiction, a memoir entitled *What Becomes of the Brokenhearted,* which was also a *New York Times* bestseller.

Harris won numerous accolades and prizes for his work. *Just As I Am* was awarded the Novel of the Year Prize by the Blackboard African American Bestsellers, Inc. *If This World Were Mine* was nominated for an NAACP Image Award and won the James Baldwin Award for Literary Excellence. *Abide with Me* was also nominated for an NAACP Image Award. His anthology *Freedom in This Village* won the Lambda Literary Award in 2005. In 1999, the University of Arkansas honored Harris with a Citation of Distinguished Alumni for outstanding professional achievement, and in October 2000 he was inducted into the Arkansas Black Hall of Fame. He has also been named to *Ebony*'s "Most Intriguing Blacks" list, *Out* magazine's "Out 100" list, *New York* magazine's "Gay Power 101" list, and *Savoy*'s "100 Leaders and Heroes in Black America" list. Other honors have included the Sprague Todes Literary Award, the Harvey Milk Honorary Diploma, and the Silas Hunt Award for Outstanding Achievement from the University of Arkansas, Fayetteville. E. Lynn Harris died on July 23, 2009.

Karen Harris Tate

Karen Harris Tate is originally from North Little Rock and is a graduate of Little Rock Central High School. She received her BS in engineering in 1985 from the University of Arkansas, Fayetteville. Tate has worked in engineering for Arkansas Power and Light Company and for Baptist Medical Systems in Little Rock, Arkansas. A career change in 1990 led to positions in television and radio news in Little Rock and in Washington, D.C., at the television show, *America's Most Wanted.* In 1993, Tate worked briefly as a communication director for a member of the House of Representatives on Capitol Hill before becoming a full-time mother. For two years, Tate held the position of Weekend Edition news host for WDUQ in Pittsburgh, a National Public Radio affiliate.

She has written and reported freelance for small publications and radio news.

Karen currently resides in northern Virginia with Cornelius, her husband of seventeen years, and their three daughters, Gabrielle, Breana, and Jillian.

Kenneth "Muskie" Harris

Kenneth "Muskie" Harris is a fourth-generation Little Rockian, and he graduated from Little Rock Central High School. His achievements include being a four-year letterman in football at the University of Arkansas, Fayetteville. Harris was the first black man to attend the University of Arkansas on an athletic scholarship from Little Rock Central. He was also one of the first black board members on the Arkansas Sports Hall of Fame board of directors. He was the first black to become the Republican nominee for lieutenant governor in 1990, running with Sheffield Nelson against the Democratic challengers Bill Clinton and Jim Guy Tucker. Harris was the first black Arkansan to win a statewide campaign. Harris was also the first black on the University of Arkansas Alumni Association board of directors, serving 2 four-year terms. He has served on numerous boards, has organized charity functions, and is active in city affairs. He attends the Lewis Street Church of Christ.

For the past thirteen years, Mr. Harris has worked closely with the judicial/legal community, serving as director of Community Relations for Sober Living and now continues this work with his own facility, Sobriety Center, in Pine Bluff.

Tracy Holmes Sr. and Rhonda Bell Holmes

Tracy Holmes Sr. and his wife of twenty-nine years, Rhonda, are 1979 graduates of the University of Arkansas, Fayetteville. Tracy Holmes's thirty-year career has focused in sales and sales management. He is currently the director of sales for Kerusso—a leading manufacturer of Christian-themed apparel in Berryville. He also volunteers with the couple's church, Valley Harvest Ministries in Bentonville, as an usher and prayer counselor.

Rhonda Bell Holmes has worked many years in the information systems field for the state of Arkansas and various companies and has also volunteered in various capacities—most recently with the Peace at Home Shelter in Fayetteville—which serves victims of domestic violence. In 2005, she volunteered with the U of A Black Alumni Reunion Planning Committee, and she currently volunteers with the couple's church as a Bible study leader, greeter, and prayer counselor.

Of late, Tracy and Rhonda have become business owners. Their business, Holmes and Holmes, has as its first product their recently released book: *The WORD Diet—30 Days of Faith—Creating Your Extraordinary Life with the Spoken Word,* by Rhonda Bell Holmes, with a foreword by Kathy Ireland. The book has received favorable reviews from authors Janis Kearney and E. Lynn Harris (www.theworddietbook.com; www.theworddiet.blogspot.com).

They have two children. Khiela graduated in 2007 from the University of Alabama, Tuscaloosa, with a PhD in clinical psychology, is completing a postdoctoral fellowship at the University of Michigan-Ann Arbor, and is scheduled to join the faculty of the University of Arkansas for Medical Sciences Psychiatry Department. Tracy Holmes II is in his fourth year of graduate school at Stanford University where he pursuing an MS in medicine and a PhD in chemical engineering. He is a co-owner and the chief accounts executive of dN Group, LLC (www.dangerousnegro.com—Black Empowerment Apparel). He is newly wed to Audrey Austrie-Holmes, a graduate of Vanderbilt University, a songwriter, performer, and minister to children and adults.

Lynda Jackson Browne

Lynda Jackson Browne, the eldest daughter of Dr. John H. and Dr. Verna W. Jackson, was born in Macon, Georgia, and grew up in Denver, Colorado. She graduated from the University of Arkansas, Fayetteville, with a BS in education in 1973 and began working for Arkansas Power and Light Company, where she was the first African American female to hold a position in the sales and marketing department.

Enrolled in a higher education administration class at the University of Arkansas, she was offered a fellowship and full scholarship to pursue the master's degree. A year later, in 1976, she graduated with highest honors with a master's degree in vocational education.

After accepting a newly created position at the University of Arkansas in the admissions department, in 1978, she became the youngest African American female to hold the position of assistant dean of students. She worked as a human resources administrator and director of the Cooperative Education program for Florida Power and Light Company and worked there for seven years. She then joined her husband at his mental health clinic as director of administrative services.

With her husband of twenty-seven years, Reginald Browne, she has established New Wineskin Family Ministries. Their ten-year weekly radio program, "Back to Eden," has allowed them to reach hurting people and, from a biblical perspective, provide godly council. The school the couple owns works with the underserved and at-risk populations in the community. The Brownes' son, Zachary Jackson Browne, is a freshman pre-pharmacy student.

Hannibal B. Johnson

Hannibal B. Johnson is a graduate of Harvard Law School. He did his undergraduate work at the University of Arkansas, where he completed a double major in economics and sociology. Johnson is an attorney, author, and independent consultant (www.hannibalbjohnson.com).

Johnson has also served as an adjunct professor at the University of Tulsa College of Law (legal writing; legal ethics), Oklahoma State University (leadership and group dynamics; business law), and the University of Oklahoma (ethics; cultural diversity in the world; race and reason).

Johnson is past president of Leadership Tulsa; the Metropolitan Tulsa Urban League; and the Northeast Oklahoma Black Lawyers Association. He is the director of Anytown, Oklahoma, a statewide human relations camp for teens sponsored by the Oklahoma Conference for Community and Justice. Johnson served as chairman of the board of directors of the Community Leadership Association, an international leadership organization (2001–2002). He is a founding director of the Oklahoma Appleseed Center for Law and Justice and serves on the board of directors of the Oklahoma Department of Libraries and Planned Parenthood of Arkansas and Eastern Oklahoma. Johnson also serves on the advisory board of the Mayborn Literary Nonfiction Writers Conference of the Southwest. He serves on the Institutional Review Board for Oklahoma State University Center for Health Sciences. In 2004, Mr. Johnson graduated with the inaugural class of the national "Connecting Community Fellowship Program" based in Richmond, Virginia.

Johnson's books include *Black Wall Street: From Riot to Renaissance in Tulsa's Historic Greenwood District*; *Up From the Ashes: A Story About Community*; *Acres of Aspiration: The All-Black Towns in Oklahoma*; *Mama Used To Say: Wit & Wisdom From The Heart & Soul*; *No Place Like Home: A Story About an All-Black, All-American Town*; and *IncogNegro: Poetic Reflections on Race & Diversity in America*.

Janis F. Kearney

Arkansas native Janis F. Kearney is a writer, lecturer, and oral historian. She is one of nineteen children born to Arkansas delta sharecroppers, Thomas James and Ethel Curry Kearney. Kearney served as personal diarist to President William Jefferson Clinton for five years. Before that, she published the award-winning *Arkansas State Press* newspaper, founded by Arkansas civil rights legends Daisy and L. C. Bates. Since leaving the White House, she has served as a W. E. B. Du Bois Fellow at Harvard University, Chancellor's Lecturer at Chicago City Colleges, Humanities Fellow and part-time faculty at DePaul University, and Humanities scholar and visiting professor at Arkansas State University, Jonesboro.

In 2004, the author completed her first book, *Cotton Field of Dreams: A Memoir*, which chronicles her childhood experiences in the southeast Arkansas delta, and the beginning of her journey from that existence. She founded Writing our World Press, a small book publishing company, in Chicago that year. In 2006, Kearney completed and published *Conversations: William Jefferson Clinton*, an oral biography, which features conversations with a diverse array of black Americans who share their insights into William J. Clinton's legacy—in particular, his lifelong relationship with the African American community, his presidency, and his historical positions on America's racial conflicts. *Quiet Guys Can Do Great Things, Too: A Black Accountant's Success Story*, the life story of Frank Ross, one of America's first black corporate accountants at a Big Four accounting firm, was coauthored by Kearney, and published by Writing our World Press in 1996.

Kearney relocated Writing our World Press, janis@writingourworldpress.com, to her home state in 2008. The Arkansas native continues to share her story nationally and internationally. Her first novel and the second installment of her personal memoir were released in November 2008.

Terry G. Lee

Terry Lee was born in Holly Grove and graduated *cum laude* from Holly Grove High School. He graduated from the University of Arkansas, Fayetteville, with a BA in political science. He has a graduate of claims administration degree from the Insurance Institute of America. He received his JD from John Marshall Law School in Atlanta, Georgia.

Terry Lee began his career as a claims representative with Farmers Insurance Group, the third-largest U.S. insurance company. During his twelve years of employment in the insurance industry, he held the positions of staff specialist, branch claims supervisor, branch claims manager, and regional claims manager for Kansas, Iowa, and Missouri. He received numerous awards for outstanding claims service and customer relations. Under his leadership, the Mission Regional Office rose from being ranked last place to first in the nation.

In 1994, Lee started his own business in Georgia, T. Lee Associates, specializing in tax and financial services for individuals and small businesses. Lee's business operates from two locations in Marietta, Georgia, serving clients in seventeen states. He plans to open two more offices in the metro Atlanta area. He also serves as the chief financial officer of the Marietta Redevelopment Corporation, which oversees redevelopment projects estimated at more than five hundred million dollars.

Lee has been happily married for twenty-six years to Cozetta Woolfolk Lee, a graduate of the School of Engineering, University of Arkansas, Fayetteville. They have one daughter, Candice Lee, a junior at Georgia Southern University.

Charles Magee

Charles Magee is a native of Prentiss, Mississippi. He received his early education in the Jefferson Davis County public school system and graduated from J. E. Johnson High School. Dr. Magee went on to receive a BS in general agriculture (animal science) in 1970 from Alcorn State University, an MS in agricultural engineering in 1973 from the University of Minnesota, and a PhD in agricultural and biological engineering in 1980 from Cornell University.

Dr. Magee's professional career began in 1973 as a research associate/instructor in the Department of Plant Science and Technology at North Carolina A&T State University in Greensboro. After receiving his PhD, he accepted a position as assistant professor of agricultural engineering at the University of Arkansas. Dr. Magee was the first African American professor to be employed in this department, and is believed to be the first in the College of Agriculture at the University of Arkansas.

In May 1984, Dr. Magee was lured to Fort Valley State University (FVSU), an 1890 land-grant university in Fort Valley, Georgia. During his eleven and a half years at FVSU, Dr. Magee received the first United States patent in the history of the university. In October 1995, Dr. Magee moved to Florida A&M University (FAMU) as professor and director of agricultural and biological engineering. Under Dr. Magee's leadership, the Board of Regents for the State University System of Florida granted FAMU a BS program in biological and agricultural systems engineering (BASE). Only two historically black universities have engineering programs of this kind.

Dr. Magee is a charter member of the national society for Minorities in Agriculture, National Resources and Related Sciences (MANRRS) (www.manrrs.org) and drafted its original constitution. MANRRS presently has chapters on the campus of more than one hundred colleges and universities across the nation. Some of Dr. Magee's other scholarly accomplishments include five United States patents and numerous publications.

Angela Mosley Monts

Angela Mosley Monts resides in Springdale. She is the wife of Howard P. Monts and the proud mother of Melisa Diamond, Megan Dionne-Denise, and Melanie D'Angela Monts. She is the grandmother of Areli Carter.

She is currently employed by the University of Arkansas with the Arkansas Alumni Association as an associate director and as the Black Alumni Society coordinator. She oversees alumni relations in the state of Arkansas and the Black Alumni Society.

Monts has had an extensive career in the consumer packaged goods industry. She worked in the industry for fourteen years. She received several awards for her excellent marketing, sales, and management leadership skills. She combines her skills from corporate America and academia to create out-of-the-box programs for her constituent groups, utilizing sales and marketing techniques.

Monts serves as a staff advisor for the University of Arkansas Gateway to Hope College Ministry, Black Graduate Students Association, Kappa Iota Chapter of Alpha Kappa Alpha Sorority, Inc., and the National Pan-Hellenic Council. She assists with the Black Students Association and the King Team of Northwest Arkansas. She also is a member of the UA Greek Hall of Fame.

She has a BA from the University of Arkansas and an MBA from Webster University in St. Louis, Missouri. She will receive an MA degree in ministry in May 2009 from John Brown University. She also is a licensed minister. She is a member of St. James Missionary Baptist Church and sits on the ministerial staff.

Lloyd A. Myers

Lloyd A. Myers received his bachelor of architecture degree in 1981 from the University of Arkansas, Fayetteville, and has done postgraduate summer studies at Harvard School of Design in urban housing and mixed-use projects and master planning in 2000.

Myers's expertise in project management and his commitment to team excellence is illustrated by the following awards for the Promenade, a project involving the management of a nine-member design firm team, a complex public-private partnership, and more than $16 million of construction. He is the winner of the Georgia Landscape Architecture Design Award, Georgia American Institute of Landscape Architecture; the City of Atlanta Urban Design Commission Award of Excellence for Urban Design, the Atlanta Urban Design Commission; the Award of Excellence for Urban Design and Community Participation Georgia, the American Institute of Architects and the Department of Transportation.

Prior to founding L. A. Myers Architecture, Lloyd founded LAM Design in 1990, and served as design manager for Atlanta's town center, Underground Atlanta. He also provided retail design expertise on urban marketplaces developed by the Rouse Company, including the New Orleans Riverwalk and Jacksonville Landing in Florida. In 1991, Lloyd provided concept planning and programming expertise to Disney Development Company for Disney's Boardwalk and urban design and project management for the 1996 Olympic Games. Other projects include the John Hope Homes Master Plan, retail planning and design for the 1996 Centennial Olympic Village. In 1992, LAM Design worked as a member of the Kohn Pederson Fox/Turner architectural team for the Federal Plaza office complex in Atlanta.

C. Calvin Smith

C. Calvin Smith received his BA in history and government from Arkansas AM&N College in 1966. His MSE in social science was received from Arkansas State University in 1970 and his PhD in history from the University of Arkansas in 1978.

Dr. Smith was the first African American faculty member hired by Arkansas State University. He was hired as an instructor of history at Arkansas State University in 1970 and worked his way through the ranks to presidential distinguished professor of Heritage Studies (PhD program), 2002–2004. He received the honorary doctor of humane letters from Arkansas State University in 2005.

He is the author of two books: *War and Wartime Changes: The Transformation of Arkansas, 1940–1945* in 1986 and *Educating the Masses: The Unfolding History of Black School Administrators in Arkansas, 1900–2000* in 2003. He has published more than thirty articles in professional journals. He also participated as a co-sponsor of two charter chapters of Omega Psi Phi Fraternity, the Alpha Zeta Chapter at Arkansas State University in 1973, and the Gamma Eta Chapter at the University of Arkansas in 1974. Dr. Smith died on December 24, 2009.

Charlie L. Tolliver

Charlie L. Tolliver received his PhD in electrical engineering from Iowa State University, an MS in electrical engineering from Purdue University, and a BS in electrical engineering from Southern University in Baton Rouge, Louisiana. He is currently a tenured professor in the Department of Electrical Engineering at Prairie View University. Prior to taking the position at Prairie View University, he was the first African American professor of engineering at the University of Arkansas (1976–1984).

In addition to his teaching responsibilities, he is also an entrepreneur with several U.S. patents registered in his name. He has received funding for grants and research from the Army Research Laboratory for such projects as development and demonstration of a highly efficient hybrid vehicle with better than zero emissions; k-band antennas, time-domain microwave imaging for robotics vision applications; and for the police probe for Homeland Security. The most notable grant for the University of Arkansas is the Transition Retention Minority Engineering Program in 1980 with the Winthrop Rockefeller Foundation to increase the number of minority engineering majors.

Dr. Tolliver has served in the following capacities: United States Air Force; associate engineer providing design modification for the Sidewinder (missile) on the F-4D Phantom Aircraft, design of electrical interfaces and control for the communication and radar system aboard the Gemini spacecraft with McDonnell Aircraft Corporation in St. Louis; interim department head and associate professor in electrical engineering at Tennessee A&I State University, Nashville; assistant professor of electrical engineering, University of Arkansas; associate director of the Minority Introduction to Engineering (MITE) program and director/originator of the Transition Retention Minority Engineering Program (TRMEP), University of Arkansas; vice president for student affairs and professor of electrical engineering, Prairie View A&M University.

Dr. Tolliver is the author of several professional papers and publications. Among his awards are two in research from the National Aeronautics and Space Administration (NASA) and the American Society for Engineering Education.

Trent A. Walton

Trent "T. A." Walton was valedictorian and class president of his graduating high school class of 1977 from Forrest City High School. He entered the University of Arkansas, Fayetteville, in the fall of 1977. He received his BS and MS degrees in chemical engineering from the University of Arkansas, Fayetteville.

As a graduate student, Walton was an R. C. Edwards Graduate Fellow, National Science Foundation Graduate Fellow, and DuPont Graduate Fellow. He performed postgraduate work at Clemson University after completing his MS. Walton was also third-place Heavyweight Division Intramural Boxer in 1979 and Intramural Campus Shot Put Champ that same year.

Prior to his work with Procter & Gamble (P&G), Walton served with W. R. Grace in their Cryovac division as a research and development engineer, meat bag development, and with E. I. DuPont photo products division as a process control engineer.

Walton recently retired from P & G as a group manager, human resources (HR) systems improvement leader. Prior experience with P & G includes Wal-Mart global customer team senior account executive, baby care—Pampers and Luvs Wipes; Wal-Mart global customer team HR manager and work process improvement leader; Tide Laundry site work system/OE manager; Charmin paper-making production system owner; ER/OD manager; Jif Peanut Butter plant HR, safety and quality assurance leader; Puritan and oils deodorizer/cost inbound quality manager; and Duncan Hines frosting/Angel Food packaging manager.

Walton has received numerous certifications and special training throughout his career. He is also the recipient of many awards and recognitions, including the Augusta, Georgia, Chronicle Father of the Year Award, Rotary International Eagle Volunteer Award, and the 2006 Northwest Arkansas MLK Committee Individual of the Year Award. He is active in church and community work.

Lonnie R. Williams

Lonnie Ray Williams is from Stephens, where he attended the Carver Schools from first through tenth grades. He presently serves as the associate vice chancellor for student affairs at Arkansas State University, Jonesboro. Prior to Arkansas State University, he served at the University of Arkansas, Fayetteville, in the following positions: assistant vice chancellor for student affairs and director of the UA multicultural center; assistant dean of students and coordinator of multicultural affairs; director and associate director of minority engineering programs; night manager of the student union; and police officer with the university police.

Dr. Williams has served on the board of trustees for Arkansas Baptist College (chairperson 2009–2010), the board of directors for the Jonesboro Church Health Clinic, and as the state representative for Arkansas North for the Ninth District of Omega Psi Phi Fraternity. He has served on the executive board of directors for the Association of Black Culture Centers, the Arkansas College Personnel Association, the Arkansas Counseling Association, and the Yvonne Richardson Center.

The following awards and recognitions were received in 2008 and represent a partial listing of Williams's numerous awards and recognitions: Outstanding Person for April 2008 by STAND-News of Central Arkansas; President's Award for Dedicated Service, presented by the Strong-Turner Alumni Chapter of Arkansas State University's Alumni Association; and the Thomas E. "Pat" Patterson Education Award, presented by the Arkansas Democratic Black Caucus.

Dr. Williams is a co-owner of *African American Perspectives* magazine of northeast Arkansas. He resides in Jonesboro with his wife, Mary, an alumna of Arkansas State University and the University of Arkansas. They have a blended family of seven children—Tina, Tyrone, Stacy, Rayshawn, Landra, Kevin, and Keaton and several grandchildren.

Chapter 5

LaTonia Clark George

LaTonia Clark George is currently employed at Wal-Mart Stores, Inc., Sam's Club division, as a market human resource manager. She is responsible for the execution of human resource initiatives in employment practices, performance management, staffing, development, and associate relations. Prior to this position, George served as senior management recruiter, director of policy and employment verification compliance, corporate human resource manager, and legislative/recruiting manager for the company.

George joined Wal-Mart in 2000. Before joining Wal-Mart, she served as a budget analyst for the Department of Finance and Administration, State of Arkansas; senior claims analyst at the Woodson Walker Law Firm; and as an auto claims representative for State Farm Insurance Company.

She obtained a bachelor's degree in public administration from the University of Arkansas, Fayetteville. In addition, she earned a master's degree in public administration from the University of Arkansas, Little Rock. George is a diamond life member of Delta Sigma Theta Sorority, Inc., and a current member of the Northwest Arkansas Area Alumnae Chapter. She is a board member of the University of Arkansas Vice Chancellor's Alumni Advisory Council, Division of Student Affairs. She is also a member of the Society for Human Resource Management (SHRM).

George enjoys networking, shopping, reading, and sports. Her lifetime goal is to be a life/career coach. She is a native of Pine Bluff, where she graduated from Watson Chapel High School. She currently resides in Bentonville with her sports enthusiast son, Anthony George.

Dexter L. Howard

Dexter L. Howard is the founder and senior pastor of Life Harvester Church in Fayetteville. His trailblazing leadership and successful efforts at reaching and serving those in need have gained him recognition as one of northwest Arkansas's top-forty leaders under the age of forty. He has been the recipient of several community service awards. In addition to leading a rapidly growing church, Howard also serves on several boards, including the University of Arkansas Alumni Association and the United Way, and as a chaplain for the Arkansas Razorback football team.

Howard is a native of Little Rock, where he was the only child of a single mother, Maxine Webb. After graduating from Central High School, he attended the University of Arkansas and earned a full athletic scholarship as a letterman with the Arkansas Razorback football team. He graduated with a bachelor's degree in communications. After the death of his father and several major failures, Howard fully surrendered his life to Christ in 1991 at Power Team Outreach. He began preaching the Gospel shortly thereafter. He met and married his wife, the former Genette Seawood, in 1994. They are the parents of six daughters: Alexa, Bethany, Celeste, identical twins Destiny and Eden, and Faith.

Howard founded Life Harvester Church in 1998. Having overcome striking challenges through the Word, Howard's fuel is his compassion for the lost and the broken. He received his doctoral degree in pastoral ministry from Minnesota Graduate School of Theology. He is a motivator, encourager, and anointed teacher. His visionary and trailblazing leadership have earned him the loyalty and admiration of his thriving congregation, as well as the respect of his peers.

Reena M. Jackson Holmes

Reena M. Holmes, CPA, is the daughter of Mr. and Mrs. Marion Jackson Sr. of Gilmore. She presently resides in Turrell with her husband, Floyd Holmes, and their daughters, Kristen and Payton.

Holmes is a graduate of the Turrell Public School System. She received her BS in business administration from the University of Arkansas, Fayetteville, and holds an MBA from Arkansas State University, Jonesboro. She is a licensed certified public accountant in the state of Arkansas.

Holmes and her husband, Floyd, are the owners and operators of Four H Farms Partnership, and she is also currently employed by the state of Arkansas as an auditor. Previously, she worked for Coastal Unilube, Inc., and for Mid-South Community College in West Memphis.

She is a professional member of the American Institute of Certified Public Accountants, the Arkansas State Board of Public Accountancy, and a member of Alpha Kappa Alpha Sorority, Inc.

Holmes is an active member of the Union Grove Missionary Baptist Church in Gilmore, where she serves as a door greeter. She enjoys traveling, planning family gatherings, relaxing with her family, and bargain shopping.

Merike Manley

Merike Manley has a degree in political science from Philander Smith College. She also has attended USC, University of Arkansas, and UALR. Presently, she is two classes away from having a master's in public administration and is in the process of writing a book.

Manley is CEO of MRSM Productions. The acronym consists of the initials of her name along with those of her sisters, Ritchie Manley Bowden and Sydnee Manley. Her work has entailed a little bit of everything from being a legal secretary to a flight attendant. Currently, she is a business development representative for a company in the service industry in Kansas, Missouri.

She is the mother of one daughter, Michelle Manley, who is a student at Bennett College for Women.

Karen Mathis Mongo

Karen Mathis Mongo, a native of Forrest City, came to the University of Arkansas, Fayetteville, in fall 1984. She declared a major in communication and ultimately earned her BA and MA in 1988 and 1990.

She moved to the Dallas–Fort Worth metropolitan area and began work with Dallas County Community College District as an adjunct instructor in speech communication and an instructional associate in writing. At Texas Woman's University, she directed the speech communication program and was an affiliate faculty member in women's studies. For twenty years, she has taught various courses, including introduction to speech communication, public speaking, business and professional communication, organizational communication, political communication and women of color, voice and articulation, developmental writing, and British literature.

Presently, she is the coordinator of the speech communication program at El Centro College and serves as co-chair of the college's learning outcomes and assessment committee. Mongo is married with four young children.

Roderick J. McDavis

Roderick J. McDavis became Ohio University's twentieth president on July 1, 2004. A native of Dayton, Ohio, he received a bachelor's degree in social sciences in secondary education from Ohio University in 1970, making him only the second university alumnus to lead the university as president. He received a master's degree in student personnel administration from the University of Dayton in 1971, and a doctorate in counselor education and higher education administration from the University of Toledo in 1974.

Dr. McDavis served as provost and vice president for academic affairs and professor of education at Virginia Commonwealth University in Richmond, Virginia, from 1999 to 2004. He was dean of the College of Education and professor of education at the University of Florida from 1994 to 1999. He was dean of the College of Education and professor of counselor education at the University of Arkansas, Fayetteville, from 1989 to 1994, and the first black dean of any college at the university. He was a professor of education in the Department of Counselor Education at the University of Florida from 1974 to 1989 and an associate dean of the graduate school and minority programs at the University of Florida from 1984 to 1989.

Dr. McDavis has served as a consultant and keynote speaker for universities, community colleges, public school systems, human service agencies, professional associations, community organizations, and churches. In 1995, Dr. McDavis was named Person of the Year in Education by the *Gainesville Sun*. He was named the 1996 Outstanding Alumnus of the College of Education at Ohio University. He also received the Post-Secondary Outstanding Educator Award from the North Central Florida Chapter of Phi Delta Kappa in 1996. Dr. McDavis received the 1997 Black Achiever's Award in Education from the Florida Conference of Black State Legislators.

This biography was taken from Ohio University's Office of the President's Web site: http://www.ohio.edu/president/mcdavis.cfm.

Katina Revels

Katina Revels, a Dallas native, received her bachelor's degree in print journalism/magazine from the University of Arkansas in 1994. She began her career in visual journalism on the photo desk of the *Fort Worth Star-Telegram* after a short stint as an intern. As a night assistant photo researcher, she was involved in the coverage of local, state, and national news.

A longtime visual journalism advocate, Revels joined the Associated Press as a photo editor in Washington, D.C., working with the state photo center. She later took a position with the *Detroit Free Press* where she helped advance the paper's print, online and multimedia coverage, gaining notice for, among other things, the Detroit Pistons' 2004 NBA championship. Revels also edited Iraq photographs and helped plan team photo and reporting coverage for the funeral of civil rights icon Rosa Parks, both in Alabama and in the days leading to the final service in Detroit.

In 2005, the Michigan Professional Photographers Association awarded her third place for Picture Editor of the Year. In 2006, she and her co-workers received accolades when the *Free Press* photo editing team won third place in the Best of Photojournalism annual contest for coverage of Rosa Parks (*Newspaper News Project—Not a Natural Disaster*) and honorable mention for Multi-Page Newspaper Documentary-Photojournalism Project.

Returning to the Associated Press in 2007, Revels was promoted to her current position as the Top Stories Desk picture editor in New York. The award-winning picture editor has aided many young journalists through her work within the National Association of Black Journalists (NABJ). She shares her commitment to visual journalism excellence and journalism excellence in her current role as the NABJ Visual task force chairperson.

Cedric E. Williams

Cedric Williams is a 1993 graduate of the University of Arkansas, Fayetteville. He received a BSBA degree in computer information systems-qualitative.

He is employed by State Farm Insurance. He started his career in 1995 as an auto representative in Pine Bluff. He later joined the Fire National Catastrophe team for three years. After completing his time with Fire National Catastrophe, Cedric returned to Pine Bluff as a fire field representative. He currently serves as a Fire Complex representative in Little Rock.

Williams has furthered his career by completing the following continuing education classes: AIS, AIC, AIM, ALMI, and CPCU designations. He also has achieved CTM and ATM-B designations in Toastmasters International.

He is actively involved in community service activities. He is a member of the Black Alumni Society of the University of Arkansas, Fayetteville, and was chairperson of the 2009 Black Alumni Reunion Committee. He holds several positions with his local church (New St. Hurricane Missionary Baptist Church), including those of deacon, Sunday School teacher, Bible study teacher, and vice president of the men's laymen group. Williams also is a member of Alpha Phi Alpha Fraternity, Inc., and St. John Masonic Lodge #456.

Chapter 6

Celia Anderson

Celia Anderson is an author. Her stories and articles both educate and inspire.

Anderson holds a master's degree from the University of Arkansas. She plans to continue her education to earn a PhD in critical and cultural media.

The former basketball player for the Lady Razorbacks also played professionally in Greece before working for the *New York Times* bestselling author, E. Lynn Harris. In the acknowledgments of his novel, *I Say a Little Prayer*, Harris referred to Anderson as a "brilliant young writer whom the world will soon discover." She has had a manuscript accepted by Random House—a compilation of short stories with Harris, slated for future publication.

Anderson also teaches freshman communication at Northwest Arkansas Community College.

Anderson's first novel, *Love Ocean*, was released January 2009. Currently, she speaks across the nation to youth, writes, and prides herself on being the best mother in the world to her only daughter, Gabrielle Simone.

Eddie Armstrong

Eddie Armstrong is founder and CEO of Armstrong and Davis Consulting in Little Rock. He is also founder of the Eddie Armstrong Scholarship Foundation, which focuses on providing minority students from single-parent households with scholarships to attend the University of Arkansas.

He is an experienced public speaker, having served as the national spokesperson for Boys and Girls Clubs of America and National Youth of the Year, including several major national events with audiences of more than five thousand. He has shared the stage with General Colin Powell, Denzel Washington, Dr. Alvin Toussaint, Shaquille O'Neal, Dan Marino, and Kurt Douglas, to name a few. He was included in Denzel Washington's *A Hand to Guide Me* in 2006 and, in 2007, was noted as one of *Ebony* magazine's top thirty on the rise in America.

Born in Little Rock, he attended the University of Arkansas, and became the second African American to be elected student body president. In 2001, he received his BA in political science. He has since worked in government relations for the nonprofit Boys and Girls Clubs of America national office, and in the corporate world, for Tyson Foods. He has served on the boards of Washington Regional Hospital Foundation, Just Communities (formally NCCJ), and is currently serving as a member of the Arkansas Governor's Mansion Association and the North Little Rock City Planning Commission.

Since leaving Tyson Foods in 2006, Armstrong has dedicated his time to developing the nonprofit Eddie Armstrong Scholarship Foundation, committed to providing educational opportunities to students and funding a scholarship for targeted students to attend the University of Arkansas. He has joined with Kim Davis of New Orleans to further develop Armstrong and Davis Consulting, Inc., a corporate, government, and community affairs firm.

Johnetta Cross Brazzell

Johnetta Cross Brazzell joined the University of Arkansas in January 1999 as the vice chancellor for student affairs. She received her PhD in higher and adult continuing education from the University of Michigan in 1991, her MA in American history (with an emphasis on the African American experience) from the University of Chicago in 1972, and her BA in history and political science from Spelman College in 1969. Dr. Brazzell has served in numerous roles for a number of professional organizations and on educational and community boards, including the National Association of Student Personnel Administrators; Association of American Colleges and Universities; National Association of State Universities and Land-Grant Colleges; the Higher Learning Commission NCA board of trustees; Project on the Future of Higher Education; the History of Education Society; the Walton Arts Center board of directors; LeaderShape board of directors; and the Northwest Arkansas Diversity Council.

Dr. Brazzell joined Spelman College in Atlanta, Georgia, in 1993, where she held the position of vice president for student affairs and also served as a member of the college faculty. Dr. Brazzell's experience also includes three years (1990–1993) with the University of Arizona in Tucson as associate dean of students and subsequently as the interim dean of students. From 1988 to 1990, she served as the assistant to the associate vice president of academic affairs/vice president for student affairs at the University of Michigan. From 1973 to 1987, she served as the director, Placement and Career Services; director, Urban Affairs Center; associate director, Urban Affairs Center; director of Community Programs, and adjunct faculty at Oakland University. Dr. Brazzell retired from the University of Arkansas as vice chancellor of student affairs on January 31, 2009.

Kevin Dedner

Kevin Dedner serves as the Section Chief for the HIV/STD Hep C Section for the Arkansas Department of Health, where he is responsible for overseeing Arkansas's efforts to prevent HIV and sexually transmitted diseases. Prior to joining the Arkansas Department of Health, Dedner served as the director-state government relations and public policy for the Mid-South division of the American Cancer Society. He was responsible for managing the public policy agenda for the six-state division. Some of his successes include helping to pass laws in Arkansas and Louisiana that prohibit smoking in public places and one of the most comprehensive colorectal cancer control laws in the country.

Dedner has also enjoyed a stint in the political arena, including being appointed director of the African American outreach effort for Al Gore's presidential run. He also was the director of outreach for the Arkansas Democratic Party.

Dedner serves the community as a member of the Arkansas Society of Association Executives and the Bio-Ethics Committee of Arkansas Children's Hospital. He has also served on the Arkansas Tobacco Control Board.

Dedner is a graduate of the University of Arkansas with a degree in political science and also holds a master of public health degree from Benedictine University. Dedner has received many awards and accolades, including *Powerplay* Magazine's Next Top Powerplayers Under 30 (2006); *Arkansas Business's* Forty under Forty (2007); and the University of Arkansas Medical Sciences/Arkansas Cancer Community Network 2007 Health Policy Award.

Dedner is a member of St. John Missionary Baptist Church. He is the charmed husband of the former Olivia Walton. The Dedners are blessed with a son, Davis Gibson Dedner, and a daughter, Ella Marie Dedner.

William Jeffrey "Giovanni" Flanigan

Jeff "Giovanni" Flanigan wears many hats. The Magnolia native and 1999 BSE graduate of the University of Arkansas is the proud father of twin boys, Jaden Ellis Franklin Flanigan and Jordan Ellis Franklin Flanigan. He is currently the pastor of the Harmony CME Church in Saratoga, Arkansas. He is currently the head boys' basketball coach and head boys' track coach at Ashdown High School in Ashdown. He teaches science to grades 5–12 at the Ashdown School District's Alternative School.

After graduating with a master of arts in teaching degree from the University of Arkansas in 2000, Flanigan became the first assistant women's basketball coach at Southern Arkansas University. In 2002, he moved to Division I, where he became the head assistant women's basketball coach and recruiting coordinator at the University of Arkansas, Little Rock, for legendary Hall of Fame Coach Joe Foley.

Flanigan left collegiate athletics in July 2004 to become the head football coach and head girls' basketball coach at Henderson Health Science Magnet Middle School. From 2005 to 2007, he was the assistant baseball coach at Parkview High School. In 2007–2008, Flanigan was named the Teacher of the Year by his colleagues at Henderson Health Science Magnet Middle School.

Flanigan is also a National Recording Artist for House Records in Houston, Texas (www.house-productions.net & www.myspace.com/giovanniontherise), where he records under the stage name "Giovanni." In October 2008, Giovanni was nominated for three Grammy awards. The House Records compilation album *Live in the Spirit of Joy* was nominated for Best Traditional Gospel Album. Giovanni is the lead contributor on this album with five songs. His song *I Know,* which is featured on the audio book for the publication *The Other Side of the Coin* by Robert Howard, was nominated for Record of the Year and the African American anthem, *We Need,* was nominated for Best Rap Song.

Crystal D. Hendricks Green

Crystal Green is an Arkansas native from North Little Rock. She graduated from North Little Rock High School in 1996. Upon graduation, she attended the University of Arkansas.

While at the university, she had the honor of being selected as the first recipient of the Coca-Cola Foundation Scholarship. Among other things, she was also honored as a Razorback Classic.

Green graduated from the University of Arkansas in 2001 with a BS in chemical engineering. After graduation, she went to work for Phillips Petroleum Company in Bartlesville, Oklahoma. Phillips Petroleum Company merged with Conoco, and after spending a little more than a year in Bartlesville, she was transferred to Ponca City, Oklahoma. Green spent five years with ConocoPhillips Company in a range of assignments.

In July 2005, she made her home in Tulsa, Oklahoma. Green left ConocoPhillips and began her career with Syntroleum Corporation in July 2006.

Green continued her education at Oklahoma State University where she received her MBA in 2008. Green is a member of Delta Sigma Theta Sorority, Inc. She has been a member of Kiwanis Club International, National Society of Black Engineers, and Leadership Ponca City. Green is married to Brandon Green and they have a daughter, Trinity.

Tanisha L. Joe-Conway

Tanisha Joe-Conway is from Stephens, Arkansas. Upon completion of her degree from the University of Arkansas, she began her professional career with the Arkansas Educational Television Network (AETN) and has spent more than ten years working with public affairs television. She has developed, produced, and coordinated public affairs programming for AETN. Her job includes live call-in programming, on-air promotion, taped specials, documentaries, and crew supervision.

Joe-Conway's work encompasses a variety of topics. She is instrumental in putting together shows like *Arkansas Week; Arkansans Ask: Governor Mike Beebe; Fighting Fat; El Latino; Election 2006: The Debates; Bringing U.S. Foreign Policy Home; Unconventional Wisdom,* and other programs of political and social significance.

Joe-Conway's work has won numerous other awards including a Videographer's Award of Distinction and the Arkansas Press Association Award for Community Service. Her work has also been screened at the Hot Springs Documentary Film Festival. She was recently named one of Arkansas's Forty under Forty professionals by Arkansas Business Publishing Group.

In addition, Joe-Conway is the associate producer on AETN's regional EMMY-winning documentary *Precious Memories: Our Vanishing Rural Churches.* She co-produced the regional EMMY-nominated documentary *Mothers in Prison: Children in Crisis.* The documentary won several awards, including the Worldfest Houston Gold Special Jury Award and the PASS Award from the National Council on Crime and Delinquency. Projects in production include *Growing Roots: Arkansas Immigrants in the Land of Opportunity; Healing Minds, Changing Attitudes;* and a project on the Arkansas Delta. Tanisha Joe-Conway is married to Charley Conway, and they have two children.

Monica M. Jones

Monica Jones is an academic counselor in the athletic department at the University of Arkansas. She returned to Arkansas in December 2008 after six years at the University of Louisville.

While at the University of Louisville, Jones worked as the assistant director of the Center for Advising and Student Services in the College of Arts and Sciences. She advised students, coordinated staff training, and coordinated the college's orientation course. In addition, Jones served as the assistant director for campus life. Under that title, she administered the nonacademic disciplinary process, assisted with diversity programs, and served as an advisor to both the National Pan-Hellenic Council, as well as the Student Government Association's supreme court.

While at Arkansas, Jones was the director of multicultural student services and an academic advisor in the College of Education and Health Professions. She earned a BA in psychology in 1995 from the University of Arkansas and an MS in counseling in 1999. She is pursuing her PhD in educational leadership and organizational development at the University of Louisville, with an anticipated graduation date of December 2010.

Trenia Miles

Trenia Miles holds a BA in psychology and an MS in counseling from the University of Arkansas. Her doctoral degree in higher and adult education is from the University of Memphis.

Dr. Miles has over fifteen years of experience in higher education. She has worked with diverse populations, including students with disabilities, at-risk students, adolescents, abused children, and adults. Her areas of expertise include teaching and training adults, student retention, counseling and career development, and student learning and engagement. She is currently employed as the director of retention services, academic program coordinator, and faculty member at Mid-South Community College. She serves as the chair of the retention committee, where she oversees academic advising, a mentoring program, Welcome Week, and an early alert retention program. In addition, she provides training in conflict resolution, customer service, mentoring, retaining students, and topics related to student learning and engagement.

Dr. Miles is a founding board member of the Power Center Academy Charter School in Memphis, Tennessee, a charter member of the Northwest Arkansas Area Alumnae Chapter, and a lifetime member of Delta Sigma Theta Sorority, Inc. Dr. Miles received the 2008–2009 National Institute for Staff and Organizational Development (NISOD) Excellence Award and the Mid-South Community College's Outstanding Faculty Award in 2009. In her spare time, she enjoys traveling, reading, exercising, swimming, and cooking.

Cynthia E. Nance

Cynthia Nance became dean of the University of Arkansas School of Law on July 1, 2006, making her the first woman and first African American to lead the Law School. Prior to becoming dean, as a University of Arkansas law professor, her teaching and research focused on labor and employment law, poverty law, and torts. She earned her JD with distinction and her MA in finance from the University of Iowa.

Prior to teaching law, Dean Nance worked as a labor educator at the University of Iowa Labor Center and was a faculty fellow in the law school there. Dean Nance has presented academic papers at Yale University, the University of Illinois, George Washington University Law School, and Franklin Pierce Law Center. She is licensed in Iowa and is a member of the American, National, Arkansas, and Washington County Bar Associations, and the Arkansas Association of Women Lawyers.

Dean Nance is also a member of the Arkansas Bar Association's Commission on Diversity and the Lawyers Helping Lawyers Committee, Phi Delta Phi, and the W. B. Putman American Inn of Court. She is co-chair of the American Bar Association's Section of Labor and Employment Law's Ethics and Professional Responsibility Committee. She is a former board member of the Law School Admissions Council and a former board member of the Lutheran Immigration and Refugee Service.

Dean Nance was a recipient of a 2007 American Association for Affirmative Action Arthur A. Fletcher Award and the 2006 NIA Professional Achievement Award. She was also honored as the 2005 Arkansas Bar Association Outstanding Lawyer-Citizen. In 2004, Dean Nance received the University of Arkansas Alumni Association's Faculty Distinguished Achievement Award for Public Service and was recognized in 2003 as a Northwest Arkansas Woman of Distinction. . She is past chair of the American Association of Law Schools (AALS) Employment Discrimination and Labor and Employment Law Sections.

At the University of Arkansas, Dean Nance has been a faculty advisor to the Kappa Iota Chapter of Alpha Kappa Alpha Sorority and an advisor to the Black Law Student Association. She is also a member of Good Shepherd Lutheran Church.

Ebony Oliver Wyatt

Ebony Oliver Wyatt graduated from Fort Smith Northside High School in 1999. She attended the University of Arkansas, Fayetteville, from 1999 to 2003 and graduated with a bachelor's degree in finance in 2003. Wyatt was an active student leader, serving as president of Delta Sigma Theta Sorority and vice president of the Student Ambassadors (a University of Arkansas tour guide group). She graduated from the university's Emerging Leader program and completed two internships, one a summer internship for General Mills and the other a co-op program for Hershey Foods USA.

After graduating in 2003, Wyatt took a full-time sales position with General Mills in Atlanta, Georgia. After working for two years, she was promoted to retail manager on the General Mills Wal-Mart team in Rogers. In 2007, Wyatt relocated to Charlotte, North Carolina, with General Mills as a customer account manager, working with two North Carolina–based retailers. In December 2008, Wyatt was promoted to category development manager for General Mills's baking division, relocating to Minneapolis, Minnesota. Wyatt is currently the highest-ranking African American female in sales at General Mills.

At General Mills, Wyatt is currently serving as the president of the Sales Black Champions Network (Sales BCN). Prior leadership experience at General Mills has included serving as a member of the Sales Diversity Council and as a member of the Bakeries and Food Service Diversity Council. Wyatt is also former chairperson for the Sales BCN Retention and Development Committee.

In 2006, Wyatt was headlined and featured in Arkansas's $300K minority recruiting ad campaign, which included a thirty-second television commercial and a radio commercial. This ad campaign ran for approximately one year. In 2009, during the ninth Black Alumni Society reunion, Wyatt was presented with the Young Alumni award for her contributions to the university and her career successes.

Wyatt is married to William Wyatt.

Terry N. Perkins Rolfe

Terry Rolfe is a native of North Little Rock. She attended the University of Arkansas from 1990 to 1994. While at the university, Rolfe was involved in various activities, including being a member of the Inspirational Singers and Delta Sigma Theta Sorority. She graduated from the university in 1994 with a bachelor's degree in microbiology. After graduation, Rolfe began her professional career with the Arkansas State Crime Laboratory in Little Rock. In 1995, she started her career as a forensic serologist. A few years later, Rolfe was promoted to chief forensic DNA examiner. She provided DNA examination and expert testimony in criminal investigations for the entire state of Arkansas. After thirteen years with the Arkansas State Crime Laboratory, Rolfe resigned her position to stay home and care for her small children. Rolfe is married to Lott Rolfe IV, also a University of Arkansas graduate and local attorney. They reside in Maumelle with their two beautiful children, Taylor and Austin.

La Tina Watkins Washington

La Tina Watkins Washington graduated from the University of Arkansas in 1994 with a BS in computer systems engineering. Since graduation, she has been employed with Acxiom Corporation in Conway as a software developer. Her family consists of her husband of eleven years, Lee, and two children, India and Joshua.

Lisa Williams

Lisa Williams is a respected researcher, national columnist, and award-winning speaker. She is the president and CEO of Williams Research, Inc., and the author of the book, *Leading Beyond Excellence*. She is also president and CEO of EPI Books, a publishing firm producing positive, uplifting books for adults and children. A subdivision of EPI Books, EPI Kid's Books Division, is Wal-Mart's premier supplier of ethnic children's books.

As a former professor at Penn State University and a two-time endowed chair holder, she has dedicated her life to educating and developing excellence in future and current leaders. Major corporations and President Clinton's Commission on Critical Infrastructure Protection have sought her advice. Dr. Williams's research has practical and global implications, and she has spoken to audiences in the United States, Belgium, Austria, Canada, London, and Australia.

Dr. Williams has been given the highest honor bestowed upon a faculty member—an endowed chair. Actually, Dr. Williams has been given this honor not once but twice in three years. As the first female to hold a multimillion-dollar endowed chair in her field, the first African American female to graduate from The Ohio State University's Department of Marketing and Logistics, and the second woman in her discipline to become a full professor, she has committed herself to exceptional scholarship. Her accomplishments were recognized when she was given the American Marketing Association PhD Project Trailblazer Award.

Her peers and students alike recognize her as a leader in the field of business and supply chain management. She has received many teaching awards and much recognition from The Ohio State, Penn State, and the University of Arkansas. Dr. Williams has been ranked by the most prestigious journal in the field for the number of articles published. While featured in many magazines for her expertise in business, she is also known for her ability to motivate executives, future leaders, and audiences of all sizes.

This biography was taken from her Web site: http://www.keyspeakers.com/bio.php?Lisa_Williams.

Chapter 7

Randy Dorian Brown Jr.

Randy Dorian Brown Jr., the son of Maria Jackson and Randy Brown Sr., was born in North Little Rock.

Brown has assumed numerous leadership roles from his first position as student council vice president in the fourth grade to president of the senior class in the twelfth grade. Brown's senior year highlight was being selected as Arkansas Boys and Girls Club Youth of the Year, which provided a full scholarship for him to the University of Arkansas, Fayetteville.

Brown entered the university in 2001 and immediately became involved in Pomfret Hall's government by representing Pomfret as one of its senators for the Associated Student Government (ASG). Brown served ASG in many capacities, but his final duties were served as the student body president. Brown is a member of Omega Psi Phi Fraternity, Inc., initiated in fall 2002. Although he was enrolled in the Sam Walton School of Business and maintained a solid grade-point average, Brown's university experience was largely vested in his extracurricular interests. Brown was exposed to the Minority Undergraduate Fellowship Program (MUFP) and developed a passion and interest in student affairs. Upon graduation in 2005, Brown attended graduate school at the University of Vermont in the higher education and student affairs program and acquired an assistantship in the department of residence life. He completed his master's degree in the spring of 2007.

Brown currently works as the residence coordinator for university housing at Florida State University. Brown lives with his eleven-year-old brother Joseph and volunteers with Joseph's baseball and basketball teams and school advisory board.

Synetra Gilmer

Synetra Gilmer is a 2003 University of Arkansas graduate. She recently received her MBA from Webster University in May 2006. She currently resides in northwest Arkansas. Gilmer began working for Wal-Mart in 2002. She is now employed by Abbott Laboratories, Ross Products division.

Gilmer works with the youth of St. James Missionary Baptist Church in Fayetteville, chaperoning the youth attending the Southern Regional Youth Convention in the Bahamas. She also works very closely with the youth minister at St. James.

As the former president of the Kappa Iota Chapter of Alpha Kappa Alpha Sorority, Inc., Gilmer assisted with the group's highway cleanup campaign, visited Rochier Heights Nursing Home, organized the Unity Step Show, participated in the MLK March, and developed student activities focusing on women's issues, health awareness, economics, and politics.

Gilmer has continued her community service involvement in the Phi Alpha Omega Chapter of Alpha Kappa Alpha Sorority, Inc. She works with the Seven Hills Homeless Shelter and highway cleanup campaign. She continues to organize programs that focus on building self-esteem and confidence for youth in northwest Arkansas.

Gilmer has worked with the Black Alumni Society since 2002 and was appointed as student representative to the BAS. In 2003, Gilmer became a BAS board member. She represents BAS at the Black Symposium and student/alumni events.

She was a member of the 2005 and 2007 BAS reunion planning committees, chairing the entertainment committee, working on the registration committee, and organizing photo shoots. She has volunteered more than three hundred hours for the society. In 2007, she received the Black Alumni Society's Community Service Award.

Quantrell Willis

Quantrell Willis is currently the academic services coordinator of educational supportive services at Kansas State University in Manhattan, Kansas. He is also pursuing his PhD in student affairs in higher education at Kansas State University. He received his master's degree in higher education from the University of Arkansas in August 2007 and his bachelor's degree in sociology/African American studies from the university in May 2005.

Before going to Kansas State University, Willis held several leadership positions at the University of Arkansas. As a graduate student, he served as the president of the Black Graduate Students' Association and as an executive board member of the University of Arkansas Black Alumni Society. He was also the vice president of the Northwest Arkansas Alumni Chapter of Phi Beta Sigma Fraternity, Inc., and currently serves as a co-advisor to the Black Students Association at Kansas State University. While an undergraduate, he was involved in numerous activities and organizations. He played an important role, along with Trevin Ware, Justin Grimes, Dwight Hall, and Dr. Joe Seabrooks, in helping form what is now Student African American Brotherhood (SAAB).

Willis was the Black Student Association president (2004–2005), an Emerging Leaders mentor, and an Emerging Leaders facilitator. He participated in various activities ranging from working as an after-school program supervisor with the Fayetteville Boys and Girls Clubs to assisting fifth graders at Jefferson Elementary. Because of his involvement during his undergraduate career, Willis received an Excellence in Leadership Award upon graduation from the University of Arkansas.

Willis has had the opportunity to speak to numerous audiences on topics ranging from leadership to academic, personal, and professional excellence. He currently volunteers with Big Brothers and Big Sisters of Manhattan, Kansas. He also provides mentorship to Manhattan High School students as an empowerment advisor as part of the USD 383's REAL Scholars Program.

Willis is married to Dr. Kellee Willis, and a father to their son Jaalon Willis and daughter Charlee Willis. Willis has also provided recollections of his life in Lewis W. Diuguid's book, *Discovering a Real America: Toward a More Perfect Union.*

Appendix B

African American Enrollment at the University of Arkansas

YEAR	AFRICAN AMERICAN STUDENTS	TOTAL NUMBER OF STUDENTS
1983	738	14,508
1984	699	13,987
1985	646	13,887
1986	656	13,976
1987	637	13,856
1988	630	14,001
1989	673	14,281
1990	684	14,600
1991	697	14,351
1992	707	14,734
1993	708	14,407
1994	713	14,655
1995	797	14,765
1996	834	14,577
1997	837	14,384
1998	880	15,060
1999	945	15,226
2000	965	15,396
2001	980	15,795
2002	1,022	16,035
2003	1,005	16,449
2004	981	17,269
2005	982	17,821
2006	946	17,926
2007	1,023	18,648
2008	1,024	19,194
2009	1,040	19,849

Information provided by University of Arkansas Office of Institutional Research.
The earliest enrollment data were tracked by race is 1983.

Appendix C

African American Timeline at the University of Arkansas

NAME	YEAR	REFERENCE
Joseph C. Corbin, an African American, is the first president ex-officio of U of A Board of Trustees at the formation of the university.	1871	*Spirit of the Legacy,* 4
James McGahee is the first black student to enroll.	1872	*Arkansas Democrat Gazette,* April 28, 2006
Executive Committee of Board of Trustees of UA declares institution "open to all without regard to race, sex, or sect."	1873	*Spirit of the Legacy,* 4
Scipio Africanus Jones is the first black to attempt to enroll in the Law School.	1887	*Remembrances in Black,* Introduction
Black teachers enroll in correspondence courses taught by the U of A.	1927	*Spirit of the Legacy,* 5
The Cooperative Extension Service, a sister unit of the U of A System Division of Agriculture, offers "practical demonstration" courses, terracing, and poultry house construction, to blacks.	1928	*Spirit of the Legacy,* 5
J. R. Jewell, U of A College of Education, dean, teaches extension classes to black teachers.	1930	*Spirit of the Legacy,* 5
Donald Murray is first to challenge out-of-state entry into Law School.	1934	*Spirit of the Legacy,* 5
Dr. Nolin M. Irby teaches graduate-level classes to blacks at AM&N College.	1936–1937	*Spirit of the Legacy,* 5
Edward Lewis Jacko Jr. attempts to enter Law School, but is not admitted.	1938	*Remembrances in Black,* Introduction
Clifford Davis files petition to enter Law School.	1946	*Remembrances in Black,* Introduction
Clifford Davis is admitted to U of A Law School, is accepted, but does not attend.	Jan. 30, 1948	*Spirit of the Legacy,* 6

NAME	YEAR	REFERENCE
Silas Hunt is the first African American student to enroll at U of A Law School.	Feb. 4, 1948	*Spirit of the Legacy*, 6
Wiley Branton applies to U of A School of Business as an undergraduate and is denied admission.	1948	*Remembrances in Black*, Introduction
Edith May Irby is first African American admitted in UAMS in Little Rock.	1948	*Spirit of the Legacy*, 6
The U of A offers graduate work for blacks in Pine Bluff. The first graduate degrees awarded to blacks by U of A are earned and presented there.	1948–1950	*Spirit of the Legacy*, 7
Residence Center is established in Little Rock to provide graduate training for black students.	Fall 1949	*Remembrances in Black*, ch. 1
U of A allows black males to live in Lloyd Hall.	1950	*Remembrances in Black*, ch. 1
Benjamin Franklin Lever is first black graduate student in residence.	1950	http://uark.edu/admin/urelinfo/SilasHunt/history.html
Jackie Shropshire is first African American to graduate from U of A School of Law.	1951	*Spirit of the Legacy*, 7
Peter Faison is a graduate student enrolled in the College of Agriculture.	Fall 1951	*Remembrances in Black*, ch. 2, Faison
George Howard is first black to be elected president of any student organization when elected president of Lloyd Hall.	1952	*Spirit of the Legacy*, 8
U of A purchases a large residence near campus and converts it into housing for black women.	1953	*Remembrances in Black*, ch. 1
Thelma O Betton receives a master's in home economics.	1954	H. Betton (personal communication, 2007, and UA Senior Walk)
Sanford Tollette III receives a master's in education.	1954	*Remembrances in Black*, ch. 2, Tollette

NAME	YEAR	REFERENCE
John M. Howard is first black university instructor (art teacher off campus).	1955	*The Edge of Campus*, 172
Joe Louis Flowers applies but is denied admission as undergraduate.	1955	*Remembrances in Black*, ch. 2
Maxine Sutton, Billie Rose Whitfield, and **Marjorie Wilkins** are first African American undergraduates admitted to U of A.	1955	*Spirit of the Legacy*, 9
Maxine Sutton, Billie Rose Whitfield, and **Marjorie Wilkins** play with marching band, but are not allowed to travel or accompany band away from campus.	1955	*Remembrances in Black*, ch. 2, Sutton Cannon, Whitfield Jacobs, and Wilkins Williams
Gordon Morgan, sociology, and **George Wesley**, theater, are master degree recipients.	1956	*Spirit of the Legacy*, 9
Ruth Bradford and **Clifton Claye** are doctoral graduates (EdD).	1958	*The Edge of Campus*, 173
Melvin Eugene Dowell is the first Fayetteville African American resident to enter U of A.	1959	*The Edge of Campus*, 173
George Whitfield serves as teaching assistant and teaches general speech course.	1961	*Remembrances in Black*, ch. 3, G. Whitfield
Joanna P. Edwards and **Robert Whitfield** file lawsuit to live in residence halls.	1964	*Spirit of the Legacy*, 9
Students are allowed to live in residence halls.	1965	*Remembrances in Black*, ch. 3, H. Betton and D. Brown
Darrell Brown is first to play on the Shoats (freshman football team).	1965	*Remembrances in Black*, ch. 3, D. Brown
Thomas "TJ" Johnson is first African American nonvarsity basketball recruit.	1967	*Forty Minutes of Hell*, 145
Black students rally at Hill Hall, the office of the *Arkansas Traveler*, to protest negative stereotypes published in the student newspaper.	1968	*Spirit of the Legacy*, 9
James Seawood is first president of the newly formed Black Americans for Democracy.	1968	*Spirit of the Legacy*, 10
Almer Lee is first varsity scholarship basketball player.	1969	*Spirit of the Legacy*, 11

NAME	YEAR	REFERENCE
Jon Richardson is first football scholarship player.	1969	*Spirit of the Legacy*, 11
Joe Tave is named assistant dean of students.	1969	*The Edge of Campus*, 173
Nigerian **Hillary Nwokeji** is first African student.	1969	*Spirit of the Legacy*, 10
Marion Anthony Wright organizes BAD choir.	1969	*Spirit of the Legacy*, 10
BAD, first "Black Emphasis Week."	1969	*Spirit of the Legacy*, 10
Darrell Brown is shot during week of "Dixie" protests.	1969	*Spirit of the Legacy*, 10
George and Sharon Bernard Miller are the first black couple to receive law degrees.	1969	*Remembrances in Black*, ch. 3, Bernard and Miller
Harold Betton receives BS in agriculture.	1969	*Remembrances in Black*, ch. 3, H. Betton
Margaret Clark and **Gordon Morgan** are the first black faculty members hired.	1969	*Spirit of the Legacy*, 10
Hiram McBeth is the first to play in Red-White spring game.	1969	*Remembrances in Black*, ch. 3, McBeth
Viralean Coleman graduates with PhD.	1969	*The Edge of Campus*, 173
Harold Betton and **James Haymon** organize first Ms. BAD and Ms. Black Collegiate of Arkansas pageants.	1970	*Remembrances in Black*, ch. 3, H. Betton
David Cooksey is chosen as financial aid director.	1970	*The Edge of Campus*, 173
Sanford Tollette IV is chosen as drum major.	1971	*The Edge of Campus*, 173
Adolph Reed becomes political science professor.	1971	*The Edge of Campus*, 173
Linda Taylor joins Phi Beta Kappa.	1972	*The Edge of Campus*, 173
Gene McKissic is voted student body president.	1972	*The Edge of Campus*, 173
Delois Gibson is appointed education professor.	1972	*The Edge of Campus*, 173
Samuel Massey is awarded honorary doctorate.	1972	*The Edge of Campus*, 173
Willie Willingham earns chemistry doctorate.	1972	*The Edge of Campus*, 173
John Gilmore earns engineering doctorate.	1972	*The Edge of Campus*, 173
Brenda Mobley becomes psychology professor.	1972	*The Edge of Campus*, 173
Willie Freeman is first black to join fraternity by pledging Tau Kappa Epsilon.	1972	*Spirit of the Legacy*, 12

NAME	YEAR	REFERENCE
Frank Falks is hired as assistant football coach.	1973	*The Edge of Campus*, 173
Clifford Monroe joins ROTC staff.	1974	*The Edge of Campus*, 173
Raymond Miller Sr., M.D., becomes board of trustee member.	1974	*The Edge of Campus*, 173
Delta Sigma Theta is first black sorority chartered.	Spring 1974	*Remembrances in Black*, ch. 4, Gant
Omega Psi Phi is first black fraternity chartered.	Fall 1974	*Remembrances in Black*, ch. 4, L. Williams
Vernon Murphy is first scholarship athlete to finish with a degree.	1975	*Remembrances in Black*, ch. 3, Murphy
Pobbi Asmani (Ghana) becomes staff member.	1975	*The Edge of Campus*, 173
Donna Lee becomes Uarkette member.	1975	*The Edge of Campus*, 173
E. Lynn Harris is chosen Cardinal Twenty.	1975	*Remembrances in Black*, ch. 4, E. Harris
Merlin Augustine becomes assistant to the president in first executive cabinet position.	1975	*Remembrances in Black*, ch. 4, L. Williams
Mazo Price earns PhD in agriculture.	1976	H. Reed (personal communication, 2010).
Charlie Tolliver is appointed electrical engineering professor.	1976	*Remembrances in Black*, ch. 4, Tolliver
Natalie Dyer wins title of yearbook beauty.	1976	*The Edge of Campus*, 173
George Knox becomes law professor.	1976	*The Edge of Campus*, 174
Alex Ford is named architecture professor.	1976	*The Edge of Campus*, 174
Nudie Williams is named history professor.	1976	*The Edge of Campus*, 174
Dionne Harold is Pom-Pom girl.	1977	*The Edge of Campus*, 174
Billy Lewis, E. Lynn Harris, Dionne Harold, and **Kim Nichols** become cheerleaders.	1977	*The Edge of Campus*, 174
Dinah Gail Gant is engineering graduate.	1977	*The Edge of Campus*, 174
Steve Sullivan (Kappa Alpha Psi), although white, pledges African American fraternity.	1977	*The Edge of Campus*, 174
Karen Johnson Williams earns BS in black studies.	1978	L. Williams (personal communication, 2010)
Shifton Baker becomes assistant track coach.	1978	*Spirit of the Legacy*, 45

NAME	YEAR	REFERENCE
Sidney Moncrief (basketball) is named All-American.	1978	*The Edge of Campus*, 174
Patricia Greene Griffen earns psychology doctorate.	1979	*The Edge of Campus*, 174
Charles Magee becomes agricultural engineering professor.	1979	*Remembrances in Black*, ch. 4, Magee
John Anderson earns business doctorate.	1979	*The Edge of Campus*, 174
Lloyd Myers, president, presides when BAD changes name to STAND.	1979	*Spirit of the Legacy*, 13
Chip Hooper (tennis) is national champion male athlete.	1979	*The Edge of Campus*, 174
Diann Ousley (600-meter track) becomes national champion female athlete.	1979	*The Edge of Campus*, 174
Wiley Branton receives Distinguished Alumnus Award.	1980	*The Edge of Campus*, 174
Charlie Tolliver, director, creates the Transition Retention Minority Engineering Program (TRMEP).	1980	*Remembrances in Black*, ch. 4, Tolliver
Bill Brown becomes assistant basketball coach.	1981	*Spirit of the Legacy*, 45
Cynthia Greer, bachelor's degree holder, earns PhD.	1981	*The Edge of Campus*, 174
Merlin Augustine serves as interim vice chancellor for student affairs.	1981–1982?	*Remembrances in Black*, ch. 4, L. Williams
Karen Harris is Miss Washington County.	1982	*The Edge of Campus*, 174
Merike Manley is voted homecoming queen.	1982	*The Edge of Campus*, 174
Hazell Reed receives PhD in horticulture and forestry.	1983	H. Reed (personal communication, 2010)
Mike Conley, Silver Medal, is first Olympian.	1984	*Spirit of the Legacy*, 43
Kenneth "Muskie" Harris becomes Arkansas Alumni Association Board of Directors member.	1985	M. Harris (personal communication, 2010)
Patrisha Young is Miss University of Arkansas.	1985	*The Edge of Campus*, 174
Naccaman Williams, Minority Affairs representative, is hired for the College of Education.	1988	N. Williams (personal communication, 2010)

NAME	YEAR	REFERENCE
Roderick McDavis (Education) is appointed academic dean.	1990	*Spirit of the Legacy*, 14
Lonnie R. Williams coordinates Black Alumni Reunions to begin on UA campus.	1990	*Spirit of the Legacy*, 14
Linda Joshua is African American Holmes Scholar in College of Education.	1991	L. Williams (personal communication, 2010)
Genette Seawood Howard (Business), **Carl Riley** (Fulbright), Minority Affairs representatives, are hired for School of Business and Fulbright.	1992	C. Riley (personal communication, 2009)
Kimbra Bell is awarded Senior Honor Citation by Arkansas Alumni Association.	1992	L. Williams (personal communication, 2010)
Kimbra Bell receives Black Alumni Reunion scholarship award.	1992	L. Williams (personal communication, 2010)
Tanisha Joe-Conway is first Black Alumni Reunion scholar (renewable), first named Randall Ferguson Jr. scholarship, later changed to Black Alumni Scholarship in 1995.	1993	*Remembrances in Black*, ch. 5, Conway-Joe
Nolan Richardson (coach) wins NCAA Basketball Championship.	1994	*Spirit of the Legacy*, 14
Willyerd Collier is chosen as affirmative action officer.	1994	W. Collier (personal communication, 2010)
Multicultural Center opened on Arkansas Ave. in temporary location, moved to permanent location in 2001.	1995	C. Kenner (personal communication from Multicultural Center director, 2010)
Crystal Hendricks is chosen as a Coca-Cola Foundation Scholar.	1996	C. Hendricks (personal communication, 2010)
Mrs. Daisy L. Gatson Bates is the first recipient of Black Students Association "Living Legacy Award."	1996	*Remembrances in Black*, ch. 5, Dedner
George Washington Carver Project.	1997	*Spirit of the Legacy*, 15

NAME	YEAR	REFERENCE
LeQuinta Wilson is the first Yvonne-Keaton Martin scholar.	1997	C. Kenner (personal communication from Multicultural Center director, 2010)
Wendell Griffen is voted president of the newly established Black Alumni Society.	1998	*Spirit of the Legacy,* 15
Lisa Williams is made endowed chair faculty member.	1999	*Remembrances in Black,* ch. 5, L. Williams
Johnetta Cross Brazzell becomes vice chancellor for student affairs.	1999	*Spirit of the Legacy,* 16
Arlene Cash is chosen dean of enrollment services.	1999	L. Williams (personal communication, 2010)
Derrick Gragg, associate athletic director, is promoted to senior associate director in 2003 and to deputy athletic director in 2006.	2000	D. Gragg (personal communication, 2010)
Carolyn Allen is chosen dean of university libraries.	2001	*Spirit of the Legacy,* 17
Joe Seabrooks (staff), **Quantrell Willis,** and other students form the Student African American Brotherhood.	Summer 2005	*Remembrances in Black,* ch. 7, Willis
First Silas Hunt Legacy Award.	Apr. 2006	*Spirit of the Legacy,* 4
Cynthia Nance is appointed Law School dean.	July 2006	*Remembrances in Black,* ch. 5, Nance
Gerald Jordan is appointed president of Arkansas Alumni Association Board of Directors.	July 2008	A. Monts (personal communication, 2010)
Charles Robinson is appointed as vice provost for diversity.	2009	C. Robinson (personal communication, 2009)

References

Bradburd, R. *Forty Minutes of Hell: The Extraordinary Life of Nolan Richardson.* New York: HarperCollins Publishers, 2010. 145.

Branam, C. "School's 1st black identified." *Northwest Arkansas Democrat Gazette,* April 28, 2006, Northwest Arkansas sec., 13.

Morgan, G., and I. Preston. *The Edge of Campus: A Journal of the Black Experience at the University of Arkansas.* Fayetteville: University of Arkansas Press, 1990.

Personal communications to the editors of this volume.

Robinson, C., and L. Williams, eds. *Remembrances in Black: Personal Perspectives of the African American Experience at the University of Arkansas, 1940s–2000s.* Fayetteville: University of Arkansas Press, 2010.

Spirit of the Legacy: The University of Arkansas Silas Hunt Legacy Award Report. Fayetteville: University of Arkansas, Office of University Relations, 2006.

Notes

Introduction

1. See *Spirit of the Legacy: The University of Arkansas Silas Hunt Legacy Award Report,* a special publication produced by the University of Arkansas, Fayetteville, April 2006.

2. Thomas Rothrock, "Joseph Carter Corbin and Negro Education at the University of Arkansas," *Arkansas Historical Quarterly* 30 (winter 1971): 277–314.

3. Geofrey Jensen, *Forgotten,* unpublished paper, April 2006.

4. See *Spirit of the Legacy,* 4, and Tom W. Dillard, "Scipio A. Jones," *Arkansas Historical Quarterly* 31 (Autumn 1972): 201–19.

5. For information on Edward Willis Jacko Jr.'s correspondence to NAACP about the University of Arkansas, see NAACP Papers, Box 1: C270, Folder 4. For information relating to correspondence and agricultural extension courses for black students, see *Spirit of the Legacy.*

6. Richard Kluger, *Simple Justice: The History of* Brown v. Board of Education *and Black America's Struggle for Equality* (New York: Vintage Books, 1977), 202–4, 258–66.

7. "University President, A. M. Harding to Governor Homer M. Adkins," December 10, 1941. Found in University Archives President's Office AC211/250, Box 1, "Negro Letters," Special Collections, University of Arkansas.

8. Robert A. Leflar, *The First 100 Years: Centennial History of the University of Arkansas* (Fayetteville: University of Arkansas Foundation, 1972), 277–78.

9. See Kluger, *Simple Justice,* 258–66.

10. Leflar, *The First 100 Years,* 278–82.

11. Leflar, *The First 100 Years,* 278–82.

12. Leflar, *The First 100 Years,* 278–82.

13. Guerdon D. Nichols, "Breaking the Color Barrier at the University of Arkansas," *Arkansas Historical Quarterly* 27 (spring 1968): 14–16.

14. "Lewis Webster Jones to R. H. Delaney," February 14, 1948. Found in University Archives President's Office AC211/250, Box 1, "Negro Letters," Special Collections, University of Arkansas.

15. Guerdon D. Nichols, "Breaking the Color Barrier at the University of Arkansas," 15–18. Also see "Lewis Webster Jones to R. H. Delaney," February 14, 1948. Found in University Archives President's Office AC211/250, Box 1, "Negro Letters," Special Collections, University of Arkansas. Jones reports, "In accepting a Negro student in our School of Law, the University took careful precautions to see that he is segregated from white students . . . he studies alone and recites alone and does not mix with white students or participate in the activities of white students."

16. Nichols, "Breaking the Color Barrier at the University of Arkansas," 15–18.

Chapter 1: In the Beginning

1. "William J. Good to James R. Goodrich," October 15, 1948. Found in University Archives President's Office AC211/250, Box 1, "Negro Letters," Special Collections, University of Arkansas.

2. "William J. Good to James R. Goodrich," October 15, 1948.

3. "William J. Good to James R. Goodrich," October 15, 1948.

4. "Lewis Webster Jones to James A. Dombrowski," October 18, 1949. Found in University Archives President's Office AC211/250, Box 1, "Negro Letters," Special Collections, University of Arkansas.

5. "Lewis Webster Jones to James F. Miller," May 26, 1951. Found in University Archives President's Office AC211/250, Box 1, "Negro Letters," Special Collections, University of Arkansas.

6. "William J. Good to James R. Goodrich," October 15, 1948, and "William J. Good to Dr. Benjamin Fine," January 11, 1954. Found in University Archives President's Office AC211/250, Box 1, "Negro Letters," Special Collections, University of Arkansas. These letters contain information about the year the university founded the Graduate Center at Little Rock and the approximate numbers of black students who attend or have attended it.

7. In one of his letters discussing desegregation at the university, President John T. Caldwell stated, "The problem of housing Negroes on the campus was one of the factors back of the University's decision to open a graduate residence in Little Rock." "John T. Caldwell to Dr. Henry H. Hill," November 24, 1953. Found in University Archives President's Office AC211/250, Box 1, "Negro Letters," Special Collections, University of Arkansas.

8. "Lewis Webster Jones to Wiley Lin Hurie," May 17, 1949. Found in University Archives President's Office AC211/250, Box 1, "Negro Letters," Special Collections, University of Arkansas.

9. Leflar, *The First 100 Years*, 284. On the first day of the new policy, a small wooden railing was placed around Shropshire to further segregate him. After one day, the railing was taken down.

10. Memorandum by Robert A. Leflar, September 23, 1948. Found in University Archives President's Office AC211/250, Box 1, "Negro Letters," Special Collections, University of Arkansas.

11. Kluger, *Simple Justice*, 267–70, 283–83.

12. "John T. Caldwell to Eugene B. Hale," October 15, 1952, and "John T. Caldwell to Dr. Henry H. Hill," November 24, 1953. Found in University Archives President's Office AC211/250, Box 1, "Negro Letters," Special Collections, University of Arkansas. Also see *Arkansas Gazette*, October 11, 1952.

13. "John T. Caldwell to Dr. Henry H. Hill," November 24, 1953. Found in University Archives President's Office AC211/250, Box 1, "Negro Letters," Special Collections, University of Arkansas.

14. Morgan, *Edge of Campus*, 17–22.

15. "John T. Caldwell to Dr. Henry H. Hill," November 24, 1953.

16. "William J. Good to James R. Goodrich," October 15, 1948.

17. "William J. Good to Dr. Benjamin Fine," January 11, 1954.

Chapter 2: Taking the Moderate Path: Desegregation in the 1950s

1. "John T. Caldwell to Ervin Canham," April 6, 1956. Found in University Archives President's Office AC211/250, Box 1, "Negro Letters," Special Collections, University of Arkansas.

2. "John T. Caldwell to Ervin Canham," April 2, 1956. Found in University Archives President's Office AC211/250, Box 1, "Negro Letters," Special Collections, University of Arkansas.

3. "John T. Caldwell to Ervin Canham," April 2, 1956.

4. Memorandum to the Board of Trustees, "Negro Students in the School of Nursing," January 8, 1954. Found in University Archives President's Office AC211/250, Box 1, "Negro Letters," Special Collections, University of Arkansas.

5. Memorandum to the Board of Trustees, "Negro Students in the School of Nursing," January 8, 1954.

6. "Memorandum to Dean Julia Miller, School of Nursing," March 24, 1954. Found in University Archives President's Office AC211/250, Box 1, "Negro Letters," Special Collections, University of Arkansas.

7. Kluger, *Simple Justice*, Appendix: Text of Decisions. For information about the "Southern Manifesto," see Elizabeth Jacoway, *Turn Away Thy Son: Little Rock, The Crisis That Shocked The Nation* (New York: Free Press, 2007), 25–26.

8. Memorandum to Board of Trustees, "Negro undergraduate applicants to the University of Arkansas," January 25, 1955. Found in University Archives President's Office AC211/250, Box 1, "Negro Letters," Special Collections, University of Arkansas.

9. Raymond D'Angelo, *The American Civil Rights Movement: Readings & Interpretations* (New York: McGraw-Hill/Dushkin, 2001), 226.

10. *Arkansas Democrat,* August 3, 1955.

11. Memorandum to Dr. Louis H. Rohrbaugh, Vice President and Provost, "Negro Applicants for Undergraduate Enrollment," August 11, 1955. Found in University Archives President's Office AC211/250, Box 1, "Negro Letters," Special Collections, University of Arkansas.

12. "James Flowers to John T. Caldwell," October 4, 1955. Found in University Archives President's Office AC211/250, Box 1, "Negro Letters," Special Collections, University of Arkansas.

13. "William J. Good to Joe Flowers," October 18, 1955. Found in University Archives President's Office AC211/250, Box 1, "Negro Letters," Special Collections, University of Arkansas.

14. "William J. Good to Joe Flowers," October 18, 1955. Good telephoned Fendler to apprise him of Flowers's letter. Apparently, Good was concerned that Flowers had been "sponsored" by some organization to write his letter. Fendler investigated Flowers and found him to be "very courteous" and "very ambitious." Fendler also reported that Flowers was "merely seeking information." "Oscar Fendler to William Good," October 14, 1955. Found in University Archives President's Office AC211/250, Box 1, "Negro Letters," Special Collections, University of Arkansas.

15. For the number of black students on the Fayetteville campus, see "Memorandum to the Board of Trustees," October 5, 1956. Found in University Archives President's Office AC211/250, Box 1, "Negro Letters," Special Collections, University of Arkansas. For numbers of summer enrollment in 1956, see "John T. Caldwell to Marcus Halbrook, Director of the Legislative Council," February 4, 1957. Found in University Archives President's Office AC211/250, Box 1, "Negro Letters," Special Collections, University of Arkansas. It is also important to note that the university refused to admit black out-of-state students as well.

16. A few black speakers/entertainers came to the university in the 1950s. See *Arkansas Traveler,* April 22, 1952; February 4, 1953; December 15, 1954. Also, Dr. Ralph Bunche, the director of the United Nations Division of Trusteeship, spoke at the university in July 1954. Apparently, Bunche was misquoted in a *New York Times* article as making some remark about the university having gone so far as to send "runners all the way to Little Rock and Pine Bluff to drum up Negroes to make the showing . . . that was carrying desegregation too far." Caldwell was so bothered by the article that he wrote Bunche asking for a clarification of his remarks. Bunche assured Caldwell that he had been misquoted and that he had the highest respect for the university and their desegregation efforts. See "John T. Caldwell to Ralph Bunche," July 21, 1954. Found in University Archives President's Office AC211/250, Box 1, "Negro Letters," Special Collections, University of Arkansas. Also, "Ralph Bunche to John T. Caldwell," July 29, 1954. Found in University Archives President's Office AC211/250, Box 1, "Negro Letters," Special Collections, University of Arkansas.

Chapter 3: To Prevent "Irreparable Harm": Desegregation and the 1960s

1. *Arkansas Traveler,* November 4, 1968.

2. Ark. Acts 1958, 2nd Ex. Sess., Act 10, printed in Acts of 1959, p. 2018. Also see Leflar, *The First 100 Years,* 198–202.

3. John T. Caldwell to James E. Pomfret, "Act 115 of 1959." Found in University Archives President's Office AC211/250, Box 1, "Negro Letters," Special Collections, University of Arkansas.

4. "Memo." Found in University Archives President's Office AC211/250, Box 1, "Negro Letters," Special Collections, University of Arkansas.

5. *Arkansas Traveler,* December 18, 1962.

6. *Arkansas Traveler,* October 27, 1961; October 31, 1961; November 20, 1963; December 3, 1963; March 31, 1965; April 17, 1968. The University of Arkansas Board of Trustees on November 22, 1963, voted not to follow the lead of the University of Texas and integrate athletics. "Minutes of the University of Arkansas Board of Trustees Meeting," November 22, 1963, Special Collections, University of Arkansas.

7. Peter Irons, *Jim Crow's Children: The Broken Promise of the* Brown *Decision* (New York: Viking Penguin, 2002), 192–93.

8. *Arkansas Gazette,* January 26, 1964.

9. *Arkansas Gazette,* August 18, 1964; August 19, 1964; September 5, 1965; September 6, 1964.

10. *Arkansas Traveler,* October 31, 1966.

11. *Arkansas Gazette,* January 6, 1967.

12. *Arkansas Gazette,* March 11, 1968.

13. *Arkansas Traveler,* April 5, 1968; April 6, 1968; April 7, 1968; April 8, 1968; April 9, 1968; April 10, 1968; May 15, 1968.

14. *Arkansas Traveler,* November 6, 1968; December 11, 1968; December 18, 1968.

15. Terry Frei, *Horns, Hogs, and Nixon Coming: Texas v. Arkansas in Dixie's Last Stand* (New York: Simon & Schuster, 2002), 92–94, 174–77.

Chapter 4: BAD Challenges Desegregation in the 1970s

1. *Arkansas Traveler,* December 9, 1970.

2. *Arkansas Traveler,* February 25, 1969.

3. *Arkansas Gazette,* January 8, 1971.

4. *Arkansas Gazette,* January 8, 1971; November 7, 1971.

5. *BAD Times,* November 1972.

6. *BAD Times,* April 6, 1973.

7. *BAD Times,* November 18, 1975.

8. See *BAD Times,* May 7, 1973; November 18, 1975; *Arkansas Traveler,* October 17, 1971; April 19, 1973; November 7, 1973; November 21, 1975; January 21, 1977.

9. *BAD Times,* April 6, 1973; *Arkansas Traveler,* March 25, 1974.

10. *Arkansas Traveler,* September 14, 1978.

11. *Arkansas Gazette,* May 25, 1974.

12. *Arkansas Traveler,* September 14, 1978.

13. See Morgan, *Edge of Campus,* 33–45.

14. *Arkansas Gazette,* September 23, 1970. *Arkansas Traveler,* October 9, 1970; October 14, 1970; January 18, 1972; November 19, 1973.

15. *Arkansas Gazette,* September 23, 1970; *Arkansas Traveler,* September 24, 1970.

16. *Arkansas Traveler,* April 10, 1974.

Chapter 5: Making an Honest Effort: Desegregation and the University of Arkansas in the 1980s

1. *Arkansas Traveler,* October 16, 1979.

2. *Arkansas Traveler,* October 16, 1979.

3. See William Julius Wilson, *The Bridge over the Racial Divide: Rising Inequality and Coalition Politics* (Berkeley and Los Angeles: University of California Press, 1999).

4. *Arkansas Traveler,* April 10, 1980.

5. *Arkansas Traveler,* April 17, 1980.

6. *Arkansas Traveler,* September 30, 1980; January 16, 1981.

7. *Spirit of the Legacy,* 13, 14; *Arkansas Traveler,* October 15, 1981; December 10, 1982.

8. *Student Enrollment,* Institutional Research, 1982–1989. *Arkansas Traveler,* December 10, 1982.

9. *Arkansas Traveler,* May 2, 1986.

10. *Arkansas Traveler,* December 10, 1982.

11. *Arkansas Traveler,* December 10, 1982.

Chapter 6: Desegregation Work Still in Progress: The University of Arkansas in the 1990s

1. *Arkansas Traveler,* March 4, 1994.

2. *Arkansas Traveler,* March 4, 1994.

3. *Arkansas Traveler,* March 4, 1994.

4. *Arkansas Traveler,* March 4, 1994; February 16, 1994.

5. *Spirit of the Legacy,* 15, 16.

6. University of Arkansas, Institutional Research, Enrollment Report Detail, 1981–2006, www.uark.edu/admin/ensvinforeports/erd/htm.

7. *Spirit of the Legacy,* 49.

8. *Arkansas Traveler,* April 9, 1993.

9. *Arkansas Traveler,* October 19, 1995.

10. *Arkansas Traveler,* January 31, 1990; January 20, 1993; March 3, 1993.

11. *Arkansas Traveler,* September 6, 1995.

Chapter 7: Destination: Diversity and Desegregation in the 2000s

1. John A. White, "State of the University Address, 2007." Fayetteville: University of Arkansas, found at http://chancellor.uark.edu/13130.php.

2. John A. White, "State of the University Address, 2005." Fayetteville: University of Arkansas, October 13, 2005.

3. *Spirit of the Legacy,* 40, 47.

4. Diversity Task Force, *Diversity Plan For The University of Arkansas Fall, 2002-Fall, 2005, Part I.* University of Arkansas, 1–49.

5. The year of Carmen Coustaut's appointment is mentioned in University of Arkansas, *Daily Headlines,* March 24, 2009.

6. See *Spirit of the Legacy.* With regard to the growth of the African American Studies Program, contact the Fulbright College Office, 525 Old Main, on the campus of the University of Arkansas.

7. University of Arkansas, Institutional Research, Enrollment Report Detail, 1981–2006, www.uark.edu/admin/ensvinforeports/erd/htm.

8. *Spirit of the Legacy,* 49.

9. See UPI.com "Sports News," March 1, 2002; *New York Times,* March 20, 2002; December 20, 2002.

10. University of Arkansas, Institutional Research, Enrollment Report Detail, 1998–2008, www.uark.edu/admin/ensvinforeports/erd/htm.

Charles F. Robinson III is vice provost for diversity at the University of Arkansas, where he is also an associate professor of history and director of African American Studies. He is the author of *Dangerous Liaisons: Sex and Love in the Segregated South* (University of Arkansas Press) and *Forsaking All Others: A True Story of Interracial Sex and Revenge in the 1880s South*.

Lonnie R. Williams is associate vice chancellor for student affairs at Arkansas State University, Jonesboro. Prior to that he was assistant vice chancellor for student affairs and assistant dean of students for multicultural affairs at the University of Arkansas, Fayetteville. In 2010 he was awarded the Silas Hunt Legacy Award from t he University of Arkansas, Fayetteville. The award recognizes African Americans for their significant contributions to the community, state, and nation.